Peru
a travel survival kit

Rob Rachowiecki

Peru – a travel survival kit
1st edition

Published by
  Lonely Planet Publications
  Head Office: PO Box 88, South Yarra, Victoria 3141, Australia
  Also: PO Box 2001A, Berkeley, California 94702, USA

Printed by
  Colorcraft, Hong Kong

Photographs
  Rob Rachowiecki (RR), cover
  Tony Wheeler (TW)

Illustrations
  Dennis Sheehan

Published
  July 1987

Although the author and publisher have tried to make the information as accurate as possible, they accept no responsibility for any loss, injury or inconvenience sustained by any traveller using this book.

National Library of Australia
Cataloguing in Publication Data

Rachowiecki, Rob
Peru, a travel survival kit

  Includes index.
  ISBN 0 908086 96 2.

  1. Peru – Description and travel – 1981 – Guide-books. I. Title.

918.5'04633

Rob Rachowiecki

Rob Rachowiecki was born near London and became an avid traveller while still a teenager. He has visited countries as diverse as Greenland and Thailand. He spent several years in Latin America, travelling, mountaineering and teaching English, and he now works there part time as a leader for Wilderness Travel, an adventure tour company. His first book, with Hilary Bradt, was *Backpacking in Mexico & Central America* (2nd edition, 1982) and he has also authored *Climbing & Hiking in Ecuador* (2nd printing 1987, Bradt Publications), and Lonely Planet's *Ecuador & the Galapagos Islands – a travel survival kit* (1986). For 1987, he plans trips to Newfoundland, the UK, Ecuador and Peru. When not travelling, he lives in the US with his American wife, Cathy, and is at present studying for a degree in biology. His dream is to some day sail around the world.

Dedication

For Cathy, whom I met in Peru.

Editor	Peter Turner
Maps	Fiona Boyes
Design	Peter Flavelle
	Valerie Tellini
Cover Design	Fiona Boyes
Illustrations	Valerie Tellini

Acknowledgements

Many people in Peru, travellers and residents, Peruvians and gringos, helped me gather the information for this book. In Lima, the manager of the South American Explorers Club afforded me immeasurable help, information, friendship and a home away from home. Connor and Mary Nixon provided me with hospitality in both Lima and Yarinacocha and shared their knowledge of almost a decade of living in the Peruvian rain forest. Sandra Ratto Risso and her staff at Chasquitur ably solved my many air travel problems. Carlos Milla Vidal and José Correa Castro shared with me both their friendship and their knowledge of the Cuzco area. The government-run Tourism Offices in the major cities were helpful with maps and information. Cristina Kessler-Noble gave me interesting insight into Quechua place names. Jim Bartle, Hilary Bradt, Peter Frost and Andrea Heckman shared information and/or travel experiences with me. I would also like to thank the Huarmey Tourist Authority.

In Australia, Tony Wheeler calmly 'reannounced' the book when I was unable to meet my overly optimistic deadlines and Fiona Boyes drew the maps from my rough sketches.

During the past five years I have authored four guide books, naively thinking that the work would become easier with practice. I was wrong. I owe my greatest thanks to Cathy who not only put up with me but also constantly cheered me on during my depressed bouts of 'I can never get this done' and shared my joy of finally finishing the book. Thank you all very much.

A Request

All travel guides rely on new information to stay up to date and one of the best sources of this information is travellers on the road. At Lonely Planet we get a constant stream of letters and postcards that help us keep in contact with the latest travel developments. So if you find that things have changed, write to us and let us know. Corrections, suggestions, improvements and additions are greatly appreciated and the best letters will get a free copy of the next edition or another Lonely Planet guide of your choice.

Contents

Introduction

Peru is a wonderful country. Anyone from an archaeologist to a zoologist will be fascinated by Peru, and the discerning traveller cannot fail to be impressed by the great variety of culture, geography and exciting travel possibilities that Peru has to offer.

Peru is frequently referred to as 'the Land of the Incas' yet it could equally be called 'the land of the Moche' (or the Chavín or the Wari). It is true that the Incas formed the greatest empire on the continent and left us with mysterious cities such as Machu Picchu, the magnificent ruins of which we can visit today. Less well known, but equally true, is that the Incas were the last in a long series of Peruvian civilisations spanning several thousand years and that the ruins of many of these earlier civilisations can also be visited.

The Peruvian Andean mountains are arguably the most beautiful and accessible on the continent and the Cordillera Blanca has become world famous among trekkers, hikers and mountaineers. There are several other ranges in Peru which are less visited but no less magnificent. Many of the precipitous glacier-clad mountains have peaks of over 6000 metres and the high valleys between are the haunts of a host of rarely seen animals.

Visitors may glimpse mammals such as the graceful vicuña or the inquisitive viscacha, and birds ranging from the tiny Andean Hummingbird to the giant Andean Condor which, soaring effortlessly on a wingspan that can exceed three metres and with a weight of over 10 kg, is the largest flying bird in the world.

But the Peruvian Andes are not just the scene of remote wilderness, they are also home to millions of highland Indians who still speak their ancient tongue of Quechua (or Aymara) and preserve much of their traditional way of life. Town and village markets are thronged with herds of produce-laden llamas led by Indians wearing their typical ponchos, which provide effective protection against the climatic extremes of this environment. The larger cities also preserve the legacy of the Spanish conquistadors and colonial churches and mansions with their dazzling ornamentation can also be seen.

The traveller could easily spend weeks or months among the Peruvian highlands and yet he would only be visiting a small portion of the country. Over half of Peru's area lies in the verdant Amazon Basin where air or river is often the only means of transportation. Exotic plants and animals amaze and intrigue the observant visitor. The dense tropical rain forest on the eastern edges of the Andes houses the greatest variety of birds on earth. Peru, although less than twice the size of Texas, is home to more than twice the number of bird species than in the entire North American continent. It is a naturalist's paradise and, because it has been so little studied, a giant natural laboratory as well.

The Andes and the Amazon are but two of Peru's diverse geographical regions. There is a third, no less different or spectacular. The entire coastal strip of Peru is desert. Lima, the capital, lies totally surrounded by bare rock and sand. Rivers from the Andes flow through this desert to the Pacific Ocean, creating small oases which have supported a variety of civilisations through the ages. To the north lie the ruins of Chan Chan, the greatest adobe city in the world and capital of the Chimu Empire. To the south, the mysterious Nazca Lines – giant stylised animal shapes etched into the desert many hundreds of years before the Spanish conquest. The etchings, as big as football fields, are visible only from the air. How and why the Nazca Lines were made remains shrouded in mystery – just one of the many fascinating features you will encounter on a journey to that most intriguing of all Andean countries, Peru!

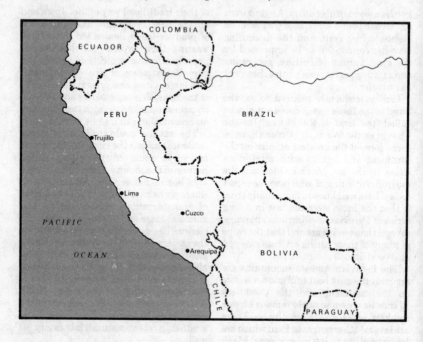

Facts about the Country

ARCHAEOLOGY & HISTORY

For many travellers, Peruvian history means 'Inca'. Certainly, the Inca civilisation is the best known and most studied of all the pre-Columbian cultures of South America and it is the one that most travellers will experience more than any other. But the Incas are merely the tip of the archaeological iceberg. Peru had many pre-Columbian cultures, some preceding the Incas by many centuries.

The concept that the many archaeological sites of Peru date from different eras and hence belonged to distinct cultures was first seriously proposed by E G Squier, an Englishman who travelled throughout Peru in the 1870s. Since then, archaeologists have slowly pieced together a chronological framework for the cultures of the Peruvian area, but it has been a difficult task. This is because none of the cultures are known to have had any written language and so their record lies entirely in archaeological excavation. Furthermore, as one culture succeeded another, they tended to impose their new values and attempted to eliminate the old – as happened when the Spanish conquered the Inca nation. The one difference with the Spanish conquest is that they did produce a written record of their exploits which gives us some insight into the Incas.

Peru is unequalled in South America for its archaeological wealth and many archaeologists find Peru's ancient sites and cultures as exciting as those of Mexico, Egypt or the Mediterranean. For many travellers, learning about and visiting these centuries-old ruins is one of the highlights of their journey and even those with little interest in archaeology usually enjoy visiting one or two of the major sites. With this in mind, this section is written as a brief overview of archaeology in Peru.

With the lack of written records, one of the main sources of information for archaeologists has been the realistic and expressive decorations found on the ceramics, textiles and other artefacts of Peru's pre-Columbian inhabitants. These relics often depict everyday life in some detail and so it is well worth your while to inspect many of these artefacts in Peru's museums. One of the best ways of visualising the overall cultural chronology is to visit *The National Museum of Anthropology & Archaeology* in Lima, where the exhibits are labelled and displayed chronologically.

Note that the sites and cultures italicised below are described in greater detail in the travel section of the book. The traveller especially interested in archaeology should check the bibliography in the Books & Bookshops section.

The Stone Age

Human beings are relatively recent arrivals in the New World. Until 1986 it was thought that they spread throughout the Americas after migrating across the Bering Strait some 20,000 years ago. In 1986, however, there was a report in the British journal *Nature* claiming the discovery of human fossils in Brazil which date back 32,000 years – still recent compared to the Old World but nevertheless a major discovery if it is substantiated. All human remains found in the Americas belong to *Homo sapiens*; there is no evidence of the presence of more primitive hominids such as are known in the Old World.

The first inhabitants of Peru were nomadic hunter/gatherers who roamed the country in loose-knit bands. They hunted fearsome animals which are long since extinct, such as giant sloths, sabre-toothed tigers and mastodons. They lived

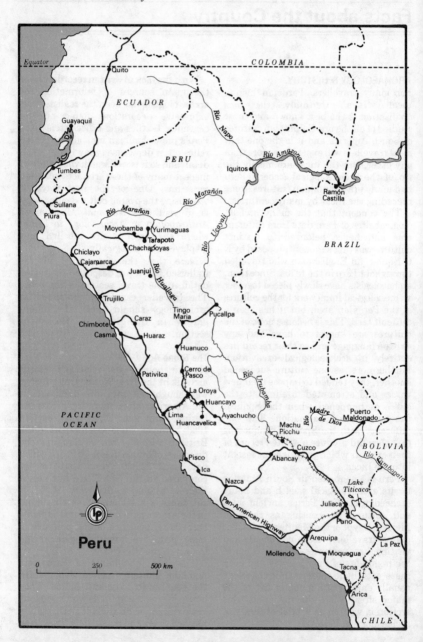

Peru

in caves and one of the oldest known of these is at Pikimachay in the Department of Ayacucho. Human remains here have been dated as 10,000 to 20,000 years old.

From the earliest arrivals until about 4000 BC, cultural development consisted mainly of improving stone implements for hunting. People knew how to make fires, wore animal skins and made simple tools and weapons from stone and bone. As their prey became extinct they began hunting animals we know today – such as deer, vicuña, guanaco and llamas. Hunting scenes were recorded in cave paintings at Lauricocha near Huánuco, and Toquepala near Tacna.

Early Agriculture

About 4000 BC, people began planting seeds and learning how to improve crops by simple horticultural methods such as weeding. In those days, the coastal strip was wetter than today's desert and a number of small settlements were established, thus changing the status of the people from nomadic hunter/gatherers to settled agriculturalists and fishermen. Several of these settlements have been excavated, with the garbage mounds yielding the best information about life at that time. Although these places can be visited, there are no on-site museums or explanations and so going to look at ancient garbage mounds is an activity with little to recommend it unless you're a professional archaeologist.

Some of the best known sites are Huaca Prieta in the Chicama valley near Trujillo, Chilca and Asia, south of Lima. Chilca was inhabited about 4000 BC and the other two sites about 2000 BC. The inhabitants fished with nets or with bone hooks and collected seafood such as crabs and sea urchins. Various crops were cultivated including cotton which appeared early on (about 3000 BC) as well as chili peppers, beans, squashes and, about 1400 BC, corn. The cotton was used to make clothing, mainly with the simple techniques of twining and later by weaving. The people lived in primitive one-room dwellings, which were lined with stone in Huaca Prieta, or they had branch or reed huts as in Asia. Ceramics and metalwork were still unknown although jewellery made of bone, shell, etc was used.

Roughly contemporary with these coastal settlements was the enigmatic site of *Kotosh* near *Huánuco* – one of the earliest ruins in highland Peru. Little is known about the people who lived here, but their buildings were the most developed for that period, and the pottery fragments found here predate those found in other parts of Peru by several hundred years.

Early Formative Period

This period extends from roughly 1250 BC to 850 BC and is known mainly from remains found in the Virú Valley and Guañape area, about 50 km south of Trujillo on the north coast. During this time, ceramics developed from rude undecorated pots to sculpted, incised and simply coloured pots of high quality. Weaving, fishing and horticulture also improved and simple funerary offerings have been found.

Chavín Horizon

This period is named after the site of *Chavín de Huantar*, 40 km east of Huaraz in the Department of Ancash. It is also known as the middle formative period and lasted from about 850 BC until 300 BC. It is termed a 'horizon' because its artistic and religious influences can be seen in several contemporary cultures, including the Cupisnique ceramics of the *Lambayeque* region (north of Trujillo) and the early pottery of *Paracas Cavernas* (south of Lima). Thus the Chavín influence was felt in a huge area covering most of the northern two-thirds of Peru's highlands and coast. The salient feature of the Chavín influence is the repeated representation of a stylised jaguar, hence the Chavín is often termed a jaguar-worshipping cult. Most importantly, this period represents the greatest early development in weaving, pottery, agriculture, religion and architecture – in a word, culture. Many archaeologists see the Chavín Horizon as the most important cultural development of pre-Columbian Peru.

Late Formative Period

Around 300 BC the Chavín style suddenly and inexplicably disappeared and there was little unity in the cultures found in Peru over the next 500 years. Although none of these cultures were individually outstanding or widespread, several were locally important. The best known are the Salinar culture of the Chicama Valley area near Trujillo and the *Paracas Necropolis* south of Lima. The Salinar ceramics show advanced firing techniques, whilst the textiles of the Paracas Necropolis are markedly improved and different from the earlier Paracas Cavernas; these textiles are considered the finest pre-Columbian textiles to have been produced anywhere in the Americas.

Regional Development

This period lasted from about 100 AD to 700 AD and as its name suggests, it was not marked by any single unifying horizon but by local development in several regions. Pottery, metalwork and weavings reached a pinnacle of technological development throughout Peru and hence this period is often referred to as either the 'Florescent' or 'Classic'.

Two distinct cultures of this period are particularly noted for their exceptional pottery; the *Moche* from the *Trujillo* area and the *Nazca* people from the south coast. These cultures recorded their ways of life in intricate detail on their ceramics and so provide archaeologists with an invaluable reference tool. Many of Peru's major museums have good collections of Nazca and Moche pottery. These two

cultures also left us with some interesting sites which are worth visiting. The Moche built massive pyramids such as the *Temples of the Sun and Moon* near Trujillo and the Nazca made their enigmatic giant petroglyphs in the desert. These last are known as the *Nazca Lines* and are best appreciated from the air in one of the many overflights in small airplanes available in the town of Nazca.

Other cultures of importance during this period include the Lima culture with its major site at *Pachacamac*, 30 km south of Lima. There was also the Recuay culture whose ceramics can be seen in the regional museum at *Huaraz* and the *Cajamarca, Kuelap*, Gallinazo and Tiahuanaco cultures.

The Wari Empire

The ruin of the highland city of *Wari* (also Huari) is found about 25 km north of *Ayacucho*. Wari was the capital of the first expansionist empire known in the Andes. Unlike the earlier Chavín Horizon, expansion was not limited to the diffusion of artistic and religious influence. The Wari were vigorous military conquerors and they built and maintained important outposts throughout much of Peru. These included *Piquillacta* near Cuzco, *Cajamarquilla* near Lima, *Wilkawain* near Huaraz, Wariwillka near Huancayo, Wiracochapampa near Huamachuco and Los Paredones near Cajamarca. The Wari culture was the first strongly militaristic and urban culture of Peru. Also, it was influenced by the Tiahuanaco religion from the Lake Titicaca region.

The Wari attempted to subdue the cultures they conquered by enforcing their own values and suppressing regional self-expression and local oral traditions. Thus from about 700 to 1100 AD, Wari influence is noted in the art, technology and architecture of most areas in Peru. More significantly, from an archaeologist's point of view, any local oral traditions which may have existed were forbidden by the conquerors and slowly forgotten. With no written language and no oral traditions, archaeologists must rely entirely on the examination of excavated artefacts to gain an idea of what life was like in the early Peruvian cultures. The Wari too, in their turn, were overthrown and their culture obliterated.

The Regional States
Because of their cultural dominance and oppression, it is not surprising that the Wari were generally not welcomed, despite their improvements in urban development and organisation. By about 1100 AD they had been overthrown, not by a new conquering force but by individual groups in their local areas. During the next three or four centuries these separate regional states thrived. The best known of these is the *Chimu* kingdom in the *Trujillo* area. Their capital was the huge adobe city of *Chan Chan* which is often referred to as the largest adobe city in the world. Chan Chan can easily be visited from Trujillo and is thoroughly described in that section.

Roughly contemporary with the Chimu was the Chachapoyas culture of the Utcubamba River basin in the Department of Amazonas. They left us with *Kuelap*, one of the most mysterious highland ruins which is reasonably accessible to the traveller (by 'reasonably' I mean half a day's walk from the nearest dirt road). Also contemporary with the Chimu were the Chancay people from the Chancay valley just north of Lima. The best collection of Chancay artefacts is at the excellent *Amano Museum* in Lima. Further south there was the Ica-Chincha culture whose artefacts can be seen in the *Ica Regional Museum*. There were also several small altiplano tribes who lived near Lake Titicaca and were frequently at war with one another. They left us with impressive, circular funerary towers dotting the bleak landscape – the best are to be seen at *Sillustani*. There were also

the Chanka who lived in the Ayacucho-Apurímac area, and, of course, there was the Kingdom of Cuzco which was the predecessor of the greatest pre-Columbian empire on the continent.

The Inca Empire
The Inca Empire, for all its greatness, existed for barely a century. Prior to 1430 the Incas, whose emperor was believed to have descended from the sun, ruled over only the valley of *Cuzco*. The Cuzqueños were at war with the Chankas for some time and the hostilities culminated in the 1430s with a major victory for the Cuzqueños. This marked the beginning of a remarkably rapid military expansion. The Inca Empire, known as Tahuantinsuyo (the four corners), conquered and incorporated the cultures mentioned in the preceding section as well as most of the cultures in the area stretching from southern Colombia to central Chile. As with the Wari Empire before them, the Incas imposed their way of life onto the peoples they conquered. Thus when the Spanish arrived, most of the Andean area had been thoroughly homogenised by Inca rule.

The Spanish Conquest
After Columbus' first landfall in 1492, the Spanish rapidly conquered the Caribbean islands and the Aztec and Mayan cultures of Mexico and Central America. By the 1520s, the conquistadors were ready to turn their attentions to the South American continent. In 1522 Pascual de Andagoya sailed as far as the San Juan River in Colombia. Two years later Francisco Pizarro headed south but was unable to reach even the San Juan. In November 1526, Pizarro again headed south, and by 1528 he had explored as far as the Santa River in Peru. He noted several coastal Inca settlements, became aware of the richness of the Inca Empire and returned to Spain to raise money and recruit men for the conquest. Pizarro's third expedition south left Panama in late 1530. He landed

on the Ecuadorean coast and began to march overland towards Peru. Finally, in September 1532, Pizarro founded the first Spanish town in Peru – San Miguel de Piura. Then he marched inland into the heart of the Inca Empire. In November 1532, he reached *Cajamarca*, captured the Inca emperor, Atahualpa, and thus effectively put to an end the Inca Empire.

Colonial Peru

The Inca capital of Cuzco was of little use to the Spaniards who were a sea-faring people and needed a coastal capital to maintain communication with Spain. Accordingly, Pizarro founded Lima in 1535 and this became the capital of the Viceroyalty of Peru, as the colony was named. The next three decades were a period of turmoil with the Incas still fighting against their conquerors and the conquistadors fighting among themselves

The Mercenary Friars operated workshops and often mistreated the Indians (Waman Puma)

for control of the rich colony. Almagro was assassinated in 1538 and Pizarro suffered the same fate three years later. Manco Inca tried to regain control of the highlands and was almost successful in 1536, but by 1539 he had retreated to Vilcabamba in the jungle where he was killed in 1544. Succeeding Incas were less rebellious than Manco Inca until the rebellion of Tupac Amaru in 1572. He was defeated and executed by the Spaniards.

The next two centuries were relatively peaceful. Lima became the major political, social and commercial centre of the Andean nations. Cuzco became a backwater and its main mark on the colonial period was in the development of the 'Cuzqueño School of Art' resulting from a unique blend of Spanish and highland Indian influences. Cuzqueño canvases can be admired today in Lima's museums as well as the many colonial churches which were built in Lima and the highlands during the 17th and 18th centuries.

The rulers of the colony were the Spanish-born viceroys appointed by the Spanish crown. Immigrants from Spain had the most prestigious positions whilst Spaniards born in the colony were generally less important. In this way the Spanish crown was able to better control its colonies. *Mestizos* or those of mixed Indian-Spanish stock, came still further down the social scale and lowest of all were the Indians themselves who were exploited and treated as serfs, at best, and often as expendable slaves. This led to an Indian uprising in 1780 under the self-styled Inca, Tupac Amaru II. The uprising was quelled and its leaders cruelly executed.

Independence

By the early 19th century, the inhabitants of Spain's Latin American colonies were dissatisfied with the lack of freedom and high taxation imposed upon them by Spain. Not only Peru, but the entire continent was ripe for revolt and independence. For Peru the change came from two directions. José de San Martín liberated Argentina and Chile, and in 1821 entered Lima. Meanwhile, Simón Bolívar had freed Venezuela and Colombia and in 1822 sent Field Marshall Sucre to defeat the Ecuadorian Royalists at the battle of Pichincha. San Martín and Bolívar met in Guayaquil in a private meeting whose events still remain unknown. As a result of this meeting, San Martín left Latin America to live in France and Bolívar and Sucre continued with the liberation of Peru. The two decisive battles of Peruvian independence were fought in 1824 at Junín on 6 August and Ayacucho on 9 December. A few royalists held out in the Real Felipe fortress near Lima until 22 January 1826, but Peru was essentially independent.

As an independent state, Peru had a brief war with Spain in 1866, which Peru won, and a longer war with Chile from 1879 to 1883, which Peru lost. The war was over the nitrate rich areas of the northern Atacama desert and as a result of the war, Chile annexed a large portion of coastal southern Peru. The area around Tacna was returned in 1929. Peru went to war with Ecuador over a border dispute in 1941. A treaty drawn up at Rio de Janeiro in 1942 gave Peru jurisdiction over what is now the northern sections of the Departments of San Martín and Loreto, but Ecuador disputes this border and armed skirmishes occur between the two countries every few years.

The government for the most part has been one of military coups and dictatorships with shorter periods of civilian rule. The most recent of these began in 1980 with the election of President Belaúnde Terry. He was defeated in the 1985 elections by Alán García Pérez. Since February 1986, Peru has been under martial law in an attempt to eradicate the Maoist *Sendero Luminoso* guerrilla movement. This basically means that there is a curfew in Lima from 1 am to 5 am but otherwise few, if any, conse-

quences are felt by the traveller. Peru is generally a safe country to travel in, as it has been for many years.

Visiting Archaeological Sites

Visiting Peru without seeing the Inca ruins in the Cuzco area (especially Machu Picchu) is a bit like visiting Egypt without seeing the Pyramids. If you're interested in more than just the Inca Empire, however, I recommend the following. Trujillo is an excellent base for seeing Chan Chan (the huge adobe capital of the Chimu) as well as Moche pyramids and good museums. If you have any spare time in Huaraz, the 2500-year-old ruins of the Chavín are worth a day trip. The artefacts of Paracas are best seen in museums and the Nazca Lines can only be appreciated properly from the air. The funerary towers at Sillustani, near Lake Titicaca, are worth seeing if you have a spare day in Puno. Kuelap is great if you have the energy to go to such a remote area. Other sites, whilst worthwhile if you are particularly interested in archaeology or if you have plenty of time in Peru, don't offer as many rewards as do the ones I've mentioned.

PEOPLE

Peru's population is approaching 20 million and almost half of it is concentrated in the narrow coastal desert. Lima alone has a population of almost six million and the second and third cities of Peru, Arequipa and Trujillo, are also both in the coastal region and have populations of about 750,000 each.

About half of the population is found in the highlands and these people are, for the most part, rural Indians or mestizos who practice subsistence agriculture. There are few large cities in the highlands. The highlanders prefer to be called *campesinos* (country-people or peasants) rather than the term Indians, which is considered to be insulting. Because of the very poor standard of living in the highlands, many campesinos have migrated to the coast. This contributes to an increasing overpopulation problem, and their lot rarely improves.

Over 60% of Peru lies in the Amazon Basin east of the Andes. This region is slowly becoming colonised but as yet only 5% of the population lives there.

About half the population is Indian and a further third is mestizo. About 12% is white and 5% is black. Most of the blacks live on the coast and a few in the Amazon region. There is a small Asian population and Chinese restaurants (called *chifas*) are found throughout Peru.

GEOGRAPHY

Peru covers 1,285,215 square km and is the third largest country in South America. It is more than five times as large as the United Kingdom. It is bounded on the north by Ecuador and Colombia, to the east by Brazil and Bolivia, to the south by Chile, and to the west by the Pacific Ocean. It lies entirely within the tropics with its northernmost point being only a few km away from the equator and its southernmost point just over 18° south.

Geographically, Peru is divided into three major regions – a narrow coastal belt separated from the Amazon rain forest by a wide mountain range. The narrow coastal strip is mainly desert and at the southern end it merges into the Atacama desert, one of the driest places on earth. The extreme northern end, near Ecuador, is mangrove swamp. This coastal desert contains Peru's major cities and its best highway, the Pan-

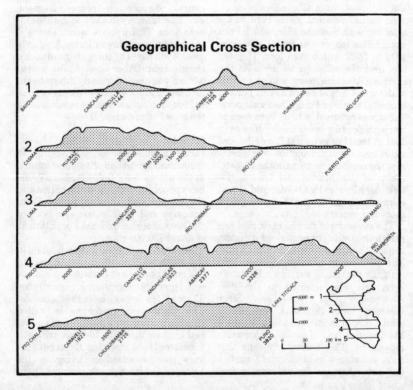

Geographical Cross Section

American, which runs the entire length of Peru and is asphalted for most of the way. The desert is irrigated in places by rivers running down the western slopes of the Andes; about 40 oases are formed in this way and they are agricultural centres.

The Andes mountains, the second greatest mountain chain in the world after the Himalaya, jut rapidly up from the coast. Heights of 6000 metres are reached just 100 km inland. The Andes are a young range still in the process of being uplifted as the Nazca plate (under the Pacific) slides under the South American plate. The Andes don't stop at the coast; 100 km offshore there is an ocean trench which is as deep as the Andes are high. Huascarán, 6768 metres above sea level, is Peru's highest mountain and the highest mountain anywhere within the tropical world. Most of Peru's Andes lie between 3000 and 4000 metres and support half the population. It is a rugged and difficult landscape with jagged ranges separated by extremely deep and vertiginous canyons. Although the roads are often in terrible condition, the traveller is rewarded by spectacular scenery.

The eastern slopes of the Andes are less precipitous, though no less rugged. They receive much more rainfall than the dry western slopes and so are clothed in a mantle of green cloud forest. As elevation is lost, the cloud forest becomes the rain forest of the Amazon Basin. This region has been penetrated by few roads and those which do exist only go in for a short distance. The traveller wishing to continue through the Amazon Basin to Colombia or Brazil must do so by river or air.

RELIGION

In common with that of most Latin American countries, the religion is predominantly Roman Catholic. Some of the older towns have splendid colonial Catholic churches. Although churches of other faiths can be found, they form only a small minority. The Indians, while outwardly Roman Catholic, tend to blend Catholicism with their traditional beliefs.

FESTIVALS & HOLIDAYS

Many of the major festivals are oriented to the Roman Catholic liturgical calendar. These are often celebrated with great pageantry, especially in highland Indian villages where the Catholic feast day may well be linked with some traditional agricultural festival (such as spring or harvest) and be the excuse for a traditional Indian fiesta with much drinking, dancing, rituals and processions. Other holidays are of historical or political interest, for example National Independence on 28-29 July. On the days of the major holidays, banks, offices and other services are closed and transportation tends to be very crowded, so book ahead if possible.

The following list describes the major holidays, but they may well be celebrated for several days around the actual date. Those marked by an asterisk * are official public holidays when banks, etc are closed; others are more local holidays.

1 January*
  New Year's Day
2 February
  Candlemas or the Virgin of Candelaria – especially in the highlands.
February-March
  Carnaval – usually held on the last few days before Lent, the Carnival is often celebrated with water fights, so be warned. It's a particularly popular feast in the highlands with the Carnaval de Abancay being one of the biggest.
March-April*
  Easter – Maundy Thursday afternoon and all of Good Friday are public holidays. Holy Week is celebrated with spectacular religious processions almost every day with Ayacucho being recognised as having the best in Peru. Cuzco is also good for Easter processions.

Making beer by chewing grain and spitting it into a pottery vat for fermentation

1 May*
Labour Day

June
Corpus Christi – the ninth Thursday after Easter. The processions in Cuzco are especially dramatic.

24 June
Inti Raymi – also St John the Baptist. Inti Raymi celebrates the winter solstice and is the greatest of the Inca festivals. It is certainly the spectacle of the year in Cuzco and attracts many thousands of Peruvian and foreign visitors. Although it is getting commercialised, it is still worth seeing the street dances, parades and the pageant held in Sacsayhuaman.

29 June*
St Peter and St Paul

16 July
Virgin of Carmen – This is mainly celebrated in the southern Sierra, with Paucartambo and Pisac near Cuzco and Pucara near Lake Titicaca being especially important.

28 July*
Peru's Independence – This is celebrated throughout the country but in the southern Sierra can begin three days ahead with the feast of St James on 25 July.

30 August*
St Rose – Patron saint of Lima and of the Americas. Major processions in Lima.

8 October*
Battle of Angamos

18 October

Lord of the Miracles – Celebrated with major religious processions in Lima; people wear purple.

1 November*

All Saint's Day – This is an official public holiday.

2 November

All Soul's Day – Celebrated with gifts of food, drink and flowers being taken to family graves, especially colourful in the Sierra. The food and drink is consumed and the atmosphere is festive rather than sombre.

5 November

Puno Day – Spectacular costumes and street dancing in Puno.

8 December*

Feast of the Immaculate Conception

25 December*

Christmas Day

There are local fiestas and festivals held somewhere in Peru every week. Many are mentioned in the individual town descriptions.

LANGUAGE

For the traveller, Spanish is the main language. In the highlands, most Indians are bilingual, with Quechua being their preferred language in most areas except around Lake Titicaca where Aymara is spoken. For most Indians, Spanish is a second tongue and between one and two million are estimated not to speak Spanish at all. These people live in very remote areas and it is rare for the traveller to encounter Indians who speak no Spanish at all. Although English is understood in the best hotels, airline offices and tourist agencies, it is of little use elsewhere.

If you don't speak Spanish, take heart. It is an easy language to learn. Courses are available in Lima (see Lima section) or you can study books, records and tapes while you are still at home and planning your trip. These study aids are often available for free from many public libraries or you might want to consider taking an evening or college course. Once you have learned the basics, you'll find that you'll be able to talk with people from all over Latin America because – apart from Brazil which is Portuguese-speaking – most of the countries use Spanish.

Spanish is easy to learn for several reasons. First, it uses Roman script. Secondly, with few exceptions, it is spoken as it is written and vice versa. Imagine trying to explain to someone learning English that there are seven different ways of pronouncing 'ough'. This isn't a problem in Spanish. Thirdly, many words are so similar to English that you can figure them out. *Instituto Geográfico Nacional* means the National Geographical Institute, for example.

Even if you don't have time to take a Spanish course, at least bring a phrase book and dictionary. Don't dispense with the dictionary, because the phrase book limits you to asking where the bus station is and won't help you translate the local newspaper. My favourite dictionary, incidentally, is the paperback *University of Chicago Spanish-English, English-Spanish Dictionary*. It's inexpensive, small enough to travel with, and yet has

many more entries than most pocket dictionaries. It also contains words used in Latin America but not in Spain.

Although the Spanish alphabet looks like the English one, it is in fact different. 'Ch' is considered a separate letter, for example, so *champú* (which simply means 'shampoo') will be listed in a dictionary after all the words beginning with just 'c'. Similarly, 'll' is a separate letter, so a *llama* is listed after all the words beginning with a single 'l'. The letter 'ñ' is listed after the ordinary 'n'. Vowels with an accent are accented for stress and are not considered separate letters.

Pronunciation is generally more straightforward than it is in English. If you say a word the way it looks like it should be said, the chances are that it will be close enough to be understood. You will get better with practice of course. A few notable exceptions are 'll' which is always pronounced 'y' as in 'yacht', the 'j' which is always pronounced 'h' as in 'happy', and the 'h' which isn't pronounced at all. Thus the phrase *hojas en la calle* (leaves in the street) would be pronounced 'o-has en la ka-yea'. Finally, the letter 'ñ' is pronounced as the 'ny' sound in 'canyon'.

Word order in Spanish is generally similar to English sentence construction with one notable exception. Adjectives follow the nouns they qualify instead of preceding them as they do in English. Thus 'the white house' becomes *la casa blanca*. Confused? Just remember that the most important phrase in Spanish is *Una cerveza helada, por favor*.

Facts for the Visitor

VISAS & DOCUMENTS

Many travellers entering Peru as tourists do not require visas. Notable exceptions are Australians, New Zealanders, French, Chileans, Venezuelans, and citizens of most communist, African and Asian countries, except Japan. Travellers from those countries can normally obtain the required visas from the capital cities of neighbouring countries if they are travelling around South America. Alternatively, apply for one at the Peruvian embassy at home before you leave.

Your passport should be valid for six months or more. A tourist card is given to everybody on arrival in Peru. There is no charge for this card, but don't lose it as you will need it for stay extensions, passport checks, and leaving the country. If you should lose it, you can get another at the immigration office in Lima and other major cities or at the exit point from the country. It is better to get a new tourist card in a major city because the immigration officials hassle you if you try to exit without one and a bribe is sometimes necessary to obtain one when leaving the country.

On arrival you are normally asked how long you want to stay, and if you're lucky and the duty officer is in a good mood, you may get the maximum of 90 days. It depends on your nationality. I can usually get 90 days with my British passport but my American wife can only get 60. Don't ask me why. Some nationalities get even less. You are given an identical stamp in both your passport and tourist card which indicates how long you can stay. If you have a ticket out of the country you can usually get enough days to last until you leave, but make sure you show the duty officer your ticket as soon as you start dealing with him, and before your passport is stamped as they don't want to change it afterwards.

In addition to your passport and tourist card, you officially need a ticket out of the country but evidence of sufficient funds for your stay is not normally required. It's rare to be asked for an exit ticket, unless you're one of those travellers that requires a visa in which case you may be asked to show it. If you buy an airline ticket for use as an exit ticket it can normally be refunded if you don't want to use it. Alternatively, buy an MCO (Miscellaneous Charges Order) from an airline belonging to IATA (International Air Transport Association). This can be used for any flight on an IATA airline or it can be refunded if it hasn't expired. Bus tickets can be bought at land borders but these are usually expensive and are not transferable or refundable. If you don't have an exit ticket it's best to not worry about it. You probably won't be asked to show one anyway.

You should always carry your passport when you are out of your hotel (or at least a photocopy of the pages with your photo and passport number) and your tourist card as there are occasional document checks on public transport – you can be arrested if you don't have identification. Another document you can use for identification is a drivers' licence (as long as it is of the type with a photo on it) or any similar official looking document that has a recent photo of you. If you are travelling between towns, you should always carry your passport because there are passport controls at the entrances and exits of most major towns, whether you arrive by bus, taxi, air, rail or boat.

Other Paperwork

International vaccination certificates are not required by law, but vaccinations are advisable. See the Health section.

Student cards are very useful indeed. They save you money at most archaeological sites, museums, etc, and occasionally in youth hostels or even for buying airline tickets. Entrance charge discounts of 50% are common. It has to be a bona fide card because almost everyone knows what the card is supposed to look like and it's difficult to get away with anything that doesn't have your photograph and an official looking seal from the school or college. They check expiry dates too.

MONEY

Until the end of 1985, the Peruvian currency was the sol, valued at S/17,300 to the US dollar. In 1986 a new currency was introduced by the simple (and, in Latin America, common) expedient of slashing the last three digits. The new currency is the Inti, worth I/17.30 to the US dollar when it was introduced. It is interesting to note that *sol* is the Spanish word for 'sun' and that *inti* means the same thing in Quechua, the Andean Indian dialect.

Cash in both soles and intis is circulating, but as the sol notes become worn out, intis will take over and by the late 1980s intis will be used exclusively. Inevitably, prices will be quoted in both currencies for some time, which will add to the traveller's confusion. Just remember that one inti is worth 1000 soles.

To make the soles to intis transfer easier to deal with, bills of equal value are the same colour and size. Thus the 10,000 sol bill is blue, as is the 10 inti bill which is worth exactly the same. The following bills are circulating: a small multicoloured 500 sol bill, and larger bills worth 1000 soles (green), 5000 soles (maroon), 10,000 soles or 10 intis (blue), 50,000 soles (orange) and 100 intis (brown). One, 5 and 50 inti bills of the appropriate colours are planned, as well as new bills of 200 and 500 intis.

The inti is divided into 100 centimos. There are coins of 5, 10 and 50 centimos which look about the same as the coins of 50, 100 and 500 soles – they are interchangeable. There is also a new 1 inti coin.

The Peruvian currency is frequently devalued. When I first visited Peru in early 1982, I received about 500 soles for the US dollar. Four years later, the figure was 17,300 soles! Since President Alan García came into office in mid-1985, the currency has stabilized somewhat and has been pegged at S/17,300 for the last months of 1985 and at the equivalent I/17.30 for the first few months of 1986. It has dropped only slightly since then and the most recent exchange is I/17.45 to the US dollar. This slow rate of devaluation is

very unusual for Latin American currencies and I expect the bubble to burst sooner or later. As it is unlikely that this financial stability will continue, all prices in this book will be quoted in US dollars.

The easiest currency to exchange is the US dollar. Although hard currencies such as other dollars, pounds sterling, French and Swiss francs and German marks are exchangeable in the main cities, the US dollar is always preferable and sometimes the only currency you can change easily in the smaller towns. It is best to exchange as much money as you think you'll need in the major cities because exchange facilities may be worse or non-existent elsewhere.

There are various rates of exchange. The 'official' exchange is currently at I/14.50 and the 'financial' rate is I/17.45. Obviously, you want to change at the higher financial rate, which is generally available for foreign exchange – but some banks will only give the official rate. So shop around. The financial rate is used for most foreign exchange transactions within Peru whilst the official rate is supposed to be used for international transactions, so if you pay for something with a foreign credit card, you'll be receiving the lower rate. The system can work to your advantage in some cases, however. For example, if you have to buy an international airline ticket it will be priced in dollars which you can pay for in intis at the lower official rate after exchanging your dollars at the higher financial rate. This is a relatively recent situation and, as so often happens with Peruvian currency exchange rules, could change at any time. The best source of information is your fellow traveller who has been there for a while.

Money can be changed in banks, *casas de cambio* (exchange houses) or with street changers. First class hotels and restaurants will also accept dollars. The best place to change varies and there are no hard and fast rules. In the early 1980s the *Banco de la Nación* was the best place

to change money but for the last couple of years only a few branches such as the one at Lima airport provided good service. Other branches varied – some changed at the unfavourable official rate or not at all. Because this is the country's major bank, and because the future situation may revert to what it used to be, I have marked this bank on the city maps. Recently, I have found that the *Banco de Crédito* has been consistently giving the best rates, especially for travellers' cheques which are often exchanged at a considerably lower rate elsewhere. Equally good rates for cash can be obtained from casas de cambio but their rate for travellers' cheques is lower. Their advantage is longer business hours. Street changers do not give a better rate and are definitely not worth the hassle except on the borders where they may be all that is available. If you do change with street changers, count your money very carefully before handing over the dollars – not all of the street changers are honest.

Banking hours are erratic. During the summer (January to March) banks are open only from 8.30 to 11.30 am. During the rest of the year they are open longer – sometimes into the afternoon but you can't count on it. Expect long lines and delays in banks and try and go fairly early in the morning for the most efficient service. Casas de cambio are often open from 9 am to 6 pm, or later in tourist areas such as Cuzco, but tend to close for a couple of hours at lunchtime.

There is an advantage to carrying cash dollars. During the summer of 1985, travellers' cheques were getting about 20% less than cash. Recently travellers' cheques were being changed at a loss of about 3% in most places, although the *Banco de Crédito* was a notable exception. Because travellers' cheques are refundable in the event of theft or loss, it is worth carrying at least some of your money in this form, although a certain amount of cash is always useful. Most major brands of travellers' cheques are accepted but I definitely do not recommend using Citibank cheques. They took over a year to reimburse me for US$200 in stolen cheques and had the gall to charge me about US$20 for 'handling'. American Express are much easier to deal with.

If you run out of money, it is a simple matter to have more sent to you, assuming that you have someone at home kind enough to send you money. A bank transfer is most quickly done by telex, although this will take at least three days. All you need to do is pick a Peruvian bank which will co-operate with your bank at home and telex your family, friend or bank manager to deposit the money in your name at the bank of your choice. If you use the *Banco de Crédito* you can receive your money in the currency of your choice (US dollars!). You should check with them first – I found that they provided me with this service and charged only 0.6% commission when I had money sent from home.

If you change more money than necessary, you can buy back dollars at a slight loss when leaving the country. The loss depends on fluctuations of the dollar; it's usually a few per cent. There are money changers working the major land borders whenever they are open, and the airport in Lima has a *Banco de la Nación* open for all international departures. Try not to get left with a lot of excess cash though, because it is not unheard of for Peruvian currency to be frozen and then the banks won't buy back intis. This happens for a few days every couple of years.

COSTS

Costs in Peru are low. If anything, the costs of travel basics such as hotels, meals and transportation have fallen in the 1980s. All good things come to an end, however, and with the recent exchange freeze on the inti I began detecting a slow price increase just before I left. I've used US dollars in all my price quotes because this is much more stable than the unpredictable Peruvian currency.

If you're on a very tight budget, you'll find that you can get by on the classic bare bones budget of US$5 per day, but that means staying in the most basic of hotels and travelling very slowly. Most budget travellers spend closer to an average of US$10 per day mainly because of the large distances that have to be covered to properly visit Peru.

If you can afford to spend a little more, however, you'll probably enjoy yourself more. The luxury of a simple room with a private hot shower and a table and chair to write letters home can be had for as little as US$2 or US$3 per person if you know where to go – this book will show you where. Saving time and energy by flying back from a remote destination which took you several days of land travel to reach is also recommended if you can afford a bit more.

Travelling hard, eating well, staying in rooms with a private bath, taking an occasional flight, seeing a movie once in a while, and drinking a couple of beers with dinner most nights sounds expensive – almost decadent – to the 'purist' budget traveller. I did that for several months whilst researching this book, and averaged US$17 a day. Even if you demand the best available, in most parts of Peru it will cost much less than wherever home may be.

I sometimes meet travellers who spend most of their time worrying how to make every penny stretch further. It seems to me that they spend more time looking at their finances than looking at the places they're visiting. Of course, many travellers are on a grand tour of South America and want to make their money last, but you can get so burned out on squalid hotels and bad food that the grand tour becomes an endurance test. Six months travelling comfortably and enjoyably can be more rewarding than a full year of strain and sacrifice.

WORKING

Officially, you need a work visa to work in Peru. You can, however, get a job teaching English in language schools, usually in Lima. They occasionally advertise for teachers in the newspapers, including the English language weekly, *The Lima Times*. They expect you to be a native English speaker and the pay is usually abysmal. *Fermath Ingles* at Tudela y Varela 215, Miraflores, pay just over a dollar an hour and that's above average. Another place is *TRANSLEX* on the Paseo de Republica in Miraflores. They pay a little more and have quite a high standard. If, in addition to speaking English like a native, you actually have a *bona fide* teaching credential, so much the better. Various American and British Schools will sometimes hire teachers of maths, biology and other subjects and often help you get a work visa if you want to stay on. They also pay much better than the language schools.

CLIMATE

Peru's climate can be divided into two seasons – wet and dry – though the weather varies greatly depending on the geographical region.

The desert coast is, as you'd expect it to be, arid. During their summer (late December to early April) the sky is often clear and the weather tends to be hot and sticky. This is the time Peruvians go to the beach. During the rest of the year the grey coastal mist known as the *garua* moves in and the sun is rarely seen. I find the weather on the coast rather depressing during most of the year. It doesn't feel like the tropics!

As you go inland, you soon rise above the coastal mist. Nazca, for example, is some 60 km inland and 600 metres above sea level, high enough to avoid the *garua* and thus hot and sunny for most of the year. Generally, the western slopes of the Andes have weather like that of Nazca.

As you get into the Andes proper, you begin experiencing the wet and dry seasons. If you're interested in trekking or hiking the Inca Trail to Machu Picchu, you'll probably want to go in the dry season which is from May to September. Although at that altitude it can be cold at night, with occasional freezing temperatures in Cuzco (3326 metres or 10,917 feet), the dry weather provides beautiful sunshine during the day. Because of this, the dry season in the Andes is known as the summer and the warmer wet season is called the winter. This leads to general confusion – when it's the summer on the coast it's the winter in the highlands and vice versa. Confused? It gets even worse when you listen to a Limeño (inhabitant of Lima) arguing with a Serrano (sierra or mountain dweller) about whether it's summer or winter. More important is whether it is the wet or dry season. The wet season in the mountains is from October to May but it usually doesn't get really wet until late January. But you can never tell for sure until you go!

As you head down the eastern slopes of the Andes it gets wetter. The driest months are the same as in the highlands, but the wet season tends to be more pronounced. The wettest months are January until April and during these months roads on the eastern slopes of the Andes are often closed due to landslides or flooding. A similar weather pattern exists in the Amazon lowlands.

HEALTH

It's true that most people travelling for any length of time in South America are likely to have an occasional mild stomach upset. It's also true that, if you take the appropriate precautions before, during, and after your trip, it's unlikely that you will become seriously ill. In six years of travelling in Latin America, I'm happy to report that I've picked up no major illnesses.

Vaccinations

Vaccinations are the most important of your pre-departure health preparations. Although the Peruvian authorities do not, at present, require anyone to have an up-to-date international vaccination card to enter the country, you are strongly advised to read the following list and receive the ones appropriate for your trip. Pregnant women should consult with their doctor before taking these vaccinations.

Yellow Fever vaccination is very important if you are planning a trip to the eastern slopes of the Andes or the Amazon basin, but not necessary if you intend to avoid the eastern lowlands altogether. This vaccination lasts 10 years.

Typhoid vaccination consists of two injections taken four weeks apart and so you have to think ahead for this one. This vaccine makes some people feel unwell and often gives you a sore arm, so try not to schedule the last shot for the day you're packing. You should get a booster shot every three years, but this doesn't normally feel so bad.

Most people in developed countries get a diptheria-tetanus injection and oral polio vaccine whilst they are at school. You should get boosters for these every 10 years.

A cholera vaccination is only necessary if an epidemic has been declared in Latin America. Protection only lasts six months.

Smallpox was eradicated worldwide in 1978 and protection is no longer necessary.

Hepatitis

The diseases mentioned above are dangerous but relatively uncommon. A depressingly common disease is hepatitis A, which is caused by ingesting contaminated food or water. Salads, uncooked or unpeeled fruit, unboiled drinks, improperly washed utensils and dirty syringes (even in hospitals) are the worst offenders. Infection risks are minimised by using bottled drinks, washing your own salads with purified water, and paying scrupulous attention to your toilet habits.

If you get the disease you'll know it. Your skin and especially the whites of your eyes turn yellow, and you feel so tired that it literally takes all your effort to go to the bathroom. There is no cure except for bed rest. If you're lucky, you'll be on your feet in a couple of weeks. If you're not, expect to stay in bed for a couple of months. Research is currently underway to find a 100% effective prophylaxis; meanwhile you are strongly advised to get a gamma globulin shot as close to departure as possible. Although it is not 100% effective, your chances of getting hepatitis A are minimised. The shot should be repeated every six months, although some authorities recommend more frequent shots.

If you do get hepatitis A, it's not the end of the world. You may feel deathly ill but people almost never suffer from permanent ill effects. If you're on a long trip, you don't have to give up and go home. Find a hotel that has a decent restaurant and get a room which isn't two flights of stairs and three hallways away from the nearest bathroom. Arrange with the hotel staff to bring you meals and drinks as you need them, and go to bed. Chances are that you'll be fit enough to travel again within a month.

Malaria

This is another disease to think about before leaving. Malarial mosquitoes don't live above 2500 metres and so if you plan on staying in the highlands you needn't worry about them. If you plan on visiting the jungle you should purchase antimalarial pills in advance because they have to be taken from two weeks before until six weeks after your visit. Dosage and frequency of pill taking varies from brand to brand, so check this carefully. Chloroquine is recommended for short term protection. Long term use of Chloroquine can cause side effects and travellers planning a long trip into the Amazon basin should discuss this risk against the value of protection with their doctor, especially pregnant women who are at higher risk when taking antimalarials. Fansidar is now known to cause sometimes fatal side effects and use of this drug should be only under medical supervision.

Thus people who spend a great deal of time in tropical lowlands may prefer not to take anti-malarial pills, on a semi-permanent basis. In this case remember that malarial mosquitoes bite at night and you should wear long sleeved shirts and long trousers from dusk until dawn, use frequent applications of an insect repellent and sleep under a mosquito net. Sleeping under a fan is also effective; mosquitoes don't like wind. The most effective ingredient in insect repellents is diethyl-metatoluamide also known as 'Deet'. You should buy repellent with 90% or more of this ingredient; many brands, including those available in Peru, contain less than 15%, so buy it ahead of time. I find the rub on lotions are the most effective, and sprays are good for spraying

Do you eat gold? The Incas could not understand the Spaniards' greed for gold (Waman Puma)

clothes, especially at the neck, wrist, waist and ankle openings.

Other Precautions

Several other things must be thought about before leaving home. If you wear prescription glasses, make sure you have a spare pair and the prescription. The tropical sun is strong, so you may want to have a prescription pair of sunglasses made. Also buy sun-tan lotion as the lotions available in Peru are not very effective. A minimum sunblocking factor of 10 is recommended, or 15 if you are fair or burn easily. Ensure that you have an adequate supply of the prescription medicines you use on a regular basis. If you haven't had a dental examination for a long time, you should have one rather than risk a dental problem in Peru.

However fit and healthy you are, *do* take out medical insurance, preferably one with provisions for flying you home in the event of a medical emergency. Even if you don't get sick, you might be involved in an accident.

Diarrhoea

The drastic change in diet experienced by travellers means that they are often susceptible to minor stomach ailments, such as diarrhoea. After you've been in South America for a while, you tend to build up an immunity.

The major problem with diarrhoea is fluid loss leading to severe dehydration – you can actually dry out to the point of death if you go for several days without replacing the fluids you're losing. So drink plenty of liquids. Caffeine is a diuretic, so the best drinks are weak tea, mineral water and caffeine-free soft drinks. Avoid milk. If you can, fast. By giving your body plenty of fluids and no food, you can often get rid of diarrhoea naturally in about 24 to 36 hours. Rest as much as you can.

If it's important (eg just before a flight or journey that has to be done), you can stop the symptoms of diarrhoea by taking

Lomotil or Imodium. These pills will not cure you however, and it is likely that your diarrhoea will recur after the drug wears off. Rest, fast and drink plenty of fluids.

Dysentery

If your diarrhoea continues for several days and is accompanied by nausea, severe abdominal pain and fever, and if you find blood in your stool, it's likely that you have contracted dysentery. Although many travellers suffer from an occasional bout of diarrhoea, dysentery is fortunately not very common. There are two types: amoebic and bacillary. It is not always obvious which kind you have and if you contract dysentery, you are recommended to seek medical advice.

Altitude Sickness

This occurs when you ascend to high altitude quickly, for example if you fly from sea level into Cuzco (3326 metres). The best way to prevent altitude sickness is to spend a day or two travelling slowly to high altitudes, thus allowing your body time to adjust. Even if you don't do this, it is unlikely that you will suffer greatly in Cuzco because it is still relatively low. A few people do become seriously ill, but most travellers experience no more than some shortness of breath and headache. If, however, you travel higher than Cuzco, you may well experience much severer symptoms, including vomiting, fatigue, insomnia, loss of appetite, a rapid pulse and irregular (Cheyne-Stokes) breathing during sleep.

The best thing you can do upon arriving at high altitude is to take it easy for the first day, and to avoid smoking and alcohol. This will go a long way in helping you acclimatise. If you feel sick, the best treatment is rest, deep breathing, an adequate fluid intake, and a mild pain killer such as Tylenol to alleviate headaches. If symptoms are very severe, the only effective cure is oxygen, best obtained by descending to a lower altitude.

Heat & Sun

The heat and humidity of the tropics make you sweat profusely and can also make you feel apathetic. It is important to maintain a high fluid intake and to ensure your food is well salted. If fluids and salts lost through perspiration are not replaced, heat exhaustion and cramps frequently result. The feeling of apathy that some people experience usually fades after a week or two.

If you're arriving in the tropics with a great desire to improve your tan, you've certainly come to the right place. The tropical sun will not only improve your tan, it will also burn you to a crisp. I know several travellers who have enjoyed themselves in the sun for an afternoon, and then spent the next couple of days with severe sunburn. An effective way of immobilizing yourself is to cover yourself with suntan lotion, walk down to the beach, remove your shoes, and badly burn your feet (which you forgot to put lotion on and which are especially white). The power of the tropical sun cannot be overemphasized. Don't spoil your trip by trying to tan too quickly; use strong (sun protection factor 10 or higher) suntan lotion frequently and put it on all exposed skin. Peru doesn't sell strong suntan lotion – bring it from home. Wearing a wide-brimmed sun hat is also a good idea.

Insect Problems

Insect repellents go a long way in preventing bites (see Malaria section). When you do get bitten, avoid scratching; unfortunately this is easier said than done. To alleviate itching, try Hydrocortisone cream, calamine lotion, or soaking in baking soda. Scratching will quickly open bites and cause them to become infected. Skin infections are slow to heal in the heat of the tropics and all infected bites as well as cuts and grazes should be kept scrupulously clean, treated with antiseptic creams and covered with dressings on a daily basis.

Another insect problem is infestation by lice or crabs and scabies. Lice or crabs crawl around in your body hair and itch. To get rid of them, wash with a shampoo which contains benzene hexachloride, or shave the affected area. To avoid being reinfected, wash all your clothes and bedding in hot water and the shampoo. It's probably best to just throw away your underwear if you had body lice or crabs. Lice thrive on body warmth; clothing which isn't worn will cause the beasties lurking within to die in about 72 hours.

Scabies are mites which burrow into your skin and cause it to become red and itchy. To kill scabies, wash yourself with a benzene benzoate solution, and wash your clothes too. Both benzene hexachloride and benzoate are obtainable from pharmacies in Peru.

Scorpions and spiders can give severely painful – but rarely fatal – stings or bites. A common way to get bitten is to put on your clothes and shoes in the morning without checking them first. Develop the habit of shaking out your clothing before putting it on, especially in the lowlands. Check your bedding before going to sleep. Don't walk barefoot, and look where you place your hands when reaching to a shelf or branch. It's extremely unlikely that you will get stung, so don't worry about it.

Snakebite

This is also extremely unlikely. Should you be bitten, the snake may be a non-venomous one. Expert opinions vary on the best treatment for snake bite. The traditional method involves applying a tourniquet just above the bite and then slashing the bite and applying suction with a rubber cup. This is not recommended for those inexperienced in treating snakebite. Greater damage can be done if circulation is cut off completely, and injudicious slashing of the bite can cause the poison to spread more rapidly through the body.

The best procedure to follow in the unlikely event of being bitten is to attempt, as far as possible, to kill the offending creature for identification or at least try and see what it looks like. If a venomous snake is suspected, get the victim to a doctor as soon as possible. Constantly reassure the victim and try to keep him as calm and motionless as possible. Keep the bitten area below the level of the heart and immobilized. Even deadly snakes only succeed in killing a small percentage of their victims.

In Australia, which has a fair amount of snakebite experience, a new method of treatment is now recommended. This is to simply immobilize the limb where the bite took place and bandage it tightly (but not like a tourniquet) and completely. Then with the minimum of disturbance, particularly of the bound limb, get the victim to medical attention. Keep the limb below heart level.

Rabies

Rabid dogs are more common in Latin America than in more developed nations. If you are bitten by a dog, try and have it captured for tests. If you are unable to test the dog, you must assume that it has rabies which is fatal and so you cannot take the risk of hoping that the dog was not infected. Rabies doesn't develop for several weeks, so if you are bitten, don't panic. You've got plenty of time to get treated. Treatment consists of a long series of injections which used to be painful but modern techniques are quicker and less painful.

Rabies is also carried by vampire bats, who prefer to bite the toes of their sleeping human victims. So don't stick your toes out from your mosquito net or blanket if you're sleeping in an area where there are bats.

Medical Attention in Peru

If you've taken the precautions mentioned in the previous sections you can look forward to a generally healthy trip. Should something go wrong, however, you can get good medical advice and treatment in the major cities. The best treatment is definitely in Lima and if you are seriously ill you should try and get there. Addresses of clinics or doctors are given in the sections on the main cities. Medical treatment is generally much cheaper than in more developed countries so it's usually worth going to the best available. Some doctors speak English.

Many prescription drugs are available in Peru, some of which are sold over the counter. If you need to buy any, make sure that they haven't expired and that they have been kept in a cool or refrigerated storage area.

First-Aid Kit
How large or small your first-aid kit should be depends on your knowledge of first-aid procedures, where and how far off the beaten track you are going, how long you will need the kit for, and how many people will be sharing it. The following is a suggested checklist which you should amend as required.

Antiseptic cream
Aspirin or similar
Lomotil for diarrhoea
Antibiotics such as ampicillin and tetracycline
Throat lozenges
Ear and eye drops
Antacid tablets
Motion-sickness medication
Alcohol swabs
Water purifier
Lip salve
Foot and groin powder
Thermometer in a case
Surgical tape, assorted sticky plasters (band-aids), gauze, bandages, butterfly closures
Scissors
First-aid booklet

A convenient way of carrying your first-aid kit so that it doesn't get crushed is in a small plastic container with a sealing lid, such as Tupperware.

Water Purification
If you use tap water for drinking or washing fruit and vegetables, you should purify it first. The most effective method is to boil it continuously for 20 minutes which is obviously inconvenient. Various water-purifying tablets are available but most of them aren't wholly effective – the hepatitis virus often survives. Also, they make the water taste strange and are not recommended for frequent and long-term use. The most effective method, and one that doesn't make the water taste as bad, is to use iodine. You can use a few drops of prepared iodine solution but the problem is that it's difficult to know exactly how strong the solution is in the first place and how many drops you should use. The following method is one that I learnt at the South American Explorers Club in Lima. I find it eliminates these problems and works very well.

Get hold of a small, 25 ml (one ounce) glass bottle and put about two to three mm of iodine crystals in it. Don't use a plastic bottle as the iodine will make it brittle and cause it to crack. Both iodine crystals and suitable glass bottles can be obtained from pharmacies. When you need a purifying solution, fill the glass bottle with water and shake it well for about a minute and then let the crystals settle to the bottom. Only a minute amount of the crystals actually dissolve in the water and you now have 25 ml of saturated (not concentrated) iodine solution which is always the same (saturated) strength. Carefully pour the saturated iodine solution into a litre (or quart) of water and leave it for 15 minutes to produce clean drinking water. The advantage of this method is that only the iodine solution is used to purify your drinking water and the crystals are left at the bottom of the 25 ml bottle; they can be used and reused hundreds of times. This is a safe and recommended method except for pregnant women and people with thyroid problems. Be sure to transfer only the 25 ml of saturated solution to your drinking water and not the actual crystals. Accidentally swallowing a whole iodine crystal will not do you any good at all.

BOOKS & BOOKSHOPS

There are several good bookshops in Lima which sell books in English. The best place for guidebooks is the South American Explorers Club at Avenida Portugal 146. Other shops are listed in the Lima section.

Outside of Lima, the choice is more limited. Books in English are not so easily available except in Cuzco and Arequipa but most of the larger cities have magazines such as *Time* or *Newsweek*.

Guidebooks

Apart from months of legwork, I used a great many books in compiling the information in this guidebook. Most of them are listed below. The books about Peru are often excellent but are either limited to just the tourist highlights or tend to be specialized – I hope this book fills the gap by being the most comprehensive general guide to Peru. There are also some good books on South America in general which have chapters on Peru. They are mainly recommended for the traveller who wants one book for his 'grand tour' of Latin America.

For the budget traveller, *South America on a Shoestring* by Geoff Crowther (Lonely Planet, 3rd edition, 1986) is recommended for its many maps and money-saving information, as well as its interesting synopses of the historical/political situation of Latin countries.

A broader approach is available in *The South American Handbook*, edited by John Brooks and published annually by Trade & Travel Publications, Bath, UK. It has been referred to as the 'South American Bible' by some travellers and it weighs about as much as one and is quite pricey. Its main drawbacks are sometimes overdue updates and lack of good city maps. It is suitable for everyone from budget travellers spending a year in Latin America to businesspeople on expense accounts visiting the major capitals, so there is a lot of extraneous information for most readers. Nevertheless, it is the best general book to the continent.

Another book which I enjoyed and thoroughly recommend is Lynn Meisch's *A Traveler's Guide to El Dorado & the Inca Empire* published by Penguin Books. Lynn is a weavings expert and has travelled professionally in Latin America to collect and document many of the traditional techniques. Her book is full of fascinating details on the crafts, cultures, markets, fiestas, and archaeology of Colombia, Ecuador, Peru and Bolivia and has good background information for the traveller. However, it doesn't set out to help with specific information on hotels, restaurants or transport.

A recent general guidebook is *The Rough Guide to Peru* by Dilwyn Jenkins (Routledge & Kegan Paul, 1985). Although its maps and hard travel information are not very detailed, it has some interesting background on Peru.

The Sierra Club have gotten into the South American guidebook market with their *Adventuring in the Andes* by Charles Frazier, 1985. It also has some interesting background but lacks good maps and tries to cover too much in too few pages.

One of my favourite guidebooks covers only the Cuzco area but does that entertainingly and in some detail. *Exploring Cuzco* by Peter Frost (Bradt Publications, 3rd edition, 1985) is highly recommended for anyone planning on spending any length of time in the Cuzco area – all the major sites are described. The book is available in Lima and Cuzco as well.

Various other guidebooks are available in Peru. The best is Reparaz's *Guide to Peru*, 5th edition, published by Ediciones de Arte Rep, Lima. Although it deals only with conventional tourism and limits itself to brief mentions of only a few major hotels, it does nevertheless give detailed descriptions of many churches, historic buildings and museums, as well as giving road descriptions for those tourists travelling by private car. There are also various books in Spanish, again aimed at the tourist visiting the conventional sites.

Many of the other books available are of the coffee table variety; fun to look through in the store and suitable as a souvenir or present rather than a travelling guide book.

There are also 'mainstream' guides by Frommer, Waldo, Birnbaum, Fodor, etc which seem to cater to the 'today's Tuesday, so it must be Rio' crowd, and are fine if that's what you're looking for.

The Outdoors

There are several books for hikers and climbers. A good all round book is *Backpacking & Trekking in Peru & Bolivia* by Hilary and George Bradt. The hikes in the 1980 3rd edition are becoming outdated but Bradt Publications is planning a new edition with updates for 1987 and it should be excellent. It has a wealth of fascinating background information as well as entertaining descriptions and maps of over a dozen good backpacking trips in Peru and Bolivia. These include classic treks such as the Inca Trail to Machu Picchu and the Llanganuco/Santa Cruz loop in the Cordillera Blanca as well as some little known hikes in less visited areas for you to discover.

If you want information about backpacking in only the Blanca and Huayhuash ranges then the book to get is Jim Bartle's *Trails of the Cordilleras Blanca & Huayhuash of Peru*. It is available from the South American Explorers Club in Lima; in the US from specialist bookshops or the author at 771 West Dry Creek Rd, Healdsburg, CA 95448; and in Europe from Bradt Publications, 41 Nortoft Rd, Chalfont St Peter, Bucks SL9 OLA, England. This detailed book is full of maps and all the information you'll need for hiking in this most beautiful region. Jim Bartle is also an accomplished photographer and his postcards are available in Peru. He has written and illustrated a beautiful and inexpensive book of colour photographs, mainly of mountains, called *Parque Nacional Huascarán* which was published bilingually in 1985 in co-operation with the Asociación Peruana para la Conservación de la Naturaleza.

Climbers will want to get *Yuraq Janka* by John F Ricker, published jointly in 1977 by the the American Alpine club and the Alpine Club of Canada. Although this book doesn't give detailed climbing routes, it has a wealth of background information and is the best book available for climbers wanting information about the Cordilleras Blanca and Rosko. Again, get this at the SAEC in Lima or mail order from Bradt Publications.

For travelling in the lowlands, Bradt Publications has two books called *South America: River Trips – Volumes I & II*. As their names suggest, they deal not with just Peru but with the whole continent. Volume I, 1981, by George N Bradt, covers a little more in Peru but lacks the excellently detailed and expert background information found in Volume II, 1982, by Tanis and Martin Jordan.

Natural History

There are no comprehensive guides to the flora and fauna of Peru. Bird-watchers are served best by various helpful books.

An Annotated Checklist of Peruvian Birds by Parker III, Parker, and Plenge, (Buteo Books, 1982) is a checklist plus information on bird-watching in Peru.

For field guides try *The Birds of the Department of Lima, Peru* by Maria Koepcke, translated by Erma J Fiske (Harrowood Books, 2nd Edition, 1983). The Department of Lima stretches for 350 km along the Peruvian desert coast and up into the Andes for 100 km, encompassing within this boundary a large area of Andean altiplano. Therefore, although the book covers only a relatively small area of Peru, it is very useful for bird-watching along most of the desert coast and the western and central parts of the Andean highlands.

For the eastern slopes of the Andes and the Amazonian lowlands the best book is considered to be the beautifully illustrated *A Guide to the Birds of Venezuela* by R M de Schauensee and W H Phelps Jr, (Princeton University Press, 1978). Although over 600 km of rain forest separates the borders of Peru and Venezuela, many of the bird species are the same. Brand new in 1986 is *A Guide to the Birds of Colombia* by S L Hilty and W L Brown, also from Princeton University Press. Both books are illustrated with comprehensive colour plates by Guy Tudor. Because Colombia has a land border with Peru, this book will probably replace the Venezuela book as the most useful for birders in Peru. Also useful is *South American Land Birds – A Photographic Aid to Identification* (Harrowood Books, 1982). This has colour photographs of about 40% of South America's birds, but there are no water birds.

Other books can be expected in the future. Barry Walker is working on a book on the birds of Machu Picchu National Park and some Danish ornithologists are working on a guidebook to Peruvian birds.

Guidebooks on different aspects of Peruvian wildlife are not available. There are, however, several excellent books on South American natural history which contain some information on Peru. My favourite is Michael Andrews' *Flight of the Condor* and Tony Morrison's *Land Above the Clouds* and *The Andes* are also very good. *The Living Planet* by David Attenborough includes sections on the Amazon basin and the Andes of Peru. There are also several books from National Geographic which are good.

Archaeology & History

One book stands out as the most readable account of the pre-Inca history of Peru. *The Ancient Civilisations of Peru* by J Alden Mason was published by Plata in 1975, although the first edition dates back to 1957 and is hence a little out of date. Despite this, I haven't seen a better book for the non-specialist about pre-Inca Peru.

Two books are recommended to the serious student of Peruvian archaeology. Both are scholarly works by professional archaeologists specialising in Peru and both have detailed references. *The Peoples & Cultures of Ancient Peru* by Luis G Lumbreras, translated by Betty J Meggers (Smithsonian Institution Press, Washington DC, 1974) and *Everyday Life of the Incas* by Ann Kendall (Batsford, London) and (Putnam's, New York, 1973).

Mason's book also deals with the Incas, as do a host of other books. Going back to the arrival of the Spanish conquistadors, the best book is undoubtedly John Hemming's excellent *The Conquest of the Incas* (Harcourt, Brace, Jovanovich, 1970, available as a Penguin paperback). I must confess to not being particularly interested in history (I came to South America originally to climb mountains and look at wildlife) but Hemming's lucid and well-written account kept me fascinated. If you read only one book on the Incas, make this the one. Mention should also be made of Hemming's *Monuments of the Incas* which is a coffee table style book, magnificently illustrated with Edward Ranney's black and white photographs of the major Inca ruins.

Another good choice is *The Royal Commentary of the Incas* written in the early 1600s by Garcilazo de la Vega. This historian was born in Cuzco in 1539 of an Inca princess and a Spanish soldier. His book is the most widely translated, easily available and readable of the contemporary accounts of Inca life.

Several books by Victor W von Hagen cover Inca history. They are getting a little outdated but aren't bad. *Realm of the Incas* (New York, 1957) is a simple general account and *Highway of the Sun – A Search for the Royal Roads of the*

Incas, 1955, republished by Plata in 1975, is an account of a 1953 expedition to trace as many of the Inca's roads as possible. Another rather interesting account of archaeological exploration is Gene Savoy's *Antisuyo* (published as *Vilcabamba* in Britain) – but professional archaeologists claim that his work is sensationalist. Makes a good read, though.

The mysterious topic of the Nazca lines has generated several books, including Erich von Daniken's *Chariots of the Gods* in which he claims that the lines and other archaeological sites were built by or for prehistoric spacemen. More sober ideas come from María Reiche in *Mystery on the Desert* (Lima, 1949) and Tony Morrison's *Pathways to the Gods* (Harper & Row, 1978). A theory that the Nazca people used hot air balloons is described by Jim Woodman in *Nazca, The Flight of Condor 1* (Murray, 1980).

The llama family consists of the domesticated llama and alpaca (pictured above) and the wild vicuña and guanaco. The alpaca is bred primarily for its fine wool and the llama is used as a pack animal. The meat is also eaten and even the dried dung is used for fuel. Their natural habitat is above 2500 metres.

Travel & Adventure

My favourite travel book about Peru is Ronald Wright's *Cut Stones & Crossroads: A Journey in the Two Worlds of Peru* (Viking Press, 1984, now available in Penguin paperback). It gives the reader a good idea of what Peru and travelling around it are really like.

Of the many good books about Amazon travel, the following two are recommended. As with the others, they don't deal with Peru alone but with the Amazon region as a whole. They are *The Rivers Amazon* by Alex Shoumatoff (Sierra Club Books, 1978) and *Passage Through El Dorado* by Jonathan Kandell (William Morrow, 1984).

The classic account of the 'discovery' of Machu Picchu in 1911 also makes a good read. Hiram Bingham's *Lost City of the Incas* has been published several times by various publishers.

Literature

Peru's most famous novelist is the internationally recognised Mario Vargas Llosa whose books have been translated into various languages including English. Among the best are *Aunt Julia & the Scriptwriter* and *The Green House* both available in English translation from Avon Books.

Pablo Neruda, a Chilean poet, describes Machu Picchu as 'Mother of stone and sperm of condors' which is only one of the many powerful images he uses in his epic poem, *The Heights of Machu Picchu*. A 1966 translation by N Tarn is available from Farrar, Straus, & Giroux, New York.

Maps

The bookshops have a limited selection of Peruvian maps. The best selection is to be had from the *Instituto Geográfico Nacional* at Avenida Aramburu 1190. Few city maps are published, and except for perhaps a detailed map of the whole of Lima, you'll find the city maps in this book are generally the best available. The South American Explorers Club has a good selection of hiking maps and a general country map.

NEWSPAPERS & MEDIA

Although it is a small country, there are literally dozens of newspapers available in Peru. Most towns of any size publish a local newspaper which is useful for finding out what's playing in the town cinemas and reading the local gossip, but has little national news and even less international news. The best newspapers are available in Lima, although many of these are sensationalist rags which luridly portray traffic accident victims on the front page whilst relegating world affairs to a few columns behind the sports section.

There are good newspapers, and one of the best is *El Comercio* published in Lima. It comes in several sections and keeps you up to date with cultural and artistic events in the capital as well as national and international news. A shorter version (missing the events sections) is available in other cities.

There is one English language tabloid called *The Lima Times* which is published weekly. Foreign newspapers and magazines are available at good bookstores and street stands.

Peru has five major television channels plus cable, but the programming leaves much to be desired. Apart from interminable sports programmes, you can watch very bad Latin American soap operas or reruns of old and equally bad North American sit-coms. The news broadcasts every evening are quite good, especially for local news. Occasionally, a National Geographic special makes its way to the screen. These kinds of programmes are advertised days ahead in the better newspapers.

If you carry a portable radio when you travel, you'll find plenty of stations to choose from. There is more variety on the radio than the TV, and you can listen to programmes in Quechua as well as

Spanish. The BBC World Service and the Voice of America can both be picked up in Peru if you have short wave.

FILM & PHOTOGRAPHY

Definitely bring everything you'll need. Camera gear is very expensive in Peru and film choice is limited. Some good films are unavailable, eg Kodachrome slide film. Others are kept in hot storage cabinets and are sometimes sold outdated, so if you do buy any film in Peru check its expiry date.

Don't have film developed in Peru if you can help it. Processing is shoddy. On the other hand, carrying around exposed film for months is also asking for washed-out results. It is best to send it home as soon after it's exposed as possible. The mail service isn't totally reliable so what I normally do is send film home with a friend. You'll often meet people heading back to whichever continent you're from and they can usually be persuaded to do you this favour, particularly if you offer to take them out to dinner. I always buy either process-paid film or prepaid film mailers so I can place the exposed film in the mailer and not worry about the costs. The last thing you want to do on your return from a long trip is worry about how you're going to find the money to develop a few dozen rolls of film.

Tropical shadows are very strong and come out almost black on photographs. Often a bright but hazy day gives better photographs than a very sunny one. Taking photographs in open shade or using fill-in flash will help. The best time for shooting is when the sun is low – the first and last two hours of the day. If you are heading into the Amazon lowlands you will need high speed film, flash, a tripod, or a combination of these if you want to take photographs within the jungle. The amount of light penetrating the layers of vegetation is surprisingly low.

The Peruvian people are both pictur-esque and varied. From a charmingly grubby Indian child to the handsomely uniformed presidential guard – the pos-sibilities of 'people pictures' are endless. However, most people resent having a camera thrust in their faces and people in markets will often proudly turn their backs on pushy photographers. Ask for permission with a smile or a joke and if this is refused don't become offended. Some people believe that bad luck can be brought upon them by the 'evil eye' of the camera. Others are just fed up at seeing their pictures used in books, magazines, and postcards and realising that somebody is making money at their expense. Sometimes a 'tip' is asked for. This is especially true in the highly visited Cuzco area. Here, many locals will dress up in their traditional finery and pose against Andean backdrops. Some even bring their llamas into Cuzco's main square. These people consider themselves to be posing for a living and become angry if you try to take their picture without giving them a few cents. Be aware of people's feelings – it is not worth upsetting someone to get your photograph.

POST

The Peruvian postal service roughly tripled its rates in mid-1985 and the service has improved somewhat since then. It is still a lot cheaper than in more developed countries. The majority of your letters will arrive safely but you can never be totally sure. For a few cents extra, you can send them *certificado* which is safe and gives you peace of mind. Although I haven't experienced a loss mailing them this way, there doesn't seem to be much you can do if it doesn't arrive.

The post office in each town is marked on the town maps. In some smaller towns it is often just part of a house or a corner of a municipal office. In Lima there are several post offices dotted around town. Opening hours are very convenient. In many towns the post office is open from 9 am until 8 pm on weekdays, and a half day on weekends including Sundays. In Lima the post office usually closes by 7 pm.

Mailing parcels of over one kg is not very convenient. They first have to be checked by customs which may not exist in most towns. In Lima, customs is at the main post office from 9 am to 3 pm on weekdays. Lunch is from 12 noon until 1 pm. You get sent from counter to counter, filling out customs declarations, buying stamps, paying export taxes and so on. Finally, you are usually required to sew up the parcel (after it has been inspected) in a cloth sack. A real pain. Regulations change from year to year. To make matters worse, many parcels are lost, stolen or damaged. This is especially true of incoming parcels which are frequently pilfered – try not to have anything valuable or interesting sent to Peru.

There are several places where you can receive mail but most travellers use either the post office or American Express. Sometimes embassies will hold mail for you, but some embassies refuse to do so and will return it to the sender. Ask before using your embassy. You can also have mail sent c/o your hotel, but it's liable to get lost. If you have mail sent to the post office, remember that it is filed alphabetically and so if it's addressed to John Gillis Payson Esq, it could well be filed under 'G' or 'E' instead of the correct 'P'. It should be addressed, for example, to John PAYSON, Lista de Correos, Correos Central, Lima, Peru. Ask your loved ones to clearly print your last name and avoid witticisms such as 'World Traveller Extraordinaire' appended to your name. American Express will also hold mail for their clients at John PAYSON, c/o American Express, Lima Tours, Casilla 4340, Belén 1040, Lima. (My sincere thanks to my father-in-law for letting me use his name.)

TELECOMMUNICATIONS

ENTEL-Peru is the place to go for long distance national and international telephone, telex, and telegram services, with the exception of Lima where the telephone company is La Compañía Peruana de Teléfonos. You will find the ENTEL office locations marked on all the street plans in this book. The bigger towns have telex and telegram services; the smaller towns have only the phone. Even the most remote villages can often communicate with a major city and so connect you into an international call. These cost about US$7 for three minutes to the US and about US$10 to Europe. You have to leave a deposit in advance and this is often more than the call will cost. You are given a receipt and the difference is returned to you at the end. The system is slow but it works. Waiting time can sometimes be as short as 10 minutes, though it can also take an hour or more to get through. You may have to wait a further 15 minutes for your refund. Rates are cheaper on Sundays and in the evenings after 9 pm. ENTEL offices are usually open from 8 am to 10 pm but the Peruvian Telephone Company in Lima is open only until 9 pm. The best hotels can connect international calls to your room at almost any time. Collect or reverse charge phone calls are possible to many countries which have reciprocal agreements with Peru – ask at the nearest ENTEL office. A (returnable) deposit is needed for these calls.

Local calls (within the town that you are in) are not as straightforward as putting a coin in a public telephone. There are not very many public telephones and they are limited to the major cities. They don't operate on coins. Instead, you have to buy discs called *Fiches RIN* which are available from street sellers, particularly newspaper vendors. Fiches RIN cost a few cents each. The ENTEL office usually has public phones available for local calls. If you can't find a public phone, you can often call from a small store or restaurant and pay for the call.

Telephone directories are available at ENTEL offices and with private phones (ie stores and restaurants). There are also yellow pages if you can read Spanish.

ELECTRICITY
Peru uses 220 volts, 60 cycles AC, except Arequipa on 50 cycles.

TIME
Peru is five hours behind Greenwich Mean Time. Although Peru is almost on the equator (from roughly 0° to 18°South) and the days are roughly of equal length year round, Peru recently introduced daylight saving time from December to March. It may or may not continue. When it first occurred a couple of years ago, there was utter chaos in the airports with no one knowing when the flights were taking off.

It is appropriate here to mention that punctuality is not one of the things that Latin America is famous for.

MEASUREMENTS & CONVERSIONS
Peru uses the metric system exclusively and I have done so throughout this book. For those travellers who still use miles, ounces, bushels, pecks, gills, leagues, roods, magnums, stones and other quaint and arcane expressions, the following table may be of use:

To Convert:	Multiply By:
Inches to centimetres	2.54
Centimetres to inches	0.3937
Yards to metres	0.9144
Metres to yards	1.094
Miles to kilometres	1.609
Kilometres to miles	0.6214
US gallons to litres	3.785
Litres to US gallons	0.264
Ounces to grams	28.35
Grams to ounces	0.03527
Pounds to kilograms	0.4536
Kilograms to pounds	2.205

To convert °Centigrade to °Fahrenheit, multiply by 1.8 and then add 32.

INFORMATION
The government tourist information agency *La Dirección General de Turismo* have offices in the major cities of Lima, Arequipa, Ayacucho, Cajamarca, Cuzco, Huancayo, Huaraz, Ica, Iquitos, Piura, Puno, Tacna and Trujillo – the location of each of these is listed under the appropriate towns. They usually don't have anyone who speaks English (with the notable exceptions of Lima and Cuzco) but they are friendly and try to help. Maps are sometimes available. Often, the office doesn't appear to be frequently visited by travellers and they're happy to see you.

ACCOMMODATION
There is much variety and no shortage of places to stay in Peru. They come under various names such as *pensión, residencial* and *hostal* as well as simply *hotel* but there is no rule which tells you that one type is better or worse than the others. It is almost unheard of to arrive in a town and not be able to find somewhere to sleep, but during major fiestas or during the high tourist season, accommodation can be rather tight. For this reason, I have marked as many hotels as possible on the town maps in this book. The fact that a hotel is marked on a city map does not necessarily imply that I recommend it, particularly the cheapest and very basic accommodation which I include in my descriptions. Read the Places to Stay sections for descriptions of the hotels. If you are going to a town specifically for a market or fiesta, try and arrive a day or more early if possible.

Sometimes it's a little difficult to find single rooms, and you may get a room with two or even three beds. In most cases though, you are only charged for one bed and don't have to share, unless the hotel is full. You should ensure in advance that you won't be asked to pay for all the beds or share with a stranger if you don't want to. This is no problem 90% of the time. If you are travelling as a couple or in a group, you can't automatically assume that a room with two or three beds will be cheaper per person than a room with one bed. Sometimes it is and sometimes it isn't. If I give a price per person, then usually a double or triple room will cost two or three times a single. If more than one price is given, this indicates that double and triples are cheaper per person than singles. Travellers on a tight budget should know that rooms with four or more beds are available in many cheap hotels and these work out cheaper per person if you're travelling in a group. I don't give these prices in my descriptions because of space considerations. Couples sharing one bed *(cama matrimonial)* are usually, though not always, charged a little less than a double room with people in separate beds. To avoid making my figures instantly obsolete because of inflation, I have used US dollars for costs.

Remember to look around a hotel if possible. The same prices are often charged for rooms of widely differing quality, even in the dollar-a-night cheapies. If you get shown into a horrible airless box with just a bed and a bare light bulb, you can ask to see a better room without giving offence simply by asking if they have a room with a window, or explaining that you have to write some letters home and is there a room with a table and chair. You'll often be amazed at the results. *Never* rent a room without looking at it first. In most hotels, even the cheapest, they'll be happy to let you see the room. If they aren't, then it usually means that the room is filthy. Also ask to see the bathroom and make sure that the toilet flushes and the water runs. If the shower looks and smells as if someone threw up in it, the staff obviously doesn't do a very good job of looking after the place. There's probably a better hotel at the same price a few blocks away.

Bathroom facilities are rarely what you may be used to at home. The cheapest hotels don't always have hot water. Even

if they do, it might not work or might be turned on only at certain hours of the day. Ask about this if you're planning on a hot shower before going out to dinner – often there's only hot water in the morning. Another intriguing device you should know about is the electric shower. This consists of a cold water shower-head hooked up to an electric heating element which is switched on when you want a hot (more likely tepid) shower. Don't touch anything metal whilst you're in the shower or you may discover what an electric shock feels like. The power is never high enough to actually throw you across the room, but it's unpleasant nevertheless. I managed to shock myself by simply picking up the soap which I had balanced on a horizontal water pipe (there wasn't a soap dish). Some hotels charge extra for hot showers and some simply don't have any showers at all. You can always use the public hot baths – available in most towns.

As you have probably gathered by now, Peruvian plumbing leaves something to be desired. Flushing a toilet creates another hazard – overflow. Putting toilet paper into the bowl clogs up the system and so a waste receptacle is often provided for the paper. This may not seem particularly sanitary, but it is much better than clogged bowls and water on the floor. A well-run hotel, even if it is cheap, will ensure that the receptacle is emptied and the toilet cleaned every day.

Most hotels will give you a key to lock your room and theft is not very frequent. Nevertheless, carrying your own padlock is a good idea if you plan on staying in the cheapest hotels. Once in a while you'll find that a room doesn't look very secure – perhaps there's a window that doesn't close or the wall doesn't come to the ceiling and can be climbed over. It's worth looking for another room – assuming you're not in some tiny jungle town where there's nothing else. This is another good reason to look at a room before you rent it.

You should never leave valuables lying around the room. It's too tempting for a maid who earns US$2 a day. Money and passport should be in a secure body pouch, other valuables can usually be kept in the hotel strongbox. (Some cheaper hotels might not want to take this responsibility.) Alternatively, pack valuables out of sight at the bottom of a locked bag or closed pack. Don't get paranoid though. In several years of travelling in Peru, only once did I have something taken from my hotel room – and it was partly my fault. I left my camera on the bed instead of at the bottom of a closed pack and it was gone when I got back. I rarely hear of people who have been ripped off from their hotel rooms, particularly if they take basic precautions.

If you're really travelling off the beaten track, you may end up in a village that doesn't even have a basic *pensión*. You can usually find somewhere to sleep by asking around, but it might be just a roof over your head rather than a bed so carry a sleeping bag or at least a blanket. The place to ask at first would probably be a village store – the store owner usually knows everyone in the village and who is in the habit of renting rooms or floor space. If that fails, you can ask for the mayor *(alcalde)* or at the *policía*. You may end up sleeping on the floor of the school house, the jail or the village community centre, but you'll probably find somewhere if you persevere. People in remote areas are generally hospitable.

In smaller towns, I usually lump the accommodation together in one section. In larger towns, however, I separate them into groups. *Bottom end* hotels are the cheapest, but not necessarily the worst. Although they are usually quite basic, with just a bed and four walls, they can nevertheless be well looked after, very clean and good value for money. They are often good places to meet other travellers, both Peruvian and foreign. Prices in this section range from just under US$1 to about US$2 or US$3 per person. Hotels in this section are usually arranged in ascending order of price. Often I include them for the sake of completeness, but a listing does not imply a recommendation – if a hotel has something more than a roof and a bed to recommend it then I mention that in the brief descriptions. Every town has hotels in the bottom end price range and in smaller towns that's all there is. Although you'll usually have to use communal bathrooms in the cheapest hotels, you can sometimes find rooms with a private bathroom for under US$2 per person.

Youth hostels as we know them in other parts of the world are not very common in Peru. The cheaper hotels make up for this deficiency. There are rarely campsites in the towns; again, the constant availability of cheap hotels make town campsites redundant for travellers on a budget.

Hotels in the *middle* sections usually cost from about US$2.50 to US$8 per person, and are also arranged in ascending order of prices. They are not always better than the best hotels in the bottom end prices. However, you can find some very good bargains here. My wife and I stayed in some really pleasant places in this range. For example, a carpeted room with a beautiful mountain view, large and comfortable bed, writing desk and a clean private bathroom with gallons of hot water cost a princely US$6 for the two of us. Even if you're travelling on a budget, there are always special occasions (your birthday?) when you can indulge in comparative luxury for a day or two.

Top end hotels are still very cheap by western standards. This section is not always found in smaller cities. The government-run *Hotel de Turistas* is often the best place in many towns. Sometimes they can be pricey, but usually you'll find them within the middle price range. If you want reasonable comfort and would like to plan your trip before you leave Lima, you can stay in the *Hotel de Turistas* in most towns and make reservations for your entire itinerary at the ENTURPERU office at Avenida Javier Prado Oeste 1358, San Isidro, Lima (telephone 721928, telex 20393). The only drawback is the lack of flexibility in your itinerary.

Luxury hotels costing around US$25 to US$50 per person are found only in a few of the major cities.

LAUNDRY

There are no self service laundry machines in Peru. This means that you have to find someone to wash your clothes for you or wash them yourself. Many hotels will have someone to do your laundry and this can cost very little in the cheaper places (under a dollar for a full change of clothes – much more in the expensive hotels). The major problem is that you might not see your clothes again for two or three days, particularly if it is raining and they can't be dried. There are laundromats (lavanderías) in the main cities but you still have to leave the clothes for at least 24 hours. Most lavanderías only do dry cleaning anyway. If you wash them yourself, ask the hotel staff where to do this. Most of the cheaper hotels will show you a huge cement sink and scrubbing board which is much easier to use than a bathroom wash-basin. Often there is a well-like section full of clean water next to the scrubbing board. Don't dunk your clothes in this water to soak or rinse them as it is used as an emergency water supply in the case of water failure. Use a bowl or bucket to scoop water out instead, or run water from a tap.

FOOD

If you're on a tight budget, food is undoubtedly the most important part of your trip expenses. You can stay in rock-bottom hotels, travel 2nd class and never consider buying a souvenir, but you've got to eat well. This doesn't mean expensively, but it does mean that you want to avoid spending half your trip sitting on the toilet.

The worst culprits for getting you sick are salads and unpeeled fruit. With the fruit, stick to bananas, oranges, pineapples, etc that you can peel. With unpeeled fruit or salads, wash them yourself in purified water. It actually can be a lot of fun getting a group of you together and heading out to the market to buy salad vegies and preparing a huge salad. You can often persuade someone in the hotel to lend you a suitable bowl, or you could buy a large plastic bowl quite inexpensively and sell or give it away afterwards.

As long as you take heed of the salad warning, you'll find plenty of good things to eat at reasonable prices. You certainly don't have to eat at a fancy restaurant; their kitchen facilities may not be as clean as their white tablecloths. A good sign for any restaurant is to see if the locals eat there – restaurants aren't empty if the food is delicious and healthy.

If you're on a tight budget you can eat from street and market stalls if the food looks hot and freshly cooked, though watch to see if your plate is going to be 'washed' in a bowl of cold greasy water and wiped with a filthy rag – it's worth carrying your own bowl and spoon. Also worth remembering (if you're trying to stretch your money) is that chifas or Chinese restaurants often offer good value. The key word here is tallarines which are noodles. Most chifas will offer a tallarines dish with chopped chicken, beef, pork or shrimp for well under a dollar. Other dishes are also good but not quite as cheap. Many restaurants offer an inexpensive set meal of the day (especially at lunch time) which is usually soup and a second course. This is called simply el menú.

Typical Peruvian dishes are tasty, varied and regional. This stands to reason – seafood is best on the coast whilst the Inca delicacy, roast guinea-pig, can still be sampled in the highlands. A description of each region's dishes is given under the

Places to Eat sections of the major cities. Spicy foods are often described by the term *a la criolla*. A brief overview of some of Peru's most typical dishes is given below.

Lomo Saltado is chopped steak fried with onions, tomatoes, potatoes and served with rice. This is one of the most standard dishes served everywhere, especially at long distance bus meal stops.

Cebiche de Corvina is a white sea bass marinated in lemon, chile and onions and served cold with a boiled potato or yam. It's delicious. *Cebiche de Camarones* is the same thing made with shrimps. These dishes are appetisers rather than full meals. If I was to single out any one dish as most typical of Peru, it would be Cebiche de Corvina.

Sopa a la Criolla is a lightly spiced noodle soup with beef, egg, milk and vegetables. It's hearty and filling.

Palta a la Jardinera is avocado stuffed with cold vegetable salad; *a la Reyna* is stuffed with chicken salad. This is one of my favourite appetisers and can make a light meal.

Most things which are available at home are available in one form or another in Peru. The following basic glossary will help you get started in translating Peruvian menus.

Almuerzo	Lunch
Arroz	Rice
Azúcar	Sugar
Cabro, cabrito	Goat
Calamares	Squid
Camarones	Shrimp
Cangrejo	Crab
Carne	Meat
Cena	Supper
Cerdo, Chancho	Pork
Cordero	Mutton
Choclo	Corn on the cob
Churrasco	Steak
Desayuno	Breakfast
Empanadas	Pastries filled with meat or cheese
Ensalada	Salad
Estofado	Stew
Frutas	Fruit
Helado	Ice cream
Huevos fritos/ revueltos	Eggs fried/ scrambled
Langosta	Lobster
Lomo	Beef
Mantequilla	Butter
Mariscos	Seafood
Pan	Bread
Papas fritas	French fried potatoes
Pescado	Fish
Pollo	Chicken
Postre	Dessert
Queso	Cheese
Sopa, Chupe	Soup
Torta	Cake
Tortilla	Omelet
Trucha	Trout
Verduras	Vegetables

DRINKS

I don't recommend drinking tap water anywhere in Latin America. *Agua potable* means that the water comes from the tap but it's not necessarily healthy. Even if it comes from a chlorination or filtration plant, the plumbing is often old, cracked and full of crud. (Salads washed in this water aren't necessarily clean.) One possibility is to carry a water bottle and purify your own water. (For more about this see Health.) If you don't want to go through the hassle of constantly purifying water, you can buy bottled mineral water (*agua mineral*) very cheaply. Unfortunately, it's always of the fizzy variety – if you prefer the non-fizzy water you'll have difficulty in finding it. The advantage of buying a bottled drink in a store is that it is usually cheaper than in a restaurant; the disadvantage is that you have to drink it at the store because the bottle is usually worth more than the drink inside. (Canned drinks cost up to three times more than bottles.) You can pay a deposit, but you have to return it to the store you bought the bottle from; a different store won't give you any money for it. What many travellers do is pay a deposit on (effectively buy) a bottle of pop, beer or mineral water and then trade it in every time they want to buy a drink in a different place.

All the usual soft drinks are available, as are some local ones with such tongue twisting names as *Socosani* or the ubiquitous *Inca Cola* which is appropriately gold coloured and tastes like fizzy bubble gum. Soft drinks are collectively known as *gaseosas* and the local brands are very sweet. Seven-up is simply called *seven*, so don't try calling it 'siete arriba' or no one will have any idea what you're talking about. You can also buy Coca-Cola, Pepsi Cola, orange Fanta or crush (called *croosh*) and Sprite – the latter pronounced *essprite*! Ask for your drink *helada* if you want it out of the refrigerator, *al clima* if you don't. Remember to say *sin hielo* (without ice) unless you really trust the water supply. Diet soft drinks have just become available in Lima although the concept of third world countries paying for a drink with no calories is a little absurd.

Juices *(jugos)* are available everywhere and are usually better than *gaseosas* to my taste, but they cost more. Make sure you get *jugo puro* and not *con agua*. The most common kinds are *mora* (blackberry), *naranja* (orange), *toronja* (grapefruit), *piña* (pineapple), *maracuya* (passion fruit), *sandía* (watermelon), *naranjilla* (a local fruit tasting like bitter orange) or *papaya*.

Coffee is available almost everywhere but is often disappointing. A favourite way of making coffee is to boil it for hours until only a thick syrup remains. This is then poured into cruets and diluted down with milk or water. It doesn't taste that great and it looks very much like soy sauce, so always check before pouring it into your milk (or over your rice)! Instant coffee is also served. Espresso and cappuccino is sometimes available but only in the bigger towns. *Café con leche* is milk with coffee, and *café con agua* or *café negro* is black coffee. Tea *(té)* is served black with lemon and sugar. If you ask for tea with milk, British style, you'll get a cup of hot milk with a tea bag to dunk in it. Hot chocolate is also popular.

Finally we come to those beverages which can loosely be labelled 'libations'. The selection of beers is limited to about a dozen kinds, but what there is is quite palatable and inexpensive. Beer comes in either large ⅔ or small ⅓ of a litre bottles. A large bottle costs as little as 40c in the cheaper bars but fancy restaurants often charge about US$1 for a small bottle. Either light lager-type beers or sweet dark beers are available. On the coast you find *Pilsen* which is made either in Callao or Trujillo – experts claim that *Pilsen Trujillo* is better made than *Pilsen Callao* but they taste quite similar and are the strongest of the coastal beers. Slightly lighter and less strong is *Crystal*. Other light coastal beers are *Garza Real* and *Dellmen*, neither of which are remarkable. Dark beer is known as *Malta* or *Cerveza Negra*. Two highland towns are known for their beer – Cuzco and Arequipa which make *Cuzqueña* and *Arequipeña* respectively. Both are available in lager and dark. The *Cuzqueña* is Peru's best beer according to many drinkers. *Arequipeña* tastes slightly sweet. Going over into the jungle you find *San Juan* which is brewed in Pucallpa and advertises itself as 'the only beer brewed in the Amazon'. It's not a bad light beer. Imported beers are usually very expensive with the exception of the light *Paceña* from La Paz which is occasionally available.

Peru has a thriving wine-making industry and produces acceptable wines, though not as good as Chilean or Argentine varieties. The best wines are from the *Tacama* and *Ocucaje* wineries and begin at about US$3 a bottle. The usual selection of reds, whites and rosés is available – I'm afraid I'm not a connoisseur and so experts will have to experiment further themselves.

Spirits are expensive if imported and

not very good if made locally, with some notable exceptions. Rum is cheap and quite good. A white grape brandy called *pisco* is the national drink, most frequently served as a *pisco sour* – a tasty cocktail made from pisco, egg white, lemon juice, sugar, syrup, crushed ice and bitters. The local firewater, *aguardiente* or sugar cane alcohol, is an acquired taste but is also good and very cheap.

THINGS TO BUY

Souvenirs are good, varied and cheap. Although going to villages and markets is fun, you won't necessarily save a great deal of money – similar items for sale in shops are often not much more expensive. In markets and smaller stores, bargaining is acceptable, indeed expected. In 'tourist stores' in the major cities prices are sometimes fixed. Some of the best stores are quite expensive; on the other hand the quality of their products is often superior.

You can buy everything in Lima be it a blow-pipe from the jungle or a woven poncho from the highlands. Although it is usually a little more expensive to buy handicrafts in Lima, the choice is varied, the quality is high and it's worth looking around some of Lima's gift shops and markets to get an idea of the things which you'd like to buy. Then you can go to the areas which make the items you're interested in – but often the best pieces are in Lima.

Cuzco also has a great selection of craft shops but the quality is rarely as high as in Lima. Old and new weavings, ceramics, paintings, woollen clothing and jewellery are all found here. Cuzco has a good selection of the more traditional weavings.

The Puno/Juliaca area is good for knitted alpaca sweaters and knick-knacks made from the tortora reed which grows on Lake Titicaca. The Huancayo area is good for carved gourds as well as for excellent weavings and clothing in the co-operative market. The Ayacucho area is famous for modern weavings and stylised ceramic churches. San Pedro de Cajas is known for its peculiar weavings which are made of rolls of yarn stuffed with wool (you'll recognise the style instantly when you see it). The Shipibo pottery sold in Yarinacocha near Pucallpa is the best of the jungle artefacts available. Superb reproductions of Moche and Mochica pottery are available in Trujillo. Shopping for these is described in more detail under the appropriate towns.

Crafts as souvenirs or gifts are relatively cheap by western standards. A good rule of thumb is, if you really like something very much, buy it (assuming you can afford it). You may not find exactly the same thing again and if you do find a better example, you can always give the first one away as a gift.

WHAT TO BRING

As an inveterate traveller and guidebook writer, I've naturally read many guide books. I always find the What to Bring section depressing, as I'm always told to bring as little as possible. I look around at my huge back pack, my two beat up duffel bags bursting at the seams, and I wonder sadly where I went wrong. I enjoy camping and climbing, so I carry a tent, ice axe, heavy boots, etc. I'm an avid bird-watcher and I'd feel naked without my binoculars and field guides. And of course I want to photograph these mountains and birds which adds a camera, lenses, a tripod and other paraphernalia. In addition, I enjoy relaxing just as much as leaping around mountains taking photographs of birds, and so I always have at least two books to read in addition to all my indispensable guides and maps. Luckily, I'm not a music addict, so I'm able to live without a guitar, a portable tape player or a shortwave radio.

It appears that I'm not the only one afflicted with the kitchen-sink disease. In Latin America alone, I've met an Australian surfer who travelled the length of the Pacific coast with his board, looking for the world's longest left handed wave; a couple of Canadian skiers complete with those skinny boards; a black man from Chicago who travelled with a pair of metre-high bongo drums; an Italian with a saxophone (a memorable night when those two got together); a Danish journalist with a portable typewriter; a French freak with a ghetto blaster and (by my count) 32 tapes; and an American woman with several hundred weavings she planned to sell. All were budget travellers staying at least 1½ months and using public transport.

After confessing to the amount of stuff I travel with, I can't very well give the time honoured advice of 'travel as lightly as possible'. I suggest you bring anything that is important to you. If you're interested in photography you'll only curse every time you see a good shot (if only you'd brought your telephoto lens) and if you're a musician you won't enjoy the trip if you constantly worry about how out of practice you're getting.

There's no denying however, that travelling light is much less of a hassle, so don't bring things you can do without. Travelling on buses and trains is bound to make you slightly grubby, so bring one change of dark clothes that don't show the dirt, rather than seven changes of nice clothes for a six week trip. Many people go overboard with changes of clothes, but one change to wash and the other to wear is the best idea. Bring clothes that wash and dry easily (jeans take for ever to dry). Polypropylene clothing dries quickly – you can rinse out polypro underwear and it'll dry in three hours. The highlands are often cold, so bring a wind proof jacket and a warm layer to wear beneath, or plan on buying a thick sweater in Cuzco or one of the other Andean towns frequented by tourists. A down jacket (bought at home) is well worth the investment if you get cold easily. A hat is indispensable; it'll keep you warm when it's cold, shade your eyes when it's sunny and keep your head dry when it rains. A great deal! A collapsible umbrella is great protection against sun and rain.

You can buy clothes of almost any size if you need them, but shoes are limited to size 43 Peruvian which is about 10½ North American. Suffice to say that I have US size 12 feet (don't laugh, they're not that big!) and I can't buy any footgear at all in Peru. (This is also true of most Latin countries, so bring a spare pair of shoes if you're planning a long trip.)

For light travelling , I often divide my trip into segments and take what I need for that segment and leave my other gear in storage. Most hotels will do that for you and if you're a member of the South American Explorers Club you can leave your gear in their Lima club-house for as long as you want. I go to Peru every year, so I have had a couple of bags of clothes and camping gear in storage more or less permanently for several years – that alone is worth the price of membership!

The following is a checklist of small items you will find useful and probably need:

Pocket torch (flashlight) with spare bulb and batteries
Travel alarm clock
Swiss Army style penknife
Sewing and repairs kit (dental floss makes excellent, strong, and colourless emergency thread)
A few metres of cord (also useful for clothesline and spare shoelaces)
Sunglasses
Plastic bags
Soap and dish, shampoo, toothbrush and paste, shaving gear, towel
Toilet paper (rarely found in cheaper hotels and restaurants)
Ear plugs for sleeping in noisy hotels or buses
Insect repellent
Suntan lotion
Address book
Notebook
Pens and pencils
Paperback book (easily exchanged with other travellers when you've finished)
Spanish-English dictionary

Small padlock
Large folding nylon bag to leave things in storage
Water bottle
First-aid kit (see Health section)

Tampons are available in Peru, but only in the major cities and in regular sizes, so make sure you stock up with an adequate supply before visiting smaller towns and villages. If you use contraceptives, then you'll also find them available in the major cities. The choice of contraceptives is limited however, and so if you use a preferred type you should bring it from home; they don't weigh much anyway.

A sleeping bag is useful if you plan on travelling on a budget (or camping) because some of the cheaper hotels don't supply enough blankets and it can get cold at night. However, most hotels will give you another blanket if you ask, so a sleeping bag is useful but not indispensable if you're planning in staying mainly in the major tourist areas.

You need something to carry everything around in. A backpack is recommended because it is less exhausting than carrying your baggage in your hands, which are left free. On the other hand, it's often more difficult to get at things inside a pack and so some travellers prefer a duffel bag with a full length zipper, or the traditional suitcase. Whichever you choose, ensure that it is a good, strongly made piece of luggage or you'll find that you spend much of your trip replacing zippers, straps and buckles. If you bring a backpack, I suggest one with an internal frame. External frames snag on bus doors, luggage racks and airline baggage belts and are liable to be twisted, cracked or broken.

SAFETY & SECURITY

Peru has a reputation for thievery and, unfortunately, it is a fully warranted one. There's no denying that many travellers do get ripped off. On the other hand, if you take some basic precautions and exercise a reasonable amount of vigilance, you probably won't get ripped off. What normally happens is that travellers are so involved in their new surroundings and experiences that they forget to stay alert and that's when something gets stolen. It's good to know that armed theft is not as frequent as sneak theft and you should remember that crowded places are the haunts of pickpockets. This means ill-lit bus and train stations or bustling markets.

Thieves look for easy targets. Tourists who carry a wallet or passport in a hip pocket are asking for trouble. Leave your wallet at home; it's an easy mark for a pickpocket. Carrying a small roll of bills loosely wadded under a handkerchief in your front pocket is as safe a way as any of carrying your daily spending money. The rest should be hidden. Always use at least an inside pocket or preferably a body pouch, money belt or leg pouch to protect your money and passport.

You should carry the greater proportion of your money in the form of travellers' cheques. These can be refunded if lost or stolen, often within a few days. Some airlines will also reissue your ticket if it is lost. You have to give them details such as where and when you got it, the ticket number and which flight was involved. Usually a reissuing fee (about US$20) is charged, but that's much better than buying a new ticket.

Pickpockets are not the only problem. Snatch theft is also common so don't wear gold necklaces and expensive wristwatches or you're liable to have them snatched from your body. I've seen it happen to someone walking with me and by the time I realised that something had been stolen the thief was 20 metres away and jumping onto a friend's motorcycle. Snatch theft can also occur if you carry a camera loosely over your shoulder or place a bag down on the ground for just one second.

Thieves often work in pairs or groups. Whilst your attention is being distracted, one thief is robbing you. Ways that I have seen this happen include a bunch of kids fighting in front of you, an old lady 'accidentally' bumping into you, someone dropping something in your path or spilling something on your clothes – the possibilities go on and on. The only thing you can do is to try, as much as possible, to avoid being in very tight crowds and to stay alert, especially when something out of the ordinary occurs.

To worry you further, there are the razor blade artists. No, they don't wave a blade in your face and demand 'Your money or your life!' They're much too gutless for that kind of confrontation. They simply slit open your luggage with the razor blade when you're not looking. This includes a pack on your back or luggage in the rack of a bus or train, or even your trouser pocket. Many travellers carry their day packs on their chests to avoid having them slashed during day trips to markets, etc. When walking with my large pack, I move fast and avoid stopping which makes it difficult for anyone intent on cutting the bag. If I have to stop, at a street crossing for example, I tend to gently swing from side to side so I can feel if anyone is touching my pack and I look around a lot. I don't feel paranoid – walking fast and looking around on my way from bus station to hotel has become second nature to me, and I never place a bag on the ground unless I have my foot on it.

One of the best solutions to the rip-off problem is to travel with a friend and to watch one another. An extra pair of eyes makes a lot of difference. I often see shifty-looking types eyeing luggage at bus stations but they notice if you are alert and are less likely to bother you. They'd much rather steal something from the tired and unalert traveller who has put his bag on a chair whilst buying a coffee. Ten seconds later he has his coffee – but no bag!

It is a good idea to carry an emergency packet somewhere separate from all your other valuables. This emergency packet could be sown into a jacket (don't lose the jacket!) or even carried in your shoe. It should contain a photocopy of the important pages of your passport in case it is lost or stolen. On the back of the photocopy you should list important numbers such as all your travellers' cheque serial numbers, airline ticket numbers, credit card or bank account numbers, telephone numbers, etc. Also keep one high denomination bill with this emergency stash. You will probably never have to use it, but it's a good idea not to put all your eggs into one basket.

Definitely take out travellers' insurance. But don't get paranoid; stay alert and you can spend months in Peru without getting anything stolen.

Getting There

There are four ways of getting to Peru: by air from anywhere in the world, by land from the neighbouring South American countries, by river boat up the Amazon from Brazil, and by sea.

AIR

Jorge Chávez International Airport in Lima is the main hub for flights to the Andean countries from Europe and North America and so it is easy to fly to Peru from those continents. There are also some international flights to Iquitos in Peru's Amazon region.

The ordinary tourist or economy class fare is not the most economical way to go. It is convenient, however, because it enables you to fly on the next plane out and your ticket is valid for 12 months. If you want to economise further, there are several options.

Students with valid international student cards and those under 26 can get discounts with most airlines. Whatever age you are, if you purchase your ticket well in advance and stay a minimum length of time, you can buy an advance purchase excursion (APEX) ticket which is usually about one third cheaper than the full economy fare based on round-trip purchase. Several restrictions normally apply. You must purchase your ticket at least 21 days (sometimes more) in advance and you must stay away a minimum period (this varies from seven to 21 days) and return within 180 days (sometimes less, occasionally more). APEX tickets normally do not allow stop-overs and there are extra charges if you change your dates of travel or destinations. Individual airlines have different restrictions and these change from time to time. A good travel agent can tell you about this. Stand-by fares are another possibility. Some airlines will let you travel at the last minute if they have available seats just before the flight. These stand-by tickets cost less than an economy fare but are not usually as cheap as APEX.

The cheapest way to go is via the so-called 'bucket shops', which are legally allowed to sell discounted tickets to help airlines and charter companies fill their flights. These tickets are usually the cheapest of all, particularly in the low seasons, but they often sell out fast and you may be limited to only a few available dates. While APEX, economy and student flights are available direct from the airlines or from a travel agent (there is no extra charge if you buy from an agent rather than direct from the airline), discount bucket shop tickets are available only from the bucket shops themselves. Most of them are good and reputable companies, but once in a while a fly-by-night operator comes along and takes your money for a super-cheap flight and gives you an invalid or unusable ticket, so check what you are buying carefully before handing over your money.

Bucket shops often advertise in newspapers and magazines; there is much competition and a variety of fares and schedules are available. Fares to South America have traditionally been relatively expensive, but bucket shops have recently been able to offer increasingly economical fares to that continent.

It is worth bearing in mind that round-trip fares are always much cheaper than two one-way tickets. They are also cheaper than 'open jaws' fares – an 'open jaws' ticket enables you to fly into one city (say Lima) and leave via another (say Rio de Janeiro).

From North America

From Canada, there are flights with Canadian Pacific from Vancouver or Toronto to Lima. From the United States, however, flights are not so straightforward. Since Braniff went bankrupt in 1984, there has been an 'air war' between US and Peruvian airlines over who should operate the flights previously provided by Braniff. As a result Peru has denied landing rights to US airlines and the US has retaliated by denying landing rights to Peruvian airlines. This means that you cannot fly direct from the US to Peru with either US or Peruvian airlines. The 'air war' has continued for three years, though there is talk of direct flights resuming in 1987.

Meanwhile, US travellers have two choices. One is to fly with an airline from a country other than the US or Peru. Airlines such as Aerolineas Argentinas, LAN-Chile, Ecuatoriana, etc will provide direct flights from Miami, New York or Los Angeles to Peru – the main drawback is that these flights are more expensive.

The cheaper alternative is to fly with AeroPeru or Faucett (the two international Peruvian carriers) who have made arrangements with airlines from Mexico or the Caribbean to fly passengers to Mexico City, Jamaica or Grand Cayman Island. Connections are then made with an AeroPeru or Faucett flight to Lima. Although this is obviously less convenient, it is the cheapest way to go and may make you eligible for a free additional flight within Peru.

Generally speaking, the US does not have such a strong bucket shop tradition as Europe or Asia, so it's harder getting cheap flights from the US to South America. Sometimes the Sunday travel sections in the major newspapers (*The Los Angeles Times* on the west coast and *The New York Times* on the east coast) advertise cheap fares to South America, although these are sometimes no cheaper than APEX fares.

A travel agent which can find you the best deal to Peru (and anywhere else in the world) is Council Travel Services which are a subsidiary of the Council on International Educational Exchange (CIEE). You can find their address and telephone numbers in the telephone directories of Berkeley, La Jolla, Long Beach, Los Angeles, San Diego and San Francisco (all in California), Amherst, Boston and Cambridge (in Massachusetts), New York City, Portland (Oregon), Providence (Rhode Island), Austin (Texas) and Seattle (Washington).

There are three gateway cities from the US to Peru. Typical APEX fares are US$460 from Miami, US$600 from New York and US$760 from Los Angeles. These fares are all round-trip fares and may include an internal flight from Lima to a city of your choice. People are often surprised that fares from Los Angeles in southern California are so much higher than from northerly New York. A glance at the world map soon shows why. New York at 74° west is almost due north of Miami at 80° and Lima at 77°. Thus planes can fly a shorter, faster and cheaper north-south route. Los Angeles, on the other hand, is 118° west and therefore much further away from Lima than New York.

From Europe

Bucket shops generally provide the cheapest fares from Europe to South America. Fares from London are often cheaper than from other European cities and also there are more bucket shops here. For this reason some European budget travellers buy their tickets from London bucket shops. This is especially true of travellers from Scandinavian countries, where cheap fares are difficult to find.

In London competition is fierce. Bucket shops advertise in the classifieds of newspapers ranging from *The Times* to *Time Out*. I have heard consistently good reports about Journey Latin America (JLA), 16 Devonshire Rd, Chiswick, London W4 2HD (tel 01 747 3108) who specialise in cheap fares to the entire continent as well as arranging itineraries for both independent and escorted travel.

They will make arrangements for you over the phone. Another reputable budget travel agency is Trailfinders, 42-48 Earl's Court Rd, London W8 6EJ (tel 01 937 9631). The useful travel newspaper *Trailfinder* is available from them for free. Typical round-trip fares from London are just under £500.

From Australia

There is no real choice of routes between Australia and South America and there are certainly no bargain fares available. The most direct route is to fly from Australia to Tahiti with UTA or Qantas and connect from there with the weekly LAN-Chile flight to Santiago. From Chile you can then fly or travel overland to Peru.

Qantas has once weekly Melbourne-Sydney-Tahiti flights. UTA fly once weekly Sydney-Tahiti. Both connect with the LAN-Chile flight to Santiago with the option of a stop-over on Easter Island.

The cheapest one-way APEX fare from Sydney is A$1180, from Melbourne or Brisbane it is A$1236. Economy class return from Sydney is A$1915 (off peak) and A$2170 (peak), from Melbourne or Brisbane costs A$1981 and A$2238. For more information contact the LAN-Chile office on the 10th Floor, American Express Tower, 388 George St, Sydney 2000.

It is also possible to fly via New Zealand to Argentina with a combination of Air New Zealand and Aerolíneas Argetinas. The flight to Buenos Aires goes via the southern Argentinian city of Río Gallegos, which is a convenient point for travelling to Chile. A return excursion fare from the east coast of Australia to Buenos Aires will cost around A$2200.

The other alternative is to fly to the US west coast and fly from there or make your way overland. The return APEX fare from Australia to Los Angeles or San Francisco ranges from A$1392 (low season), A$1749 (shoulder) to A$1938

(high season); one-way fare is A$1013. By shopping around you should be able to obtain a better deal, though not on the LAN-Chile flights. Check the ads in the travel sections of the Melbourne *Age* or the *Sydney Morning Herald*. Student Travel Australia (STA) has offices in all states and is a good place to look for cheap fares. In Melbourne they are at 220 Faraday St, Carlton 3053 (tel (03) 347 6911); 1A Lee St, Railway Square, Sydney 2000 (tel (02) 212 1255); Shop 2, Societe General House, 40 Creek St, Brisbane 4000 (tel (07) 221 9629); Level 4, The Arcade, Union House, Adelaide University, Adelaide (tel (08) 223 6620); Hackett Hall, University of WA, Perth (tel (09) 380 2302); Union Building, University of Tasmania, Hobart (tel (002) 34 1850). In Melbourne, Sydney and Brisbane it is also worth trying the Flight Shops: Melbourne (tel (03) 67 6921), Sydney (tel (02) 233 2296) and Brisbane (tel (07) 229 9958).

Because of the high cost of flying to the Americas, the other option is a Round-the-World ticket. Some excellent deals are available, often for less than a return ticket to South America. They are usually valid for six months or a year with a number of stop-overs, usually five, depending on the price of the ticket.

LAND

If you live in the Americas, it is possible to travel overland. However, if you start from North or Central America, the Pan American highway stops in Panama and begins again in Colombia, leaving a 200 km roadless section of jungle known as the Darien Gap. This takes about a week to cross on foot and by canoe in the dry season (January to mid-April) but is much heavier going in the wet season. Most travellers going by land fly around the Darien Gap.

From South America it is straightforward to travel by public bus from the neighbouring countries of Ecuador, Chile and Bolivia.

RIVER BOAT

It is possible to travel by river boat all the way from the mouth of the Amazon at Belém in Brazil to Iquitos in Peru. Normally, travellers will need to break the journey up into several stages because very few boats do the entire trip.

The easiest way is to take one boat from Belém to Manaus in central Brazil and then a second boat from Manaus to Benjamin Constant on the Brazilian side of the Peruvian-Brazilian-Colombian border. At this point you can take local motor boats across the border to the small Peruvian port of Ramón Castilla. You can also reach Ramón Castilla by local motor boat from Leticia on the Colombian side of the tri-border. From Belém to Benjamin

Constant will take about two weeks depending on the currents and which boat you are on. From Ramón Castilla on to Iquitos takes a further two or three days. The entire trip will cost roughly US$70 or less if travelling on the lower decks. Further information about river travel in Peru is found in the Getting Around and Amazon Basin chapters.

SEA

It is possible to arrive in Lima's port of Callao by both expensive ocean liners and cheaper freight vessels. Few people arrive by sea, however, because services are infrequent and are normally more expensive and less convenient than flying.

Getting Around

Peru is a big country and so you'll need several months to visit it all overland. If your time is limited, you'll have to choose the areas which are the most important to you. Public buses are frequent and reasonably comfortable on the major routes and they are the normal form of transport for everybody. Less travelled routes are served by older and less comfortable vehicles. There are two railway systems which can make an interesting change from bus travel. Those in a hurry or desiring greater comfort or privacy can hire a car with a driver which is often not much more expensive than renting a self-drive car. Air services are widespread and particularly recommended for those short on time. In the jungle regions, travel by river boat or air is normally the only choice.

Whichever form of transport you use, remember to have your passport on your person and not packed in your luggage or left in the hotel safe. You need to show your passport to board most planes. Buses have to go through a transit police check upon entering and leaving major towns; again, passports must usually be shown. If your passport is in order, these procedures are no more than cursory. If you're travelling anywhere near the borders you can expect more frequent passport controls.

AIR

Even the budget traveller should consider an occasional internal flight because they are not very expensive. One-way tickets are usually half the price of a round-trip ticket and so you can travel one-way overland and save time by returning by air. Until recently, there were two fare structures on internal flights; one for residents and one for foreign tourists. Naturally, the 'foreign' fare was almost twice the cost of the 'resident' fare. This system was abolished in 1985 and at this time there is one fare structure for everybody. Should the dual structure be reinstated, bear in mind that in the smaller towns they don't check your resident status very carefully. I used to fly as a resident by making up any seven figure *cédula* (ID) number – this didn't normally work in Lima and Cuzco.

If you are arriving in Lima (or Iquitos) with one of Peru's two international airlines, Faucett or AeroPeru, remember to ask about their internal flights before making your reservation. Usually they'll include a free trip from Lima to the city of your choice, but the ticket must be bought outside of Peru. They also sometimes offer 'Visit Peru' tickets for US$180 which allow you unlimited air travel within Peru. Again, the ticket must be bought outside of the country and you may have to decide upon an itinerary in advance. Faucett and AeroPeru only fly to and from countries in the Americas.

Once you have arrived in Peru, you'll find the same two airlines serving most of the major towns. You can get a small discount (usually 7%) if you have a valid student ID. Both companies normally charge the same fare so use the one whose schedule most closely matches yours. Tickets can usually be signed over from one company to another if you want to change your schedule. This involves having the ticket 'released' by one airline before the other airline will accept it. In addition to Faucett and AeroPeru, you'll find several local airlines which tend to serve the smaller jungle towns with light aircraft. The military, known as *Grupo Ocho*, occasionally provide flights but these are only a few dollars cheaper than the regularly scheduled flights and are not normally worth waiting for.

The following cities are served by scheduled air services with either Faucett

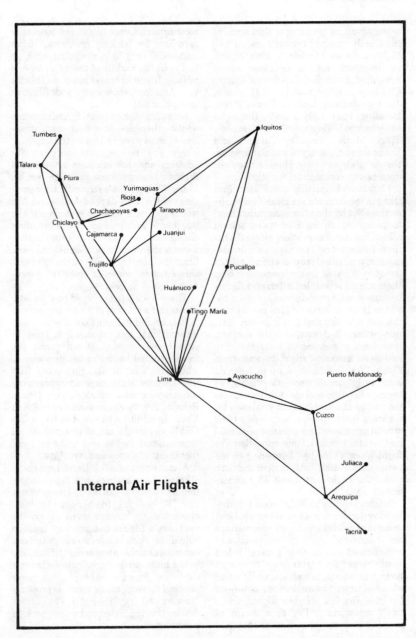

Internal Air Flights

or AeroPeru, or both. Note that some of the smaller towns have only one or two flights per week. Further details are given in the 'Air' sections of these cities: Arequipa, Ayacucho, Cajamarca, Cuzco, Chachapoyas, Chiclayo, Huánuco, Juanjui, Juliaca, Iquitos, Lima, Piura, Pucallpa, Puerto Maldonado, Rioja (for Moyobamba), Tacna, Talara, Tarapoto, Tingo María, Trujillo, Tumbes and Yurimaguas. Contrary to popular opinion, the Anta airport near Huaraz does not operate any commercial flights.

Flights are frequently late. Flights first thing in the morning are more likely to be on time but by the afternoon things tend to have slid an hour or more behind schedule. AeroPeru offer more flights than Faucett and, perhaps as a consequence, tend to be late more frequently. If flying in or out of Cuzco, remember that there are no scheduled afternoon flights because weather conditions are often too windy later in the day. This means that the last morning flight, if it is very late, may be cancelled because of the weather, thus leaving passengers stranded. Try and book an early flight to and from Cuzco. You should show up at least an hour early for all domestic flights, as baggage handling and check-in procedures tend to be chaotic. It is not unknown for flights to leave up to an hour *before* their official departure time because predicted bad weather would have cancelled the flight later. (This has happened to me twice in about 100 flights in Peru and both times the flight left about 15 minutes early.)

Flights tend to be fully booked during holiday periods so make reservations well in advance. Make sure all reservations are confirmed and reconfirmed and reconfirmed again. As a general rule I would reconfirm flights both 72 and 24 hours in advance, as well as a week or two ahead of time. The airlines are notorious for bumping you off your flights if you don't reconfirm – I've even heard of people being bumped off even after they had

reconfirmed. Cuzco flights are especially notorious for booking problems. If it's impossible for you to reconfirm because you're in the middle of nowhere, have a reliable friend or travel agent do this for you. And don't show up for your flight at the last minute.

Some flights have seating assignments whilst others are on a first-come, first-seated basis when you get on the airplane. There are no separate sections for smokers and non-smokers on internal flights. Non-smokers have to suffer. Many flights have extraordinarily good views of the snow-capped Andes and it is worth getting a window seat even if the weather is bad, because the plane often rises above the clouds giving spectacular views of the mountains. When flying from Lima to Cuzco try and sit on the left hand side for great views of the 6271-metre-high peak of Salcantay.

There is a 9% tax charged on domestic flights and a massive 21% on international tickets bought in Peru. So it is best to buy international tickets ahead of time in your home country. If you want the freedom of not having to decide where or when you want to fly, remember that international flight taxes in neighbouring countries are substantially lower – 16% in Bolivia, 10% in Ecuador and only 2% in Chile. In addition to ticket taxes, a flat US$10 departure tax is charged on all international flights and US$2 on local flights out of Cuzco and Arequipa.

A maximum of 20 kilos of luggage is allowed. Lost luggage is a depressingly frequent problem (although I must admit that it has yet to happen to me). Normally the luggage turns up on the next day's flights but try and include valuables such as camera gear and essentials such as a warm coat (if heading to the highlands) or medications in your carry on luggage. Always lock your checked luggage, make sure it is properly labelled and try to see that the correct destination tag is tied on by the check-in personnel.

If you fly with one of the small jungle airlines, the normal rule is to just show up at the airport in the morning and buy a seat on the next plane leaving for your destination. They leave as soon as they are full, which doesn't take long with a six-seater going to a popular destination. Less common destinations may be served only every few days. If you have a lot of luggage, you may be charged extra. Fifteen kilos is about the most you can get away with in a small airplane – if you're lucky. Travel light!

BOAT

Although Peru has a long coastline, travel along the coast is almost entirely by road or air and there are no coastal passenger steamer services, although international cruise ships arrive in Callao once in a while.

In the highlands there are boat services on Lake Titicaca, the highest navigable lake in the world at just over 3800 metres. Boats are usually small motorised vessels that take about 20 passengers from Puno to visit the various islands on the lake. There are departures every day and costs are low. There used to be a couple of larger steamships crossing the lake from Puno to Bolivia but this service no longer exists. Instead there is a hydrofoil which is very expensive and can be booked through travel agents. It is much cheaper to take a bus from Puno to La Paz, Bolivia, which gives you the opportunity to 'cross' Lake Titicaca by a ferry over the narrow Strait of Tiquina.

It is in Peru's eastern lowlands that boat travel becomes of major importance. This is mainly of two types – small dugout canoes or larger cargo boats. The dugout canoes are usually powered by an outboard engine and act as a water taxi or bus on some of the smaller rivers. Sometimes they are powered by a strange arrangement which looks like an inboard motorcycle engine attached to a tiny propeller by a three-metre-long propeller shaft. These are called *peke-pekes* and are a slow and rather noisy method of transportation but are OK for short trips. They are especially common on Lake Yarinacocha near Pucallpa and are sometimes a bit bigger than a dugout canoe. As one gets further inland and the rivers widen, larger cargo boats are normally available.

Dugout Canoes

Dugout canoes often carry as many as two dozen passengers and are the only way to get around many roadless areas. Wherever they are found, you can hire one yourself to take you anywhere, but this is very expensive. If you take one with other passengers then its much cheaper but not as cheap as bus travel over a similar distance. This is because an outboard engine uses much more fuel per passenger/km than does a bus engine.

Many of the boats used are literally dugouts, with maybe a splashboard added to the gunwales. They are long in shape but short on comfort. Seating is normally on hard, low, uncomfortable wooden benches accommodating two people each. Luggage is stashed forward under a tarpaulin, so carry hand baggage containing essentials for the journey.

If it is a long journey you will be miserable if you don't take the following advice, which is worth the cost of this book! *Bring seat padding.* A folded sweater or towel will make a world of difference to your trip. Pelting rain or glaring sun are major hazards and an umbrella is excellent defence against both. Bring suntan lotion and wear long sleeves, long pants and a sun hat – I have seen people unable to walk because of second degree burns on their legs from a six-hour exposure to the tropical sun. As the boat motors along, the breeze tends to keep insects away and it also tends to cool you down so you don't notice the burning effects of the sun. If the sun should disappear or the rain begin, you can get quite chilled, so bring a light jacket. Insect repellent is useful during stops along the river. A water bottle and food will complete your hand luggage. Remember to stash your spare clothes in plastic bags or they'll get soaked by rain or spray.

A final word about dugout canoes – they feel very unstable! Until you get used to the motion, you might worry about the whole thing just rolling over and tipping everybody into the piranha, electric eel or boa constrictor infested waters. Clenching the side of the canoe and wondering what madness possessed you to board the flimsy contraption in the first place doesn't seem to help. But dugouts feel much more unstable than they really are, so don't worry about a disaster; it almost never happens. I've ridden many dugouts without any problems, even in rapids. Nor have I met anyone who was actually dunked in.

River Boats

This is the classic way to travel down the Amazon – swinging in your hammock aboard a banana boat piloted by a grizzled old captain who knows the waters better than the back of his hand. You can travel from Pucallpa to the mouth of the Amazon in this way,

although the number of boats doing the entire trip are extremely few and far between. More likely you'll spend a couple of days getting to Iquitos where you'll board another, slightly larger boat and continue for a further couple of days to the border with Brazil and Colombia. From there, more boats can be found for the week-long passage to Manaus (Brazil) in the heart of the Amazon Basin.

Although cargo boats ply the Ucayali from Pucallpa to Iquitos, and the Marañon from Yurimaguas to Iquitos, they tend to leave only once or twice a week. The boats are small, but with two decks. The lower deck is normally for cargo and the upper for passengers and crew. Bring your own hammock. Food is usually provided, but it is basic and not necessarily very hygienic. You may want to bring some of your own. To get a passage, go down to the docks and just start asking around until you hear of a boat going where you want to go. Find out who the captain is and arrange a passage – it's usually worth asking around about the approximate cost, though often the captains will charge you the same as anybody else. Departure time is, more often than not,

Inca Balsa raft

dependent on a full cargo and *mañana* may go on for several days if the hold is only half full. Sometimes you can sleep on the boat whilst you are waiting for departure, thus saving on hotel bills.

Boats to Iquitos are relatively infrequent and rather small, slow and uncomfortable. Beyond Iquitos, however, services are both more frequent and more comfortable. Things are generally more organised too; there are chalk boards at the docks with ship's names, destinations and departure times displayed reasonably clearly and accurately. You can look over a boat for your prospective destination and wait for a better vessel if you don't like what you see. Some boats even have cabins, though these tend to be rather grubby airless boxes and you have to supply your own bedding. I prefer to use a hammock. Food is usually included in the price of the passage, and may be marginally better on some of the bigger and better ships. If you like rice and beans – or rice and fish, or rice and tough meat, or rice and fried bananas – you'll be OK. If you don't like rice, you'll have a problem. Bottled soft drinks and beers are usually available – ask about this before the boat leaves because you definitely don't want to drink the water. Sanitary facilities are basic but adequate. A pump shower is usually aboard.

Occasionally, boats from Iquitos go all the way to the mouth of the Amazon, though this is very rare these days. However, the very fact that ocean going vessels are capable of reaching Iquitos, indicates how vast this river is. Many people have misconceptions about sailing down the Amazon watching monkeys swinging in the tree tops, snakes coiled among the branches, and parrots and macaws flying across the river in front of you. In reality, most of the banks have been colonised and there is little wildlife there. Also, the boats often navigate the mid-stream, and the shoreline is seen only as a rather distant green line. In fact, some people find the monotonous diet

and long days of sitting in their hammocks to be boring and they don't enjoy the trip.

I travelled this way from Iquitos all the way to Manaus and had a great time. I was already aware of and prepared for the lack of wildlife, and so I came prepared with a couple of very thick books. Yet I found I barely had the time to read them, there was so much to do. Quarters were close on the passenger deck, and my elbows literally touched my neighbour's when I was in my hammock. Friendliness and an easy-going attitude are essential ingredients for a river trip. Most of the passengers are friendly and fun, and you can have a great time getting to know them. The views of the great river stretching all around were often very beautiful, particularly during the misty dawns and the searing sunsets.

On the first evening of a seven-day trip, I was sitting in the bow enjoying the cooling breeze and watching the sun go down. Soon, a small crowd of Peruvian and Brazilian passengers and crew gathered, and a rum bottle and guitar appeared. Within minutes, we had a first rate party going with singing, dancing, hand clapping, and an incredible impromptu orchestra. One of the crew bent a metal rod into a rough triangle which he pounded rhythmically, someone else threw a handful of beans into a can and started shaking, a couple of pieces of polished wood were clapped together to interweave yet another rhythm, a mouth harp was produced, I blew bass notes across the top of my beer bottle and everyone had a great time. A couple of hours of rhythmic music as the sun went down became a standard part of the ship's routine and gave me some of my most unforgettable moments of South American travel.

Once or twice a day, the boat would pull into some tiny Amazonian port to load or offload passengers and cargo. The arrival of a big boat was often the main event of the day in one of these small river villages, and the entire population might come down to the riverbank to swap gossip and watch the goings on. This, too, added to the interest of the trip.

For some people, boating down the Amazon is a monotonous and sweaty endurance test. For others it's a great experience – I hope my descriptions help you decide whether this is something you'd like to attempt or want to avoid.

RAIL

There are two railway networks in Peru, which do not connect. Both go from the coast to the highlands and were major communication links between the Sierra and the coast before the advent of roads and later air travel. Trains are less used today but nevertheless still play an important part in Peru's transport system.

There are two classes. Second is very cheap and very crowded and uncomfortable. First is about 25% more expensive, much more comfortable and still cheaper than a bus journey of comparable length. In addition, there are buffet and Pullman cars which require a surcharge. They are heated and give access to food service. There is also a more expensive tourist train from Cuzco to Machu Picchu. Generally, train travel is slower and cheaper than buses for a journey of equal length, but what you lose on speed you gain in the comfort of being able to stand up and stretch your legs.

In addition to the normal train, there is a faster electric train called an *autovagon*. This is smaller and more expensive than the ordinary train and runs on only a few routes.

The Central Railroad runs from Lima to the mining town of La Oroya. Here it branches north and south. The north-bound line goes to Cerro de Pasco but has been closed since the early 1980s. The southbound line goes to Huancayo and there are direct trains from Lima to Huancayo but frequency of service changes from year to year – there is never

more than one train a day, however. This trip takes a whole day and passes through the station of Galera, which is at 4781 metres above sea level and the highest standard gauge railway station in the world. In Huancayo you can change railway stations and then continue to Huancavelica. The autovagon also runs the Huancayo-Huancavelica section.

The Southern Railroad runs from the coast at Mollendo through Arequipa to Lake Titicaca and Cuzco. With the decline of importance of Mollendo as a shipping port and the construction of the asphalted Pan-American Highway from Arequipa to Lima, the short Mollendo-Arequipa section is now closed. The Arequipa-Lake Titicaca-Cuzco section is, however, the longest and busiest section of Peru's railways. Trains from Arequipa to Puno, on the shores of Lake Titicaca, run every night and three days a week. You can change at Juliaca, about 40 km before Puno, for daily trains to Cuzco. Services don't run on Sundays. The Arequipa-Juliaca (or Puno) service takes a whole day or night; the Puno-Cuzco service also takes a whole day. In Cuzco there are two train stations; one for the service described above and the other for service to Machu Picchu. You cannot go directly from Arequipa or Lake Titicaca to Machu Picchu at this time; there are plans afoot to extend the track and make this possible in the future. There are several train and autovagon services from Cuzco to Machu Picchu every day.

The last segment of Peru's southern railway is found in the extreme south of the country. It is a border train which runs several times a day between Tacna in Peru and Arica in Chile.

The main drawback to travelling by train is thievery. The night train from Arequipa to Puno is especially notorious, particularly in crowded and ill-lit 2nd class carriages where a dozing traveller is almost certain to get robbed. Dark train stations are also the haunts of thieves, who often work in pairs or small groups.

The answer to the problem is to travel by day and stay alert, to travel with a friend or group, and to travel in 1st class. Above all, stay alert. (The Tacna-Arica train is safer than the others.)

For all services it is advisable to buy tickets in advance – the day before is usually best. This way you don't have to worry about looking after your luggage whilst lining up to buy a ticket at a crowded booking office window.

BUSES
Long Distance

Without a doubt, buses are the most frequently used form of public transport in Peru. They go just about everywhere except for the deep jungle and Machu Picchu (trains or foot only). This is hardly surprising when one considers that the average Peruvian is too poor to be able to afford a car and yet many can afford to travel by bus. Bus fares are cheap because the cost of labour (booking office clerks, drivers and mechanics) is very low and because buses tend to run full and sell all their seats.

There are dozens (if not hundreds) of competing bus companies and they all have their own offices. Therefore there is no central bus terminal. In some towns, the different bus companies have their offices clustered around a few city blocks whilst in other towns the terminals are scattered all over. I have tried to mark as many of these as possible on my city maps and the accompanying text will tell you which destinations are served by which companies.

It is always a good idea to buy your ticket in advance. This guarantees you a seat and also means that you can check out the schedules and prices of different companies without being encumbered by your luggage. There is sometimes a separate 'express' ticket window for people buying tickets for another day. Schedules and fares change frequently and vary from company to company; because of this I only give an approximate

idea of how frequently buses leave and the average fares. Exact fares and schedules would be obsolete within a very few months. Students with international student cards are officially allowed a 10% discount although some companies will simply not sell discounted tickets.

When you buy your ticket, try and avoid the seats at the back of the bus because the ride is nearly always much more bumpy. On some of the rougher mountain roads you can literally be thrown out of your seat in the back of the bus. Also try and avoid those seats which come over the wheel wells because you'll lose leg space. When you buy your ticket, always be sure to ask where the bus is leaving from because the ticket office and bus stop are sometimes on different streets.

When waiting in bus terminals, watch your luggage very carefully. Snatch theft is common and thieves work in pairs – one may distract you whilst the other grabs your bag. Razor blade artists abound, too. Whilst you're dozing off, leaning against your pack, somebody may try to slash through the pockets. Keep luggage where you can see it and stay alert. I hear depressingly frequent stories of theft in bus stations. I have been able to avoid losing my gear during many thousands of km of bus travel simply by staying alert. Thieves are looking for an easy rip off – they won't bother you if you look on top of things. They will bother you if you leave your pack leaning against the wall for 15 seconds when you're buying a bar of chocolate. Turn around with your chocolate and – no pack!

During the journey your luggage, unless it is small enough to carry on, will travel in the luggage compartment. This is normally reasonably safe. You are given a baggage tag in exchange for your bag which should be securely closed and locked if possible. I like to watch my pack getting loaded onto the bus and I usually exchange a few friendly words with the loader (who is often the driver's assistant) just to make sure that my bag is properly loaded and going to the right destination. During a long trip I get off and check my bag at stops and generally maintain a high profile. Of course, if you're on a night bus you'll want to sleep but I've not had any problem with anyone claiming my luggage in the middle of the night. Your hand luggage is a different matter. If you're asleep with a camera around your neck you may well wake up with a neatly razored strap and no camera at the end of it. I sleep with my carry on bag (usually a day pack) strapped on to my person and with my arms around it.

Distances are large in Peru and you'll probably take some trips at night. The buses running up and down the paved Pan-American Highway are reasonably comfortable and have reclining seats. The same kinds of buses are often used on the rougher roads into the mountains but they are generally less comfortable because the constant bumping and jarring has often broken the reclining mechanism on some of the seats – how good a seat you get is largely a matter of luck. On the more remote highways, the buses are often of the uncomfortable 'school bus' type. An irritating habit that bus companies have is to shift all the rows of seats forward so that they can get another row or two in the bus. This is fine if you're short or medium sized, but can be a real pain if you're six foot one, as I've found. The heating in buses doesn't always work and it can literally get down to freezing *inside* the bus when travelling in the mountains at night, so bring a blanket, sleeping bag or warm clothes as hand luggage. Conversely, the air conditioning doesn't always work and so it can get very hot and sweaty on some of the lowland trips, especially if the windows can't be opened.

Long-distance buses stop for at least three meals a day. The driver will announce how long the stop will be but it's usually worth asking again unless you're sure you heard right. *Diez minutos*

and *treinta minutos* sound very much alike when the driver mumbles the words whilst stifling a yawn. And it's your responsibility to be on the bus when it leaves. Many companies have their own special rest areas and these are sometimes in the middle of the desert so you don't have any choice but to eat there. The food is generally inexpensive but not particularly appetising. I generally eat the *lomo saltado* (chopped beef fried with vegetables and served with rice) and find it's one of the standard, more edible dishes. Some travellers prefer to bring their own food.

These rest stops double as lavatory stops. Some of the better long-distance buses do have toilet cubicles aboard but don't rely on them. Sometimes they don't work and are locked, at other times they are used as an extra luggage compartment and, if they do work, somebody invariably vomits over the whole thing just before you go to use it. Rule number one of travel in Peru is to always carry your own roll of toilet paper because you will never find any in the toilets. Most rest stop areas have somewhere to buy essentials like toilet paper, toothpaste, chocolate and other snacks.

If you're travelling during long holiday weekends or special fiestas, you may find that buses are booked up for several days in advance, so book as early as you can for these periods. Whichever time you travel, be prepared for delays and don't plan on making important connections after a bus journey. Innumerable flat tires, a landslide, or engine trouble can lengthen the two-day journey from Lima to Cuzco to a four-day odyssey. Such lengthy delays are not very common, but a delay of several hours can be expected quite frequently.

If you want to travel immediately, remember that you can often flag down a bus almost anywhere, even if it is a long distance one. Recently, Cathy and I decided to go to Huaraz from Lima and as we were walking towards the Ormeño bus terminal, I saw a bus marked *Huaraz* standing at a traffic light. We quickly crossed the street, waving at the driver as we ran, and he let us onto the bus thus saving us a walk to the terminal and a wait for the next bus. Of course, long distance buses are less likely to stop if they are full or travelling at high speed.

A useful thing to carry on an overnight bus is a flashlight, because the driver nearly always shuts off the interior lights when the bus is underway. Being so close to the equator, it is dark for 12 hours and a flashlight enables you to read a book for a few hours before going to sleep. And when you do decide to sleep, ear plugs are a good idea.

Local Buses
Local buses are usually slow and crowded, but very cheap. You can get around most towns for about 10c. Local buses often go out to a nearby village and this is a good way to see an area. Just stay on the bus to the end of the line, pay another 10c and head back again, usually sitting in the best seat on the bus. If you make friends with the driver, you may end up with an entertaining tour as he points out the local sights, in between collecting other passengers' fares.

When you want to get off a local bus, yell *Baja!*, which means 'Down!' Telling the driver to stop will make him think you're trying to be a back seat driver, and you will be ignored. He's only interested if you're getting off, or down from the bus. Another way of getting him to stop is to yell *Esquina!*, which means 'Corner!' He'll stop at the next one.

Trucks
In remote areas, trucks often double as buses. Sometimes they are pick-up trucks with rudimentary wooden benches and at other times they are ordinary trucks; you just climb in the back, often with a cargo. I once had a ride on top of a truck carrying two bulls - for 12 hours my feet dangled just cm away from a pair of impressively large horns! If the weather is OK, you can get fabulous views as you travel in the refreshing wind (dress warmly). If the weather is bad you hunker down underneath a dark tarpaulin with the other passengers - unless the cargo happens to be two bulls in which case you stay on top and get soaked to the bone. It certainly isn't the height of luxury, but it may be the only way of getting to some areas, and if you're open minded about the minor discomforts, you may find these rides among the most interesting in Peru.

Payment for these rides is usually determined by the driver and is a standard fare depending on the distance. You can ask other passengers how much they are paying; usually you'll find that because the trucks double as buses they charge almost as much.

TAXI
There are many different kinds of taxis ranging from shared *colectivos* running a set route between two towns, to expensive *remisse* taxis parked in the stands outside a fancy hotel. Whatever kind of taxi you take, there are two things to remember: fares are invariably cheaper than in North America or Europe and you *must* always ask the fare in advance because there are no meters. It is quite acceptable to haggle over a taxi fare - drivers often double or triple the standard rate for an unsuspecting foreigner. Try and find out what the going rate is before taking a cab. About US$1 is fare for the cheapest and shortest run in Lima, a little less in other cities.

For short hops around a city, just flag down one of the many taxis which seem to be everywhere. They are recognisable by the small red TAXI sticker in the windshield. The cars themselves can be of almost any model and colour - Volkswagen Beetles are among the most popular. The black *remisse* taxis outside the expensive hotels are usually the most convenient, comfortable and reliable, and some of their drivers speak English. They do a brisk trade in taking well-heeled tourists to the airport or Gold Museum. They are also the most expensive and have set rates which are often two or three times the rate of a taxi flagged down on the street.

Shared taxis are called *colectivos* and do set runs. One of the best known runs is along Avenida Arequipa between downtown Lima and the suburb of Miraflores – there is a set fare (about 15c) and the driver drives along with one hand out of his window holding up as many fingers as the number of seats he has available. You can flag him down on any corner and get off wherever you like. Other colectivo taxis work for *comités* and have a set run between major cities. These cost about twice as much as a bus fare and are about 25% faster than an express bus. Comités are labelled on all my city maps and are worth investigating as an alternate form of long distance transport. They will often pick you up from your hotel if this is prearranged.

Note that the term *colectivo* is also used to denote a bus, especially a minibus or van.

Finally, you can hire a taxi with a driver for several hours or even days. The cost varies depending on how far you expect to drive in a day and on how luxurious a vehicle you get. If you speak Spanish and make your own arrangements with a driver you could start around US$30 to US$40 for a whole day, if you're not driving non-stop on bad roads. On the other hand, a tourist agency could arrange a comfortable car with an English-speaking driver for about twice as much. Often, your hotel can help arrange a taxi for you. If you hire one for several days, make sure that you discuss eating and sleeping arrangements. Some drivers will charge enough to be able to make their own arrangements, whilst others will expect you to provide a room and three meals.

Tipping is not the norm, especially for short hops within the city. If you hire a driver for the day and he is particularly helpful or friendly, you may want to tip but this isn't considered obligatory.

CAR RENTAL

You can drive yourself, but this tends to be expensive. The cheapest car rental I found was from National Car Rental who have Volkswagen Beetles for US$19 per day plus 18c per km plus US$4 per day for (optional) insurance. The insurance covers accidents but not theft. This means that if you decided to rent a car for three days to go from Lima to Nazca and back (about a six-hour drive without stops) you would have to pay about US$150 plus gas (which is just over US$1 per gallon). If you rent by the week it's slightly cheaper – US$220 per week plus insurance and gas but your first 1000 km are free. Bear in mind that this is for a VW Beetle with an 'economical' company. Their Nissan Patrol 4WD Jeep runs US$470 per week including 1000 free km. Budget, Avis and Hertz also have offices in Peru. Rental car agencies have offices at the major airports (Lima, Cuzco, Arequipa) and also downtown in the major cities.

If you decide that you want to drive yourself despite the expense, you need to be over 25 and must use a credit card charge as a deposit, although some agencies will accept US$200 cash. A valid driver's licence from your home country is normally accepted. Bear in mind that the condition of the rental vehicles is often not very good, roads are badly potholed (even the paved Pan-American Highway) and drivers extremely aggressive. Road signs, where they exist, are often small and unclear. Gas stations are few and far between. Theft is all too common and so you should not leave your vehicle parked in the street or you'll lose your hubcaps, windscreen wipers, even your wheels. When overnighting, park the car in a guarded lot (the better hotels have them). As a general rule, I do not recommend self-drive car rental.

YOUR OWN CAR

You cannot drive your own car to Peru from North America because of the roadless rain forest of the Darien Gap between Panama and Colombia. Therefore you have to either ship your vehicle to South America or buy a car there. Both alternatives are expensive and fraught with problems – but it certainly is done, and once in a while you'll meet someone touring South America in their own VW bus. Read the warnings in the last paragraph of the Car Rental section. If that doesn't deter you, get a copy of a book about driving in third world countries. A good one is *Overland & Beyond* by T & J Hewat, published by Lascelles of London. There are others.

HITCHHIKING

Hitching is not very practical in Peru because there are few private cars, because public transport is relatively cheap, and because trucks are used as public transport in remote areas, so trying to hitch a free ride on one is the same as trying to hitch a free ride on a bus. Many drivers of *any* vehicle will pick you up but will also expect payment. If the driver is stopping to drop off and pick up other passengers, ask them what the going rate is. If you are the only passenger, the driver may have picked you up just to talk with a foreigner, and he may wave aside your offer of payment. If you do decide to try hitching, make sure in advance of your ride that you and the driver agree on the subject of payment.

FOOT

By 'Foot' I mean either two (your own) or four (with a mule). Peru is certainly a good destination for adventurous treks in the Andes. Both the Inca Trail to Machu Picchu and the Cordillera Blanca have justly become world famous for hiking and backpacking. Several excellent guidebooks have been published specifically for foot travellers – see the the list in the Books & Bookshops section.

Walking around cities is generally safe, even at night, if you stick to the well lit areas. Always be on the alert for pickpockets, though, and make local enquiry before venturing into an area you don't know.

Lima

If you read the *Paddington Bear* books when you were young, as I did, you may remember that Lima is in 'darkest Peru', which conjures up images of an exotic city located in the heart of a lush tropical jungle. Unfortunately, this is far from the case. The city is mainly a modern one, sprawled untidily on the edge of the coastal desert. It has a host of urban problems but despite this, most visitors find it interesting, if nerve racking, to visit.

Lima, Peru's capital, was founded by Francisco Pizarro on 6 January 1535, which coincides with the Catholic feast of Epiphany, or the Day of the Kings. Hence the first proud name of Lima was the City of the Kings and many of the old colonial buildings can still be seen in the capital. Unfortunately, much of Lima's original colonial charm has been overwhelmed by a recent uncontrolled population explosion.

For almost four centuries Lima remained a small city until unprecedented growth began in the 1920s. The urban population of 173,000 in 1919 more than tripled in the next two decades and from 1940 until the present, it has multiplied a further ninefold. Almost a third of the nation's 19 million inhabitants are now trying to live in Lima and most of the city is overcrowded, polluted and noisy. Much of this growth can be attributed to the influx of very poor people from other areas of Peru, especially the highlands. They come searching for a better life with a job and perhaps opportunities for their children. Most end up living in the *pueblos jovenes* (literally 'young towns') which are shanty towns surrounding the capital and lacking electricity, water and adequate sanitation. Jobs are scarce and the most common form of 'employment' is to work as an *ambulante* or street vendor selling anything from chocolates to clothes pins. The profits are barely enough to feed the ambulantes and the possibilities of improving their lot are very low.

Lima's location in the centre of Peru's desert coastline gives it a climate and environment that can only be described as dismal. From April until December, the city suffers from the coastal fog known as *garua* which blots out the sun and blankets the buildings in a fine grey mist. Unless they are repainted on a yearly basis, the buildings soon take on a ghostly pallor from the incessant mist and a look at any of the city's rooftops will reveal a thin concrete-like layer of hardened grey sludge. Even during the few short months of Lima's summer the situation is barely improved; although the sun does come out, the smog makes walking the downtown streets a sticky and unpleasant activity and the beaches are overcrowded cesspools. The waste products of over five million inhabitants have to go somewhere and most of them end up in the Pacific – there are daily health warnings in the newspapers during the summer months.

Having read this far you might well be thinking of ways to avoid Lima. If you plan on doing any kind of extensive travelling in Peru, however, you will find it is virtually impossible to avoid the desert coastline and in turn, Lima.

Despite the capital's drawbacks there are reasons for visiting the city other than because you have to. The inhabitants are generally friendly and hospitable, there are plenty of opportunities for dining, nightlife and other entertainment, and, perhaps most important of all, there is a great selection of museums including some of the best in Peru. So try and ignore the traffic jams and the crowds and get to know some of the people and the culture of Peru.

Warnings

With literally millions of very poor and unemployed people in Lima, it is hardly surprising that the city suffers from a crime problem. Don't worry – you are unlikely to be mugged or otherwise physically hurt but many travellers do have their belongings stolen. Please re-read the section on Safety & Security in Facts for the Visitor before arriving in Lima.

Travellers have gotten sick by drinking tap water and your best bet is to stick with bottled drinks or to purify your own water. Remember that the salads in the cheaper restaurants (and some of the fancier ones) are often washed in the same tap water that you don't want to drink and so it's safest to avoid uncooked vegetables.

Occasionally there are reports in the foreign press of bombings, blackouts and demonstrations in Lima. Whilst these undeniably occur, in five years of travelling in Peru I've come to the conclusion that Lima is as safe as any other major city. However, in February of 1986 a curfew was imposed in Lima. It may have ended by the time you read this so make local enquiries. Curfew hours are from 1 to 5 am and you are not allowed to walk or drive anywhere in the city without a *salvo conducto* or safe conduct pass. If your international flight arrives at the airport during these hours you are given a pass, but the cab drivers charge about US$15 to US$20 to take you downtown. Salvo conductos are available at the National Stadium, Door 1, on the 700 to 900 blocks of the Paseo de la República, from 9 am to 12 noon on Mondays to Saturdays and from 2 to 5 pm on Mondays to Fridays. In case of emergency, drive with interior lights on, do not exceed 35 km per hour, carry a white flag in a prominent place and obey orders to stop.

Information

Tourist Information The Ministry of Industry & Tourism runs Tourist Information Offices in all major Peruvian cities. In Lima, their office (tel 323559) is át Jirón de la Unión 1066 (also known as Jirón Belén) about half a block from the Plaza de San Martín. Hours are from 9 am to 5 pm, Monday to Friday. Some of the staff speak English and they have a wealth of up-to-date information about transportation, hotels and sightseeing throughout the more popularly visited parts of Peru. There is also a Tourist Information Office at the airport but it is not as good; they will help you find a hotel by phone, however.

A most useful source of general information is the *Peru Guide* which is a free booklet published monthly by Lima Tours, whose office is at Belén 1040, a few doors from the Tourist Office. The booklet can also be found at some of the better hotels, restaurants and tourist spots in Lima, as well as at the South American Explorers Club.

South American Explorers Club For many long term travellers and ex-pat residents of Peru, this club has become somewhat of a legend. Since it was founded by Don Montague and Linda Rojas (née Rosa) in 1977, it has been involved in anything ranging from the clean-up of the Inca Trail in 1980 to the clean-up of erroneous media reports about discoveries of 'lost' Peruvian cities in 1985. Its primary function, however, is as an information centre for travellers, adventurers, scientific expeditions, etc and the club's headquarters in Lima can provide a wealth of advice about travelling anywhere in Latin America, with an emphasis on Peru.

The club has an extensive library of books, maps (some published by the club) and trip reports left by other travellers. A variety of the most useful books and maps are for sale and there are trail maps for the Inca Trail, the Mt Ausangate area, the Cordilleras Blanca and Huayhuash as well as general maps of South America. Useful current advice can be obtained

"INDIAN MARKET" - MIRAFLORES.
"GOLD MUSEUM."

MUSEO ARQUELOGICO - MAGDALENA - LARCO MUSEUM - + AMANO MUSEUM."

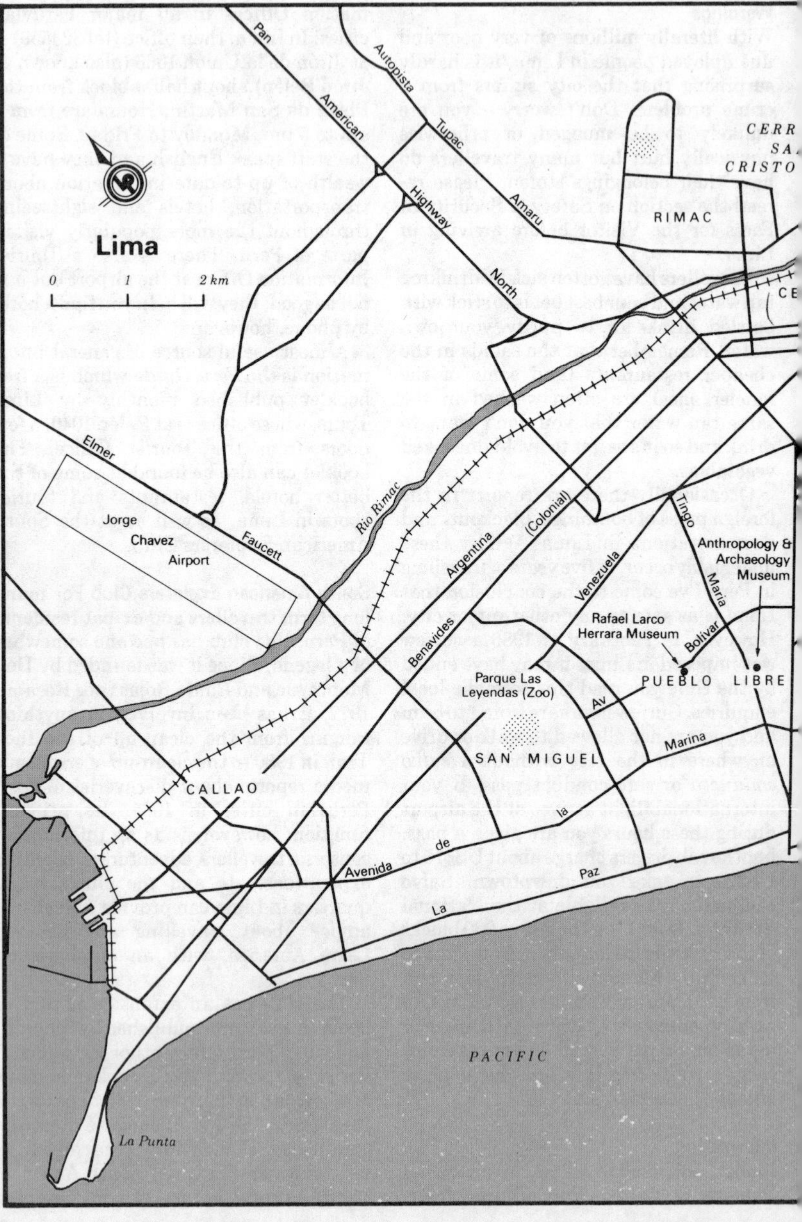

Lima

0 1 2 km

Pan American Highway

Autopista

Tupac Amaru

North

CERRO SAN CRISTO

RIMAC

CE

Elmer

Jorge Chavez Airport

Faucett

Rio Rimac

Argentina (Colonial)

Venezuela

Tingo Maria

Anthropology & Archaeology Museum

Rafael Larco Herrara Museum

Bolivar

PUEBLO LIBRE

Benavides

Parque Las Leyendas (Zoo)

Av

Marina

SAN MIGUEL

CALLAO

Avenida   de   la   Paz

La

La Punta

PACIFIC

"La Rosa Nautica" – Restaurant Lima 67

Lima Tours - near hotel

about travel conditions, currency regulations, weather conditions and so on.

The club is an entirely member-supported, non-profit organisation. Membership costs US$25 per individual (US$35 for a couple) and lasts for four issues of their excellent and informative *South American Explorer* magazine, which, as they'll tell you, is officially a quarterly but in fact comes out at surprisingly irregular intervals – so your US$25 membership is usually good for about two or three years. In addition to four issues of the magazine, members receive full use of the club house and its facilities which include: an information service and library; introductions to other travellers and notification of expedition opportunities; storage of excess luggage (anything ranging from small valuables to a kayak); storage or forwarding of mail addressed to you at the club; a relaxing place to read and research, or just to have a cup of tea and a chat with the friendly staff; a book exchange; buying and selling of used equipment; discounts on the books, maps and gear sold at the club and other services. Non-members are welcome to visit the club but are asked to limit their visit to about half an hour and are not eligible for membership privileges until they cough up their US$25. Paid-up members can hang out all day – a welcome relief from the madhouse bustle of Lima.

If you're already in Lima you can just go to the club house and sign up. Otherwise, you can mail your US$25 and any questions you may have direct to the club at Casilla 3714, Lima 100, Peru. The street address is Portugal 146, on the 13th block of Alfonso Ugarte in the Breña district of Lima, about a 10 or 15-minute walk from the Plaza San Martín. The club is open from 9.30 am to 5 pm on Mondays to Fridays and has been known to open on Saturdays too. You can call 314480 for current hours.

There is also a US office (tel (303) 320 0388) at 1510 York St, Denver, CO 80206.

This is where the magazine is published and if you're not sure whether or not you want to join, send them US$4 for a sample copy of the *Explorer* and further information.

Immigration Lima is one of the easiest places in Peru to have your tourist permit extended. Most European nationalities receive 90 days upon arrival which can be extended for a further 90 days. A few nationalities (including the US) are given only 60 days but they can renew twice to give the same 180 day total. Those nationalities which require tourist visas (France, Australia and New Zealand are notable examples) can also renew for 60 days. Once your maximum of 180 days is up you must leave the country but there is no law against crossing the border to a neighbouring country and returning the next day to start the process over again.

The Lima Immigration Office is on the 500 block of Paseo de la República and 28 de Julio. They open about 8 am on weekdays and it's best to go first thing in the morning if you want to get your extension the same day. It used to be that you needed specially stamped paperwork but this is no longer required as of 1986. What you do need is your passport and the white immigration slip which you received upon entry (it's not a disaster if you lose it but the process becomes more time consuming and expensive). You also need a *solicitud* or written request for an extension. This can be obtained from one of the itinerant typists in the street outside – they know all the jargon and charge about a dollar for the service. These documents are presented with a fee of US$20 which can be payed in intis at the official rate thus saving you about 20%. Sometimes a ticket out of the country is asked for though you can get around this by showing enough money. The more affluent you look the less hassle you'll have. Remember that regulations change frequently in Latin America and Lima is no exception!

Note that a bus ticket from Lima to the Ecuadorian, Bolivian, or Chilean borders will cost you less than the US$20 renewal, so if you're on a tight budget you might want to spend your money travelling towards a convenient border and re-enter the country instead of renewing in Lima.

A final word about student visas. If you're studying in Peru you can get one but they're usually more hassle than they're worth and many foreign students prefer to just use tourist permits.

Embassies Travellers from most nations can enter the neighbouring countries of Ecuador and Chile simply by showing their passports and obtaining a tourist card at the border. If you wish to check this you'll find the Ecuadorian Embassy (tel 228138) at Las Palmeras 356, San Isidro, from 9 am to 1 pm on weekdays and the Chilean Embassy (tel 407965) at Javier Prado Oeste 790, San Isidro, from 8.45 am to 12.30 pm on weekdays.

To enter the neighbouring countries of Bolivia and Brazil, citizens of France, the USA, Australia, New Zealand and some others require visas. Most western European countries do not require visas. The Bolivian Embassy (tel 228231) is at Los Castaños 235, San Isidro, from 8.30 am to 1.30 pm on weekdays. The Brazilian Embassy (tel 452421) is at Comandante Espinar 181, Miraflores from 9 am to 1 pm on weekdays.

All other South American countries can be reached from Peru only by air or occasionally ship. The principal countries with diplomatic representation are:

Argentina
Pablo Bermudez 143, Jesus María, (tel 729920 or 245984), from 8 am to 1 pm on weekdays
Colombia
Arequipa 2685, Lince, (tel 407835), from 9 am to 12.30 pm on weekdays
Venezuela
Salaverry 3005, San Isidro, (tel 415948), from 9 am to 12 noon on weekdays

Most major English speaking and European countries are represented in Peru. The main ones are:

Belgium
Angamos 380, Miraflores (tel 463335), from 8.30 am to 3 pm on weekdays
Canada
Libertad 130, Miraflores, (tel 463890), from 8.30 to 11 am on weekdays
France
Arequipa 3415, San Isidro, (tel 704968), from 9 am to 12 noon on weekdays
Ireland
Carlos Povias Osores 410, San Isidro, (tel 230808)
Israel
Washington Building, 6th floor, 600 block of Arequipa, Lima, (tel 321005), from 10 am to 1 pm on weekdays
Italy
Petit Thouars 369, (tel 223477)
Japan
San Felipé 356, Jesus María, (tel 630000), from 9 am to 12.30 pm and 3.30 to 5.30 pm on weekdays
The Netherlands
Avenida Principal 190, San Borja, (tel 751548), from 9 am to 12 noon on weekdays
New Zealand
Salaverry 3006, San Isidro (tel 621890)
Norway
Canaval Moreyra 585, San Isidro, (tel 416377), from 9 am to 12 noon on weekdays
Spain
República de Chile 120, Lima, (tel 310420), from 9 am to 12 noon on weekdays
Switzerland
Salaverry 3240, San Isidro, (tel 624090), from 9 am to 12 noon on weekdays
UK
Washington Building, 12th floor, 600 block of Arequipa, Lima, (tel 283830), from 10 am to 3 pm on Mondays to Thursdays and to 1 pm on Fridays
USA
Grimaldo del Solar 346, Miraflores, (tel 443621), from 8.15 to 11 am on weekdays except Wednesdays, (there is also the embassy office on the 1400 block of Garcilazo de la Vega and Avenida España downtown – call 286000)
West Germany
Arequipa 4210, Miraflores, (tel 459997), from 9 am to 12 noon on weekdays

Money Exchange As you will have gathered from the Facts for the Visitor chapter, changing money can be problematic in Peru. Lima is the best place in the country to change money, but it's by no means a straightforward procedure, especially if you're changing travellers' cheques. One of the few places in town which gives the same rate for travellers' cheques as for cash is the Banco de Crédito, whose main office is at Jirón Lampa 399 in Lima. They are open from 8.30 to 11.30 am on weekdays throughout the year. In addition they open in the afternoon from 4 to 6 pm from April to December. As always, these hours are subject to change. Until recently, only the main office would change travellers' cheques but the Miraflores and San Isidro offices have started to do so.

Few of the other banks change money and often if they do so it is at the unfavourable official rate. Casas de cambio or exchange houses usually give the good free rate for cash but pay several per cent lower for traveller's cheques. Casas de cambio are found near the Plaza San Martín, especially on Colmena going north-west. They are also found on Larco in Miraflores. Their main advantage is that they are open for longer hours than the banks but, as always, shop around particularly if exchanging a large amount of money.

Street changers are often found hanging out around the casas de cambio. The corner of Plaza San Martín and Ocoña is a favourite spot and on some days it seems as if every person on the block is buying or selling dollars. There is no real advantage to changing money with street changers – they never give more than the best rates in banks or casas de cambio.

There is a Banco de la Nación at the airport which sometimes changes money but you can't rely on it. There are usually a couple of casas de cambio operating near the international arrivals exit. Exchange rates at the airport are usually 2% lower for cash and 10% lower for travellers'

cheques than the best rates downtown – these are approximate figures which fluctuate.

If you need to receive money from home, one of the best places to have it sent is the Banco de Crédito which charges less than 1% in service fees and allows you to have your money in US dollars. Check with the main office for the telex number to have money sent to you. Other banks may charge high fees or pay you only in intis at the unfavourable official rate.

Although you can usually change excess intis back to dollars at a slight loss when you leave the country, this is not always reliable so try not to be left with a huge wad of intis when you leave. The last time I left Peru through Lima's International Airport, I was told that the Peruvian government had suspended trading on the inti and that I couldn't change my excess intis back to dollars. 'Sorry, that's what el presidente says.'

If you lose your travellers' cheques, I hope that they're American Express. Their office is at Lima Tours (tel 276624), Belén 1040, from 9.15 am to 4.45 pm on weekdays. American Express are one of the easiest companies to deal with for refunds – usually within 72 hours. Other travellers cheques often take longer, notably (First National) Citibank which took about a year to process my claim for about US$200 in stolen cheques. I definitely do not recommend using them. They're at Colmena 1070 in Lima, (tel 273930) – good luck. The Bank of America (tel 717777) is at Augusto Tamayo 120, San Isidro. Visa is represented at the Banco de Crédito and Mastercard at the Banco Latino. Diners Club (tel 414272) is at Canaval Moreyra 535, San Isidro and Thomas Cook (tel 278353) is at Wagons-Lit, Ocoña 174, Lima. If you lose other travellers' cheques, go into any major bank and ask for assistance. They'll usually be able to tell you where to go to make a claim.

Note that during the Lima summer, from January to March, banks are open only in the mornings from 8.30 to 11.30 am. In 1986 the government tried to introduce afternoon banking but popular opinion didn't allow this to happen. Everyone wants to go to the beach on hot summer afternoons. During the rest of the year, most banks are open in the afternoons but hours vary depending on the bank.

Post The main post office is inside the city block on the north-west corner of the Plaza de Armas. This is where to go for mail sent to you at Lista de Correos, Correos Central, Lima. There are also branch post offices in various districts of Lima. The main office is open from 8 am to 6 pm from Monday to Saturday and from 8 am to 12 noon on Sunday mornings. The branch post office on Colmena is open until 8 pm from Monday to Saturday. There is an office at the airport which is open from 8 am to 6 pm from Monday to Saturday and one in Miraflores on the corner of Larco and 28 de Julio which is open the same hours.

American Express clients can have mail held for them at Amex, c/o Lima Tours, Belén 1040, Lima. Mail can be picked up from 9 am to 12 noon and from 3 to 5 pm in the afternoon on weekdays. Bring identification for mail collection, both at Amex and the post office.

Members of the South American Explorers Club can have mail held for them at Casilla 3714, Lima 100, Peru.

Having parcels sent to you is a problem; many are opened or stolen. Sending parcels abroad is reasonably safe if you send them *certificado* but it is time consuming. First one must take the parcel (weighing less than 20 kilos) to the *Aduana* (customs) office in the main post office. This is open from 9 am to 12 noon and from 1 to 3 pm on weekdays. After customs approval, you can then go to the post office to buy stamps and then return to customs for final clearance and payment of taxes (usually about 5% of the declared value). You often have to leave a photocopy of your passport, so bring one with you and make sure that the page(s) have your picture, name and passport number on them. Only now are you allowed to close the parcel up, so don't go with a neatly wrapped parcel as it won't be accepted. Large parcels have to be sewn up in a cloth bag and you have to supply the bag, needle and thread. It usually takes a couple of hours and a lot of patience for the whole procedure but remember that postal rules and regulations change frequently.

Telephone, Telex & Telegrams Long distance and international telephone calls are made from the usually crowded and chaotic telephone office on Plaza San Martín, to the right of the Cine Metro. Whereas most of Peru is served by ENTEL, Lima is served by the Peruvian Telephone Company which keeps shorter hours and seems less efficient. They supposedly have direct dialling but it's usually out of order. You have to place your call through the receptionist, pay a big deposit at the cash register (bring extra money), wait for up to an hour or more for your call to be announced over the loudspeakers, make your call, and then wait for up to half an hour for the balance of your deposit to be returned. It's not always that bad but it gets very crowded indeed in the evenings. They are open from about 9 am to 9 pm from Monday to Saturday.

If you want to make a local call, you'll need to buy tokens called *fiches RIN*, available from vendors on many street corners. These cost a few cents each and are used instead of coins. Public telephone booths are scattered around the city.

Telegrams and telexes can be sent from the office on the corner of Lampa and Emancipación in Lima. The first class hotels can connect you with the international operator or send telexes.

Bookshops The best selection of guidebooks in English is to be found at the

South American Explorers Club. The ABC bookstores, of which the main branch is at Colmena 689, three blocks from the Plaza San Martín, have a good but expensive selection of English, German and French newspapers, magazines, coffee table books, guidebooks, etc. Also good for books about Peru is the Librería AYZA on Jirón Unión – they're slightly cheaper. Bear in mind that most English books about Peru are much cheaper in Britain or the US than they are in Peru.

The Lima Times, the capital's English language weekly, advertises a good selection of books about Peru. They can be obtained from their offices at Carabaya 928, 3rd floor.

There is a good selection of paperback novels at the Librería El Pacifico under the cinema of the same name in Miraflores. Used paperback novels in English can be bought or exchanged at the Book Exchange at Ocoña 211, two blocks from the Plaza San Martín. They have a good selection of 1000-page blockbuster novels which will help you while away interminable waits for late buses and planes. Members of the South American Explorers Club will find a free book exchange at the clubhouse.

Maps Again, the South American Explorers Club is a good place to begin looking for maps. They have trail maps of the main hiking areas, road maps of Peru and detailed street and bus maps of Lima. If they don't have the maps you want, they'll know where you can get them.

For topographical maps, go to the Instituto Geográfico Nacional (IGN) (tel 451939) at Aramburu 1198, Surquillo. They are open from 8 am to 3 pm on weekdays and you need to have your passport to get in. The Servicio Aerofotográfico Nacional at Las Palmeras Air Force base in Chorrillos can sell you aerial photographs from 8.30 am to 12 noon and from 2 to 4 pm on weekdays. Some of these aerial photos are available from the IGN.

Lima is such a huge city that it is impossible to do more than indicate the main downtown area in a book such as this one. You are strongly advised to buy a street/bus map of the city if you want to spend a few days looking around. The best is published by Lima 2000.

Many maps are sold by street vendors around the Plaza San Martín area. The selection varies from good to bad and the prices tend to be high so try bargaining.

Medical The best general clinic, but also the most expensive, is considered to be the Clínica Anglo-American (tel 403570) on the 3rd block of Salazar, San Isidro. In San Borja try the Clínica San Borja (tel 413141) at Avenida del Aire 333. In Lima there's the Clínica Internacional (tel 288060) at Washington 1475. All three of these have 24-hour service and some English-speaking staff. Cheaper and also good, is the Clínica Adventista (tel 459040) at Malecón Balta in Miraflores.

If you're bothered with intestinal problems an English speaking doctor, who has been recommended to me, is Dr Alfredo Calderón at Carabaya 928, 3rd floor, Lima.

A highly recommended dentist is Dr Gerardo Aste (tel 417502), Antero Aspillaga 415, office 101, San Isidro. He speaks excellent English and did a very careful, thorough and painless job of replacing a filling which I broke in Peru.

If you wear glasses and have your prescription with you, you can have a spare pair of glasses made up very cheaply at one of the numerous opticians in Lima. There are several along Cailloma, downtown, and around Schell and Larco in Miraflores. Having your eyes examined for a new prescription is also cheap but some ophthalmologists practising in Peru have archaic equipment and don't do very good jobs. If you need a new prescription, ask at your embassy for an ophthalmologist they can recommend.

Tourist Police For emergencies ranging from robbery to rabies you can contact the tourist police for advice and assistance. They have been recommended to me by several people for their courtesy and helpfulness. They usually have English-speaking police available and they can cut down on a lot of red tape if you need a police report to make an insurance claim or a travellers' cheque refund. The Policía de Turismo (tel 237225 or 246571) is found at Salaverry 1156, Jesus María.

Laundry Many hotels can have your laundry done for you. The more expensive the hotel, the more expensive the laundry! Lima, indeed Peru, does not have coin-operated laundromats where you can do your own wash and dry. Instead, you must leave your clothes with a *lavandería* or laundry and pick them up later, usually the next day though same day service can be arranged by paying extra.

Many lavanderías are only for dry cleaning and others charge by the item instead of by the load. The lavandería that I use most often is *LavaQuick* at Benavides 604 and La Paz in Miraflores. They charge about US$2 for a four kilo load, washed, dried and folded and can give 24-hour service, or same day if you pay a tip. They are open from 9 am to 6 pm on Mondays to Saturdays but close at 1 pm on Thursdays. Ask at your hotel for directions to the lavandería nearest you if you don't want to go to Miraflores.

Spanish Courses Perhaps because Lima is not so attractive a city as, say, Quito in Ecuador, fewer people stay here to learn Spanish. Courses are offered however. One place that I've heard recommended is the Centro de Idiomas at 956 Camaná, 2nd floor. They have small classes at three different levels and they are relatively small – 10 is about the maximum but classes often have only four or five students. They meet for two hours per day on weekdays and costs are a modest US$16 a month.

Working The most frequent job opportunities are for English teachers but pay is usually very low. If you make US$1 per hour you're doing fairly well. Native English speakers can try Fermath Inglés, Tudela y Varela 215, Miraflores or TRANSLEX which is on the Paseo de la República in Miraflores.

If you actually have a teaching qualification, you might do better. The American school, the Colegio Roosevelt (tel 350590) in Monterrico, pays as much as US$20 per day for substitute teachers. Bona fide teachers often hang out in Brenchley's Pub (see under Places to Eat) and you might make further contact there. American and British oil workers also drink there, though oil-related jobs are not easy to find unless you have some experience and qualifications.

Travel & Tour Agencies There are many travel agencies in Lima which can, apart from sell you airline tickets and make your hotel reservations, provide you with tour services. For guided tours of Lima, the city, the churches, the museums, Lima by night tours, tours of the nearby archaeological sites such as Pachacamac, and so on, *Vista Peru* is one of the best, although their tours aren't particularly cheap, starting at US$10 per person. Comfortable transportation and English speaking guides are provided. Reservations and information about *Vista Peru* can be obtained at *Lima Tours*, Belén 1040.

Tourist departures to Cuzco and Machu Picchu are also available – these are three days and two nights, cost about US$140 plus airfare, but are not recommended unless you are in a great hurry. Other companies can provide you with similar services and may be cheaper, for example *Turicentro* at José Pardo 497, Miraflores which does the Cuzco/Machu Picchu trip for US$90 plus airfare. There are many travel and tour agencies in Lima along and near Colmena, north-west of the Plaza San Martín.

For adventure tourism, two companies

have Lima offices. *Expediciones Mayuc* at Conquistadores 199, San Isidro, can take you river running on the Cañete, 150 km south of Lima. They specialise in river running and trekking in the Cuzco area and have their main office in Cuzco but the San Isidro office can also give you information. *Explorandes* at Bolognesi 159 in Miraflores also specialises in trekking and river running adventures. These tours tend more towards the top end of the market; cheaper tours can be joined by travelling to the area you're interested in and making contact there.

Things to See

There is a wealth of museums, churches and colonial houses to visit in Lima, enough to keep you occupied for several days. Most of these are described below. Unfortunately, opening hours are subject to frequent change and you may want to check with the Tourist Office at Belén 1066 for up-to-date times. Hours are often shortened drastically during the January to March coastal summer season with January being one of the most difficult of months to find places open all day. Mornings are generally the best time to go anywhere during the summer.

Museums
Museo Nacional de Antropología y Arqueología This is both one of the cheapest and one of the best museums in Lima and should be high on the list of anyone at all interested in the archaeology of Peru. The collection is well laid out and traces the prehistory of Peru chronologically from the earliest archaeological sites to the arrival of the Spaniards. Chavín stone carvings, Nazca ceramics and Paracas weavings are all displayed here along with collections showing the best artefacts of all the major Peruvian cultures. The section on the Archaeology of Peru in the first chapter of this book is essentially based upon a visit to this museum and so you may want to re-read it before you go.

Entrance to the museum is 30c, plus another 30c if you want to use a camera. It is open from 10 am to 6 pm on Tuesdays through Sundays. It is at Plaza Bolívar, at the intersection of Avenida San Martín and Vivanco in Pueblo Libre, but there are plans to move it to a larger location near Avenida La Marina in the Maranga district sometime in 1987, so you may want to check with the tourist office first.

Museo Nacional de la República Better known as the National Museum of History, this building once housed the revolutionary heroes San Martín (1821-22) and Bolívar (1823-26). The museum contains late colonial and early republican paintings, furnishings and independence artefacts and is mainly of interest to students of the Peruvian revolution. It's next door to the Anthropology & Archaeology Museum in Plaza Bolivár and is open the same hours. Entrance is 25c.

Museo de Oro del Peru The Gold Museum actually houses two separate museums in the same private building which is owned by the Mujica Gallo family. The incredibly rich gold museum itself is in a huge basement vault. There are literally thousands of gold pieces ranging from ear plugs to ponchos embroidered with hundreds of solid gold plates. In addition there are numerous other artefacts of silver and precious stones such as lapis lazuli, emeralds and pearls.

The top half of the building houses an Arms Museum which is reputed to be one of the best in the world. Even if you are fairly uninterested in guns, as I am, you'll probably be fascinated by the thousands of ancient and bizarre firearms from all over the world which are displayed here. One of my favourite exhibits is a huge and ornately decorated blunderbuss which is about two metres long with a five cm bore and flaring trumpet-like muzzle. It dates from the 1800s and although it looks more suitable for hunting elephants, it is labelled as a duck hunting rifle!

The two museums are found at Alonso de Molina 100, in the outlying suburb of Monterrico, east of downtown Lima. Hours are from 12 noon to 7 pm daily. The Gold Museum is a private collection and high on the 'must see' list for many tourists visiting Peru on guided tours and so the admission is correspondingly high at US$4 per person. This allows you to view both the Gold and Arms Museums; separate tickets for the two are not sold. Photography is not permitted but postcards and colour slides are for sale.

Museo Rafael Larco Herrera This is also a private museum and consists of one of the most incredible collections of ceramics to be found anywhere. Many of these items were collected by a former vice-president of Peru in the 1920s and there are said to be about 55,000 pots in the collection. Entering the first rooms is like walking into a museum store room; one is completely overwhelmed by shelf after shelf, stacked to the high ceilings with literally thousands of ceramics grouped roughly into categories such as animals, people, medical practices and so forth.

Going further into the museum one finds rooms with the best pieces exhibited in the uncluttered manner that they deserve. In addition to the ceramics there are exhibits of mummies, a small gold room, a small cactus garden, textiles made from feathers and also a Paracas weaving which contains 398 threads to a linear inch – a world record. In a separate building one finds the famous collection of pre-Columbian erotic pots which detail, with a remarkable explicitness, the sexual practices of several Peruvian cultures. All in all, this is a museum not to be missed by the ceramicist and is highly recommended to everyone.

The museum is at Bolívar 1515 in Pueblo Libre and is open from 9 am to 1 pm and 3 to 6 pm daily except Sunday when it is open only until 1 pm. Entrance is about US$4 and photography is not allowed. If you take a cab, make sure the driver knows where he is going because many drivers confuse this museum with the nearby Museum of Anthropology & Archaeology.

Museum of Art Housed in a very handsome building, Lima's art museum is far more wide-ranging than just art; it houses everything from colonial furniture to pre-Columbian artefacts in addition to canvases covering four centuries of Peruvian art. It's well worth a visit.

The museum is located at Paseo de Colón 125, Lima and is open from 9 am to 6 pm on Tuesdays to Sundays. Admission is about 60c (recent reports are that this price has gone up to US$1.50) and photography is not allowed.

Amano Museum Those interested in Peruvian archaeology will find this museum well worth making the effort to see. It houses a fine private collection of ceramics which is arranged chronologically to show the development of pottery through Peru's various pre-Columbian cultures. The museum specialises in the little known Chancay culture of which it has a remarkable collection of textiles. Entrance is in small groups and by appointment only. All groups are met at the door by a guide who will show you around in exactly an hour – it is best if you understand Spanish or at least have someone along to translate. You have to form your own group. You cannot wander the museum at will but by listening to the guide you'll end up learning a good deal about the development of pottery in Peru and about the Chancay culture.

The tours are free but you must make an appointment by phoning 412909. Tours are available on weekdays at 2, 3, 4 and 5 pm. The museum is a little out of the way at Retiro 160 which is off the 11th block of Angamos in Miraflores so give yourself plenty of time to get there – these people are extremely punctual, unlike the rest of Peru.

Central Lima

1	Bullring & Museum	45	Hotel Richmond
2	Hotel San Sebastian	46	Cine Excelsior
3	Sanctuary of Santa Rosa	47	Church of La Merced
4	Peña Hatuchay	48	'No Name' Restaurant
5	Cine Imperio	49	L'eau Vive del Peru Restaurant
6	Church of Santo Domingo	50	Church of San Pedro
7	Main Post Office	51	Turismo Chimbote Bus
8	Francisco Pizarro Monument	52	Cine Tauro
9	Government Palace	53	Booke Exchange
10	Cine Central	54	Cine Plaza
11	Teatro Municipal	55	Cine Adan y Eva
12	Hotel Residencial Roma	56	International Telegrams
13	Hotel Savoy	57	General Market
14	Hotels Comercio & Pacifico	58	Faucett Airline & Hotel Bolívar
15	Bar Cordano	59	Gran Hotel
16	Church of San Francisco & Catacombs	60	Parrilladas San Martín
		61	1900 Restaurant
17	Cine Venecia	62	Lima Tours & American Express
18	Cine Lido	63	Tourist Information Office
19	Cine Tacna	64	AeroPeru
20	Hotel Granada	65	Hostal Belén
21	Church of San Agustín	66	Cine Metro & International Telephone Office
22	Pension Union & Cine Bijou		
23	Cathedral	67	Bus to Chosica
24	Hostal Wiracocha & Peruvian Health Sciences Museum	68	Olano Bus
		69	Cine República
25	Hotels Europa & San Francisco	70	Transportes Rodriguez
26	Expreso Huaral	71	Santa Catalina Convent
27	Museo de la Cultura Peruana	72	South American Explorers Club
28	Cine Portofino	73	Sheraton Hotel
29	Hotel Claridge	74	TEPSA Bus
30	Teatro Seguro	75	Palace of Justice
31	La Naturaleza (Health Food)	76	Ormeño Bus Company
32	AYZA Bookstore	77	Empresa Huaraz
33	Asociacion Naturista Peruana	78	Buses to Pachacamac & Pucusana
34	Hotel Damascus		
35	Cafe Adriatico	79	Museum of Italian Art
36	Museo del Banco del Reserva	80	Expreso Sud Americano
37	Banco de Crédito	81	Comité 12 to Huancayo
38	Torre Tagle Palace	82	Cine Conquistador
39	Museum of the Spanish Inquisition	83	US Embassy
40	Congress Building	84	Museum of Art
41	Hotel Crillón	85	Morales Moralitos Bus
42	Post Office	86	Circuito de Playas Beach Bus
43	Hostal El Sol	87	Immigration
44	Hotel La Casona	88	León de Huánuco Bus

Museo del Banco Central de Reserva This is another specialist archaeological museum which is well worth knowing about because it is located in the heart of downtown and makes a quiet and welcome relief from the hustle and bustle of changing money or reconfirming airline tickets. Last time I was there admission was only 3c. It is well worth visiting in its own right and specialises in ceramics from the Vicus culture, as well as housing a small collection of other pre-Columbian artefacts and 19th and 20th century Peruvian art. It is found in the Central Reserve Bank at the corner of Ucayali and Lampa and is open from 10 am to 5 pm on Tuesdays to Saturdays and 10 am to 1 pm on Sundays.

Museum of the Inquisition This is housed in the building used by the Spanish Inquisition from 1570 to 1820. It subsequently became the senate building and is now a university library. Visitors can walk around the basement where prisoners were tortured. There's a rather ghoulish exhibit of life-size waxworks of unfortunates on the rack, or having their feet roasted.

The museum is at Junín 548 opposite the Plaza Bolívar in Lima (not the same plaza as in Pueblo Libre). It is open from 9 am to 7.30 pm on weekdays and from 9 am to 4.30 pm on Saturdays and admission is free. There's a remarkable wooden ceiling in the library upstairs.

Museo de Ciencias de la Salud The Peruvian Health Sciences Museum has a unique collection of pre-Columbian artefacts ranging from mummies to pots which show the extent of medical practices known to pre-Hispanic cultures. Exhibits show how various injuries and diseases were known and cured. Another part of the museum traces cultural developments in Peru from the stone age inhabitants through to the Incas. Medical instruments from the 18th and 19th century are also displayed. This museum is of interest to everyone but should particularly be visited by health professionals. The exhibits are well labelled in both Spanish and English.

Apparently, the museum will arrange pre-Columbian banquets – meals consisting solely of the kind of food which would have been available before the arrival of the Spaniards. You must have a group to arrange a banquet. Call the museum (tel 270190) for full details. I've never tried this so if you can get a group together let me know how the food is!

The museum is just off the Plaza de Armas at Junín 270 and is open from 9 am to 5 pm daily except Sunday. Admission is US$1.

Museo de la Cultura Peruana This small museum concentrates on those items which are more closely allied to popular art or handicrafts than to archaeology and history. Ceramics, carved gourds, recent art and traditional folk art, and costumes from various periods and places are exhibited here.

The museum is at Alfonso Ugarte 650 and charges 10c admission with an extra fee for photography. Hours are from 10 am to 5 pm on weekdays and 9.30 am to 5 pm on Saturdays.

Museo de Historia Natural The natural history museum has a modest collection of stuffed animals but is well worth a visit by anyone wishing to familiarise themselves with the fauna of Peru. Mammals, birds, reptiles, fish, insects, etc are all represented.

The museum is at Arenales 1256 and is open from 8.30 am to 3.30 pm on weekdays, 8.30 am to 12 noon on Saturdays, and Sundays by previous arrangement. Admission is 15c.

Museo Etnográfico de la Selva This is a small but interesting collection of jungle artefacts collected by Dominican missionaries in the south-eastern parts of Peru. Indian items such as clothes, headpieces, pottery, basketwork, jewellery and household items are displayed and there are many photographs showing the items in use.

The museum is in the grounds of the Santuario de Santa Rosa de Lima on the first block of Avenida Tacna. It is open daily from 9.30 am to 1 pm and from 3.30 to 7 pm and admission is 10c.

Museo de Arte Italiano Housed in a fairy-tale building in a park on the 2nd block of the Paseo de la República, the museum of Italian art is more attractive to look at than it is to look inside. The exhibits are badly labelled and are mostly reproductions but if you like Italian art it's open daily except Mondays from 9 am to 7 pm and admission is about 30c.

Museo Numismatico del Banco Weise If you're interested in the collection and study of coins, then this is the place to go. The museum exhibits Peruvian coins, bills and medals from colonial days to the present. You don't need any coins to get in (it's free) and opens from 9 am to 1 pm on weekdays. The Banco Weise is at Cuzco 245 and the numismatic collection is on the 2nd floor.

Philatelic Museum Housed appropriately in the Central Post Office on the corner of the Plaza de Armas in Lima, the museum gives you opportunities to examine, buy or trade Peruvian postage stamps. There is also a small exhibit of the Inca 'Postal System'. The collection of Peruvian stamps is not complete and can be seen from 8 am to 1.30 pm and 2 to 4 pm on weekdays, 8 am to 1.30 pm on Saturdays, and 8 am to 12 noon on Sundays. Admission is free.

If you are interested in acquiring any stamps for your collection, you'll find the museum shop open from 8 am to 12 noon and from 2 to 3 pm on weekdays. Collectors and dealers meet at the museum on the last Sunday of the month to sell, buy and trade stamps.

Museo Taurino The bullfight museum is at the Plaza de Acho, Lima's bullring, at Hualgayoc 332 in the Rimac district. If you're interested in bullfighting then it's well worth the trip. If you're anti-bullfighting then you might want to go anyway just to see the matadors' relics which include a holed and bloodstained costume worn by a famous matador who was gored and killed in the Lima bullring some years ago. Chalk one up for the bull! There are actually some very good paintings and engravings of bullfighting scenes by various artists, notably Goya, which are worth seeing. Entrance is 20c and the museum is open on weekdays from 9 am to 1 pm and from 3 to 6 pm.

Religious Buildings

There are many churches, monasteries and convents in Lima and they make a very welcome and quiet break from the noisy traffic and incessant crowds of Lima. Opening hours tend to be even more erratic than the museums so you have to take your chances – churches are often closed for restoration, religious services, or because the caretaker is having an extended lunch.

The Cathedral The original Cathedral was finished on the south-east side of the Plaza de Armas in 1555, but was soon deemed too small and another was planned in its place. Work on the new Cathedral began in 1564 but the building was still unfinished when it was consecrated in 1625. It was more or less finished by 1649 but badly damaged in the earthquake of 1687 and almost totally destroyed in the earthquake of 1746. The present building is a reconstruction based upon the early plans.

The interior is stark compared to many Latin American churches. Of particular interest is the coffin and remains of Francisco Pizarro, to be seen in the mosaic-covered chapel just to the right of the main door. For many years there was controversy over whether the remains actually were those of Pizarro. Recent investigation shows that the remains previously shown were of some other, unknown, conquistador. Pizarro's remains were discovered in the crypt in the early 1980s and transferred to the chapel and now most authorities agree that the exhibit is authentic. Also of interest is the well-carved choir and the small religious

Top: Cathedral, Lima (TW)
Left: Guards outside the Presidential Palace, Lima (RR)
Right: Buildings of Virgins of the Sun, Pachacamac Ruins, near Lima (RR)

museum in the back of the Cathedral.

The Cathedral's opening hours have changed regularly over the years. At the last check, they were from 10 am to 1 pm and from 2 to 5 pm daily. Entrance was 30c and included the religious museum. Photography was not allowed but colour slides and postcards were for sale.

San Francisco The Franciscan church and monastery is famous for its catacombs, which can be visited. It is less known for its remarkable library where thousands of antique texts can be seen, some dating back to the time of the conquistadors.

The church is one of the best preserved of Lima's early colonial churches. It was finished before the earthquake of 1687 which badly damaged most of Lima's churches. San Francisco withstood both this quake and the one of 1746 better than most churches but the quake of 1970 caused considerable damage. Much of the church has, however, been well restored in its original baroque style with Moorish (Arab) influence and is well worth a visit.

Guided tours are available in both English and Spanish. It is highly recommended that you join a tour as this will enable you to see the catacombs, library, cloister and a very fine museum of religious art which non-guided visitors are not allowed to see. The underground catacombs are estimated to contain 70,000 burials; the faint of heart may find it slightly unnerving to enter the bone-filled crypts.

The church is at the corner of Lampa and Ancash and is open daily from 10 am to 12.45 pm and from 3 to 5.45 pm. Entrance is 60c and includes the guided tour. Spanish-speaking tours leave several times an hour and tours in English at least once an hour.

Convento de los Descalzos This infrequently visited convent and museum lies at the end of the Alameda de los Descalzos, an attractive if somewhat forgotten avenue in one of the poorer areas of Lima. It is found in the Rimac district and is safe to visit. The visitor can see old wine-making equipment in the 17th century kitchen, the refectory, the infirmary, typical cells of the Descalzos (literally, the barefooted, a reference to the Franciscan friars), and some 300 colonial paintings of the Quito and Cuzco schools.

Entrance to the convent and museum is 30c and Spanish-speaking guides will show you around. A tour lasts about 40 minutes and the doors are open from 9.30 am to 1 pm and 3 to 6 pm daily except Tuesdays.

Santuario de Santa Rosa de Lima Saint Rose is the first saint of the western hemisphere and is particularly venerated in Lima, where she lived. There is a peaceful garden and a small church built roughly on the site where the saint was born. A small adobe hut, built by Saint Rose in the early 1600s as a private room for prayer and meditation, is the sanctuary itself. Perhaps of greater interest is the Museo Etnográfico de la Selva which is in the same grounds. (See Museums above for further information about opening hours and location.) Admission to the sanctuary is free.

Santo Domingo This is one of Lima's most historic churches, for it was built on the land that Francisco Pizarro granted in 1535 to the Dominican Friar Vicente Valverde, who accompanied Pizarro throughout the conquest and was instrumental in persuading Pizarro to execute Atahualpa after the Inca had been captured and ransomed in Cajamarca.

Construction of the church of Santo Domingo was begun in 1540 and finished in 1599. Although the structure survived the earthquakes reasonably well, much of the interior was modernised in the late 1700s. The tombs of Saint Rose and the black Saint Martin de Porras (also of Lima) are to be seen in the church. There is an alabaster statue of Saint Rose which was presented to the church by Pope Clement in 1669. There is also fine tilework showing the life of Saint Dominic and pleasantly quiet cloisters to walk around and relax in.

The church is on the first block of Camaná across from the Central Post Office. The church itself is open from 7 am to 1 pm and 4 to 8 pm daily. The monastery and tombs are open from 9.30 am to 12.30 pm and 3.30 to 5.30 pm on Mondays to Saturdays and in the morning on Sundays and holy days. Entrance is 30c.

La Merced Another historic church, La Merced has a long and colourful history. It was built on the site of the first mass said in Lima in 1534, before the city had been officially founded by Pizarro in 1535. The original building was a temporary affair and was soon replaced by a larger church which in turn was torn down and a third building was constructed beginning in 1628. This was seriously damaged by the 1687 earthquake but reconstruction soon began. The 1746 quake badly damaged the facade and a new one was begun. Further damage to the church occurred in 1773 when a fire destroyed all the paintings and vestments in the sacristy. Thus most of today's church dates to the 1700s. An attempt was made to modernise the facade in the early 1900s but this was restored back to its original appearance in 1936. Inside the church there is an ornately carved chancel and an attractively decorated cloister.

Most visitors to Lima pass the church several times because it is located on the busy pedestrian street of Jirón Unión at Miro Quesada. The church is open daily from 7 am to 12.30 pm and from 4 to 8 pm and the cloister is open from 8 am to 12 noon and from 3 to 5.30 pm.

San Pedro This small church is considered by many experts to be one of the finest examples of early colonial architecture to be seen in Lima. It is a fairly small baroque church, consecrated by the Jesuits in 1638 and little changed since then. The interior is sumptuously decorated with gilded altars, Moorish-influenced carvings and an abundance of beautiful glazed tilework. It's well worth seeing. Opening hours are from 7 am to 12.30 pm and from 6 to 8 pm daily and admission is free. The church is on the corner of Azangaro and Ucayali in the old centre.

San Agustín In contrast to San Pedro, the church of San Agustín is one of the more changed of Lima's early churches. The churrigueresque (an elaborately and intricately decorated Spanish style common in colonial Latin America) facade, which dates from the early 1700s, is the oldest part of the church to have stayed intact and is worth seeing. Much of the church was reconstructed at the end of the 19th century and then again after the extensive damage of the 1970 earthquake. The church is at Ica 251 and Camaná and can be visited daily from 8.30 am to 12 noon and from 3.30 to 5.30 pm.

Las Nazarenas This church was built in the 18th century and is not in itself of great interest. The site it was built on, however, plays a part in one of Lima's most passionate and traditional religious feasts.

The site used to be a shanty town inhabited mainly by liberated black slaves. One of the walls of the shanty town was painted with an image of the Crucifixion of Christ in the early 1600s by one of the ex-slaves. The area was destroyed by an earthquake in 1655 but the wall with the mural survived. This was considered a miracle and the church of the Nazarene was later built around the mural. A copy of this crucifixion, known as the Lord of the Miracles, is carried around in a huge procession of many thousands of the faithful on 18 October every year. The procession continues for two or three days with the holy image being taken from church to church before being returned to Las Nazarenas.

The church is at the corner of Huancavelica and Tacna and can be visited from 7 to 11.30 am and 4.30 to 8 pm daily. Admission is free.

Other Sights

Whilst the museums and religious buildings are undoubtedly the places where the visitor will spend the most time sightseeing, there are many plazas, buildings and other sites of interest.

Plaza de Armas The central and most important plaza in any Peruvian town is likely to be its Plaza de Armas. Lima is no exception. This large plaza, 140 metres square, was the original heart of Lima but none of the original buildings remain. The oldest part still to be seen is the impressive bronze fountain which was erected in the centre in 1650. The Cathedral is the oldest building on the plaza, reconstructed after the 1746 earthquake.

The exquisitely balconied Archbishop's Palace to the left of the Cathedral is a relatively modern building dating to 1924. The Government Palace on the north-east side of the plaza dates from the same period. The handsomely uniformed presidential guard is on duty all day and the ceremonial changing of the guard takes place daily at 12.45 pm. The other buildings around the plaza are also modern: the Municipalidad (town hall) built in 1945, the Unión Club and various stores and cafés.

There is an impressive statue of Francisco Pizarro on horseback (he was actually only a mediocre horseman) on the corner of the plaza opposite the Cathedral. The story goes that the equestrian statue was once in the centre of the plaza, but the clergy took a dim view of the fact that the horse's rear end was facing the Cathedral and so the whole statue was moved to its present location.

Plaza San Martín One of the major plazas in downtown Lima, the Plaza San Martín dates from the early 1900s. The bronze equestrian statue of the liberator, General San Martín, was erected in 1921.

Jirón Unión Five blocks of this street join the two plazas mentioned above. These five blocks are a pedestrian precinct containing several good jewellery stores, bookshops, movie theatres and the church of La Merced. Consequently it is always very crowded with shoppers, sightseers, ambulantes, and, inevitably, pickpockets. Few visitors to Lima miss this street though, and it is perfectly safe as long as you keep your valuables in an inside pocket or money belt.

Palacio Torre Tagle Built in 1735, this mansion is considered to be the best surviving colonial house in Lima. It has recently become the offices of the Foreign Ministry and entrance during weekdays is either prohibited or restricted to the patio. On Saturdays you can enter the building from 9 am to 4 pm and a tip to the caretaker usually ensures that you can go upstairs to inspect the fine rooms and balconies. The house is at Ucayali 363.

Casa Aliaga This is one of Lima's most historic houses, being built on the land given to Jerónimo de Aliaga by Pizarro in 1535 and having been occupied by the Aliaga family ever since. It is furnished completely in the colonial style and can be visited only with Vista Tours, who charge US$10 for a half-day city tour, including the Aliaga house. Vista Tours (tel 276624) is a subsidiary of Lima Tours at Belén 1040 in Lima. The Aliaga house is at Jirón Unión 224.

Other Colonial Houses The following are houses that are easier to visit although not as important as the above. The Casa Pilatos, now housing the National Culture Institute, is at Ancash 390 and is open from 8.30 am to 4.45 on weekdays. The

Casa de la Riva, run by the Entre Nous Society, is at Ica 426 and is open from 10 am to 5 pm daily. The Casa de Riva-Aguero, housing the Catholic University library and a small folk art collection, is at Camaná 459 and is open from 5 to 8 pm on weekdays. The Casa de Ricardo Palma is the home of the Peruvian author of that name and can be visited for a small fee from 10 am to 12.30 pm and from 4 to 7 pm on weekdays and from 10 am to 12 noon on Saturdays. The house is at Gral Suarez 189, Miraflores.

The Zoo This is found in the Parque las Leyendas between Lima and Callao. The zoo is divided into three areas representing the three major geographical divisions of Peru: the coast, the sierra (or Andes) and the Amazon basin. Mainly animals from Peru are shown, although there are a few examples of more typical zoo animals such as elephants. The zoo has been modernised recently and is worth a visit by anyone interested in learning about Peru's wildlife. Admission is about 30c and hours are from 9 am to 5 pm daily except Monday.

Sport

Soccer (called *futbol*) is the national sport, closely rivalled by volleyball, which is of a high standard. Peru's National Stadium off the 7th, 8th and 9th blocks of the Paseo de la República is the venue for the most important soccer matches and other events. The national team is quite good and qualified for the World Cup in Madrid in 1982.

Horse racing is popular and takes place most weekends and some weekday evenings at the Monterrico Racetrack at the junction of the Pan-American Highway South with Avenida Javier Prado. I've never gone but I understand that if you're reasonably well dressed and take your passport you can use the members stand.

The typically Hispanic sports of bull-fighting and cockfighting both have their aficionados in Lima. The bullfighting season is in late October through November and tickets are sold well in advance. The bullring is at Acho in Rimac. Famous foreign matadors fight in the Acho bullring and the bullfights are well advertised in the major newspapers. There is also a short season in March. Cockfighting occurs year round at the Coliseo de Gallos at Avenida Sandia 150 just off the Parque Universitario.

Swimming and surfing are both popular during the summer months of January to March. However, the water is heavily polluted at all the Lima beaches and newspapers warn that swimming and surfing pose a severe health hazard.

There are several tennis and golf clubs in Lima. The 1st class hotels and tour agencies can help organise a game for you. Sudex agency at Carabaya 933 can help with tennis and golf in Lima and Lima Tours at Belén 1040 has three buses a day to El Pueblo Inn, a country club 11 km east of Lima on the Central Highway. The bus costs US$1 and entrance to the country club is US$1.50. Tennis, golf, riding, swimming and bowling are available.

You can go 10-pin bowling and play pool at the Brunswick Bowl at Balta 135, Miraflores.

Miraflores

This is the Lima suburb most frequently visited by tourists. Until the 1940s, it was a beachfront community separated from the capital by countryside and haciendas. With Lima's recent population boom this countryside has become the fashionably elegant residential district of San Isidro, and Miraflores has become one of Lima's most important shopping, entertainment and residential areas.

Many of the capital's best restaurants and nightspots are found here and the pavement cafés are the places to hang out, to see and be seen. As can be expected, prices and quality of everything ranging from a sweater to a steak will be higher in Miraflores than other parts of the city. Miraflores is connected with Lima by the tree-lined Avenida Arequipa, where frequent colectivos and buses run.

Street Markets

There are several of these ranging from the incredibly crowded general market in downtown Lima to the leisurely and relaxed artists' market in Miraflores. Some of the most important are described.

Lima's main market is at Ayacucho and Ucayali to the south-east of Avenida Abancay. Although it officially occupies a whole city block, this is not even close to being large enough and stalls and vendors completely congest the streets for several blocks around. You can buy almost anything here, but be prepared for extreme crowding and watch your valuables. It's an eye-opening experience to come here and many people enjoy a visit despite the discomfort.

The streets behind the Central Post Office are the centre of a black market known as *Polvos Azules* (literally, blue powders, don't ask me why). It's just as crowded as the main market and you should watch your wallet just as closely. This is the place to come if you're looking for smuggled luxuries such as ghetto blasters or perfume, as well as a remarkable variety of other consumer goods.

Lima's main flower market is found at the south end of the National Stadium (9th block of Paseo de la República) and is a kaleidoscopic scene of beautiful flowers at bargain prices. The best selection is in the mornings. Spend a dollar on a dozen red roses and make someone's day!

The Indian Artisans' Market is found along the north side of Avenida de la Marina on the 600 to 1000 blocks. There is a great selection of handicrafts here but the quality and prices vary a good deal so shop carefully. This is perhaps one of the less tourist oriented of the handicraft markets but, obviously, any handicraft

market relies upon tourist consumption. Better quality at greater expense can be found at various handicraft stores in Lima and Miraflores (see the Things to Buy section).

Finally, the artists' market found most afternoons and evenings on Parque Kennedy in the heart of Miraflores is a good place to see local artists' work. This ranges from garish oil 'painting by number' monstrosities to some surprisingly good water colours.

Places To Stay

There are literally scores of hotels to choose from in Lima, ranging from US$1 per night cheapies to luxury hotels which could cost you a hundred times as much. It is impossible and unnecessary to list them all but the following selection should provide you with something suitable.

Generally speaking, hotels are somewhat more expensive in Lima than in most other cities. Most of the cheapest are to be found right downtown with some well-known budget hotels being located within a very few blocks of the Plaza de Armas. The downtown area is slightly less safe at night than some of the fancier neighbourhoods such as Miraflores, and it is dirtier and noisier. However, I have often stayed downtown and there's no real problem as long as you don't parade around with a gold chain on your neck and a wallet peeking out of your hip pocket.

Mid-priced and expensive hotels are found all over Lima, with some excellent luxury hotels being located in both the heart of downtown and in Miraflores.

The one type of hotel which is not found in Lima is the government-run ENTURPeru Tourist Hotel. These are found in all major cities in Peru except the capital, probably because the capital already has so many good hotels to choose from. ENTURPeru's main reservation office, however, is found in Lima and you can plan a complete Peru travel itinerary staying in good hotels at this office. Reservations are free and the cost of the room is no higher than going direct to the hotel in whichever cities you want to visit. Over 40 cities have hotels which can be reserved at ENTURPeru, Avenida Javier Prado Oeste 1358, Lima 27, Peru. Phone numbers are 721928 or 728227, telex is 20393. They are in the San Isidro district.

Places to Stay - bottom end

One of the best known of Lima's budget hotels is the *Hotel Europa* (tel 273351) at Ancash 376. It's a rather shabby old place but it is safe and reasonably clean and so it's often full by mid-afternoon. They charge US$1.20/2.20 for singles/doubles and there are bigger rooms with up to six beds. There is sometimes hot water in the communal showers. Nearby are the equally cheap but much grimier and less pleasant *Hotel Comercio* and *Hotel Pacifico* on the first block of Carabaya.

Perhaps the cheapest place in town is the *Hotel Richmond* on Jirón Unión at Cuzco. It has a reasonably attractive old-fashioned lobby with marble stairs but the rooms are grimy and the water erratic. They charge about 60c per person or about US$1 per person in rooms with a private bath. Further along the same street at Unión 442, 3rd floor (go through the bookshop and café) is the basic but friendly and clean *Pensión Unión* which charges US$1 per person and sometimes has hot water in the evenings. It was damaged by fire recently but I understand it has reopened. Also very near to the centre is the *Hostal Damasco* at Ucayali 199 which is fairly clean and friendly. They charge about US$3.40 for a double room and a little more for a double with a private bath. There's usually hot water.

The *Asociación de Amistad Peruano/Europeo* has dormitory-style accommodation (no privacy) on the 7th floor of Camaná 280. Baggage lockers are provided and the association is an information source, but sleeping here is no cheaper than the cheap hotels. There is also a *Youth Hostel* in Miraflores at 1247 Larco which charges about US$3 per person and is the cheapest place to stay in Miraflores. I have not heard any good reports about this hostel.

The *Gran Hotel* on Abancay 546 has spacious rooms but is old and has seen better days. They charge US$2 per person in rooms with private bath and a few cents less in rooms with communal baths. There is occasional hot water. The *Hostal Belén* at Belén 1049 opposite the Tourist Information office has fairly reliable hot water and is reasonably clean. Rooms are US$2.50/3.50. The *Hostal Universo* at Azangaro 754 is fairly close to several bus terminals and is safe although not very clean. They charge US$2.50/4 in rooms with private bath and hot water sometimes.

The *Hotel Wilson* at Chancay 633 is another cheapish possibility at US$4.80 for a double room with bath. The *Hostal Wiracocha* at Junín 270 has been recommended, although to me it doesn't seem particularly special. Rooms are US$4/5 with private bath and hot water. Rooms without private bath are about US$1 less but there's cold water only in the communal showers.

If you want to stay with a family try calling the Rodriguez at 236465. They rent rooms for US$3 per person at Colmena 730.

Places to Stay - middle

Two hotels on Ica have recently gained a lot of popularity among discriminating budget travellers. The *Hotel San Sebastian* at Ica 712 charges US$4/7 for singles/doubles. There are many bathrooms with hot water, the rooms are clean, there is a helpful English-speaking landlady, left luggage facilities and a roof-top terrace. Definitely pleasant. Also popular is the *Hotel Residencial Roma* at Ica 326 which is clean and central and provides double rooms with private bath and hot water for US$8, or US$6 for rooms with shared baths.

La Casona at Moquegua 289 has a very pleasant lobby with plants and flowers. The carpeted rooms are shabby but not too bad and the hot water is reliable. They charge about US$7/10 for rooms with private bath but discounts can be arranged if staying for a few days.

A very attractive converted mansion with a view of the Pacific is the *Hostal Barranco* (tel 671753) at Malecón Osma 104 in the Barranco suburb, just beyond Miraflores. The rooms vary from simple to very good and the prices also vary from about US$8 to US$22 a double room. Some are with private bath. There is a garden, pool and games room.

There are plenty of good mid-range hotels in Miraflores where a clean room with private bath will run about US$10 to US$18 single. All of the following have been recommended for pleasantness and good service; English is spoken at most of them. They include the *Residencial Inn* (tel 471704) at General Borgoño 280 for US$13 single including breakfast; the *Residencial Waldorf* on the 3rd floor of Schell 121 (no sign, ring bell) with clean rooms for US$10 single and US$16 double; *La Alameda* at Pardo 931 for US$20 a double including breakfast; the *Hostal Residencial Aleman* at Arequipa 4707 which charges US$17 single and US$26 including an excellent breakfast; the *Hostal Torreblanca* at José Pardo 1543 for US$18 single and US$25 double, again including breakfast and the similarly priced *Hostal El Ejecutivo* at 28 de Julio 245, including breakfast and with a telephone in your room.

Also recommended is the *Hostal Miramar* at Malecón Cisneros 1244 which has some rooms with ocean view. Singles/doubles are US$20/30 including breakfast.

There are several similar mid-priced hotels in downtown Lima. All are with private bath and hot water. The *Hostal El Sol* at Rufino Torrico 773 is US$10 per person, centrally located but reasonably quiet. The *Hotel Grand Castle* is con-veniently located opposite the Ormeño bus terminal at Zavala Loayza 218 and charges US$12/16 and has been recommended for good service. Also good is the *Hostal Residencial Los Virreyes* at Cañete 826 near the Plaza 2 de Mayo. They charge US$16/23 including breakfast. Cheaper, with clean spacious rooms but rather old and run down, is the *Hotel Claridge* at Cailloma 437 which charges US$10/15. New, pleasant, quiet and recommended is the *Hostal Granada* at Huancavelica 323. They opened in 1985 charging US$20 for a double including breakfast, but the price may go up if business picks up.

In the San Isidro residential district, midway between downtown Lima and Miraflores, several quiet mid-priced hotels are to be found. These include the *Hostal Residencial Firenze* at S Tellería 203 and Chinchón, good value at US$10/12 for singles/doubles. Also good is the *Hostal Residencial Collacocha* at Andrés Reyes 100 at the end of the Paseo Parodi which charges US$12/16.

Places to Stay - top end

Many of the mid-priced hotels in the previous section are better than the top end hotels in most Peruvian cities. Lima is one of the few places where you can get real 1st class or luxury hotels if you really feel that you need one (and can afford it!). It's worth enquiring about discounts at many of these top end hotels. All rates given include taxes.

The street with the greatest selection of fancy downtown hotels is Colmena in the four blocks north-west of the Plaza San Martín. Cheapest is the *Hostal San Martín* (above the Parrilladas San Martín right on the Plaza) which charges US$35 for a double room with air-con, telephone, carpeting and a private bar in your room. Next door is the new and modern *El Plaza* which charges US$37/45 for singles/doubles.

Across the street is the venerable *Gran Hotel Bolívar* which is the oldest 1st class hotel in town and is a delight to wander around in. They reputedly serve one of the better Pisco Sours in town and if you can't afford a room you can luxuriate with a drink in the bar. A string quartet plays light classical pieces in the beautiful, stained-glass domed rotunda during afternoon tea (pricey but charming). If you stay here, get rooms on the 2nd or 3rd floors if you can. The upper floors seem less used and slightly musty. Rooms are US$65 for singles, US$85 for doubles. Similarly priced, but much more modern, is the excellent *Hotel Crillón* at Colmena 589. They have a Sky Room restaurant (on the top floor, about the 21st) with stupendous views of Lima.

Other 1st class downtown hotels are the *Lima Sheraton* at Paseo de la República 170 for about US$75 a room and the more modest *Gran Hotel Maury* at Ucayali 201, only one block from the Plaza de Armas and reputedly the hotel which invented the Pisco Sour. Their rooms are US$35/47.

On the way to Miraflores, in San Isidro, is the *Hotel Sans Souci* at Arequipa 2670. It is pleasant looking and has been recommended, though I found the management distinctly unfriendly when I went to look at it. Rooms are US$25/30 for singles/doubles. A reasonably priced 1st class hotel in Miraflores is the *Hostal Ariosto* at La Paz 769. A surprising number of famous people stay here, ranging from jazz musicians to writers, as well as a fair sprinkling of international business people and tourists. Rooms are about US$35 single and US$45 double but discounted rates can be arranged for large groups or long stays.

Luxury hotels include the *El Pardo* at Pardo 420 with rooms for US$61/80 and the *Miraflores César* at La Paz and Diez Canseco which holds the dubious distinction of being Miraflores' (and probably all of Peru's) most expensive hotel with singles for US$97 and doubles for US$115.

Places to Eat

As with hotels, Lima has a vast selection of restaurants of every price range and quality. There is one notable gap, however. There are no 24-hour restaurants and nothing seems to be open before 7.30 am except for street vendors. So if you want an early breakfast, you're out of luck (unless you are staying at one of the top hotels).

Cheap Eats Starting with the cheaper restaurants, there are several which can be recommended to the budget traveller. If you're staying in the *Hotel Europa* there are two good and popular ones on the same block. Try the unnamed chifa at Ancash 306 for large portions of *tallarines* (noodle dinners) for about 60c – it's a popular place. A few doors away is the *Restaurant Machu Picchu*, also cheap and good.

My favourite restaurant in the area is *El Cordano*, a pink building at Ancash 202, opposite the railway station. It's a little more expensive but has an interesting '20s decor, excellent espresso coffee and a very varied menu of typical Peruvian snacks and meals. They are also one of the few places in town which serve a good variety of different Peruvian beers as well as a good choice of local wines and piscos. A bottle of their house wine costs less than a dollar and is rough but drinkable. It's a good place to meet people. Hours are from about 9.30 am to 9 pm.

A very clean and reasonably priced place which I tried recently is the *Café Adriatico* at Ucayali 239. They have good and inexpensive lunches and are also good for light breakfast if you like espresso coffee.

A good street for cheap places to eat is Quilca, between the Plaza San Martín and Avenida Garcilazo de la Vega. Here you'll find about a dozen inexpensive restaurants to choose from. Another cheap possibility, with private curtained booths, is the *Chifa Restaurant Nakasone* at Alfonso Ugarte 1360 and convenient for the South American Explorers Club. There are plenty of other cheap restaurants all over Lima.

Vegetarian Food If you like vegetarian food, you'll find several places to choose from. The *Asociación Naturista Peruana* at Ucayali 133 and the *La Naturaleza* at Camaná 489 are both in Lima and very inexpensive. There are also two vegetarian restaurants in Miraflores which are only a little less cheap. One is the *Govinda* at Schell 630, run by the Hare Krishnas, and a block away at Schell 598 is *Bircher Berner* which has a nice garden to sit in whilst you wait for your food – this restaurant gets my special award for the slowest service in Lima.

Italian Food Italian food lovers will find several pizzerias to choose from on Olaya and Diagonal streets by the Parque Kennedy. The most expensive is *La Pizzería* but it's overpriced; the other places are cheaper but none of them are outstanding. Some folks tell me that the *Pizza Hut* at Espinar and 2 de Mayo in Miraflores has the best pizza. There are a number of quite reasonable pizzerias in Miraflores.

Mid-Range Restaurants A good lunch time restaurant popular with Lima's business-men is the *Raimondi* at Miró Quesada 110. I like it because there's no sign and the outside gives no indication of the spaciousness and comfort within. The food is good and although you'll pay a little more here it's not too expensive.

If you'd like to dine in elegant and special surroundings, then there are several reasonably priced restaurants (US$5 to US$10 for a meal) which are housed in some of Lima's historic buildings. One of my favourites is the *L'Eau Vive* at Ucayali 370. The food is prepared and served by a French order of nuns and features dishes from all over the world as well as some exotic cocktails. It's extremely quiet and prices are moderate. They are

open daily except Sunday from 12 noon to 2.45 pm and from 8.15 to 10.15 pm.

Another good moderately priced choice is the *1900* at Belén 1030 which has live folklórico music in the evenings. They are open from 10 am to 10 pm and the evening music starts about 7.30 pm. Two expensive (about US$20 for a full meal) restaurants also housed in attractive old houses are the *Tambo de Oro* at Belén 1066 in Lima and the *Los Condes de San Isidro* at Paz Soldan 290 in San Isidro. Both are open for lunch from 12 noon to 3 pm and for dinner from 7 to 11 pm. *El Tambo de Oro* is closed on Sundays.

Cafés & a Pub There are many pavement cafés to be found in Miraflores. One of the best known is the *Haiti* on the traffic circle next to the El Pacifico cinema. Its main attraction is its excellent location – good for a coffee and watching the world go by, the food at best is only mediocre. Across the other side of the traffic circle is the much better *La Tiendecita Blanca* which has a superb pastry selection. Nearby, at Ricardo Palma 258, is *Vivaldis* which appears to be one of the more 'in' places for young Mirafloreños and, on the same block, is *Liverpool* which is a similar café but always seems to be less crowded. There are several pavement cafés along Larco of which the *La Sueca* at Larco 759 is particularly good for its excellent pastries.

The Brenchley Arms is, as its name would suggest, a British pub. It's as genuine as you'll find in Peru and is run by the thoroughly British Mr Brenchley and his charming (unless you don't pay your bar tab) Peruvian wife. They have a small but excellent dinner menu with such delights as pork or lamb chops, liver and onions (my favourite), hot pies and curries. Prices are surprisingly moderate and beer consumption is correspondingly high – British beer is not imported into Peru but the local Pilsen and Crystal seem to do the trick. There is a dart board and you can read the British newspapers.

This is the haunt of British and American expats who work for oil companies, schools or the embassies and they will be delighted to tell you about Peru's, ah, problems. English is spoken. Spanish is not. The pub is at Atahualpa 174, a block from the El Pacifico cinema, and they are open from 6 pm to closing time which varies from 11 pm to ... ? Meals are served from 7 to 10 pm – snacks only on Sunday when the cook gets his day off. Cheers!

First Class Restaurants There are many 1st class restaurants in the Lima area and prices, although high by Peruvian standards, are still very reasonable when compared to a fancy meal in a European or North American restaurant. If you want to spend US$20 or US$30 per person (including tax, tips and drinks) in a really luxurious place, then the following can all be recommended.

There are three excellent restaurants in the little shopping mall between the 6th block of La Paz and the 4th block of Alcanfores in Miraflores. The *Carlin*, *El Suche* and *El Condado* all have good food, service and ambience. One of my favourite places for a special meal is *La Rosa Nautica* which serves good seafood and is located at the end of a pier at Costa Verde in Miraflores. The ocean is floodlit and surfers sometimes surf through the pilings. You should take a taxi to get there.

Limeños have given me several recent recommendations for a newer ocean-front restaurant which supposedly has better seafood. It's the *El Salto De Fraile* which means 'the priest's leap' – you can guess the story. It's at the Herradura beach in Chorrillos; again, take a taxi. In Barranco, *El Otro Sitio* at Sucre 317 has been recommended for its romantic location next to the Bridge of Sighs, its good Peruvian food and its live music in the evenings. There are many more 1st class restaurants to choose from once you've exhausted these possibilities.

Most of these restaurants are open for lunch and dinner and closed from about 3 to 7 pm.

Entertainment

To find out what's going on, the best newspaper to get is *El Comercio* which lists cinemas, theatres, art galleries and music shows. If your Spanish is not up to handling this, then read the English weekly *The Lima Times* which has an abbreviated listing of what's going on. Generally speaking, most nightlife starts late and goes on until 3 or 4 in the morning and so tends to be more popular at weekends. Cultural events such as the theatre or the symphony start earlier and films run from early afternoon.

Cinemas One of the cheapest forms of entertainment is a film. With several dozen cinemas to choose from, you can usually find something worth seeing. Foreign (ie non-Peruvian) films are normally screened with their original sound track and Spanish sub-titles. Admission is typically well under a dollar. One can often see the latest Oscar nominees or Cannes winners along with the usual selection of horror, porn and kung fu. There are some cinema clubs which show better films – these are listed in the newspapers' cultural events section, separately from the ordinary cinema listings.

Theatre & Music The best place in Lima for cultural events is the *Teatro Municipal* at Ica 300, downtown. This is the venue for the symphony, opera, plays and ballet. The best seats are expensive and even the cheap tickets will cost you several dollars. Another good venue is the *Teatro Segura* on the 200 block of Huancavelica. The *Teatro Arequipa* on the 800 block of Avenida Arequipa has revues in Spanish. For surprisingly good plays in English, see the local theatre group *The Good Companions* which is run by the British Council. They seem to have something new going every month and they advertise in *The Lima Times*. Or call them on 479760 for information.

Peruvian Music Live Peruvian music is performed at *peñas* where you can often sing along or dance. Drink and sometimes food is served. There are two types – *folklórico* or *criolla*. The first is more typical of the Andean highlands and so it is less popular in Lima whilst the second is more coastal. The peña with the best reputation among budget travellers, and deservedly so, is the *Hatuchay* at Trujillo 228 in Rimac, just across the bridge behind the presidential palace. It's in a huge barn of a place. The music is mainly folklórico and there is plenty of audience participation and dancing (during the second half). Typical Peruvian snacks are served as well as drinks. Peñas are generally fairly pricey but this one is inexpensive at around US$1 cover charge and no minimum consumption. Doors open about 9 pm and music gets under way about 10 pm. Get there early or reserve ahead to ensure a good seat.

Another reasonably priced peña is the *Wifala* at Cailloma 633 in Lima. They play folklórico music. The *Karamanduka* at Benavides 621, Miraflores, plays criolla music, is much more expensive, and caters to the richer Limeños. In Barranco is the *La Estación de Barranco* at Pedro de Osma 112 where a variety of both folklórico and criolla music can be heard. Also in Barranco, next door to the *El Otro Sitio* restaurant at Sucre 315, is the *El Buho Pub* which plays criolla music. These places are a little cheaper than in Miraflores but are still fairly pricey. Hours are the typical late night Friday and Saturday times – from about 10 pm to the early hours.

Bars There are many good bars for a drink and, sometimes, music. The best are mainly in Miraflores. *The Brenchley Arms* pub at Atahualpa 174 is a good place to meet English-speaking locals –

see under Places to Eat for more information. The *Johann Sebastian Bar* at Schell 369 is a quiet place with classical music, expensive drinks and a pleasant ambience.

There are two excellent but expensive bars in Miraflores which feature live jazz most nights; the *Lions Club* at 338 Madrid (by the Plaza Bolognesi) and the newer and highly recommended *Satchmo's* at La Paz 538. Internationally famous musicians are sometimes featured and cover can be as high as US$15 plus a two drink minimum.

Discos There are several American-style discotheques which tend to be dark and expensive. Some have a members only or couples only policy but you can often get around this by showing your passport and telling the doorman that you're a tourist. One of the best known (but by no means best) is the *Arizona Colt* below the El Pacifico cinema in Miraflores – it's a pick-up joint as much as anything else, which is probably true of most discos. *La Miel* across the street under the *Indianapolis* café at José Pardo 120 is perhaps better. *Faces* at the Centro Comercial Camino Real, Level A 68/72, by the intersection of Camino Real and Choquehuanca in San Isidro, is a fairly new and popular dancing spot.

Other possibilities for dancing in the San Isidro area are the *Unicorn* at Paseo de la República 3030, *La Manzana* at Miguel Dasso 143, *Ebony Sicodelico* at Las Magnolias 841, and the *Las Rocas Club* at Rivera Navarrete 821. I'm not a disco fan so I haven't been to any of these. I'll be happy to send a free copy of the next edition of this book to whoever sends me the best list of discotheques to publish in my next edition.

Getting There
Air Domestic flights are almost exclusively with AeroPeru or Faucett. Their flight tickets are often interchangeable if they are endorsed from one airline to the other.

The following cities are served from Lima with flights by both airlines unless otherwise indicated. Prices given are approximate one-way fares. Schedules and prices change frequently but this information will give you a general idea of costs and frequencies of service.

Arequipa: two flights a day, US$40.

Ayacucho: one flight every morning with AeroPeru, US$22.

Cajamarca: three flights a week with AeroPeru, US$43.

Cuzco: three or four flights every morning, US$40.

Chachapoyas: one flight on Mondays with AeroPeru, US$36.

Chiclayo: one or two flights a day, US$29.

Huánuco: four flights a week with AeroPeru, US$25.

Juanjui: two flights a week with AeroPeru, US$32.

Juliaca: one flight a day via Arequipa with AeroPeru, US$54.

Iquitos: four or five flights a day, US$42.

Piura: one or two flights a day, US$36.

Pucallpa: two flights a day, US$30.

Puerto Maldonado: one or two flights a day, US$47.

Rioja: four flights a week, US$37.

Tacna: two flights a day, US$44.

Talara: two or three flights a day, US$37.

Tarapoto: two or three flights every day, US$31.

Tingo María: daily except Tuesdays with AeroPeru, US$26.

Trujillo: two or three flights a day, US$22.

Tumbes: one flight a day, US$38.

Yurimaguas: four flights a week, US$38.

Flight information, buying tickets, and reconfirming flights is best done at the airline offices rather than at the airport counters where things can be chaotic. You can buy tickets at the airport on a space-available basis, however, if you want to leave for somewhere in a hurry. *AeroPeru* (tel 317626 for domestic flights and 322995 for international flights) and *Faucett* (tel 275000 for domestic flights and 283210 for international flights) both have their offices in the Plaza San Martín, Lima.

Aerocóndor (tel 329050 ext 117) has an office at the Hotel Sheraton for Nazca Lines overflights but their flights are much cheaper if booked in Nazca. *Grupo 8* is the military airline. They have an information desk in the domestic section of the airport. Most of their flights are into the jungle regions and are a little cheaper than the commercial airlines. The main drawbacks to flying with them are that departures are infrequent (about once a week) and you can only fly by arriving at the airport early on the day of the flight and buying tickets on a space-available basis.

About a score of international airlines have offices in Lima, especially along Colmena. Check the yellow pages under Transportes Aereas for telephone numbers and call before you go. Offices change addresses frequently.

If departing internationally, first check-in (two hours early is usually suggested, as many flights are overbooked) and after you have obtained your boarding pass, go to the Banco de la Nación where you must pay a US$10 international departure tax. Travellers' cheques are not accepted, only cash (intis or US dollars). Then you can go through the immigration desk (where your tax stamp, passport and entry slip are all checked) and into the international departure lounge.

If leaving on a domestic flight, there is no departure tax. Again, overbooking is the norm, so be there an hour early. On all flights, domestic and international, it is essential that you *reconfirm* several times. Officially, you should reconfirm 24 to 72 hours in advance but it's best to reconfirm upon arrival and then both 72 and 24 hours in advance and perhaps a couple of other times as well. Flights get changed or cancelled with depressing frequency and so it's worth calling the airport or airline just before going to the airport to see if your flight is still leaving.

If you are going to be travelling in some remote part of Peru 72 hours in advance of your flight, try and find a responsible travel agent or other person to reconfirm for you. Passengers are often stranded for days because they failed to reconfirm, were bumped off their flight, and found that the flights for several days were all full. This is especially true during the busy months of July and August when tourists are literally driven to tears when trying to get flights, particularly to and from Cuzco. *Reconfirm!* And if you are reconfirmed, then *reconfirm* again. Get to the airport at least an hour ahead of your flight. And, obnoxious as this may sound, push if you have to. It can get very crowded.

Buses Most travellers will use the long distance bus services to visit other cities in Peru. The most important road in the country is the Pan-American Highway which runs north-west and south-east from Lima, roughly paralleling the coast and at times coming right down to the Pacific Ocean. It is paved for most of its length and comfortable, long distance north and southbound buses leave Lima every few minutes; it takes approximately 24 hours to drive to the Ecuadorean border in the north and the Chilean border in the south. Other buses ply the much rougher roads inland into the Andes and even across the Andes and down into the eastern jungles.

Although buses play a major part in long distance transportation, there is no such thing as a city bus terminal. Instead, each bus company runs its own office and bus terminal. This section should get you pointed the right way; if the destination you want isn't mentioned (and most of them are) then ask the tourist office to help you.

Generally, you can buy tickets well in advance of your planned travel date and this is highly recommended, particularly if you want to travel at weekends or holidays. Lima's bus stations are notorious for thievery and it makes a lot of sense to find the station and buy your tickets unencumbered with luggage. Then, when it's time to leave, you can just go to the terminal and climb on the bus without trying to look after your luggage while you're in a crowded line waiting to buy a ticket. Always ask if the bus leaves from where you bought the ticket; occasionally the terminal isn't at the same place.

It pays to shop around if you are on a budget. TEPSA is generally one of the fastest and most reliable companies but they have fewer departures than some other companies and are the most expensive. Ormeño has many buses, frequent departures, and is medium priced; their service is fair. Morales Moralitos also has many departures and medium prices but their service is often poor. Some of the cheapest companies, though their service is slow and more subject to breakdowns, can cost you only half of a TEPSA fare. Special or promotional cheap fares are offered by various companies at various times. By the same token, fares can also go up for peak periods or holidays.

The biggest bus company in Lima is Ormeño at Carlos Zavala 145. There are various subsidiaries at the same address: Expreso Ancash, Expreso Continental, Expreso Chinchano and Transportes San Cristobal. Between them they have frequent departures for Ica, Arequipa, Tacna, Ayacucho, Cuzco, Trujillo, Chiclayo, Tumbes, Huaraz, Caraz and various intermediate points. This is the company I always use if travelling overland along the coast or to Cuzco. For the Huaraz area you can also try Transportes Rodriguez at Roosevelt 354 or Empresa Huaraz at Montevideo 655.

TEPSA is on Paseo de la República 129 and has buses to Ica, Arequipa, Tacna,

Huánuco, Tingo María, Pucallpa, Trujillo, Chiclayo, Tumbes and Cajamarca. This is the most comfortable and reliable choice for Pucallpa, but it's also the most expensive.

Léon de Huánuco at 28 de Julio 1520 is a cheaper but less reliable choice for Huánuco, Tingo María, Pucallpa, Juanjui and Tarapoto. Another possibility for Pucallpa is Nor-Oriente at 28 de Julio 2195.

Olano at Apurímac 543 has buses to the northern coast, mountains and jungles. Their buses go to Trujillo, Chiclayo, Chachapoyas and Moyobamba. Empresa Transportes Chinchaysuyo at Grau 525 also has northbound buses for Casma, Trujillo, Piura and Tarapoto.

For the Huancayo area try M Caceres at 28 de Julio 2195 (same terminal as Nor-Oriente). For the Tarma/Chanchamayo area there's the choice of Transportes Chanchamayo at Luna Pizarro 453 or Empresa Los Andes at 28 de Julio 2405.

Morales Moralitos is at Grau 141 and has many subsidiary companies at the same address. Morales Moralitos goes to Nazca and Cuzco; Transportes CIVA goes to Huancabamba in the north; SOYUZ goes to Ica; ETUCSA goes to Huancayo and Ayacucho; and Cruz del Sur goes to Arequipa, Puno and Cuzco. Another company to try for Arequipa and Puno is Jacantaya at Colmena 1631, although they probably aren't much better.

Buses can be very much delayed during the rainy season. This is less of a problem along the coast, where it rarely rains (although the violent floods of the 1983 El Niño year closed the Pan-American Highway in the northern part of Peru for several weeks) but it is an annual problem in the highlands and jungles. If travelling there in the rainy season, especially from January to April, journey times can double or even triple because of landslides and bad road conditions.

For approximate fares and journey times, see under the appropriate city.

Colectivos These are an alternative to buses for long distance overland drives. The colectivo taxis are generally about 20% faster than most buses but cost almost twice as much. Speed is their main advantage. They are not really much more comfortable than buses when six or seven passengers and a driver squeeze inside. Departures are less frequent than the bus companies. If you want to pay for all the seats, you can get an *expreso* and often you can leave right away.

Companies which run colectivo taxis are called *Comités*. The main ones in Lima include Comité 11 at Leticia 587 which goes to Huaraz and Caraz. Comité 12 at Montevideo 736 goes to Huancayo and Ayacucho. Comité 13 at Cotabambas 347 goes to Trujillo and Cajamarca. Comité 14 at Leticia 604 goes to Huaraz. Comité 30 at Bolívar 1587 goes to Huancayo.

Rail Peru has two railway systems. The train from Lima goes inland to Huancayo and does not connect with the train linking Arequipa, Lake Titicaca, Cuzco and Machu Picchu.

Lima's train station is Desamparados on Avenida Ancash, behind the Presidential Palace. There used to be daily train service but this was recently disrupted when terrorists blew up a bridge on the mountainous route. Service has been suspended indefinitely; the tourist office or railway station can inform you if it has restarted by the time you read this.

Assuming the train is running again you'll find that tickets to Huancayo cost about US$3 in 1st class and US$2.20 in 2nd. Tickets can be bought the day before and sell out quickly in 1st class. The train departs at 7.40 am and takes about 10 hours. Food is available and the journey reaches 4780 metres above sea level. The journey can be broken at Chosica (see Around Lima), Matucana where there are a few basic hotels, or La Oroya which is an ugly and cold mining town a little over half way to Huancayo. Most people go all the way to Huancayo from where, if you wish, you can continue to Huancavelica on another train. The railway north from La Oroya to Cerro de Pasco has been out of service for some years.

Sea Lima's port is Callao, only 15 km from the city centre, but very few travellers arrive in Peru by ship. Most of the vessels docking at Callao carry freight rather than passengers. The docks area is not particularly attractive and has a reputation of being somewhat dangerous to the unwary.

Getting Around

Airport Transport Lima's Jorge Chávez International Airport is in Callao, about 12 km from downtown or 16 km from Miraflores. An ordinary taxi will take you from downtown to the airport for about US$3 if you bargain; a black *remisse* taxi of the kind found parked outside the main hotels will charge you two or three times as much.

Colectivo taxis, taking about six passengers for 50c each, can be found on the north side of the 700 block of Colmena near Cailloma, downtown. There is an extra charge for luggage and they leave when full from about 6 am to 6 pm. Airport buses, costing about US$2 per passenger, can be booked at Trans Hotel at Camaná 828 in Lima or Ricardo Palma 280 in Miraflores. Fares are higher if they pick you up from your hotel.

The cheapest way to get to the airport is on a city bus. No 35, which runs along Alfonso Ugarte, passes the airport and charges a few cents. If you have a pile of luggage, this isn't recommended.

If you're trying to get out of the airport, you'll find plenty of airport cabs charging anywhere from US$10 to US$17 (or more during the curfew). You can bargain these down to half price with some insistence. If you can carry your luggage about 200 metres, then walk out of the one main

gate of the airport parking area and flag down one of the street taxis outside. You can get a ride for US$3 if you bargain.

There is also an airport bus which charges about US$4 per passenger and will take you to your hotel. There is a hotel booking agent in front of the international arrivals gate – they can help you make a telephone booking and get you on the airport bus, but you may have to wait an hour before the bus leaves. Hotel bookings can be made in the mid-priced and top hotels but not in the very cheapest ones. There is also a cheaper bus which leaves from in front of the national arrivals section, but recent increases in airport security may mean that buses are no longer allowed to park in front of the airport – ask.

Airport Facilities The airport is divided into two sections. To the right, as you look at the building, is the national arrivals and departures; to the left is the international section. If arriving on an international flight, especially during the day, look for a tourist information booth *before* you go through immigration. They can advise you about current exchange rates and transport out of the airport.

At immigration, ask politely for as many days as you need to avoid getting a standard 30 days. Keep the entry slip as you need to surrender it when leaving Peru. In the baggage claim area, avoid a porter unless you want to have your luggage trundled 20 metres outside the door and dumped into the most expensive taxi in town. Going through customs, the far right lanes are usually the most hassle-free for tourists. When several flights arrive at once, it can be a real zoo. Keep your wits and your luggage about you!

Facilities at the airport are not very good. The Banco de la Nación will not change travellers' cheques and sometimes won't even change cash dollars or excess intis back into dollars. Regulations change frequently. Casas de cambio will usually give you about 2% less than the best rates downtown for US$ cash and 10% less for travellers' cheques. There is a cafeteria over the domestic flight lounges which is open during the day but not for early morning or evening flights. There is a very small coffee shop in the middle of the ground floor which is open most of the time but offers little beyond coffee and stale plastic-wrapped objects masquerading as sandwiches. There is a post office and long-distance telephone office open during the day. There is a 24-hour left luggage room which charges about US$2 per piece per day. There are gift shops and a not particularly well-stocked duty free area.

Buses Taking the local buses around Lima is rather a challenge. Buses are often slow and crowded, but they get you there very cheaply along with the literally millions of Lima's commuters who rely upon the capital's bus service every day. Fares are generally about 10c and bus lines are identifiable by their destination cards, numbers and colour schemes.

If you want to use Lima's bus system then you should buy a *Guía de Transportes de Lima Metropolitana* which is a detailed bus map published by Lima 2000 and available from bookstores and map shops. This guide will show you where every bus line goes, tell you whether it's a large omnibus or a small minibus, and describe the bus's colour scheme and route number. At last count there were over 180 bus lines listed in the guide so it's beyond the scope of this book to list them all.

At the time of going to press, Avenida Quilca has been paved over and is now a pedestrian precinct. The bus guides still show the buses to Miraflores going along it although a 1987 edition (if printed) may show the changes. The tourist office is only a couple of blocks from Quilca and Plaza San Martín so ask them where the new bus lines run.

There are a few colectivo lines that operate cars or minibuses without any numbers or colour schemes and simply drive up and down the same streets all day long. The one that is the most useful goes along Avenida Arequipa and joins Lima with Miraflores. The vehicles are identifiable by the driver waving his hand in the air – the number of fingers held up indicates the number of seats available. One of these lines runs along Avenidas Tacna, Garcilazo de la Vega and Arequipa. You can flag them down anywhere along their route and get off anywhere you want. Fare is about 12c.

It takes a certain sense of adventure to use Lima's bus system but it's a lot of fun if you can put up with the crush and bustle. Whatever you do, don't forget to keep your money in a safe place – pickpockets haunt the crowded buses and thefts are common.

Taxi If you can't face the crowded buses then you'll find that the taxis are generally reasonably priced and efficient. If there's three or four of you it can be quite cheap. It's good if you speak some Spanish and are prepared to bargain because taxis don't have meters and so you have to agree the price with the driver before you get in. As a rough guide, the cheapest ride will be under a dollar and a ride from downtown to Miraflores will be about US$2 but gringos are often, though not always, charged more.

Taxis are identifiable by a red and white TAXI sticker on their windshield. Otherwise they can be any make or colour with Volkswagen beetles being the most common. The black *remisse* taxis parked outside of the best hotels and restaurants always charge two or three times more than the other cabs.

In late 1986 there have been movements to introduce meters into taxis. How long this will take to come into effect is a moot point.

Car Rental The major car rental companies such as Hertz, Avis, Budget and National

Top: Library of Church of San Francisco, Lima (TW)
Left: Torre Tagle Palace, Lima (TW)
Right: Church of San Francisco, Lima (TW)

are all represented in Lima. Their desks can be found at the airport. National is usually the least expensive but car rental is generally not cheap. There are plenty of hidden charges for mileage (per km), insurance, etc so make sure that you read the rental agreement carefully before hiring a car. A credit card charge is usually required for a deposit. Your driver's licence is normally adequate for driving in Peru. Renters normally need to be over 25. Beware of the bad roads, aggressive drivers and make sure you leave your car in a safe, guarded parking place at night. Never leave any valuables locked inside the car whilst you aren't in it.

Things to Buy

Markets are not the best places in Lima to shop for souvenirs and handicrafts, with the possible exception of the Indian artisans' market described in the Markets section. A better selection is found in shops and shopping arcades. The prices tend to be high but variable and so it pays to shop around. Two very similar looking wall hangings, for example, may cost US$30 and US$40 in two different shops. Quality is usually good in the places mentioned in this section. Although prices are fixed in some stores, you can bargain in others. If buying several items in one place, it's always worth asking for a discount.

Two of my favourite shopping arcades in Lima are both on Belén; the smaller one at 1066 where the tourist information office is and a larger one at 1030 where the 1900 restaurant is. An excellent variety of handicrafts from all over Peru can be found here. These include tightly woven rugs and wall hangings from Ayacucho; tapestries made of rolls of stuffed wool from San Pedro de las Cajas; hangings called *arpilleras* which are scenes made from little cloth dolls; carved gourds from Huancayo; spears, feather ornaments, blow pipes, etc from the jungle; carved stone buildings from Ayacucho; carved and colourfully painted wooden boxes

which open up to reveal incredibly intricate scenes of Peruvian life; tooled leatherwork; and the usual assortment of ponchos, sweaters and rugs. Don't be put off by the high prices in some of the stores – others are much more reasonably priced.

Jewellery is also popular and reasonably priced. Gold, silver and turquoise is common although it's much too heavy for my taste. There are several good jewellery stores along the pedestrian section of Jirón Unión. Remember to always carry your cash in a safe inside pocket when shopping. Cash dollars and sometimes travellers' cheques can be used in some of the better stores and exchange rates are often within 1% of the best rates in town. Don't use your credit card, though, because you'll end up paying about 25% more than you do with cash.

There are plenty of other handicraft stores downtown, especially along Colmena, but I like the places on Belén most of all. There are also some very nice shops in Miraflores but they do tend to be expensive, although the quality and the shopping atmosphere is as good as you'll find anywhere. Highly exclusive jewellery and handicrafts stores are to be found in the very attractive *El Suche* arcade, off the 6th block of La Paz in Miraflores. The 5th block of La Paz is also good with *La Gringa* having an excellent selection and the *El Alamo* shopping arcade is also recommended. The fact that Peru's most expensive hotel, *Césars*, is on this block will give you an idea of what to expect.

Around Lima

There are several nearby excursions that can be made as day trips or weekend jaunts. Those that follow can all be done using public transport.

PACHACAMAC

These ruins are the closest major archaeological site to Lima and they are the most frequently visited. They are about 31 km south of the capital and are easily reached by public transport.

Although Pachacamac was an important Inca site and a major city when the Spanish arrived, it predated the Incas by roughly 1000 years and had long been a major ceremonial centre on the central coast before the expansion of the Inca empire. Most of the buildings are now little more than walls of piled rubble except for the main temples which are huge pyramids. These have been excavated but, to the untrained eye, they look like huge mounds with rough steps cut into them. One of the most recent of the complexes, the Mamacuña or House of the Chosen Women, which was built by the Incas, has been excavated and reconstructed and gives some idea of Inca construction. It is surrounded by a garden, and houses innumerable swallows' nests in the roof beams and so is of interest to the ornithologist as well as the archaeologist.

The site is extensive and a thorough visit takes some hours. Near the entrance is a visitors' centre with a small museum and a cafeteria. From there a dirt road leads around the site. Those with a vehicle can drive from complex to complex, leaving their car in various parking spots to visit each section. Those on foot can walk around the site in an hour at a leisurely pace but without stopping for long at any of the sections. Although the pyramids are badly preserved, their size is impressive and you can climb the stairs to the top of some of them, from where you can get excellent views of the coast on a clear day.

Guided tours to Pachacamac are offered by Vista (information at Lima Tours, Belén 1040). Tours cost US$15 per person and include round-trip transportation, an English-speaking guide and a visit to the Archaeology & Anthropology Museum in Lima. Tours are daily except Monday.

Those wishing to visit Pachacamac without a guided tour can do so by catching a minibus from the corner of Colmena and Andahuayalas near the Santa Catalina convent in Lima. The buses are line 120, light blue in colour with orange trim, and they leave two or three times an hour as soon as they have a load. Fare is about 25c and the journey takes roughly an hour. Tell the driver to let you off near the *ruinas* or you will end up at Pachacamac village, about a km beyond the entrance.

The ruins are open daily, except Monday, from 9 am to 5 pm. Entrance is about 30c and a bilingual booklet describing the ruins is available for US$1. When you are ready to leave, flag down any bus outside the gate. Some come by full but you can usually get on a bus within half an hour or so. It's advisable not to leave it to the last minute.

THE CENTRAL HIGHWAY

This is the road which heads directly east of Lima and into the foothills of the Andes, following the Rimac river valley. There are several places of interest along the first 80 km of the road east of Lima. Various, confusing systems of highway markers and distances are given in different guide books but bus drivers usually know where you need to get off. The road continues to the high mining town of La Oroya which is described in the Central Peru chapter.

Puruchuco

This pre-Inca chief's house has been reconstructed and there is a small museum on the site. Although it's only a minor site, the museum is quite good and worth a visit and the drive out gives a look at some of Lima's surroundings. Puruchuco is about five km out of Lima on the Central Highway (using the highway distance markers) and about 13 km from downtown Lima. It is found in the suburb of Ate, just before the village of Vitarte and there is a clear signpost on the highway. The site is several hundred metres along a road to the right. Opening hours are from 9 am to 5 pm from Tuesdays to Saturdays. Admission is 30c. See below for how to get here.

Cajamarquilla

This large site dates to the Wari culture of 700 to 1100 AD. It consists mainly of adobe mud walls and some sections are being restored. Entrance is from 9 am to 5 pm on Tuesdays to Saturdays and admission is 30c. There is a road to the left at about km 10 (18 km from downtown Lima) which goes to the Cajamarquilla zinc refinery, almost five km from the highway. The ruins are roughly halfway along the refinery road and then to the right along a short poor road. They aren't very clearly marked (though there are some signs) so ask.

Santa Clara

This village, at about km 12 (20 km from downtown Lima) is the site of two well-known resorts, the *Granja Azul* and *El Pueblo*. The first is more of a restaurant and has dancing in the weekends and the second is more of a country club and features a swimming pool, golf course, tennis courts, etc.

Chaclacayo

This village is at km 27 and is about 660 metres above sea level – just high enough to rise above Lima's coastal *garua* or sea mist. You can normally bask in sunshine here while about six million people in the capital below have to languish in the grey fog. There are several vacation hotels such as *Centro Vacacional Huampani* and *Centro Vacacional Los Cóndores* where you can expect to pay about US$30 for a double cabin. There are pleasant dining, swimming and horse riding facilities.

Chosica

The resort town of Chosica at 860 metres above sea level is almost 40 km along the central highway. It was very popular with Limeños at the turn of the century but today its popularity has declined somewhat, although escapees from Lima's *garua* will still find it to be the most convenient place to find a number of variously priced hotels in the sun.

Getting There

Buses to Chosica leave frequently from Lima and can be used to get to the other intermediate places mentioned above. The majority of buses leave from near the intersection of the 15th block of Colmena with the 9th block of Ayacucho. The 200a green and red bus leaves from the 15th block of Colmena for Chosica. The 200b silver bus with red trim leaves from the 15th block of Colmena for Chosica and continues to the village of Ricardo Palma a few km beyond. The 200c dark green bus with white trim leaves from the 15th block of Colmena for Chosica and continues to the fruit-growing area of Santa Eulalia. The 201 cream and red bus leaves from the 15th block of Colmena for the village of San Fernando, passing through all points to Chaclacayo but not going to Chosica. The 202a bus leaves from the 8th block of Ayacucho for Santa Clara. The 202b green and blue bus leaves from the 12th block of Colmena (Parque Universitario) for Santa Clara and stops at the Granja Azul. The 202c bus leaves from the 8th block of Ayacucho for Jicamarca via Vitarte and Huachipa and takes you near Cajamarquilla. The 202d bus leaves from the 8th block of Ayacucho for Cajamarquilla refinery. The 204 bus goes from the 10th block of Ayacucho to Chosica. Fares are about 50c to Chosica.

The South Coast

The entire coastal lowlands of Peru are a desert interspersed with oases clustered around the rivers which flow down the western slopes of the Andes. The Pan-American Highway runs through these desert lowlands joining the Ecuadorian border in the north with the Chilean border in the south – a driving distance of approximately 2675 km. Most of this is paved and it is the best highway in the country. Lima lies roughly in the middle of the Peruvian coastline.

The south coast is generally more visited by travellers than the north. This is because the Pan-American Highway south of Lima goes through many places of interest, and it is the route for travelling overland through Arequipa to those popular destinations for the traveller in South America – Lake Titicaca and Cuzco. The main points of interest for travellers along the south coast are: Pisco for the nearby wildlife, Ica for its museum and wine-making industry, Nazca for the famous Nazca lines, the beautiful colonial city of Arequipa nestling under a perfect cone-shaped volcano, and Tacna for travellers heading to Chile. There are, of course, many other places to visit for the traveller with extra time to spare.

PUCUSANA

This small fishing village, 68 km south of Lima, is a popular beach resort. From January to April it can get very crowded, especially at weekends, but during the rest of the year you often have the place to yourself.

Beaches

There are four beaches. Pucusana and Las Ninfas beaches are small and on the town's seafront, and so tend to be the most crowded. La Isla is a beach on an island in front of the town. You can wade out there at very low tides. Frequent boats go there from the small harbour. The fare is just a few cents if there are several passengers. You can also hire boats by the hour for about US$2 or US$3 but you must bargain for the best rates. The most isolated beach is Naplo which lies almost a km away and is reached by walking through a tunnel. There are good views from the cliffs around the town.

Places to Stay

There are four hotels, none of them very fancy. The best is the new *Salón Blanco*. There is also an old *Salón Blanco* which is not so good. The *Hotel Bahía* is also quite good and its restaurant is recommended. The cheapest is the *Hotel Delicias*. They are all found on or within a block of the seafront as are several seafood restaurants. Hotel prices are between US$1 and US$2 per person but usually go up during the busy summer weekends which are best avoided.

Getting There

Because Pucusana is about eight km off the Pan-American Highway, the major companies running along the coast don't normally stop here. From Lima you have to take a Pucusana colectivo 97 which leaves frequently from the corner of Colmena and Andahuaylas near the Plaza Santa Catalina. The colectivos are red and blue with white trim and charge about 75c for the trip which can take up to two hours.

CAÑETE

The full name of this small town, about 144 km south of Lima, is San Vicente de Cañete. Although the site predates the Incas, it is now of little interest except to river runners who sometimes take inflatable rafts or kayaks down the Río Cañete.

River Running

In late 1985 *Expediciones Mayuc* began weekly Sunday river trips in inflatable rafts down the Cañete. The trip costs about US$16 per person including all equipment, boatmen and transportation from the Cañete Plaza de Armas. It is a pleasant adventure suitable for beginners. The trip takes several hours so bring a picnic lunch. Get further information and reservations in their office (tel 225988) at Conquistadores 199, San Isidro, Lima. They also organise treks and river running around the Cuzco area, as well as jungle expeditions. (See under Cuzco.)

Places to Stay & Eat

The best hotel is *La Casona* on the Plaza de Armas which charges about US$2/3 for singles/doubles with a cold shower. It is often full. A couple of blocks away is the *Hotel Genova* which is basic but adequate for US$1.60/2.

There are several restaurants on the plaza of which the *Paris* is one of the best.

Getting There

Expreso Chinchano, which is part of the Ormeño bus company in Lima, has buses every hour or two for US$1.50. The journey takes about 2½ hours from Lima. For journeys out of Cañete it is easiest to stand on the Pan-American Highway, about four blocks from the plaza, and wait for a passing bus.

CHINCHA

The small town of Chincha Alta is the next landmark, some 55 km beyond Cañete. The small Chincha Empire flourished in this area during the 'Regional States Period' around the 13th century and was conquered by the Incas in the late 14th century. They retained importance within the Inca Empire and the Lord of Chincha was present at Cajamarca in 1532 when the Inca Atahualpa was captured by the Spaniards.

Today there is little to see and few travellers stop here unless they have a passionate interest in archaeology. The best of the surviving ruins are at Tambo de Mora on the coast some 10 km west of Chincha and at the nearby temple of La Centinela.

Places to Stay

There are a few simple hotels in town and a better one on the outskirts. In town are the basic *Hostal Residencial San Francisco* at Callao 154 and the *Hotel Sotelo* at Benavides 260. They charge about US$1.50 per person. Better, but a dollar per person more, is the *Hostal Residencial Majestic* on Diego del Almagro 114.

Just north of Chincha at km 197.5 on the Pan American highway is the fancier *Hostal El Sausal* running about US$8 per person.

PISCO

Pisco gives its name to the white grape brandy produced in this region and is the first town south of Lima frequently visited by travellers. It is a fairly important port of about 82,000 inhabitants and lies some 235 km south of the capital. Most visitors use Pisco as a base to see the wildlife of the nearby Ballestas Islands and Paracas Peninsula but the area is also of considerable historical and archaeological interest.

Note that the resort village of Paracas is about 15 km south of Pisco but because accommodation is expensive and limited, most travellers stay in Pisco and make day trips out to Paracas and the Ballestas Islands. In the following sections on archaeology and wildlife, the Pisco-Paracas area is described as a whole.

Archaeology

Pisco is an oasis watered by the river of the same name but the surrounding countryside is barren and sandy desert typical of Peru's coast. Until the beginning of this century, no one suspected that the drifting dunes of this arid area had

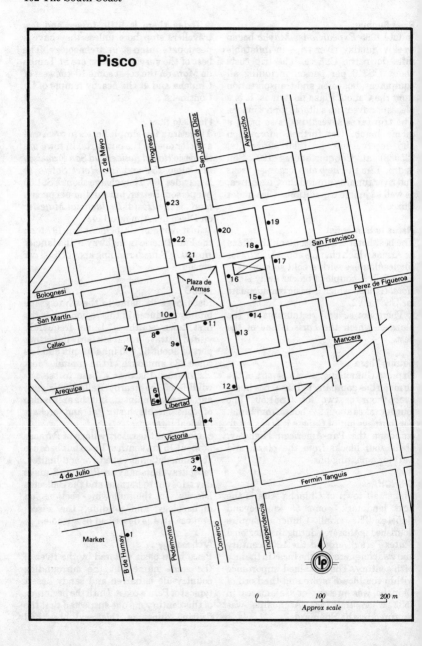

Pisco

2 de Mayo

Progreso

San Juan de Dios

Ayacucho

•23

•20   •19

•22   •18   San Francisco

21•   •17

Plaza de   •16
Armas

Bolognesi

San Martín   15•

10•   •14

8•   •11   13•

7•   9•   Mancera

Callao

Arequipa   12•

6•
5•   Libertad

•4

Victoria

3•
2•

4 de Julio   Fermín Tanguis

Market   •1

B de Humay

Pedemonte

Comercio

Independencia

Perez de Figueroa

0   100   200 m

Approx scale

1	Comité 9M to Paracas
2	Expreso Oropesa
3	Hostal Mi Casa
4	Hostal Grau
5	Comité 2M to San Andrés
6	Hostal Peru
7	Hostal Angamos
8	Hostal Callao
9	Hotel Embassy, Hotel Comercio & Restaurant Candelabrum
10	Empresa José de Martín
11	Banco de Crédito
12	Comité 7 M to San Clemente
13	Teatro Solar
14	Teatro Solar (another entrance)
15	Paracas Express
16	Cathedral
17	Church of La Compañía
18	Ormeño Bus Station
19	Hostal Josesito Moreno
20	Cine Pisco
21	Hostal Pisco
22	Hostal Progreso
23	Post Office

covered the site of a well-developed culture which predated the Incas by over 1000 years. It was not until 1925 that the Peruvian archaeologist J C Tello discovered burial sites of the Paracas culture which existed in the area from approximately 1300 BC until 200 AD. These people are considered to have produced the finest textiles known in the pre-Columbian Americas.

Paracas Antiguo is the name given to the early centuries of the culture about which little is known except that it was influenced by the Chavín Horizon. Most of our knowledge is about the later Paracas culture from about 500 BC to 200 AD. This is divided into two periods known as Paracas Cavernas and Paracas Necropolis, named after the two main burial sites discovered. Cavernas is the earlier (500 to 300 BC) and is characterised by communal bottle-shaped tombs which were dug into the ground at the bottom of a vertical shaft, often to a depth of six metres or more. Several dozen bodies of varying ages and both sexes – possibly

family groups – were buried in some of these tombs. They were wrapped in relatively coarse cloth and accompanied by funereal offerings of bone and clay musical instruments, decorated gourds and well-made ceramics.

Paracas Necropolis (300 BC to 100 AD) is the site which yielded the treasure trove of exquisite textiles for which the Paracas culture is known today. This burial site is about 20 km south of Pisco and can still be seen although drifting sands have all but covered it. It is near the J C Tello Museum on the north side of Cerro Colorado on the isthmus joining the Paracas Peninsula with the mainland.

The Necropolis consisted of a roughly rectangular-walled enclosure in which over 400 funerary bundles were found. Each consisted of an older mummified man (who was probably a nobleman or priest) wrapped in many layers of weavings. It is these textiles which are marvelled at by visitors today. They average about a metre by 2½ metres in size although one measuring four metres by 26 metres has been found. This size is in itself remarkable because weavings wider than the span of the weaver's arms (a bit over a metre) are rarely found in Peru. The textiles consist of a wool or cotton background embroidered with multicoloured and exceptionally detailed small figures. They are repeated again and again until often the entire weaving is covered by a pattern of embroidered designs. Motifs connected with the nearby ocean are popular, for example fish and seabirds, as well as other zoomorphic and geometric designs. No written description, at least by this writer, can do them justice – they really have to be seen to be appreciated.

It is best to visit the Lima museums for a look at the Paracas mummies, textiles and other artefacts. The National Museum of Archaeology & Anthropology and the Rafael Larco Herrera Museum are particularly recommended. In the region, visit the J C Tello Museum in the Paracas

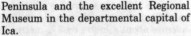
Garments from the Paracas Necropolis

Peninsula and the excellent Regional Museum in the departmental capital of Ica.

Our knowledge is vague about what happened in the area during the 1000 years after the Paracas culture disintegrated. A short distance to the southeast, the Nazca culture became important for several centuries after the disappearance of the Paracas culture. This in turn gave way to Wari influence from the mountains. After the sudden disappearance of the Wari Empire, the area became dominated by the Ica culture which was similar to and perhaps part of the Chincha Empire. They in turn were conquered by the Incas.

About this time a remarkable settlement was built by the expanding Incas, one of which is perhaps the best preserved early Inca site found in the desert lowlands today. This is Tambo Colorado, so called for the red-painted walls of some of the buildings. Hallmarks of Inca architecture such as trapezoidally shaped niches, windows and doorways are evident, although the buildings were made not from rock but from adobe bricks. It is

about 50 km inland from Pisco and although not as spectacular as the Inca ruins in the Cuzco area, nevertheless it is worth visiting by archaeology enthusiasts or travellers with some extra time.

Wildlife

The Paracas Peninsula and the nearby Ballestas Islands are the most important wildlife sanctuary on the Peruvian coast. The area is particularly known for its bird and marine life. The birds nest on the offshore islands in such numbers that their nitrogen-rich droppings (guano) collect in quantities large enough to be commercially exploited for fertiliser. This practice dates from at least Inca times. Large sea lion colonies are also found on the islands.

The most common guano-producing birds are the Guanay Cormorant, Peruvian Booby and the Peruvian Pelican. These are seen in colonies of several thousand birds. Less frequently seen, but of particular interest, are the Humboldt Penguins on the Ballestas Islands and the Chilean Flamingoes in the Bay of Paracas. The Andean Condor occasionally comes down to the coast and may be seen gliding majestically on the cliff thermals of the peninsula. The most useful guidebook to the coastal birds is *The Birds of the Department of Lima, Peru* by Maria Koepke. It is available from Harrowood Books, Newtown Square, Pennsylvania, USA, and sometimes from bookstores in Lima or at the Hotel Paracas.

Apart from the birds and sea lions, other seashore life is evident. The most obvious are the jellyfish, some reaching ⅔ of a metre in diameter and with stinging tentacles trailing a metre or more behind them. One calm day when the sea was glassy smooth I was crossing the Bay of Paracas and saw a huge flotilla of jellyfish gently floating in the upper layers of the ocean. There must have been hundreds of them. Often they get washed up onto the shore where they will quickly dry out in the hot sun and form beautiful mandalic patterns on the sand. Sea hares, ghost crabs and seashells are also found by beachcombers strolling along the shore. Swimmers should take great care because of the jellyfish.

The Ballestas Islands

Except for the people collecting guano, it is prohibited to land on the islands and so the only way to visit the bird and sea lion colonies is to go on an organised boat tour. If you're the sort of person who shudders at the thought of an organised tour, take heart. These trips are fun, inexpensive and definitely worthwhile.

Various places in Pisco offer tours but basically they are all the same. Everybody gets lumped into one group irrespective of where they sign up (except those who take the more expensive Hotel Paracas tour). Most hotels in Pisco will sign you up for the tour but you may as well go to the Hostal Pisco because that's where they usually start from.

The tours leave daily around 7 am and cost about US$4 per person. Usually you will be picked up from your hotel in a minibus and when everyone is collected

you are driven to Paracas. Here you board rather ancient and slow boats for the excursion – there's no cabin so dress appropriately against the wind and spray. The outward boat journey takes about 1 ½ hours and en route you will see the so-called *Candelabra* which is a giant figure etched into the coastal hills rather like the figures of the Nazca lines. No one knows who made the hill drawing or what it signifies although you'll hear plenty of theories.

About an hour is spent cruising around the islands once you get there. You can't fail to see plenty of sea lions on the rocks and swimming around your boat. Bring a camera and binoculars if you have them. Although you do approach the wildlife close enough for a good view, some species, especially the penguins, are a little less visible. If you show some interest the boatman will usually try to point out and name some of the various species (in Spanish). Wear a hat – there are a lot of birds in the air and it's not unusual for someone to receive a direct hit!

On your return trip ask to see the flamingoes. They are usually found in the southerly part of the bay (see map) and not on the direct boat route. Sometimes the boatman will ask for a small tip to pay for the extra fuel and time needed to see them. They aren't always there – the best times are supposedly in June and July but I've seen them in January too.

Once you return to the mainland, a minibus will take you back to Pisco in time for lunch. If you want to stay on in Paracas, you'll have to make your own way back.

The Paracas Peninsula

Tours to the Paracas Peninsula are not organised so frequently from Pisco. The Hotel Paracas will organise an expensive tour but you could just hire your own taxi in Pisco, particularly if you can get a group together. A half-day taxi hire would cost about US$25. Alternatively,

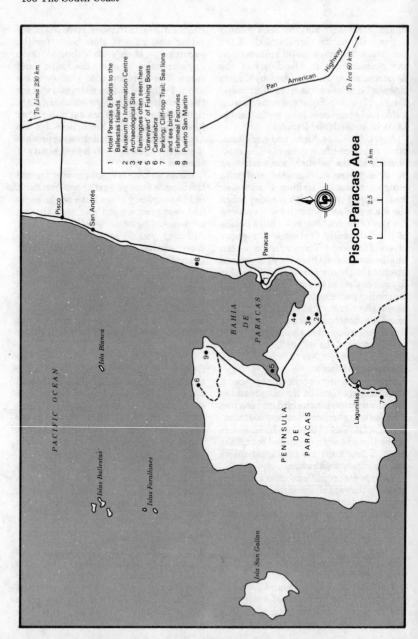

Pisco-Paracas Area

1 Hotel Paracas & Boats to the
   Ballestas Islands
2 Museum & Information Centre
3 Archaeological Site
4 Flamingoes often seen here
5 'Graveyard' of Fishing Boats
6 Candelabra
7 Parking; Cliff-top Trail; Sea lions
   and sea birds
8 Fishmeal Factories
9 Puerto San Martin

To Lima 230 km

Pan American Highway

To Ica 60 km

Pisco

San Andrés

PACIFIC OCEAN

Isla Blanca

Islas Ballestas

Islas Farallones

Isla San Gallan

BAHIA
DE
PARACAS

Paracas

PENINSULA
DE
PARACAS

Lagunillas

0   2.5   5 km

you can catch the colectivo into Paracas and walk, but allow yourself plenty of time. Bring food and, more importantly, plenty of drinking water.

Near the entrance to Paracas is an obelisk commemorating the landing of the liberator San Martín. The bus continues further in and will drop you in front of the Hotel Paracas if you ask the driver. It's worth going into the hotel for a look at their large-scale wall map and the books for sale in their gift shop. You continue on foot either along the tarmac road south of Paracas or, better still, walk along the beach from the hotel and look for seashore life.

About three km south of the hotel on the road is a park entry station where a small fee may be charged though it's not always open. You can see it from the beach. There is a park centre about two km beyond the entrance. Here you'll find an information centre and the J C Tello Museum. The information centre is free and the museum costs about 70c to get in. Unfortunately, the best pieces were stolen a few years ago but a small collection of weavings and other artefacts remains. A few hundred metres behind this complex is the Paracas Necropolis, though there's not much to see. In the bay in front of the centre one can often see flamingoes.

Beyond the park centre the tarmac road continues around the peninsula, past a 'graveyard' of old fishing boats, to Puerto San Martín which is a smelly and uninteresting fishmeal plant and port on the north tip of the peninsula. It's best to forget the tarmac road and head out on one of the dirt roads crossing the peninsula.

The first dirt road branches left from the tarmac a few hundred metres beyond the park centre. Six km later it reaches the little fishing village of Lagunillas where you probably will find someone to cook you some fresh fish. The road continues for another five km, parallel to the coast, to a parking lot from where a footpath leads to a cliff-top lookout. Here there are grand views of the ocean with a sea lion colony on the rocks below and plenty of seabirds gliding by. You can continue further in if you're adventurous.

You can also take a rough track to the Candelabra, although it's a long way. Shortly before Puerto San Martín a dirt road branches from the tarmac and heads for the site, about 13 km away. If you want to spend a lot of time exploring the Paracas Peninsula you should get the topographic map 28-K, available from the Instituto Geográfico Nacional in Lima.

Tambo Colorado

The easiest way to visit this early Inca coastal site is to hire a taxi in Pisco for half a day – about US$25. Otherwise you can take the Oropesa bus which leaves Pisco for Huancayo every morning at 10 am. The road goes right through the middle of the site so you can't miss it. Once you get to the site, ask the locals about when to expect a return bus from the mountains – there's usually a couple every afternoon. The on-site caretaker will answer your questions and collect a few cents.

Places to Stay – bottom end

Because of the nearby fishing industry, Pisco is occasionally full of fishermen, hotels are booked up and prices rise. This is unpredictable because to avoid over-fishing, short seasons are periodically declared. These last a few days every few months and that's the time to avoid if you can – but no one knows for sure when an open season will be declared.

There are several basic cold water hotels charging about a dollar per person per night. These include, in roughly descending order of attraction, the *Hostal Angamos, Progreso, Peru, Callao, Grau* and *Mi Casa*. A little more expensive is the *Hostal Josesito Moreno* which claims to have hot and cold running water in the rooms but looks pretty grimy.

Places to Stay – middle

The *Hostal Pisco* used to be a popular cheap hotel. I paid a dollar to stay there in mid-83 but now singles/doubles are US$4/6 or US$8/12 with a private bath. I think it's way overpriced and not good value. The best place in town for my money is the *Hotel Embassy* which is clean and good. They charge about US$3/5 for singles/doubles with private bath and tepid water. There is a bar on the roof if you want to hang out in the evenings. Next door is the *Hotel Comercio* which isn't great – they only have doubles at US$4 with private bath and cold water and the place could do with a clean-up.

Places to Stay – top end

Paracas, 15 km south of Pisco, is a resort town full of private seaside villas which are empty for most of the year. There are two hotels. The *Hotel Paracas* on the bay is the best with an excellent, though expensive, dining room and a garden complete with swimming pool and games. They charge about US$22/30 for singles/doubles. They organise trips to the Ballestas Islands which cost about twice as much as the ones from Pisco – the only advantage is their better and faster boats. The hotel is open to non-residents and has a small gift shop where books about the area can be bought, as well as large-scale wall maps to study.

The other hotel is the medium priced *El Mirador* which is situated in sand dunes at the entrance to town. It didn't seem to be doing a great deal of business when I was last there but I've heard it's quite good.

Places to Eat

For early risers heading for the Ballestas Islands, the *Hotel Pisco* serves a small and overpriced breakfast. You can sometimes find cheaper cafés open early on the Plaza de Armas. For main meals, the best place is the *Restaurant Candelabrum* next to the Hotel Embassy. They are friendly and serve a good variety of food. There are several restaurants on the Plaza de Armas of which the *As de Oro* has received frequent recommendations from other travellers but I found it had mediocre service and a limited menu last time I visited it, but at least it's reasonably priced. There is often seafood to be had in the restaurants. One local speciality is turtle (tortuga) cooked in a variety of ways.

If you want to eat seafood fresh from the sea go to the fishing village of San Andrés which is about five km south of Pisco. There are several cheap restaurants lining the shore and although it's not fancy, the food is good.

Getting There

Bear in mind that Pisco is some five km west of the Pan-American Highway and many coastal buses travelling between Lima and Ica or Nazca don't stop there. There are direct buses to Pisco from both Lima and Ica but if you're not on a direct bus make sure you ask if the bus goes into Pisco or you may be left on the turn-off with five km to walk or hitch.

The Ormeño bus company has a terminal a block away from the Plaza de Armas. Buses leave for Lima (US$2.50, four hours) and Ica (60c, one hour) approximately every hour. Ormeño also has four buses a day to Nazca (US$2, 3½ hours) and Arequipa (US$9, 16 hours). A couple of buses a day go up to Ayacucho (US$9) and tickets can be bought for Cuzco, but a change of bus is involved.

Other long distance bus companies include Paracas Express (three buses daily to Lima), Empresa José de Martín (six daily to Lima) and Expreso Oropesa which runs a daily bus at 10 am to Huancavelica and Huancayo (US$10.50, up to 24 hours).

To get to Paracas it's best to first go to Pisco and then catch a local bus, although Paracas Express will go on to Paracas from Lima if there's enough demand.

Getting Around

There are two local buses to know about.

Comité 9M to Paracas leaves from the market about every half hour and costs 25c. Comité 2M to San Andrés leaves every few minutes for 10c. Note that the buses usually leave when full and so if you go to San Andrés and then try and continue to Paracas you may wait a long time. It's often better to return to Pisco and take the Paracas bus from the market.

ICA

Ica is a pleasant colonial town of about 150,000 inhabitants. It was founded by Jerónimo Luis de Cabrera in 1563 and is the capital of the department of Ica. It lies about 305 km south of Lima and 80 km from Pisco. The Pan-American Highway heads inland from Pisco, rising gently to 420 metres above sea level at Ica. Because of this, the town is high enough to rise above the coastal *garua* (sea mist) and the climate is dry and sunny. The desert surrounding Ica is noted for its huge sand dunes.

Many visitors stop here. Ica is irrigated by the river of the same name and the oasis is famous for its grapes. There is a thriving wine and pisco-producing industry and the distilleries and wineries can be visited. There are some excellent museums, attractive colonial churches and several annual fiestas.

Information

Tourist Information To help you keep up with what's going on there is a tourist office at Cajamarca 179. It's open from 7.30 am until 3 pm on Mondays through Fridays.

Money Exchange There are two or three casas de cambio which are open erratically, usually only change dollars cash at lower rates than Lima and don't always have money. Street changers hang around outside. You can also try the Banco de Crédito which sometimes will change money. The Hotel de Turistas changes money at the unfavourable 'official' rate.

Ica is not reliable for money changing so change in Lima or Arequipa if you can.

Wineries

Wineries and distilleries are known as *bodegas*. They can be visited year round but the best time is from late February until early April which is the time of the grape harvest. At other times they're not working and there's not much to see.

The best of Peru's wine comes from the Tacama and Ocucaje wineries. Unfortunately, these are among the most difficult to visit because they are fairly isolated. The Vista Alegre winery makes reasonable wine and is the easiest of the large commercial wineries to visit. A number of smaller family-run wineries can also be visited.

To get to the Vista Alegre winery, walk across the Grau bridge and take the second left. It's about three km; all the locals know it. Alternatively, the No 8 or 13 city buses go near there. They pass the main plaza. The entrance to the winery is a large yellow-brick arch and they're open from 9 till 5 on weekdays but it's recommended to go in the morning. About eight km further on is the Tacama winery but there aren't any buses so you have to hire a taxi if you don't want to walk that far. The Ocucaje winery is about 36 km south of Ica and a little distance off the Pan-American Highway. Again, you need to hire a taxi to get there although it might also be possible to take a bus bound for Nazca and get off at the Ocucaje turn-off.

The easiest of the small local *bodegas* to visit are in the suburbs of Guadalupe, about three km before Ica on the road from Lima. There are frequent city buses from opposite the Hostal Europa in Ica. In Guadalupe you'll find the Bodegas Peña, Lovera and El Carmel within a block or two of the plaza. There are many stalls selling huge bottles of various kinds of piscos and wines. Also recommended is the Bodega Mejía, which is 17 km south of Ica and reached by a bus which leaves

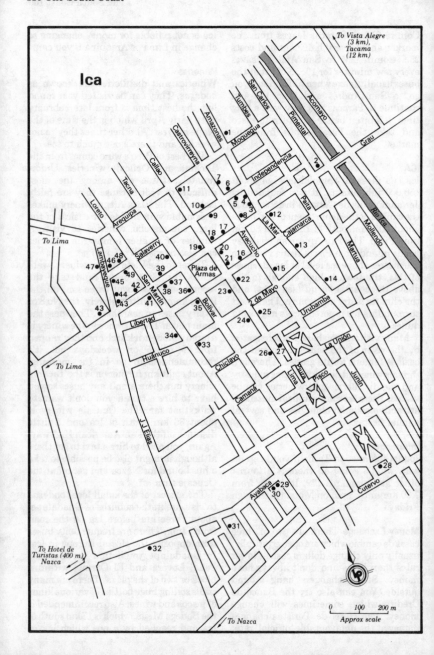

Ica

To Vista Alegre
(3 km),
Tacama
(12 km)

To Lima

To Lima

Plaza de
Armas

To Hotel de
Turistas (400 m)
Nazca

To Nazca

0   100   200 m
Approx scale

from the market about every hour. It has a sign for San Juan Olivo.

If you just want to buy some local wine or pisco without going to the source, a good place to go is the east side of the Plaza de Armas which has several liquor shops.

Museums

There are two museums in Ica; both of them are interesting and one is a 'must see'.

Don't miss the Regional Museum in the south-western suburbs about 1½ km from the centre. You can take a No 17 bus from the Plaza de Armas but it's a pleasant walk. The museum is open from 8 am to 6 pm daily except Sunday when it closes at noon. Entrance is 65c with an extra 35c camera fee. It is one of the best small regional museums in Peru. There are excellent collections of artefacts from the Paracas, Nazca and Inca cultures. You will see some superb examples of Paracas weavings as well as textiles made from feathers, beautiful Nazca ceramics, well preserved mummies, trepanned skulls and trophy heads, *quipus* (the knotted strings used by the Incas as mnemonic devices) and many other objects.

Perhaps the weirdest exhibit is a re-hydrated mummy hand. This centuries-old dried out hand was placed in a re-hydrating saline solution so that it could be examined microscopically and checked for diseases that the owner of the hand may have had. It's a very informative and well laid out museum and because it's fairly small you don't feel overwhelmed and can learn a great deal. Interesting maps and paintings can be bought as souvenirs.

The second museum is the Cabrera stone museum on the Plaza de Armas. There's no sign but you'll find it at Bolívar 170. It's one of the strangest museums you'll ever see and consists of a collection of 11,000 carved stones and boulders showing 'pre-Columbian'

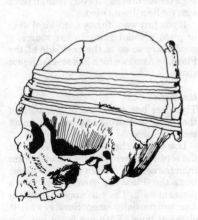

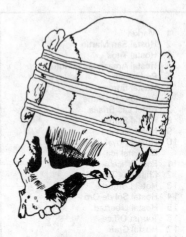

Pre-Incan method of beautifying skulls

surgical techniques, and day-to-day living. The owner, Dr Javier Cabreras (who is descended from the city founder) claims that these stones are hundreds of years old but most authorities don't believe him. You can see some of the stones in the museum entrance but for a proper look at them along with a guided tour and explanation you have to shell out US$5! The museum is open from 9 am to 1 pm and 4 to 8 pm.

Churches
The rather bare church of San Francisco has some fine stained-glass windows. The church of La Merced was rebuilt in 1874 and contains finely carved wooden altars. The Cathedral contains the tomb of a local priest, Padre Guatemala, to whom miracles have been attributed. The church of El Señor de Luren boasts an image of the Lord which is venerated by pilgrims bi-annually.

Fiestas
Ica has more than its share of fiestas. The most famous is the wine harvest festival held every March. It's called the *Festival Internacional de Vendimia*, or the Vintage

Festival. There are processions and beauty contests, cockfights and horse shows, arts and crafts fairs, music and dancing, and of course the pisco and wine flow freely.

In October the religious pilgrimage of the Lord of Luren culminates in a traditional all night procession on the 3rd Monday of the month. This festival is repeated in March and sometimes co-incides with Holy Week celebrations.

The Carnival of Yunza takes place in February. Participants dress in beautiful costumes and there is public dancing. One dance involves circling a tree until it is pulled down. As in most Latin American carnivals, water is thrown.

The founding of the city on 17 June 1563 is celebrated every June during Ica week. The more important Ica tourist festival is held in the latter half of September.

Nazca Lines
It's much cheaper to fly over the Lines from Nazca but if you're in a hurry you can do it from Ica for about US$90 per person with a minimum of three needed. There is an AeroIca office.

Places to Stay - bottom end

Bear in mind that the prices below are average costs and that even the cheapest hotels raise their prices substantially during the festivals, especially the March harvest festival when hotels are often fully booked.

Of the super cheapies the *Hostal Europa* is quite good for 80c per person. The rooms are basic but the beds are clean and there's a wash basin in each room. Three similarly priced hotels which are conveniently located together are the *Hostal Royal, Diaz* and *Ica*. The last one is supposed to be the best and has an annex a few blocks away if the main hotel is full, but they're all just basic cold water cheapies though quite a few budget travellers stay there. Other hotels for under US$1 per person include the *Hostal Amazonas*, which is clean and has rooms with private baths (cold water) but no singles, and the less attractive *Hostal Grau* which has some rooms with private cold water bath but again no singles. The friendly *Hostal Sol de Oro* charges US$1 per person or US$1.60 for rooms with private baths. They have hot water and single rooms.

If all of these are full and you're on a tight budget, you can try the *Hostal San Martín, Titos, Libertad* or *Lima* but they are very basic.

For the slightly more affluent budget traveller there's the clean *Hotel Olimpia* which charges US$1.30 per person but only has communal showers with cold water, though there is a cheap restaurant. The new *Hostal La Viña* is US$1.70 per person in rooms with private bath and cold water. The *Hotel Jacaranda* charges about the same or a few cents more for a room with private bath and there is hot water.

The *Hotel Confort* has clean, simple rooms with the kind of tepid electric shower which may give you a shock if you're not careful. They charge US$2/3.70 for singles/doubles. Similarly priced is the ever-popular *Hotel Colón* which is a rambling old building right on the Plaza de Armas. It certainly has some character, though check the water – it didn't work in the mornings last time I was there. They have an inexpensive restaurant. The *Hotel Presidente* looks quite good for US$2.30 per person in rooms with private bath, hot water and a sauna next door.

Places to Stay - middle

The clean *Hotel Las Brisas* is recommended for those who want inexpensive comfort – good beds and hot showers for US$3.30/5.30. Also good are the remarkably fancy looking hotels *Siesta* and *Silmar* which charge US$5/7.50 if it's not harvest festival. Both hotels have the expected clean rooms and private baths with hot water.

If you're looking for peace and quiet, you can try the *Hostal San Isidro* away from the town centre near the Regional Museum. They charge US$2.70 per person but not all the rooms have private showers or hot water.

Some way out of town is the *Hostal Medanos* (tel 231666) at km 300 on the Pan-American Highway. They have a swimming pool and charge US$6 per double.

Places to Stay - top end

There are no really good hotels in the town centre, though the government-run *Hotel de Turistas* comes fairly close – it's about two km from the Plaza de Armas. It's a very modern building and they charge US$11/15 for singles/doubles, including continental breakfast.

Out on the Pan-American are two more good hotels. The *Hostal El Carmelo* (tel 23191) at km 301 is US$8/11 while the luxurious *Hotel Las Dunas* (tel 231031) at km 300 is US$36/40. All of these hotels have swimming pools and restaurant facilities, and the *Las Dunas* offers tennis, golf, horse riding and Nazca Lines overflights if you have the money.

Places to Eat

If you're staying in one of the better hotels you'll find the food is good, if expensive. Cheaper restaurants are to be found in the town centre but none of them are first class.

The best is the *Pizzería Venezia* which has decent coffee, is open for (latish) breakfasts, and serves a lot more than just pizzas. It's moderately priced. Several guidebooks recommend the *Restaurant Mogambo* but they were only open for drinks when I tried it. The *Restaurant San Isidro* on the way to the Regional Museum is good for meat.

There are several chifas and other restaurants on Calle Lima; the *Chifa Hong Kong* is good. For dining with a 2nd floor view of the main street, try *Chifa Las Terrazas*. For economy, the *Hotel Colón* restaurant has been recommended and there are several other cheap restaurants along Calle Grau heading east from the Plaza de Armas.

Getting There

Ica is a major bus destination on the Pan-American Highway and is easy to get to from Lima, Nazca and Arequipa.

Buses Most of the bus companies are clustered around a little park at the west end of Salaverry, so it's easy to wander around comparing prices and schedules. Several companies run frequent buses up and down the Pan-American and charge approximately the same with the exception of TEPSA which charges about 25% more and is said to be the most efficient although they have less frequent departures.

Northbound to Lima costs about US$3.80 and takes about five hours – hourly departures with Ormeño, eight daily with Señor de Luren, four daily with Cruz del Sur, hourly slow buses (US$3.30) with SOYUZ, and departures with other companies. For north of Lima change in Lima. For Pisco (60c, one hour) there are many more buses in the morning than

afternoon. Make sure your bus goes into Pisco and not just the turn-off from the Pan-American Highway.

Southbound to Nazca costs US$2 and takes about three hours. Most companies go there once or twice a day. If you're in a hurry to get to Lima or Nazca take a colectivo taxi. They leave from the Plaza de Armas as soon as they have a car load. Fares are US$6 to Lima and US$3.30 to Nazca.

To Arequipa costs US$8 and takes about 15 hours – though most travellers stop at Nazca. Ormeño has four departures daily and Cruz del Sur two buses every night. One of the latter continues to Tacna on the Chilean border.

If you're heading to the highlands you can get to Cuzco with Ormeño for US$13. Departures are every two days. Cóndor de Aymares has buses to Abancay most days. Many of the other companies will get you to Cuzco but expect you to change buses. Make sure you're on a direct bus if you don't want to stay overnight somewhere.

A *quipu* or calculating device (Waman Puma)

HUACACHINA

This is a tiny resort village nestled in huge sand dunes about five km west of Ica. There's a small lagoon which Peruvians swim in because it's supposed to have curative properties, though it looks murky and uninviting to me. The surroundings are pretty though – graceful palm trees, colourful flowers, attractive buildings in pastel shades, and the backdrop of giant sand dunes. It's a pleasant side trip from Ica and a very quiet place to rest.

Places to Stay & Eat

There are two hotels, both around the lagoon. Just to the right of the bus stop is the attractive pink building of the *Hotel Mossone*. There's no sign. They charge US$6/10 for singles/doubles with bath. A little further around the lagoon is the blue *Gran Hotel Salvatierra* which charges about US$3 per person in simple but clean rooms with cold water showers.

The hotels will prepare your meals (ask in advance) or you can eat simply at the *Bar-Recreo Curasi* which is a block away from the lagoon and serves cheap Peruvian meals. There are also vendors by the lagoon or bring a picnic lunch.

Getting There

The red bus marked *Huacachina* leaves two or three times an hour from the church of Señor de Luren in Ica, heads along Calle Lima, past the Plaza de Armas and out to the village – about 15 minutes and 10c.

NAZCA

From Ica, the Pan-American Highway heads roughly south-east, passing through the small oasis of Palpa, famous for its orange groves, and rising slowly to Nazca at 598 metres above sea level and about 450 km south of Lima. Although only a small town of some 30,000 inhabitants, it is frequently visited by travellers interested in the Nazca culture and the world famous Nazca Lines.

Information

The Hotel Nazca is the main local information source but you can also get information at a bookshop a block from the Plaza de Armas. Money changing in Nazca is not very easy, though you can pay for services on the airlines and in the better hotels with cash dollars (at the unfavourable official rate). There is a cinema and sometimes music in the restaurants on weekends.

Archaeology

Like the Paracas culture to the north, the ancient Nazca culture was lost in the drifting desert sands and forgotten until this century. In 1901, the Peruvian archaeologist Max Uhle was the first to excavate Nazca sites and to realise that he was dealing with a separate culture from other coastal peoples. Before his discovery, only five Nazca ceramics were known in museums and no one knew how to classify them. After 1901, thousands of ceramics were found. Most were discovered by *huaqueros* or grave-robbers who plundered burial sites and sold their finds to interested individuals or museums. Despite the amateurish and destructive excavations of the *huaqueros*, archaeologists have constructed a fairly accurate picture of the Nazca culture.

The Nazca culture appeared as a result of the disintegration of the Paracas culture around 200 AD. It is divided into three periods; early (200 to 500 AD), late (500 to 700 AD) and terminal (700 to 800 AD). These periods coincide with the types of ceramics studied by archaeologists. Ceramics, because they are preserved so much better than items made of cloth or wood and because they are often decorated with representations of everyday life, are the most important tool for unravelling Peru's ancient past. The designs on the Nazca ceramics show us their plants and animals, their fetishes and divinities, their musical instruments and household items, and the people themselves.

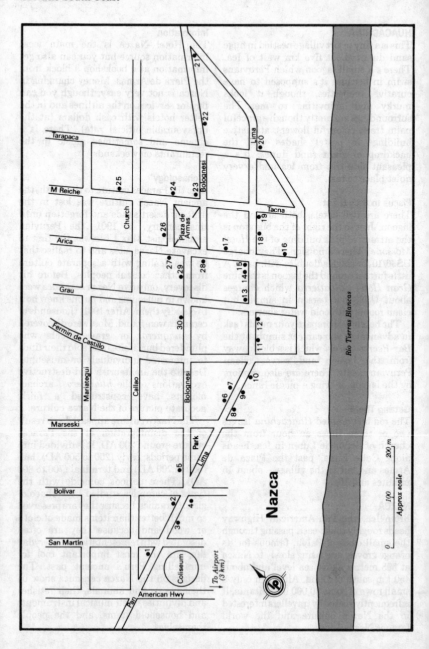

Nazca

To Airport
(3 km)

Pan American Hwy

Coliseum

San Martín

Bolívar

Marseski

Fermin de Castillo

Grau

Arica

M Reiche

Tarapaca

Church

Plaza de
Armas

Mariategui

Callao

Bolognesi

Park

Lima

San Martín

Bologneesi

Velasco

Tacna

Lima

Rio Tierras Blancas

0   100   200 m

Approx scale

1	Hotel Montecarlo
2	Aero Ica
3	Ormeño Bus
4	Aero Cóndor
5	Hotel de Turistas
6	La Fontana Restaurant
7	ENTEL
8	La Taberna
9	Cruz del Sur Bus
10	Hotel Royal
11	Hotel Nazca
12	Morales Moralitos Bus
13	Market
14	Hostal Konfort
15	Comité 12 to Ica
16	Hostal San Martín
17	Hostal Central
18	Hostal Acapulco
19	Roggero Bus
20	Post Office
21	Banco de la Nación
22	Hostal Oropeza
23	Hotel Lima
24	Hostal El Sol
25	Hotel Internacional
26	Museum
27	Hostal Roman
28	Sr de Lurén Bus
29	Cinema
30	Tourist Information & Bookshop

The early Nazca ceramics are characterised by being very colourful and having a greater variety of naturalistic designs. Pots with double necks joined by a 'stirrup' handle are frequently found, as well as shallow cups and plates. In the late period, the decoration was more stylised. (The decorations are, in all cases, much more stylised than the vigorously natural styles of the contemporary Moche culture of the northern coast.) The designs painted on the ceramics of the terminal period are poorer and influenced by the Wari culture from the highlands.

Even the most casual observer will soon learn to recognise the distinctive Nazca style. The colours are vivid and the stylised designs are painted directly onto the ceramic rather than being moulded.

The effect is strong and attractive. Nazca ceramics can be seen in the museums of Lima and Ica, as well as in the small local museum in Nazca itself.

The Nazca Lines

Once, whilst travelling on a bus to Nazca, I was amazed to find that one of my (gringo) travelling companions hadn't heard of the Nazca Lines. I naively thought that anyone going to Nazca would have heard all about them but evidently, such is not the case. So .... what are the Nazca Lines?

Actually, no one really knows. They are huge geometric designs drawn in the desert and visible only from the air. Some designs represent a variety of giant animals such as the 180-metre-long lizard, a 90-metre-high monkey with an extavagantly curled tail, or a condor with a 130-metre wing span. Others are simple but perfect triangles, rectangles or straight lines running for several km across the desert. All in all, there are several dozen different figures. They were made by the simple expedient of removing the sun-darkened stones from the surface of the desert and piling them up on either side of the lines, thus exposing the lighter coloured stones below. The best known lines are found in the desert some 20 km north of Nazca.

The questions remain, who constructed the lines and why? How did they know what they were doing when the lines can only be properly appreciated from the air? Maria Reiche, a German mathematician, has spent most of her life studying the lines and thinks the lines were made by both the Paracas and Nazca cultures over the period 900 BC to 600 AD with some additions by the Wari settlers from the highlands in the 7th century. She considers the lines to be an astronomical calendar.

This is by no means accepted by other writers. Tony Morrison considers the lines to be ritual walkways linking *huacas* or sites of ceremonial significance. Jim

Woodman thinks that the Nazca people knew how to construct hot-air balloons and that they did, in fact, observe the lines from the air. Von Daniken thinks that the lines are extraterrestrial landing sites. There are plenty of other theories. If you're interested, see the Books section in Facts for the Visitor. Maria Reiche gives evening talks at the Hotel de Turistas if there are enough people, but she is now well into her 80s and sometimes indisposed.

Seeing the Nazca Lines

The best way to fully appreciate this giant archaeological mystery is to take a flight over the lines. Most people fly from Nazca because flying from Lima or Ica is very expensive. Although you can make reservations in Lima, it's cheaper to make arrangements when you arrive in Nazca. You can almost always fly on the day you want.

Flights are taken in light aircraft (three to nine seats) in the mornings. There's no point in expecting punctuality because the flights depend on the weather. The planes won't take off until there is reasonable visibility and there's often a low mist over the desert until it warms up around 9 or 10 am. Strong winds in the afternoon make flying impractical. Passengers are usually taken on a first come first served basis, with priority given to those who have made reservations in Lima. Don't worry – nine times out of 10 there's room for everyone.

There are three main companies vying with one another and it's best to check all three to find the best deal. They're all close to one another. You want to know the cost (sometimes it's cheaper to pay in intis though they quote in dollars), what size plane is used (the larger ones have middle seats which give unfavourable views), how long the flight is (usually 30 to 45 minutes), and what is included in the price. You should get free transportation to and from the airport. Sometimes a light breakfast is included after the

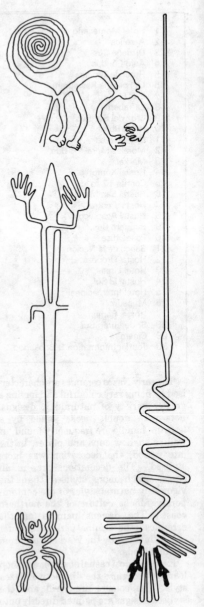

Nazca Lines

flight – you should eat very lightly before the flight unless you're used to small airplanes making tight turns. When I was last there, AeroCondor were charging US$18 for a 35-minute flight, AeroIca US$20 for a 40-minute flight, and Montecarlo were charging US$21 but threw in a free night in their rather nice hotel.

Stop Press Recent reports have reached me that the Peruvian government has regulated Nazca Line flights and that fares are now a standard US$40 per passenger (at the official rate). You can change at the free street rate and buy tickets in Intis, which is equivalent to about US$32 per passenger.

If you can't or don't want to fly, you can get an idea of what the lines look like from the observation tower built on the side of the Pan-American Highway about 20 km north of Nazca. From the top of the tower you get an oblique view of three of the figures (lizard, tree and hands) but it's not very good. Don't go walking around on the lines because it damages them and you can't see anything anyway. To get to the tower either take a taxi or catch a northbound bus in the morning and hitchhike back. Don't leave it too late as there's little traffic.

Other Excursions

Many people come to Nazca, take an overflight, and go on, but there's a lot more to see in the area. You should hire a taxi for this, it's not very expensive. The best place to go for information is the Hotel Nazca. They will organise a taxi for you with a driver who knows the ruins – they have set up a guide co-operative which is both inexpensive and good.

One of the most interesting tours is to the Cemetery of Chauchilla, 30 km away. Here you'll see bones, skulls, mummies, pottery shards and fragments of cloth dating back to the late Nazca period. Although everything of value has gone, it's quite amazing to stand in the desert and see tombs surrounded by bleached skulls and bones that stretch off into the distance. The tour takes about 2½ hours and costs US$3 per person with a minimum of three passengers.

If you want to inspect the Nazca Lines from ground level, and climb a nearby hill as well as the viewing tower, you can do the Nazca Lines-Mirador tour for the same price.

Also US$3 per person is the tour to the Inca Paredones ruins and Cantallo aqueduct, and a smaller Nazca cemetery. The ruins are not very well preserved but the underground aqueducts, built by the Incas, are still in working order and provide irrigation to the nearby fields. These sites are closer to Nazca and you can walk there if you have several hours. Cross the river on the Arica bridge and go straight on for a couple of kms to the Paredones and a further couple of kms to the Cantallo aqueduct, which is found in the grounds of the Hacienda Cantallo. I haven't done this walk, so check locally first.

West of the Lines is Cahuachi, the most important known Nazca centre, and you can go there on a four-hour tour for US$4. Here there are several pyramids and a site called El Estaquería which consists of rows of logs half buried vertically in the ground – their function is a mystery. The site is being excavated and it may be closed to visitors.

A six-hour tour costing US$45 for five people is 113 km to Sacaco to look for fossils, though I don't know anyone who has done it. If you want to do an all-day trip to see the vicuña sanctuary at Pampas Galeras, high in the mountains 90 km east of Nazca, it'll cost you US$80 for five people. You'll see it much more cheaply if you take a bus to Cuzco via Abancay. Other tours can be arranged if you know where you want to go.

On the plaza is the small town museum which is open daily from 9 am to 7 pm and costs 15c to visit.

Places to Stay - bottom end

The most popular hotel for budget travellers is the friendly *Hotel Nazca* run by the Fernandez family who organise the excursions listed above. Basic but clean rooms are US$1.40/2.50 for singles/doubles and there is hot water in the communal showers. Other hotels in this price range include the family run *Hostal El Sol* which has a cafeteria for breakfasts, and the recently remodelled *Hostal Lima*, which also has a restaurant and rooms with private baths for US$2.20/3.30, as well as cheaper rooms with communal showers.

If these sound too expensive there are plenty of cold water cheapies - in Nazca's heat the lack of hot water is no real hardship. The *Hostal Konfort* is reasonable and charges US$1.10/2 for singles/doubles and the *Hostal San Martín* is similar. Other cold water cheapies which look less attractive are, in roughly descending order of attraction, the *Acapulco, Oropeza, Royal, Central* and *Roman*.

Places to Stay - middle

The *Hotel Internacional* looks quite good and charges US$3/5 for singles/doubles with private bath. The *Hotel Montecarlo* has a swimming pool, bar and cafeteria

and is good value at US$5/7 or about US$2 extra if you stay in one of their bungalows. If you fly over the Nazca Lines with them they'll give you a free night at the hotel (the night before the flight only) so if you plan on doing this check in early and spend the afternoon luxuriating around the pool.

Places to Stay - top end

The best hotel in Nazca itself is the government-run *Hotel de Turistas* which costs US$18/26 for singles/doubles including continental breakfast and use of the swimming pool. At about the same price is the lovely converted hacienda *Hotel de la Borda*, which has pretty gardens, a pool and serves knock-out pisco sours in their bar. It's a few kms out of town by the airport - take a taxi.

Places to Eat

The best hotels serve good food but are expensive. Cheaper meals can be found all over Nazca; there seems to be a restaurant on every block. Two places currently popular with travellers are *La Fontana* and *La Taberna* which are opposite one another on Calle Lima. The latter sometimes has live music on Saturday night. There are plenty of cheap restaurants where the locals go but many of them seem to close down or change hands every couple of years.

Getting There

Buses & Colectivos Nazca is a major destination for buses on the Pan-American Highway and is easy to get to from Lima, Ica or Arequipa. Ormeño has the most frequent departures with several a day to Lima (US$4.20, eight hours) as well as intermediate points. They also have two or three buses a day to Arequipa (US$5.80, 10 hours) and Tacna (US$7, 14 hours).

Buses to Cuzco leave every two days and cost US$13 for the 30 to 40-hour trip. Roggero has slightly cheaper fares to Lima, Arequipa and Tacna but their buses travel exclusively at night, which is

a drag if you want to see the scenery. Several other companies are found along the main street and they have similar destinations and prices.

Comité 12 has fast colectivo taxis to Ica.

CHALA

The first town of any importance on the Pan-American Highway south-east of Nazca is the fishing village of Chala about 170 km away. In Inca times, fresh fish were sent by runners from here to Cuzco – an amazing effort. Chala's main attractions are fresh seafood and the opportunity to break the long journey to Arequipa, but most travellers just tough it out and keep going. Maybe that's a good reason to stop – you won't see too many tourists.

Places to Stay

The best place is the government-run *Hotel de Turistas* at Calle Comercio 601 at the south end of the beach. The verandah faces the ocean but the bedrooms don't. Opposite is the *Hostal Otero*. Neither are very expensive. A cheaper place on the beach is reported.

CAMANÁ

From Chala, the Pan-American Highway runs close to the coast until it reaches Camaná, about 220 km away. The views of the ocean are often very good as the highway torturously clings to sand dunes dropping down to the sea.

Camaná is 175 km from Arequipa but the road is paved and so it is a popular summer beach resort with Arequipeños. The beaches are good but are five km from the centre and so you have to take the local bus to La Punta to visit them. At La Punta there are private holiday bungalows but no tourist facilities.

Places to Stay

The reasonably priced, government-run *Hotel de Turistas* at Calle Lima 138 has a garden. The hostals *Central* and *Velarde* on Calle 28 de Julio are cheaper.

MOLLENDO

The Pan-American Highway leaves the coast at Camaná and heads inland for 135 km to the junction of Repartición. Here, a major branch road heads east into the Andes for 42 km to Arequipa. The Pan-American turns south towards the coast and, after a further 15 km, divides again. The south-eastern branch goes on towards the Chilean border while the south-western road heads to Mollendo.

This small port of 15,000 inhabitants is about 110 km south-west of Arequipa and is a popular beach resort for Arequipeños during the January to March summer season but is very quiet for the rest of the year. Mollendo is normally reached by road from Arequipa and the traveller passes through interesting desert with delicate brown, pink and grey colours, particularly attractive in the oblique light of early morning. Near La Joya there are some extraordinary crescent-shaped grey sand dunes which look as if they had been deliberately poured in unlikely positions on the pinkish rock.

Mollendo is a pleasant town with several plazas and attractive hilly streets.

The beach is good. There are many customs agencies and shipping offices but most ships now dock in Matarani, 15 km to the north-west.

Information
The Banco de Crédito changes dollars at the unfavourable official rate so you should change money at Arequipa. One of the best reasons to visit Mollendo is to go to the nearby nature reserve at Mejía.

Places to Stay
During the high season singles are more difficult to obtain. There are plenty of cheap and basic hotels such as the *Hostal Aller* at US$1/1.70 for singles/doubles. Some doubles are US$2.30 and include a private cold water shower. Cheaper still, and not as good, are the basic *Hostal Verona, Hotel Royal* and *Hotel San Martín*.

For a little more money, a good clean hotel is the *Hostal La Cabaña* which charges US$1.20 per person (communal bathrooms) or US$1.80 per person in rooms with private baths. There is hot water in the mornings and/or evenings. For US$2 per person, the clean *Hostal Salermo* is recommended. All rooms have private showers and hot water. The modern *Mollendo Hotel* (no sign) charges US$5/8 for rooms with a private bath but they drop their rates substantially in the off season.

Places to Eat
The hostals *Salermo* and *La Cabaña* both have good reasonably priced restaurants. There are several cafeterias around the Plaza de Armas, including the *Toldo Pizzería* for Italian and other food. Cheap restaurants are found along Calle Arequipa near the market. The *Chifa Tun Fung* is good for Chinese food and the *Heladería Venecia* for ice cream and snacks. The *Sea Room* is a rather funky bar with the best view of the ocean.

Getting There
The passenger train from Mollendo to Arequipa no longer runs, though some freight trains keep this route open.

The quickest way to get to and from Arequipa is by shared colectivo taxis which charge US$2.30 per person and take about two hours. Comités 1, 11 and 20 provide this service and all of them have departures at the same times in the morning, midday and evening.

The buses to Arequipa are cheaper (US$1.70 per person) and slower (three hours). Empresa Aragon has six buses daily to Arequipa, Ormeño has three daily, and Cruz del Sur has one afternoon bus daily. TEPSA runs four buses a week direct to Lima (US$12).

Comité 5 has frequent colectivo taxis to the port of Matarani, and Comité 3 goes to the beach resort of Mejía for 30c. Neither company has an office – go to the street corner indicated on the map and wait. Empresa Aragon has five buses daily through Mejía to the Tambo river valley and Empresa Bustinza has buses at 7 am, 12.30 and 6 pm through Mejía, La Curva and Cocachacra to El Fiscal (70c, 1½ hours). This company also has a daily bus to Tacna.

MEJÍA & THE TAMBO RIVER VALLEY
This is an interesting area and easily visited from Mollendo. Mejía is a summer beach resort for Arequipeños and is a ghost town from April to December. There are plenty of private homes but no hotels, a couple of snack bars and an excellent beach.

About six km south-east of Mejía along the coastal road is the little known Lagunas de Mejía nature reserve. These coastal lagoons cover over 100 hectares in area and are the largest permanent lakes in 1500 km of desert coastline; hence they attract great numbers of coastal and migratory bird species. Bird-watchers can go on one of the morning buses from Mollendo to the Tambo valley or El Fiscal and get off at the reserve. There's no sign,

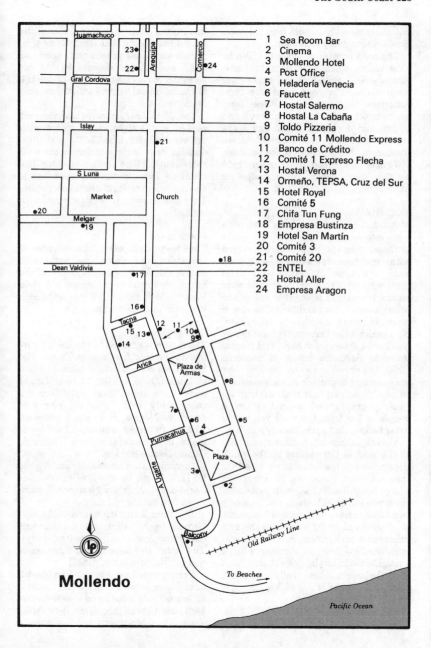

1   Sea Room Bar
2   Cinema
3   Mollendo Hotel
4   Post Office
5   Heladería Venecia
6   Faucett
7   Hostal Salermo
8   Hostal La Cabaña
9   Toldo Pizzeria
10 Comité 11 Mollendo Express
11 Banco de Crédito
12 Comité 1 Expreso Flecha
13 Hostal Verona
14 Ormeño, TEPSA, Cruz del Sur
15 Hotel Royal
16 Comité 5
17 Chifa Tun Fung
18 Empresa Bustinza
19 Hotel San Martín
20 Comité 3
21 Comité 20
22 ENTEL
23 Hostal Aller
24 Empresa Aragon

Huamachuco
Arequipa
Comercio
Gral Cordova
Islay
S Luna
Market
Church
Melgar
Dean Valdivia
Tacna
Arica
Pumacahua
A Ugarte
Plaza de Armas
Plaza
Balcony
Old Railway Line
To Beaches
Pacific Ocean

Mollendo

but you can see the lagoons from the road. Buses return every afternoon.

The road continues along the Tambo river valley which is an important irrigation project with rice and sugar-cane plantations. The road joins the Pan-American Highway at El Fiscal from where buses return to Mollendo at 5 and 10 am and 4 pm. El Fiscal has a gas station and an overpriced flyblown restaurant. It's the only place in about 100 km of desert road. You can wait here to flag down buses to Arequipa or Moquegua.

MOQUEGUA

Moquegua is a dry and dusty town with some interesting-looking buildings. Many of them, even the cathedral, are roofed with sugar-cane stalks covered with dried mud – a type of wattle and daub construction. Although the town is built on the Moquegua River it is one of the driest towns in Peru and feels almost as if it should be in the middle of the Sahara. No wonder – the Peruvian coastal desert reaches its driest point here, and merges into the Atacama desert of northern Chile, the driest in the world. The river does manage to provide enough moisture to be able to carry on some agriculture (mainly grapes and avocados) but a couple of km from the river you would never believe that agriculture is possible.

Moquegua has a population of about 10,000 and is the capital of the small department of the same name. It is 1412 metres above sea level and 220 km south-east of Arequipa. At the north-east end of town is a small hill which can be easily climbed for an excellent view of Moquegua (and the mud roofs) as well as the arid mountains surrounding it. The pleasant and shady Plaza de Armas, with a wrought iron fountain, is a welcome relief from the desert. There really isn't much to do, but I found it ... different.

Places to Stay

There are about eight hotels, most of them quite basic with cold water in the shared bathrooms. The *Hostals Cornejo, Torata* and *Comercio* are quite good and clean and charge about US$1.30 per person. Slightly cheaper are the *Hospedaje El Ovalo, Hostal Central* and *Alojamiento Moderno*.

The *Hostal Los Limoneros* has a pleasant garden and simple clean rooms with private bath for US$3/5.30 for singles/doubles or a little less for rooms with shared bath. There's only cold water. The *Hotel de Turistas* has hot water but is about three km from the town centre. They charge about US$5/8 for rooms with bath.

Places to Eat

The cheapest places are, as usual, around the market but there are better restaurants on Avenida Moquegua, north-east of the Plaza. My favourite restaurant is *A Todo Vapor*, which means 'full steam ahead!'. It's clean and good value.

Getting There

The easiest way to get to Moquegua is by bus from either Arequipa or Tacna. The bus offices are around the market. Buses to Lima (about US$10, 19 to 23 hours) leave three times daily with Ormeño, twice daily with Cruz del Sur and Angelitos Negros, and once a day with TEPSA (more expensive). These buses make intermediate stops at Camaná, Chala, Nazca and Ica.

Arequipa is 3½ hours away and it costs US$1.70 to get there with Cruz del Sur (eight daily), Angelitos Negros or Ormeño (both five daily).

To Tacna is two hours and US$1 with Ormeño (eight daily), Cruz del Sur (four daily) and Angelitos Negros (two daily). The latter also have two or three buses daily to Ilo (two hours, US$1).

Transportes Lacustre and San Martín have buses several times a week over a little used rough road and a 4600-metre-high pass (Abra Choquijarani) to Puno. Transportes Moquegua has five buses a

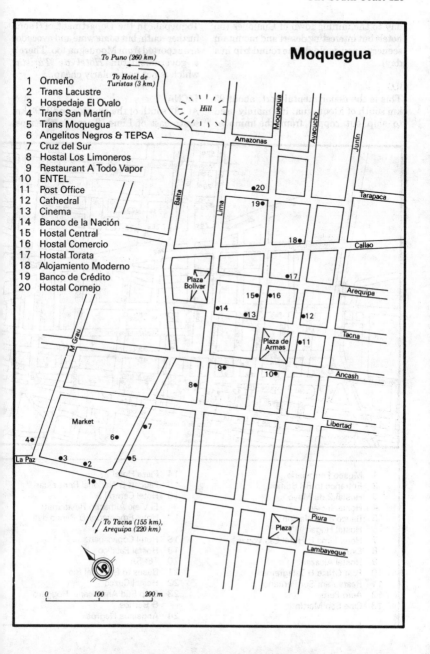

1 Ormeño
2 Trans Lacustre
3 Hospedaje El Ovalo
4 Trans San Martín
5 Trans Moquegua
6 Angelitos Negros & TEPSA
7 Cruz del Sur
8 Hostal Los Limoneros
9 Restaurant A Todo Vapor
10 ENTEL
11 Post Office
12 Cathedral
13 Cinema
14 Banco de la Nación
15 Hostal Central
16 Hostal Comercio
17 Hostal Torata
18 Alojamiento Moderno
19 Banco de Crédito
20 Hostal Cornejo

Moquegua

To Puno (260 km)
To Hotel de Turistas (3 km)
Hill
Amazonas
Moquegua
Ayacucho
Junín
Tarapaca
Callao
Balta
Lima
•20
19•
18•
Plaza Bolívar
•17
Arequipa
15• •16
•14 •13
•12
Tacna
Plaza de Armas
•11
M Grau
9•
10•
Ancash
8•
Libertad
Market
7•
6•
•5
4•
•3 •2
La Paz
1•
To Tacna (155 km), Arequipa (220 km)
Piura
Plaza
Lambayeque
0   100   200 m

day to the mining town of Cuajones (no hotels but interesting desert and mountain scenery – you could do the round trip in a day).

ILO

This is the departmental port, about 95 km south of Moquegua. It's mainly used to ship out copper from the mine at

Toquepala in the Department of Tacna further south, but some wine and avocados are exported from Moquegua too. There's a government-run *Hotel de Turistas* which is not particularly cheap.

TACNA

At 18° south of the equator and 1293 km south-east of Lima, Tacna is the most

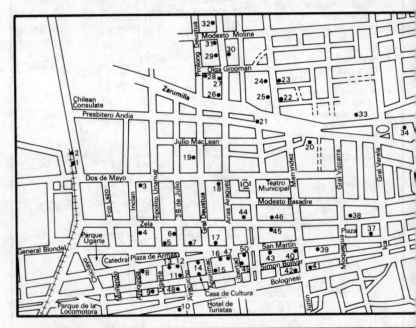

1   Museo Ferroviario
2   Entrance to RR Station
3   Hostal 2 de Mayo
4   Hostal Inclan
5   Banco de la Nación
6   Hostal Hogar
7   Hotel Lima & Hotel Las Vegas
8   Expreso Tacna
9   Hostal Alcazar
10 Post Office & Telegrams
11 Restaurant Sur Peruano
12 Aero Peru
13 Cine San Martín
14 Plaza Hotel
15 Faucett & National Rent-a-car
16 Hotel Central &
    El Viejo Almacén Restaurant
17 Hotel Emperador & Banco de
    Crédito
18 Hotel Copacabana
19 Hostal Pacífico
20 TEPSA
21 Buses to Boca del Río
22 Hostal Cuzco
23 Emp Sud Americano, Roggero
    & Berrios
24 Angelitos Negros

southerly major town in Peru. It is the capital of its department, has a population of about 46,000 and lies 560 metres above sea level. Tacna is only 36 km from the Chilean border and has strong historical ties with that country. It became part of Chile in 1880 during the War of the Pacific and remained in Chilean hands until 1929 when its people voted to return to Peru.

Tacna has some of the best schools and hospitals in Peru – whether this is because of the Chilean influence is a matter of opinion.

Tacna is a clean and pleasant city but a little more expensive than the rest of Peru. The main reason to go there is to cross the land border which is well served by road and rail. The most interesting

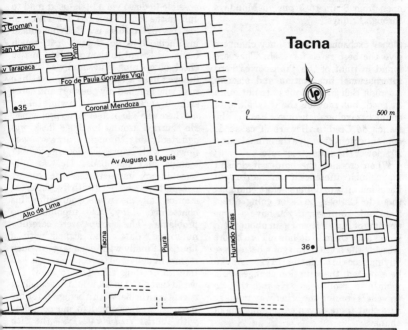

25	Hostal Don Abel
26	Cruz del Sur (2 offices)
27	Ormeño
28	Hostal
29	Hostal San Pedro
30	Hostal Tauro & Hostal Paris
31	Cruz del Sur (2 offices)
32	Sur-Peruano
33	Hotel Don Quijote
34	Taxis to Arica, Hostal Imperio & Nevado
35	Trans Peru (to Arica)
36	Tourist Office
37	Hostal El Inca
38	El Paraíso Vegetarian Restaurant
39	Hotel Camino Real
40	Hostal Junín
41	Hostal Premier
42	Hostal La Alameda
43	Chifa Say Wa
44	San Cristobal Hotel
45	ENTEL
46	Hostal Lider
47	Bolivian Consulate
48	El Pollo Pechogon
49	Pizzeria Pino
50	Café Genova

thing to see in Tacna is the railway museum. Most people find that a day is more than enough to stay in Tacna.

Information

Tourist Information The Tourist Office (tel 713501) is about two km east of the town centre at Avenida Bolognesi 2088 (there's no number on the building). They are open from 8 am to 3 pm on Mondays through Fridays.

Money Exchange Street money changers give the best rates for cash. They are found in front of the Transportes Peru Internacional bus station and also on Avenida Bolognesi. Banks are not quite as good, but may be the only place to change travellers' cheques. Best is the Banco de Crédito. Beware of casas de cambio which often give the official rate – 20% lower than the street rate.

When crossing the border it doesn't make much difference if you change your Peruvian intis to dollars before changing them to Chilean pesos or going direct from intis to pesos. If you have a large amount of intis left you gain about 2% if you change them to dollars in Peru before crossing the border. You get a better rate buying pesos in Chile than in Peru. As can be expected, the situation changes from month to month so try and talk to travellers coming the other way to make sure that there haven't been any major changes.

Consulates Both Bolivia and Chile are represented by consulates in Tacna and it's worth checking with them if you're crossing the border to ensure that there hasn't been some recent change in regulations.

Entering Chile is generally straightforward for most travellers who simply receive a tourist card at the border. This is normally valid for 90 days and is free for most Europeans (except Finns who pay US$10 and the Swiss who pay US$2), Canadians, US citizens, Australians,

New Zealanders and most other nationalities. Visas (US$5.25) are available for one entry only and are required for French nationals and citizens of communist or African countries. The Chilean Consulate is open from 8 am to 12.30 pm, Mondays through Fridays.

Few travellers enter Bolivia from Tacna without stopping at Puno, but it is possible to do so via a little-used road to Juli on the south shore of Lake Titicaca. For this reason there is a Bolivian consul in Tacna but he doesn't get much business. I went to the consulate just to check on opening times and was almost dragged in by a very excited squirrel-like man who grabbed my passport and short sightedly peered at it, all the while telling me there was 'No problema, no problema'. He scurried around his huge desk and agitatedly dug through a drawer overflowing with impressive looking rubber stamps and ink pads. He carefully selected an immaculate page in my passport and covered it with five different stamps, all the while continuing his chattering litany, 'No problema, no problema'. The stamps were carefully numbered, dated and signed with a flourish. Finally wielding a large wooden stamp, he delivered the coup de grace – an imprint reading GRATIS to show the world that he, at least, would not consider accepting a bribe. With a benign smile my passport was returned to me complete with Tourist Visa No 027-85 – the 27th visa he had issued that year. It was December. I hadn't the heart to tell him that I wasn't going to Bolivia.

So ... he's open from 9 to 11.30 am and 4 to 5 pm on Mondays to Fridays. For details about documents required for entry to Bolivia, read the section for Puno which is on the more frequently used route into Bolivia.

National Railway Museum

The Museo Ferroviario is located at the railway station and is open from 8 am to 3 pm on Mondays to Fridays. Admission

Top: Desert Coast (RR)
Bottom: Peruvian Boobies, Ballestas Islands (RR)

Top: Sea Lions, Ballestas Islands (RR)
Left: Mummies at Chauchilla Nazca Cemetery (RR)
Right: Cathedral, Plaza de Armas, Tacna (RR)

was 3c last time I was there! It's a 'must see' for railway enthusiasts and even if you're not crazy about trains there is an interesting display of turn of the century engines and other rolling stock. They also have a philatelic section displaying stamps with railway themes from all over the world.

Parque de la Locomotora
A British locomotive built in 1859 and used as a troop train in the War of the Pacific is the centrepiece of this pleasant downtown park.

History Museum
This small museum is located in the *Casa de Cultura* and is officially open from 10 to 12 noon and 4 to 8 pm from Monday to Saturday. In reality it's often closed though you can find someone to open it up if you ask in the offices. The main exhibit deals with the War of the Pacific which is explained by paintings and maps. There are a few archaeological pieces.

Plaza de Armas
The main feature of the plaza is the huge arch – a monument to the heroes of the War of the Pacific. It is flanked by larger than life bronze statues of Admiral Grau and Colonel Bolognesi. Nearby, the six-metre-high bronze fountain was designed by the French engineer, Eiffel. The fountain supposedly represents the four seasons. Eiffel also designed the Cathedral which is noted for its clean lines, fine stained-glass windows and onyx high altar. The plaza is a popular meeting place for Tacneños in the evenings and has a patriotic flag raising ceremony every Sunday morning.

Around Tacna
Pocollay is a suburb five kms from Tacna and can be reached by walking east on Avenida Bolognesi or taking a bus along that street. It is popular with Tacneños for its typical restaurants which are especially busy on Sundays. Dishes served include *Patasca a la Tacneña* which is a thick spicy vegetable-and-meat soup; *Picante de Guatita* or hot peppered tripe (better than it sounds!); *Cazuela de Ave* or a thick chicken-and-vegetable soup; *Choclo con Queso* or hot corn on the cob with cheese; *Chicharrones de Chancho* or deep-fried chunks of pork, usually served with pop corn; *Asado de Chancho* or roast pork; *Cordero a la Parilla* or barbecued lamb; and that most typical of Peruvian highland dishes, *Cuy Chactado* or fried guinea pig, usually spicier than that served in the mountains.

Continuing north-east of Tacna, are the villages of Calana, Pachía, and Calientes which are 15, 17 and 24 km from Tacna respectively. The area is known for its pleasant climate and countryside (by desert standards). There is a good typical restaurant, the *Bochio*, in Pachía and hot springs in Calientes.

Tacna's main seaside resort is Boca del Río, about 55 km south-west of the city. Buses go from Tacna along a good road, but there are no hotels although Tacneños have built summer homes there. The beach is reportedly good.

The modern copper-mining centre of Toquepala is near a cave in which rock paintings dating to 8000 BC have been found. They clearly illustrate a guanaco hunt among other things. It's not easy to get here and there's no hotel, although the people at the mine may be able to help with floor space.

Places to Stay – bottom end
Hotels in Tacna sometimes suffer from water shortages and the cheapest hotels had no water when I was last there. Maybe the situation has changed but the following hotels are dry: hostals *Imperio* and *Nevado* charging about 60c per person and hostals *San Pedro, Tauro* and *Paris* charging about 80c per person.

The *San Cristobal Hotel* managed to keep its water running and charged only 60c per person. Convenient for the railway station is the basic but clean

Hostal 2 de Mayo which charges US$1/1.60 for singles/doubles and sometimes manages to produce hot water in the communal showers. Other basic cold water cheapies include the *Hostal Pacifico* for US$1.05 per person, the *Hostal Lider* for US$1.20 per person, the *Hostal Cuzco* and *Hostal Don Abel* for US$1.20/1.80 and the clean *Hostal Junín* for US$1.30/2.

A basic clean hotel that has been recommended by travellers is the *Hotel Las Vegas* which charges US$1.30 per person and has a good and inexpensive restaurant. The *Hostal La Alameda* and *Hotel Don Quijote* also charge US$1.30 per person or if you prefer a private bath it's US$1.60 each. Similarly priced is the unfriendly *Hotel Alcazar*. There's also an often full hotel with no sign by the Ormeño bus depot which charges US$2.30 for a double room with cold shower – no singles.

Places to Stay - middle

The *Hotel Copacabana* is clean and good and has rooms with private bath at US$2/2.70 for singles/doubles; still only cold water though. Also good and clean is the *Hostal Inclan* for US$2/3 with bath and they have hot water in the evenings. The *Hostal Premier* costs a few cents more but they have only cold water. The *Hostal Hogar* is simple, friendly and clean and has hot water sometimes. They have rooms for US$2.30/3 or with private bath for US$3/4. The new looking *Hostal El Inca* is also good and charges US$2.70/4.30 for rooms with private bath and hot water. The clean *Hotel Lima* charges US$3/5 for singles/doubles but their baths are, at best, tepid. They have a good, reasonably priced restaurant.

Clean and reasonably comfortable are the *Hotel Emperador* and *Hotel Central*, both of which charge US$3.70/6 for rooms with hot showers. The *Central* has room phones if you need to place a call. The *Plaza Hotel* is the best of the mid-priced hotels for US$4.70/8 singles/doubles.

Places to Stay - top end

There are two good hotels and both have restaurant and bar facilities. The government run *Hotel de Turistas* charges US$8.30/11.30 which includes a continental breakfast. They have a small swimming pool. The modern *Hotel Camino Real* has a discotheque and charges US$8.30/12 for singles/doubles.

Places to Eat

One of the best and most popular restaurants in town is the Italian style *El Viejo Almacen* which runs about US$2 to US$3 for a meal and has good steaks, pasta, ice cream, espresso coffee, cheap local wine and desserts. Nearby are the cheaper *Pizzería Pino* and the *Café Genova* with pavement tables and good coffee.

If you don't want Italian food then try the *Restaurant Sur Peru* which is inexpensive and popular with the locals especially at lunch time. They are open from 7 am to 3 pm and 6.30 to 9 pm on Mondays to Saturdays. Wash down some of their local food with a ½ litre pitcher of the rough and hearty *Vino de Chacra* (literally 'field wine') which costs only 50c.

Good Chinese food is to be had at the *Chifa Say Wa*. There is a vegetarian restaurant, the *El Paraiso*, which I haven't tried. For chicken try *El Pollo Pechugon* where half a grilled chicken and French fries will cost you about US$1.30. The restaurants at the *Lima* and *Las Vegas* hotels are quite good and not expensive.

Getting There

Tacna is the end point of some buses southbound from Lima, although there are more frequent buses from Arequipa. There is air service from Lima and Arequipa. It is easy to get here from Arica, Chile.

Air There are daily flights to Arequipa continuing to Lima with either AeroPeru or Faucett. Both have offices in downtown Tacna. All flights leave in the early morning and you must stay overnight in Arequipa if you wish to connect to Cuzco or Juliaca. Approximate fares to Arequipa are US$17 and to Lima US$50.

Buses Several companies run buses to Lima (21 to 26 hours). The cheapest is Sud Americano which charges US$9.50 on their nightly service. Cruz del Sur also have a nightly bus and charge US$11.50 but sometimes give special fares of about US$10 in the low season. Ormeño also has four services daily for US$11.50. Other companies to try are Sur Peruano, Angelitos Negros and Roggero. TEPSA are the most reliable but the most expensive with two daily departures for US$15.50 and their presidential non-stop service every Saturday for US$21. These companies will sell you tickets to Camana, Chala, Nazca or Ica.

Buses to Arequipa take six to seven hours and cost about US$2.70. Ormeño, Angelitos Negros and Cruz del Sur all have five departures daily. These companies all have buses to Moquegua (2½ hours, US$1.30).

Cruz del Sur has the only direct bus to Cuzco, leaving daily at 6.30 am (24 hours, US$11.50). Sur Peruano sells tickets for Puno (US$8) but the trip entails a full day stop-over in Arequipa (leave Tacna 9.30 pm, arrive Arequipa 4 am, leave Arequipa 4 pm and arrive in Puno at 5 am). Empresa Berrios has a bus (three hours, US$1.70) to Toquepala .

Buses to the coastal resort of Boca del Río leave when full from where Avenida Leguia turns into Zarumilla. Fares are 70c for the one-hour journey.

The international buses to Arica (Chile) leave hourly all day long from Transportes Peru. The trip costs US$1.30 and the bus stops at the border – it often takes a long time to cross if there are many passengers. There are a couple of other companies nearby but Transportes Peru has the most comfortable service.

Colectivos Shared taxis to Arica (five passengers) cost US$2.30 per person and are the most efficient way of getting to Chile. They stop at the border and the driver helps you through. There are several companies (see map) which leave as soon as the car is full, so ask around to find out which car is going next. Make sure you tell the driver you have a passport because locals with 'salvo conductos' (passes) have different and faster border formalities.

Expreso Tacna have a daily taxi to Arequipa at about noon which costs US$6 per passenger.

Rail Trains go from Tacna to Arica and back several times a day and this is the cheapest way to cross the border. Turn-of-the-century locomotives can be seen in the Tacna railway station while you wait for the train. There are two departures in the early morning and two more in early and mid afternoon. Tickets cost 80c and the trip takes 1½ hours. Your passport is stamped at the train station, there is no stop at the actual border, and you receive your entry stamp when you arrive. There are four daily return trains from Arica and so you can make a day trip of it if you want to see a little of Chile. Note that there are no money changers at the railway station.

Getting Around
Airport Transport There is no airport bus and you have to take a taxi (US$1.50) or walk about five km.

GOING TO CHILE
Border crossing formalities are relatively straightforward in both directions. Taxis are the quickest way of going whilst trains are the cheapest. A casa de cambio in Arica is at 18 de Septiembre 330. They'll change both intis and dollars into pesos. You used to gain about 2% by changing your excess intis into dollars in Peru before arriving but ask other travellers for current details.

From Arica you can continue south into Chile by air or bus or north-east into Bolivia by air or one of the two trains a month. There are plenty of hotels and restaurants; Arica is quite a lively place.

Go to the Chilean Tourist Office (tel 32101) which is on the 2nd floor of Avenida Prat 305, above the post office, for information about travel further in Chile, or consult Lonely Planet's *Chile – a travel survival kit*.

Arequipa

Arequipa is 2325 metres above sea level in the mountainous desert of the western Andes and therefore is a city of the highlands rather than one of the coastal lowlands. It is, however, better connected with the coastal transportation network than it is with the highlands and is, therefore, often included with the south coast in many guidebooks.

AREQUIPA
The Pan-American leaves the coast at Camaná and heads east to Repartición, 135 km away. Here, the Pan-American swings south but another highway continues for 40 km to Arequipa, capital of its department and the major city of southern Peru. Arequipeños claim it is Peru's 2nd largest city, but with 700,000 people it is a very close 3rd behind Trujillo.

It certainly is a beautiful city surrounded by spectacular mountains. The most famous of these is the volcano El Misti which is 5822 metres high and has a beautiful conical peak, topped by snow. It rises majestically behind Arequipa's cathedral and is clearly visible from the Plaza de Armas. To the left of El Misti is the higher and more ragged Chachani (6075 metres) and to the right is the lower peak of Picchu Picchu.

Many of the city's buildings date to colonial times. They are often built with a very light-coloured volcanic rock called *sillar*. The buildings dazzle in the sun which shines almost every day and hence Arequipa has earned the nickname of 'the white city'.

Arequipa has a long history. There is archaeological evidence of pre-Inca settlement by Aymara Indians from the Lake Titicaca area. Some scholars consider that the Aymaras named the city – *Ari* means 'peak' and *quipa* means 'lying behind' in Aymara and hence Arequipa is 'the place lying behind the peak' (probably referring to the conical peak of Misti). Other people claim that it is a Quechua name. An oft-heard legend has it that the fourth Inca, Mayta Capac, was travelling through the valley and was enchanted by it. He ordered his retinue to stop, saying, '*Ari, quipay*' which translates into 'Yes, stay.'

The Spaniards refounded the city on 15 August 1540 and the date is remembered with a week long fair in Arequipa. The fireworks show in the Plaza de Armas on 14 August is particularly spectacular. Unfortunately, the city is built in an area highly prone to earthquakes and none of the original buildings remain. Arequipa was totally destroyed in the earthquakes and volcanic eruptions of 1600. Further major earthquakes occurred in 1687, 1868 and more recently, in 1958 and 1960. For this reason, many of the city's buildings are built low to withstand earthquakes. Despite these disasters, several 17th and 18th century buildings survive and are frequently visited. Without doubt, the most interesting of these is the Santa Catalina monastery.

Information
Tourist Information The Tourist Office is half a block from the Plaza de Armas at La Merced 117. It is open from 8 am to 3 pm on Mondays to Fridays.

Bookshops The ABC bookshop at Avenida Santa Catalina 217 has a selection of English novels, magazines, and books about Peru. There is a map store on Mercaderes half a block from the Plaza. You can buy topographic maps of the mountains if you want to go mountaineering.

Money Exchange Rates are pretty close to what they are in Lima. The Banco de Crédito has been giving as good a rate as

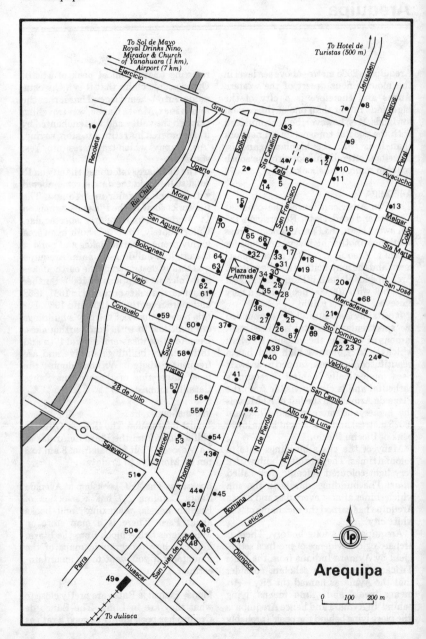

To Sol de Mayo
Royal Drinks Nino,
Mirador & Church
of Yanahuara (1 km),
Airport (7 km)

To Hotel de
Turistas (500 m)

Arequipa

0   100   200 m

To Juliaca

anywhere, so give them a try. There are plenty of other banks and casas de cambio.

Churches

Visiting hours for churches in Arequipa are erratic. They vary every time I visit the city. The Tourist Office usually can tell you when specific churches are open to visitors, but even they can't keep up with all the changes. Those churches whose hours are not listed below are normally open from 7 to 9 am and from 6 to 8 pm.

Convent of Santa Catalina This place wins my 'most fascinating colonial religious building in Peru' award so even if you're burned out on visiting churches, you should try and see this convent. Actually,

1	La Recoleta Monastery & Museum
2	Santa Catalina Convent
3	Hostal Santa Catalina
4	Municipal Museum & Crafts Shops
5	Romie's Peña
6	San Francisco Church
7	Hotel Jerusalen
8	Hostal La Casa de mi Abuela
9	Peña Jatuchayin
10	Residencial Guzman
11	Govinda Restaurant
12	Conresa Tours
13	Santa Teresa Church
14	El Quinque Steak House
15	ABC Bookstore
16	Hotel Crismar
17	Post Office
18	Carnaby Discotheque
19	Restaurant Bonanza
20	Hostal Roma
21	Hotel Crillon Serrano
22	Hotel Viza
23	Cine Concord
24	Mountain Guide
25	Jorge's Hotel, Monza Italian Restaurant & Chifa Ha Wa Yan
26	Hostal Imperial & La Taberna Restaurant
27	Hostal V Lira
28	Banco de Crédito
29	Hostal Mercaderes
30	Hostal Excelsior
31	Map Store
32	Cathedral
33	Casa Ricketts
34	Hostal El Mirador
35	Hotel & Cinema El Portal
36	La Compañía Church
37	ENTEL
38	Expresos Victoria del Sur & Sur Peruano
39	Hostal Royal
40	Hotel San Francisco
41	Cine Ateneo
42	Angelitos Negros, Empresa Nieto Emp Aragon, Emp Sudamericano, Emp Cruz del Sur, Trans Palma, TEPSA, Trans Jacantaya & other transport companies, Pensión Tacna & Hostal San Juan
43	Hostal Virrey, Comité 20, Emp Valdivia & Cruz del Sur
44	Ormeño
45	Hostal Florida
46	Comité 1
47	Hostal Extra
48	Hostal Premier
49	Railway Station Entrance
50	Hostal Europa & Hostal Paris
51	Hostal Parra
52	Comité 3
53	Comité 4
54	Comités 2 & 15
55	Gran Hotel
56	Hostal Americano, Hostal Ejercicios & Cine Variedades
57	Hostal La Merced
58	La Merced Church
59	Empresa San Augustin
60	Goyenache Palace
61	Tourist Office
62	Cinema
63	Hospedaje Cuzco, Balcony Restaurant, Hotel Maison Plaza, Aero Peru & Faucett
64	El Cerroje & Pizza Nostra
65	Lima Tours
66	National Rent-a-car
67	Hotel Presidente
68	Hotel Conquistador
69	Santo Domingo Church
70	Casa de Moral

it's not just a religious building, it's a good sized complex, almost a city within a city. It was built in 1580 and enlarged in the 17th century. The convent is surrounded by imposing high walls and the 450 nuns who lived within led a completely secluded life and never ventured outside the convent. Accordingly, the place was shrouded by an aura of mystery for almost four centuries until it was finally opened to the public in 1970.

Now, the few remaining nuns continue to live a cloistered life but remain in only the northern corner of the complex. The rest is open to the public and you are free to wander around as you will. It's like stepping back in time to a forgotten world of narrow twisting streets and tiny plazas, beautiful courtyards and nuns' simple quarters. Santa Catalina has been completely and excellently restored and the delicate pastel colours of the buildings are attractively contrasted with bright flowers, period furnishings, and religious art. It is a paradise for photographers who often spend all day here as the moving sun makes subtle changes in the lighting. It's a wonderful place to just relax and wind down, write your journal and perhaps reflect upon your trip.

There are two ways of visiting Santa Catalina. One is to wander around slowly, discovering for yourself the intricate architecture of the complex; getting slightly lost and finding your way again, and revisiting those areas you enjoyed the best. This is the way that I recommend as being the most fun. Alternatively, you can hire a guide. Just ask for a guide when you buy your entrance ticket and they'll give you the next available one. It helps if you speak Spanish. Guide services are free but a tip is appreciated. Entrance costs US$1.30 and it's open from 9 am to 4 pm daily. There is a small cafeteria which sells delicious home-made snacks cooked by the nuns.

The Cathedral The imposing cathedral stands on the Plaza de Armas. The original structure, dating from 1656, was destroyed by fire in 1844. The second building was toppled by the earthquake of 1868 and so most of what you see has been rebuilt since then. The outside is impressive but the inside is surprisingly bare. As with many of Arequipa's churches, the interior emphasises an airy spaciousness and luminosity and the high vaults are much less cluttered than churches in other parts of Peru.

La Compañía Just off the south-eastern corner of the Plaza de Armas, this church is one of the oldest in Arequipa and noted for its ornate main facade which bears the inscription *Año 1698*, although the side porch dates even earlier, to 1654. This Jesuit church was so solidly built that it withstood the earthquakes that toppled the Cathedral and other buildings. Inside, many of the original murals were covered with plaster and white paint by 19th century restorers but the polychrome cupola of the San Ignacio chapel survived and is worth visiting. Opening times vary from year to year. Recently the church was open from 8 am to 12 noon and from 3 to 8 pm and costs 10c to visit.

San Francisco This church was originally built in the 16th century and has been damaged by earthquakes. It still stands and visitors can see a large crack in the cupola – testimony to the power of the quakes. There is an impressive silver altar but the rest of the church has a relatively simple interior (by Peruvian standards).

La Recoleta A short walk from the centre is the monastery of La Recoleta, built on the west side of the Chili River in 1648 by the Franciscans and now completely rebuilt. For me, this is the most interesting place to visit in Arequipa after Santa Catalina. The Franciscans were among the most active of the Catholic missionaries and study and education played a large part in their activities. I was fascinated by their huge library of over 20,000 books, many of which are centuries old. They have several *incunables* or books dated before 1550 and their oldest volume dates to 1494. There is also a museum of Amazonian exhibits collected by the missionaries. These include a large exhibit of stuffed birds and animals, as well as objects made by the Indians. There is also an extensive collection of preconquest artefacts and religious art of the Cuzqueño school. You can visit the cloisters and monks' cells.

The monastery is open from 9 am to 1 pm and from 3 to 5 pm on Mondays through Fridays and on Saturdays in the morning. Admission is 30c. A Spanish speaking guide is available (tip expected) and worth engaging to make sure that you don't miss the library, especially if you're a bibliophile.

Other churches If you're particularly interested in colonial churches then you could also visit the churches of Santo Domingo, Santa Teresa and La Merced.

Museums

For a city of its size, Arequipa doesn't have a good selection of museums. One of the best is in the monastery of La Recoleta (see above). The Municipal Museum has a few paintings, historical documents, photographs, maps and other paraphernalia pertaining to the city's history. It is open from 9 am to 6 pm on Mondays through Fridays and admission is a few cents. There is an archaeological collection at the University of San Agustín on Avenida Ayacucho east of the centre but it was closed for restoration when I was last there. Ask at the Tourist Office to find out if it has reopened.

Colonial Houses

Many beautiful colonial houses are now being used as art galleries, banks, or offices and can be visited. One of the best is the Casa Ricketts, built in 1738, which was first a seminary, then the archbishop's

palace, then a school, before passing into the hands of one of Arequipa's upper crust families and finally being sold to the Banco Central. It now houses a small art gallery and museum, as well as bank offices. Entry is free and it's open from 8 am to 12 noon and from 3 to 6 pm, Mondays through Fridays. Also worth a look are the Casa de Moral, now owned by the Banco Industrial, and the Goyaneche Palace.

Yanahuara

This suburb is within walking distance of the town centre and makes a good excursion. Go west on Avenida Grau over the bridge and continue on Avenida Ejército for about six or seven blocks. Turn right on Avenida Lima and walk up five blocks to a small plaza where you'll find the church of Yanahuara which dates from 1750. At the end of the plaza is a *mirador* or viewing platform with excellent views of Arequipa and El Misti.

Head back along Avenida Jerusalén, which is the next street parallel to Avenida Lima, and just before reaching Avenida Ejército you'll see the well known *Picantería Sol de Mayo* where you can stop for an excellent lunch of typical Arequipeño food. The whole walk should take about 1½ hours round trip from the town centre but if you get tired there's the green Yanahuara No 152 city bus which returns from Yanahuara Plaza to downtown every few minutes.

Cayma

A little way beyond Yanahuara is Cayma, another suburb with an often visited church. To get there continue along Avenida Ejército about three blocks beyond Avenida Jerusalén and then turn right on Avenida Cayma and climb up this road for about a km. The church of San Miguel Arcángel is open from 9 am to 4 pm and the church warden will take you up the small tower for a tip – excellent views, particularly in the afternoon. Buses marked Cayma go there from Arequipa along Avenida Grau.

Tingo

Five km south of Arequipa, this is another of the frequently visited suburbs of Arequipa. There's a small lake, swimming pools and typical restaurants which are popular with Arequipeños on Sundays but it's pretty dead during the rest of the week. Catch a No 15 Tiabaya bus from the corner of Avenidas Palacio Viejo and La Merced.

Places to Stay – bottom end

The *Gran Hotel* and *Hostal Roma* are among the cheapest at 65c per person but they're dirty and have only cold water. The *Pensión Tacna* for 90c and the *Hostal San Juan* for US$1 per person are a little better but they're by the bus offices and therefore noisy. The best of the really cheap and basic hotels is the *Hotel Crillon Serrano* which is friendly and has hot water in the mornings. They charge 80c single or US$1.50 double and have rooms with private bath for 20c more.

There are several hotels charging about US$1/1.70 for singles/doubles. These include the clean *Hostal Mirador* which only has cold water in the shared bathrooms but a few rooms (not singles) have great views over the Plaza de Armas. For the same price, the reasonably clean and friendly *Hostal Royal* does have hot water, as does the *Hostal Virrey* which has some rooms with private baths for US$1.70/2.30. The *Hotel San Francisco* has hot water in the mornings and charges US$1 per person.

One of the most popular hotels for budget travellers is the well-known *Residencial Guzman* which charges US$1.30/2.30 for singles/doubles. They're friendly and helpful (especially with train information and tickets) and there's a nice courtyard where they'll serve you early breakfasts if you have a schedule to keep. They have some cheaper dormitory-style rooms but the lines to the hot showers can get a bit long when the place is full. Similarly priced and also with hot water is the popular *Hostal Mercaderes* just off the Plaza. Right on the Plaza is the *Hospedaje Cuzco* which is clean and has hot water but none of the rooms have Plaza views. They have a cheap balcony restaurant which does have views. Similarly priced is the basic *Hostal V Lira* which has hot water.

For a few cents more try the good and friendly *Hostal Extra* which has a garden, rooms with private showers and hot water, and a convenient location for the Ormeño bus station. It's a bargain and is often full. Also friendly is the *Hostal Excelsior* which has hot water and a few rooms with private showers. Fairly close to the railway station is the *Hostal Parra* which has hot water in the mornings and is clean. Closer to downtown is the *Hotel Imperio* which has hot showers and a few doubles with private bathrooms.

The *Hostal Americano* charges US$1.70/2.70 for singles/doubles, is basic but clean and friendly and has hot water. There are beautiful red geraniums in the passageways. Next door is the similarly priced *Hostal Ejercicios* which is clean but only has cold water. *Jorgé's Hotel* charges the same and also has rooms with private bath for US$2.30 and US$4.30 single and double. It is central and provides both hot water and tourist information. The *Hotel Florida* charges about the same and is reasonable.

The *Hostal Santa Catalina* near the

convent charges US$2/3 for singles/doubles with shared bath and is popular with German-speaking travellers. It has been reported as clean and friendly but with an erratic hot water supply. *Hostal Europa* and *Hostal Paris* are next to one another and convenient for the railway station but are fairly basic and have hot water only in the mornings. They charge US$2 per person in rooms with private bath and a little less in rooms with shared showers. The *Hostal La Merced* has large clean rooms with private baths and hot water for US$2.70/4.30. The *Hostal Premier* is similarly priced and has some slightly cheaper rooms without private baths but the communal showers don't look too clean.

Places to Stay - middle

My favourite hotel in Arequipa is the charming and very respectable *La Casa de Mi Abuela* which charges US$4/6 for singles/doubles with private shower and hot water. There's an attractive garden full of singing birds, and tables and chairs are provided so you can eat breakfast. They'll also serve you breakfast in bed (!) and it's not very expensive. Each room includes a radio and a 'bar' with beer and soft drinks which you pay for when you leave. It's clean and well run and very secure – you have to ring a bell to get in. It's at Jerusalén 606 and the sign is very small.

Several good hotels charge US$5.50 for singles and US$8 for doubles. They are all fairly modern, clean and comfortable establishments which are rather similar to one another. All rooms are with private bath and hot water. One traveller recommends the *Hotel Conquistador* as the best value hotel in Peru. Similar are the newish *Hotel Crismar*, the *Hotel Viza* which has carpeted rooms with telephones but is a bit run down – not bad though, and the *Hotel Jerusalén* which has a restaurant and provides the luxury of a sit-down bathtub in some of their rooms if you're fed up with showers.

Places to Stay - top end

The *Hotel Maison Plaza* is on the Plaza de Armas and charges US$9/12 for singles/doubles with bath, but only two of its rooms have plaza views. Also on the Plaza is the very modern *Hostal El Portal* which charges US$16/22 and adds a 50% surcharge on rooms with a plaza view. This is probably the best run and most comfortable hotel in town and even boasts a roof-top swimming pool.

Slightly cheaper is the government run *Hotel de Turistas* which is in an attractive building surrounded by gardens in the Selva Alegre suburb about 1½ km north of the town centre. The modern *Hotel Presidente* is similarly priced.

Places to Eat

There are many restaurants around the Plaza de Armas, particularly on the Santa Catalina side. The *Balcony Restaurant* of the Hospedaje Cuzco is great for views; the food is OK and cheap. Below the balcony are several more restaurants including the cheap and good *El Cerrojo* which serves excellent espresso coffee and the *Pizza Nostra* for Italian food.

For coffee drinkers, there are two cafés on the first block of San Francisco which have good espresso, cappuccino and snacks. The best coffee, and also the most expensive, is at *Monzas*.

For local food my favourite place is the *Sol de Mayo* which is at Jerusalén 207 in the Yanahuara district. See directions to get there under Yanahuara. It is open only for lunch and serves good and reasonably priced Peruvian food. Try *rocoto relleno* (hot peppers stuffed with meat, rice and vegetables), *cuy chactado* (seared guinea pig), *ocopa* (potatoes with a spicy hot sauce and fried cheese), *chupe de camarones* (shrimp soup), *chancho al horno* (suckling pig), *anticucho* (shish kebab of beef or beef hearts), *cebiche* (marinated seafood), and wash it down with *chicha* (fermented maize beer). A lunch time visit to the *Sol de Mayo* should be combined with a visit to the Mirador de Yanahuara.

Near the *Sol de Mayo*, on the 10th block of Avenida Ejército, is the recently opened *Royal Drinks Niño* which is the new name and location of the old downtown favourite, *Chez Niño*. Good international food is served from 12 noon to 3 pm and from 6 pm onwards. Another worthwhile restaurant is the *Bonanza* which serves a good variety of reasonably priced dishes and is popular with Arequipeños. Vegetarians might want to try the *Govinda* which is good, very cheap, and run by the Hare Krishnas. Carnivores should try the *El Quinqué* steak house which has a pleasant ambience and folk music on some evenings (closed Sundays). If you want Chinese food, the *Chifa Ha Wa Yan* is good. The nearby *La Taberna* has reasonable steaks for about US$2 or US$3.

Entertainment

Things are generally pretty quiet mid-week. An irritating habit of some places is to advertise a nightly *peña* but in fact there's rarely anything going on except for Friday and Saturday nights.

Romie's Peña by the San Francisco church has long been popular. It's a very lively but tiny bar so you have to get there before they close the doors. It's a fine art; at 9 pm they may be empty and by 10 be full to overflowing. The music is usually good but eat first because they only serve drinks.

Another place to try is *Peña Jatuchayin* which has meals but is unreliable with the music. They promise music which doesn't arrive on weekdays but weekends are usually OK. It's a bit expensive and there's a small cover charge, so make sure the musicians are there before paying.

The *El Quinque* steak house also has good live folk music once or twice a week, and a good atmosphere. There are other places which you'll see advertised but don't believe everything you read.

There are several discotheques if you like to disco – one is Carnaby Discotheque and is open mid-week, though don't expect crowds! There's also the usual selection of movie theatres, some of which show English-language movies with Spanish subtitles.

Getting There

Air There are three direct flights to Lima, two to Tacna, one or two to Cuzco and one to Juliaca every day. Juliaca is presently served only by AeroPeru whilst the other cities are served by both AeroPeru and Faucett. Both airlines have offices on the Plaza de Armas and their fares are usually the same. One way to Lima is about US$48, to Cuzco US$26, to Juliaca US$19 and to Tacna US$16.

All non-Peruvian passengers have to pay a US$2 departure tax at the airport.

Buses The majority of bus and colectivo offices are on San Juan de Dios, particularly around the 600 block (between Alto de La Luna and Salaverry).

Lima is 17 to 21 hours away. TEPSA has the fastest service on its daily non-stop Presidential bus which is the most expensive at about US$12. The regular service, with stops, takes three or four hours longer and costs about US$9. Ormeño has eight daily buses to Lima and Sur Peruano two buses which are often the cheapest and slowest. Expreso Victoria has four departures daily but is usually more expensive. Also try Cruz del Sur with three daily buses, Angelitos Negros with one, and others.

For intermediate points, most buses stop in Nazca (US$5) as well as Camaná, Chala, and Ica but remember that Pisco is about five km off the Pan-American Highway and not all buses go there. Change in Ica if necessary. For north of Lima, change in Lima.

If you're going inland to Lake Titicaca, try Transportes Jacantay. They have two afternoon buses daily to Juliaca (12 hours) and one to Puno (13 hours, US$5).

Sur Peruano also goes to Puno. Cruz del Sur has the only direct service to Cuzco (about 21 hours via Imata – a wild and rough route, US$9, 4 and 6 pm daily). Bear in mind that Cruz del Sur has four or five offices scattered along San Juan de Dios so find out where the bus leaves from. (The majority of travellers heading to these places prefer to use the train.)

Transportes Aragon has five departures daily for the coast at Mollendo. Many of their buses go on to Mejía. Cruz del Sur has afternoon departures to Mollendo and there are others. For Ilo, there are buses with both Cruz del Sur and Angelitos Negros.

If you're heading for Moquegua or Tacna (for Chile), Angelitos Negros has five daily departures for Moquegua (3½ hours, US$1.60) and seven departures for Tacna (six hours, US$2). Other companies which do this route are Ormeño (five daily to Tacna) and Cruz del Sur (five to Tacna and eight to Moquegua).

For sightseeing in the Department of Arequipa try Empresa Nieto which has daily dawn departures for Chivay (five hours, US$1.60). Their bus goes on to Yanque, Achoma and Maca on the upper Colca Canyon. Transportes Palma also has daily early morning buses to Chivay which continue on to Cabanaconde (10 hours, US$3.20). Empresa Jacantay have a 6.30 am departure for Cabanaconde via Huambo (a round trip to the Colca Canyon via Sihuas, Huambo, Cabanaconde and Chivay can therefore be done using public transport). The Jacantay bus leaves a couple of streets away from their office so get precise directions when you buy the ticket.

For buses to Corire (three hours, US$2) to visit the Toro de Muerte petroglyphs, go with Transportes San Antonio who have three daily buses. (This company is presently on Avenida Consuelo, well away from the others.) Cruz del Sur has occasional buses on through Corire to Aplao and Cotahuasi where there is a basic hotel.

Colectivos These shared taxis take five passengers and cost 1½ to two times more than a bus. They are faster, but not necessarily more comfortable. Usually they'll pick you up from your hotel. Comité 4 goes to Lima daily at 2 pm (17 hours, US$15). Comité 3 has a daily service at 10 am to Puno (nine hours, US$10) but ensure that you've made it perfectly clear that you're going to Puno because many passengers go only as far as Juliaca and the driver may be reluctant to continue the 44 km to Puno with only one passenger. Comités 1 and 20 have three or four cars a day to Mollendo (two hours, US$2.30) and Comités 2 and 15 have two departures daily to Majes (US$3) and Chuquibamba (five hours, US$5.50) for visits to the Majes Canyon irrigation project and Corire.

Rail The Arequipa-Juliaca route is bleak but most travellers find the views of the altiplano are interesting and you may see flamingoes, vicuñas, alpacas, and llamas. This journey is much more comfortable by train than by bus. If you want to travel in daylight, there are three departures from Arequipa each week at 7.40 am on Mondays, Wednesdays and Fridays. They all go to Juliaca and Puno but not to Cuzco.

There is also a night train which leaves Arequipa at 9 pm each evening and arrives at Juliaca at 6 am the following day. This train continues to Puno, an hour away, or you can connect with the day train to Cuzco which leaves Juliaca at 9 am. Thus it is possible to buy a through ticket to Cuzco from Arequipa and you arrive at 6 pm.

An extremely high number of people have their bags slashed or stolen or their pockets picked on the night train, particularly in the overcrowded and ill-lit 2nd class and, to a lesser extent, in 1st class. There are also a large number of thieves mingling with the crowds, waiting for the night train in the bustling Arequipa train station. Watch your baggage carefully and constantly. You are safest buying the buffet or pullman class tickets in addition to your 1st class ticket. The buffet car has food available but this isn't included in the price of your ticket. The pullman car has comfortable reclining seats so you can sleep. Both these carriages are heated (it gets very cold on the altiplano at night and most of the journey is at altitudes over 4000 metres). There are attendants who keep the doors locked and allow only ticket holders into the carriages and they keep an eye on the luggage. Oxygen is available if you get sick from the altitude. Note that if you buy a pullman ticket to Cuzco you may have to change carriages in Juliaca in the morning as the pullman car doesn't normally continue to Cuzco. You continue in 1st class.

The 1st class fares from Arequipa are US$6 to Juliaca, US$6.70 to Puno, and US$12.70 to Cuzco. The fares in 2nd class are about 25% lower. There is a flat surcharge of US$2.50 for Buffet and US$3 for Pullman class (on top of the 1st class fare).

It's best to buy your tickets in advance rather than trying to do so whilst guarding your luggage in the pre-departure crowds. The ticket office for 1st class tickets is open from 10 to 11 am and from 3 to 5 pm on Mondays to Saturdays and from 3 to 6 pm on Sundays. Second class tickets are sold from 7 am to 12 noon, 3 to 6 pm, and 8 to 10 pm on weekdays, 8 am to 12 noon and 4 to 10 pm on Saturdays, and 9 am to 12 noon and 3 to 10 pm on Sundays. Unfortunately these hours change frequently. The departure times of the trains also change but not drastically. You can rely on three day trains and six or seven night trains each week.

I've occasionally heard talk of starting a comfortable sleeper service on the night train, using quaint old-fashioned sleeper coaches. It sounds like a nice way to go but I rather doubt that anything will ever come of these ideas.

Getting Around

Airport Transport There are no airport buses, although the No 3 Zevallo-Aeropuerto bus goes along Grau and Ejército and passes within a km of the airport – ask the driver where to get off. A taxi from downtown costs about US$1.50.

Tours Various tourist agencies advertise city tours but it's easy enough to visit the most interesting places yourself – they're all within walking distance.

Around Arequipa

Several long distance excursions can be made from Arequipa. The most popular is the tour of the Colca Canyon. Others include climbing the volcano El Misti and other mountains, visiting the Majes canyon and the petroglyphs at El Toro Muerto, and hiking in the Valley of the Volcanoes. Although many of these places can be visited by public transport this is often inconvenient and taking a tour is sometimes worth the extra money – unless, of course, you have time on your hands and prefer the adventure of taking infrequent ramshackle buses to remote areas. The main advantage of taking a tour is that you can stop at the most interesting points for sightseeing and photography, whilst on public transport the bus just keeps on going.

If you decide to go on a guided tour you'll have many options – there are dozens of tour companies operating out of Arequipa and some of them aren't very good so make sure that you discuss exactly what to expect before parting with your money. Guides should be able to produce a Tourist Guide card.

The greatest variety of excursions are offered by Anthony Holley. He is an Englishman and long time resident of Arequipa who knows the area extremely well and personally conducts all his groups using four-wheel drive Land

Petroglyph from Toro Muerto

Rovers. He charges about US$20 per person per day (sometimes more for very long trips) but requires a minimum of six people. He'll take you anywhere you want to go and is a great source of useful information. When not on tour he parks his blue Land Rover in front of the Santa Catalina monastery every morning and uses his vehicle as a mobile 'office'. At other times he can be contacted at home (tel 224452) or you can call his wife, Señora Maureen (tel 212525), between 8 am and 3.30 pm on weekdays. Or write to Casilla 77, Arequipa, Peru.

Holley's Unusual Excursions will take you everywhere except the Colca Canyon – this tour is offered by several other tour operators. Most of these operators will lump their clients together in one group. *Conresa* tours at Jerusalén 409 often provides the vehicle and the lowest price, about US$12 for the day trip with a full bus. Unfortunately, the minibuses used don't have adequate leg room for tall people unless you're lucky enough to get one of the front seats. Guides don't always speak English. Many companies also advertise other trips but these rarely go due to lack of interest. The most expensive and comfortable tours are offered by *Lima Tours*.

Finally, you can drive yourself. National Car Rental will rent a VW for US$19 per day and 19c per km or a small Toyota Jeep for US$26 per day and 26c per km. Larger vehicles are available and they sometimes have special tariffs or weekly rates. Minimum age is 25 and minimum deposit is US$200 or a credit card.

COLCA CANYON

Controversy rages about whether or not this is the world's deepest canyon. The sections which you can see from the road on a standard guided tour are certainly very impressive but are not the deepest parts of the canyon. To see the deepest sections you have to make an overnight trip and hike in. Some measurements of the depth of the canyon are taken only from the north rim which is higher than the south – decide for yourself if this is ethical. Anyway, does it really matter whether it is the deepest in the world? It certainly warrants a visit if you have the time.

Most guided tours leave Arequipa (2325 metres) at dawn and climb northwards through desert scenery and over the pass separating Chachani and El Misti. The road continues through the nature reserve of Pampas de Cañihuas (about 3850 metres) where vicuñas and sometimes guanacos are sighted. Later in the trip domesticated alpacas and llamas are frequently seen and so it is possible to see all four members of the South

American cameloid family in one day – something which it is not normally easy to do. After two to three hours a breakfast stop is made at Viscachani (4150 metres). The road continues through bleak altiplano over the high point of about 4800 metres from where the snowcaps of Ampato (6288 metres) are seen. Then the road drops spectacularly to Chivay (see next section) which is about 160 km from Arequipa.

The thermal hot springs of Chivay are normally visited (bring swimming gear and towel) and the tour bus continues west following the south bank of the upper Colca Canyon. The landscape is remarkable for its Inca and pre-Inca terracing which goes on for many km and is the most extensive I've seen in Peru. The journey is worthwhile to see the terracing alone. Along the route are several villages whose inhabitants are involved in agriculture and continue using the terraces today. At Yanque an attractive church which dates from the early 1700s is often visited.

About 20 km beyond Chivay, and about four km before Achoma is the *Colca Tourist Lodge* where lunch is taken either on the way in or out. Soon after the lodge the bus often stops for the driver to point out a small carved boulder which is supposed to represent a pre-Columbian map of the terracing. The end point of the tour is at the lookout known as Cruz del Cóndor, about 60 km beyond Chivay and an hour before you get to the village of Cabanaconde. As the name suggests, Andean Condors are sometimes seen here – early morning or late afternoon are the best time for this. From the lookout the view is impressive with the river flowing 1200 metres below you. Mt Mismi, on the other side of the canyon, is about 3200 metres above the canyon and some guides will tell you that the depth measurement should be taken from Mismi's summit. In fact, deeper sections can be seen if you go further in but this requires leg work from Cabanaconde (see next section).

Most tours go back the way they came and the return trip takes about 10 to 12 hours. It is possible to continue through Cabanaconde and Huambo to the Pan-American Highway at Sihuas. The road is in very bad shape and not shown on all maps.

Places to Stay

Chivay, at an altitude of about 3700 metres, is the capital of the province of Caylloma and has a couple of cheap and basic *pensións*. One is the *Hotel Moderno* on the Plaza de Armas. When in Chivay don't neglect to visit the hot springs which are five km to the north-east of the village by road. There is a clean swimming pool and changing rooms, a basic cafeteria, and an admission fee of 5c.

The government-run *Colca Tourist Lodge*, near Achoma about 20 km beyond Chivay, is the most comfortable place to stay in the Colca river valley. Although it is some distance from the canyon itself, it is a good centre for walking and inspecting the pre-Columbian terracing. They charge US$7/10 for singles/doubles with bath and hot water. Meals are available. The place is often empty but if you want to make a reservation call ENTURPERU (tel 721928) in Lima or try at one of the better travel agencies in Arequipa.

Cabanaconde has one basic *pensión* which charges 75c a night. Ask here for directions to walk to the canyon – it takes about six hours one-way so you should be prepared to camp.

Getting There

If you don't want to take a guided tour, see the Buses section under Arequipa for details of the two companies which have daily dawn departures to Chivay. One continues from Chivay past the tourist lodge (where you can get off) and on to Cabanaconde. The section of road between Cabanaconde and Huambo veers away from the canyon. It is also the roughest part of the road and there is little transport. Jacantay bus company in

Top: Church of San Agustin, Arequipa (TW)
Left: Santa Catalina Convent, Arequipa (RR)
Right: Santa Catalina Convent, Arequipa (RR)

Top: Plaza de Armas, Cathedral & Volcán Misti, Arequipa (RR)
Left: Cloister of La Compañía, Arequipa (TW)
Right: Church of Yanahuara, Arequipa (TW)

Arequipa does the trip to Cabanaconde through Huambo, and this may be the best way to go, though I've never tried it.

RIVER RUNNING

An excellent guide to the Colca Canyon is in *Kayak Through Peru* by the Polish Canoandes expedition, 1981. It can be obtained in bookshops in Lima, but is not easy to find. The Colca Canyon is a dangerous and difficult river and not to be undertaken lightly. A few commercial outfitters do rafting trips through portions of the river in August. These trips are expensive, but are the only option unless you are fully equipped and experienced in river rafting. Try Mayuc Expediciones, Apartado 596, Cuzco, Peru.

CLIMBING EL MISTI

This 5822-metre-high volcano is technically one of the easiest ascents of any mountain of this size in the world. Nevertheless it is hard work and you normally need an ice axe. It is recommended that you talk to Señor Zamire Landoval who works in the photo studio at Calle Santo Domingo 416. He is an expert on climbing El Misti and other mountains and can provide you with up-to-date information, rent you equipment and put you in contact with a guide if you wish. I've also heard that Carlos Vargas at Bolívar 220 is a recommended guide though I haven't met him.

To get to the mountain by public transport take a bus to Chiguata. Buses leave about 6 am and 1 pm from Avenida Sepulveda in the Miraflores district and take about an hour to Chiguata for a fare of 25c. From Chiguata to the base camp takes about eight hours or more along rough trails. It's a hard uphill slog and there's little if any water en route. From the base to the summit and back takes about a further eight hours and there's no water. The downhill hike from the base camp to Chiguata takes three hours or less.

If you hire a vehicle you can get much higher up the mountain than by public transport and it saves you having to hassle with your luggage on a crowded public bus. Anthony Holley is used to dropping climbers off at the highest and most convenient place (above the Aguada Blanca dam at 4000 metres) but the service is expensive. I've heard that *Turandes* at Calle Mercaderes 130 also provide this service but I don't know how reliable they are.

If you're a beginner climber then please note that people have died in these mountains and it's not as easy a climb as it looks. The main problems are the lack of water, the altitude, and extreme weather conditions. Carry plenty of drinking water and cold weather gear and be aware of the main symptoms of altitude sickness. If in doubt, go back down.

TORO MUERTO

This is a magnificent and unusual archaeological site in the high desert. It consists of hundreds of carved boulders spread over about two square km of desert. Archaeologists are uncertain of the cultural origins of this site but it is thought that it was made by the Wari culture about 1200 years ago.

To get to the site by public transport, take a San Antonio bus to Corire (US$1.40, four hours) and then walk for about 1½ hours. In Corire there is one basic hotel, the *Hostal Willy* which charges about a dollar per night and can give you information on reaching the site.

The Toro Muerto petroglyphs can also be visited more conveniently but expensively on full day tours from Arequipa. Anthony Holley does the round trip, along with stops at other sites of interest, for US$20 per person.

VALLEY OF THE VOLCANOES

This unusual valley is covered with scores of small and medium sized volcanic cones and craters – a veritable moonscape. The

65-km-long valley is located around the village of Andagua near the snowcapped mountain of Coropuna which, at 6305 metres, is the highest peak in southern Peru. It is a weird and remote area which is seldom visited by travellers. Perhaps that's a good reason to go.

To get there you can take a Delgado bus from Arequipa through Corire on to Andagua. At present it only runs three times a week, out on Sunday, Wednesday and Friday, and back on Monday, Thursday and Saturday. There are no hotels in Andagua but the people are friendly and you can camp there.

Lake Titicaca

Generations of school children have been taught that Lake Titicaca, at 3820 metres above sea level, is the highest navigable lake in the world and this fact alone seems to be a tourist attraction. In fact there are many navigable lakes of over 4000 metres, such as Lake Junín in Peru's central Andes, but Lake Titicaca gets the distinction of being the world's highest simply because it has frequent passenger boats and it is the best known. And if you like trivia, amaze your friends with the facts that Lake Titicaca, at over 170 km in length, is also the largest lake in South America and that it is the world's largest lake at over 2000 metres in elevation. At this altitude the air is unusually clear and the deep blue of the lake is especially inviting. Various interesting boat trips can be made on the lake from Puno, Peru's major port on Lake Titicaca. This is one of the main reasons why travellers spend a night in Puno en route to either Cuzco or Bolivia.

There are many other reasons to spend more time in the area. Not the least of these is simply the incredibly luminescent quality of the sunlight on the altiplano. It seems as if horizons are limitless and the earthy tones of the scenery are as deep as the lake itself. These colours are reflected in the nut-brown faces of the people of the altiplano as well as in their colonial churches and archaeological monuments, several of which are well worth visiting. The Department of Puno is also famous for its folk dances which are the wildest and most colourful found in the Peruvian highlands. And if this isn't enough, there are fascinating Andean animals to see such as huge herds of the domesticated alpacas and llamas as well as sparkling highland lakes full of Giant Andean Coots or various species of rosy coloured flamingoes.

JULIACA

With a population of some 100,000 Juliaca is the largest town in the Department of Puno and has the department's only commercial airport. It is also an important railway junction with connections to Arequipa, Puno and Cuzco. Located at an elevation of 3822 metres, Juliaca is the first altiplano town visited by many overland travellers en route from the coast to either Cuzco or Lake Titicaca. Unfortunately it is of comparatively little interest and most people prefer to go on to Puno where there are better hotels and a view of Lake Titicaca.

If you arrive from the coast, especially by air, remember to take it easy for a day or two – see Altitude Sickness in the Health section in Facts for the Visitor.

The main reasons why you might stay here are to make train or plane connections, to take the rarely travelled northerly route into Bolivia, or to visit the Monday market. There is also a daily market along the railway tracks – you can buy almost anything here if you look. The selection of both sheep and alpaca woollen goods is good and prices are very competitive with Puno and Cuzco.

Information

The best hospital in the Department of Puno is the Clínica Adventista de Juliaca. Money changing facilities are limited – for cash dollars try the *ferretería* (hardware store) shown on the map. Otherwise go to Puno. There is an ENTEL for long distance and international phone calls. The cinema may help you while away an evening.

Places to Stay - bottom end

There are several cheap, basic, cold water places by the railway station. The *Hotel Benique* at 65c single and US$1.10 double

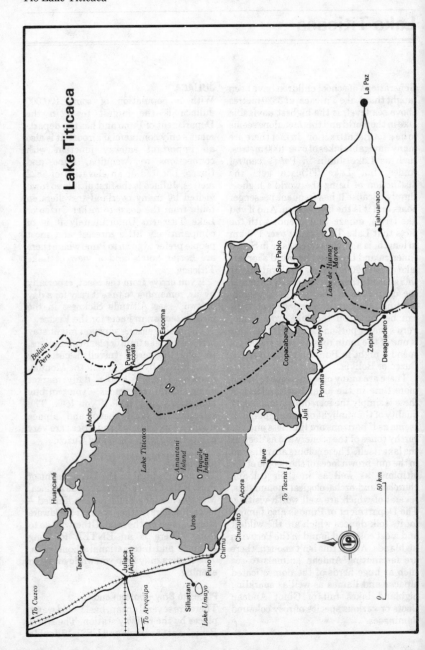

Lake Titicaca

La Paz

Tiahuanaco

Lake de Huaiñay Marca

San Pablo

Copacabana

Zepita

Desaguadero

Yunguyo

Pomata

Bolivia
Peru

Escoma

Puerto
Acosta

Juli

Ilave

Moho

Acora

Lake Titicaca

Amantani Island

Taquile Island

Chucuito

Huancané

Uros

Chimu

To Tacna

Taraco

Puno

Juliaca (Airport)

Sillustani

Lake Umayo

To Cuzco

To Arequipa

50 km

0   50 km

and the slightly more expensive *Hostal Loreto* have little to recommend them other than their cheapness and closeness to the railway station. Other basic cheapies are the *Hotel del Sur, Juliaca,* and *Ferrocarril* all of which charge around 75c per person. The *Hostal San Antonio* has been recommended as the best of the supercheapies but it isn't up to much either.

For a little more money you can find a more agreeable hotel. My recommendation for a cheap hotel is the clean and friendly *Hotel Yasur* which has rooms with communal baths for US$1.50/2.50 for singles/doubles or if you want a room with a private bath you'll pay about US$2.20/3.50. They have hot water in the mornings and evenings but unfortunately this is unreliable. This hotel fills up fast so get there as early as you can. Another place to try is the *Hostal Sakury* which charges US$1.40 per person in single rooms with shared baths or US$2/3 for rooms with private baths. They claim to have hot water, but again this is unreliable.

Places to Stay - middle

The *Hostal Peru* is conveniently close to the railway station and charges US$2.70/4.70 for rooms with shared bathrooms and US$3.70/5.70 for rooms with private bath. It's clean and comfortable and has hot water in the evenings. If you're looking for greater comfort, try the government-run *Hotel de Turistas* which will charge you about twice as much as the Hostal Peru and includes continental breakfast. They're located on the outskirts of town so take a taxi.

Places to Eat

There seems to be a simple restaurant on every block in Juliaca's town centre so you won't starve. None of the restaurants are anything to write home about. The best choice might be the *Pollería Riko Riko* which sometimes has live music at the weekends.

Getting There

Air Juliaca airport serves both Juliaca and Puno. AeroPeru has a flight every morning to Arequipa with same day onward connections to Lima or Tacna. Daily flights from Lima via Arequipa to Juliaca are also available. There are no direct flights to Cuzco, although on some days it is possible to fly the long way round via Arequipa. This is expensive. There are also no flights to Bolivia.

Fares to Arequipa are about US$19 and to Lima about US$66. Both AeroPeru and Faucett have offices in Juliaca but Faucett doesn't currently service Juliaca.

Buses Services are available to most points in southern Peru. The cheapest long distance services are with Transportes Jacantaya who have daily buses at 5 pm for Arequipa (10 hours, US$4.70) and Lima (26 hours, US$13). Cruz del Sur charge a few cents more and also have a 5 pm bus to Lima and three buses a day to Arequipa. They have three buses a day to Cuzco (11 hours, US$5.20). Sur Peruano have a late-afternoon bus to Arequipa with connections to Lima and Tacna. These companies also have services to Puno but it is much more convenient to take the colectivo service.

Colectivos Shared taxis frequently ply the 44 km route between Juliaca and Puno and provide a good service. The vehicles of Comité 1 charge just under a dollar per passenger and take about ¾ of an hour to drive on the good road to Puno. They leave from the railway plaza as soon as they are full – about two or three times an hour.

Rail Juliaca is the busiest railway crossroads in Peru. The single train station serves Puno to the south, Cuzco to the north-west and Arequipa to the southwest. Naturally, you can get off at intermediate points but these are of little interest to most travellers. If you want to take the train on to Machu Picchu you have to change train stations in Cuzco – there is no direct service from Juliaca to Machu Picchu.

Tickets are often sold out in advance in 2nd class and almost always in 1st class (which has numbered and reserved seats) so think ahead. The ticket windows are open from 7 to 10 am, 4 to 7 pm, and 8 to 10 pm every day except Sunday when they're open from 7 to 10 am and 4 to 6 pm.

First class fares are about US$6.60 to Cuzco, US$6.10 to Arequipa and 60c to Puno. Second class fares are approximately 25% lower. Travellers pay an extra charge of US$2.50 on top of the 1st class fare in buffet class and an extra US$3 in pullman class.

Departure times to Puno are about 7 am and to Cuzco about 8.30 am. There is no Sunday service to these towns. Night trains to Arequipa leave about 8.45 pm every night and day trains leave at 8.30 am on Tuesdays, Thursdays and Saturdays. Times are approximate because the trains don't originate in Juliaca and so it depends on whether they arrive on time from their points of origin.

Passengers arriving on the overnight train from Arequipa and continuing to Cuzco normally have a couple of hours to wander around between trains. There are many salespeople at the train station selling alpaca sweaters and ponchos and you can do your buying right through the carriage windows if you want. Bargain hard – prices tend to drop just before the train leaves.

Beware of thieves. Read the warnings in the Arequipa train section and watch your gear with an eagle eye.

Getting Around
Airport Transport There is no airport bus at present. Bargain for a taxi and expect to pay about US$1.50 to US$2.

THE NORTHERN ROUTE INTO BOLIVIA
Decrepit but interesting old 3 de Mayo

buses full of Andean Indians go from Juliaca to Huancané several times a day. The journey takes three hours and costs about 75c. The company has no office and you just show up and pay on the next available bus. Occasionally some buses continue to Rasapata or Moho – the latter on the route to Bolivia. Huancané has a basic hotel near the Plaza de Armas. I'm told there's a basic *pensión* in Moho but I've never been there.

There is a bus from Huancané to Moho on most days. It takes one day on foot. From Moho there is a truck to Bolivia once a week (usually Saturday). The nearest Bolivian town is Puerto Acosta which is a day's foot travel from Moho. In Puerto Acosta you'll find the Bolivian immigration, a couple of basic hotels and bus connections with La Paz. This is a little travelled and adventurous route into Bolivia and recommended only for experienced off-the-beaten-track travellers with little concern for time or comfort. I'd

1	Comité 1 Colectivos to Puno
2	Railway Station
3	Hostal Loreto
4	Hostal Peru
5	Hotel Benique
6	Hostal Sakury
7	Aquarius Discotheque
8	Aero Peru
9	Sur Peruano Buses
10	Cinema
11	Hotel del Sur
12	Money Exchange (in Ferretería)
13	Hotel Juliaca
14	Pollería Riko Riko
15	Hotel Yasur
16	Faucett
17	Cruz del Sur Buses
18	Post Office
19	Transportes Jacantaya
20	Transportes 3 de Mayo
21	ENTEL Peru
22	Hostal San Antonio
23	Hostal Ferrocarril

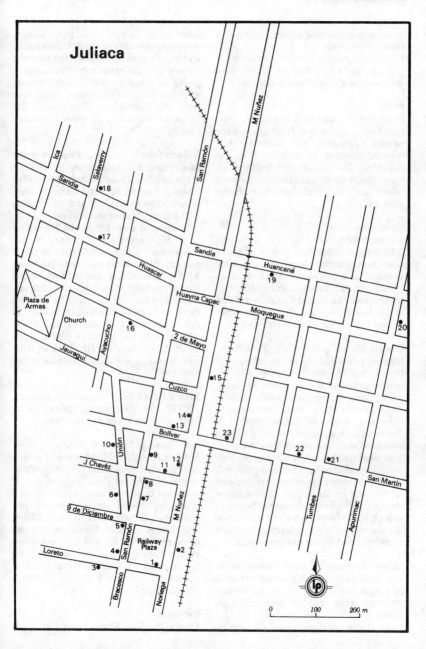

be interested in hearing from anyone who takes this route.

Note that the nearest Bolivian consul is in Puno. See under that town for further information about entering Bolivia.

PUNO

Puno was founded on 4 November 1668 near the site of a now defunct silver mine named Laykakota but there are few colonial buildings to see other than the cathedral. The town itself is drab and not very interesting but there's a good selection of hotels and plenty to see in the environs.

Information

Tourist Information There is a tourist information office but it has changed address at least three times in the last few years. The most recent location is at Cajamarca 527. There is still an office on Melgar near the Hostal Florida but it was closed last time I was there. They may reopen the old location at Deusta 342.

Climate For many travellers, Puno is the highest place they'll be spending any time in and the weather at this altitude can be extreme. It's very cold at night, particularly during the winter months of June through August when the temperatures may drop well below freezing. If you're cold, buy one of the thick alpaca sweaters from the market – they're cheap. The rainy season is October through May with December to April being the wettest. Roads are sometimes closed then because of flooding or landslides although the train normally keeps running. The sun at this altitude is very strong and sunburn is a common problem so remember to wear a wide brimmed hat or use sunscreen.

Money Exchange If you're going to or coming from Bolivia it's easiest to buy or sell your Bolivian pesos at the border, although they can be exchanged in Puno.

To change dollars, casas de cambio were giving better rates than banks. There are several of these on Calles Junín and Independencia – it's worth shopping around because rates vary. Banks were giving lower rates or not changing money at all but they won't necessarily stay that way. The Banco de la Nación is on the Plaza de Armas and the other banks are near by.

Bolivian Consul The consul's office is not easy to find in its location on the top floor of the building above the AeroPeru office. There is a small sign and they are open from 8.30 am to 12.30 pm and from 2.30 to 4.30 pm on Mondays to Fridays.

Citizens of non-communist European countries (except France), Canada and Israel do not require visas or tourist cards and can enter Bolivia with just a passport. All others need a tourist card or, in the case of nationals of communist countries, a visa. The tourist card is free, valid for 30 days, and can be renewed in Bolivia. It can be obtained from the consul in Puno within 24 hours. If you're planning on entering Bolivia it's worth checking with the consul to see if the situation has changed.

Other Offices Puno has a post office and an ENTEL for international phone calls. Both are open seven days a week.

Hot Showers Many of Puno's cheaper hotels have only cold showers and at this altitude most people find them downright unpleasant rather than invigorating. If you want to economise you can stay in a cheap hotel and use the public hot showers. The best is on Avenida El Sol and charges about 25c for a 30-minute hot shower between 7 am and 7 pm every day except holidays. You can also try the Gymnasium on Calle Deusta which is open from 7 am to 3 pm on Tuesdays through Sundays.

Cathedral

On the Plaza de Armas is the Cathedral

which dates to 1757. The lower part of the main facade is well sculpted but the interior is more spartan than the facade suggests. There is a silver plated main altar.

Museum

Just off the plaza is the town's main museum, once a private collection but now bequeathed to the city since the owner's death. The Museo Carlos Dreyer is open from 9 am to 7 pm on Mondays through Fridays and costs about 50c to visit. Opening hours change frequently and it's best to go in the mornings.

Views

There are two good spots for views. The best is Huajsapata Park, a little hill about 10 minutes to the south-west of town. It is topped by a larger-than-life white statue of the first Inca, Manco Capac, looking out at the legendary site of his birth, Lake Titicaca . The view of the town and the lake is excellent but unfortunately the park is badly looked after and frequently used as a latrine so you have to watch where you step. Another good spot for views is from near the arch on Calle Independencia.

Market

The market is always interesting especially in the mornings when the salespeople are setting up. It's full of Indian ladies hunkered down behind piles of potatoes or peanuts and it's also a good place to buy woollen clothes.

Fiestas & Folklore

The Department of Puno is noted for its wealth of traditional dances – some sources count about 100 different varieties. Some are rarely seen by tourists and others are performed in the streets during the various annual fiestas. Many of the

1	Tourist Office	31	Perla del Altiplano (Bus)
2	Tranextur	32	Hostal San Carlos
3	Plaza de Armas	33	Hostal Europa
4	Cathedral	34	Transturin
5	Carlos Dreyer Museum	35	Hostal Lima, Sol Mar Tour
6	Samana Bar		& Colectur
7	Samary Restaurant	36	Hostal Venecia & Hostal Central
8	La Hostería Bar	37	Hostal Colón, Comité 3
9	Hostal Monterrey		& Coop 2 de Febrero
10	Restaurant Ambassador	38	Hostal Taurino
11	Casa de Cambio	39	Hostal Roma & Hotel Internacional
12	Hostal Colonial	40	Delta Café, Club 31,
13	Parque Pino (or San Juan)		Restaurant Internacional
14	Hotel Sillustani		Restaurant Sillustani and
15	Hotel Arequipa & Casa de Cambio		Misky's Restaurant
16	Bolivian Consul, Aero Peru	41	Hostal Extra
	& Casa de Cambio	42	Post Office
17	Twin Cinemas	43	Hostal Nesther
18	Hotel Centenario	44	Hostal Rosario
19	Hostal Italia	45	Hotel Tumi
20	Hostal Los Uros	46	ENTEL
21	Las Rocas Restaurant	47	Comité 2 & Sur Peruano Bus
22	Market	48	Hostal Posada Real
23	Hotel Ferrocarril	49	Hot Showers (Gymnasium)
24	Comité 1 (to Juliaca)	50	Hostal Florida
25	Railway Station	51	Public Hot Showers
26	Hostal Don Miguel	52	Hostal Real
27	Hotel Embajador	53	Port (Boats to Uros & Taquile)
28	Hotel Los Incas		
29	Jacantay & Cruz del Sur (Bus)		
30	Morales Moralitos (Bus)		

dances have specific significance and if you make friends with the locals they'll explain this to you. Although the dances often occur during processions celebrating Catholic feast days they usually have roots in completely different pre-conquest celebrations. These are often tied in with the agricultural calendar and may celebrate planting or harvesting, for example. Even if you have difficulty in understanding the meaning of the dances, you'll be fascinated by the costumes used for them. These are extremely rich, ornate and imaginative and are often worth more than an entire household's ordinary clothes. Included in this show of colour and design are grotesque masks, dazzling sequinned uniforms and animal outfits , to mention a few.

In addition to the elaborately outfitted dancers there are musicians playing a host of traditional instruments. Some, such as most of the brass and string instruments, have obvious Spanish influence. Many of the percussion and non-brass wind instruments, however, have changed little since Inca times. These include hand drums or tambourines (*tinyas*) and larger drums (*wankaras*) as well a host of different shakers, rattles and bells. Inca wind instruments include the very typical and well known panpipes which come in a variety of lengths ranging from tiny high-pitched ones to base panpipes almost as tall as the musician. These are often made from bamboo and are known as *antaras, sikus* or *zampoñas* depending on their size or range. Flutes

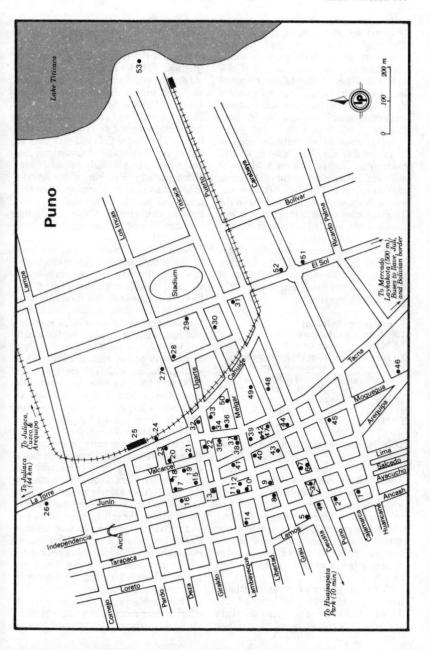

Puno

Lake Titicaca

To Juliaca (44 km)

To Juliaca, Cuzco & Arequipa

To La Torre

To Mercado Laykakota (500 m); Buses to Ilave, Juli, and Bolivian border

To Huajsapata Park (10 min)

(*flautas*) are also seen at most fiestas. The most common are simple bamboo penny whistles called *quenas*, whilst others are large wooden blocks that look as if they've been hollowed out of a metre length of two by four. The most esoteric of these flutes is the *piruru* which is carved from the wing bone of the Andean Condor.

Seeing a street fiesta with dancing can be planned or may be a matter of luck. Sometimes celebrations are held in one town and not another and at other times, such as carnival, there are fiestas everywhere. It's always worth checking in the Tourist Office to see if they know of any fiestas worth visiting in the surrounding area.

Apart from the major Peruvian fiestas listed in the Facts about the Country chapter, the following are a selection of the fiestas particularly important in the Lake Titicaca region.

6 January	Epiphany
2 February	Candlemas
7-8 March	Saint John
2-4 May	Alacitas (Puno miniature handicrafts fair)
	Holy Cross (Huancané, Taquile, Puno)
25 July	Saint James (Taquile)
24 September	Our Lady of Mercy
1-7 November	Puno week

This is only a selection – there are others.

Places to Stay – bottom end

Many of the nicer hotels fill up quickly when the trains arrive in the evenings so try and find a room as soon as possible. The prices given are low – they may rise during fiestas and sometimes in the evenings, although hotels are supposed to display a board with the prices of their rooms.

There are plenty of cheap and basic hotels near the corner of Libertad and Tacna. Most of them are none too clean and have only cold showers. Even if they claim to have hot water it doesn't always work. One of the best of the super cheapies is the *Hostal Torino* at 50c for singles and 90c for doubles – cold showers only in the communal bathrooms. Other similarly priced dives are the *Hostal Venecia, Central* and *Centenario*. The *Hostal Rosario* and *Hostal Roma* cost a few cents more but don't offer anything better. The *Hostal Colonial* isn't too bad at 75c per person and it sometimes has hot water. The similarly priced *Hostal Extra* usually has hot water in the evenings and has a reasonably attractive courtyard which is unusual in Puno hotels. The *Hostal Colón* is similar but dirtier and its security has been questioned.

For a little more money you can have hot water but, because of water shortages, this is usually limited to certain hours of the day, usually in the evenings. If you like a hot shower in the mornings your choice is more limited. The *Hostal San Carlos* often has hot water in the evenings and has reasonable rooms for 90c single and US$1.50 double. The *Hostal Europa* is similarly priced and in addition has singles/doubles with private baths for US$1.50/2.25. This hotel has built up a reputation among budget travellers as *the* place to stay in Puno and so it's often full. It's clean, has left luggage facilities and hot water in the evenings.

Another good similarly priced hotel is the quiet *Hostal Los Uros* which has a cafeteria open for early breakfasts and claims to have hot water during most of the day. It has no single rooms but there are plenty of triples and even quads which work out very cheaply if there's a group of you travelling together. In fact, most of Puno's hotels have plenty of large shared rooms and the *Hotel Los Incas* has mostly triples and quads for about US$1 per person. There is sometimes hot water in their communal showers.

There are several quite good hotels offering clean rooms with private baths in the US$2 single and US$3.25 double price range. The *Hostal Nesther* has hot water from 7 to 9.30 am in the mornings, the popular *Hostal Monterrey* in the evenings and the clean and central *Hostal Lima* both mornings and evenings although the water was barely lukewarm when I took a morning shower there. The *Hotel Arequipa* is supposed to be similar to the above but the service is lousy. Also in this price range is the *Hostal Posada Real* which has received good reports.

Places to Stay - middle

The cheapest place in this category is the *Hotel Tumi* at US$3/5 for singles/doubles with private bath but the rooms are not much better than the best hotels in the bottom end price range. The *Hotel Internacional* is US$4.50/7.50 with private bath but complaints have been made about the service.

Although most hotels in this category have fixed prices, often in US dollars, you can always try bargaining. For example, the *Hotel Embajador* halved it's official rates of US$9/14 for some travellers I met. They have good comfortable rooms with round-the-clock hot water in the private bathrooms.

For US$8/11 for singles/doubles you can stay at the clean *Hotel Ferrocarril* which is conveniently located across from the railway station. Each room has central heating and a private bath with one of those shocking electrical showers that you have to use with care – make sure it's working properly before taking the room. They have a reasonably priced restaurant with folk music every evening at 7.30 pm and some travellers report receiving a free welcome pisco sour when they stayed there.

Also in this price range is the good clean *Hostal Italia* which will provide you with a room heater if you suffer from the cold. You can bargain here but make sure that your hot shower works because a few of the cheaper rooms on the ground floor have no hot water. Similarly priced are the *Hostal Real* and *Don Miguel*.

Places to Stay - top end

The best place in Puno itself is the fairly new *Hotel Sillustani* which charges US$12/16 for clean carpeted singles/doubles with private bath and hot water all day. They have a reasonable restaurant and breakfast is usually included in the price of the room.

The expensive government-run *Hotel Isla Esteves* is attractively located on an island in the western part of Lake Titicaca. It is connected to Puno via a five km road over a causeway but there are no buses and so it's a pain to get to and from. Taxis charge an exorbitant US$1.50 for the trip. Many of the rooms look out directly on the lake and the exceptionally beautiful views are the hotel's main attraction. The restaurant is no more than mediocre. Prices are about US$25 single and US$40 double including continental breakfast.

Places to Eat

There are five restaurants at the corners of Moquegua and Libertad which provide a good choice. The *Delta Café* and *Misky's* are both cheap cafés and recommended for early breakfasts. The *Restaurant Sillustani* and *Internacional* are among the best in town – I much prefer the *Sillustani* for its ambience and good value. The *Samary Restaurant* is also good and has a varied menu. The *Restaurant Las Rocas* has good food and is reasonably priced.

Several other cheap restaurants are found along Avenida Lima – the *Restaurant Ambassador* is good. The *Hotel Ferrocarril* has a medium priced Italian restaurant with folk music around 7.30 pm every evening.

Entertainment

The cinema has two separate theatres and thus two different shows each day. English language movies with Spanish sub-titles are sometimes shown.

For nightly folk music try the *Hotel Ferrocarril Peña* at 7.30 pm. All other places are pretty much a question of luck though weekends are always the best times to hope for running into a good musical evening. The *Restaurant Sillustani* sometimes has music, particularly at weekends, and you might hear of other restaurants with a show.

My favourite bar is the *Samana*. Its thatched roof and wooden benches provide a pleasant atmosphere, and there is live music most weekends. The tiny *La Hostería Bar* doesn't look big enough to hold both a band and an audience but somehow it packs them in – don't drink too much beer as the toilet facilities are limited! Both these places are popular with travellers.

Getting There

Air The nearest airport is in Juliaca, about 44 km away. There is an AeroPeru office at Arequipa 130 in Puno. See the Juliaca section for further information about the flights.

Buses The roads are in bad shape and most people prefer to travel by train for greater comfort. If you prefer travelling by bus the following services are available:

For Cuzco try Cruz del Sur or Jacantaya which are conveniently located next to one another. Between them they have about four or five buses to Cuzco but most of them are overnight. Fares are about US$5 for the 11-hour trip. These companies also have services to several other major cities including Arequipa (13 hours, US$5.30) and Lima (32 hours, US$13.30). SurPeruano has a cheaper service to Arequipa for about US$4. La Perla del Altiplano has buses to Tacna on Mondays and Fridays at 5.30 pm for US$5.40. Morales Moralitos' terminal was closed but may reopen.

For buses to the towns on the south side of the lake and the Bolivian border go from the Laykakota market.

Colectivos The main colectivo service is

Comité 1 which leaves frequently from in front of the railway station for Juliaca. They charge about 80c per person for the 45-minute trip and leave when full.

Comités 2 and 3 have shared taxi service to Arequipa every morning for about US$10, nine hours.

Rail The first few km of the journey out of Puno follows the shores of Lake Titicaca and the views are good. At Juliaca there is a junction and the train continues to Cuzco or branches down to Arequipa. The Cuzco train leaves daily except Sunday at 7.25 am. The Arequipa night train leaves daily at 7.45 pm and the day train leaves on Tuesdays, Thursdays and Saturdays at 7.25 am. Be alert for thieves in the dimly lit train station, especially early in the mornings and in the evenings. Be particularly careful on the night train – see the warnings under the Arequipa train section.

The ticket office is open from 6.30 to 8 am, 9.30 to 11.30 am, 2 to 5 pm and 7 to 8.30 pm on weekdays and on Sundays from 6.30 to 8 am, 2 to 4 pm and 7 to 8.30 pm. First class fares are US$6.70 to Arequipa and US$7.20 to Cuzco. Second class fares are approximately 25% lower. There is a US$2.50 surcharge for buffet class and US$3 for pullman class (over the 1st class fare). See the Arequipa train section for more details about these classes.

You can usually buy your ticket the night before but sometimes, especially for the Cuzco train, the numbered 1st class seats get sold out. The problems are that the ticket office is reluctant to sell tickets earlier than the night before and tour companies often buy up blocks of tickets for their tours. You can try and buy a ticket early at the train station or at least find out the earliest that they can be sold (sympathetic ticket sellers may sell you a ticket early if you look worried enough). Otherwise you may have to check on the tour agencies and see if they have any spare tickets – they often do.

Around Puno

There are four main excursions to be made out of Puno. Two of them are lake trips; one to the floating islands of Los Uros and the other to the island of Taquile. The other two are land trips; one to the archaeological site of Sillustani and the other is a drive along the southern shores of the lake to visit various small towns which are famous for their colonial churches and their fiestas.

All of these excursions can be done cheaply using public transport. Also, tour companies will arrange guided trips which are more expensive and not necessarily worth the extra money. I went on a guided visit to the archaeological site of Sillustani because there is little literature about the site and I wanted to learn as much as I could about it. I was with a group of about half a dozen non-Spanish-speaking travellers who were particularly interested in Sillustani and wanted as informative a visit as possible. I arranged an excursion with Rey Tours of Puno. They charged us US$10 each and promised us a private vehicle to pick us up from the hotel and an English-speaking guide to explain the ruins to us. The old bus that picked us up was almost an hour late, they picked up two more small groups along the way as well as a few friends of the driver, they charged us an extra fee for admission to the site and to crown it all the guide knew very little about the ruins that we didn't already know, and didn't speak any English so I ended up translating for him.

Of course, anyone who has spent any time travelling in Latin America knows that these things happen and to expect and accept them. It's not quite as easy to accept when you're paying for it though. So if you take a guided tour you might want to sign a written agreement or not pay until the trip is underway.

SILLUSTANI

The Inca Empire was known as *Tahuantinsuyo* or 'the land of four quarters'. The southern 'quarter' was called *Collasuyo* after the Colla tribe which, along with the rival Lupaca tribe, dominated the Lake Titicaca area and later became part of the Inca Empire.

Not a great deal is known about the Colla people. They spoke Aymara instead of Quechua, they were a warlike tribe, and they had unusual burial customs for their nobility. Their dead were buried in funerary towers called *chullpas* which can be seen in various places in the area. The most impressive are the *chullpas* of Sillustani.

The tallest of these reaches a height of about 12 metres and there are several others which are almost as high. They are located on a small hilltop in the peninsula of Lake Umayo and look very impressive against the bleak landscape. The towers are either round or square and inside them were found the remains of Colla nobility, who were buried in family groups, complete with food and belongings for their journey into the next world. The only opening into the towers was a small hole facing east, just large enough for a man to crawl through. After a burial was completed, the entrance was sealed. Nowadays nothing remains of the burials, but the *chullpas* are well preserved and worth seeing, both for their architecture and for their impressive location.

The outside of the towers are of massive coursed blocks reminiscent of Inca stonework but it should be realised that they were not built by the Incas. Archaeologists consider the architecture to be more complicated than that of the Incas. Some of the *chullpas* of Sillustani are unfinished. Carved but unplaced blocks and a ramp used to raise them to the correct height are among the points of interest at the site. A few of the blocks are decorated – the carving most often noticed by visitors is that of a lizard.

Sillustani is surrounded by Lake Umayo

which is an interesting Andean lake with a good variety of plants and water birds. Bird-watchers should particularly look for the Giant Andean Coot, the White-tufted and Silvery Grebes, the Puna Ibis, the Andean Goose, the Black-crowned Night-Heron, the Speckled and Puna Teals, the Yellow-billed Pintail, the Andean Lapwing, the Andean Gull (strange to see a 'sea' gull so far from the ocean) and, if you're lucky, perhaps one of the three species of flamingoes found in the Andean highlands.

Getting There

The site is about 30 km north-west of Puno and there is a daily bus run by Tranextur from Puno's Plaza de Armas. The bus leaves at 2.30 pm and costs US$2 for the round trip which takes about 3½ hours and allows about 1½ hours at the ruins. This is convenient because the afternoon light is the best for photography. Admission to the ruins costs a further 25c and there is a small on-site museum – this is not a guided tour. Dress warmly for the trip and bring sun protection.

If you would prefer to spend more time at the site you could hire a taxi for about US$10 to US$15. This isn't much more expensive than the Tranextur bus if you can get a group together.

Camping by the lake is reportedly possible though there are no facilities.

THE FLOATING ISLANDS

The excursion to the floating islands of the Uros people is the one most frequently undertaken by visitors to Puno and hence has become somewhat over-commercialised. Despite this it remains popular because there is nothing quite like it anywhere else.

The Uros people used to speak their own language but nowadays speak Aymara – most have intermarried with Aymara-speaking Indians and no pure blooded Uros exist today. They were always a small tribe and began their unusual floating existence centuries ago in an

Mummy being carried to its crypt (Waman Puma)

effort to isolate themselves from the Collas and the Incas. About 300 people live on the islands at present but the attractions of shore life are slowly eroding away even this small number.

The Uros' lives are totally interwoven with the *tortora* reed which grows abundantly in the shallows of Lake Titicaca. They harvest these reeds and use them to make everything from the islands themselves to little model boats to sell to tourists. The islands are constructed from many layers of reeds which rot away from the bottom and are replaced at the top. The 'ground' is soft and springy and care must be taken where you tread as it's easy to put your foot into a rotted out section. The biggest of the islands contains several buildings including a school. The walls are constructed of *tortora* but some of the roofs are now of tin.

The Uros build canoe-like boats from tightly bundled reeds. They are used for both transportation and fishing. A well constructed boat can carry a whole family and will last for about six months before beginning to rot. You can usually persuade

Top: Boat to Amantaní on Lake Titicaca (RR)
Left: Reed boat at Uros Islands, Lake Titicaca (TW)
Right: Puno boat dock, Lake Titicaca (RR)

Top: Fiesta, Department of Puno (RR)
Bottom: Sillustani chullpas, near Puno (TW)

one of the Uros to give you a ride on a boat but be prepared to pay. Also be prepared to give a 'tip' for taking photographs.

There are always plenty of women trying to sell you their handicrafts such as models made from *tortora* and embroidered wall hangings. Many visitors find it annoying to be constantly pestered to buy the souvenirs, to give presents to the kids and to hand out money every time you lift your camera. Begging and selling is more common here than in any other part of Peru that I've been to, so if you find this difficult to deal with you'd be better off going elsewhere. If you prefer, you can give food instead of money – the islanders particularly like fresh fruit. I went with a sack of oranges and became a hit with the kids.

Getting There

It's easy to get there. Just go down to the docks and hang around – you'll be propositioned to take a trip to the islands within minutes of arriving. You can hire an (expensive) private boat or go with the next group. Boats generally leave about every half hour throughout the day starting about 7 am and continuing through early afternoon. The standard trip takes about four hours and visits the main island and perhaps one other. The boats leave as soon as there are about 15 or 20 passengers and a fixed price is charged – usually around US$2.50 per person. All the boats are small and rather decrepit motorboats and there are no life jackets – though I have never heard of an accident.

En route you may well see the Uros paddling around in their reed boats, fishing or gathering *tortora* reeds. Various species of birds are to be seen on the lake (see under the Sillustani section). Even if the Uros and their floating islands are rather sad the ride on the lake can be beautiful in good weather.

TAQUILE ISLAND

This is a real island as opposed to a floating one and it is less frequently visited. It's a long trip and best done overnight although day trips from Puno are entirely possible.

Taquile is the most fascinating island I've ever been on. The people wear colourful traditional clothes which they make themselves. The men always seem to be walking around the island knitting the tightly woven woollen caps which they wear constantly. These look like floppy nightcaps and can only be described as cute. The women weave the elegant-looking men's waistcoats which, when worn with their caps, rough-spun white shirts and thick calf-length black pants, give the men a very raffish air. The women themselves, in their many layered skirts and delicately embroidered blouses, also look very handsome. These clothes, which are among the best made traditional clothes in Peru, can be bought at the island's co-operative store.

The people speak Quechua rather than the Aymara of most Titicaca Indians and maintain a strong air of group individuality. They don't often marry with non-Taquile people and their lives are untrammelled by such modernities as roads or electricity. There are no vehicles, not even bicycles, on the island and more surprisingly there are no dogs. No barking to wake you up at night.

Taquile is very peaceful but the islanders are by no means content to let the world pass them by. When enterprising individuals from Puno began bringing tourists to visit the island they fought against this invasion. It wasn't the tourists that they didn't want – it was the entrepreneurs from Puno. Now the passenger boats that go to Taquile are owned and operated by the islanders themselves. This enables them to control tourism and keep it at what they consider to be reasonable levels. This may be the key to maintaining a respectful and co-operative relationship between the locals and the tourists – something which is sadly lacking on the floating islands of the Uros.

The scenery of the island is beautiful. The soil is a deep earthy red colour which, in the strong highland sunlight, contrasts magnificently against the intense blue of the lake. The backdrop of Bolivia's snowcapped Cordillera Real on the far side of the lake completes a splendid picture. The island is about six to seven km long and has several hills with Inca terracing on the sides and small ruins dotting the tops. Visitors are free to wander around to explore these ruins and enjoy the peaceful scenery.

If you're in the area in July remember that St James Day (25 July) is a big feast day on Taquile. Dancing, music and general carousing go on for several days through to the beginning of August when the Indians traditionally make offerings to the mother earth, *Paccha Mama*. New Year's Day is also generally festive and rowdy.

Places to Stay

Some people elect to stay overnight. From the island dock there is a steep stairway (lovely views) to the island centre. The climb takes about 20 minutes or more if you're not acclimatised. It is strongly recommended that you don't do this climb immediately after arriving from the coast – climbing stairs at 4000 metres is a painful, breathless experience if you're not used to it. In the centre you are greeted by a group of the inhabitants who will arrange accommodation for you if you wish. Individuals or small groups are assigned to an island family who will put you up in their houses. These are pretty rustic and there are no hotels as such. There is a standard charge of about 50c per person and gifts of fresh food are appreciated. You are given some blankets but you should bring a sleeping bag as it gets very cold at night. Beds are pretty basic and facilities are minimal. You do what the locals do – wash in cold water out of a bucket and use the fields as a latrine. If you like a little comfort, overnighting in Taquile is not for you.

If you do decide to stay the night remember to bring a flashlight as there is no lighting. Be careful to get the lie of the land while it's still light. Some friends of mine became completely lost on the island one night and couldn't find the house they were staying at. They ended up having to rough it for the night.

There are a few simple restaurants in the centre selling whatever is available: fresh lake trout if you're lucky – boiled potatoes if you're not. Bottled drinks are normally available but have been known to run out. Boiled tea is usually safe to drink but it's worth bringing a water bottle and water purifying tablets if you have them. Also bring extra food unless you're prepared to take potluck on what's available in the restaurants. Bring small bills because change is limited and there's nowhere to change dollars. And bring extra money – many travellers are unable to resist the high quality and uniqueness of the woven and knitted clothes for sale in the island co-operative store.

Although conditions are primitive by western standards it's a wonderful experience and some travellers stay for several days. The people are friendly and the lifestyle peaceful and relaxed. I remember staying there once at the time of a full moon. I watched the sunset and moonrise from a small Inca ruin at the top of one of the island's hills. It was windless and still. The mirror-like lake darkened slowly until I felt that Taquile was it's own little world, completely detached from the rest of the earth. When the moon came up over the 7000-metre snowcaps of the Cordillera Real it seemed twice as bright and much larger than normal in the crystalline air over the lake. An unforgettable evening.

Getting There

A boat for Taquile leaves from the Puno dock every day. If there is enough demand there's often a second boat. Departure time is usually about 8 or 9 am; you can either go down to the dock on the previous day to find out when it's currently leaving or show up by 7.30 am or so and see what is available. The 24-km passage takes approximately four hours and costs US$4 for the round trip. You get about two hours on the island and the return trip leaves at 2.30 pm, arriving in Puno around nightfall. Remember to bring adequate sun protection for this long trip – the power of the tropical sun bouncing off the lake at almost 4000 metres can cause severe sunburn.

AMANTANÍ

This island is a few km north of Taquile and similar to it. Because it is further away from Puno it is less often visited by travellers and there are fewer facilities. Basic food and accommodation is available but it tends to be more limited and dearer than in Taquile. Boats to Amantaní leave from Puno's dock in the mornings several times a week – ask around for the next departure. The boat Atún has been recommended for this trip.

THE ISLANDS OF THE SUN & MOON

The Island of the Sun is the most famous island on Lake Titicaca because it is the legendary birthplace of Manco Capac, the first Inca. Both the Island of the Sun and of the Moon have Inca ruins. They are in the Bolivian portion of the lake and to visit them you should go from the Bolivian port of Copacabana which is about 11 km beyond the border town of Yunguyo.

THE SOUTH SHORE TOWNS

An interesting excursion by bus can be made to the towns of Chimu, Chucuito, Ilave, Juli, Pomata and Zepita on the south shores of the lake. If you started early enough you could visit all of them in one day and be back in Puno for the night, or you can stay in some of the towns themselves, or continue on to Bolivia.

Getting There

To get to any of these places go to Puno's Mercado Laykakota on the Avenida El Sol side. Cheap and very slow buses, slightly dearer and faster minibuses, or more expensive colectivo taxis leave from here to the south shore towns and the Bolivian border. Buses are more frequent to the nearer towns such as Ilave but if you are patient you should be able to leave for the town of your choice within an hour or so. Minibus fares to the border are less than US$2 and closer towns are proportionately less.

CHIMU

The road east of Puno closely follows the margins of the lake. After about eight km you reach the village of Chimu – hikers might find this a pleasant lakeshore walk. Chimu is famous for its *tortora* reed industry and its inhabitants have close ties with the Uros. Bundles of reeds can be seen piled up to dry and there are always several of their reed boats in various stages of construction. Although this is an interesting sight, I found that the villagers were not particularly friendly to sightseers.

CHUCUITO

About 18 km east of Puno the village of Chucuito is reached. There are two attractive colonial churches – La Asunción and Santo Domingo, the latter has a small museum. Opening hours are erratic. The town was of some importance as a major Lupaca centre and a pre-colonial stone sundial can be seen in the main plaza. East of town there is a trout hatchery.

Places to Stay

On the outskirts of Chucuito is the expensive *Tambo Titikaka Motel* which charges about US$12 per person. Its main attraction is the superb view of the lake.

ILAVE

Near Chucuito the road turns south-east and away from the lake although the waters can usually be seen in the distance. The village of Platería, once famous for its silverware, is soon passed. About 40 km from Puno the road passes through the straggly community of Molleko. The area is noted for the great number of mortarless stone walls snaking eerily over the bleak altiplano.

Ilave is 56 km from Puno and has a Sunday market. It doesn't have the interesting colonial architecture of the other towns but its positioning on the crossroads gives it some importance. There is a daily bus on the little used road to Tacna. Unfortunately it leaves at 4 pm and so much of the scenery is missed. The journey takes about 14 hours and costs US$5.50.

JULI

The road returns to the lake near the bay of Juli where flamingoes are sometimes seen. Juli is 80 km from Puno and is famous for its colonial churches. There are four and they are all in a greater or lesser state of disrepair although they are being slowly restored as funds become available. San Juan Bautista is the oldest, dating from the late 1500s, and contains richly-framed colonial paintings of the lives of St John the Baptist and St Teresa. This church is now a museum but opening hours are erratic – best to try in the morning.

The church of La Asunción was finished in 1620 and has a large courtyard from where there are excellent vistas of Lake Titicaca. Its belfry was struck by lightning and shows extensive damage. San Pedro on the main plaza is in the best condition whilst Santa Cruz has lost half of its roof. It is interesting to see the churches in their unrestored states to get some idea of what the magnificent colonial churches in the highly-visited tourist centres such as Cuzco would look if they had not been carefully and extensively restored.

Juli has a small port with infrequent and irregular service to Bolivia. There is both a boat and a hydrofoil; the latter costs about US$50 per passenger. Further information can be obtained at Transturin in Puno.

Market day in Juli is Thursday.

Places to Stay

There are two hotels. The *Hotel Los Tréboles* is on the main square, charges about 50c a night, and is pretty grungy. There is a better *Hotel Turistas* about 20 minutes out of town by the lake, charging about US$4 per person.

POMATA

From Juli the road returns to the lake shore again and continues to Pomata, 106 km from Puno. As you arrive in Pomata you'll see the Dominican church which was founded in 1700. It's dramatically located on top of a small hill and is known for its great number of baroque carvings and for its windows made of the translucent stone, alabaster. As with the other churches in the region, you can never tell exactly when it will be open.

Just beyond Pomata the road forks. The main road continues south-east through Zepita (where there is another colonial church) to the Bolivian border at Desaguadero whilst a side road hugs the shore of Lake Titicaca and goes to the other border crossing at Yunguyo.

Places to Stay

There is one cheap hotel here, the *Hotel Puma Uta*. I'm told it's OK.

GOING TO BOLIVIA

For many travellers Puno and Lake Titicaca are a stepping stone to Bolivia, which borders the lake to the south.

Going to Bolivia – Water

Until recently there was a steamer service from Puno to the Bolivian port of Guaqui leaving Puno weekly at 8 pm on Wednesdays. This connected with trains between Cuzco and Puno and between Guaqui and La Paz. This service was recently discontinued but I'm told that it may start up again. The voyage took about 11 hours and cost US$27.50 including supper, breakfast and a bunk. Check with a travel agent to find out if it's sailing again.

There is also a boat and (expensive) hydrofoil service from Juli to Copacabana in Bolivia. This used to be run by Crillón Tours but, like the steamers, has been out of operation. Ask at the tourism office or one of the travel agencies such as Transturin about the current situation.

Going to Bolivia - Land

There are two ways to go; via Yunguyo and via Desaguadero. They both have their advantages and both will be described.

The Yunguyo route is the more attractive and has the added interest of the boat crossing at the Strait of Tiquina. It is a little more complicated and longer than the Desaguadero route and so in the past some travellers preferred to go via Desaguadero. Extensive flooding in early 1986 temporarily closed the Desaguadero route and it remains a very slow trip because of severe road damage.

For more information about Bolivian entrance formalities, see the Bolivian Consul information in Puno.

Via Yunguyo You can get buses from the Laykakota Market in Puno to the border town of Yunguyo for about US$1.50. The trip takes three hours and Cruz del Sur also does this route. At Yunguyo there are a couple of basic hotels but most people continue to Bolivia as there is little of interest in Yunguyo. There are money changers in the main plaza and on the street by the border which is about two km away. Count your money carefully. It's best to change a small amount to just get you to La Paz. The border is open from 8 am to 6 pm. There are several huts to visit – ask the officials where to go next.

There are Bolivian immigration formalities 11 km beyond Yunguyo in Copacabana. Transportation ranging from trucks to buses is available. Sunday is market day in Yunguyo and there is more frequent transport on that day. On weekdays you may have to wait an hour or two. Copacabana is a much more pleasant place than Yunguyo so if you want to break your journey do so here. There are several hotels to choose from. Remember that Bolivian time is one hour ahead of Peru.

There are about three buses a day from Copacabana to La Paz which take about five hours including a boat crossing of the Strait of Tiquina. You have to register with the Bolivian navy to cross – a simple formality but don't miss your bus!

If you leave Puno early in the morning you can reach La Paz in one day. If you can afford an extra couple of dollars it is much more convenient to buy a Puno-La Paz ticket with a company such as Colectur. They will drive you to Yunguyo, stop at the money exchange, show you exactly where to go for exit and entrance formalities, and drive you to Copacabana where you are met by a Bolivian bus which will take you to La Paz. Although this costs about US$6 the service of guiding you through the border formalities and providing a through service makes it worthwhile for some travellers.

If you are in La Paz and heading for Puno you can find agents for this through service in the Residencial Rosario at Illampu 704. For some reason the La Paz-Puno route costs US$16, much more expensive than the same journey from Puno to La Paz.

An expensive tour is offered twice a week by Transturin. For about US$55 they'll take you in a comfortable coach to Juli and Pomata to visit the churches, cross the border in Yunguyo, provide lunch in Copacabana, take you on a 3½-hour boat trip to the Island of the Sun, and continue by bus to La Paz. You are accompanied by a guide throughout.

Via Desaguadero Buses from Puno's Laykakota market leave every hour or two for Desaguadero (US$1.80, three hours). At Desaguadero there are two basic hotels. The *Hotel Montes* charges about 70c per person but is not good. A little better is the *Hotel Bolívar* which is right next to the border on the Bolivian side and charges US$1.50 per person. The best restaurant in town is in this hotel. The border is open from 8 am to 12 noon and 2 to 5 pm daily. Outside of these hours you can cross back and forth easily enough if, for example, you want to eat at the *Bolívar*. There are money changers at the border and a casa de cambio around the corner. When I crossed this border some years ago there were several different offices to visit but now there appear to be one on each side of the border. Always ask the officials where you should go next. The border officials here have been repeatedly criticised for their corruption so keep your wits about you.

There used to be (before the 1986 floods) several buses a day from Desaguadero to La Paz passing the ruins of Tiahuanaco. You can break your journey here if you wish. Travellers arriving from La Paz will find minibuses back to Puno running until mid afternoon.

Sometimes companies in Puno will offer through bus trips to La Paz via Desaguadero but this service was suspended because of road damage when I was last in Puno.

Entering Peru from Bolivia

Usually there's little hassle at either border and you can get 90 days without difficulty. This is good if your tourist card has almost expired – just go to La Paz for an evening and come back to Peru the next day. See Visas and Documents in Facts for the Visitor.

Cuzco

This chapter covers the Department of Cuzco which includes the city of Cuzco and many smaller towns, villages, nearby archaeological sites and the Inca Trail to Machu Picchu. In addition the most direct road link from here to the coast is described. This road goes through Abancay, the capital of the Department of Apurimac, then on through the southern part of the Department of Ayacucho and joins the Pan-American near Nazca.

The Department of Cuzco lies in exceptionally beautiful Andean scenery. This beauty is not the main reason why the area is visited, however. Almost every visitor to Peru comes to Cuzco to see the heart of the once mighty Inca Empire which has left us with the most fascinating and accessible archaeological ruins in the continent.

CUZCO

Cuzco is the hub of the travel network in South America. In this respect it is reminiscent of Kathmandu in Nepal. Both cities attract thousands of travellers and tourists who flock not just to visit a unique destination, but also to travel back in time and experience a centuries-old culture very different to our 20th century western way of life. Most of Cuzco's central streets are lined with massive stone walls built by the Incas in the 15th and 16th centuries and now form the foundations of colonial or modern buildings. The streets are often stepped and narrow and thronged with Quechua-speaking descendants of the Incas. It is the archaeological capital of the Americas and also the oldest contin-uously inhabited city in the continent.

Cuzco is the capital of its department. Figures for its population vary between 140,000 and 400,000 – the lower figures are probably better estimates. The city is 3326 metres above sea level and visitors should take care not to overexert themselves during the first few days, particularly if they fly in from Lima at sea level.

History

Cuzco is a city steeped in history, tradition and legend. Indeed, it is often difficult to distinguish where fact ends and myth begins. When Columbus arrived in the Americas, Cuzco was the thriving and powerful capital of the Inca Empire. Legend tells us it was founded in the 12th century by the first Inca, Manco Capac, who was the sun of the sun and born in Lake Titicaca. During his travels, he plunged a golden rod into the ground until it disappeared. This point was *cuzco* or Quechua for 'the earth's navel' and here he founded the city which became the heart of the great Inca empire.

So much for the legend. Parts of it are undoubtedly true; the Inca Empire did have its origins around the 12th century, Cuzco did become the capital and one of the earliest Inca leaders was named Manco Capac. But the archaeological record shows that the area was occupied by other cultures for several centuries before the rise of the Incas. Very little is known about these pre-Incas except that some of them belonged to the Wari expansion of the 8th and 9th centuries.

The Incas had no written language and their history was entirely oral, passed down through the generations. Their early history is obviously more legend than fact. The empire's main expansion occurred roughly in the hundred years before the arrival of the conquistadors and the oral history of that important later period is relatively accurate. Hence our knowledge of the history of Cuzco dates back to about the mid-1400s. The Spaniards, under Francisco Pizarro,

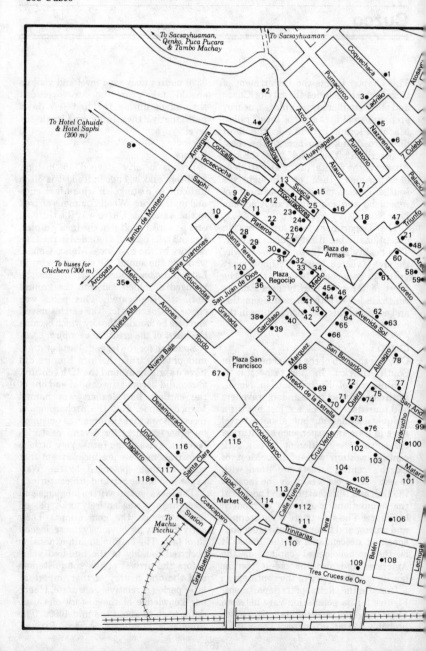

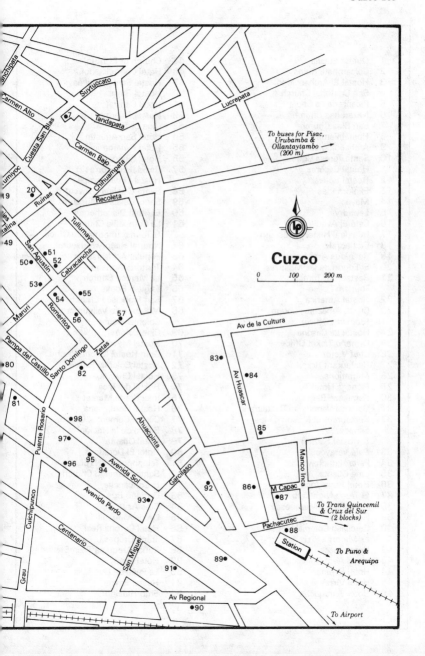

1	Quinta Eulalia	47	Church of El Triunfo
2	Colcampata Ruins	48	Hotel Conquistador
3	Hostal El Archaeologo	49	Hostal Santa Catalina
4	San Cristobal Church	50	Hostal Royal
5	Picantería La Chola	51	Hotel Central
6	Nazarenas Church	52	Hostal Palermo
7	San Blas Church	53	Cine Cuzco
8	Hostal Familiar	54	Hotel San Agustín
9	Archaeological Museum	55	Hotel Panamericano
10	Santa Teresa Church	56	Hotel Libertador
11	Hostal Caceres	57	Residencial Torres &
12	Hostal Bolívar		Hostal Limaqpampa
13	Explorandes	58	Santa Catalina Convent
14	Mayuc	59	Santa Catalina Museum
15	Laundry	60	El Muki Discotheque
16	Café El Ayllu	61	La Compañía Church
17	Regional History Museum		& Tourist Information Office
18	Cathedral	62	Natural History Museum
19	Religious Art Museum	63	Popular Art Museum
20	El Fogon de las Mestizas	64	Trattoria Adriano
21	Restaurant Tumi &	65	La Merced Church
	Tourism Police	66	English Books
22	Hostal America	67	San Francisco Church
23	Cuzco Amazonic Lodge	68	Marqués de Valleumbroso
	(Booking Office)		Colonial House
24	Hostal La Casona	69	Cine Colón
25	Ormeño Ticket Office	70	Hostal Mesón
26	Chef Victor	71	Gran Hostal Machu Picchu
27	Restaurant Roma	72	Hostal Colonial Palace
28	Migrations	73	Hostal Chavín
29	Picoaga Hotel	74	Hostal del Inca
30	Kamikaze Bar	75	Inka Crafts Market
31	Govinda Vegetarian Restaurant	76	Hostal Qorikancha
32	Restaurant El Mesón de los	77	Centro Comercial Cuzco
	Espaderos	78	Banco de la Nación
	& Hostal Samari	79	Hotel Ollanta
33	Café Varayoc	80	Hotel El Dorado
34	Peña Hatuchay	81	Telephones, ENTEL
35	Cine Ollanta	82	Santo Domingo Church
36	Hotel Royal Inca		& Coricancha
37	El Truco Nightclub	83	Ormeño Bus
38	Hotel de las Marquesas	84	Cine Azul
39	Hotels Garcilaso 1 & 2	85	Urcos Minibus
40	Garcilaso Colonial House	86	Hotel Corona Real
41	La Mamma Pizzería	87	Trans Oropesa
42	Hotel Cusco	88	Puno/Arequipa Train Station
43	Lloyd Aero Boliviano	89	Hotel Savoy
44	Hotel Espinar	90	La Peña de Don Luis
45	Hotel Virrey	91	Hostal Raymi
46	Hotel Wiraqocha	92	Emp Hidalgo

93	Post Office
94	Cuzco Centre of Native Art
95	Aero Peru
96	Peruvian Andean Treks
97	Hostal Alhambra 2
98	Faucett
99	Hotel El Sol
100	Tambo Hotel
101	Hostal Los Portales
102	Hostal Inti
103	Hostal Colonial
104	Hostal Monarco
105	Hostal Aragon
106	Morales Moralitos Bus
107	Hotel Kancharina
108	Trans Sr de los Animas & Hotel Belén
109	Hostal Tambo Real
110	Hostal San Martín
111	Hostal Trinitarias
112	Hostal La Posada
113	Hostals Comercio & San Pedro
114	Hostal Tupac Amaru
115	Santa Clara Church
116	Hotel Peru
117	Cine Unión
118	Hotel Imperio
119	San Pedro Church
120	Cross Keys Pub

reached the city in 1533 and from that point on, written records (the so-called chronicles) were kept. These included accounts of Inca history as told to the Spanish chroniclers by the Incas. The most famous of these accounts was written by Garcilaso de la Vega, born in Peru in 1539, who was the son of an Inca princess and a Spanish conquistador. He lived in the Cuzco area until the age of 21 and then moved to Spain where he died in 1616. Although his writings and that of the other chroniclers cannot be considered to be entirely accurate, they do give us a good overall idea of Inca history.

The seven Incas who succeeded Manco Capac governed a small tribe which was one of several groups living in the Andean highlands during the 13th and 14th centuries. They left little for us to remember them by although the remains of some of their palaces can still be seen in Cuzco. These Incas, and the location of some of their palaces, are listed below in chronological order. They span a period from roughly the 12th century to the early 15th century.

1. Manco Capac – The Palace of Colcampata is traditionally attributed to the first Inca but some sources claim that it was built by Huascar shortly before the arrival of the Spaniards. The massive retaining walls with eleven niches can be seen next to the church of San Cristobal on a hill in the north-western outskirts of Cuzco. The walls seem, at least to my untrained eye, to be too well made to be attributable to the first Inca but the legend persists.
2. Sinchi Roca – The Palace of Cora Cora; some of the walls can be seen in the courtyards of the houses on the right of Calle Suecia as you walk uphill from the Plaza de Armas.
3. Lloque Yupanqui
4. Mayta Capac
5. Capac Yupanqui
6. Inca Roca – The huge blocks of this Inca's palace now form the foundations of the Museum of Religious Art and include the famous twelve-sided stone of *Hatunrumiyoc*.
7. Yahuar Huacac
8. Viracocha Inca – His palace was demolished to make way for the present Cathedral on the Plaza de Armas.

The ninth Inca, Pachacutec, began the great expansion of the empire. Until his time the Incas dominated only a small area close to Cuzco and frequently skirmished with, but did not conquer, various other highland tribes. One of these was the expansionist Chancas who occupied a region about 150 km to the east of Cuzco. By about 1438 the Chancas were on the verge of conquering Cuzco and Viracocha Inca and his eldest son, Urcon, believed that their small empire was lost. Viracocha Inca's third son refused to give up the fight and rallied the Inca army with the help of some of the older generals. In a desperate final battle they managed to defeat and rout the Chancas. The victory was unexpected and the legend is that the boulders on the battlefield turned into warriors and fought on the Inca's side.

The younger son who defeated the Chancas took the new name of Pachacutec and proclaimed himself the new Inca over his father and elder brother. Buoyed by his victory over the Chancas he began the first wave of the expansion which was eventually to form the Inca Empire. During the next 25 years he conquered most of the central Andes between the two great lakes of Titicaca and Junín.

In addition to being a mighty military figure, frequently compared by historians to the likes of Alexander the Great or Genghis Khan, Pachacutec was a great urban developer. He devised the famous puma shape of the city and diverted the Sapphi and Tullumayo rivers into channels which crossed the city, providing water and keeping the the city clean. He built agricultural terraces and many buildings, including the famous Coricancha temple and his palace on what is now the western corner of the Plaza de Armas. Parts of the walls may be seen whilst dining in the *Roma* restaurant.

There was, of course, no Plaza de Armas before the arrival of the Spanish. Instead there was an even greater square divided by the Sapphi canal. The area now covered by today's Plaza de Armas was known as *Aucaypata* and on the other side of the Sapphi, in the area now called the Plaza Regocijo, was the *Cusipata*. Together, these formed a huge central plaza which was the focus of social life for the population.

Pachacutec was fortunate in having a son who was every bit as great a leader as his father. During the 1460s, Tupac Yupanqui, the tenth Inca, helped his father subdue a great area to the north which included what is now the northern Peruvian and southern Ecuadorian Andes as well as the northern Peruvian coast. Tupac Inca took over as Inca in 1471 and the empire continued to expand dramatically. By the time of Tupac Inca's death around 1493, the empire extended from Quito in Ecuador to south of Santiago in Chile.

Huayna Capac assumed power as the eleventh Inca upon his father's death and was the last to rule over a united empire. By the time he assumed power the empire was by far the greatest that had ever been known in the western hemisphere and there was little left to conquer. Despite this, Huayna Capac marched (he would, in fact, have been carried in a litter) to the northernmost limits of the empire, in the region today marked by the Ecuadorian/Colombian border. Here, using Quito as his main base of operations, the Inca fought a long series of inconclusive campaigns against the tribes of Pasto and Popayán. He sired a son, Atahualpa, who was born of a Quitan mother.

By this time Europeans had already discovered the New World, and various epidemics, including smallpox and the common cold, swept down from Central America and the Caribbean faster than the conquerors. About 1525 Huayna Capac died in such an epidemic. Shortly before his death he divided his empire giving the northern part around Quito to Atahualpa and the southern Cuzco area to another son, Huascar.

Both sons were well suited to the powerful position of ruling an empire; so well suited that neither wished to share his power, and civil war followed. Huascar was the most popular of the two contenders. He had lived in Cuzco for most of his life and had the following of the people. Atahualpa on the other hand, had spent most of his life in the outposts of the empire and had little support in the Cuzco area. However, he had the support of the army that had been fighting the northern campaigns. After several years of warfare, Atahualpa's battle-hardened troops defeated and captured Huascar outside of Cuzco in 1532 in the major battle of the civil war. The new Inca retired to rest in Cajamarca.

Meanwhile, Francisco Pizarro had landed in northern Ecuador and had marched south in the wake of Atahualpa's conquests. Although Atahualpa was undoubtedly aware of the Spaniards' presence, he was too busy fighting the civil war to worry about a small band of foreigners. By the autumn of 1532 however, Pizarro was in northern Peru, Atahualpa had defeated Huascar, and a fateful meeting was arranged between the Inca and Pizarro.

On 16 November 1532, the meeting which was entirely to change the course of South American history took place in Cajamarca. The Inca was ambushed by a few dozen Spaniards and the armed conquistadors succeeded in capturing Atahualpa, killing thousands of unarmed Indians, and routing tens of thousands more. The conquest of the Incas had begun.

The conquest succeeded for two main reasons. Pizarro, realising that the emotions of the recent civil war still ran high, decided to turn it to his use. Accordingly, he marched into Cuzco after holding Atahualpa prisoner (and then murdering him) and was thus accepted right into the heart of the empire by a people whose support lay more with the defeated Huascar than Atahualpa.

The second reason was the superior Spanish weaponry. Mounted on a horse, protected by armour and swinging a steel sword, a Spanish cavalryman was virtually unstoppable. The Spaniards hacked dozens of unprotected Indians warriors to death during a battle. The Indians responded with their customary weapons of clubs, spears, slingshots and arrows but these were rarely lethal against the mounted, armour-plated conquistadors.

Battle dress   Ceremonial dress   Judicial dress

Uniforms of the Inca emperor

Additionally, in the early battles, the Indians were terrified of the Spaniards' horses and primitive firearms, neither of which had been seen in the Andes before.

It took Pizarro almost a year to reach Cuzco after capturing Atahualpa. In an attempt to regain his freedom, the Inca offered a ransom of a roomful of gold and two rooms of silver. This was to be brought from Cuzco. To speed up the process, Pizarro sent three of his soldiers to Cuzco in early 1533 and they proceeded to strip *Coricancha*, the Gold Courtyard, of its splendid and rich ornamentation. Pizarro himself entered Cuzco on 8 November 1533, after winning a series of battles on the road from Cajamarca. By this time Atahualpa had been killed and Pizarro appointed Manco, a half brother of Huascar, as a puppet Inca. For almost three years the empire remained relatively peaceful and was 'ruled' by Manco Inca and Pizarro.

In 1536, Manco Inca realized that the Spaniards were there to stay and decided to try and rid his empire of them. He fled from the Spanish and raised a huge army estimated at well over 100,000 men. He laid siege to the Spaniards in Cuzco and almost succeeded in annihilating them. Only a desperate last ditch breakout from Cuzco and violent battle at Sacsayhuaman saved the Spaniards from complete loss and Manco Inca retreated to Ollantaytambo and then into the jungle at Vilcabamba.

The Inca Empire was an Andean one and so situating the capital at Cuzco in the heart of the Andes made a lot of sense. The Spaniards, however, were a seafaring nation and needed to maintain links with Spain. Therefore in 1535 Pizarro founded his capital in Lima on the coast. Although Cuzco remained very important during the first post-conquest years, once it had been captured, looted and settled, its importance declined. By the end of the 1500s, Cuzco was a quiet colonial town with all the gold and silver gone and many

The execution of Tupac Amaru I in Cuzco (Waman Puma)

of the Inca buildings pulled down to make room for churches and colonial houses. Despite this, enough of the Inca foundations are left to make a walk around the heart of Cuzco a veritable journey back through time.

Few events of historical importance have occurred in Cuzco since the conquest. There have been two major earthquakes and one important Indian rising. The earthquakes, in 1650 and 1950, brought colonial and modern buildings tumbling down whilst most of the Inca walls were completely unaffected. The only Indian revolt which came at all close to succeeding was led by Tupac Amaru II in 1780 but he too, was defeated by the Spaniards. The battles of Peruvian Independence in the 1820s achieved what the Inca's armies had failed to do but it was the white descendants of the conquistadors which wrested power from Spain and life in

Cuzco after Independence continued much as it had before.

The single event which has affected Cuzco the most since the conquest occurred this century. With the discovery of Machu Picchu in 1911 and the development of international tourism in the second half of the century, Cuzco has changed from being a provincial backwater to Peru's foremost tourist centre. Until the 1930s, Cuzco's main link with the outside world was via the long train journey to Lake Titicaca and thence to Arequipa. Now there is a modern international airport with daily flights to Lima and other destinations, as well as road links with the coast. Visiting Peru and missing Cuzco is as unthinkable as visiting Egypt and not seeing the pyramids.

Information

Tourist Information The official Ministry of Tourism on Calle Tecsecocha doesn't normally deal with tourist enquiries. The Tourist Information office is on the Plaza de Armas next to the church of La Compañía. They are open from 8.30 am to 12.30 pm daily except Sunday and from 2.30 to 5.30 pm Mondays to Fridays. There is a Tourist Information office at the airport but it's usually closed.

There's usually someone on duty who speaks English and they can give you up-to-date information about train schedules, opening hours, festivals and so on. They also have left luggage facilities and will sell you entrance tickets to the various sites around Cuzco.

Visitor Ticket It is difficult to buy an individual entrance ticket to most of the major sites in and around Cuzco. Instead, you have to buy the so-called 'Visitor Ticket' which gives access to fourteen different sites. This costs US$10 (US$5 for students with cards), is obtainable from the tourist office or from one of the sites and is valid for 10 days. This is good value if you want to visit most of the sites

but expensive if you want to go to just a couple of them. It is valid for the following places within Cuzco: the Cathedral, Santo Domingo and Coricancha, San Blas, Santa Catalina, the Historical Museum and the Religious Art Museum. In addition it is valid for Sacsayhuaman, Qenko, Puca Pucara, Tambo Machay, Pisac, Chinchero, Ollantaytambo and Pikillacta, all of which are outside of Cuzco. The biggest draw-back to the Visitor Ticket is that each site can only be visited once. Other museums, churches and colonial buildings in and around Cuzco can be visited for free or by paying a modest individual admission charge.

Student Cards Of all places in South America, Cuzco is probably the best place to have an international student card. Many admission fees into the ruins and other sites are quite expensive but you can usually get a discount of up to 50% if you present an unexpired student card with photograph. Wherever you go make sure to ask about student reductions.

Books The best source of general information about Cuzco and the surrounding area, including maps of the Inca Trail, Machu Picchu, and all the other sites, is the highly recommended book *Exploring Cuzco* by Peter Frost. It is available in bookstores in Cuzco or at the South American Explorers Club in Lima.

Two other highly recommended books are by John Hemming. The first is *The Conquest of the Incas* and the other is his large coffee table book *Monuments of the Incas* which is illustrated with superb black and white photographs by Edward Ranney.

Tourist Police Their office is on the north-eastern corner of the Plaza de Armas and they are open 24 hours. Some English is spoken and they're trained to deal with problems pertaining to tourists. However, they don't investigate cases. If you have something stolen they'll help you with the official police reports needed for insurance claims and will also tell you how to place a radio announcement offering a reward for the return of your property, particularly if it has little commercial value (eg exposed camera film, your journal or documents).

Money Exchange For the last couple of years I have found casas de cambio to give consistently better service than banks – better exchange rates and less fuss. There are several on the Plaza de Armas and along Avenida Sol. They are usually found in or next to souvenir stores or travel agents and so they tend to remain open for as long as the store is open – often till after dark and on Sundays. It's worth shopping around, particularly if you exchange a large amount, as exchange rates can vary. Many hotels will accept dollars but their exchange rates are not usually as favourable as the casas de cambio. Street money changers can be found outside the banks and casas de cambio but their rates aren't any better and so there's little point in changing money on the streets. The Banco de la Nación used to be the only place you could change money and occasionally, particularly during times of major financial flux, the casas de cambio close down. In this case try the bank.

American Express All travellers' cheques can be exchanged in the casas de cambio. The American Express agent is at Lima Tours but they don't sell or exchange travellers' cheques, nor will they refund lost or stolen travellers' cheques. These services can only be had in Lima. Lima Tours will hold American Express client mail addressed c/o American Express, Lima Tours, Casilla 531, Cuzco, Peru. Their street address is Avenida Sol 567 (next to Faucett airline) but they are open for mail collection only from 3 to 5 pm on Mondays to Fridays and so it's more convenient to have your mail sent to the General Delivery at the Post office.

Post Office The Post Office is open from 8 am to 7 pm daily except Sundays and holidays when it is open from 8 am to 12 noon. They will hold mail for up to 3 months if it is addressed to you c/o Lista de Correos, Correos Central, Cuzco, Peru. For some strange reason they have two sections for letters – a male and female one. So it's worth checking both sections in case your letter gets misfiled.

Photography Good selections of film are available in Cuzco but they are much more expensive than at home.

The best lighting is in the early morning and late afternoon when the sun is low. The shadows tend to come out very black in the middle of the day.

Some of the local inhabitants dress up in their traditional finery and lead their llamas past the most photogenic spots. This is not a coincidence! They will expect a tip for posing and consider this to be their job as a 'model' rather than begging. About 10c seems to be standard for a quick shot. Some tourists object to paying for these photographs – in which case they shouldn't take them. On the other hand, if you make friends with your potential model they will co-operate in getting you some professional looking shots which are worth paying for.

If you want to take some natural looking unposed shots please be sensitive and discreet. I hate to say it, but I often see travellers who are more concerned with getting a good photograph than about their subject's feelings. Not every one takes all that kindly to being constantly photographed doing such mundane things as selling vegetables, breast feeding their children, or loading up their llama. How would you feel if there were hordes of photographers taking your picture at the supermarket check-out stand, or whilst you were washing your car and wearing your oldest and grungiest jeans, or as you were trying to commute to work? It gets very old very quickly.

Top: Cathedral towers & colonial rooftops, Cuzco (RR)
Left: Plaza de Armas & Church of La Compañía, Cuzco (RR)
Right: Cathedral, Cuzco (RR)

Top: Llamas in front of the Cathedral, Plaza de Armas, Cuzco (TW)
Left: Blind musician on the Inca street, Hatunrumiyoc, Cuzco (TW)
Right: La Compañía floodlit at night, Cuzco (TW)

Laundry There are good laundry facilities in Cuzco. Two places will take your clothes in the morning and have them ready the next day, or the same evening if they're not too busy. They charge by the load rather than by the item so it's not too expensive. I usually use the *Lavendería Splendor* on Calle Suecia. There is another laundry on Procuradores. Both are within half a block of the Plaza de Armas.

Immigration If your tourist card is about to expire you don't have to go to Lima to renew it. You can do so at the *Migraciónes* office at Calle Santa Teresa 364 – there's only a small sign. This may cost you US$20 and they may only give you a 30 day extension so if you have the time you should consider going to Bolivia for a day and getting 90 days for free on your return.

Medical The best clinic is at the Regional Hospital on the Avenida de la Cultura (tel 223691).

Warnings

The two things to be careful of are the altitude and thieves. It's worth rereading the sections on Altitude Sickness and Security in the Facts for the Visitor chapter.

1986 Earthquake

The 1986 earthquake, while not severe enough to cause large loss of life, substantially damaged many of Cuzco's buildings. The ones which were hardest hit were generally on the streets running on a south-east to north-west axis. For some reason, the seismic waves caused much less damage to buildings on streets running on the south-west to north-east axis. Several buildings lost their entire upper floors and many lost their roofs. Many buildings are being supported by temporary pilings whilst repairs are being undertaken. Some of the hotels and other buildings mentioned in this book are now

closed, although most hope to reopen some time in the future. The most famous of the badly damaged buildings are the churches of Santo Domingo (over the Inca temple of Coricancha) and La Compañía on the Plaza de Armas. These were closed to the public during 1986 although it is hoped that they will reopen soon.

Things to See

There are four things to remember when sightseeing. First, buy your Cuzco Visitor Ticket. Second, carry a student card if you have one. Third, don't get so excited by what you're seeing that you forget about your pockets and your camera – thieves congregate in the same places that sightseers do. And fourth, opening hours are erratic and can change for any reason ranging from the caretaker wanting to have a beer with his friends to feast days such as Corpus Christi.

The Plaza de Armas This was the heart of Inca Cuzco (although in Inca times it was twice as large and named *Huacaypata*) and remains the heart of the modern city. Two flags are often seen flying above the Plaza. One is the red and white Peruvian flag and the other the rainbow coloured flag of *Tahuantinsuyo* – the four quarters of the Inca Empire. The Plaza is surrounded on all four sides by colonial arcades. On the north-eastern side is the Cathedral, fronted by a large flight of stairs and flanked by the churches of Jesus María and El Triunfo. On the south-eastern side is the very ornate church of La Compañía. Some Inca walls remain, notably the palace of Pachacutec found in the *Roma* restaurant on the western corner. The pedestrian alleyway of Loreto is a quiet and pleasant way to enter or leave the Plaza. Both sides of Loreto have Inca walls.

Churches

Cuzco's colonial churches are numerous, much more ornate and better preserved than in other cities – a direct correlation with the importance of the tourist industry in Cuzco. There are literally scores of churches and so only the most important are described. Visiting hours for churches are given below but they do tend to vary. A good time to visit is in the early morning when the churches are open for services. Officially, they are not open to tourists at this time but if you go in quietly as one of the congregation you can see the church as it is supposed to be – a place of worship rather than just a tourist site.

Religious festivals are a superb time to see the churches. I remember visiting the Cathedral at Corpus Christi one year when the church had been completely cleared of pews. In their place were huge pedestals supporting larger than life statues of various saints in rich vestments. Each saint was being venerated by candle light and there were literally thousands of candles illuminating the ornate interior of the church. The place was absolutely thronged with people including several bands of musicians who wandered around in the smoky atmosphere playing mournful Andean tunes in the saints' honour. As with many highland feast days it was a fascinating combination of ancient and colourful pagan festivities, sombre and prayerful Catholic rites, and the usual Latin American dose of modern mayhem.

Remember though, that these are places of worship so act accordingly, especially if you go when a service is underway. Photography is normally not allowed, particularly flash photography because the intensity of repeated flashes seriously damages the pigments of the centuries-old art inside the churches.

The Cathedral Begun in 1559 and taking almost a century to build, the Cathedral is not only Cuzco's main church but also one of the city's greatest repositories of colonial art. There are hundreds of canvases, many from the Cuzco school of painting. This is a style which combines the art of 16th and 17th century Europe

with the imagination of Andean Indian artists who had only a few Spanish canvases to guide them in what was considered to be artistically acceptable.

The Cathedral has been combined with two other churches. To the left as you face it is the church of Jesus María dating from 1733 and to the right is the church of El Triunfo. This right hand church is normally used as the entrance into the whole three-church complex. El Triunfo is the oldest church in Cuzco and dates from 1536. As you go in, look to your right to see a large painting of the great earthquake of 1650. The city of those days, as shown in the painting, is recognisable as Cuzco even today. The inhabitants are parading around the plaza with a crucifix, praying for an end to the quake. Miraculously, the earthquake stopped (don't they all?) and the city was saved. That particular crucifix has been venerated ever since and it can be seen in the main part of the Cathedral.

Right in front of the entrance there's a vault which contains the remains of the famous Inca historian, Garcilaso de la Vega, who was born in Cuzco in 1539, the son of a Spanish conquistador and an Inca princess. He left Peru in 1560 and died in Spain in 1616. His remains were returned to Cuzco just a few years ago by the King and Queen of Spain.

As you go into the main part of the Cathedral turn right. In the far corner is the entrance to the sacristy which often smells of fresh cedar and you can sometimes see wood carvers doing restoration work. The sacristy is covered with paintings of Cuzco's bishops starting with Vicente de Valverde, the bloodthirsty friar who accompanied Pizarro during the conquest. Look for Manuel de Mollinedo, Bishop of Cuzco from 1673 to 1699 and one of the most influential supporters of the Cuzco school of art. Behind an iron grille is a crucifixion attributed to the Flemish painter, Van Dyck.

In the corner of the Cathedral next to the sacristy is a huge painting of the Last

Supper. This is a fine example of the Cuzco school – a European style of painting with Indian influence. The supper consists of the Inca delicacy *cuy* or roast guinea pig.

At the very back of the Cathedral is the original wooden altar, behind the present silver altar which stands some 10 metres in front of the rear wall. Directly opposite the silver altar is the magnificently carved choir, dating from the 17th century and one of the finest in Peru.

There are many splendid side chapels. Some contain the elaborate silver trolleys used to cart the religious statues around during processions. Others have intricate altars. One of the most interesting is to the left of the choir as you face it and contains *El Señor de los Temblores* (the Lord of the Earthquakes) which is the crucifix carried around the plaza during the 1650 earthquake. It is blackened from countless votive candles which have been lit beneath it – nowadays the candles are kept well away from the statue to prevent further smoke damage.

The Cathedral is open for tourism from 10 am till 12 noon and from 3 to 6 pm.

Entrance is with the Visitor Ticket via the side chapel of El Triunfo. The main doors are open for worship from 6 am to 10 am.

La Compañía This church is also on the Plaza de Armas and is often lit up at night. It can be seen from the train as you come in from Machu Picchu after dark – a splendid sight. It's foundations contain stones from the palace of Huayna Capac, the last Inca to rule over an undivided and unconquered empire.

The church was built by the Jesuits – hence the name: the church of the Company of Jesus. Work was begun in 1571 but the church was destroyed by the 1650 earthquake. Reconstruction began almost immediately and the Jesuits planned on making it the most magnificent church in Cuzco. The Bishop of Cuzco complained that its splendour shouldn't rival that of the Cathedral and finally Pope Paul III was called upon to arbitrate. His decision was in favour of the Cathedral but by the time final word reached Cuzco the Compañía was almost complete. It has an incredibly baroque facade and is one of Cuzco's most ornate churches.

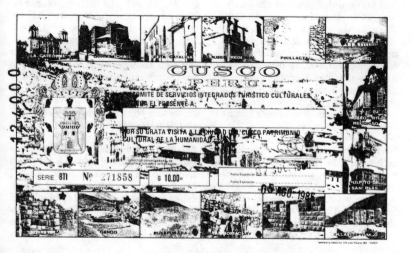

The interior has the usual array of fine paintings and richly carved altars. Two large canvases found near the main door show early marriages in Cuzco and are noteworthy for their wealth of period detail.

Before the 1986 earthquake, La Compañía was open for tourism from 11 am to 12 noon and from 5 to 6.30 pm. Entrance was free. Since the earthquake, the church has been temporarily closed.

La Merced This is generally considered Cuzco's third most important colonial church. It too was destroyed in the 1650 earthquake and rebuilt – the present structure dates from 1654.

There are two sections. The church itself is open for worship from 7 to 9 am and 5 to 7.30 pm. To the left of the church, at the back of a small courtyard, is the entrance to the monastery with a museum which is open from 8.30 am to 12 noon and from 2.30 to 5.30 pm daily except Sunday. Entrance is about 50c.

The order of La Merced was founded in Barcelona by San Pedro Nolasco in 1218 and paintings showing his life are hung around the walls of the beautiful colonial cloister. On the far side of the cloister is the church which contains the tombs of two of the most famous conquistadors, Diego de Almagro and Gonzalo Pizarro. Also on the far side of the cloister is a small religious museum which contains vestments said to have belonged to the conquistador/friar Vicente de Valverde. The museum's most famous exhibit is a priceless solid gold monstrance about a metre in height and covered with hundreds of jewels.

San Francisco This church and monastery, dating from the 16th and 17th centuries, is more austere than many of the other churches in Cuzco but nevertheless there is a large collection of colonial religious paintings and a well-carved, cedar wood choir. One of the paintings measures nine by 12 metres and is supposedly the largest painting in South America. It shows the family tree of St Francis of Assisi, the founder of the order. His life is depicted in the paintings hung around the colonial cloister.

Also of interest are the crypts which are not totally underground. There are two of them. Inside there are plenty of human bones, some of which have been artistically arranged to form phrases designed to remind the visitor of the transitory nature of life.

The monastery is open from 9 am to 12 noon and from 3 to 5 pm daily except Sunday. Entrance costs about 30c and you can have a Spanish-speaking guide (tip expected). San Francisco is not visited as often as the other major churches and you can often have the place to yourself.

Santa Clara This church is part of a strict convent and it is difficult to visit. Seeing it became a minor challenge for me and I finally found that you can usually get in for mass if you go around 6 or 7 am. Worth the effort because it's one of the more bizarre churches in Cuzco, indeed, in the whole of Peru.

It also dates from the 16th century. Inside, almost the entire interior is covered with mirrors. I've heard that the mirrors were used by the early clergy to entice the local Indians into church for worship. The nuns provide the choir during mass. They sit at the very back of the church, separated from the priest and the rest of the congregation by an ominous looking grille of very heavy metal bars which stretch from wall to wall and floor to ceiling.

San Blas This church is a comparatively small and simple one made of adobe. The main reason to visit it is to see the exquisitely carved pulpit which has been called the finest example of colonial wood carving in the Americas. Legend claims that it was carved by an Indian who miraculously recovered from a deadly disease – he subsequently dedicated his life's work to carving this pulpit for the church. Supposedly, his skull is seen nestled in the top most part of the carving. In reality, no one knows for certain the identity of either the skull or the wood carver.

San Blas is open from 10 am to 12 noon daily except Sunday and from 3 to 6 pm daily. Entrance is with the Cuzco Visitor Ticket.

Santa Catalina This convent is reputedly a beautiful building although I've never seen it because it has been closed for restoration during most of the 1980s. It has recently reopened – ask at the tourist office about hours of admission. There is also a colonial and religious art museum here. Entrance is with the Cuzco Visitor Ticket.

Santo Domingo This church is more famous as the site of Coricancha – the major Inca temple in Cuzco. The church has been twice destroyed; first by the earthquake of 1650 and later by the earthquake of 1950. (It was again damaged in the 1986 earthquake and is currently closed for restoration.) In the entrance there are photographs showing the extent of the 1950 damage. It is interesting to compare the state of the colonial building with the Inca walls which survived these earthquakes with minimal effects. Also in the entrance one can see a carved doorway in Arab style – a result of centuries of Moorish domination in Spain. Inside the cloister are the Inca temple remains. Round the outside of the courtyard are colonial paintings of the life of Saint Dominic. It is interesting to note the several representations of dogs holding torches in their jaws. These are God's dogs or, in Latin, *dominicanus* – hence the name of this religious order.

Entrance to both the cloister and the Inca ruins is by Cuzco Visitor Ticket. Opening hours are 9 am to 12 noon and 2 to 5 pm daily except Sunday (check to see if the church has reopened since the earthquake).

Inca Ruins in Cuzco

The majority of Inca ruins are outside the city and will be dealt with separately. The main ruin to visit within Cuzco is Coricancha. Other ruins have been converted into colonial or modern buildings but their walls can still be seen.

Coricancha This Inca ruin forms the base of the colonial church of Santo Domingo.

Coricancha is Quechua for 'the golden courtyard'. It used to be the richest temple in the Inca Empire but all that remains is the stonework – the conquistadors looted all the precious stones and metals.

In Inca times, Coricancha was literally covered with gold. The walls of the temples were lined with some 700 solid gold sheets weighing about two kg apiece. There were life-size gold and silver replicas of corn which were ritually 'planted' in agricultural ceremonies. Various other treasures made of solid gold were reported including altars, llamas, babies and a replica of the sun which was lost. Within months of the arrival of the first conquistadors all of this incredible wealth had been melted down.

The temple was used for various religious rites. The mummified bodies of several of the previous Incas were kept here and brought out into the sunlight every day. Food and drink were offered to them and then ritually burnt. Coricancha was also an observatory where priests kept track of major celestial activities.

The modern visitor must leave all this to the imagination. At least much of the stonework remains and it ranks among the finest Inca architecture in Peru. The most famous part of Coricancha is a perfectly fitted, curved wall which can be seen from outside the site. This six-metre-high wall has withstood the violent earthquakes which destroyed most of the colonial buildings of Cuzco.

Inside the site, the visitor enters a courtyard. In the middle is an octagonal font which was once covered with 55 kg of solid gold. There are Inca side chambers to either side of the courtyard. The largest are to the right and were said to be temples to the moon and to the stars. These were perhaps covered with more appropriately coloured sheets of solid silver, but the conquistadors' looting of the temples' riches was so fast and thorough that records are hazy. The walls are perfectly tapered upwards, and with the niches and doorways are excellent examples of Inca trapezoidal architecture. The fitting of the individual blocks is so precise that it defies the oft-quoted criterion of inserting a knife blade between them. Indeed, in some places you cannot tell where one block stops and the next begins when you glide your finger over the joint.

Opposite these chambers, on the other side of the courtyard, are the smaller temples dedicated to thunder and the rainbow. In this section three holes are carved through the walls to the street outside. The purpose of these is not known but various theories have been advanced. Perhaps they were drains, either for sacrificial *chicha* or even blood, or more mundanely for rainwater. Alternatively they may have been speaking tubes connecting the inner temple with the outside. Another noteworthy feature of this side of the complex is the floor in front of the chambers, which dates from Inca times and is carefully cobbled with pebbles.

The buildings described cover only two sides of the square. There was a larger chamber at either of the remaining two sides but only small segments of the foundations of these remain.

After the conquest, Coricancha was given to Juan Pizarro but he was not able to enjoy it for long. He was killed in the battle at Sacsayhuaman in 1536. In his will he bequeathed it to the Dominicans and the site has been in their possession

since then. Today's site is a rather bizarre combination of Inca and colonial architecture, topped with a modern protective roof of glass and metal. Visiting hours are as for the church of Santo Domingo.

Other Inca Walls in Cuzco None of the other Inca buildings in Cuzco are visitor sites in themselves but they can still be admired, mainly from the outside.

Walking south-east and away from the Plaza de Armas along the narrow alley of Loreto, you have Inca walls on both sides. The right hand side belongs to *Amarucancha* or the courtyard of the serpents. Perhaps its name derives from the pair of snakes carved on the lintel of the doorway near the end of the enclosure. Amarucancha was the site of the palace of the eleventh Inca, Huayna Capac. After the conquest, the church of La Compañía was built here and behind the church there is now a school. On the other side of Loreto is the longest surviving Inca wall in Cuzco, and also one of the best. It belonged to the *Acllahuasi* or the house of the chosen women. Interestingly enough, after the conquest the building became part of the closed convent of Santa Catalina and so it went from housing the Virgins of the Sun to housing the pious Catholic nuns.

Heading north-east and away from the Plaza de Armas along Calle Triunfo you soon come to the street of *Hatunrumiyoc* named after the great twelve-sided stone which seems to be on every sightseer's itinerary. The stone is on the right about half way along the second city block and can usually be recognised by the small knot of Indians selling their souvenirs next to it. This excellently fitted stone belongs to a wall of the palace of the sixth ruler, Inca Roca. Although technically brilliant, it is by no means an unusual example of polygonal masonry. In Machu Picchu there are stones with an excess of 30 angles (although these are corner stones and therefore are counted in three dimensions) and a block with 44 angles in one plane has been recorded at Torontoy, a minor ruin roughly half way between Machu Picchu and Ollantaytambo.

It is interesting to note the great difference between the wall of Hatunrumiyoc and that of the Acllahuasi. The first is made of polygonal stone blocks with no regular pattern whilst the second is made from carefully shaped rectangular blocks which are 'coursed' or layered in the manner of bricks today. Both styles were common in Inca architecture. As a rough rule of thumb, the polygonal masonry was considered stronger and thus used for retaining walls in terraces, whilst the coursed masonry was more aesthetically appealing to the Incas and was used for the walls of their temples and palaces.

Museums & Colonial Buildings

These are lumped together because many of the museums are in colonial houses and seeing the interiors is often as interesting as seeing the exhibits.

Archaeological Museum Housed in a fairly recent colonial mansion, the archaeological museum is the most interesting in Cuzco. The exhibits are steadily being relabelled in English, which is a great help to the visitor. There is a small but good collection of gold and turquoise miniatures, a large and creaky mummy room, and an extensive exhibit of ceramics. There are also paintings of the last Incas and some Inca clothing. Admission is 30c (but a price rise can be expected in the near future) and it's open from 7.45 am to 12.15 pm and from 3 to 5.45 pm on Mondays to Fridays.

Regional History Museum This building rests on Inca foundations and is also known as the admiral's house after the first owner, Admiral Francisco Aldrete Maldonado. It was badly damaged in the 1650 earthquake and rebuilt by Pedro Peralta de los Rios, the Count of Laguna, whose crest is above the porch. Further

damage occurred during the 1950 earthquake but it has now been fully restored and counts among Cuzco's finest colonial houses.

The architecture has several features to look out for; a massive stairway guarded by sculptures of mythical creatures, a corner window column which looks like a statue of a bearded man until you go outside when it appears to be a naked woman, and the plateresque facade. (Plateresque is an elaborately ornamented 16th century Spanish style which is suggestive of silver plate.) The interior of the building has been restored in colonial style and is filled with period furniture and paintings arranged in chronological order.

Entrance is with the Cuzco Visitor Ticket and the museum is open from 9 am to 12 noon daily except Sunday and from 3 to 6 pm on Mondays to Fridays.

Religious Art Museum This building was first the palace of the Inca Roca and then used as the foundation for the residence of the Marquis of Buenavista. Later it became the Archbishop's Palace and that is the name that it is still often called today. The church donated the mansion to house a good religious art collection. Many of the paintings are noted for their accuracy of period detail, particularly a series which shows Cuzco's Corpus Christi processions in the 17th century. The interior is also noteworthy for its colonial tilework.

Entrance is with the Cuzco Visitor Ticket and the museum is open from 9.30 to 12 noon and from 3 to 6 pm daily except Sunday when it is open only in the afternoon.

Other Museums There are two more small museums next to one another on Avenida Sol. The Natural History Museum has an uninspiring collection of stuffed animals and the Popular Art Museum has some rather undistinguished recent canvases.

The Tourist Information Office can

inform you of any special exhibits in town. Once in a while one of the banks brings a travelling show to Cuzco or there is some other exhibit of a temporary nature.

Things to Buy

The best area to see local crafts being made and sold is around the Plaza San Blas and the streets leading up to it from the Plaza de Armas. The San Blas area has built up a reputation as Cuzco's artisan quarter and it's interesting not only to see them at work but also to see the interior of some of the buildings. Prices vary greatly but so does quality, so shop around. The very best artisans may charge 10 times more for what, superficially, appears to be the same item as sold in a store on the Plaza de Armas, but the difference in quality is noticeable.

Bargaining is expected, except for a few of the more expensive stores where prices are fixed. Going to the general market to buy crafts isn't a good idea – neither the prices nor the quality are any better than elsewhere and thieves abound. If you like to shop in a market atmosphere then you can go to a crafts market – there's one on the corner of Quera and San Bernardo and another behind the Faucett airline office on Avenida Sol. You will frequently be approached by people on the street who want to sell you all kinds of crafts. This can become a little wearisome when you're not in a buying mood – the only thing to do is to say 'No, gracias' as firmly as possible and show absolutely no interest. The slightest spark of interest will inevitably result in your being pestered for five minutes. Finally, there is a nightly crafts market held under the arches around the Plaza de Armas.

Some of the best (not the cheapest) places are as follows: Taller Olave, to the left of Plaza San Blas, for reproductions of colonial sculptures and precolonial ceramics; Taller Mérida, Carmen Alto 133, for earthenware statues of Indians; and Josefina Olivera, Santa Clara 501, by the Machu Picchu train station, for old ponchos and weavings.

Tour Agencies

These are roughly divided into two classes. One provides standard tours of Cuzco and the various other ruins in the area and the other provides adventure tours: trekking, climbing or river running.

The standard tours include the following. A half day city tour; a half day tour of the nearby ruins (Sacsayhuaman, Qenko, Puca Pucara and Tambo Machay); a half day tour to visit the Sunday markets at either Pisac or Chinchero; a full day tour to the Sacred Valley (Pisac and Ollantaytambo and perhaps Chinchero); and a full day to Machu Picchu. There are many tour companies and most of them do a pretty good job. If you decide to take a tour, ask questions before you pay. Is there an English-speaking guide? Will there be a large number of non-English-speaking people resulting in the guide having to repeat everything in two or three languages? How big a group will it be? What kind of transportation is used?

Costs vary and so it's worth shopping around. The cheaper tours are liable to be crowded multilingual affairs whilst the more expensive ones can be tailored to the individual needs of one person. Kantu Tours and Pisac Tours on the Plaza de Armas run fairly cheap tours which are quite good. Milla Turismo, located in the Centro Comercial Cuzco building on the corner of San Bernardo and Ayacucho, is run by the extremely knowledgeable Carlos Milla who speaks excellent English and will provide you with a private vehicle and driver as well as a guide if this is required. He can tailor an itinerary to suit you. This isn't as cheap as going on a standard tour but if you form a small group it's quite reasonable. Various expensive agencies with offices in Lima also have their office in Cuzco. They cater mainly to private groups and include

Exprinter and Dasatour in the Hotel Cusco, Receptor and Universal Tours at the Hotel Savoy, and Lima Tours at Avenida Sol 567. There are many other agencies. It's as well to remember that anyone with a little extra time can visit all the places mentioned using public transport. This is very cheap and details are given further in this chapter.

There are also a large number of agencies which run adventure trips. One of the most frequently taken trips is rafting down the Urubamba for one or two days at about US$20 a day. The Inca Trail is another popular adventure. You can hire porters, cooks and guides or you can just rent some equipment and carry it yourself. Equipment available for rent in Cuzco includes tents, sleeping bags, backpacks and stoves – everything you might need for hiking. These items usually cost around US$1 to US$2 per item per day. On the whole, I've found that the better agencies don't just rent equipment. They prefer to organise their tours and provide porters and guides. However, the cheaper agencies will just rent equipment, so ask around if the first place you come to doesn't have what you want. There are several cheap agencies on Procuradores and around the Plaza de Armas.

The agency that I have used frequently over the years is Expediciones Mayuc, Calle Procuradores 354. They have a Lima office at Conquistadores 199, San Isidro, tel 225988 and 460028. They aren't very cheap but they provide excellent services for rafting the Urubamba, Tambopata and Colca Rivers. They also cover all the trekking routes in the area and they go to Manu. English is spoken. Another excellent general adventure agency is Explorandes on Procuradores 372, and in Lima at Bolognesi 159, Miraflores, tel 469889 and 450532. They are the oldest established and among the most expensive. If you're interested in mountaineering, then contact Peruvian Andean Treks on Avenida Pardo. They

have the some of the best guides and equipment for climbing the local snow-peaks.

You may have noticed that I haven't included lists of the cheapest agencies. Whilst you can get some good trips with them, they change names and owners quite often and are less stable than the more expensive outfitters. Your best bet is to check them out yourself and ask around other budget travellers for reports on how good or bad the cheapest agencies are.

Places to Stay

As befits the most visited city in Peru, Cuzco has about a hundred hotels of all types. Cuzco gets rather crowded during the dry season, which coincides with North American and European summer holidays, and so accommodation can be a little tight from June to August, especially during the 10 days before the major annual summer solstice festival of Inti Raymi held on 24 June. Nevertheless you will always be able to find somewhere to stay even though the best hotels are often fully booked for Inti Raymi. During the rest of the year it is a buyer's market and it is well worth bargaining for better rates – many hotels are almost empty.

Many travellers will want to spend some time visiting nearby villages or perhaps hiking the Inca Trail. Most hotels in Cuzco will be happy to store your excess luggage for a few days so you don't have to lug it around. Always ensure your luggage is securely locked and clearly labelled. Within a hotel it's unlikely that anyone will razor blade your pack open but light fingers may (rarely) dip into unlocked luggage. Don't leave any valuables in long term storage and ask for a receipt.

Bear in mind that several of the hotels mentioned below will be temporarily or perhaps permanently closed after the 1986 earthquake.

Places to Stay - bottom end

The cheapest place in town is the basic *Hostal Bolívar* which is often described as a classic gringo dive. This makes it sound undeservedly intriguing – but all it is, is the cheapest place in town. They charge about 30c each and the place occasionally gets checked by the police for drugs or passport violations. Most other cheap places charge a lot more. You'll pay about 80c each at the basic *Hostal Royal*, *Residencial Torres* and *Hotel Central*. Of these the last is the best and will store luggage for you. For about US$1 per person (doubles, triples, and quads only) you can try the centrally located *Hostal La Casona* which has a couple of rooms with balconies facing the Plaza de Armas. These rooms aren't easy to get but they're fantastic when there are processions in the plaza. They'll store your luggage and there's even hot water in the communal showers. Other basic hotels with hot water in the US$1 single and US$1.70 double price range are the *Hostal Colonial* and *La Posada*. The *Hotel Imperio* also has hot water, is right next to the Machu Picchu train station and charges US$1 per person or US$1.50 in rooms with private showers.

One of the best cheap hotels is the *Hostal Familiar* which charges US$1.30 per person in basic rooms. It is clean and friendly, has a pleasant courtyard and provides hot showers and safe luggage storage. A few rooms have private showers. The *Hostal Caceres* has singles/doubles for US$1.30/2.30. It is clean and has hot water and left luggage facilities but there aren't very many bathrooms. Similarly priced is the *Hostal Palermo* which has some Inca walls and serves breakfast. They have hot water and will store luggage. Also in this price range you can try the basic *Hostal Samari* or the *Hostal Panamericano* and *Hostal Limaqpampa* which are not so good.

For US$2 per person the *Hostal El Archaeologo* is popular with backpackers. It is clean and has a pleasant garden, but

there are no single rooms. Hot water and kitchen facilities are available. Similarly priced and also good is the *Gran Hostal Machu Picchu* which is a colonial-style building around a courtyard. There is hot water and some rooms have private bathrooms for US$4 per person. Other hotels for about US$2 single and US$3.30 double include the *Hostal Trinitarias* which has hot water and some rooms with private showers (rooms with communal showers are cheaper). It's reasonably clean and they'll store your luggage. Also the *Hotel Corona Real* which is friendly and convenient for the Puno train station and the *Hotel Peru* which is popular with Peruvians and is convenient for the Machu Picchu train station. These last two hotels have had recent problems with their hot water so check first if you want a hot shower. The *Hostal Belén* has rooms with baths and hot water for US$2 per person, but it is shabby and run down. Similarly priced is the *Hostal Monarco*.

Places to Stay - middle

The *Hotels Saphi* and *Cahuide* have been made into one hotel and offer simple but comfortable rooms with private bath and hot water for singles/doubles US$3/5 – bargain in the off season. It's a huge rambling building with a roof top garden to sit in, left luggage facilities and a breakfast cafeteria. The *Hotel America* (also known as *Plateros*) is clean and popular, has luggage storage and charges US$2.70/4 for singles/doubles in rooms with communal baths and has a few rooms with private baths for US$3.30/4.70. The *Hostal Los Portales* is clean but has an erratic water supply – ask for hot water an hour before taking a shower. They charge US$3/4 for singles/doubles with communal bath and US$4/6 with shared bath. They have several rooms with four beds.

There are several places for US$3.30 single and US$5.70 double; they're OK but not particularly good. The *Hostal Koricancha* has rooms with private baths and occasional hot water, but is rather dingy and run down. The *Gran Hostal Chavín* rarely has hot water and many rooms are without private bath. The *Hostal Meson* looks reasonably clean and has some cheaper rooms with communal showers.

The *Hostal Tambo Real* charges US$4/6 with bath, is clean and friendly, but has hot water only from 6 pm to 10 am. The *Hostal Aragon* charges about the same in the low season and is very good – their prices at least double during the high season.

There are several good hotels which charge about US$5.50/8 singles/doubles with private bath and hot water. The clean and friendly *Hostal Raymi* is recommended. It has carpeted rooms, is convenient for the Puno train station, has a small garden and is very quiet. Closer to downtown are the *Hotel Ollanta* and *Hotel El Sol*, both of which are good. The *Hotel Virrey* is right on the Plaza de Armas and has two rooms with plaza views. Similarly priced is the *Hostal de Inca* and the *Hostal Santa Catalina* – the last is old and somewhat run down, has an erratic water supply and you should bargain. It's friendly though.

The *Hotel Garcilaso II* charges US$6/10 singles/doubles with bath and hot water – don't confuse it with the more expensive *Garcilaso I* up the street. The *Hotel de las Marquesas* has wonderful colonial ambience and charges US$7 single and US$12 double for attractively furnished rooms around a beautiful courtyard. It's excellent value but often full. Similarly priced are the *Hotel Mantas* next to the church of La Merced and the *Hostal Loreto* which is at the Plaza de Armas end of the Loreto alley. Both are good.

Places to Stay - top end

The *Hostal Wiracocha* is on the corner of the Plaza de Armas but has no rooms with plaza views. There is a reasonable restaurant with excellent espresso coffee.

Rooms are about US$10/16 singles/doubles. The pleasant and friendly *Hostal Inti* has heated, carpeted rooms with a telephone. They charge US$14/22 and include breakfast in that price. At about the same price you can stay at the *Tambo Hotel*, the colonial style *Hostal Colonial Palace*, or the modern *Hotel Garcilaso I*. All are good. The *Hotel Espinar* is friendly and centrally located and charges US$15/22 but bargain in the low season.

Getting into the luxury class are the *Hotel Conquistador* for US$21/39 singles/doubles and the recently renovated *Hotel Internacional San Agustín* for US$26/37.

There are half a dozen first class hotels in Cuzco which all charge around the US$40 single and US$60 double figure. Despite the high cost, many of these are booked out by tour groups during the high season so if you want luxury book ahead through a travel agent. These hotels include the *Hotel Libertador* which is considered to be the best and most expensive; the *Hotel El Dorado* with an interesting lobby and a good though expensive restaurant with musicians; the new *Hotel Royal Inca* with no two rooms alike; the old, but good and central *Hotel Cusco*; the modern *Picoaga Hotel* and *Alhambra 2*; and the *Hotel Savoy* which, despite its five star rating, is the poorest of the first class hotels.

Places to Eat

As befits a city with such a cosmopolitan range of visitors, Cuzco has a great variety of restaurants and there is something for every taste and budget. With literally hundreds of eateries to choose from, I have limited this section to places I have tried personally. They can be very popular, especially during the busy season, so be prepared to wait for a table or make a reservation, particularly at the better restaurants.

Breakfast & Snacks Starting at the

beginning of the day with breakfast, one of the best choices is the simple and reasonably priced *El Ayllu* café next to the Cathedral. They always play classical music and have a great selection of juices, coffee, tea, yogurt, cakes, sandwiches and other snacks. It is a popular meeting place throughout the day. Two other restaurants on the plaza serve very strong espresso coffee for coffee addicts – the *Hotel Wiracocha* restaurant and *Chef Victor*. The latter serves huge and reasonably priced meals throughout the day and is good value. Other cafés which are good for breakfasts, snacks, and meeting people are the *Piccolo Bar* near *Chef Victor* and the *Café Varayoc* on Plaza Regocijo.

Local Food Several restaurants serve typical Peruvian food, are very inexpensive, often have outside patios and are usually open only for lunch or afternoon snacks. Monday seems to be the day off for many of them. The food is tasty and authentic, but people with very finicky stomachs might question the hygiene. Personally, I really enjoy eating lunch in one of these places and if you stick to cooked food it's unlikely that you'll get sick.

If you want to try something really Andean, then order *cuy* or roast guinea pig which is a delicacy dating to Inca times. Often this has to be ordered a day in advance. Other typical local dishes include *Anticucho de Corazon* which is a shish-kebab from beef hearts, *Rocoto Relleno* or spicy bell peppers stuffed with ground beef and vegetables, *Adobo* or a spicy pork stew, *Chicharrónes* which are deep fried meat chunks, usually of *chancho* or pork ribs and sometimes of *gallina* or chicken, *Lechón* or suckling pig, *Choclo con Queso* or corn on the cob with cheese, *Tamales* or boiled corn dumplings filled with cheese or meat and wrapped in a banana leaf, *Cancha* or toasted corn, and various *locros* or hearty soups and stews. The meal is often washed down with *chicha* which is either a fruit drink or a fermented and mildly alcoholic corn beer.

The local restaurants serving these Andean specialities are often called *picanterías* (literally spicy places) or *quintas* which are literally country houses, but here they are inns in the nearby suburbs. Often they have a *sapo* which is a popular *picantería* game, rather like darts in an English pub or pool in an American bar. The *sapo* is a metal toad which is mounted on a table – players have to toss a metal disc as close to the toad as possible with top points for throwing the disc into the toad's mouth. Men will sometimes spend the whole afternoon drinking beer or *chicha* and competing at this old test of skill.

One of the best *quintas* and closest to downtown is the *Quinta Eulalia* which has a colourful courtyard. Further afield is the *Quinta Zárate* with a nice garden on Calle Tortera Paccha in the eastern outskirts of town and the *El Mirador* on the longer eastern approach road towards Sacsayhuaman. Both places have good views of the city but aren't easy to find; take a taxi there and walk back. *Picanterías* within walking distance include *La Peña de Don Luis* and *El Fogon de las Mestizas* – both highly popular with Peruvians. Finally, the *Picantería La Chola* is supposedly the most 'typical' of Cuzco's restaurants and most nearly approaches a Cuzqueña *chichería* or Andean chicha tavern. It has been rather watered down to cater to gringo tastes – the best places are totally unsigned holes-in-the-wall which are best visited with Peruvian friends.

International Food Most of the restaurants in this section serve Peruvian food as well as international. There are several Italian places. My favourite, and the favourite of many travellers judging by the lines during the high season, is the medium priced *Trattoria Adriano*. They often have delicious dessert cake as well as great pasta dishes. *La Mamma Pizzería* serves ... you guessed it, and it's quite good though not especially cheap.

If you are economising, try the *Govinda* vegetarian restaurant run by the Hare Krishnas – don't worry, it's a restaurant and not a recruitment centre. The food is good, cheap and wholesome, and their bread lasts for several days if you want to take some on a trek.

Also fairly cheap are the Chinese restaurants of which one of the best is the *Chifa Hong Kong* near the *Hotel Ollanta* on Avenida Sol.

Dedicated carnivores with an extra dollar to spend should try *El Mesón de los Espaderos* which serves steaks, steaks or steaks. Get there early and sit in the attractively carved balcony overlooking the Plaza de Armas.

Peruvian Food Places included in this section defy precise descriptions as either local or international. Several clean restaurants on the Plaza de Armas serve a wide variety of good and reasonably priced Peruvian and international food. *Chef Victor* lacks ambience but makes up for it with huge servings. *Restaurant Roma* and *El Paititi* both have genuine Inca walls to dine next to, if that's what turns you on. *El Paititi* was part of the House of the Chosen Women and now offers slightly overpriced food in a white table cloth environment. Many people like it but I feel it looks better than it is. The *Roma* was part of the Inca Pachacutec's palace which after the conquest became the house of Francisco Pizarro. It was one of the first of Cuzco's 'good' restaurants and although it has since been eclipsed by slightly better ones, it still remains a good and reasonably priced choice. They often have local musicians in the evenings for which there may be a small cover charge. Tucked away and almost forgotten in the corner of the plaza behind the Cathedral is the rather undistinguished looking *El Tumi* restaurant which is moderately priced and good.

Gringo Alley This nickname is given to Procuradores (tax-collector's street) which is the alley leaving the Plaza de Armas on the north-west side. It has a good selection of cheap bars, pizzerías, restaurants, cafés and places to hang out in. It's popular with backpackers and is a good place to meet people. I can't honestly single out any place which is particularly good because names and owners seem to change periodically but it's a good street to check out if you're on a budget.

Most Expensive Some of the best hotels have excellent restaurants. Prices are high and often charged in dollars rather than intis. The food is rather too bland for my liking but it's popular with tourists who have particularly delicate stomachs and want to absolutely minimise their health risks. Local musicians often play. The best two hotel restaurants are at the *El Dorado* or the more expensive *Libertador*.

The fanciest non-hotel restaurant is the *El Truco* which has a nightly dinner and show (from 8.30 to 10.30 pm) and is actually quite good value. Reservations are worth making in the high season because it is a 'must' for tour groups. The food is good, the show is good and it makes a pretty fancy night out. They charge about a dollar cover for the music and about another dollar for 'table charge' (you have to sit at a table). The cheapest plates are also about a dollar so even budget travellers sometimes go for a look at the smoother end of Cuzco's night life.

Night Life

The *El Truco* and *Roma* restaurants mentioned above have live entertainment with dinner every night. But if you'd rather listen to your music in a slightly looser (and cheaper) bar environment then you'll find several places to choose from.

One of my favourite night spots is a dive on the Plaza de Armas across the square from the cathedral. It's the *Peña Hatuchay* and you can hear the lively music coming out of an upstairs window on the corner at the little street of Media. The entrance is not very obvious – it's up a small dark stairway in the middle of the block – ask anyone. The *Hatuchay* is to the left and at the back of the building. It's very popular with both locals and travellers and its main attraction is non-stop live *folklorico* music with several different bands playing during the evening. It's the longest running of Cuzco's cheaper night spots – many of the others change names, locations, or owners every year or two but the *Hatuchay* has been providing a good and consistent scene for at least five years that I know of. They serve only small glasses of beer or pisco with lemon and so the reason to come here is for the local music and the raucous atmosphere. There's dancing and it gets very crowded indeed. Be warned in advance that the toilet facilities are not for the sensitive – arrive with an empty bladder!

There are two more night spots in the same building. Just to the left of the stairs is the *Do-Re-Mi* which is a *criolla peña*, more popular with locals than foreigners. The music has a coastal influence and the singer keeps up a constant stream of terrible jokes and satirical comments – OK if you understand Spanish. One of their main attractions was a very flamboyant, tall and skinny black guy with huge hands who played the *caja* – literally a box that the musician sits on and drums with his hands. He would arrive around midnight wearing a pink suit and a wild grin and he had a great scatty voice to go with his appearance. The *Do-Re-Mi* was really fun in 1984/85 but seemed to go downhill in 1986, so go and decide for yourself.

Also in the same building is the *Los Violines* which attempts to be the poor man's *El Truco*, though it is usually almost empty. These places open about 9 pm but don't get going until after 10 and,

on a busy night, may stay open until two or three in the morning.

Other places on the Plaza de Armas include the new *Do-Re-Mi* which is on the corner of the Plaza and Calle Suecia and seems to be a cross between the *Roma* and *El Truco* but no better than either of them. Nearby is an upstairs club/bar which you enter through a guarded grille gate near the *Piccolo* bar about half way along the block. This club has gone through four name and owner changes in the last few years. In its most recent incarnation it's quite a good dancing bar with a member's only rule. Most travellers can get in by showing their passport. The club has an attractive balcony which looks out on the Plaza.

Another place that goes through frequent name changes is the club up the stairs at the north-western corner of the Plaza Regocijo, a block away from the Plaza de Armas. It's most recent name is the *Kamikaze* and it's a sixtyish sort of freak dive with a great variety of live music. I went there frequently in 1985 and was impressed by their performers – guitarists singing protest songs from Chile, traditional Bolivian highland groups, jazz musicians, local bands and classical guitarists among others. I hope the place stays open.

A block up from Plaza Regocijo, on Siete Cuartones, is a new English pub called the *Cross Keys* which is easily identifiable by the huge metal keys hanging outside. Inside, there's a dart board, English-speaking staff and a pub-like ambience. The pub is run by a British ornithologist, Barry Walker, and his Peruvian wife. A good place for a beer and a natter.

For people who like disco dancing, there are several places. Apart from the club/bar mentioned above, there is the *El Muki* which is just off the Plaza and in front of the *Hotel Conquistador*. It's a dark and smoochy sort of place with plenty of alcoves – they have a couples only rule at the door though they don't usually count if there's a mixed group going in. It's fairly expensive. There's also *Las Quenas* which is in the *Hotel Savoy* basement and is popular with Peruvians. Finally, mention must be made of the famous *Abraxas Bar* which used to be on the Plaza above the *Piccolo* and then moved to Herrajes 171 near the Religious Art Museum. It used to be *the* place to go for late night dancing but it recently has gone way downhill and caters to the less salubrious of Cuzco's nightlifers. It's near the police station, too!

Getting There

Rail Cuzco has two train stations which are not within easy walking distance of one another. The one near the end of Avenida Sol serves Puno and Arequipa whilst the station next to the main city market serves Machu Picchu and Quillabamba. Because of this, it has been impossible to travel from Arequipa or Puno directly to Machu Picchu. You must change stations in Cuzco. Note, however, that there are plans afoot of linking the Machu Picchu train line with the Arequipa station. If this should ever happen, then the Machu Picchu station will become obsolete.

The train for Puno leaves at 8 am daily except Sunday and takes about 10 hours. It passes through Juliaca at about 5 pm and so you can connect with the nightly train from Juliaca to Arequipa which leaves about 8.45 pm.

Tickets for the Puno train are often sold out in 1st class and so it's worth buying a ticket on the previous day if possible. The ticket office is open from about 6.30 am on Mondays to Saturdays to buy tickets for the train of the day. For advance sales try from 9.30 to 11 am and 3 to 5 pm on Mondays to Saturdays, and from 8 to 10 am on Sundays. The morning hours tend to be erratic. First class fares are about US$6.60 to Juliaca, US$7.20 to Puno and US$12.70 to Arequipa. Second class fares are about 25% less. Buffet and Pullman

classes cost an extra US$2.50 and $3 respectively, on top of the 1st class fare. For further descriptions of the classes see Arequipa. As always with Peruvian trains, be careful of thieves.

The Machu Picchu train, with several departures a day, is the most frequently used train in Peru. This fact, combined with the station's location near the crowded and busy central market, makes it a prime target for thieves. In recent years the Peruvian police has increased patrols around the station and on the trains. This has greatly minimised the risk of rip-offs, but you still have to be very vigilant because it's so crowded.

There is a bewildering variety of trains to choose from. Some go only as far as Machu Picchu and others continue to Quillabamba, which is the end of the line. Some are express and others are local, stopping everywhere. The *autovagon* is an electric train which is generally smaller, faster and more expensive than the other trains. Some services are designated for tourists only and are better guarded, have reserved seating and are much more expensive. To make matters even more complicated, schedules change very frequently and so the following information can only be used as a rough guide – you must check at the station before you travel to determine current services. Often an extra train gets laid on during the height of the tourist season (June to August). And of course, trains tend to be late very frequently, with the exception of the autovagon which is on time surprisingly often. Finally, bear in mind that there are plans of linking the Machu Picchu line with the Puno/ Arequipa train station.

If you'd rather use some other way of getting to Machu Picchu – you can't. There are no roads and the helicopter service of a few years ago has been stopped because the vibration of the choppers was damaging the ruins. Even if you want to walk in along the Inca Trail you must take a train to Kilometre 88 which is the starting point of the trek. So everyone uses the train to go to and from Machu Picchu.

Apart from Cuzco, the following stations are of interest to travellers; they are given in order away from Cuzco.

Ollantaytambo station can be reached by road and this enables travellers to visit the Sacred Valley ruins by bus and then continue from Ollantaytambo to Machu Picchu without returning to Cuzco. All trains stop here.

The halt at *Kilometre 88* is where hikers get off the train to begin the Inca Trail. Only the local train stops here.

The next important station is at Aguas Calientes but is misleadingly called *Machu Picchu* station. This station is served by all trains except the tourist train and is the place to go if you want to spend the night near the ruins without staying at the very expensive Machu Picchu hotel.

The closest train station to the Machu Picchu ruins themselves is called *Puentes Ruinas* and is two km beyond the Machu Picchu station. All trains stop here except for the Quillabamba autovagon – although they do sometimes if you ask in advance. The tourist train doesn't go beyond Puentes Ruinas so you must travel on the local train or the Quillabamba autovagon if you plan on continuing beyond here.

Santa Teresa station is 18 km beyond Puentes Ruinas and there is a tenuous road link with Cuzco (about 15 hours in a truck). It is also the end of Mollepata – Santa Teresa trek (see *Backpacking in Peru & Bolivia* by Hilary & George Bradt). There is a basic hotel.

The jungle edge town of *Quillabamba* is the end of the line.

A new train station is being built in Urubamba and may be operational by 1987.

The local train is the cheapest and stops everywhere. It is also the one with the worst reputation for robbery and you are better off travelling in 1st class. It leaves Cuzco daily at 5.30 am and 2 pm

and takes about four hours to Machu Picchu and seven hours to Quillabamba. First class fares to Machu Picchu are US$1.90 and to Quillabamba US$3. Second class is about 20% cheaper.

The autovagon to Quillabamba leaves daily at 1.30 pm and takes three hours to Aguas Calientes and 5½ hours to Quillabamba. The fare is about US$3.90 to Machu Picchu and US$6 to Quillabamba. Vendors are not allowed aboard and the autovagon doesn't stop at many stations so bring some food.

The tourist train and autovagon stops only at Ollantaytambo and Puentes Ruinas (for the Machu Picchu ruins). Normally, only round trip tickets are sold and the idea is that you go in the morning, spend two or three hours at the ruins, and return in the afternoon – a tiring day with inadequate time at the ruins. Nevertheless, this is the way that many, if not most, people visit Machu Picchu. It is difficult but not impossible to buy tourist train tickets to travel on separate days – it's best to go via a travel agent if you plan on doing this. The tourist train leaves at 8.20 am, takes about 3½ hours and costs US$16.50 for the round trip. The tourist autovagon leaves at 7 and 8 am, takes about three hours and costs about US$18.50 for the round trip. Students get about a 20% discount on these fares. Make sure to ask if the ticket includes entry into the ruins as this will cost you a further US$5.

There are two entrances with separate ticket windows. The right hand entrance serves the tourist trains and the ticket office is open from 6.30 to 8.30 am and from 10 am to 12 noon every day and from 2 to 4 pm every day except Sunday. The left hand entrance is for the local train and the Quillabamba autovagon. The ticket office for the train is open from 6 to 7 am and 11 am to 2 pm every day and from 4 to 5 pm from Monday to Friday. There is a separate window for the Quillabamba autovagon which is open from 12 noon to 1.30 pm daily and sells

Top: Inti Raymi Festival, Sacsayhuaman (RR)
Left: Chinchero Market (RR)
Right: A deformed & trepanned skull from Inca times (RR)

Top: River running on the Urubamba (RR)
Bottom: Llamas & Sacsayhuaman ruins overlooking Cuzco (TW)

same day tickets only. Note that the station entrance for the Quillabamba autovagon is to the side of the building – ask where when you buy your ticket.

Buses There is no central bus terminal. For buses to the Sacred Valley (Pisac, Urubamba and Ollantaytambo) go about one km east on Avenida Recoleta. You'll see a line of minibuses waiting to leave at frequent intervals throughout the day. This is rather far from the centre and thus inconvenient. Again, as with many things in Cuzco, there are plans afoot to change the Sacred Valley bus stop to a more central location. Ask at the tourist office or your hotel to see if they still leave from Avenida Recoleta. Many buses go only as far as Pisac and you should try and leave in the morning if you want to make sure of reaching Ollantaytambo. All fares are under a dollar. These buses will also drop you off at the Inca site of Tambo Machay so that you can walk back from there to Cuzco and visit the other nearby ruins en route.

For Chinchero there is a service from Avenida Arcopata. There are frequent trucks and minibuses leaving on Sunday mornings for the market; the fare is about 30c. On other days of the week you should go as early as possible and be prepared to wait, as service is infrequent and erratic. Trucks for Mollepata and Abancay and other destinations leave from here most mornings but, as is usual with truck services, there is no set time. Ask around for departure information.

For the road south-east of Cuzco there are frequent minibuses from Avenida Huascar to Oropesa and Urcos. These are the buses to take to visit the ruins of Tipon, Piquillacta and Rumicolca.

For the jungle try Transportes Quincemil which has several trucks a week to Puerto Maldonado. It is a wildly spectacular but difficult journey. The road is in bad shape and there are no buses. It takes two to three days in a truck from Cuzco and costs about US\$10. The journey could be broken at Ocongate or Quincemil where there are basic hotels. I've never gone beyond Ocongate except by air to Puerto Maldonado. I'd be interested in hearing from anyone who does this trip.

Next to the Transportes Quincemil office is Cruz del Sur which provides the south of the country with bus services. They have three buses daily to Sicuani (US\$1.60) and a bus every evening to Juliaca (US\$4.80, 11 hours) and Puno (US\$5.25, 12 hours). Most people prefer the marginally more expensive but much more comfortable day train. Cruz del Sur also has a nightly service to Arequipa via Imata. This is a rough journey on a little travelled road. It takes about 21 hours and costs US\$9. The service continues to Lima (42 hours, US\$17.50).

A cheaper but not quicker route to Lima is via Abancay (8 hours), Puquio and Nazca (33 hours). This is the most frequently travelled bus route between Cuzco and the capital. Ormeño provides this service every other day. You buy the tickets (US\$14 to Lima, US\$4 to Abancay) from their office on the Plaza de Armas but the buses leave from the station on Avenida Huascar. Morales Moralitos and Señor de los Animas has a similarly priced service but their buses don't look as good.

Empresa Hidalgo has two or three buses a week along the inland Andean route to Ayacucho. This is a very rough but spectacular road. Many consider it the most impressive (and difficult) route between Cuzco and the coast.

Note that all of these times are average, for good conditions. In the wettest months of the rainy season, especially January through April, long delays are possible.

Air Cuzco's airport claims international status because of the twice weekly flights to La Paz, Bolivia. All departures and arrivals are in the morning because frequent afternoon winds make landing and takeoff difficult.

Flights to Bolivia cost US$122 but you can pay with intis at the official rate which saves you about 20%. Departures are with LAB (Lloyd Aereo Boliviano) at 9.40 am on Tuesdays and Saturdays.

There are direct flights at least once a day to Lima (US$48), Arequipa (US$25) and Puerto Maldonado (US$21) with Faucett and AeroPeru airlines. AeroPeru sometimes has direct flights to Ayacucho (US$26) depending on the time of year. (All fares are approximate.) Same day connections are possible to Juliaca or Tacna via Arequipa and to most northern cities via Lima. Contrary to popular opinion, there are no direct flights from Cuzco to Iquitos; you have to fly to Lima and connect from there.

LAB, AeroPeru and Faucett all have offices in downtown Cuzco and don't normally sell tickets at the airport counters. The military airline, *Grupo 8*, does sell tickets at the airport. They have flights to Lima and Puerto Maldonado, usually on Thursdays. These don't always go, cannot be booked in advance and are often full. Although they are somewhat cheaper than the (already cheap) commercial airline fares, the inconvenience makes them hardly worth considering. The exception is if you want to fly past Puerto Maldonado to Iberia or Iñapari for the Brazilian border in which case you should enquire at the *Grupo 8* desk at the airport to determine when the next flight is (usually Thursdays) and show up packed and ready to go.

Airport departure tax is US$10 for international flights and US$2 for internal flights with the exception of flights to Puerto Maldonado which are not taxed. I'm told that this is because Puerto Maldonado is a developing area.

Flights tend to be overbooked, especially during the busy season, so confirm your flight when you arrive in Cuzco, reconfirm 72 hours in advance and then reconfirm again 24 hours in advance. If you buy your ticket from a travel agent in Cuzco they'll reconfirm for you. Ensure that your flight is properly and frequently reconfirmed and then check in at least a full hour ahead of departure time (two hours early is even better). Check-in at Cuzco airport is often chaotic and even people with confirmed seats and boarding passes have occasionally been denied boarding because of overbooking errors. (Don't get overly paranoid; this doesn't happen ALL the time.) During the rainy season, flights can be postponed for 24 hours because of bad weather. When flying from Cuzco to Lima, it's worth checking in as early as possible to get a seat on the right hand side for the best views of the 6271-metre peak of Salcantay – some of the pilots like to fly quite close to the mountain and the views are stupendous. From Lima to Cuzco, sit on the left. Occasionally, a different route is taken over Machu Picchu, but not often.

A taxi from the airport to downtown Cuzco costs a little over a dollar whilst the local bus costs a few cents.

Around Cuzco

THE NEARBY RUINS

This is the name given to the four ruins closest to Cuzco. They are often visited in one day and entrance is with the Cuzco Visitor Ticket. The ruins are Sacsayhuaman, Qenko, Puca Pucara and Tambo Machay. The most convenient, cheapest way to visit them is to take a Sacred Valley bus to Pisac and get off at Tambo Machay, which is the ruin furthest from Cuzco and at 3700 metres, the highest. From here you can walk the eight km back to Cuzco, visiting all four ruins along the way. Colourfully dressed locals and their llama herds often hang around near the sites hoping to be photographed. Tipping is expected (about 10c) and photographers trying for a free shot will meet with an unfriendly reception.

Tambo Machay

This small ruin is about 300 metres from the main road and consists of a beautifully wrought ceremonial stone bath and hence is popularly called 'El Baño del Inca'. Opposite it is a small signalling tower from where the next ruin of Puca Pucara can be seen. There is usually a guard at Tambo Machay who will punch your Visitor Ticket for this site and Puca Pucara as well.

Puca Pucara

Returning from Tambo Machay you'll see this small site on the other side of the main road. In some lights the rock looks very red and the name literally means Red Fort. It is the least interesting and least visited of the four ruins.

Qenko

This small but fascinating ruin is variously written qenqo, qenco, q'enqo, etc. It translates into zigzag. It consists of a large limestone rock completely covered with carvings, including the zigzagging channels which give the site its name. These are thought to have been used for the ritual sacrifice of chicha or perhaps blood. Tunnels are carved below the boulder and there's a mysterious looking cave with altars carved into the rock, so it's worth bringing a light. This ruin is on the left hand side of the road as one descends from Tambo Machay, about four km before Cuzco.

Sacsayhuaman

This huge ruin is the most impressive in the immediate Cuzco area. The name means Satisfied Falcon but most local guides cannot resist telling visitors that the long Quechua name is most easily remembered by the mnemonic Sexy Woman.

The most interesting way to reach the site is to climb the steep street of Resbalosa, turn right at the top, pass the church of San Cristobal and continue until you come to a hairpin bend in the road. Here you'll find the old Inca road joining Cuzco with Sacsayhuaman. Climb it to the ruins which are to the left at the top. This also makes a good descent route when returning from visits to the other nearby ruins. It is a short but steep climb taking almost an hour from Cuzco so make sure you are acclimatised before attempting it. The site is open from dawn till dusk and the guards are very active in demanding to see your Cuzco Visitor Ticket. Arriving at dawn will give you the site to yourself – tour groups begin arriving in mid-morning.

Sacsayhuaman may seem huge but what today's visitor sees is roughly only 20% of the original structure. Soon after the conquest the Spaniards tore down many walls to use the blocks for building their own houses in Cuzco. But they left the largest and most impressive of the original rocks, one of which weighs in excess of 300 tons. Most of them form the main battlements.

The Incas envisioned Cuzco as having the shape of a puma. Sacsayhuaman formed the head. The site is essentially three different areas, the most obvious being the three-tiered zigzag walls of the main fortifications. These 22 zigzags form the teeth of the puma and also are a very effective defensive mechanism – an attacker must expose a flank when attacking any wall. Opposite is the hill called Rodadero, with retaining walls, curiously polished rocks and a finely carved series of stone benches known as the throne of the Inca. In between the zigzag ramparts and Rodadero Hill lies a large flat parade ground which today is used for the colourful tourist spectacle of Inti Raymi, held every 24 June. The site is actively being excavated following the recent discovery of seven mummies behind the Rodadero Hill.

The magnificent zigzag walls still remain the major attraction of the site even though much of this fortification has been destroyed. Three towers once stood above these walls. Only the foundations

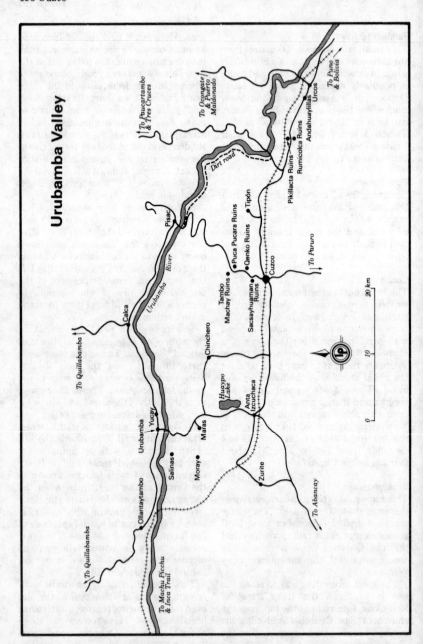

Urubamba Valley

To Paucartambo & Tres Cruces

To Ocongate & Puerto Maldonado

To Puno & Bolivia

Urcos

Andahuaylillas

Rumicolca Ruins

Pikillacta Ruins

Dirt road

Tipón

Pisac

Puca Pucara Ruins

Qenko Ruins

Urubamba River

To Paruro

Tambo Machay Ruins

Cuzco

Calca

Sacsayhuaman Ruins

To Quillabamba

Chinchero

Huaypo Lake

Yucay

Urubamba

Anta Izcuchaca

Maras

Salinas

Moray

Zurite

To Abancay

Ollantaytambo

To Quillabamba

To Machu Picchu & Inca Trail

0   10   20 km

remain but the 22-metre diameter of the largest, Muyuc Marca, gives an indication of how large they must have been. Muyuc Marca, with its perfectly fitted stone conduits, was used as a huge water tank for the garrison. Other buildings within the ramparts provided food and shelter for an estimated 5000 warriors. Most of these structures were torn down by the Spaniards.

The fort was the site for one of the most bitter battles of the conquest. About 2½ years after Pizarro's entry into Cuzco the rebellious Manco Inca recaptured the lightly guarded Sacsayhuaman from the Spanish and used it as a base to lay siege to the conquistadors in Cuzco. Manco was very nearly successful in defeating the Spaniards and it was only a desperate last ditch attack by 50 Spanish cavalry led by Juan Pizarro that finally succeeded in recapturing Sacsayhuaman and putting an end to the rebellion. Although Manco Inca survived and retreated to the fortress of Ollantaytambo, most of his forces were killed. The thousands of dead littering the site attracted swarms of carrion-eating Andean condors. This is the reason for the inclusion of eight condors in Cuzco's coat-of-arms.

THE SACRED VALLEY

The Vilcanota/Urubamba river valley, about 15 km north of Cuzco as the condor flies, is a beautiful place and worth visiting for a few days. The climate is pleasant because of the elevation (600 metres lower than Cuzco) and there is much to do – visit Inca ruins, bargain in Indian markets, stroll through Andean villages, or take an exciting river running trip down the Sacred Valley.

The most important points of interest in the valley are the ruins at Pisac and Ollantaytambo, both of which require the Cuzco Visitor Ticket for admission. Other lesser sites can also be visited. Accommodation is available in the towns of Pisac, Calca, Yucay, Urubamba and Ollantaytambo. Various tour companies

in Cuzco run half and full day guided bus tours of the Sacred Valley, visiting the Pisac and Ollantaytambo sites, but if you have a few days, taking local buses and staying in the valley itself is a rewarding experience.

River Running

One of the most pleasant ways to begin a visit to the Sacred Valley is to spend a day running the river in an inflatable rubber raft. Several companies do this almost every day. One which I have frequently used is Mayuc in Cuzco. For about US$25 per person they'll pick you up from your hotel in Cuzco, drive you to the village of Huambutio where the run begins, provide you with an experienced river guide, life jacket, paddles and lunch, and at the end of the day take you into Pisac. All your luggage can be safely left aboard their vehicle whilst you are on the river. The rapids are exciting (you'll get wet!) but not dangerous and you'll have a wonderful time. The views are splendid. Mayuc also have more ambitious river running trips on the Urubamba near Ollantaytambo, as well as trips of several days on the Tambopata, Colca and Manu rivers. There are other companies which also offer good trips.

PISAC

Pisac is 32 km from Cuzco by paved road and is the most convenient starting point for visiting the Sacred Valley. There are two Pisacs. One is the colonial and modern village lying alongside the river and the other is the Inca fortress located on a mountain spur about 600 metres above the river.

For most of the week, colonial Pisac is a quiet Andean village with little to do except sit and relax in the Plaza or go down to the bakery and buy some bread fresh from the old-fashioned clay oven. The village comes alive on Sundays, however, when the famous weekly market takes place. This attracts both tradition-ally dressed locals from miles around and garishly dressed tourists from all over the world. Despite being a big tourist attraction, this bustling, colourful market retains at least some of its traditional air. Selling and bartering of produce goes on alongside the stalls full of weavings and sweaters for the gringos. Many of the stall holders come from Cuzco and even after hard bargaining, prices in Pisac are no lower than Cuzco. The main square is thronged with people and it becomes even more crowded after the mass (said in Quechua), when the congregation leaves the church in a colourful procession led by the mayor holding his silver staff of office. Things start winding down about lunch time and by evening the village returns to its normal somnolent state. Note that there is a smaller market on Thursdays.

The ruins above the village are among my favourite Inca sites, partially because the walk there is so spectacular and partially because it is one of the less visited ruins on the tourist circuit and (except on Sundays) you don't see too many people there. The ruins are reached either by a new 10 km paved road climbing up the Chongo valley or by a shorter but steep footpath from the Plaza. There is little traffic along the road but it is possible to hire a pick-up truck in Pisac to drive you up to the ruins. The footpath to the ruins leaves town from the left hand side of the church. There are many crisscrossing trails but as long as you generally head towards the terracing you'll get to the ruins without much difficulty. Allow roughly 1½ hours for the climb.

The ruins are located on a hilltop with a gorge on either side. The west one (to the left of the hill as you climb up on the footpath) is the Kitamayo gorge and to the right or east is the Chongo gorge where the road ascends. Pisac is particularly well known for its agricultural terracing which sweeps around the south and east flanks of the mountain in vast, graceful curves. They are almost unbroken by stairs which would promote erosion, take up valuable cultivation space, require greater maintenance and make walking and working along the terraces more difficult. Instead, the different levels of terracing are joined by diagonal flights of steps made of flagstones set into the walls of the terraces. The terracing is in use today.

Above the terraces are some cliff-hanging footpaths which are well defended by massive stone doorways, steep stairs and at one point, a tunnel carved out of the rock. It is exciting to walk along these paths – the views are wonderful and a pair of caracara hawks often accompanies you. This highly defensible site guards not only the Urubamba Valley below but also a pass into the jungle to the north-east. Near the top of the terraces is Pisac's main religious centre with extremely well built rooms and temples. Some new excavations are under way at the back (north end) of the ruins; you can see a series of ceremonial baths being reconstructed. Remember to look across the Kitamayo gorge when you're at the back of the ruins and you'll see the cliff wall honeycombed with hundreds of holes. These are Inca tombs which unfortunately were robbed before being examined by archaeologists. The site is large and requires several hours, or a whole day, for a good look around. People occasionally camp near the ruins but there is no water. If you decide to spend the night, please don't light fires which are illegal; use a stove for cooking or bring cold food. A recent fire ruined a large portion of the vegetation above the terraces.

Places to Stay

Pisac is a small village and accommodation is limited, especially before market day, so get there early or do a day trip from Cuzco. The most popular place for budget travellers is the *Hostal Pisaq* on the square, which charges about US$1.70/2.30 singles/doubles, is reasonably clean and friendly and provides occasional and

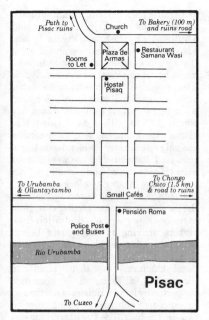

Pisac

erratic hot showers and meals. Cheaper but dirtier is the *Pensión Roma* by the bridge which has a few doubles for US$2 and dormitory-style accommodation for about 60c per person. A few houses rent rooms, there's one on the square near the *Hostal Pisaq*. The fanciest place is the *Chongo Chico* in an old farmhouse about 1½ km away from town. It has beautifully carved furniture and good home made meals, but the hot water supply is erratic. They charge about US$20 for a double room with breakfast.

Places to Eat
There are several very basic cafés. The best is the *Samana Wasi*. The *Hostal Pisaq* café isn't too bad. The rest have little to recommend them.

Getting There
Frequent minibuses charging about 30c leave from the stop on Avenida Recoleta in Cuzco. Some of these buses continue along the Urubamba Valley to Urubamba or Ollantaytambo. This is the cheapest way to go but also the most crowded. There are more expensive tourist buses from the many agencies in Cuzco, especially on market day, or you can hire a cab for about US$10. For returning to Cuzco or continuing down the Urubamba Valley, wait for a bus by the bridge.

CALCA
About 18 km beyond Pisac is Calca, the most important town in the valley, but of little interest to the traveller. There are some small and unspectacular ruins in the vicinity and a couple of very basic hotels. Most people go on.

YUCAY
Approximately 18 km beyond Calca is the pretty little village of Yucay with the fanciest hotel in the valley, the *Alhambra 3*, which charges about US$40 for a double room in a beautiful old hacienda. There is a small but interesting private museum. Next door is the *El Bohio* outdoor restaurant which is usually open for lunch.

URUBAMBA
About four km beyond Yucay lies the town of Urubamba, at the junction of the valley road with the Chinchero road. The town is pleasant enough, though not exceptional, and it can be used as a convenient base to explore the Sacred Valley. Continuing down the valley you come to the village of Tarabamba, about six km away. You can cross the river here and continue on a footpath climbing roughly southwards up a valley for a further three km to the salt pans of Salinas which have been used for salt extraction since Inca times. It is a little visited and incredible site.

Another interesting site is the experimental agricultural terraces of Moray. This is more difficult to get to. First you have to climb or get a ride on the steep road leaving Urubamba across the river and go as far as the church of Tiobamba. From here, take a track on the right three km to the village of Maras, and then it is a further seven km on the trail to Moray. It is sometimes possible to visit Maras by car depending on the condition of the road. There are no facilities except very basic stores in Maras, so you should be self sufficient.

Places to Stay & Eat

There are a couple of very basic cheap hotels in the town centre. The best is the *Hotel Urubamba* a couple of blocks from the central plaza and about 10 minutes from the main road. They charge less than 50c per person and are friendly. For a little luxury, try the government-run *Centro Vacacional Urubamba* which has a very cold swimming pool and comfortable, if impersonal, rooms with clean hot showers for about US$6/10 singles/doubles. There is an adequate restaurant. The best hotel is the very friendly and pleasant *Hostal Naranjachayoc* which has comfortable rooms with heaters and hot water for about US$16/22 singles/doubles. There is an attractive garden, good home made food in the restaurant and a roaring wood fire in the bar. Both these hotels are on the main valley road – the *Naranjachayoc* is on the Yucay side of town and the *Centro Vacacional* is on the Ollantaytambo side. There are simple restaurants on the main plaza.

Getting There

Minibuses leave Cuzco several times a day from the bus stop on Avenida Recoleta.

When I was last in Urubamba, a railway construction project was busily underway. It appeared that the Machu Picchu railway line was being extended to Urubamba and thus it may soon be possible to travel to Urubamba by rail.

OLLANTAYTAMBO

This is the end of the road as far as the Sacred Valley is concerned – only rail or foot traffic goes beyond. Ollantaytambo is, like Pisac, a major Inca site and admission is by the Cuzco Visitor Ticket. The site is a massive fortress and is one of the few places where the Spaniards lost a major battle during the conquest. Below it is the village of Ollantaytambo which is built on traditional Inca foundations and is the best surviving example of Inca city planning. The village is divided into blocks called *canchas* and each cancha has only one entrance which leads into a courtyard. Individual houses were entered from this courtyard and not direct from the street as in our city blocks.

The huge and steep terracing guarding the Inca fortress is spectacular enough to literally bring gasps of admiration from visitors arriving in the square below. Ollantaytambo is where Manco Inca retreated after being defeated at Sacsayhuaman. In 1536 Hernando Pizarro led a force of 70 horsemen supported by large numbers of native and Spanish foot soldiers in an attempt to capture the Inca. The steep terracing was highly defensible and Pizarro's men found themselves continuously showered with arrows, spears, stones and boulders. They were unable to climb the terraces and were further hampered when the Inca, in a brilliant move, flooded the plain below the fortress through previously prepared channels. The Spaniards' horses had difficulty manoeuvering in the water and Pizarro decided to beat a hasty retreat which well nigh turned into a rout as the conquistadors were followed down the valley by thousands of the victorious Inca's soldiers.

It is probable that the Incas themselves considered Ollantaytambo as a temple rather than a fortress but the Spanish, after their defeat, called it a fortress and it has usually been referred to as such ever since. The temple area is found at the top of the terracing. There are some extremely well built walls which were under construction at the time of the conquest and have never been completed. The stone

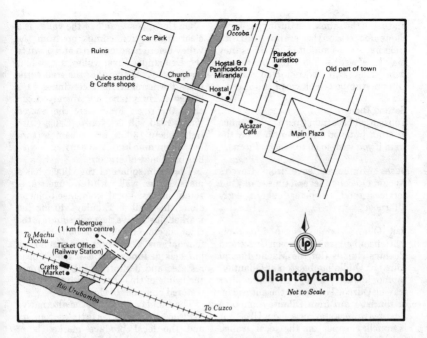

Ollantaytambo

Not to Scale

used for these buildings was quarried from the mountain side six km away and high above the opposite bank of the Urubamba river – transporting the stone blocks from the quarry to the site was a stupendous feat involving the man power of thousands of Indians.

Manco Inca's victory was short lived. Soon afterwards the Spaniards in Cuzco were relieved by the return of a large Chilean expedition and Ollantaytambo was again attacked but this time with a cavalry force over four times larger than was used for the first attack. Manco Inca retreated to his jungle stronghold in Vilcabamba and Ollantaytambo became part of the Spanish empire.

Places to Stay & Eat

The cheapest places to stay all charge about 75c per person. All are basic cold water places and include the *Hostal Miranda*, the unnamed hostal next door,

as well as a couple of double rooms for rent upstairs in the *Café Alcazar* which is also a reasonable place to eat. A better place is the *Parador Turistico* in a pleasant old building. They have the best restaurant in town, hot water sometimes and charge about US$3.50 per person. There are only 10 rooms which are often full but you can make a reservation by calling the Ollantaytambo telephone operator and leaving a message (if you speak Spanish). There are a few basic cafés on the plaza.

On the outskirts of town near the railway station, about a km from the centre, is the North American run *El Albergue*, a very clean, pleasant but rustic hostal. Washing facilities are limited to cold water buckets or the sauna. The folks who run the place have been there for many years and know the area inside out. They charge US$5 per person including continental breakfast and use of the sauna, but during the June-September season they are often full with trekking groups and at other times they may be closed, so don't rely on staying here. They can be contacted via the Ollantaytambo telephone operator.

Getting There
You can get here from Cuzco by either bus or train but you must continue on the train if you wish to go to Machu Picchu.

Buses Minibuses leave from Cuzco's Avenida Recoleta several times a day but services tend to peter out in early afternoon.

Rail Ollantaytambo is an important station and all trains between Cuzco and Puentes Ruinas (for the Machu Picchu ruins) or Quillabamba stop at Ollantaytambo about 1½ to two hours after leaving Cuzco. The fare in the autovagon or tourist train from Ollantaytambo to Puentes Ruinas station is about US$3 but is much cheaper on the local trains. Schedules change frequently and you should check at the Ollantaytambo station for exact information. Be sure to read the section on trains in Cuzco to find out which trains are running. Note that the local train is often extremely overcrowded by the time it reaches Ollantaytambo and standing room only is the rule rather than the exception in 2nd class.

CHINCHERO
This site is also visited with the Cuzco Visitor Ticket. It combines Inca ruins with an Andean Indian village, a colonial country church, wonderful mountain views and a colourful Sunday market.

The Inca ruins consist mainly of terracing, not as spectacular as at Pisac, but interesting nevertheless. If you walk away from the village through the terraces on the right hand side of the valley you'll find various rocks have been carved into seats and staircases.

On the opposite side of the valley is a clear trail which climbs up from the valley before heading north and down to the Urubamba River valley about four hours away. At the river the trail turns left (downstream) and continues to a bridge at Huayllabamba where you can cross the river. From here the Sacred Valley road will get you to Calca (turn right, about 13 km) or Urubamba (turn left, about nine km). You can flag down a bus until mid-afternoon.

The main square of the village has a massive Inca wall with ten huge trapezoidal niches. Local women sell chicha along this wall on Sundays during the market. Just above the main square is the colonial church which is built on Inca foundations. The church is in regular use but lack of funds means it hasn't been restored and it's interesting to compare the inside of this church with the highly restored churches of Cuzco.

The Sunday market is the alternative to Pisac's market. It is a little less touristy and the local produce market is of importance to inhabitants of surrounding villages. The crafts section is similarly priced to Pisac or Cuzco but the local people still dress in traditional garb which is good to see. If you come midweek, when there is no market and few tourists, you'll still see the women dressed in traditional clothing and so it's obvious that their Sunday get-up isn't just for the tourists.

Places to Stay & Eat
There is a small cheap hotel but it's not always open. The tourist office in Cuzco may have current information. The hotel may provide meals but there is no restaurant. A village store will sell very basic supplies. Camping is possible below the terracing.

Getting There
Trucks leave from Calle Arcopata in Cuzco early every morning. Minibuses leave fairly frequently on Sunday

mornings for the market. This service is slowly expanding to include one or two minibuses on weekdays.

THE INCA TRAIL

This is the best known and most popular hike on the continent and is walked by thousands of people every year. Many of these adventurers are not prepared for the trip. Every guidebook to South America at least describes the trail and most provide a map. I do the same in self defense as much as anything else. If walking to Machu Picchu has been a lifelong ambition then go ahead and enjoy yourself – it certainly is an exceptional hike. If you are an experienced backpacker looking for solitude or remote mountain villages, then I suggest hiking any one of the many other available trails.

If you do decide that the Inca Trail is not to be missed, please don't defecate in the ruins, don't leave garbage anywhere, don't damage the stonework by building fires against the walls (it blackens and, worse still, cracks the rocks), and don't pick the orchids and other plants in this National Park. I'm sure 99% of my readers wouldn't consider doing any of the above but there is the one person in a hundred who will thoughtlessly cause more damage than the other ninety nine. The South American Explorers Club organised an Inca Trail clean-up in 1980 and collected about 400 kg of unburnable garbage. Other clean-up campaigns since then record similar figures. Please carry out your empty cans and other trash and make an attempt to bury your faeces away from the trail and water sources.

You can hike with just what you can carry on your back or you can hire porters, guides and cooks. Many budget travellers elect to hire just one porter to carry a pack – this is inexpensive. You should carry a stove as wood is scarce, a sleeping pad and warm bag, and a tent or other protection against the rain. All this equipment can be rented inexpensively in Cuzco. Also bring insect repellent, suntan lotion,

water purification tablets or iodine and basic first aid supplies. I know of people who have 'done' the Inca Trail with a sheet of plastic and a bag of peanuts. Fine. They can go hungry and freeze if they want to but such behaviour is irresponsible and foolish. The trek takes three full days, the temperatures can go below freezing at night and it rains even in the dry season. There is nowhere to buy food. The ruins are roofless and don't provide shelter. Caves marked on some maps are usually wet and dirty overhangs. Although the total distance is only 33 km, there are three high passes to be crossed, one of which reaches a height of 4200 metres. The trail is often steep, so don't be lulled into a false sense of security because it is a relatively short distance. Hike prepared.

You can obtain detailed maps and information in Lima at the South American Explorers Club as well as from trekking agencies and the tourist office in Cuzco. Many maps do not include the new section of trail joining Phuyupatamarca with Huiñay Huayna. Most maps, with the notable exception of the one available from the SA Explorers Club, don't have contours marked on them. The trail is fairly obvious for most of the way and it is difficult to get lost, especially if you carry a compass. The map in this book is perfectly adequate. There have been occasional reports of robberies on the trail and you are advised to travel in a group rather than singly. The dry season from June to September is the most popular time and also the most crowded. The trail is fairly empty during the rest of the year but it is also very wet and the mud can be 30 cm deep for long stretches.

I hope this information has helped to put things into a realistic perspective. All the other things you may have read about the trail are also true. The views of snow capped mountains and high cloud forest can be stupendous, weather permitting. Walking from one beautiful ruin to the next is a mystical and unforgettable experience. Enjoy the hike but please don't spoil it for the people coming after you.

Getting There

The normal way is to take the train from Cuzco to Kilometre 88. The tourist train and autovagon don't stop here and so you have to take the local train, which has a well deserved reputation for thievery. Watch your pack like a hawk. Watch for thieves who distract your attention whilst your camera is snatched, your pack slashed or your pockets picked.

Ask where to get off because although everyone knows the stop it is very small and badly marked. At Kilometre 88 you cross the river; there is now a footbridge as well as the ski-lift-type contraption which used to be the only way across. As you cross the river you have to either buy a trail permit or present one obtained from the Ministerio de Cultura in Cuzco. It's easier to buy it at the trail head (but check with the Cuzco tourist Office for the latest in the ever-changing regulations.) The fee is about US$7 (there's a discount for students with cards) but includes entrance into Machu Picchu which itself runs at about US$5. You're ready to begin the walk.

An alternative way to begin the Inca Trail is to walk along the south bank of the Urubamba River from Ollantaytambo where the river is crossed. Although I have never done this, reports indicate that it adds a pleasant 20 km to the trip and that the trail is easy and well marked until you run into the Inca Trail at Llactapata, about a km up from Kilometre 88.

You aren't allowed to bring backpacks into Machu Picchu and doing the hike in reverse, i.e. from Machu Picchu to Kilometre 88, is not permitted.

The Hike

Quechua names are given with English translations in parentheses. It is interesting to note that various translations

are possible and often the most frequently given ones are not necessarily the best or most accurate. Anthropologist Cristina Kessler-Noble has provided me with some interesting variations.

After crossing the Urubamba River (2200 metres) and taking care of trail fees and registration formalities, you have two choices. Turn right (west) to see the little visited site of Q'ente (hummingbird) one km away, or turn left and begin the Inca Trail as it climbs gently through a eucalyptus grove for about one km. The minor ruin of Llactapata (town on hillside) is passed to your right and soon you cross the Río Cusichaca (joyful bridge) on a footbridge and head south along the east bank of the river. Although there are camping possibilities just before Llactapata, most people elect to continue to the village of Huayllabamba (grassy plain) on the first day. It's about seven km along the river to the village, climbing gently all the way and recrossing the river after about four km. Look over your shoulder for views of the snowcapped Veronica, 5750 metres.

Huayllabamba is a tiny village five or 10 minutes above the fork of the Llullucha (a type of herb) and Cusichaca rivers at an elevation of about 2750 metres. The Llullucha is crossed by a log bridge. It is possible to camp in the plaza in front of the school but beware of thieves slitting your tent at night. You can continue south along the Cusichaca to the ruins of Paucarcancha about three km away if you want to get away from the crowds. Camping is possible at the ruins but carry water up from the river.

The Inca Trail itself climbs steeply up along the south bank of the Llullucha river. After about half an hour the river forks. Continue up the left fork for 500 metres and then cross the river on a log bridge. There are several flat campsites on both sides of the bridge. The area is known as three white stones although I've never figured out exactly which boulders are referred to. This site is usually the

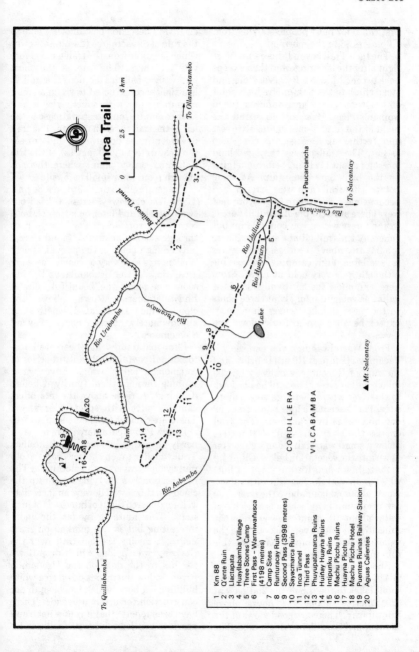

Inca Trail

0   2.5   5 km

To Quillabamba

To Ollantaytambo

To Salcantay

Rio Urubamba

Rio Pacamayo

Rio Cusichaca

Rio Llullucha

Rio Huaynuro

Rio Aobamba

Railway Tunnel

Dam

Lake

CORDILLERA VILCABAMBA

▲ Mt Salcantay

• Paucarcancha

1   Km 88
2   Q'ente Ruin
3   Llactapata
4   Huayllabamba Village
5   Three Stones Camp
6   First Pass – Warmiwañusca (4198 metres)
7   Camp Sites
8   Runturacay Ruin
9   Second Pass (3998 metres)
10   Sayacmarca Ruin
11   Inca Tunnel
12   Third Pass
13   Phuyupatamarca Ruins
14   Huiñay Huayna Ruins
15   Intipunku Ruins
16   Machu Picchu Ruins
17   Huayna Picchu
18   Machu Picchu Hotel
19   Puentes Ruinas Railway Station
20   Aguas Calientes

first camp for most people starting from Kilometre 88 in the morning.

The Inca Trail beyond this camp turns right after the log bridge and then sweeps back to the Llullucha. It is a very long and steep climb to the 4198-metre high point of the trek, the Warmiwañusca (dead woman's) Pass. It's best to spend the night at the three stones campsite to rest and further acclimatise for the steep ascent. The trail passes through cloud forest for about 1½ hours before emerging on the high bare mountain. At some points the trail and the stream bed become one – so prepare to get your feet wet. There are a couple of small flat areas in the forest where you could camp but generally the trail climbs steeply. There is a flat area above the forest where water is available and camping is possible although it is very cold at night. From here you follow the left hand side of the valley as you climb for about three hours to the pass. It takes longer than you'd expect because the altitude slows you down.

From Warmiwañusca you can see the Pacamayo (sunrise) River far below and the ruin of Runturacay halfway up the hill above the river. The trail heads down to the river where there are good campsites. The descent is a long knee straining one and takes over an hour. The trail crosses the river at about 3600 metres below a small waterfall – don't go too far down into the vegetation below. Climb up to the right towards Runturacay (egg hut) which is an oval shaped ruin with superb views, about an hour above the river. You can also camp here – there is a trickle of water about 10 minutes away from the ruins to your left as you look out into the valley. Previous campers have left this ruin in an unsavoury condition.

Above Runturacay the trail climbs to a false summit, then continues past two small lakes to the top of the 2nd pass at 3998 metres, about 1½ hours above Runturacay. There are good views of the snowcapped Cordillera Vilcabamba. The

clear trail descends past another lake to the ruin of Sayacmarca (dominant town) which is visible from the trail a km before you get there. The site is the most impressive of all this far along the trail. It is a tightly constructed town on a small mountain spur with superb views. You have to climb a long steep staircase to the left of the trail to reach the site. The trail itself continues downwards and crosses the headwaters (3600 metres) of the Rio Aobamba (wavy plain) where there is enough room for a small campsite.

The gentle climb to the 3rd pass begins. There is a causeway across a dried out swampy lake and later on a tunnel, both Inca constructions. The trail goes through some beautiful cloud forest but the high point of the pass at almost 3700 metres isn't very obvious. There are great views of the Urubamba valley and soon you reach the beautiful ruin of Phuyupatamarca (town above the clouds) which is at about 3650 metres and approximately three hours beyond Sayacmarca.

Phuyupatamarca has been well restored and contains a beautiful series of ceremonial baths which have water running through them (purify it before drinking). A ridge above the site offers camping sites with spectacular views. There are camp guards here sometimes.

From Phuyupatamarca there is a newly opened (1985) section of the Inca Trail which is much shorter than the old route which traverses the mountain. The new section is a dizzying drop into the cloud forest below, following an incredibly well-engineered flight of hundreds of Inca steps. This route is by far the more interesting but is not marked on most maps. It rejoins the old trail near the electric power pylons which drop down the hill to the dam on the Urubamba River. Follow the pylons down to a white building – a hotel which has been under construction for about a decade. There have been reports that it is now open and provides youth hostel type facilities for about US$1.30 per person. Don't rely on this though. Camping is possible nearby. A 500-metre trail behind the hotel leads to the beautiful Inca site of Huiñay Huayna which cannot be seen from the hotel.

Huiñay Huayna is normally translated as 'forever young'. An alternate and much more attractive translation was recently explained to me. Huiñay is the Quechua infinitive for 'to plant the earth' and thus a more accurate translation may be 'to plant the earth, young' – perhaps a reference to the young springtime earth of planting time. Anyway, from planting comes growing, and thus one has 'growing young' as opposed to 'growing old' and hence the popular catchall translation of 'forever young'.

Whatever it means, it is a small but exquisite place and deserves the short side trip and an hour or two of exploration. Climb down to the lowest part of the town where it tapers off into a tiny and very exposed ledge overlooking the Urubamba River far below. This ruin is about a three-hour descent from Phuyupatamarca.

From Huiñay Huayna the trail contours around through the cliff-hanging cloud forest and is very thin in places, so watch your step. It takes about 2½ hours to reach the penultimate site on the trail, Intipunku (sun gate). The first view of Machu Picchu is had here. There is room for a couple of tents but no water. This is the last point where you're allowed to camp on the Inca Trail.

From Intipunku to Machu Picchu is a ½-hour descent. Backpacks aren't allowed into the ruins and immediately upon arrival you are asked to check your pack at the lower entrance gate and have your trail permit stamped. It is rather a brusque return to rules and regulations – all you want to do is quietly explore the ruins but park guards insist that you check your pack and permit first. Remember that the pass is valid for only the day it is stamped so try to arrive in the morning. Sometimes you can persuade the guards to stamp it for the next day.

You have several choices of what to do after you've explored the ruins. You can stay at the expensive hotel near the site or camp on the road below the site (see Machu Picchu). Or you can take the six km road (buses available) down from the ruins to the railway line and go to the village of Aguas Calientes which is two km up the railway tracks. Here, there are basic and cheap hotels, restaurants and hot springs (see Aguas Calientes). Or you can take the afternoon train and be in Cuzco, Ollantaytambo or Quillabamba that evening.

MACHU PICCHU

This is without any doubt the best known and most spectacular archaeological site on the continent. During the busy dry season months of June to September, up to a thousand people daily come to visit the Lost City of the Incas, as Machu Picchu is popularly known. Despite this great tourist influx, the site manages to retain its air of grandeur and mystery and is to be considered a 'must' for all visitors to Peru.

Machu Picchu is both the best known and the least known of Inca ruins. It was not mentioned in any of the chronicles of the Spanish conquistadors and today archaeologists can do no more than speculate as to its function. Although it was known to a handful of Quechua peasants who farmed the area, the outside world was unaware of its existence until the American historian Hiram Bingham stumbled upon it almost by accident on 24 July 1911. Bingham's search was for the lost city of Vilcabamba, the last stronghold of the Incas, and he thought that he had found it at Machu Picchu. We now know that the remote and difficult to reach site of Espiritu Pampa, much deeper into the jungle, is the site of Vilcabamba and that Machu Picchu is a mysterious site which was never revealed to the Spanish and well nigh forgotten until just 75 years ago.

When the site was discovered in 1911 it was very different to what we see today. All the buildings were thickly overgrown with vegetation and Bingham's team had to be content with roughly mapping the site. Bingham returned in 1912 and 1915 to carry out the difficult task of clearing the thick forest from the ruins and he also discovered some of the ruins on the Inca Trail. Further studies and clearing were carried out by Peruvian archaeologist Luis E Valcárcel in 1934 and a Peruvian-American expedition under Paul Fejos in 1940-41. Despite these and more recent studies, our knowledge of Machu Picchu remains sketchy. Over 50 burial sites were discovered and these contained over 100 skeletal remains. About 80% of these were female. An early theory claims that this was a city of chosen women who catered to the Incas' needs but this theory has lost support. It is now thought that Machu Picchu was already an uninhabited and forgotten city at the time of the conquest. This would explain why it wasn't mentioned to the Spaniards. One thing is obvious; the exceptionally high quality of the stonework and the abundance of sites which are ornamental rather than practical, indicate that Machu Picchu must have once been an important ceremonial centre.

There have been two recent reports of new discoveries in the area. The first, in the early 1980s, was of some burial sites on Huayna Picchu mountain. The most recent, in late 1986, reports the exciting discovery of a new city about twice the size of Machu Picchu and five km to the north of it, according to a Peruvian government spokesman. Local and US archaeologists have named the city Marampata. Neither of these places are easily accessible to the general public.

Inside the Ruins

Unless you arrive on the Inca Trail, you'll officially enter the ruins through a guarded ticket gate on the south side of Machu Picchu. About 100 metres of footpath will bring you to the maze-like entrance of Machu Picchu proper – the ruins lie stretched out before you. They are roughly divided into two areas separated by a series of plazas and it is the area to the left of the plazas which contains the majority of the most interesting sites. Immediately after the entrance there are Agricultural Terraces above and below you. Beyond these terraces there is a long staircase climbing up to your left. This leads to a hut on the south-east spur overlooking the ruins and gives the best vantage point for the 'classic' photograph and most complete overall view of the site.

This hut is known as the Hut of the Caretaker of the Funerary Rock and is one of the few buildings which has been restored with a thatched roof – which makes it a good shelter in case of rain. The Inca Trail enters the city just below this hut. Behind the hut is a carved rock which may have been used to mummify the nobility and which explains the name of the hut.

If you continue straight into the ruins, instead of climbing the stairs to the hut just described, you soon come to a beautiful series of sixteen connected Ceremonial Baths that cascade across the ruins accompanied by a flight of stairs. Just above and to the left of the baths is the one round building of Machu Picchu: the Temple of the Sun. This curved and tapering tower is said to contain Machu Picchu's finest stonework. Inside is an altar and a curiously drilled trapezoidal window which looks out on the site. This window is popularly named the Serpent Window but it's unlikely that snakes lived in the holes around it. More likely the holes were used to suspend a ceremonial gold sun disk. Below the tower is an almost hidden natural rock cave which the Inca's stonemasons carefully carved with a step-like altar and sacred niches. Mummies were discovered in this site which gives it the name of the Royal Tomb.

Top: Inca trail porters in traditional clothes (RR)
Left: Descending steps on the Inca trail (RR)
Right: The train for Machu Picchu pauses in Ollantaytambo (TW)

Top: Alpaca at Machu Picchu (RR)
Left: Machu Picchu (RR)
Right: Machu Picchu, the traditional view (TW)

Climbing the stairs above the Ceremonial Baths you come to a flat area of jumbled rocks, once used as a quarry. Turn right at the top of the stairs and walk across the quarry on a short path which leads to the four-sided Sacred Plaza. The far side contains a small lookout platform with a curved wall and a beautiful view of the snowcapped Cordillera Vilcabamba above. Below, you can see the Urubamba River and the modern buildings of a hydro-electric project. The remaining three sides of the Sacred Plaza are flanked by important buildings. The Temple of the Three Windows commands an impressive view of the plaza below as seen through the huge trapezoidal windows which give the building its name. With this temple behind you, the Principal Temple is to your right. Its name derives from the massive solidity and perfection of its construction. Although the rear right corner of the temple is damaged, this is because of the ground settling below this corner rather than any inherent weakness in the masonry itself. Opposite the Principal Temple is the House of the High Priest although archaeologists cannot surely say who, if anyone, lived in this building.

Behind and connected to the Principal Temple lies a small but famous building called the Sacristy. It has many well carved niches, perhaps used for the storage of ceremonial objects, as well as a carved stone bench. The Sacristy is especially known for the two rocks flanking its entrance; they are said to contain 32 angles in each although I must admit to always coming up with a different number when I count them!

Behind the Sacristy is a staircase climbing a small hill to the major shrine in Machu Picchu, the Intihuatana. This Quechua word loosely translates into the 'hitching post of the sun' and refers to the carved rock pillar, often mistakenly called a sun dial, which stands at the top of the Intihuatana hill. This rock didn't

aid in telling the time of day but rather the time of year. The Inca's astronomers were able to predict the solstices using the angles of the pillar and thus the Inca, who was the son of the sun, was able to claim control over the return of the lengthening days of summer. Exactly how the pillar was used for these astronomical purposes remains unclear but its elegant simplicity is remarked upon by many modern observers. It is recorded that there were several of these Intihuatanas in various important Inca sites but they were all (with the known exception of this one) smashed by the Spaniards in an attempt to wipe out what they considered to be the blasphemy of sun worship.

At the back of the Intihuatana is another staircase descending down to the Central Plaza which separates the important sites of the Intihuatana, Sacred Plaza and Temple of the Sun from the more mundane areas opposite. At the lower end of this area is found the Prison Group, a labyrinthine complex of cells, niches and passageways both under and above ground. The centrepiece of the group is a carving of the head of a condor; the natural rocks behind it look like the outstretched wings of the bird. Behind the condor is a well-like hole and at the bottom of this is the door to a tiny underground cell which can only be entered by bending double.

Above the Prison Group is the largest section of the ruins, the Industrial and Residential Sectors. These buildings are less well constructed and had more mundane purposes than the buildings across the Plaza.

Walks Near Machu Picchu

There are four fairly short walks which can be done starting from and returning to the ruins.

The most famous is the climb up the steep mountain of Huayna Picchu at the back of the ruins. Huayna Picchu is normally translated as 'young peak' but it is interesting to note that *picchu* with the

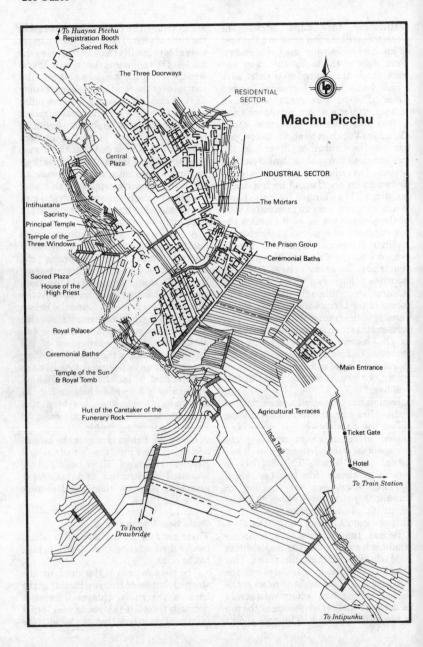

To Huayna Picchu
Registration Booth
Sacred Rock

The Three Doorways

RESIDENTIAL
SECTOR

Machu Picchu

Central
Plaza

INDUSTRIAL SECTOR

The Mortars

Intihuatana
Sacristy
Principal Temple
Temple of the
Three Windows

The Prison Group

Ceremonial Baths

Sacred Plaza
House of the
High Priest

Royal Palace

Ceremonial Baths

Main Entrance

Temple of the Sun
& Royal Tomb

Hut of the Caretaker of the
Funerary Rock

Agricultural Terraces

Inca Trail

Ticket Gate

Hotel

To Train Station

To Inca
Drawbridge

To Intipunku

correct glottal pronunciation, refers to the wad in the cheek of a coca-chewing, Quechua-speaking mountain dweller – the wad looks like a little peak in the cheek.

At first glance it would appear that Huayna Picchu is a difficult climb but there is a well-maintained trail and although the ascent is steep it is not technically difficult. You begin by walking to the very end of the Main Plaza and turning right between two open-fronted buildings. Just beyond is a registration booth where you have to sign in – it's open only until about 2 pm. The climb takes about an hour and goes through a short section of Inca tunnel. The view from the top is spectacular but if you are short on either time or energy, I feel that the view from the Hut of the Caretaker of the Funerary Rock is easily as good.

It is possible to continue from the peak down the back side of Huayna Picchu on a very poorly maintained and overgrown trail to the small Temple of the Moon but remember the descent takes over half an hour and the ascent back to the peak twice as long. Because of lack of proper trail maintenance, you do this section at your own risk.

A much less steep but very scenic walk is from the Hut of the Caretaker of the Funerary Rock, along the top of the terraces and out along a narrow cliff-clinging trail to the Inca drawbridge. The trail is marked and there is also a registration booth which is open erratically – you're supposed to register here before 3 pm. The walk takes 20 minutes and you get a good look at the vegetation of the high cloud forest as well as a different view of Machu Picchu. The drawbridge itself is less interesting than the walk to get there. You aren't allowed to walk right up to it and have to be content with viewing it from behind a barrier about a 100 metres away. Someone crossed both the barrier and the bridge a few years ago and fell to his death.

The Inca Trail ends from just below the Hut of the Caretaker of the Funerary Rock and heads back to the notch in the horizon called Intipunku or the Gate of the Sun. You can see both the trail and Intipunku by looking at the hill behind you as you enter the ruins. This hill is named Machu Picchu (Old Peak) and is what gives the site its name. It takes about 45 minutes to reach Intipunku and it's possible to continue as far as Wiñay Wayna (see the Inca Trail) if you can spare about five hours for the round trip.

The fourth walk is the most difficult and rarely done – an ascent of the hill of Machu Picchu. Take the Inca Trail for a few minutes and look for a trail to your right passing through a gap in the walls of the terraces. It's not very obvious and there's no sign. If you find the trail, it'll be very overgrown but you can force your way through the thick vegetation to the top of Machu Picchu peak. Allow well over an hour for the climb and be prepared for disappointment unless the trail has been recently cleared.

Admission

The site is open daily from 7.30 am to 5 pm and so seeing the sunrise or sunset over Machu Picchu is difficult unless you arrive via the Inca Trail and camp at Intipunku. It's not as spectacular as you may have imagined it anyway; the surrounding high mountains mean that it's already broad daylight when the sun comes up.

Machu Picchu is Peru's showpiece site and entrance fees are accordingly high. Foreigners pay about US$5 per day to get in but students with bona fide identification get a 50% discount. The site is exceptionally difficult to enter other than through the gate and the guards (who wear hard hats) are very vigilant, so resign yourself to paying.

Many visitors buy a Machu Picchu combined ticket book in Cuzco from one of the tourist agencies. This includes tickets for the round trip tourist train (or autovagon) ride, the bus to and from the ruins, entrance into the ruins and lunch at the Machu Picchu hotel. Make sure your ticket contains all these sections and shop around. The combined ticket will cost you at least US$30 but is often more depending on the agency. Most agencies will provide an English-speaking guide as well. This ticket doesn't enable you to cut corners by, for example, travelling on the cheaper local train or bringing a sandwich lunch, but if you want to go first class all the way you should consider getting the combined ticket book to save you the hassle of buying the individual tickets. The main drawback is that the combined ticket is valid for just one day and you only get to spend about two or three hours in the ruins before it's time to start returning to the train station. A cheaper version of the combined ticket is sometimes available from the train station in Cuzco. This includes train, bus and entrance fees, but no lunch or guides.

You aren't allowed to bring large packs or food into the ruins and packs have to be checked at the gate. Although you are allowed to visit all parts of the ruins, don't walk on any of the walls as this will loosen the stonework as well as unleash an angry cacophony of whistle blowing from the guards. The guards check the ruins carefully at closing time and blow their whistles loudly and so trying to spend the night is also difficult. Yes, I know it sounds depressingly over-regulated but there's not much you can do about it and getting uptight with the rules will only spoil your visit.

Often, on or around full moon, you can bribe one of the guards to unlock the ruins and accompany you around by moonlight. This is expensive unless you can organise a group, and difficult unless you speak Spanish and have the ability to bribe people without appearing to do so!

Getting There

Most visitors take the tourist train or autovagon from Cuzco getting to the Puentes Ruinas railway station at about 10.30 or 11 am. The four-hour journey begins with a climb out of Cuzco which, because it is too steep for normal railroad curves, is accomplished by a series of four back and forth zigzags. The tracks then drop gently through mainly agricultural countryside to the important station of Ollantaytambo, where all trains stop. From here you can see Mount Veronica (5750 metres) to your right and the Urubamba river gorge to your left. The train descends down the narrow gorge with superb views of the very difficult white water of the lower Urubamba.

At Puentes Ruinas station you are at about 2000 metres above sea level and the ruins of Machu Picchu lie roughly 700 metres above you. There is a fleet of buses waiting to take you up to the ruins on a six km road (the Hiram Bingham highway, opened in 1948) which zigzags thrillingly up the mountainside. Tickets for the bus cost approximately US$1 each way and are obtained at the railway station ticket office, across the platform facing the left hand side of the train as you come in. There are about a dozen buses but on a busy day you may have to wait up to an hour if you don't get out on the first wave of buses and so it's worth hustling a little bit as you get off the train.

Unfortunately, Machu Picchu is so geared to the tourist train arrival that it is sometimes difficult to get a bus up at other times. Usually there is a bus for the arrival of the local train but if you walk the two km from Aguas Calientes you may find no bus or that the driver wants to wait an hour until all the 22 seats are filled. If there's a group of you it's possible to buy all 22 tickets if you have the cash. Otherwise, you'll have to walk. Rather than climb six km on the road it's better to hike up the shorter and steeper footpath. Cross the bridge behind the railway station and turn right. You'll soon see arrows marking your path which crosses the road at several points on the ascent. Note that the drivers will not normally stop for passengers at intermediate points. The climb takes about 1½ hours from the station.

The tourist trains leave for the return trip at about 3 to 4 pm and the buses start descending from the ruins at about 2 pm. Bus lines can get very long during the busy season. Buying tickets for the tourist train can be a little problematical as the seats are often fully booked by day tripping passengers from Cuzco.

If you have the time, the most economical way to go is via the local train (1st class) or the Quillabamba autovagon to Aguas Calientes, spend the night there, spend a full day at Machu Picchu ruins, spend another night at Aguas Calientes and then return via the local train or autovagon. This avoids the tourist train completely and maximises your time at the ruins.

It's obvious, I hope, that from reading this you realise that the ruins are most heavily visited from about 11 am to 2.30 pm. Many tours combine visits of Machu Picchu with the Sunday markets at either Pisac or Chinchero and so Sundays are fairly quiet but Fridays, Saturdays and Mondays are busy. The months of June to August are the busiest. Try and plan your visit early or late in the day, especially during the dry season (the whole day is the best) and you'll have several hours of peace and quiet. An early and wet midweek morning in the rainy season will virtually guarantee you the ruins to yourself.

Post Office

There is a Post Office booth at the Puentes Ruinas train station which is usually open for the afternoon train departure. All postcards are franked with a special Machu Picchu souvenir postmark.

Museum

There is a small museum a few hundred metres behind the train station which shows photos of Hiram Bingham and gives a little information about the ruins. If you're pressed for time, you'd be better off going straight to the ruins.

Places to Stay & Eat

There is only one place to stay at Machu Picchu itself – the government-run *Hotel de Turistas*. This costs US$45/55 singles/doubles but despite the expense it's often full. If you want to stay here it's recommended that you make a reservation either through a travel agency in Lima or Cuzco or direct from the ENTURPERU office in Lima (tel 721928). You can sometimes get a room on the day you arrive, especially during the low season, but don't rely on it.

If you want to overnight so that you can spend a full day at the ruins there are two cheap choices. The best is to stay at Aguas Calientes, two km towards Cuzco on the train tracks from the Puentes Ruinas station. Alternatively you can camp, although there are no proper sites and it's illegal to camp within the ruins. You can camp along the road a short way below the tourist hotel or you can stay on the football field near the train station. Camping along the road isn't much fun and camping on the football field doesn't bring you very much closer than a cheap hotel at Aguas Calientes, plus you have a bunch of gear to look after and so the Aguas Calientes choice is definitely the most convenient.

The only place to eat at the ruins is in the hotel. There is a restaurant which serves expensive breakfast and supper and a cafeteria on the patio which serves expensive self service lunches. There is also a souvenir shop/snack bar for bottled drinks which aren't much cheaper than in the cafeteria. Bring a packed lunch and water bottle if you want to economise. It's illegal to bring food into the ruins, but small bags aren't searched and so you can smuggle a sandwich in with your camera. It's illegal because many tourists litter the site so if you do smuggle in some food, don't leave any trash whatsoever and don't eat your apple right under the guard's nose.

Cheap snacks and drinks can be purchased at the train station in the afternoon.

AGUAS CALIENTES

This village, although tiny, is the closest to Machu Picchu and so it is a frequent destination for travellers who wish to do more than just visit Machu Picchu on the standard one-day train trip from Cuzco. The scenery here is pretty and it's a good place to meet other travellers and relax in the countryside.

Hot Springs

Trekkers completing the Inca Trail may want to soak away their aches and pains in these natural thermal springs which give the village of Aguas Calientes its name. To get there just follow the path past the Youth Hostel for about 10 minutes. The hot springs are open from 5 am to 8 pm and entrance is 30c – but often there's no gatekeeper early in the mornings.

The government has tried to 'improve' the hot springs by building concrete pools (which are shallow so don't dive in), changing cubicles (no doors), and a cafeteria (usually closed). They seem to have forgotten to build a toilet so you can guess where people piss. There is a shower pipe with shampoo and soap wrappers thrown around. It's rather disappointing but definitely has the potential to improve. At the very least, it's worth going up there for the walk which is pretty. Check it out.

Places to Stay

Next to the railway tracks is the cheap *Hostal Los Caminantes*, a rambling, dark and rather dirty building. They charge 65c per person in three, four and five bed rooms or US$1.10 single and US$1.60 double. Cold water only in the dank showers. The *Hostal Qoñi* (better known as *Gringo Bill's* because of its American owner) is a better choice at about US$1.30 per person. There is only one communal bathroom with hot water but the place is expanding and rooms

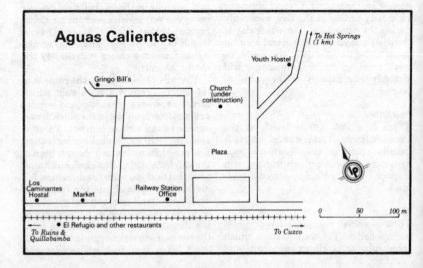

Aguas Calientes

To Hot Springs (1 km)

Youth Hostel

Gringo Bill's

Church (under construction)

Plaza

Los Caminantes Hostal

Market

Railway Station Office

0   50   100 m

● El Refugio and other restaurants

To Ruins & Quillabamba

To Cuzco

with balconies and private showers are planned, as well as a full time restaurant. They serve breakfast from 5.30 am for early risers to the ruins and there are storage facilities and information available. The management is friendly and can help with laundry and money changing, etc. Finally, the government-run Youth Hostel (Albergue Juvenil) charges US$2.25 per person in rooms usually containing four very narrow bunk beds. There is hot water sometimes in the communal bathrooms and meals are served. It's clean but rather spartan and cheerless. Many people think it's a white elephant – there are about 200 beds but it's usually ¾ empty.

There used to be cheap accommodation available in some of the houses and restaurants by the railway line but these have pretty much shut down since the huge youth hostel opened. Occasionally, Aguas Calientes gets invaded by a huge group of Peruvian students and so these other places can provide accommodation in emergencies.

Places to Eat

Most of the restaurants are clustered along the railway tracks and are not particularly good. Some have been criticised for undercooked food or unhygienic conditions and travellers get sick here more often than elsewhere. The tap water is not safe to drink. Two restaurants which I found reasonably clean are the El Refugio and the Aiko – both have good meals for under a dollar. There are several others to experiment with.

There's not much to do in the evening except to hang out in one of the restaurants and talk to other travellers over a beer. There is a kind of discotheque/cine-theatre/nightclub place called El Clave del Sol which opens occasionally. It's run by a Frenchman and he likes to show obscure French films without sub-titles – a different form of culture in the land of the Incas, I suppose. It's on the right hand

side of the path on the way to the hot springs.

Getting to Machu Picchu

Although Aguas Calientes is the nearest village to the ruins, it is still about eight km away on foot, though you can take public transport. From the village you head roughly west along the railway line. There is no road or proper footpath but with so few trains most people just walk along the track – it's only about two km and it means you get to the ruins early, before the crowds. There are a couple of tunnels so you might want to take a torch.

The next station beyond Aguas Calientes is called Puente Ruinas and is the station for the ruins. From the Urubamba river valley floor a steep six km road climbs about 600 metres to the ruins. If you're on foot you don't have to follow the road – there is a signposted footpath which is shorter, steeper and very narrow. You emerge breathless at the top about an hour later. There is also a fleet of 22-seater buses costing about a dollar per seat which go from the station to the ruins. Normally they go when they are full which means every few minutes after the tourist train comes in and rather infrequently at other times. There is also an early morning bus which takes site employees up to work. Most people walk – it's cool first thing in the morning and gives a good look at the high mountain cloud forest. Orchids often bloom along the path especially in the rainy months.

Rail It has to be trains because the road doesn't get to Aguas Calientes (nor Machu Picchu). There is a ticket office on the north side of the railway tracks. Note that the Aguas Calientes train station is known as Machu Picchu – don't ask me why. Usually only the 'local train' stops here and many people prefer to walk 2 km to Puentes Ruinas for a better selection of faster trains to Cuzco. The local trains for Cuzco stop at Aguas Calientes about 8.30

am and 5 pm, take about four to five hours and cost about US$2. The trains to Quillabamba pass through about 9.30 am and 6 pm, take about three hours and cost about US$1.

There is also a local autovagon which passes through at 7.15 am on the way to Cuzco (3¼ hours, US$4) and at 4.30 pm on the way to Quillabamba (two hours, US$2).

SANTA TERESA

This village is about 20 km beyond Aguas Calientes on the way to Quillabamba and is a point from where it is possible to find trucks to Cuzco. The rough journey takes about 15 hours during the dry season and is very difficult during the rainy months of November to April. It is also the termination point of a four day trek or hike from the village of Mollepata, through the Cordillera Vilcabamba and passing Salcantay. (See the Bradt's book *Backpacking & Trekking in Peru & Bolivia*.) There is a basic hotel here and the local trains between Cuzco and Quillabamba stop here.

SOUTH-EAST OF CUZCO

The railway and road to Puno and Lake Titicaca head out from Cuzco to the south-east. There are several sites of interest en route which can be visited from Cuzco in one day.

Tipón

This little known Inca site consists of some excellent terracing at the head of a small valley. The site is noted for its fine irrigation system. To get there take the Transportes Oropesa bus from Cuzco and ask to be set down at the Tipón turn off, 23 km beyond Cuzco and a few km before Oropesa. From the turn-off, a four-km dirt road climbs steeply to the ruins.

Pikillacta and Rumicolca

This is the only major pre-Inca ruin in the Cuzco area. Pikillacta means 'the place of the flea' and was built by the Wari culture

at around 1100 AD. Entrance is by the Cuzco Visitor's Ticket. The site is just past a lake on the left hand side of the road about 32 km beyond Cuzco. It is a large city of crumbling two storied buildings which are interesting in that all the entrances were on the upper floor for defense. A defensive wall can be seen surrounding the city. The stonework is much cruder than that of the Incas.

Across the road from Pikillacta, about a km away, is the huge Inca gate of Rumicolca. It was built on Wari foundations and you can see the cruder Wari stonework contrasting with the Inca blocks.

The swampy lakes in the area are also interesting. You can see workmen making roof tiles from the mud surrounding the lakes.

The area can be reached by taking an Urcos minibus from Cuzco.

Andahuaylillas

This village lies about 40 km beyond Cuzco and seven km before Urcos and can be reached by the Urcos minibus. Andahuaylillas is a pretty Andean village which is famous for its beautifully decorated church and attractive colonial houses. The church is compared to the best in Cuzco. It's open erratically but if you ask around you can usually find a caretaker to open it up – a tip is expected.

FROM CUZCO TO THE JUNGLE

There are three overland routes from Cuzco to the jungle. One is via the railway to Quillabamba which is described in the section on Quillabamba. The other two are poor dirt roads. It's best to travel on these in the dry months (June to September) as they can be very muddy and slow in the wet months, especially around January to April. One road heads to Paucartambo, Tres Cruces, Shintuyo and towards Manu National Park whilst the other goes through Ocongate and Quince Mil to Puerto Maldonado. These are described below.

Paucartambo

The small village of Paucartambo lies on the eastern slopes of the Andes about 115 km from Cuzco on a well maintained but very narrow dirt road. There are fine views of the Andes dropping away to the high Amazon basin beyond. The dirt road is one way and travel is from Cuzco to Paucartambo on Mondays, Wednesdays and Fridays and the return is on Tuesdays, Thursdays and Saturdays. Trucks for Paucartambo leave early on the appropriate mornings from near the Urcos bus stop in Cuzco. The journey takes about five hours.

Paucartambo is particularly famous for its very authentic and colourful celebration of the Fiesta de la Virgen del Carmen which is held annually on and around 16 July. There is much traditional street dancing and the costumed processions are especially colourful. Relatively few tourists have seen this fiesta simply because it's been difficult to get to and because once you're there you either have to camp or hope to find a local to give you floor space as there are no hotels. Tourist agencies in Cuzco are starting to realise the potential of this fiesta as a tourist attraction and are beginning to run buses specifically for the fiesta. If you go this way you may be able to sleep on the bus. A basic hotel will probably open soon – maybe by the time you read this.

Tres Cruces

About 45 km beyond Paucartambo is the famous jungle view at Tres Cruces. The sight of the mountains finally dropping away into the Amazon basin is exceptionally beautiful and made all the more exciting by the sunrise phenomenon which occurs around the time of the winter solstice (21 June). For some reason the sunrise here tends to be optically distorted and so double images, haloes and unusual colours may occur, particularly during May, June and July. During this time of year, various adventure tour agencies advertise sunrise-watching trips to Tres Cruces. You can also try taking the thrice weekly truck service to Paucartambo and asking around for a truck going on to Tres Cruces – Sr Cáceres in Paucartambo will reportedly arrange sunrise-watching trips. There are some Inca ruins within walking distance of Paucartambo – ask in the village for directions.

Manu National Park

This jungle park is the biggest in Peru and is one of the best places in South America to see a huge variety of wildlife. There are some Indian groups which continue to live as they have done for generations. One of the reasons that the park is such a success in preserving so large a tract of virgin jungle is that it is remote and difficult to get to. Visiting it requires a great deal of time, self sufficiency, money and ability to travel in difficult conditions.

Commercial adventure companies occasionally organise expensive guided expeditions into the park – this is probably the best way to go because travelling alone can be very frustrating and expensive. It costs about the same to hire a dugout canoe for a week for one person as it does for six people and so group travel makes sense. Various agencies in Cuzco run guided trips – Mayuc has been doing trips every year in July and August. If you want to set up a trip in advance you can write to Wilderness Travel, 1760 Solano Ave, Berkeley, CA 94707, USA.

If you want to form your own expedition, then I suggest you read *South America: River Trips*, Vol 1 by G Bradt and Vol 2 by T & M Jordan, both published by Bradt Enterprises and both containing sections on Manu. In Lima, the South American Explorers Club can help members obtain up-to-date information. Officially you need a permit from the Dirección General Forestal y del Fauna, Jirón Natalio Sanchez 220, Jesús María, Lima (tel 323150 and 323154) or from the CENFOR office in Cuzco at Calle Quera 235, 2nd floor, (tel 233632 and 233653). They can give up to date information and issue a permit to visit the park. I've heard it's difficult to get permits for solo travellers.

The first stage is to take a truck from Cuzco via Paucartambo (see above) to Shintuyo. This takes 24 hours, costs about US$5 and is a rough 300-km ride. About 30 km before Shintuyo is the village of Salvación where there is a Park Office and a couple of basic hotels. You can start asking around here for boats into the park. You should bring *all* supplies from Cuzco. This should include a jerry can full of gasoline (a 200-litre drum for any kind of long trip) for the boat which will make it easier to find a boatman willing to go. This can cost US$100 or more for the one way trip. The Park personnel may know if any trips are being planned in the near future and you might be able to join them if you're lucky.

If you go on to Shintuyo you're closer to the park but there are fewer facilities. There is a mission station where you can arrange to camp by talking to the priest. Reports have reached me of some adventurers who claimed that they had a small balsa raft built here for about US$10 – the priest can introduce you to a reliable carpenter. I've not been to Shintuyo myself. A friend who knows the area well and has had some river running experience tells me that the Río Alto Madre de Dios is one mean river and you'd kill yourself going down it on a balsa raft.

The boat journey takes two days down the Madre de Dios River to its junction with the Manu River. There is an airstrip at this point, known as Boca Manu, which is often the starting point for commercial trips into the park, thus eliminating the time-consuming truck and boat approach. There are no regular air services and a light plane must be chartered, usually from Puerto Maldonado.

At Boca Manu, you can turn right and continue down the fairly busy Madre de Dios, past gold panning areas, to Puerto Maldonado, but you won't see much wildlife. The virgin jungle lies a further day up the Manu River to the park headquarters at Pakitsa. There is a guard post there but no other facilities. You can walk around on jungle trails but it's best if you hire your boat to stay on for a few days and use it to take excursions further up the Manu and some of the side streams. You have to provide enough food for yourself and the boatman. It's difficult to organise, difficult to do and expensive. The possibility of observing jungle wildlife is, however, one of the best in South America. Good luck!

The Road to Puerto Maldonado

This road is almost 500 km long and takes about 2½ days to travel. Trucks leave daily from Transportes Quince Mil in Cuzco. Most people fly on the cheap daily flight linking Cuzco with Puerto Maldonado.

The road follows the south-eastern route to Puno until Urcos, where the dirt road to Puerto Maldonado begins. About 125 km beyond Cuzco you come to the highland town of Ocongate, where there are a couple of basic hotels. About an hour's drive beyond Ocongate is the village of Tinqui (you can sleep in the school) which is the beginning of a week long hike encircling Ausangate, at 6384 metres the highest mountain in southern Peru. Now the road begins to drop steadily. The next town of any size is Quince Mil, 240 km from Cuzco and the half way point. There is a hotel here but it's often full – the area is a gold mining centre. You are now less than 1000 metres above sea level (although still in the Department of Cuzco) and the road drops into the jungle for a further 100 km before the flatlands are finally reached. The last 140 km into Puerto Maldonado is flat. It's a tiring and difficult trip, but if you are used to long-haul travelling it does give a good look at the beautiful scenery on the eastern slopes of the Andes.

QUILLABAMBA

Quillabamba lies on the Urubamba River and at the end of the train line from Cuzco and Machu Picchu. At only 950 metres above sea level it is hot and humid and so can properly be called a jungle town, the only one in Peru which is reached by railway. Because it is so close to Cuzco and so accessible it makes an worthwhile destination for travellers wanting to get a glimpse of the high jungle. The town itself is quiet and pleasant, if not particularly interesting. It can be used as a base for trips further into the jungle.

Places to Stay

There are over a dozen hotels to choose from, all of them cheap and some quite good. The *Hostal Comercio* charges 50c or 60c per person depending on whether or not you have a (rather dank) private bathroom. Similarly priced are the basic *Hostal Progreso* (no singles), *Hostal San Antonio* (dormitory accommodation), *Hostal San Martín* (dirty), the *Hostal Thomas* and *Hostal Urusayhua* and the *Alojamiento Dos de Mayo*. The *Hostal Convención* charges US$1/1.30 singles/doubles, has a courtyard, some rooms overlooking the Plaza de Armas, though it's still just a basic hotel. All of these have communal bathrooms with cold water only.

A recommended clean and cheap hotel is the *Hostal Alto Urubamba* which charges US$1.10/1.80 for singles/doubles with shared bath and US$1.40/2.25 with private bath. The *Hostal Cuzco* is also clean and pleasant but has an erratic water supply. It costs US$1.70/2.30 with a private bath – cold water only but it's hot enough in Quillabamba that you can manage quite well without hot showers. The *Hostal Quillabamba* is recommended for its clean rooms and roof top restaurant. The *Hostal Lira* is also good,

though its restaurant is on the ground floor and less attractive. Both these hotels have hot water and charge about US$2 single and US$3 double with private bath.

The newest and best place in town is the *Hostal Don Carlos* which provides rooms with private bath and hot water for US$3/4 singles/doubles.

Places to Eat

The best place in town is the rooftop restaurant at the *Hostal Quillabamba* with good views and adequate meals for about a dollar, though the service is slow. The *Hostal Lira* also has a reasonable restaurant. The *El Rancho Restaurant* serves good grilled chicken and is clean. There are several *heladerías*, or ice cream parlours, serving light refreshment on the Plaza de Armas.

Getting There

Rail The train station is linked with the town by two parallel bridges. The pedestrian bridge leads to a steep flight of stairs (I counted 172 steps) which takes you to the bottom of town. If you don't feel like the climb you can take a colectivo truck or shared taxi from the station to the market place for about 25c. The ticket office at the train station is open from 4.30 to 5.40 am, 12 to 2.15 pm and 8.30 to 10.15 pm daily except on Sunday when it is open only at night. You can buy train tickets a day in advance but autovagon tickets are sold only on the morning of departure (except for the Sunday auto-vagon when you can buy tickets on Saturday). You are advised to get your autovagon tickets as early as possible because, despite assurances that it's never sold out, it sometimes is, especially at weekends.

The autovagon leaves at 5.15 am and takes about two hours to Aguas Calientes (for Machu Picchu) and 5¼ hours to Cuzco. Fares are US$2 and US$6 respectively. This is an 'express' train and so does not stop at Puentes Ruinas which is

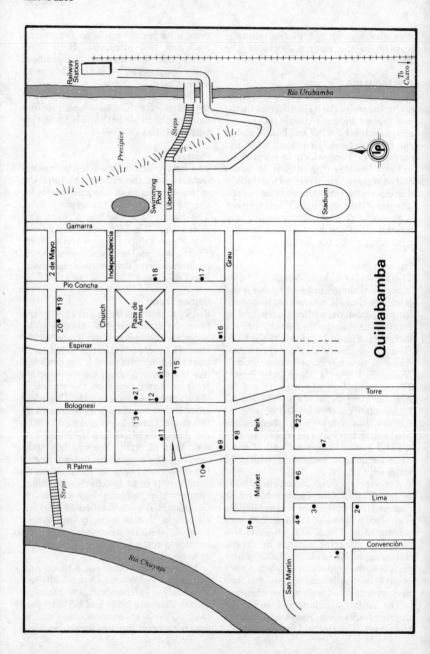

Railway Station

To Cuzco

Rio Urubamba

Precipice

Steps

Swimming Pool

Libertad

Stadium

Gamarra

2 de Mayo

Independencia

Grau

●18

●17

Pio Concha

Church

Plaza de Armas

●19

●20

●16

Espinar

●15

●14

Bolognesi

●21

●12

Torre

●13

Park

●22

●11

●8

●7

R Palma

●9

Steps

●10

Market

●6

Lima

●5

●3

●2

●4

Convención

San Martin

●1

Rio Chuyapi

Quillabamba

1	Hostal Lira
2	Trucks to Cuzco
3	Hostal Urusayhua
4	Hostal San Martín
5	Hostal Quillabamba
6	Hostal Progreso
7	Hostal Cuzco
8	Taxis
9	Trucks & Buses to Kiteni
10	Hostal Thomas
11	Hostal Comercio
12	El Rancho Restaurant
13	ENTEL
14	Hostal Don Carlos
15	Banco de Crédito
16	Banco de Los Andes
17	Hostal San Antonio
18	Hostal Convención
19	Hostal Alto Urubamba
20	Alojamiento Dos de Mayo
21	Cinema
22	Town Hall (Municipalidad)

the closest station to Machu Picchu. Vendors are not allowed on board and all that is available is warm coke, so bring your own food.

The local trains leave at 5.30 am and 2 pm. They stop at all stations and take about three hours to Machu Picchu (US$1) and 7½ hours to Cuzco (US$3). Second class is very crowded but tickets are about 20% cheaper.

Buses & Trucks Trucks leave from Avenida Lima or the market for Cuzco on an irregular basis. Ask around. The journey takes roughly 15 hours and costs about US$2. This rough route goes high over the spectacular pass of *Abra de Malaga* and is a favourite road for ornithologists who see many different species of birds as the ecological zones change from sub-tropical to sub-glacial.

Pick-up trucks (there is also one bus) leave every morning from the market to the village of Kiteni, further into the jungle. The trip takes about six hours and costs US$2.

KITENI & BEYOND

This is the end of the road as far as this section of the jungle is concerned. This small jungle town has one cheap and basic hotel. In addition there is a medium priced new lodge on the other side of the river about a km away.

It is possible to continue by river but you are advised to be self sufficient as food and accommodation are often non-existent. The first major landmark is the *Pongo de Manique* which is a steep-walled canyon on the Urubamba river. There is a basic hotel in the area. The canyon is dangerous and boats don't go through it in the rainy season when the water is too high (from November through May). Boats as far as the pongo can occasionally be found by enquiring in Kiteni.

During the dry season a few boats continue through the pongo. The river is relatively calm afterwards (though there are still some rapids) but there are few settlements until you reach the oil town of Sapahua, about two to four days beyond the pongo. There is basic food and accommodation here and the oilmen (Americans and Britons) are often interested in seeing a different face. From Sapahua there are flights to Satipo with SASA and some flights to Lima for the oilmen.

It is sometimes possible to continue down the Urubamba to the village of Atalaya, two to three days away. Here there is another airstrip with SASA air connections to Satipo. Boats can be found to continue down the river, now the Ucayali, as far as Pucallpa. From Kiteni onwards is obviously a little-travelled and adventurous route, especially beyond the Pongo de Manique, but it is possible for experienced and self sufficient travellers.

CUZCO TO THE COAST BY ROAD

Most buses between Cuzco and Lima go via Limatambo, Abancay, Chalhuanca, Puquio, Pampas Galeras and Nazca. This route is frequently taken by budget travellers who don't want to fly and who want to see some of the spectacular scenery as the road drops off from the Andes to the desert coast.

LIMATAMBO

Limatambo is a small and infrequently visited village 80 km west of Cuzco by road. Most people are too busy leaving or arriving at Cuzco to do more than just drive through Limatambo on the bus. This is a shame because it's worth a visit.

The village is named after the small but well-made Inca ruin of *Rimactambo* (speaker's inn). It was better constructed than many other tambos because it was probably used as a ceremonial centre as well as a lodging place for the Inca as he travelled the empire. There is an exceptional polygonal retaining wall with 12 man-sized niches – this wall itself is worth the trip for those interested in ruins. The site is better known as Tarahuasi, after the Hacienda on whose grounds it is located. It is about two km away from Limatambo on the road towards Cuzco and easy to find.

In Limatambo there is a basic and inexpensive hostal and a swimming pool which is popular with the locals. The village is located in pretty, mountainous countryside at the upper end of a river valley which is a headwater tributary of the Apurimac River. The hostal and swimming pool are a retreat for the citizens of Cuzco wanting to get away from the city for a weekend.

You can get there from Cuzco on the bus to Abancay or the truck to Mollepata.

MOLLEPATA

This small but old village is a few km off the main Cuzco-Abancay road and a couple of hours beyond Limatambo. It is the starting point for a trek to Santa Teresa, beyond Machu Picchu, or an alternate and longer beginning of the Inca Trail. Directions for both hikes are given in Bradt's *Backpacking & Trekking in Peru & Bolivia*. Alternatively you can do the trek simply by hiring an *arriero* or muleteer in Santa Teresa – they know the trails. Allow about five days to Santa Teresa and about four days to Huayllabamba on the Inca Trail. Mules aren't allowed on the Inca Trail so you'll have to carry your own gear after Huayllabamba or hire porters. This is feasible at Huayllabamba.

Getting to Mollepata is straightforward if not particularly comfortable. Trucks leave Cuzco from the end of Calle Arcopata early every morning, usually about 7 am. It's a dusty but scenic five-hour drive. In Mollepata you can buy basic supplies but it's best to bring everything from Cuzco. There is no hotel but you can camp if you ask around – don't leave belongings unattended. If you plan on carrying your own gear and dispense with mule drivers and guides you can leave right away.

ABANCAY

This small city is the capital of the Andean Department of Apurimac, one of the least explored departments in the Peruvian Andes. It is a sleepy rural town located about eight-hours drive west of Cuzco and at an altitude of 2377 metres above sea level. Despite its status as departmental capital and main town between Cuzco and the coast, it has no scheduled air service and has a forlorn and forgotten air about it. Some travellers use it as a resting place on the long and tiring bus journey between Cuzco and the coast or Cuzco and Ayacucho.

Things to See

Despite it's forgotten air, Abancay is not totally devoid of interest. The Carnival, held in the week before Lent, is particularly colourful and is a chance to see Andean carnival celebrations uncluttered with the normal trappings of international tourism. There is a nationally acclaimed folk dancing competition. Hotels tend to

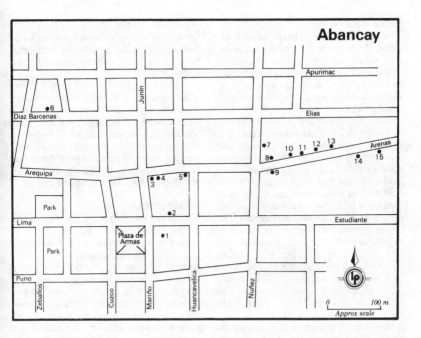

1 Cathedral
2 Municipalidad & Cine Municipal
3 Post Office
4 Cine Nilo
5 Market
6 Hotel de Turistas
7 Hostal Abancay
8 Minibuses to Cuzco
9 Sr de Huanca Buses
10 Hotel Gran
11 Morales Bus
12 Hostal & Restaurant El Misti
13 Hidalgo Bus
14 Ormeño Bus
15 Hostal Luramen

fill up early so get there a couple of days before it gets underway. Another festival is Abancay Day, 3 November.

People interested in Inca ruins may want to visit the Hacienda of Saihuite, near the turn off to Huanipaca and Cachora on the main road towards Cuzco and 45 km away from Abancay. Here are found several large carved boulders; the stones of Saihuite. They are intricately decorated and similar to the more commonly visited carved rock at Qenko, near Cuzco, but the Saihuite stones are considered the most elaborate.

The best weather is during the dry season of June to October when walkers or climbers may want to head towards the sometimes snowcapped peak of Ampoy, about 10 km north-north-west of the town and approximately 5000 metres in height. During the rest of the year the weather tends to be wet, especially in the first four months of the year.

Travellers merely passing through town can check out the two cinemas or stroll through the plazas.

Places to Stay & Eat

The best of the very cheap hotels is the *Hotel Gran* which charges about 50c per person in rooms with a shared bathroom and 75c per person in rooms with private bathroom. It's a basic cold water hotel but the rooms are reasonably large and clean. Similarly priced is the *Hostal Abancay* which has broken windows and looks very run down. A few cents more will get you a room at the *Hostal El Misti* which isn't any better then the *Gran* but it does have a restaurant of sorts. Fairly new and clean is the *Hostal Luramen* which charges US$1:30 per person in rooms with shared baths and US$2 per person in rooms with private baths. Hot water is available. The best in town is the government-run *Hotel de Turistas* found in a pleasant old-fashioned country mansion. They charge US$3.50/5.50 for singles/doubles (shared bathroom) and US$5.75/7.50 in rooms with private baths and hot water. The restaurant has meals for about US$3 each.

If you don't want to eat in one of the hotels, there are plenty of cheap cafes near the bus stations.

Getting There

The easiest town to get to is, not surprisingly, Cuzco. There are several minibuses every day which are cramped but faster than ordinary buses. They leave from the corner of Nuñez and Arenas and charge about US$5.25 for the six-hour trip. You could try these minibuses for a trip to Saihuite.

The bus companies have cheaper departures to Cuzco and Lima (via Nazca) every two days. It is one of the inexplicable lunacies of Peruvian bus travel that all the buses to the coast leave within hours of one another and you can be stuck for two days before the next slew of buses leaves. Most of the companies marked on the map on Calle Arenas serve Cuzco (US$4, eight hours), Nazca (US$13, 26 hours) and Lima (US$15, 34 hours). These are average times for the dry season; in the wet season journeys have been known to take three times as long. Señor de Huanca is the only company which runs large, cheap buses to Cuzco every day.

If instead of heading to the coast, you want to travel north-west into the Andes to Andahuaylas and Ayacucho, you will be rewarded with magnificent and wild scenery. It is a difficult route however, and transportation is rough and not very regular. Señor de Huanca provides buses to Andahuaylas and Hidalgo has a bus about every two days to Ayacucho.

ANDAHUAYLAS

This is the second most important town in the department of Apurimac and is passed through on the way to Ayacucho. It is 135 km west of Abancay. I have never stopped here so I can't tell you much about it. There is an airport here but, despite rumours to the contrary, there have been no scheduled flights for some years. The best hotel in town is the government-run *Hotel de Turistas* which is on Avenida Lozano Carrillo and is similarly priced to the Abancay tourist hotel. There are also some cheaper places. It's a very quiet little town in which to break your journey if you have a relaxed schedule and are fed up with being bounced up and down on the atrociously surfaced mountain roads. The beautiful mountain lake of Pacucha is Andahuaylas' main attraction, 10 km away from the town and reachable by car.

CHALHUANCA

This village has a basic hotel and a restaurant which is often used as a meal stop on the Cuzco to Nazca run. It is 120 km south-west of Abancay.

PUQUIO

This village is 189 km beyond Chalhuanca and also has a basic hotel and meal stop restaurant. The last 50 km before Puquio passes through an incredibly wild looking area of desolate, lake studded countryside – worth staying awake for.

PAMPAS GALERAS

Roughly 65 km beyond Puquio and 90 km before Nazca the road passes through the vicuña sanctuary of Pampas Galeras where you can see herds of vicuña from the bus. You can also get off and camp if you are self sufficient. Pampas Galeras reserve is most often visited from Nazca.

Central Peru

The central Peruvian Andes are one of the least visited and most forgotten areas of Peru. The harsh mountain terrain has made ground communications especially difficult and the region also suffers from a lack of air services. Huancayo, for example, is both the capital of the Department of Junín and Peru's fifth largest city with roughly a third of a million inhabitants – yet it lacks a commercial airport. Two of the area's other departmental capitals (Huancavelica and Cerro de Pasco) are also without commercial airports. The departmental capital of Ayacucho, founded in 1540, received its first permanent public telephone link with the outside world in 1964, at a time when there were still only a few dozen vehicles servicing the city. The neglected population of the Central Andes is mainly rural, involved in subsistence agriculture and among the poorest people in Peru.

It was in such an environment of isolation and poverty that the *Sendero Luminoso* or Shining Path, Peru's major terrorist organisation, emerged in the 1960s and grew in the 1970s. The violent activities of the Sendero, as it is simply referred to, escalated dramatically in the 1980s and headlines all over the world proclaimed Peru's internal unrest. Following reports of atrocities and mass murders in the central Peruvian highlands, committed both by the terrorists and by government troops during incompetent attempts to subdue the terrorists, tourism declined from the high levels of the late seventies. During 1983 and 1984, the Departments of Ayacucho, Huancavelica and Apurímac were almost completely deserted by travellers and tourists and Peruvian authorities strongly discouraged travellers from visiting these departments.

By 1985 however, things had quietened down considerably and tourism once again returned to these areas, albeit very slowly. I spent several weeks travelling here and found little external evidence of the Sendero. What I did find, however, were delightful colonial towns which are among the least spoilt in the entire Andean chain. The people were very friendly and frequently commented on how they were glad to see travellers again – it was a sign of the return to normalcy. The travel itself was exciting too, not only because of the magnificent mountain views but also because it took a certain amount of effort to get there. Compared to most of Peru, the region still has its communications problems, roads are bad and traversing them is a minor challenge.

Although the region has appeared to be safe for the last couple of years, the prudent traveller will make local enquiry before travelling to the Huancavelica-Ayacucho area. I found that the Tourist Information Office in Lima could give an accurate idea of whether or not the region was considered safe to travel in. My personal recommendations, assuming that the present situation continues, is definitely to visit the area if you're looking for some fairly off-the-beaten-track experiences without wanting to resort to sticking a machete through your teeth and poling a canoe in the headwaters of the Amazon! If you stay on the main highways (they're almost all spectacular but rough dirt or gravel roads) you'll have a great time. I don't suggest visiting villages that require extensive travel on back roads or mule tracks however. The Sendero is still active in the remoter regions and although foreign tourists are not their targets, there's no point in tempting providence.

The Central Highlands is certainly the area of Peru that have received the most negative publicity because of recent terrorist activities. Remember, however, that there is an extensive area north of Huancavelica-Ayacucho which is not as prone to terrorist related problems and which is also remote and visited infrequently. This includes the Department of Junín with its interesting handicrafts as seen in the weekly Sunday market at Huancayo. Many of the nearby villages are worth visiting to see the handicrafts being made at their source. North of Huancayo are many little known but worthwhile areas: the fabulous Franciscan monastery of Ocopa, the private astronomical observatory in Tarma, the bird life of the Lake of Junín and magnificent scenery everywhere. If you want to travel a lesser known part of Peru, then read on!

LA OROYA

This highland town of some 35,000 inhabitants proudly calls itself 'the metallurgical capital of Peru'. Unless you're interested in metallurgy – which in La Oroya translates into the huge, state-run, CENTROMIN smelter and refinery with its attendant slag heaps – you'll not want to linger here as it is a cold and unattractive place. However, most travellers visiting central Peru's interior at least pass through La Oroya for it is a major junction as well as being an important industrial town.

La Oroya, at over 3700 metres above sea level, is linked with Lima by a 187 km long railroad. This passes through the station of La Galera, which at 4781 metres above sea level is the world's highest station on a standard gauge track. If you do the trip from Lima, you'll find oxygen is available in 1st class and if you're not yet acclimatised, you may be glad to know it's there. Even sitting quietly in your seat is a breathless experience. The scenery during the second half of the trip is stark and bare. Llamas and alpacas are sometimes seen and the snow often comes to below 5000 metres. The scenery is awesome rather than pretty and its splendour is tarnished

by several mining operations.

As you can imagine, the huge vertical change in such a relatively short length of track makes this stretch of railway one of the most exciting in the world for train enthusiasts (not to mention ordinary travellers). The *South American Handbook* claims that along its whole length the railway traverses 66 tunnels, 59 bridges and 22 zigzags. I lost count when I did the trip but the figures seem about right. (For fares and schedules, see under Lima. Since mid 1986 this service has been temporarily suspended until further notice – terrorists blew up a bridge one night when the trains weren't running.)

From La Oroya, the railway continues north beyond Cerro de Pasco to Goyllarisquizga mine and south to Huancayo where you can change for another train to Huancavelica. The northern section has been closed for some years but the southern section had been operating fairly regularly until mid-1986. Most travellers from Lima take the train direct to Huancayo in one day and this will be the best way to go when the service is continued.

A road also links Lima with La Oroya and this is the only way to get there at present. From here you can take roads to the four points of the compass: north to Cerro de Pasco and Huánuco (and then down into the northern jungle); east to Tarma (and down into the central jungle); south to Huancayo, Huancavelica and Ayacucho (and on to Cuzco); and west to Lima. All of these central highland towns are described in this chapter.

Information

For obvious reasons, La Oroya is a place to travel through and not to. It is possible to travel from Lima to several other central highland towns in one day and therefore few travellers stop here. If you should be stranded, you'll find basic hotels and restaurants. There are two or three places near the train station. Buses also leave from near the train station. The *Hostal*

San Martín, which is about two or three km out of the centre in the direction of Lima, is said to be marginally better than the places by the station.

TARMA

This small town at about 3050 metres above sea level on the eastern slopes of the Andes is about the same size as La Oroya but much pleasanter – its local nickname is 'the pearl of the Andes'. It's only 60 km east of La Oroya and provides the best places to stay in the La Oroya/Tarma area.

Tarma has a long history. It is named after the Tarama people who inhabited the area before the Incas arrived. Both pre-Inca and Inca ruins are to be found in the hills and mountains surrounding the town, but they are overgrown and not well known. (An adventurer would have plenty of scope for discovering ruins on the nearby peaks.) The actual town seen today was founded by the Spaniards soon after the conquest, but the exact date is uncertain (I've read 1534, 1538 and 1545). Nothing remains of the early colonial era but there are a number of attractive 19th and early 20th century houses with white walls and red-tiled roofs.

Information

There is a travel agency, *Turismo Tarama*, which doubles as an information centre and can provide local guides. They have produced an informative booklet *Folleto Turistico de la Provincia de Tarma* by Rafael Cárdenas Santa María which is very useful and costs about US$1. Their office at Huaraz 537 (tel 2286) is open from 8.30 am to 12.30 pm and 2.30 to 5.30 pm daily except Sunday. Sr Cárdenas is often there to answer questions.

Things to See

The big attraction of the year is undoubtedly Easter with many processions during Holy Week, including several candle-lit ones after dark. They culminate on the morning of Easter Sunday with a marvellous procession to the Cathedral which follows a beautifully carpeted route made entirely of flower petals.

The annual fiesta of El Señor de Los Milagros (the Lord of the Miracles) takes place in late October with the 18th, 28th, and 29th being the principal feast days. (No, I don't know why there's a ten day gap.) This is another good opportunity to see processions marching over beautiful carpets of flower petals.

Other fiestas include Tarma Week near the end of July and San Sebastián on 20 January.

Also worth visiting is the small Astronomical Observatory run by the owner of the Hostal Central. Tarma is

1	Cine Ritz
2	ENTEL, Hotel Galaxia & Restaurant Chavín
3	Restaurant Conquistador
4	Banco de Crédito
5	Turismo Tarama
6	Expreso Tarma
7	Empresa Hidalgo
8	Comité 1 (Lima)
9	Trans Arellano
10	Trans Chanchamayo
11	Post Office
12	Hostal Tarma
13	Restaurant Don Vale
14	Hotel Vargas
15	Hotel Tuchu
16	Comité 20 (Chanchamayo)
17	Police
18	Bus stop to Acobamba & Palca
19	Hostal Cordova
20	Trans San Juan
21	Cooptal & Trans Palcamayo
22	Hostal Anchibaya
23	Hostal Ritz
24	Sr de Muruhuay bus stop
25	Comité 3 (Huancayo)
26	Hotel El Dorado
27	Hostal Central & Astronomical Observatory
28	Baños Del Sol

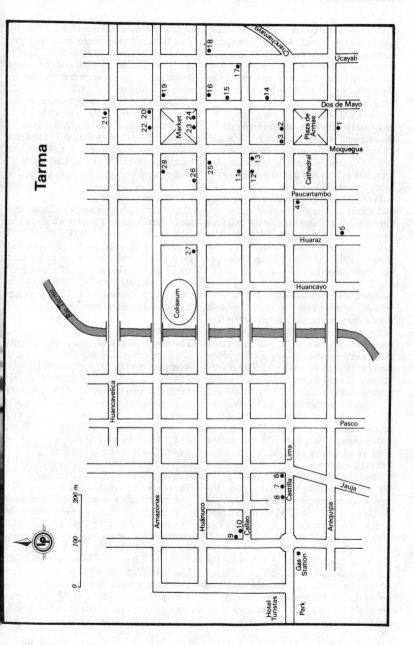

Tarma

high in the mountains and on the clear nights of June through August, some good star gazing is to be had. The owner was temporarily away when I was visiting Tarma, so I didn't get a chance to use the observatory – I'd welcome any first hand reports.

The Cathedral is modern (built in 1965) and is of interest because it contains the remains of Peru's president, Manuel A Odría, who was born in Tarma and who had the Cathedral constructed during his presidency. The clock in the clock tower dates from 1862.

There are several nearby excursions which will be described at the end of the Tarma section. These include the religious shrine of Señor de Muruhuay (9 km), the cave of Guagapo (33 km), and the weaving village of San Pedro de Cajas (50 km from Tarma).

Places to Stay – bottom end

One of the cheapest places is the basic *Hostal Ritz* on the market which charges 75c single and US$1.40 double. It has communal showers with cold water and the outside rooms are noisy. Nearby is the similar *Hostal Anchibaya*. The dingy looking *Hostal Tarma* charges 90c per person and the *Hostal Cordova* doesn't look much better at US$1.20/1.75 singles/doubles; an extra 20c for a room with a private bath. If you're staying in a cold water cheapie you can find hot public showers at *Baños del Sol*, half a block from the market.

The *Hostal Central* is old but adequate. It's an interesting place because the owner has an astronomical observatory in the hotel. Rooms are US$1.30/1.90 singles/doubles and about 25c per person extra for a room with a private bath. There is hot water occasionally.

Among the better cheap hotels are the *Tuchu*, charging US$2/3.10 singles/doubles in rooms with private bath and hot water in the mornings. The *Hotel Vargas* has spacious rooms and some hard beds if you're fed up with soft and sagging mattresses. They charge US$2.20/4 in rooms with private bath and hot water in the mornings. Similarly priced is the *Hotel El Dorado* which has the same facilities and has been recommended by some travellers.

The best of the cheaper hotels is the new and clean *Hotel Galaxia* on the Plaza de Armas. Unfortunately, it has only 16 rooms and so is often full. All rooms are with private bath and hot water in the mornings and they charge US$3.25/5.25 singles/doubles.

Places to Stay – middle

The best run place in town is the government-run *Hotel de Turistas* which can be reserved in Lima at ENTURPERU (tel 721928). The hotel is set in pleasant gardens at the west end of town and rates are US$5/8 singles/doubles in rooms with communal baths and US$9.50/13.50 in rooms with private baths. These prices include continental breakfast.

Places to Eat

There are plenty of cheap restaurants along Avenida Lima (which becomes Avenida Castilla in the west end of town). The *Restaurant Chavín* on the Plaza de Armas is good and the *Conquistador* nearby is acceptable and cheap. The best restaurant in town is *Don Vale* – they only open for meal times (11.30 am to 2.30 pm and 7 to 10.30 pm) and you can get a reasonable meal for about US$1.

Getting There

There are two areas of town from which transport leaves frequently: from near the market and from Avenida Castilla at the west end. Along Avenida Castilla, Expreso Tarma goes to La Oroya every hour for US$1.10; Comité 1 has three cars a day to Lima for US$6 and takes six hours; Hidalgo has a slower and cheaper overnight bus to Lima and also two buses a day to Huancayo (US$1.40, three hours); Transportes Arellano has a daily night bus to Lima (US$4); and Trans

Chanchamayo has a cheap and slow overnight truck to the lowland towns of La Merced and San Ramón (collectively known as Chanchamayo). Trans Chanchamayo also has buses from Lima to Chanchamayo which pass through the market soon after dawn but they are often already full.

The most convenient way to get to Chanchamayo is by the colectivo taxis of Comité 20 which leave from the market when they're full. They charge US$2.30 per passenger for the two hour precipitous descent to about 600 metres at La Merced. It's worth doing the trip just for the views. (Note that in 1986 this road was closed for repair daily except Sunday and travellers could only leave Tarma for Chanchamayo before 6.30 am or after 5 pm. Repairs should be completed by the late 1980s but make local enquiry to find out if the road is fully open by the time you read this.)

Getting Around

There are several companies which have local services from near the Market. Most of these go to Acobamba (to visit the shrine of El Señor de Muruhuay) and some continue to Palcamayo (to visit the famous Guagapo caves). Transportation to San Pedro de Cajas is irregular and cannot be relied upon – ask around. The companies marked at 18, 21 and 24 on the Tarma map are local bus companies.

ACOBAMBA

This village is 9 km from Tarma and is famous for the religious sanctuary of El Señor de Muruhuay which is visible on a small hill about 1½ km away from Acobamba. Everyone knows where it is.

The sanctuary is built around an image of Christ painted onto the rock. Historians claim that it was painted by a royalist officer after losing the Battle of Junín, which was a major battle of independence fought on 6 August 1824. Despite this, legends persist of the painting's miraculous appearance. The first building around the image was a roughly thatched hut which was replaced by a small chapel in 1835. Since then the feast of El Señor de Muruhuay has been celebrated annually every May. The third and present sanctuary was inaugurated on 30 April 1972 and is a very modern building with an electronically controlled bell tower and decorated with huge weavings from San Pedro de Cajas.

The annual festival is held throughout May and is a colourful affair. Apart from the religious services and processions, there are ample opportunities to sample local produce and see people dressed in traditional clothes. Many stalls are set up offering *chicha* (corn beer) and *cuy* (roast guinea-pig) but be wary if your stomach is not used to local food. There are dances and fireworks, and very few gringos. There are no hotels and most visitors stay in nearby Tarma.

PALCAMAYO

This attractive village is 28 km away from Tarma and serviced by several colectivos a day. From Palcamayo it is possible to visit the *Gruta de Guagapo* which is a huge limestone cave in the hills about four km away. It is one of the largest and best known caves in Peru and is officially protected as a National Speleological Area. There are also several other less well known caves in the area which would be of interest to speleologists (those who study caves).

The Guagapo cave has been explored by various expeditions from all over the world and requires caving equipment and experience for a full descent. It is well over a km long and contains waterfalls, squeezes and underwater sections. It is possible to enter the cave for a short distance but soon you need to wade. A local guide, Sr Modesto Castro, has explored the cave on numerous occasions and can provide you with ropes, lanterns, etc. He lives in one of the two houses below the mouth of the cave and has a collection of photographs and newspaper clippings describing the exploration of the cave.

To get to the cave ask in Palcamayo. You'll be shown a dirt road which winds off into the hills – it's a pleasant four km walk. The cave has a large opening in the side of the mountain to the right of the road and Sr Castro's house is on the left hand side of the road. Bottled drinks are available and prospective expeditions could camp.

The Palcamayo area is also known for the many Inca and pre-Inca ruins in the surrounding hills. They have been little explored, however, and are of little interest to the casual tourist. An adventurer equipped with camping gear could spend days wandering the hill tops looking for ruins.

SAN PEDRO DE CAJAS

This high (4040 metres above sea level) Andean village is known throughout Peru for the unique style and excellence of its tapestries which are often exported. The tapestries are made of stuffed rolls of wool (difficult to visualise until you actually see some). They can be bought from the weavers for less than you pay in Lima but the village is not oriented to selling to tourists, facilities are very limited and some basic Spanish is needed.

Sr Teofilo Oscanoa Vilches runs the one basic hotel, the *Comercio* at Calle Chanchamayo 120. A bed will cost under US$1. Not surprisingly, there are no hot showers, but the people are friendly. There are no restaurants but you can arrange simple meals at the hotel. Some weavings are available here and you can ask around if you want to see more. Change as much money as you'll need before you get here because there are no money changing facilities.

Market day is every other week on Wednesdays. It is a locally important livestock and produce market and not a crafts market.

Getting There

You can get a bus from Tarma to Palcamayo easily enough (see above) but buses continuing on to San Pedro are infrequent. You can walk or hope to hitch a ride along the 16-km dirt road which goes from Palcamayo, past the Guagapo Cave and on to San Pedro. The road climbs uphill most of the way and San Pedro is about 800 metres above Palcamayo.

If you want to try to get all the way to San Pedro by bus, ask around the north side of the market in Tarma early in the morning. There is also a bus from the La Oroya railway station at about 2 pm and there are daily buses from Junín.

JAUJA

Heading south-east along the Central Andes from La Oroya is the main road to Huancayo. Several towns of importance are passed along the way. The first of these is the historic town of Jauja which lies on a junction about 80 km south-east of La Oroya, 60 km south of Tarma and 40 km north of Huancayo.

Before the time of the Incas, the area was an important Huanca Indian community and Huanca ruins can be seen on the skyline of the hill to the south-east of town and about three km away. There are many other little known ruins in this area which is ideal for adventurous walking. Jauja is historic because it was Pizarro's first capital in Peru, although this was a short-lived honour. Little remains of the early colonial days except for some finely carved wooden altars in the main church.

About four km away from Jauja is the pleasant Laguna de Paca, a small resort which has a hostal, a few rowing boats, and fishing.

The colourful weekly market is held on Wednesday mornings.

Places to Stay & Eat

Most people who visit Jauja stay in Huancayo and travel to Jauja on one of the frequent buses joining the two towns.

If you want to stay in Jauja you'll find the basic *Hotel Ganso de Oro* in front of the railway station. They charge about US$1.25/2 singles/doubles and have hot water at times. They tend to get full by early afternoon. Similarly priced is the *Hotel Santa Rosa* on the corner of the main plaza by the church – only cold water here. The best place is the government-run *Albergue de Paca* by the lake of that name; rooms are about US$5/8 including continental breakfast. Reservations can be made in Lima at Enturperu (tel 721928).

There are several cheap and basic restaurants of which the best are the ones in the *Ganso de Oro* and *Paca* hotels.

Getting There

The train from Lima to Huancayo stops at Jauja (see under Lima and Huancayo for further train information).

ETURSA minibuses leave from Amazonas 789 in Huancayo as soon as they are full – about every ½ hour. They charge about 80c for the one-hour drive. This is the most convenient way of getting to Jauja.

CONCEPCIÓN

South of Jauja the road branches and follows either the west or east sides of the Mantara River valley to Huancayo. By taking the east side one comes to Concepción, a small village about half way between Jauja and Huancayo. Although the village itself is of no more than passing interest, the nearby Convent of Santa Rosa de Ocopa is well worth a visit.

The Convent was built by the Franciscans in the early 1700s as a training centre for their missionaries heading down into the jungle regions. It's a beautiful building set in a pleasant garden and during the years of missionary work the friars have built up an impressive collection which can be seen in their museum. This includes stuffed jungle wildlife, Indian artefacts, photographs of early missionary work, old maps, a fantastic library of some 20,000 volumes (many of them centuries old), a large collection of colonial religious art mainly of the Cuzqueño school, and many other objects of interest. It's well worth a visit.

The Convent is open daily except Tuesdays from 9 am to 12 noon and from 3 to 5 pm. Entrance is 30c. Frequent colectivo taxis leave from the Concepción Plaza de Armas for Ocopa, which is about five km away.

Places to Stay & Eat

There are a couple of basic hotels. The best is the reasonably pleasant *Hotel Real* on the main plaza which charges about US$1 per person and has hot water in the mornings. Cheaper and more basic is the *Hotel El Paisanito* about a half block from the plaza.

There are a couple of simple restaurants which tend to close soon after dark.

Getting There

The easiest way to get to Concepción is to take one of the frequent colectivo taxis from Huancayo leaving from Calixto and Ancash behind the civic centre. They charge about 60c per passenger. Alternatively, and more cheaply, take one of the buses which leave frequently from Calixto and Mantaro.

HUANCAYO

This modern city of about 360,000 inhabitants lies on the flat Mantaro River valley which is one of the most fertile in the Central Andes and supports a large rural population. At an elevation of 3260 metres above sea level and a distance of about 300 km from Lima, Huancayo is the capital of the Central Andean department of Junín and is the major commercial centre for the area. It is of great importance as a market town for the people living in the many nearby villages but it is still relatively undeveloped on a national level despite its size and departmental status.

The town itself is not of great interest but its weekly Sunday market, when both crafts and produce from the Mantaro River valley are sold, is famous among locals and travellers. In addition, Huancayo makes a good base from which to visit the many interesting villages of the Mantaro valley.

Information

The government-run *Dirección de Turismo* is on the 3rd floor of Ancash 415, just off the Plaza de Armas. It is open from 7 am to 2.15 pm Mondays to Fridays. Their office is a great source of information about sightseeing in the Mantaro valley, what there is to do and how to get there by public transport. The enthusiastic young woman whom I talked to bemoaned the fact that Huancayo always seemed to be forgotten in the tourist scheme of things and then provided me with a huge list of places in the Mantaro valley that I should see. To see everything would take a couple of weeks and I'll try and outline the best places in the pages that follow. Definitely visit this tourist bureau if you're interested in spending some time in the area, especially if you speak Spanish.

Money Exchange There are several casas de cambio between the civic centre and the Plaza de Armas on Avenida Real. These are usually the best places to

1	Hostal Dani
2	Railway Station to Lima
3	Hotel Residencial Huancayo
4	Lalos Restaurant
5	Hotel Mandarin
6	Residencial Baldeon
7	Comité 1 (to Tarma)
8	Comités 3 & 30 (to Tarma & Lima)
9	Cathedral
10	ETUCSA Bus & Duchas Tina
11	Cine Central
12	Hostal Palermo
13	Flamingo Grill
14	Banco de la Nación
15	Iglesia La Merced
16	Chifa Porvenir
17	Banco de los Andes
18	Banco de Crédito
19	Hotel Kiya & Chifa Imperial
20	Hotel Santa Felecita
21	Restaurant Olimpico & Café Giraldez
22	Casa de Cambio
23	Tourist Office
24	Plaza Amazonas (buses to Chupaca & Pilcomayo)
25	Etursa Minibus (to Jauja)
26	Buses to La Oroya
27	Iglesia La Inmaculada (buses to Hualhuas & Cochas)
28	Market
29	Buses to San Jeronimo & Concepción
30	Expreso Huaytapallana & Hotel Pierola
31	Arzapolo Bus
32	Hotel Prince
33	Taxis to Concepión
34	Hotel de Turistas
35	Casa de Cambio
36	Empresa Hidalgo
37	Hotel El Inca & Comité 22 (to Lima)
38	Hotel Centro
39	Hostal Roma
40	Comité 12 (to Lima)
41	ENTEL
42	Post Office
43	Municipalidad
44	Hotel Real & Hotel Torre Torre
45	Hostal Santo Domingo
46	Hotel El Dorado
47	Banco de Crédito
48	Cines Real & Andino
49	M Caceres Bus (to Lima)
50	Hotel Presidente
51	Alarcon Bus (to Satipo)
52	Molina Bus (to Ayacucho)
53	Trans Ayacucho
54	Percy's Hotel
55	Railway Station to Huancavelica

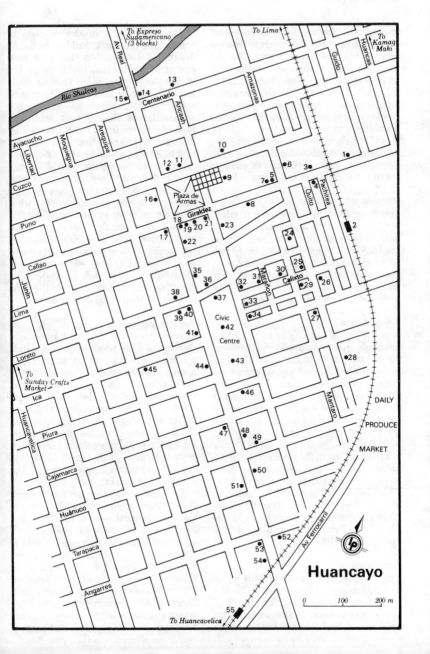

To Expreso
Sudamericano
(3 blocks)

To Lima

To Kamaq
Maki

Av Real

Río Shulcas

Centenario

13

15

14

Ayacucho

Moquegua

Arequipa

Ancash

Amazonas

Guido

Huancas

Libertad

Cuzco

Puno

Callao

Junín

Lima

Loreto

Ica

10

12 11

16

Plaza de
Armas

9

Giraldez

18

17

19 20 21

22

23

35

36

38

39 40

41

37

Civic

42

Centre

43

44

45

46

6 3

7 5

8

1

Pachitea

Quito

4

2

24

30

25

32 31

33

34

Marañón

Calixto

29 26

27

28

To
Sunday Crafts
Market

Huancavelica

Piura

Cajamarca

Huánuco

Tarapaca

Angarres

47

48

49

50

51

52

53

54

Mantaro

DAILY

PRODUCE

MARKET

Av Ferrocarril

55

To Huancavelica

Huancayo

0   100   200 m

change cash. You may find that travellers' cheques are not easy to change in casas de cambio but the banks marked on the map, especially Banco de Crédito, will often exchange travellers' cheques, but at a loss of as much as 10%. Of course, the situation varies from year to year (and even month to month) so by the time you read this you may find that changing travellers' cheques is no problem.

The major hotels will normally accept US dollars – cash and travellers' cheques – and exchange them for guests.

Warning

Huancayo has built up quite a reputation for thievery and the bus and train stations and Sunday market are said to be crawling with thieves. I found that I had no problem (admittedly I'm used to this kind of situation) but many travellers have complained about bag snatching and slashing, pickpocketing, etc.

Things to See

A good view of the city is to be had by heading north-east on Avenida Giraldez. About two km from the town centre is Cerrito de la Libertad where, apart from the city view, there are snack bars and a playground. Continuing about another two km (there is a sign pointing to the right and an obvious path) you come to the eroded geological formations known as Torre Torre.

In the city itself, the Cathedral and the church of La Inmaculada are both modern and not particularly noteworthy. The most interesting church is La Merced on the first block of Avenida Real. Although there's isn't much to see, this is where the Peruvian Constitution was approved in 1839.

Entertainment

There really isn't much nightlife to be had in Huancayo. There are three cinemas marked on the map. The *Flamingo Grill* at Ancash and Ayacucho has some kind of peña late on Friday and Saturday nights

– I've never been. In the interests of researching this book, I did go to the *El Molino Discotheque* at the north-west end of Calle Huancas by the river. It's your basic dancing place (mainly disco records) with a dark bar. There is a couples only rule but despite this fact the woman friend that I went with was hassled unmercifully. I don't much like disco and just wanted to sit at the bar and talk to Andrea about local handicrafts – the local machos figured that if I didn't want to dance with my friend then one of them could just take my place. (I offer this vignette in an attempt to show what going out in Peru may involve.) It's an OK place if you do want to disco – or if you want to meet some local drinking/dancing companions. Other dancing joints are to be found at El Tambo, which is an area about one or two km north-west of downtown and a block or two to the right of Avenida Real. Taxi drivers know it.

Markets & Shopping

There are two main markets in Huancayo. One is the daily produce market which occurs along the railway tracks and in the nearby covered market (see map). It's worth a visit. In the *Mercado Modelo* (as the indoor market is known) the meat section sells various Andean delicacies including fresh and dried frogs, as well as the more typical guinea pigs, rabbits, chickens, etc. It's very colourful. Although it's a daily market, the most important day is Sunday which coincides with the weekly crafts market.

The Sunday crafts market is held along Calle Huancavelica along five or six blocks to the north-west of Ica. There is a good variety of weavings, sweaters and other textile goods, embroidered items, ceramics, wood carvings and the carved gourds which are a speciality of the area. These are made in the nearby villages of Cochas Grande and Chico. There is also a variety of non-crafts items ranging from cassette tapes to frilly underwear. This market is colourful but you must bargain hard to get the best prices. Gourds are reputedly the best buy. This is definitely the place to watch your pockets, your wallet and your camera.

There is one excellent crafts cooperative which has a good selection of high quality goods from the departments of Junín and Huancavelica. This is *Kamaq Maki* which is Quechua for 'Creative Hand' and consists of a cooperative of several hundred local craftspeople who strive to continue traditional techniques and designs in their work. They consider themselves to be farmers first and crafts-people second, which in itself is a traditional arrangement. The quality of goods is high and prices tend to be fixed. Kamaq Maki is open from 8 am to 12 noon and from 2 to 6 pm on weekdays and from 10 am to 12 noon and from 3 to 5 pm on weekends and holidays. Their store (which is almost a crafts museum) is at Brasilia 200. (It's off my map; continue north-east along Calle Huancas three blocks beyond Centenario to San Carlos and turn right for a couple of long blocks. Brasilia is on your left.) If you're even remotely interested in crafts you should definitely visit the cooperative. They'll be happy to ship goods home for you.

Adventure Tour Guide

A local man, Luis 'Lucho' Hurtado, speaks good English and knows the surrounding area well. He can guide you on adventurous treks down the eastern slopes of the Andes and into the high jungle. You walk, ride horses or take public transport. It isn't luxurious but it's a good chance to see some of the 'real' rural Peru. His father has a ranch in the middle of nowhere where you can stay and you get to visit all kinds of local people. I met Lucho only briefly at the South American Explorers Club and he impressed me as being honest and knowledgeable. I have heard repeated recommendations for his trips which usually last from three to eight days. If you can get a group together, so much the better. If not, you may be able to hook up with another group. Costs are about US$16 per person per day, including simple food. Accommodation is rustic and camping is sometimes done. If you're interested about doing some guided off-the-beaten-track travel, look for Lucho at Calle Huancas 209. His postal address is Apartado 510, Huancayo (tel 222395). He puts signs up in the *Hostal Dani*.

Peruvian weaving

Places to Stay - bottom end

There are many cheap hotels located in the area between the railway station to Lima and the Plaza de Armas. There are also a couple of cheap hotels located in front of the railway station to Huancavelica but the central ones are better. The *Hotel Residencial Huancayo* is US$2 for a double room and there is hot water in the communal showers all day. This place is popular with travellers. Also popular, and deservedly so, is the small and simple *Hostal Dani* which has a friendly and helpful English-speaking landlady. They charge US$1.40 per person and there is also hot water all day. One of the cheapest hotels in town, and reasonably good, is the *Hostal Santo Domingo* which charges about US$1 per person and has hot water sometimes. It's close to the Sunday crafts market.

Other cheap hotels include the *Hotel Prince* which has basic rooms with private baths for US$1.80/2.80 singles/doubles. There is hot water only in the early mornings and evenings and there are some rooms with shared showers which are about 50c cheaper. Beware that some of the rooms do not have windows. Near the Civic Centre is the *Hotel Torre Torre* which is basic but reasonably clean and charges US$2.20/3 for rather dark rooms with private hot showers. There are also cheaper rooms with shared showers. Next door is the more basic *Hotel El Real* at US$1 per person.

Right opposite the Hidalgo bus station on Loreto is the *Hotel El Inca* which charges US$2.20 for a double with bath and cold shower – there is hot water in the communal showers. It's a big hotel and adequate if you arrive late at night and couldn't be bothered to look further. Near the Plaza de Armas is the *Hotel Centro* which has only cold water and doesn't seem very good; rooms are US$2 a double. Better is the *Residencial Baldeon* which charges US$1.40 per person and has hot water. They sell good home made pies.

Other cheapies include the *Hotel Mandarin* which doesn't seem too good; the *Hostal Palermo* whose main claim to fame is being on the Plaza de Armas; the *Hotel Pierola* and the *Hostal Roma*, neither of which look very good either. Near the Huancavelica railway station is the overpriced *Percy's Hotel* which charges US$3 per person in rooms with private bath but no hot water.

Slightly up market is the modern *Hotel El Dorado* which has clean and carpeted rooms with private bathroom for US$2.50 per person. The hot water supply tends to be erratic, however. It's a block from the civic centre and easy to find – it has huge signs all over the 5th floor.

If you end up staying in a hotel with no hot water and would like a hot shower, try *Duchas Tina* behind the Cathedral. They have public hot showers open all day.

Places to Stay - middle

There are two clean mid-range hotels on the Plaza de Armas. Both the *Santa Felicita* and the *Kiya* charge US$4.50/5.50 singles/doubles with private bath and hot water. Rooms have telephones, and soap and towel are provided.

The centrally located *Hotel de Turistas* is an old and pleasant-looking building with some wooden balconies. They charge US$7/10 with bath and hot water – there are some cheaper rooms with shared bath. Continental breakfast is included and the restaurant and bar is pleasant. Similarly priced and more modern is the *Hotel Presidente*.

Places to Eat

Visitors should try the local speciality *Papa a la Huancaina* which is a boiled potato topped with a tasty white sauce of cheese, milk, hot pepper and butter. The whole concoction is served with an olive and eaten as a cold potato salad. Despite the hot pepper, it's not too spicy – in fact I find that it has a distinctly peanut-like flavour.

There are several good restaurants on or near the Plaza de Armas. The best is the recommended *Restaurant Olimpico* which has good meals for about US$1, efficient service and a huge open kitchen where you can see your food being prepared. Also good is the *Chifa Imperio* (in the Hotel Kiya) for Chinese food and the *Café Giraldez* for fried chicken. If you're on a tight budget, try the *Chifa Porvenir* which looks rather divey but serves reasonable meals for 50c. Also cheap and popular, is *Lalo's*, but the service can only be described as chaotic. There are plenty of other places for you to try.

Getting There

There is no airport and the train service from Lima was suspended indefinitely in mid-1986, so bus or car is the only transport currently available from the coast. The railway may well reopen by the time you read this book, however.

Rail There are two train stations in different parts of town and they are not connected by trains (although the tracks do connect). The Central Station serves Lima. The journey takes about 10 hours and costs about US$3 in 1st class – tickets usually sell out the day before. Second class is about US$2.20. Before the service was suspended, there were three departures every week at 7 am on Mondays, Wednesdays and Fridays. It's a spectacular journey which is further described under the Lima and La Oroya sections.

The Huancavelica train station at the south-eastern end of town is the best way to get to Huancavelica because the road is not very good. There are two types of trains; the faster *autovagon* and the slower *tren*. The autovagon takes 3½ hours, costs US$2 and leaves at 7 am and 1.30 pm daily except Sunday. Try and buy tickets on the previous day if possible as this service is very popular and often full. The tren takes about five hours, leaves at 7.30 am daily except Sunday and costs US$1.50 in 1st class and US$1.20 in 2nd class. The ticket window usually opens up about 6 am and then closes when the morning trains have gone. It reopens about 12.30 pm for the afternoon autovagon and then may open again in the evening. Ticket selling hours are a bit erratic.

Buses It's worth checking around the various bus companies if you're on a tight budget as one or two of them may sometimes be offering special fares. For example, the last time that I took the bus to Lima I went with Hidalgo which had two morning buses and three night buses and charged US$3 for the nine to 11 hour trip. In comparison, ETUCSA had more frequent departures but charged US$3.50 per passenger, Expreso Sud Americano were charging US$4 each and Empresa Los Andes charged US$4.50 for the same trip. So shop around.

Hidalgo have twice daily buses to Tarma (two hours, US$1.40) and to Huancavelica (four hours, US$1.80).

Arzapalo has two or three buses (usually overnight) to Cerro de Pasco (eight hours, US$2.70).

ETUCSA was the only company which was running regular service to Ayacucho (10 hours, US$4.50, very cold and bumpy) when I was last in Huancayo. Buses left every night and every other day . The road to Ayacucho is notoriously bad so schedules and the companies running them change particularly frequently on this route. Direct service from Huancayo to Cuzco is normally not available and travellers to Cuzco should take a bus to Ayacucho and try again there. ETUCSA also has daily departures for La Merced and Satipo (in the jungle).

Alarcon has three departures a week to Satipo on the direct road which is very rugged and beautiful (I'm told). I've never done this trip and would like to hear from anyone who does.

Local buses to most of the local villages leave from the street intersections which I've shown on the map. There is rarely an office or fixed schedule. You just show up and wait until a bus is ready to leave. Ask other people waiting for the local bus for more details. The Tourist Office is good with local bus information.

If you are in a hurry to get somewhere you might consider taking one of the taxi colectivos which are about twice as expensive and 25% faster than the buses. There are usually several departures a day with each company. Comités 12, 22 and 30 go to Lima, and 1 and 30 go to Tarma.

Sightseeing along the Mantaro Valley

Two main road systems connect Huancayo with the villages of the Mantaro Valley. They are simply known as the left or right of the river, with Huancayo lying in the southern part of the valley, left translates into west and right into east. It is best to try and confine your sightseeing on any one given day to one side or the other because bridges are infrequent.

Perhaps the most interesting excursion is on the east side of the valley to the twin villages of Cochas Grande and Cochas Chico which are about 11 km away from Huancayo. These are the major centres for the production of the incised gourds for which the area is famous. Oddly enough, the gourds are mainly grown on the coast and imported into the highlands from the Chiclayo and Ica areas. Once they reach the highlands, they are dried, scorched and decorated with woodworking tools. The gourds are available at the Huancayo Sunday crafts market but, if you speak Spanish and can hit it off with the locals, you can see them being made and buy them at Cochas.

Other villages which you can visit for handicrafts include San Agustín de Cajas, Hualhuas and San Jerónimo de Tuman. Cajas is known for the manufacture of broad brimmed wool hats although it seems to be a dying industry now. Hualhuas is famous for its wool products – it's a centre for the manufacture of ponchos, weavings, sweaters and other items. San Jerónimo is known for its

filigreed silverwork. In addition it has a 17th century church with fine wooden altars. It should be noted that whilst the villages are easily visited from Huancayo, most of the buying and selling is done in Huancayo and there are few shops or other facilities. The key here is to be able to speak Spanish and make friends with the locals.

Continuing north of these east side villages one soon comes to Concepción (see before Huancayo) from where it is possible to visit the fascinating Convent of Ocopa.

HUANCAVELICA

Driving south from Huancayo for 147 km brings us to Huancavelica, the capital of the department of the same name. It's a high and remote area. Most of the department lies above 3500 metres and has a cold climate although it can get T-shirt hot during the sunny days of the dry season – May to October. The rest of the year tends to be wet and during the rainiest months from February to April the roads are sometimes in such bad shape that Huancavelica can be virtually cut off from the rest of Peru.

The city is located at nearly 3700 metres above sea level and has a population of only some 20,000 inhabitants. It is a historic place however. Before the arrival of Europeans it was a strategic Inca centre and shortly after the conquest the Spaniards discovered its mineral wealth. By 1564, the Spaniards were sending Indian slaves to Huancavelica to work in the mercury and silver mines. The present town was founded in 1571 under the name of Villa Rica de Oropesa and it still retains a very pleasant colonial atmosphere. It's a small but attractive town and you certainly won't see too many tourists.

There are eight churches of note of which Santa Ana, now in a bad state of disrepair, was founded in the 16th century and was followed in the 17th century by the Cathedral, Santo Domingo,

San Francisco, San Cristobal and La Ascension. San Sebastián came later still but appears in a worse state of repair than most of the others. San Francisco is famous for its 11 intricately worked altars. The Cathedral has been restored and contains what has been called the best colonial altar in Peru. It is certainly a magnificent church. Santo Domingo is currently under restoration.

Unfortunately, Huancavelica is suffering from the aftermath of the recent Sendero Luminoso terrorist upheaval. Most of the churches are still closed although the situation is definitely normalising. Despite assurances from the tourist office that the Cathedral would be open from 6 to 8 pm and San Francisco from 6 to 8 am I found that San Francisco didn't open at all when I was there and that the Cathedral was only open from 7 pm. I was able to visit Santo Domingo by talking to the workmen who were restoring it – it was interesting to see the restoration process under way.

Terrorism
This area, along with the department of Ayacucho, remains one of the most sensitive to terrorist problems. It seemed quiet when I was there in mid-1986 and the locals seemed to think that there was little to worry about. Despite this, it would be wise to make enquiry in the Lima or Huancayo tourist offices to ensure that the situation remains stable before embarking on a trip to this charming and remote highland town.

Tourist Information The very fact that there is a functioning Tourist Office is a good sign that things are returning to normal. It was obvious, however, that when I was there they were still not used to seeing many tourists. They weren't able to tell me when the churches would be open for example. Things will probably improve. The Tourist Office is on the second floor of Manuel Segura 122. There is no sign outside.

Police I had to register at the PIP office (see map) upon arrival. This was a quick and straightforward formality – they just wanted to see my passport and write down my name and number.

Later during my first evening in Huancavelica I was visited in my hotel room by three plain clothes policemen. I showed the proper amount of indignation and they soon left. It seemed just as well that I had already registered with the PIP. Enquire upon arrival about what the current regulations are.

Money Exchange Your best bet is to change money in Huancayo. There are no casas de cambio in Huancavelica and the banks cannot be relied upon to even change cash let alone travellers' cheques. The Banco de Crédito is your best chance, although don't rely on it.

If you're staying at the *Hotel de Turistas* you can pay your bill in dollars but at a loss.

Post The Post Office on the Plaza de Armas is worth a look because of the tumbledown old colonial building that it is housed in.

Hot Springs The San Cristobal hot springs (see map) are fed into a large though slightly murky swimming pool in which you can relax for about 5c. For 10c you can have a shower. There is a bar and café and it's reasonably pleasant. They are open from 6 am to 4.30 pm daily and will rent you towel, soap and bathing suit if you've forgotten yours (although their selection of bathing wear is limited and unlovely).

Market Market day is Sunday and although there are smaller daily markets, Sunday is the best day to see the locals in traditional dress (see the next town, Lircay). The main market area is by the river with a smaller market off the main street of M Muñoz.

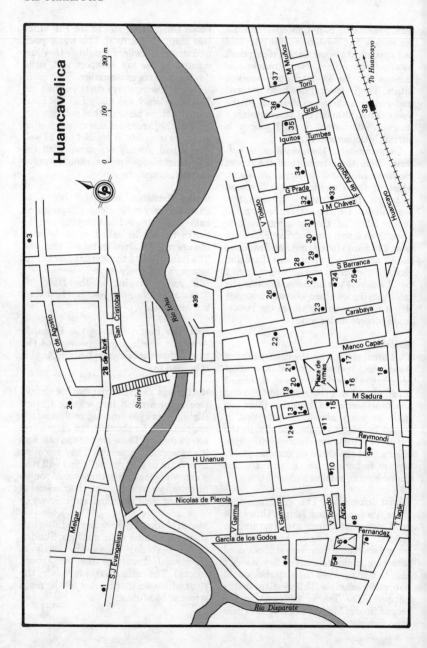

Huancavelica

Río Ichu

Río Disparate

To Huancayo

Stairs

Plaza de Armas

5 de Agosto
28 de Abril
San Cristobal
Melgar
S J Evangelista
Nicolas de Pierola
H Unanue
Garcia de los Godos
V Garma
A Gamarra
V Toledo
Arica
Fernandez
T Tagle
Raymondi
M Sadura
Manco Capac
Carabaya
S Barranca
J M Chávez
F de Arauco
G Prada
V Toledo
Tumbes
Iquitos
Grau
Toril
M Muñoz
Huancayo

1	Plaza & Church of the Ascension
2	Hot Baths (Natural)
3	Plaza & Church of San Cristobal
4	Bar Restaurant Jek
5	San Sebastian Church
6	Bolognesi Plaza
7	San Francisco Church
8	Hostal San Francisco
9	Banco de la Nación
10	Banco de Crédito
11	Restaurant Ganza de Oro
12	Recreo La Cantuta
13	Cine Tauro
14	Restaurant Joy
15	Cine Sideral
16	Cathedral
17	Hotel de Turistas
18	Hostal Mercurio
19	Tourist Information
20	Post Office
21	Town Hall
22	ENTEL
23	Hostal Tahuantisuyo
24	Hotel Savoy
25	Hostal Santo Domingo
26	Santo Domingo Church
27	Market
28	Restaurant Japonesita
29	Empresa Hidalgo
30	Litós Pollería
31	Chifa Imperio
32	Emp Trans Huascar
33	Hostal Peru
34	Expreso Huancavelica
35	PIP
36	Parque Mariscal Castillo
37	Santa Ana Church
38	Railway Station
39	Market

Places to Stay

Most hotels are very cheap and have only cold water – not a great hardship with the natural hot baths in town.

The cheapest place is the *Hostal San Francisco* followed by the very simple but reasonably clean *Hostal Peru* where you can stay for just 50c per person, or 75c for a couple sharing a bed. A little more expensive but not any better looking is the *Savoy* for 70c single and 90c double, and the *Santo Domingo* for 75c per person. The best of the super cheapies is the *Hotel Tahuantinsuyo* which has some well-lit rooms with table and chair for 90c single and US$1.50 double (add 30c for rooms with private bath). They advertise hot water but it is currently broken down and may remain so for years.

If you want hot water you can try the *Hostal Mercurio* which charges about US$1.40 per person but it jumps to around US$3 each if you want a private bath. It's clean but grim looking – rows of rooms painted an institutional green.

The best in town is, of course, the government-run *Hotel de Turistas* on the Plaza de Armas. It's a nice enough place and has hot water. They charge about US$9/13 singles/doubles for rooms with private bath – rates are about 30% lower if you take a room with shared bath. Prices include a continental breakfast.

Places to Eat

There aren't any particularly good restaurants in town. The restaurant at the Hotel de Turistas is the most expensive and no more than mediocre. Anywhere else in town you can eat for a dollar or less. There are several chicken places along M Muñoz between the two main plazas of which the best is *Litós Pollería*. There are other cheap restaurants along the same street of which the *El Dorado* and the *Chifa Imperio* are probably the best – though nothing to get excited about. Just off M Muñoz is *La Japonesita* – no, it's not a shushi place but it does serve excellent trout. This is fished from the large nearby Andean lake of Chochococha, which at 4600 metres above sea level must be one of the highest commercial fish sources in the world.

Another street to look along for food is V Toledo where you'll find the *Restaurant Joy* which has reasonable lunches and the *Ganso de Oro* which has been recommended. Just around the corner from the *Joy* is the *Recreo La Cantuta* which is a good place for an outdoors beer and meeting the locals over a game of *sapo*. This is an old Peruvian game of skill which is played by throwing brass disks at a table with an open mouthed brass toad mounted in the middle. Highest points for getting your disk in the toad's mouth and less points for near misses – you get the idea.

There are plenty of other cheap and basic places to eat but note that most close down early and some serve only lunches.

Getting There

Despite being the capital of its department, Huancavelica doesn't have a commercial airport and so you have to travel overland. The train from Huancayo is more comfortable than bus from anywhere else.

Rail There are three trains a day to Huancayo, except Sundays when there is no service. The autovagon leaves at 7 am and 1 pm, takes almost four hours and costs about US$2. The ordinary train leaves at 7.30 am and takes about six hours. Tickets are US$1.50 in 1st class and US$1.20 in 2nd. Autovagon and 1st class tickets sell out very fast and you should try and buy tickets a day in advance. Current ticket office hours are from 10 to 11 am and from 4 to 5 pm but 'helpless' gringos can sometimes sweet-talk the station master into selling tickets out of hours.

Buses Almost all major bus departures are from Avenida M Muñoz. To Huancayo takes about four to five hours, costs almost US$2, and there are two buses a day with Hidalgo and two a day with Huascar. To Lima the cheapest is Huascar at about US$6.50 but they only have Saturday and Monday departures at present. Expreso Huancavelica charge US$1 more but have a daily 5 pm

departure for the approximately 15-hour journey via Huancayo and La Oroya. They terminate in Lima's La Victoria district which is not a very good area. Hidalgo will sell you tickets to Lima but you have to change buses at Huancayo. Another company with an office on the same street is Oropesa which used to run buses to Lima but appeared to be temporarily closed when I was in town.

To get to Ayacucho it's best to go back to Huancayo as there are no direct services at present. There is a bad road linking Huancavelica with Ayacucho, though, and so it is possible that a direct service may start in the future.

Huascar runs a daily bus to Lircay. Travelling the less frequented back roads to remoter villages is not recommended at this time because of possible terrorist activities.

LIRCAY

This is a small colonial town almost 80 km south-east of Huancavelica. It's main claim to fame is being the centre for the traditional clothing of the department. This clothing can be seen at Huancavelica's Sunday market. The predominant colour is black. The men wear rainbow coloured pom poms on their hats and waists – these are supposedly love tokens from women. The women wear rainbow coloured shawls over their otherwise sombre clothing. There are a couple of basic hotels.

IZCUCHACA

Izcuchaca is the main village between Huancayo and Huancavelica. There's a pottery centre, hot springs and archaeological ruins which are accessible only on foot. Also there is an historic bridge which, legend has it, was built by the Incas and defended bitterly by Huascar during the advance of Atahualpa's troops in the civil war raging in the Inca Empire at the time of the arrival of the Spaniards. There is a basic hotel.

AYACUCHO

The small city of Ayacucho lies at 2731 metres above sea level, has a population of 31,000 and is the capital of its department. Despite its remoteness and small size, it is arguably Peru's most fascinating Andean town after Cuzco. It is well worth a visit.

Five hundred years before the Inca Empire, the Wari Empire dominated the Peruvian highlands. Their ruined capital lies 22 km to the north-east of Ayacucho with which it is now linked by a paved road and hence can be easily visited. The Spaniards founded Ayacucho in 1540 and many of the old colonial buildings have been preserved. Ayacucho played a major part in the battles for independence and a huge nearby monument marks the spot where the important Battle of Ayacucho was fought in 1824.

As described at the beginning of this chapter, the Central Andes are one of Peru's most forgotten areas. Ayacucho is no exception to this rule. For example, its first road link with the Peruvian coast was not finished until 1924 and as late as 1960 there were only two buses and a few dozen vehicles in the city. Departmental statistics show that as recently as 1981 there were only 44 km of paved roads in the department, only 7% of the population had running water in their houses and only 14% had electricity. Thus Ayacucho has retained its colonial atmosphere more than most Peruvian cities.

It is in this remote environment that the Sendero Luminoso (Shining Path) had its beginnings. It started in 1962 as the Huamanga Command of the Frente de Liberación Nacional (FLN). In 1965, the Huamanga Command broke with the national FLN organisation and in the late '60s flirted with communism. In the 1970s, the Sendero was a quiet and little known local organisation, headquartered at Ayacucho's University of Huamanga. Non-violent political discussion and dissent within the confines of the university

A Spaniard takes a young girl from her parents (Waman Puma)

campus were the main activities of the fledgling organisation.

In the early 1980s, the violence with which the Sendero has been frequently identified in the world press began. It escalated to a peak in 1982 and in 1983 strong military measures were taken in an attempt to control the organisation. These measures, whilst frequently criticised because of the killings of innocent civilians, were more or less successful in halting the spread of the Sendero and today their control is limited to a few remote regions. The Sendero's objectives appear to be to overthrow the present democratic system in Peru, to destroy all bourgeois elements in the country and to return the land to the peasant farmers. Their ideals are marked by a blind violence in the achievement of their aims and hence the Sendero has little popular support in their country.

The major towns in the area, including

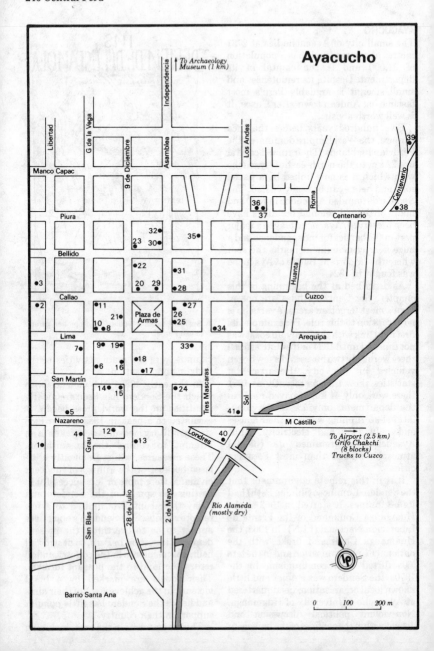

1	Ormeño Bus
2	Hostal Samary
3	Hostal Sixtina
4	Santa Clara Church
5	Hotel Santiago & Hotel La Crillonesa
6	Emp Trans Ayacucho
7	Trans Molina
8	Hostal Santa Rosa
9	Restaurant La Fortaleza
10	Faucett
11	San Francisco de Paula Church
12	Market
13	San Francisco de Asis Church
14	Trans Hidalgo
15	Banco de Crédito
16	La Compañía Church
17	Ayacucho Tours
18	Banco de La Nación
19	El Baccara Restaurant
20	Morochuco Tours & Aero Peru
21	Prefectura
22	Hotel de Turistas
23	Santo Domingo Church
24	La Merced Church
25	Cathedral, University & Consejo Municipal
26	Cinema
27	La Colmena Hotel & Alamo Restaurant
28	San Agustín Church
29	Restaurant Los Portales
30	Cinema
31	Tourist Office
32	Post Office & ENTEL
33	Hostal Central
34	Emp Trans Huamanguina
35	Restaurant La Ancla
36	Hostal Magdalena
37	Etucsa Bus
38	Statue
39	Buses for Huari, Quinua & Huanta
40	Emp Trans Fajardo Etmufa
41	Trans Cangallo

Ayacucho, have again become safe to visit, although travelling to the most remote areas is not advised. It is worth noting that tourists and travellers are not the target of Sendero attacks. To be on the safe side, the traveller should make enquiry at the Tourist Office in Lima before travelling to Ayacucho. At this time there is no requirement to register with the police upon arrival and no curfew is in force.

Information

The Ayacucho Tourist Office is at Asamblea 138 and is open from 7.30 am to 3.45 pm on Mondays to Fridays. They are a good source of information and leaflets.

Ayacucho Tours and Morochuco Tours used to organise local sightseeing tours and give information. With the recent lack of visitors, they haven't been of much use but as tourism picks up again they may be worth checking.

Money Exchange Make every effort to arrive with as much money as you'll need. The banks may or may not change cash dollars at a low rate; the two tour companies mentioned above may accept cash dollars for their services – again at a poor rate; the Hotel de Turistas will let you pay your bill in cash dollars. Straight-forward exchange is not easy.

Festivals

Ayacucho's Holy Week celebration (the week before Easter) has long been considered Peru's finest religious festival and attracts visitors from all over the country. Rooms in the better hotels are booked well in advance and even the cheapest hotels are often full.

The Tourist Bureau prints an annual brochure describing the Holy Week events with street maps showing the main processions. Visitors are advised to get this detailed information, which is free. The celebrations begin on the Friday before Palm Sunday and continue for 10 days until Easter Sunday. Each day is marked with solemn yet colourful processions and religious rites which reach a fever pitch of Catholic faith and tradition.

In addition to the religious services,

Ayacucho's Holy Week celebrations are marked by a great number of secular activities. These include art shows, folk dancing competitions and demonstrations, local music concerts and street events, sporting events (especially equestrian ones), agricultural fairs and the preparation of typical meals.

Things to See

Within the city there are many churches, colonial buildings and museums to visit. Opening hours were severely disrupted from 1982 to 1984 but are returning to normal now. You are advised to ask at the Tourist Office for current hours. Opening hours during Holy Week tend to be much longer.

Archaeology & Anthropology Museum To get there, just walk north from the Plaza de Armas along Asamblea, which soon turns into Independencia. The museum is in the *Centro Cultural Simón Bolívar* which is a little over a km from the town centre and on your right – you can't miss it.

I was told that the museum is normally open from 8.30 am to 6 pm daily except Sunday but there is a sign on the door which gives 8 am to 12 noon as the opening hours, so you'd be advised to try in the morning. Entrance is less than 10c. The major part of the small exhibit consists of Huari ceramics.

Churches The 17th century Cathedral (on the Plaza de Armas) has a religious art museum which was closed last time I was in Ayacucho. Other colonial churches from the 16th, 17th and 18th centuries are marked on the map. Their opening hours are erratic but they are well worth visiting if you can figure out when you can get in. The tourist office may have opening hours.

Colonial houses There are several old mansions which are now mainly political offices and can often be visited upon presentation of your passport. The offices of the Department of Ayacucho (the *Prefectura*) on the Plaza de Armas are a good example. The armed guard will let you in with your passport between 8 am and 12 noon on weekdays. The mansion was constructed between 1740 and 1755 and sold to the state in 1937. On the ground floor is a pretty courtyard and the visitor can see the cell of the local heroine of independence, María Parado de Bellido. Go upstairs to see some excellent tilework.

Also worth a look is the Salon de Actas in the Consejo Municipal, next to the Cathedral, from where an excellent view of the Plaza can be had. The tourist office can suggest others.

Places to Stay

The owner of the hotel I stayed in told me that tourism had dropped off completely in 1983 and 1984 and is only beginning to recover now. Hence hotel prices tended to be ridiculously cheap. The prices quoted will probably rise as tourism recovers further.

Places to Stay – bottom end

One of the cheapest is the basic *Hostal Magdalena* which is next to the ETUCSA bus terminal and charges about 60c per person. They have hot water sometimes. Better is the *Hostal Samary* which is clean and quite pleasant and has hot water in the mornings. They have rooms with private bath for US$1.30/2 singles/doubles and also cheaper rooms with shared bath. The *Hotel La Crillonesa* is also a reasonable cheap hotel with hot water in the morning and single rooms for about US$1.

The best cheap hotels in town are the *La Colmena* and the *Santa Rosa*. They charge about US$1.40/2.10 and have clean rooms with private bath and hot water at least once, and usually twice a day. Both hotels have pleasant courtyards.

Other cheap hotels to try are the *Hostal*

Central, Hostal Sixtina and *Hotel Santiago* none of which seem particularly good or bad.

Places to Stay - middle

The government-run *Hotel de Turistas* is the best in town. Reservations can be made in Lima at ENTURPERU (tel 721928). Rooms are US$7/10 singles/doubles with private bath and hot water; continental breakfast is included. Rooms with shared bathrooms are available for US$5/6.50.

Places to Eat

The *Alamo Restaurant* starts serving breakfast at 7 am and has pancakes and yoghurt as well as the usual eggs and sandwiches. They are open all day and serve good cheap food. They don't sell beer but otherwise this restaurant is recommended to budget travellers.

Marginally more expensive, but still cheap (there are no fancy or expensive restaurants in Ayacucho) is the good *Restaurant La Fortaleza* which does serve beer, and the *Los Portales* on the Plaza de Armas which is a good cafe with a sawdust-on-floor ambience. If you're in the mood for seafood you could try the *Marisquería El Ancla* which makes a reasonable cebiche and sometimes has music on a Friday night.

Nearby Excursions

Three places are often visited from Ayacucho. The village and battlefield of Quinua is normally combined with a visit to the Huari ruins. Also the Inca ruins of Vilcashuamán can be visited. The rough road from Ayacucho to the jungle settlements of San Francisco and Luisiana on the Apurimac River is considered dangerous because of terrorist activity.

Huari Ruins & Quinua

Pick-up trucks leave from the end of Avenida Centenario in Ayacucho for Quinua about once an hour. Fare is 30c for the one-hour ride. The attractive 37 km

road climbs about 550 metres to Quinua which is at 3300 metres above sea level. The ruins of Huari are passed after about 20 km. There is a sign for a small site museum which is usually closed – there are more Huari artefacts to be seen in the Ayacucho museum. There are five main sectors of the ruins which are marked by road signs. The ruins are impressive mainly for their size; they sprawl for several km along the side of the road. They are not restored however, so there isn't much for the untrained eye to see. Interested travellers may want to try and find a guide from Morochuco or Ayacucho Tours. Otherwise you can just get off the pick-up truck and scramble around yourself. The upper sites are located in rather bizarre forests of Opuntia cacti. Don't leave it too late to look for onward or return transportation as pick-ups can get hopelessly full in the afternoons.

Huari is built on a hill and the road from Ayacucho climbs through it, affording reasonable views from the pick-up truck. The road climbs further beyond Huari until the pretty village of Quinua is reached. The pick-up truck usually stops at a plaza with steps leading up to the village church from the left hand side as you arrive from Ayacucho. The church is on an old fashioned cobblestoned plaza and there is a small museum nearby which displays various relics from the major independence battle which was fought nearby. The museum is open from 8 am to 1 pm daily except Mondays and costs about 5c to visit.

To reach the battlefield, turn left behind the church and head out of the village on Jirón Sucre which, after about 10 minutes walk, rejoins the main road. As you walk, notice the red-tiled roofs which are elaborately decorated with ceramic model churches. Quinua is famous as a handicraft centre and these model churches are especially typical of the area.

The white obelisk which has been visible intermittently for several km on the approach to Quinua now lies a few minutes walk in front of you. The 40-metre-high monument is impressive and has some carvings commemorating the Battle of Ayacucho, fought here on 9 December 1824. The walk up from Quinua and the views are pleasant.

There is no accommodation and only very basic food supplies at Quinua. There is a small market on Sunday.

Vilcashuamán

Vilcashuamán, or Sacred Falcon, was a major crossroads city of the Inca Empire. It was here that the Inca road from Cuzco to the coast crossed the road running the length of the Andes and Vilcashuamán was considered as the geographical centre of the empire. Little is left of the earlier magnificence; Vilcashuamán has fallen prey to looters and many of its blocks have been used to build more modern buildings. The once magnificent Temple of the Sun now has a parish church on top of it. The one structure which remains in a reasonable state of repair is a five-tiered pyramid called an *usnu* which is topped by a huge double throne carved from stone and used by the Inca.

Vilcashuamán is near the village of Cangallo, about 120 km south of Ayacucho. Cangallo can be reached by daily trucks and occasional buses and basic accommodation is available. Morochuco and Ayacucho Tours can provide guided service.

Getting Around

Pick-up trucks, and occasionally buses, leave from beyond the statue at the east end of Avenida Centenario for many local villages including Quinua and the Huari ruins.

There are four local city buses; one goes to the airport from the Plaza de Armas.

Trucks to Cangallo leave from the *Puente Nuevo* area which is the bridge on Londres over the Río Alameda. Departures are normally in the mornings. Empresa Transportes Fajardo Etmufa and Trans-portes Cangallo, both near the Puente Nuevo, have (between them) a daily bus or truck to Cangallo continuing onto Vilcashuamán if there is enough demand. Empresa Transportes Huamanguina also does this route at irregular intervals. It takes about a half day for the trip which costs a little over US\$1.

Getting There

Ayacucho is most easily reached by air. If you come by road, be prepared for long delays during the rainy season (worst months are February to April) especially if coming from the Cuzco direction. The road between Huancayo and Ayacucho is also very bad but both routes are spectacular.

The best road to Ayacucho is from Lima via Pisco. Ormeño claims 18 hours for this trip but it is closer to 22 to 24 hours and more during the wet months. The route follows the south coast almost as far as Pisco and then swings inland to Castrovirreyna. This is a small mountain town about 12 to 14 hours from Lima. There are several basic restaurants, and buses usually stop here for meals. The road climbing to Castrovirreyna is an incredible series of hairpin bends hugging the mountain side, often with room for only one vehicle at a time which makes the journey a little more exciting.

Beyond Castrovirreyna the road climbs to about 4800 metres and passes several high Andean Lakes – blue, green and turquoise. The road flirts with the snow line for over an hour and the views of high Andean scenery and snowcaps are dramatic. Finally, the road begins to drop towards Ayacucho and forests of the dwarf polyepsis trees appear as the countryside begins to get greener. Sufferers from soroche in the high passes are relieved by the arrival at Ayacucho at a mere 2731 metres above sea level.

Buses Ormeño's service to Lima costs about US\$7.50 and leaves most days of the week. Cheaper is Hidalgo which has service most days for about US$6.50. Hidalgo also has two buses a week to Cuzco which are always full and have to be booked in advance for the 30 hour, US$8 trip. Buses to the intermediate town of Andahuaylas are available three times a week.

Transportes Molina has old buses which have daily afternoon departures to Huancayo for US$3.50. They also have three buses a week to Andahuaylas.

Transportes Ayacucho runs three buses a week to Huancayo, three to Andahuaylas, and two to Lima.

ETUCSA has a daily bus to Huancayo for US$3.50.

Note that these companies change their routes and services rather frequently.

The cheapest way to Cuzco is to wait at the Grifo (petrol station) Chakchi for a truck and ride in the back with the locals. This is slow and uncomfortable but the views are great and you will be experiencing the Andes from a very different perspective. Trucks leave most days.

Air Both AeroPeru and Faucett have offices in downtown Ayacucho. The airport is about three km from the town centre so you could walk. There are irregular buses from the Plaza de Armas and a taxi will cost about US$1.50.

Despite the presence of an office, Faucett had no flights into Ayacucho recently so you had to rely on AeroPeru who have daily flights to and from Lima for US$27 each way. Sometimes, especially during the June to September high tourist season, there are also flights to Cuzco for US$28. Enquire at any AeroPeru office about this.

NORTH FROM LA OROYA

If, instead of heading east or south from the Central Andean crossroads town of La Oroya (as has been described in the earlier parts of this chapter) you decide to go north, you will travel through the highland towns of Junín, Cerro de Pasco, Huánuco, Tingo María and end up in the important jungle town of Pucallpa. This section of Peru's central Andes is described in this part of the chapter.

JUNÍN

About 55 km due north of La Oroya is the village of Junín. I have never heard or read of a hotel here but there must be some kind of basic accommodation available. Nearby is the Pampa of Junín where an important independence battle was fought (there is a monument) and about 10 km beyond the village is the interesting Lago de Junín.

This lake is about 30 km long by 14 broad and is Peru's second largest lake after Titicaca. It is over 4000 metres above sea level and thus is the highest lake of its size in the Americas and the western world. It is known for its bird life – some authorities claim that a million birds at a time live on the lake or its shores. It is a little visited area and an excellent destination for anyone interested in seeing a good variety of water and shore birds of the high Andes.

CERRO DE PASCO

Cerro de Pasco is Peru's highest major town, the capital of its department, and a miserable place. Its elevation of 4333 metres above sea level makes it bitterly cold at night and its main reason for existence is mining. The population is about 30,000. Cerro de Pasco is about 40 km north of Lake Junín and has the closest hotels to the lake – accommodation is poor.

Places to Stay

I could find no hotels with hot water when I was there. The four or five hotels in town were all basic, cold and unattractive. On the other hand, they provide a bed and a roof over your head, which has to count for something.

The *Hotel San Pedro* and the *Hotel Santa Rosa*, both by the Plaza de Armas, are as good as any.

HUÁNUCO

Huánuco, 105 km north of Cerro de Pasco, is almost 2500 metres lower than that town and so provides a welcome relief for soroche sufferers. The elevation is only 1894 metres above sea level. Huánuco is on the upper reaches of the Río Huallaga, which is the major tributary of the Río Marañon before it becomes the Amazon. Huánuco is also the capital of its department and the site of the Temple of Kotosh (also known as the Temple of the Crossed Hands) which is one of Peru's oldest Andean archaeological sites. The town has an interesting natural history museum and a pleasant Plaza de Armas.

Information

MICTI (Ministerio de Industria, Cultura, Turismo y Integración) can provide tourist information on the 5th floor of their building on the Plaza de Armas. They are open from 7.30 am to 12.30 pm on Mondays to Fridays and also from 1 to 3.45 pm from April to December.

Money Exchange There is a casa de cambio on the corner of the Plaza de Armas as well as the Banco de Nación and Banco de Crédito. Between them you should be able to get money changed, but don't expect very good rates.

Natural History Museum

This is a surprising museum. One would not expect a museum of this calibre in a town of the size of Huánuco. It is small but well organised and what there is to see is labelled. The director of the museum, Sr Nestor Armas Wenzel, is dedicated, enthusiastic and delights in showing visitors around. He particularly likes to talk to foreign visitors and has flags and 'Welcome' in many languages decorating the entrance lobby. Admission is about 40c and the museum is open from 9 am to 12 noon and from 3 to 6 pm on weekdays and from 10 am to 1 pm on Sundays.

The Temple of Kotosh

This archaeological site is also known as the Temple of the Crossed Hands after the life-size moulding, made of mud, of a pair of crossed forearms which was discovered in the ruins by an archaeological team working in the early 1960s. The

1	Aero Peru & Hotel de Turistas
2	Post Office
3	Banco de la Nación
4	Cine Central
5	Trans Arellano Buses
6	Trans Ucayali Buses
7	ENTEL (new office)
8	ETUCSA Buses
9	Empresa La Perla Buses
10	Hostal La Pileta
11	Ministry of Tourism (5th floor)
12	Hostal Las Vegas
13	Chifa Polo Sur
14	Hostal La Cabaña
15	ENTEL (old office)
16	Empresa Nor-Oriente Buses
17	Hotel Astoria
18	Comité 5
19	Cars, minibuses & buses to Tingo Maria
20	León de Huánuco Buses
21	Etposa & La Perla del Oriente Buses
22	Hotel Triunfo
23	Hostal Huánuco
24	Hostal Viajero
25	Casa de Cambio
26	Hotel Real
27	Comité 12
28	Museum
29	San Cristobal de Huánuco
30	Comité 1
31	Banco de Crédito
32	Hostal Internacional
33	Gran Hotel Cuzco
34	Hotel Imperial
35	Hotel Europa
36	Hostal Huallaga
37	Hotel La Victoria
38	Trucks to Tantamayo
39	Trans La Acosta
40	Empresa Dos de Mayo

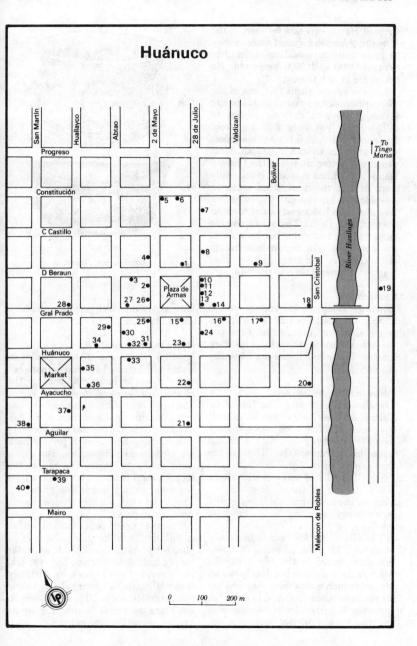

Huánuco

Crossed Hands can now be seen in the Museum of Archaeology and Anthropology in Lima and the moulding is dated to between 4000 and 5000 years old. No others are known to exist.

Little is known about this, one of the most ancient of Andean cultures. The site is overgrown and difficult to get to (although it lies only five km from Huánuco) and there is little to see unless you are very interested in Kotosh. Most people are better off seeing the Crossed Hands in the Lima museum. If you really want to visit the ruins, head south on Avenida San Martín until you come to a lake and then head west out of town on the road to La Unión. There is a stream to cross and the footbridge has been down for some time. The tourist information office can give you more precise information – I haven't been to the ruin.

Places to Stay

Hotels get filled quickly and so you are advised to start looking as early as possible. You can usually find a bed but by late afternoon the choice is very limited. Huánuco's hotels are generally not very good.

Places to Stay – bottom end

The cheapest in town is the *Hostal La Cabaña* for US$1/1.60 singles/doubles. It has received fairly good reports but I found it very basic and with a broken water supply. Perhaps they'll fix it by the time you get there.

For US$1.30/2.30 you can stay at the *Hotel Astoria, Triunfo, Huallaga* or *Viajero*. The first is probably the cleanest of an unprepossessing basic bunch of hotels.

The *Hostal La Victoria* is basic and charges US$1.70/2.70 singles/doubles. Similarly priced is the *Hotel Europa* which is also very basic but does have a lot of rooms which means there may be a bed for you later in the day. Also in this price range are the better *Hostal Internacional* and the *Hotel Imperial* both of which

Kotosh vessels, Huanuco

have some rooms with private bath which cost a little more.

Places to Stay – middle

For US$3 single and US$4.50 double in rooms with private bath and perhaps hot water if you're lucky you can try the *Hostal La Pileta* and *Hostal Las Vegas*. The *Gran Hotel Cuzco* isn't bad and has hot water during at least part of the day and a cafeteria. It's popular with Peruvian businessmen. Rooms with private bath are US$4/6 singles/doubles. For a few cents more, try ringing the bell at the secure *Hostal Huánuco* which has a good hot water supply and is also often full. They have some slightly cheaper rooms with shared baths.

The government-run *Hotel de Turistas* is on the Plaza de Armas and looks pleasantly old fashioned. Its hot water supply has been criticised however and that's perhaps why rooms are a relatively cheap US$5.70/7.70 with bath including continental breakfast. The *Hotel Real* on the Plaza de Armas is almost twice as expensive and the best in town.

Places to Eat

I looked hard but I couldn't find anywhere remarkable. The *Chifa Polo Sur* on the Plaza seemed to be one of the best.

Getting There

Huánuco is on the main Lima – Pucallpa coast to jungle highway and so there is plenty of transport here. There is also an airport.

Buses & Colectivos With about half a dozen different bus companies competing on the route to Lima you'd think that there would be a wide choice of departure times. There isn't. In one of the typically tiresome quirks of travel in Peru, you have to take a night bus or not travel at all. The best service is with León de Huánuco, which has three buses nightly to Lima (10 hours, US$6.50). Other companies which have a night bus to Lima are San Cristobal de Huánuco, Expreso Nor-Oriente, Empresa La Perla, La Perla del Oriente and Transportes Arellano in roughly descending order of reliability.

For Pucallpa it's also a 10-hour, US$6.50 trip. León de Huánuco has a 4 pm departure which gets in at the depressing time of 2 am – you might be allowed to sleep on the bus until dawn. An earlier departure is with ETPOSA/La Perla del Oriente (they share an office) who have a noon departure, though finding a hotel in Pucallpa at 10 pm is not much better.

If heading to Pucallpa you might avoid the problem of late night arrivals by travelling to Tingo María and spending the night there (although not many buses leave Tingo for Pucallpa during the day, either). There are services throughout the day to Tingo María. Comité 1 has shared taxi colectivos to Tingo during the morning and Comité 5 throughout the day (US$3.50, 2½ hours). If you walk to the general transport stop beyond the Río Huallaga bridge (10 minutes from the town centre) you'll find shared taxis, cheaper minibuses, and cheaper and slower buses with the La Marginal company all heading to Tingo.

Comité 1 has shared cars for Cerro de Pasco in the morning (US$3.50, 2½ hours). Comité 12 also has cars to Cerro de Pasco and usually one car every morning which goes on to La Oroya (four to five hours, US$6). Sometimes they have cars going all the way to Lima – particularly if a group of you takes up all the seats.

Transportes Ucayali has three overnight buses to Cerro de Pasco (US$1.50) continuing to La Oroya (US$2.80) and going on to Huancayo (9 hours, US$3.50). They have one day bus. ETUCSA also has a night bus to Huancayo.

Finally, to visit the remote towns of La Unión, Tantamayo and other villages, head for Jirón San Martín, a couple of blocks south of the market. Here you'll find Empresa Dos de Mayo with a daily morning bus to La Unión (seven hours, US$3.30). Transportes La Acosta also has vehicles for this route. For Tantamayo (12 hours to cover 150 km!) there are *mixtos* (half truck and half bus) leaving every morning from the street corner of San Martín and Aguilar. This is a good place to look for transport to other remote villages in the area.

LA UNIÓN

This town is roughly half way between Huánuco and Huaraz and it is feasible to travel this way to get to the Cordillera Blanca. La Unión has a couple of basic hotels and transportation is available from here on to Chiquian, near the Cordillera Huayhuash. From Chiquian (where there are basic hotels) one can continue to Huaraz and the Cordillera Blanca. This is a little travelled and, by all accounts, spectacular route.

About two to three hours walk from La Unión are the Inca ruins of Huánuco Viejo.

TANTAMAYO

This small and remote village is in the

mountains north of Huánuco and has a hotel where information can be obtained for visiting several ruins which are within a few hours walk. Guides can be hired.

TINGO MARÍA

The 118-km road north from Huánuco climbs over a 3000-metre pass before dropping steadily to Tingo María which lies in the lush tropical slopes of the eastern Andes at an elevation of 649 metres above sea level. The town is on the edge of the Amazon basin and is hot and humid for most of the time. Thus it could be called a jungle town yet it is surrounded by steep Andean foothills – it is typical of the somewhat arbitrary decisions a guidebook writer must make as to whether Tingo María should be included in the Central Highland section or the Jungle chapter. This debatable point will no doubt provide you and your travelling companions with material for hours of conversation as your bus slogs along this slow but spectacular section of highway!

Tingo María is a thriving market town but because one of its main products is coca (for cocaine) and, to a lesser extent, marijuana, the town is rather unsavoury and not especially friendly to tourists. It also has a bad reputation for thievery. It is definitely not a good place to 'score'. The two times that I stayed here I saw few foreign visitors; most people go on to the jungle at Pucallpa.

Money Exchange The *Librería Victoria* doubles as an exchange house and will change dollars at about 10% lower than in Lima. The banks, if they exchange at all, tend to give poorer rates still. Better exchange can be had in Pucallpa.

Things to See

The university has a botanical garden which is rather run down and overgrown but some of the plants do have labels on them so you can learn something from them. The botanical garden is often locked but there is a gate keeper living in

the shack behind the gate so if you whistle and yell he'll open it up for you.

The university (which is about three km out of town) is supposed to have a small zoo but I couldn't find anyone who knew about it.

Comité 13 has colectivos every ½ hour or so which take you out to the *Cuevas de Lechuza* (owl caves) for 50c. The caves are about eight km away and there is a US$3 'National Park Fee'. There are no facilities, however, apart from an urchin manning a few planks nailed together into a toll booth – no guides, no information, no lights. The caves are supposed to contain nocturnal parakeets – I only went as far as the toll booth.

Places to Stay

Although there seem to be a lot of hotels, they are generally of a low standard and are often full so you should look for a room as soon as you arrive. I ended up staying in one of the 'better' hotels (the *Nuevo York*) because it was the first that had a room available and I'd looked in half a dozen others. The management told me that the room wouldn't be ready for half an hour until the maid had finished cleaning it. I asked for the key so that I could go up and drop off my pack. When I reached my room I found all the doors and windows open and a very harassed looking maid attempting to clean the linoleum-tiled floor which was badly scuffed up and covered with what appeared to be bird dung. Upon enquiry, I found that the previous occupants had been a couple of machos who were in Tingo for a cockfighting competition and were travelling with their prize cocks who had evidently shared their bedroom. My opinion of cockfighting and its aficionados, never very high, took a turn for the worse. Perhaps I should be thankful that the men weren't bullfighters.

Places to Stay – bottom end

The cheapest hotels charge US$1.30/2.30 singles/doubles for basic rooms and

Top: Inca trail hikers viewing Sayacmarca (RR)
Bottom: Don Victor Delgado loads mule team, Cordillera Vilcabamba (RR)

Top: Plaza de Armas, Ayacucho (RR)
Left: Huancavelica Cathedral (RR)
Right: Gourd seller, Huancayo Market (RR)

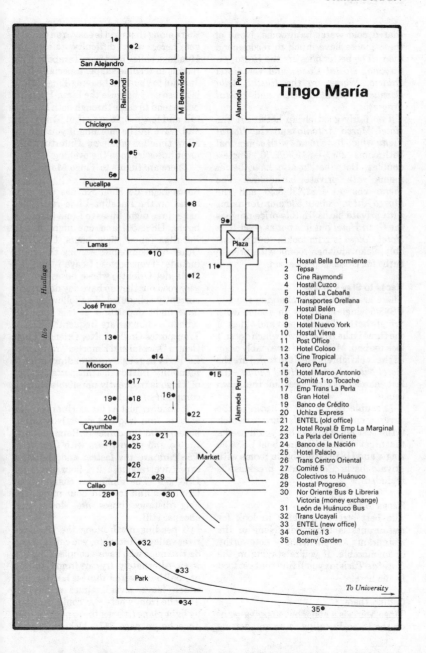

Tingo María

1 Hostal Bella Dormiente
2 Tepsa
3 Cine Raymondi
4 Hostal Cuzco
5 Hostal La Cabaña
6 Transportes Orellana
7 Hostal Belén
8 Hotel Diana
9 Hotel Nuevo York
10 Hostal Viena
11 Post Office
12 Hotel Coloso
13 Cine Tropical
14 Aero Peru
15 Hotel Marco Antonio
16 Comité 1 to Tocache
17 Emp Trans La Perla
18 Gran Hotel
19 Banco de Crédito
20 Uchiza Express
21 ENTEL (old office)
22 Hotel Royal & Emp La Marginal
23 La Perla del Oriente
24 Banco de la Nación
25 Hotel Palacio
26 Trans Centro Oriental
27 Comité 5
28 Colectivos to Huánuco
29 Hostal Progreso
30 Nor Oriente Bus & Libreria Victoria (money exchange)
31 León de Huánuco Bus
32 Trans Ucayali
33 ENTEL (new office)
34 Comité 13
35 Botany Garden

To University

shared cold water bathrooms. None of these places have much to recommend them. The better ones are the *Hostal La Cabaña*, *Hostal Cuzco* and the *Hotel Palacio*. Worse are the *Hostal Bella Dormiente*, *Hostal Belén* and *Hostal Progreso*.

Two fairly good cheap hotels are the *Hotel Marco Antonio* and the *Hostal Viena* which have rooms with communal bathrooms for US$1.70/2.70 singles/doubles. Both hotels also have better rooms with private bathrooms. The *Viena* charges US$2.30/3.30 and the *Marco Antonio* about 50c more for rooms with private baths. In this price range is the *Gran Hotel* but it is not as good. The *Hotel Coloso* is grim looking but reasonably clean and has rooms with private baths for US$2.30 per person.

Places to Stay – middle

There are three hotels charging roughly US$3/5 singles/doubles in rooms with private baths. The cheapest and oldest of the three is the *Hotel Royal* which doesn't look too bad. Modern and reasonably clean (if the cockfighters aren't in town) are the *Hotel Nuevo York* and *Hotel Diana* – the last named is the best in the town centre.

A couple of km out of town is the government-run *Hotel de Turistas* which is the best place to stay but you'll need a taxi to get there. Prices are about US$6.50 single and US$9.50 double in rooms with private bath. Continental breakfast is included.

Places to Eat

The best street on which to look for restaurants is Raimondi. None of the restaurants are particularly noteworthy or memorable. If you're staying in the *Hotel de Turistas* you'll find the best food in the hotel.

Getting There

Tingo María is a major bus stopping-point on the Lima-Pucallpa route and getting there along that road is easy. You can also get here, with difficulty, along the Huallaga valley road from Tarapoto. This road is in terrible shape, especially from Juanjui to Tocache. Leaving Tingo María is not so easy because the Lima-Pucallpa buses tend to come through both late and full and few people get off in Tingo. Try and leave in the morning if you can, to allow time for problems. Unfortunately, most buses leave in the evening.

There are flights to Tingo María.

Buses León de Huánuco has the most buses on the Pucallpa-Lima run. They have three night buses to Lima (about 18 hours, US$8.50) and one night bus to Pucallpa (about eight hours, US$5.30). Other bus companies serving this route include Transportes Ucayali and La Perla del Oriente, whose buses are not very good but they do have day departures currently scheduled. The following only have night departures at this time but schedule changes are frequent: TEPSA, Transportes Orellana, Nor Oriente, Trans Centro Oriental and Empresa Transportes La Perla in roughly descending order of reliability (although transportation out of Tingo is frequently unreliable with all companies.)

If heading just as far as Huánuco, it's easy to find frequent colectivos (minibuses) from the corner of Raimondi and Callao and shared cars with Comité 5. The cars are the fastest and the most expensive (about a 2½-hour drive for US$3.50). The minibuses charge about US$1 less and take an hour more. The long distance buses are slower and cheaper still.

If heading north along the Huallaga river valley to Tarapoto, you can try León de Huánuco who have a couple of buses a week. Alternately, try cars from Comité 1 or small buses with Empresa La Marginal which leave several times a day for Tocache from where you could continue by light plane (it's not too expensive – see Tocache on page 347). Uchiza Express also has buses to Tocache. Occasionally these companies have buses beyond Tocache.

Air AeroPeru has an office in town. The airport is about two km away. AeroPeru sometimes can be persuaded to give you a ride in their pick-up truck but don't rely on it. A taxi will cost about US$1.50. There are flights to and from Lima every afternoon except Wednesday. Fares are US$31 each way. There are no flights on to Pucallpa at this time.

If you go to the airport and ask around, you can find light aircraft flying as far as Juanjui from where buses or other light aircraft can take you to Tarapoto. (For more information about light aeroplane flights, see Tarapoto and Tocache.) There are flights on most days.

The North Coast

The scenery of the Peruvian coast north of Lima is similar to that of the south coast; both areas are part of the great South American coastal desert. The coastal drive north from Lima passes huge rolling sand dunes, dizzying cliff sides, oases of farmland, busy fishing villages, relaxing beach resorts, archaeological sites dating back thousands of years, and some of Peru's largest and most historic cities.

Few travellers are able to fully appreciate this area of Peru. Most are so wrapped up in visiting the world famous Inca ruins and Lake Titicaca to the south that the northern part of the country is largely ignored. Those who do travel north tend to either head straight to the Ecuadorean border, 24 hours away, or drive along the coast for four hours and head inland to the Callejón de Huaylas to visit the beautiful mountains of the Cordillera Blanca. Slowly travelling the north coast, however, allows greater involvement with the local people and often gets you away from the gringo 'scene'.

ANCÓN

The first town north of Lima is the big luxury resort of Ancón, about 40 km from the capital. This is the seaside resort for Lima's upper class, with clubs, fancy restaurants, and private summer homes. It's not really tourist orientated and the few hotels are expensive.

En route from Lima to Ancón, the Pan-American passes through the opposite end of Peru's social scale – the *Pueblos Jovenes* or young towns. These are shanty towns, often with no running water, electricity or other facilities. They are built by peasants migrating to Lima from the highlands in the search for jobs and a higher standard of living.

CHANCAY

Beyond Ancón, the road passes through the spectacular Pacasmayo sand dunes. There are two roads – one snakes along a narrow ledge at the bottom of the dunes and the other goes over the top. Both offer superb views of the dunes, which stretch on for some 20 km until the small village of Chancay. This area is known for the Chancay sub-culture which existed here from about 1100 to 1400 AD. This coastal culture is noted for its Black-on-White ceramic style which is best seen at the excellent Amano Museum in Lima. Chancay itself is a small fishing village of some 10,000 inhabitants and there is little to see, though there is a simple, friendly hotel.

THE CHURÍN ROAD

About 20 km north of Chancay there is a turn-off right to the small towns of Sayán, Churín and Oyón in the mountains. The road follows the Río Huaura valley and an Expreso Huaral bus from Avenida Abancay 131 in Lima goes up this road daily. About five km along this turn-off you come to the Reserve of Loma de Lachay which is a curious hill which seems to gain most of its moisture from

Chancay pot

the coastal mists, creating a unique micro-environment of a dwarf forest with small animals and birds. There are no facilities.

Between Sayán and Churín the road rises through strange rock formations and tropical scrub vegetation. Churín, 190 km from Lima, is a minor resort known for its good hot springs. There are a couple of cheap hotels on Avenida Larco Herrera, the main street. The *Hostal Internacional Churín* is the best and there is also the cheaper *Alojamiento Jardín*. Several inexpensive restaurants serve local food such as trout and *cuy* (guinea pig).

Beyond Churín the road continues through the village of Oyón and on to the southern parts of the Cordillera Raura, a remote snowcapped range of mountains. Adventurous travellers with camping gear could hike through these mountains to reach the Cordillera Huayhuash.

HUACHO

Over 140 km north of Lima the small town (population 40,000) of Huacho is passed. This lies at the mouth of the Río Huaural and buses go from here up the valley. Across the river is the village of Huaura where San Martín proclaimed Peru's independence. There are two or three basic hotels.

BARRANCA & PARAMONGA

About 190 km north of Lima, the small town of Barranca is the centre for Supe, Pativilca, Paramonga and the turn-off for Huaraz and the Cordillera Blanca, all of which lie within a few kms of Barranca. There's little to see in Barranca itself; it just happens to be the biggest town with the best facilities in the area and most buses along the coast stop here. Most everything happens on the main street which is also the Pan-American Highway.

A few km south of Barranca is the small fishing port of Supe where there are a couple of basic hotels. Nearby is the archaeological site of Aspero. Although

Chancay weaving

one of the oldest sites in Peru, there is little of interest here for the untrained eye.

A few km north of Barranca is the village of Pativilca with a very basic hotel and a few simple restaurants. Most people stay at Barranca. Just north of Pativilca is the turn-off to the right up to Huaraz and the Cordillera Blanca. This is a spectacular road climbing through cactus-laden cliff sides and is worth travelling in daylight. For many people, the Pan-American between Lima and the turn-off to the mountains at Pativilca is as much of the north coast as they get to see.

Three or four kms beyond the Huaraz turn-off is the archaeological site of Paramonga. It is a huge adobe temple attributed to the Chimu civilisation, which was the ruling power on the north coast before being conquered by the Incas in the mid-1400s. The massive temple, surrounded by seven defensive walls, is clearly visible on the right hand side of the Pan-American and is worth a visit.

Entry is about 20c and there is a small on-site museum open from 8 am to 5 pm. Local buses from Barranca to Paramonga will drop you off near the entrance.

I got to know Barranca better than I had bargained for a few years ago. For one reason or another I was in a great hurry to get from Ecuador to Lima and so I took direct long distance buses from Quito to the border and from the border to Lima. When I reached Peru I heard about a rumoured general strike but the buses were running in Tumbes and so I bought my ticket to Lima. By the time I reached the outskirts of Barranca I had been travelling pretty much non-stop for 40 hours and was beginning to breathe more easily – after all, it was only another four hours to Lima. Then the General Strike began. Logs were pulled across the Pan-American Highway and rather menacing looking groups of workers manned these barricades. No vehicles, not even taxis or private cars, were allowed through. For two full days a two-km-long line of vehicles stood in the tropical sun outside of Barranca. I understand that transportation was paralysed throughout the country during this period. Meanwhile all the passengers slept on the bus and walked into town to eat. The protest was over the rise in the cost of milk. This is a good example of why not to plan too tight a schedule when travelling in Peru!

Places to Stay & Eat
There are a couple of movie theatres and plenty of cheap restaurants of which the best is the *Chifa Lung Fung* on the main street. There are several hotels of which the best is the *Hotel Chavín* also on the main street and charging about US$6 for a clean double room with private bath. There are some cheaper places of which the *Pacífico* is quite good.

HUARMEY
The Pan-American enters a particularly deserted stretch north of Paramonga. The departmental line dividing the Departments of Lima and Ancash is soon passed. At Huarmey, 290 km north of Lima, is a government-run *Hotel de Turistas* which is the best hotel in the 420-km stretch of road between Lima and Chimbote. They charge about US$10 for a double with bath, and reservations can be made by calling ENTURPERU in Lima at 721928.

There's nothing to do in Huarmey apart from spend the night in the hotel but if you have your own transportation you'll find some excellent deserted beaches nearby.

CASMA & SECHÍN
The small town of Casma is 370 km north of Lima and the archaeological site of Sechín is about five km away and easily reached from Casma. Although this is a historical town, having once been an important colonial port which was sacked by various pirates during the 1600s, its importance has declined greatly. There's not much to do in either the port (11 km from the town) or the town itself, which was largely destroyed by the earthquake of 31 May 1970. The main reasons to be here are either to visit the ruins of Sechín or to travel to Huaraz via the Punta Callán road which gives an excellent panoramic view of the Cordillera Blanca.

Sechín
This site is one of the oldest in Peru (1500 BC) and among the more important and well preserved of the coastal ruins. It was first excavated by the renowned Peruvian archaeologist J C Tello in 1937 but has suffered some damage from grave robbers and natural disasters. It lies five km south-east of Casma and is easily reached on foot or by taxi; there are good road signs.

Head south of Casma on the Pan-American Highway for three km and then turn left on the paved road to Huara for a further two km to the site. If you're descending from Huara you can visit the ruins en route to Casma if you don't have too much gear.

At Sechín there is a small modern museum and the partially excavated site, part of which was thought to have been buried by a landslide. Only part of the area is open to visitors. This consists of three outside walls of the main temple which are completely covered with bas-relief carvings showing warriors and captives being eviscerated. The carvings are up to four metres high and are gruesomely realistic. Which warlike peoples were involved in raising this temple is a mystery – this is part of the interest of this site. Inside the main temple are earlier mud structures which are in the process of being excavated – you can't go in but there's a model in the museum which is small but worth a visit.

There are several other early sites in the Sechín area. Most of these remain unexcavated because of lack of funds. From the museum you can see Sechín Alto in the distance – a large flat-topped hill. The fortress of Chanquillo, which consists of several towers surrounded by concentric walls, can also be visited but is best appreciated from the air. Aerial photographs are on display at the museum. The museum attendant can give further directions if you wish to explore more than just Sechín and there is a detailed area map in the museum.

The Sechín ruins and museum are open daily from 9 am to 5 pm and cost 40c to visit. There is a small shady garden and picnic area but bring your own food. The entry ticket also allows you to visit the Mochica ruins of Pañamarca, which are 10 km inland from the Pan-American Highway on the road to Nepeña. This turn-off is about halfway between Casma and Chimbote. The Pañamarca ruins have been badly weather damaged.

Places to Stay

There are three hotels in Casma. The best is the pleasant *Hostal El Farol*, set in a garden and with a simple cafeteria and bar. There's a useful map in the lobby if you plan on exploring some of the ruins in the area and the staff are friendly and helpful. The hotel is just off the main road between the bus stop area and the Plaza de Armas, a couple of blocks from each – there's a sign on the main road. Rooms with communal showers are US$1.70/3 for singles/doubles and with private showers US$2.30/4.30. There's only cold water but Casma is so warm that there's no great hardship.

If you want to save a few cents you could try the basic and unattractive *Hostal Central* on the Plaza de Armas. A clean new hotel, the *Sanchez*, has just opened a block from the Plaza. Prices will probably be similar to the *El Farol*.

Places to Eat

My wife and I stayed at the *El Farol* in 1985 and wanted to have breakfast. We were the only customers in the hotel's cafeteria but were told that breakfast would be no problem. We asked what there was (you soon learn to ask what there is *(Que hay?)* before choosing in small restaurants) and the assistant replied that he'd see. He strode purposefully over to the refrigerator and swung it open and all three of us peered hopefully inside. We couldn't help but laugh; there was a half full bottle of Pepsi and a small and rather sadly wrinkled papaya. The assistant, slightly crestfallen, soon recovered and offered to go out and buy some eggs and bread and we returned half an hour later to a good breakfast, complete with papaya juice.

There aren't any particularly good restaurants in Casma. One of the best is the inexpensive *Chifa Tio Sam*, next to the Hotel Sanchez near the Plaza. There are several cheap and basic places near the main bus stops which will do if you're waiting for a bus.

Getting There

Many companies run buses north and south along the Pan-American Highway but because Casma is so small most of them don't have offices. If heading for Trujillo or Lima you can flag down buses as they come through and hope for a seat. Otherwise, Empresa Turismo Chimbote with an office on the main street has five buses daily to Lima but they only have two or three seats available in the Casma office; the rest are sold in Chimbote. It's best to book for your departure as soon as you arrive. Chincha-Suyo also has an office on the main street and a couple of buses daily to both Lima and Trujillo – a better chance for seats but the buses are old. Tepsa has an office but it's not always open. To Lima averages US$4 and six hours, to Trujillo about US$2 and three hours.

There are also frequent colectivos to Chimbote, 50 km to the north, from where there are better facilities. These take 1¼ hours and charge US$1.

Several small companies have buses to Huaraz via a dirt road over the Cordillera Negra. The trip begins with good views of the desert foothills of the western Andes and then climbs up the fertile Casma valley, finally emerging over the 4224-metre-high Punta Callán pass which is 30 km from Huaraz and from where one of the best overall panoramic views of the Cordillera Blanca can be had. It's worth doing the journey during the day with Empresa Moreno (seven hours, US$3). Empresa Chincha-Suyo has only night buses (though you might just catch the dawn from Punta Callán). Empresa Huaraz has only three buses a week. If all of these are full, try Empresa Soledad – although their offices were closed last time I was there.

Note that all the bus offices and stops are clustered together within a few blocks of one another on the main road at the junction with the Pan-American where it arrives in Casma from Lima. You won't have any difficulty in finding the buses – it's a small town.

CHIMBOTE

This is the first major town reached on the north coast; it is 420 km north of Lima. Chimbote is Peru's largest fishing port with millions of tons of fish being landed in the 1960s. The industry has declined since then due to overfishing but despite this and despite the earthquake of 1970 which destroyed much of the city, the population has continued to grow dramatically and is now close to 200,000 – about the size of Cuzco. The comparison stops there, however. Chimbote has several large fishmeal factories which give the town a pervasive and distinctive odour and there are also some steel mills. The beaches are dirty but good for watching bird life.

There's not much to do unless you're interested in the fishing or steel industries but the town can be used as a base for excursions into the Santa River valley where there are some little explored archaeological ruins. It's also a good place to stay overnight if you're headed to Huaraz via the spectacular Cañon del Pato route.

Information

The Tourist Office at Bolognesi 421 can provide you with information about touring a local steel mill if you're interested. Also ask them about visiting the ruins of the Santa valley.

Santa Valley

The Santa River flows into the ocean at Santa, about 20 km north of Chimbote. The river valley is a little explored area with not much public transport – a few buses go up this road en route to Huaraz. Aerial reconnaissance has revealed dozens of pre-Inca sites (read Gene Savoy's *Antisuyo*) including a Great Wall, about 50 km long.

Adventurous travellers could explore the valley on foot – you don't need too much gear as it doesn't rain or get cold. A blanket and sleeping pad will suffice. Climbing the hills on the sides of the valley will bring you to very rarely visited ruins. A possible place to start from is Tanguche which is the first place inland from Santa and marked on most maps. Parts of the Great Wall can be seen nearby and many more ruins lie in the hills

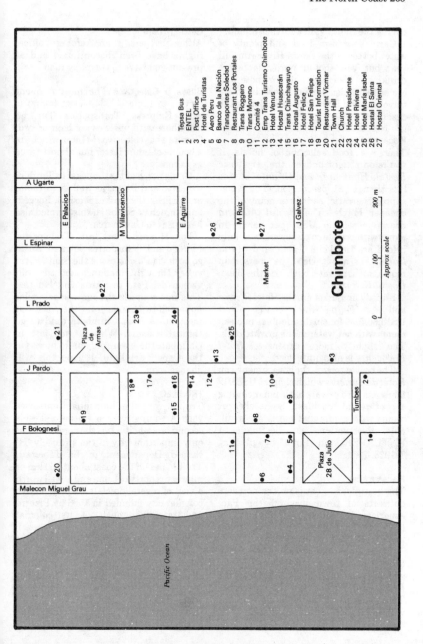

1 Tepsa Bus
2 ENTEL
3 Post Office
4 Hotel de Turistas
5 Aero Peru
6 Banco de la Nación
7 Transportes Soledad
8 Restaurant Los Portales
9 Trans Roggero
10 Trans Moreno
11 Comité 4
12 Emp Trans Turismo Chimbote
13 Hotel Venus
14 Hostal Huascarán
15 Trans Chinchaysuyo
16 Hostal Augusto
17 Hotel Felice
18 Hotel San Felipe
19 Restaurant Vicmar
20 Tourist Information
21 Town Hall
22 Church
23 Hotel Presidente
24 Hotel Riviera
25 Hotel María Isabel
26 Hostal El Santa
27 Hostal Oriental

A Ugarte

E Palacios

M Villavicencio

E Aguirre

M Ruiz

J Galvez

Chimbote

Approx scale

0   100   200 m

L Espinar

L Prado

J Pardo

F Bolognesi

Malecon Miguel Grau

Plaza de Armas

Market

Plaza 28 de Julio

Tumbes

Pacific Ocean

edging the Santa valley further inland.

Carry your own food and plenty of water bottles – the Santa River runs all year but you should purify it before drinking. This trip is only for those who are self sufficient, experienced in rough travelling and interested in exploring the desert.

Places to Stay

There's a good selection of hotels. If you're on a tight budget, the very basic *Hostals Huascarán* and *Oriental* charge less than US$1 per person. The water supply is erratic, as it is in many of the cheaper hotels. The *Hostal Augusto* charges just over US$1 per person in rooms with private cold showers. Similarly priced are the *Venus, Felic* and *María Isabel*. For about US$2 per person in rooms with private bath try the clean *Hostal El Santa*.

Slightly upmarket are the *Hotel Riviera* and *San Felipe* which charge about US$3.50/5.50 for singles/doubles in clean rooms with hot water in the private bath. The slightly more expensive *Hotel Presidente* is also quite good.

The best in town is the government-run *Hotel de Turistas* which charges US$8/12 for rooms with private bath and including a continental breakfast. Some cheaper rooms with communal baths are available. Reservations can be made at ENTURPERU in Lima by phoning 721928.

Places to Eat

The best place to eat is on the northern outskirts of town just off the Pan-American. It's called *Los Pinos* and is in the Vivero Forestal complex – taxi drivers know it. It's not too expensive.

There are no fancy restaurants downtown. A reasonable choice is *Los Portales* which is good and inexpensive. Or try the *Restaurant Vicmar* near the waterfront. Those staying at the *Hotel de Turistas* will find a good restaurant there.

Getting There

Although there is an AeroPeru office, flights have been discontinued and at present you have to travel by road.

Buses & Colectivos The most frequent service to Lima (US$4, seven hours) is with Empresa Transportes Turismo Chimbote with buses every hour or two. Comité 4 has colectivos to Lima which are a couple of hours faster but almost twice as expensive.

Going north along the coast to Trujillo, Chiclayo and Piura, as well as to Lima, are TEPSA (the most expensive), Roggero and Chinchay-Suyo. The last named also has buses to Cajamarca.

For Huaraz there are Transportes Moreno and Transportes Soledad. Buses go both via Casma or via the Santa River valley through Huallanca and the wild Cañon del Pato to Caraz and Huaraz. This last route is the most spectacular approach to Huaraz from the coast but most buses from Chimbote tend to go through Casma. When I was last in Chimbote there were only night buses via the Cañon del Pato. I hope this will change soon.

TRUJILLO

Trujillo, with ¾ million inhabitants, vies with Arequipa for the status of Peru's second largest city. It is the capital of and only important city in the strangely 'H' shaped Department of La Libertad. Trujillo lies on the coast about 560 km or nine hours north of Lima and is well worth a visit of several days. It is an attractive colonial city founded in 1536 by Pizarro and retaining much of its colonial flavour.

Nearby is the ancient Chimu capital of Chan Chan which was conquered by the Incas, as well as several other Chimu sites. Also nearby are the immense Moche Pyramids of the Sun and Moon which date back about 1500 years. If all this culture wears you out, you can relax at the pleasant beaches nearby.

Information
Tourist Information The tourist office (tel 246941) on the Plaza de Armas is run by the Tourist Police who are distinguished by their smart white uniforms. They are exceptionally friendly and helpful – more so than any policemen that I've met in six years of travel in Latin America. They have set up patrols in the major archaeological sites with the specific aim of aiding and protecting visitors. Their office is open daily from 8.30 am to 7 pm.

Money Exchange This chore is a distinct pleasure in Trujillo because some of the banks are housed in colonial buildings. One of my favourite is the Banco Nor Peru in the Casa de la Emancipación which gives good rates for both cash and travellers' cheques. You can also change money in the more modern Banco de Crédito or in one of the casas de cambio which can be found on the main street of Gamarra. If you check a few places, you should be able to find exchange rates comparable to Lima. This is the best place to change money on the north coast.

Immigration Although you won't be entering or leaving the country through Trujillo, you might need to renew your visa or tourist card. This can be done at the Migraciónes, next to the Banco de la Nación.

Medical The best place for general medical services is the Anglo-American hospital opposite Cassinelli's Museum. They don't charge very much.

Colonial Buildings
The colonial mansions and churches are most attractive and worth visiting. Unfortunately, they don't seem to have very regular opening times and the listed times may well change without notice. There are also some very worthwhile museums.

The single feature of the colonial centre which is especially distinctive in Trujillo is the beautiful wrought-iron grillwork which fronts almost every colonial building in the city. This, combined with the pastel shades that the buildings are painted, produces a very typical *Trujillano* ambience which is not found in other colonial cities in Peru.

Plaza de Armas
The main square is very spacious and attractive with an impressive central statue of the heroes of Peruvian Independence. The plaza is fronted by the Cathedral which was begun in 1647, destroyed in 1759 and rebuilt soon afterwards. It has a famous Basilica and is often open in the evenings around 6 pm.

There are several elegant colonial mansions surrounding the Plaza. One is now the Hotel de Turistas and it contains a small museum of Moche ceramics. Another is the Urquiaga Mansion, which stands next to the tourist information office and now belongs to the Banco Central de la Reserva del Peru. It has a small ceramics museum and can be visited during banking hours for free.

Churches
Apart from the Cathedral, the colonial churches of Santo Domingo, San Francisco, La Compañía, San Agustín and Santa Clara are worth a look, although getting inside is largely a matter of luck. They are close to one another and so it's easy to stroll from one to the next. San Agustín, with its finely-gilded high altar, dates from 1558 and is usually open. You certainly won't get into the church of Belén – it's completely in ruins since the 1970 earthquake but it is instructive to see what an unrestored church looks like.

Art Galleries
Several of the colonial buildings contain art galleries with changing shows.

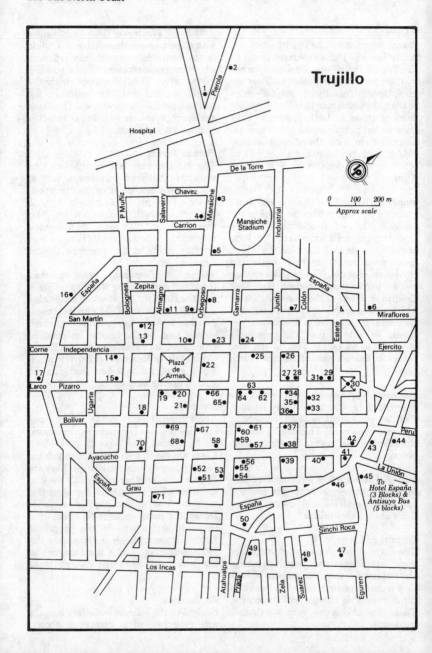

Trujillo

0   100   200 m
Approx scale

1	Cassinelli Museum	38	Exp Norpacifico
2	Pussy Cat Club	39	Hostals Central & Lima
3	Bus stop for Chiclayo	40	Comité 12
4	Comité 10	41	Hostal Peru
5	Buses to Chan Chan, Huanchaco & Arco Iris	42	Hotel Paris
6	Emtrafesa Bus	43	Hostal Las Vegas
7	San Martín Hotel	44	Exp Sudamericano
8	Cine Primavera	45	Roggero Bus & Bull Ring
9	ABC Chicken Restaurant	46	Old city wall
10	Hotel de Turistas	47	Market
11	Banco de la Nación	48	Local bus to Pyramids of the Sun & Moon
12	University Zoology Museum	49	Chinchaysuyo Bus (37)
13	La Compañía Church	50	Cine Chimu
14	Post Office	51	Hotel San José
15	Santo Domingo Church	52	Cine Star
16	Dancin' Discotheque	53	Hotel Opt Gar
17	Local bus to Buenos Aires beach	54	24 hour Restaurant
18	Aero Peru	55	Hotel Turismo, Chifa Oriental & Chifa Ak Chan
19	Tourist Information	56	Teatro Ayacucho
20	Casa Urquiaga	57	Hostal Vogi
21	Cine Ideal	58	Market
22	Cathedral	59	Hotel Continental & Hostal Acapulco
23	Santo Domingo Art Gallery	60	Hotel Premier
24	San Francisco Church	61	ENTEL
25	Casa de los Léones	62	Iturregui Palace
26	Santa Clara Church	63	El Mesón de Cervantes
27	Marcos Café & Café Romano	64	Casa de la Emancipación & Banco Nor Peru
28	Peru Express	65	Banco de Crédito
29	Tepsa Ticket Office	66	Faucett
30	Plazuela El Recreo	67	San Agustín Church
31	Pizarro & Recreo Restaurants	68	Hostal Residencial Los Escudos
32	Empresa Diaz	69	Archaeology Museum
33	Emp Antisuyo	70	Ruined Church of Belén
34	Hotel Americano & Cine Peru	71	Tepsa Bus Station
35	Hostal Colón		
36	Salud y Vigor & other vegetarian restaurants		
37	Chinchaysuyo Bus (& 49)		

Admission is normally free or a nominal few cents. The Santo Domingo art gallery, next to the church, is open from 9.30 am to 1 pm and 4 to 8.30 pm daily.

The Casa de los Léones (also known as the Ganoza Chopitea residence) has changing shows; they're open from 10 am to 1 pm and 4 to 9 pm daily. The shows can often be very good, depending on your taste of course! They make a change from the interminable religious and colonial art that are the stock of most museums – good modern Peruvian art is sometimes shown as well as rather arcane collections that you may never have a chance to see elsewhere.

Palacio Iturregui

This early 19th century mansion is unmistakable and impossible to ignore – it's painted an overpowering blue colour. Its main claim to fame is that General Iturregui lived here when he proclaimed Trujillo's independence from Spain in 1820. Trujillo was one of the first cities in Peru to declare its independence. The mansion is now used by the swanky Club Central who will allow you to visit between 11 am and 12 noon on weekdays.

Cassinelli Museum

This archaeological museum is located on the western outskirts of town in the basement of a petrol (gas) station. It's open on Mondays through Fridays from 8 to 11.30 am and 3 to 5.30 pm and admission is about 50c.

I remember visiting this museum one afternoon. I found the petrol station without any difficulty and I could see several pots and other pieces through the windows. I went inside and asked if I could see the collection and was told to wait a few minutes. I looked at the haphazardly displayed pots in the garage office and wondered if this was all there was to see. After all, what could I expect in an oily garage? After a few minutes, however, I was led through a locked door, down a narrow flight of stairs, and through a second locked door, this time a heavily armoured one. I entered the basement and was astonished by the sight of hundreds of ceramics carefully exhibited on shelves filling the entire room. The curator showed me dozens of his favourite pieces, letting me hold and examine several as he explained where they came from and what they represented.

Among the most interesting of the ceramics were the whistling pots which produced clear notes when they were blown. I was especially intrigued by a pair of pots which represented a male and a female bird – they appeared to be tinamous – which, superficially, were very similar to one another but when they were blown each produced a completely different note. These notes correspond to the different male and female calls.

The exhibits were fascinating and well set out and I was the only visitor. I was very pleased to be able handle a few of the pots myself. The whistling pots were superb. The rather bizarre location of the museum added to its uniqueness. All in all, this was among the best museum experiences I have had in Peru and I give this museum a whole-hearted recommendation.

Señor Cassinelli has also put together a collection of his best pots and exhibited them (under glass) in the front rooms of the Hotel de Turistas. It's a free show.

Archaeology Museum

This university-run museum was temporarily closed for restoration when I was last in Trujillo but it should have reopened by now. Opening hours are 8 am to 1 pm on weekdays from January to March and 8 am to 12 noon and 3 to 6 pm on weekdays from April to December and admission is free.

Zoology Museum

Also run by the university and temporarily closed recently, it should have reopened by now with the same hours as their archaeology museum.

Beaches

The beach at the Trujillo suburb of Buenos Aires is easily reached by black and white local buses which pass the stop on Larco and España several times an hour. You can swim there, although the water tends to be rough, and there are several seafood restaurants by the beach. Go in a group and have someone watch your possessions when you're in the water. Going to the beach and staying in front of the restaurants is safe enough, but walking along the beach away from the Buenos Aires area is dangerous. There is a track from Buenos Aires to Chan Chan and this is especially notorious for muggings. The tourist office map for the area calls this track a *Via de Evitamiento* which translates into 'route to be avoided.'

A much better beach is found in the village of Huanchaco, 11 km to the north. See the Huanchaco section.

Caballos de Paso

These are literally 'pacing horses' and breeding, training and watching them is a Peruvian equestrian activity. The idea is to breed and train horses which 'pace' (walk or trot) more elegantly than others. Trujillo and Lima are both centres for this upper class pastime. Trujilleños will tell you that the activity originated in their Department of La Libertad.

Fiestas

Trujillo's major festival is called *El Festival Internacional de la Primavera* or the Spring Festival. It's been held annually for some 35 years and its attractions include international beauty contests, parades, national dancing competitions, *caballos de paso* exhibitions, sports and various other cultural activities including, according to my 1985 calendar – 'Beautiful North American Cheerleaders'. Yes, well . . . The last week in September is when it all happens and better hotels are fully booked far in advance.

The last week in January is also busy with the national Marinera contest. The Marinera is a typically coastal Peruvian dance which involves much waving of handkerchiefs. Students of folk dance shouldn't miss this one.

Places to Stay – bottom end

It is perhaps because Trujillo is so far from the more heavily visited areas of Peru that its hotels are cheaper than most other major cities. The cheapest, while nothing to write home about, offer double rooms for a dollar and even the more expensive hotels are cheap in comparison with Cuzco or Arequipa.

One of the cheapest is the very basic *Hostal Peru* which costs 60c for a single and US$1 for a double. Opposite is the *Hotel Paris* for 70c and US$1. The *Hostal Lima* has, for some strange reason, become popular with gringos so stay here if you want to meet other budget travellers. It looks like a jail and is noisy. They charge 80c and US$1 single and double and the *Hostal Central* next door is similarly priced. Also in this price range is the *Hostal Colón*. None of these hotels have private showers or hot water and their standards of cleanliness aren't very high.

The best budget hotel, for my money at least, is the *Hotel Americano*. It is housed in a rambling old mansion which is rather dingy but nonetheless has character. Some of the rooms have private bathrooms with cold water. They are really basic but kept fairly clean. Singles/doubles are US$1.30/2.30 with private bath and a little less in rooms with communal bath.

Costing just a few cents more is the *Hotel Premier* which is less interesting and less friendly, though the facilities are similar. Also the *Hotel San José* which is clean and the *Hotel España* which is basic but clean and convenient for the Antisuyo bus station.

Places to Stay – middle

The *Hotel Las Vegas* looks clean but is otherwise unremarkable and charges US$2.70/4.70 with private bath. The *Hotel San Martín* has the advantage of having over 100 rooms and so is almost never full. It's characterless but reasonably clean and there's hot water in the private showers. The rooms cost US$3/5 for singles/doubles with bath. The *Hotel Turismo* is also clean and has telephones and hot water in all the rooms; they charge US$3.30/4.70 with bath. Clean, modern and good is the *Hostal Vogi* which costs US$3.30/5.30 with private bath and hot water.

The new *Hotel Continental* is also good and has clean carpeted singles/doubles with telephone, music, private bath and hot water for US$4/6. Next door is the similarly priced *Hostal Acapulco* which rates itself as a three-star hotel but looks neither as good nor as clean as its neighbour – its main attraction is the Turkish bath on the premises. Also in this price range is the pleasant *Hostal Residencial Los Escudos* which is locked and secure, so ring the bell to get in. There is a garden and continental breakfast is served. The clean and well run *Hotel Opt Gar* has a good restaurant and singles/doubles at about US$5/7.50.

Places to Stay – top end

The government-run *Hotel de Turistas* (phone ENTURPERU in Lima at 721928 for reservations) is excellent value at US$8/11 for singles/doubles with private bath and continental breakfast. There are a few cheaper rooms with shared bath. The hotel is in a beautiful building right on the Plaza de Armas and there's an excellent ceramic museum on the premises. I'd stay here if I had a few extra dollars.

The most expensive hotel in town is the modern *Hotel El Golf* which has a swimming pool and other facilities but is well away from the centre so you have to take a taxi. Stay here if you're with a convention.

Places to Eat

A good area to head for when thinking of food is the market. There are plenty of restaurants nearby and, for the impecunious, the food stalls in the market itself are among the cheapest places to eat in Trujillo. However, you'll find that restaurant prices are also very reasonable. A block away from the market are several Chinese restaurants of which the *Chifa Oriental* and *Chifa Ak Chan* are recommended. Nearby is the *Restaurant 24 Horas* which is inexpensive and always open. The *Hotel Opt Gar* on the same block serves some of the best international food in town.

Rank according to race - Spaniard, Mestizo, Mulatto and Indian (Waman Puma)

My favourite restaurants are both on the 700 block of Pizarro. The *Café Romano* has strong espresso coffee and *Marco's Café* serves delicious home-made cakes and pies as well as ice cream. Both these cafés serve a variety of good food. Ask for their set lunch or dinner if you're economising – they're well under a dollar.

A good choice for a cheap set lunch in pleasant surroundings is the *El Mesón de Cervantes*. They have an outside court-yard with shaded tables. Also cheap, though less elegant-looking, are the *Pizarro* and *Recreo* restaurants which are good value for money. If you like fried chicken, then try the *ABC* chicken restaurant which is distinguished not only by large portions but also by the man-sized chicken sitting on the roof! Vegetarians are not forgotten and Trujillo has several vegetarian restaurants to choose from. Three or four are found in the area around the 700 block of Bolívar. One of the best is the *Salud y Vigor*. And health and vigour to you, too.

Top: Reed canoes at Huanchaco near Trujillo (TW)
Left: Meeting an ancient Peruvian! Sechín Ruins Museum (RR)
Right: Children in front of Cathedral, Plaza de Armas, Trujillo (RR)

Top: Author nose to nose with warrior, Sechín ruins (RR)
Left: Carving of warrior, Sechín ruins (RR)
Right: Carvings at Huaca Arco Iris, near Trujillo (RR)

Entertainment

There are many cinemas and one of these is often the best choice for an evening out. There are plenty of bars and if you're looking for an American-style cocktail lounge you can drink at the *Pussy Cat Club* which has a fancy atmosphere, disco and good restaurant. It's also known as Billy Bob's. Another discotheque is called simply *Dancin'*.

Getting There

Trujillo is Peru's major north coast city and is served by scores of long distance buses making the 24-hour run along the Pan-American Highway between Lima and the Ecuadorean border as well as intermediate coastal points. There is also a daily air service from the capital and other cities.

Air Both Faucett and AeroPeru have offices in downtown Trujillo. Together they operate two or three flights a day to Lima. One way fares are about US$26. AeroPeru has three flights a week to Cajamarca (US$15), two flights a week to Juanjui (US$24) and two flights a week to Iquitos (US$52) via Yurimaguas (US$39) and Tarapoto (US$29). In addition, each airline operates two flights a week to Tarapoto. Faucett flies to Chiclayo five times a week for US$10. There are no flights from Trujillo to Piura or Tumbes at this time. Schedules vary so often that there is little point in giving the days on which flights operate.

Buses & Colectivos Most major companies operate up and down the coast along the Pan-American Highway. A few go inland. I have found that prices and schedules vary widely from company to company and month to month. There isn't much of a set pattern that you can rely on and so the details given below are only intended as a rough guide. TEPSA is usually the most expensive and has a ticket office well away from the bus depot (you can buy tickets at both office and depot but make sure you know where the bus is leaving from), Chinchaysuyo has two depots and Expresa Antisuyo also has two depots with the one further from town being used for more departures. (See city map for locations.)

If you're heading north your next major stop is Chiclayo. This journey costs US$2 and takes up to four hours by bus. What the locals do is stand on Avenida Mansiche outside the stadium and get on the next bus which is heading north. All northbound buses with seats available will stop here. If you'd rather not bother about watching your luggage while waiting on the side of the road, then the most frequent Chiclayo service is with EMTRAFESA which has a dozen buses a day. If you're in a hurry you can take a Comité 10 shared taxi which leaves as soon as it is full, takes about 2½ hours, and charges twice as much as a bus.

Several bus companies provide service to Piura (US$4, nine hours) and/or Tumbes (US$9, 16 hours). TEPSA and Expreso Sudamericano both have night buses to Tumbes and Roggero has a bus to Tumbes leaving in the afternoon. Roggero also has a night bus to Piura. Chinchaysuyo has both a day and a night bus to Piura.

The trip to Lima takes nine hours and when I did it in late 1985 it cost about US$6. I did the same journey six weeks later and it cost just under US$5. So if you think you've noticed dozens of price 'errors' in this book, you might begin to understand the reason why! The most comfortable service to Lima is with TEPSA but they have three night buses only. If you prefer to travel during the day then check Chinchaysuyo which has several departures for Lima daily. Other companies which go to Lima usually run only one bus a day (usually overnight) and they include Expreso Norpacifico, Expreso Sudamericano, Roggero and Peru Express. Many of these buses will sell tickets to intermediate points between Trujillo and Lima.

There are various bus services inland. Chinchaysuyo has a direct bus to Huaraz (US$6, 10 hours) but it's a night bus. If you want to travel by day you should go from Chimbote instead.

For some reason I had difficulty in finding good bus connections from Trujillo to Cajamarca. Connections from Chiclayo to Cajamarca are better so if you're planning on visiting both cities then you may want to consider going first to Chiclayo and then to Cajamarca. If you go from Trujillo then the company that goes to Cajamarca is Empresa Diaz but, frustratingly, their office is closed more often than not. The journey takes about eight hours and costs US$3.50. If you can't find a direct bus then you could take any bus to Chiclayo and get off at the Cajamarca turn-off (about 15 km past Pacasmayo) to wait for a Cajamarca-bound bus from anywhere. It's a hot place to wait but there are a couple of basic cafés for cold drinks. If you leave fairly early in the morning from Trujillo you should be able to connect with a bus from Chiclayo. Finally, if bussing seems too much of a hassle, then book a shared taxi seat with Comité 12 which charges US$6.50 for the 5½-hour drive leaving at 12.30 pm daily.

If you want to head east from Trujillo to Otuzco, Santiago de Chuco, Huamachuco, and Cajabamba (this is the much rougher and longer old route to Cajamarca) then the best regular service is with Antisuyo. Unfortunately, this attractive route is driven only at night but perhaps their schedule will change.

Chinchaysuyo has two buses a week which take the long northern route into the jungle. The buses leave at 2 pm on Tuesdays and Fridays and go via Chiclayo, Bagua Grande and Moyobamba to Tarapoto. This is an exceedingly long, rough and tiring journey which takes 24

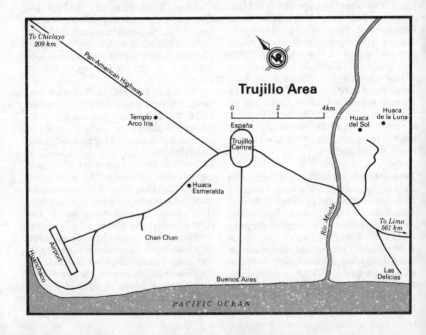

hours if the going is good – which it usually isn't. It's a spectacular route though, and well worth doing if you break it down to more manageable sections.

Getting Around

Airport Transport The airport is about 10 km north-west of Trujillo and can be reached cheaply by the bus to Huanchaco, although you'll have to walk the last km or so. Ask the driver where the airport turn-off is. A taxi to or from downtown will cost from US$2 to US$3.

ARCHAEOLOGICAL SITES AROUND TRUJILLO

The Moche and the Chimu are the two cultures which have left the greatest mark on the Trujillo area. But they are by no means the only ones. In a March 1973 *National Geographic* article, Drs M E Moseley and C J Mackey claimed knowledge of over 2000 sites in the Moche River valley, which enters the ocean near Trujillo. Many of these sites are small and well-nigh forgotten, but others include the largest pre-Columbian city in America (Chan Chan) as well as pyramids which required an incredible 50 million adobe bricks to construct.

There are five major archaeological sites which can be easily reached from Trujillo by local buses or taxis. Two of these sites are Moche, dating from about the 500 AD, and the other three are from the Chimu culture dating from about 1200 or 1300 AD.

Archaeology

One of the earliest groups studied in Peru are the Huaca Prieta people who lived at the site of that name around 3500 to 2300 BC. The people were hunter/gatherers who also began to develop simple agriculture. Cotton and varieties of beans and peppers were grown but corn, now a staple, was unheard of. Finds of simple fishing nets and hooks indicate that the Huaca Prieta people ate primarily seafood. They lived in single room shacks half buried in the ground and most of what is known about them has been deduced from their middens, or garbage piles. Hence we know that they were a pre-ceramic people, didn't use jewellery, and had developed netting and weaving. At their most artistic, they decorated dried gourds with simply carved patterns; similarly decorated gourds are produced today as a Peruvian handicraft. Hot stones may have been dropped into these gourds to be used for cooking food.

Huaca Prieta is one of the most intensively studied early Peruvian sites but, for the non-archaeologist, it's more interesting to read about it than to visit the site. After all, it's simply a prehistoric pile of garbage. If you want to go, it's about 30 km north of Trujillo on the south side of the Chicama valley by the coast. Colectivos go from Avenida España to Cartavio from where it's about a seven-km walk.

After the decline of the Huaca Prieta site, a developmental era began. Weaving improved, agriculture developed with the advent of corn and, particularly importantly, the making of ceramics began and simple funerary offerings were made. Burial sites in the Chicama and Virú Valleys gave archaeologists an insight into this development, but no specific site is particularly important to the traveller. This period is called the Guañape after a tiny fishing village near the mouth of the Virú River where burials of this era were excavated.

About 850 BC, a new major cultural influence began to leave its mark on the area. This was the cultist period, named after a feline-worshipping cult with one of its main centres at Chavín de Huantár on the eastern slopes of the Cordillera Blanca. This Chavín influence swept mainly over the northern mountains and the northern and central coasts of Peru. At its most simple, the Chavín influence consisted of a highly stylised art form based especially on jaguar motifs. The Chavín Horizon could be called the first

Cornice of the cats, Chavín de Huantár

major culture in Peru as well as one of the most artistically developed. It encompassed various groups and areas typified by their rapid development of ceramic ware, and a common art form. In the Trujillo area, the Chavín influence was represented especially by the Cupisnique culture. Examples of Cupisnique pottery can be seen in the museums of Lima and Trujillo, although there are no especially noteworthy ruins for the visitor to see.

Archaeologists identify several other geographically smaller and less important cultures which occurred in the Trujillo area and coincided with the later Cupisnique period. These include the Salinar, Vicus and Gallinazo periods.

So far, I've described a series of developments which probably have left you, the traveller, with little desire to head up to Trujillo to explore ancient sites and cities. This has been just by way of introduction. With the decline of the Cupisnique period we find the origins of the fascinating Moche period – and this culture *has* left us with impressive archaeological sites to visit and with some of the most outstanding pottery to be seen in Peru's museums.

The Moche culture is named after the river which flows into the ocean just south

of Trujillo. The term Mochica has been used interchangeably with Moche and refers to a dialect that was spoken in the Trujillo area at the time of the conquest, but was not necessarily spoken by the Moche people. Moche is now the preferred usage.

The Moche culture grew out of the Cupisnique at about the time of Christ. The Moche didn't conquer the Cupisnique; rather there was a slow transition characterised by a number of developments. Craftsmanship of ceramics, textiles and metals improved greatly, architectural techniques developed to produce huge pyramids and other structures, and there was enough leisure time to have a highly organised religion and to develop art.

As with the Nazca culture which developed on the south coast at about the same time, the Moche period is known especially for its ceramics. They are considered the most sensitively artistic and technically developed of any found in Peru. Thousands of Moche pots are preserved in museums and they are so realistically decorated with figures and scenes that they give us a very descriptive look at life during the Moche period. Pots were modelled into lifelike representations of people, crops, domestic or wild animals, marine life or model houses. Other pots were painted with scenes of both ceremonial and everyday life. By 'reading' these pots archaeologists know that the Moche was a very class conscious society. The most important people were the urban classes, especially the priests and warriors. They lived closest to the large ceremonial pyramids and other temples. They were surrounded by a middle class of artisans and then, in descending order, farmers and fishermen, and finally servants, slaves and beggars.

The priests and warriors were both honoured and obeyed. They are the people most frequently shown in ceramics which depict them being carried in litters or wearing particularly fine jewellery or clothing. Their authority is evident in pots which show scenes of punishment, including the mutilation and death of those who dared to disobey them. Other facets of Moche life which are dealt with

Moche pot

include surgical procedures such as amputation or setting of broken limbs. Sex is realistically shown; one room in the Rafael Herrera Museum in Lima is entirely devoted to (mainly Moche) erotic pots depicting most sexual practices including some rather imaginative ones! Clothing, musical instruments, tools and jewellery are all frequent subjects for ceramics. In fact, most of what we know about the Moche is from this wealth of pottery – there was no written language.

The ceramics also show us that the Moche had well developed weaving techniques but, because of rare rainstorms every few decades, most of their textiles have been destroyed. Metalwork, on the other hand, has survived. They used gold, silver and copper mainly for ornaments but some heavy copper implements have also been found.

The Moche did not live in towns as we know them. A closer description would be a high density of peasant population surrounding a central worship site such as a massive pyramid. Two of these survive next to one another a few km south of Trujillo. They are known as the *Huacas del Sol y de la Luna* (the Temples of the Sun and the Moon) and are easily visited. The Temple of the Sun is the largest pre-Columbian structure in South America and is described in more detail below.

The Moche period declined around 700 AD. The next few centuries are somewhat confusing. The Wari culture, based in the Ayacucho area of the central Peruvian Andes, began to expand and its influence was felt as far north as the Chicama valley.

The next important period in the Trujillo area was the Chimu, which existed from about 1000 to 1470 AD. The Chimu built a capital at Chan Chan, just north of Trujillo. Chan Chan is the largest pre-Columbian city in Peru, covering about 28 square km, and it is estimated to have housed about 50,000 people. The Chimu was a highly organised society – it must have been to build and support such

The Chimu god, Naymlap, who brought the desert dwellers to their homes on balsa rafts

a city as Chan Chan. Its artwork was less exciting than that of the Moche, tending more to functional mass production than artistic achievement. Gone, for the most part, is the technique of painting pots. Instead, they were fired by a simpler method than that used by the Moche and the product was the typical blackware seen in many collections of Chimu pottery. Despite its lesser quality, it still showed us life in the Chimu kingdom. Despite the decay in the quality of ceramics, metallurgy developed and various alloys were worked, including bronze. They were also exceptionally fine goldsmiths.

It is as an urban society that the Chimu are best remembered. Their huge capital contained approximately 10,000 dwellings of varying degrees of quality and importance. There were storage bins for food and other products from their empire, which stretched along the coast from the Gulf of Guayaquil to Chancay. There were huge walk-in wells, canals, workshops and temples. The royal dead were buried in mounds containing a wealth of funerary offerings. The whole city was decorated with designs moulded into the mud walls and the more important areas were layered with precious metals.

It must have been a dazzling sight. Today, only the mud walls and a few moulded decorations remain and it is the huge extent of the site which amazes the visitor as much as anything else. The Chimu were conquered by the Incas in about 1460 but the city was not looted until the Spanish arrived. Heavy rainfall has severly damaged the mud mouldings although a few have survived and others have been restored.

Huaqueros

This is a frequently heard word, especially in the Trujillo area. A *huaquero* is literally a robber of *huacas*. A huaca refers to any temple, shrine or burial area of special significance. Huacas are often characterised by their richness. Temples were decorated with sheets of precious metals and royalty was buried with a treasure trove. Huaqueros specialise in finding and opening these forgotten graves and removing the valuables within for sale to anybody prepared to pay for an archaeological artefact. Ever since the Spanish conquest, huaqueros have worked the ancient graves of Peru. To a certain extent, one can sympathise with a poor *campesino* grubbing around in the desert hoping to strike it rich but the huaquero is also one of the archaeologist's greatest enemies. So thorough has the huaqueros' ransacking been that an unplundered grave is never found by archaeologists – someone else has always been there first.

Today's visitor to Trujillo and the surrounding sites is sometimes offered a 'genuine' archaeological artefact. These are not always genuine and if they are it is illegal to export them out of Peru.

Chan Chan

This is the huge ruined capital of the Chimu Empire which most visitors want to see. Built by the Chimu around 1300 AD, it is the largest pre-Columbian city in the Americas and has also been called the largest mud city in the world. At the height of the Chimu Empire it housed an estimated 50,000 inhabitants and contained a vast wealth of gold, silver and ceramic objects. After Chan Chan was conquered by the Incas, the wealth remained more or less undisturbed. The Incas were interested in expanding their imperial control, not in amassing treasure. As soon as the Spaniards arrived, however, the looting began and within a few decades there was little left of the treasures of Chan Chan. The remnants have been pillaged through the centuries by huaqueros.

Not only the huaqueros have caused damage at Chan Chan. Devastating floods and heavy rainfall have severely eroded the mud walls of the city. Several decades can go by with almost no rain but occasionally the climatic phenomenon of El Niño can cause rainstorms and floods in the coastal desert. The most recent of these was in 1983.

The Chimu capital consisted of nine major sub-cities, each of which was built by a succeeding ruler and hence the nine areas are often referred to as the Royal Compounds. Each contained a royal burial mound where the ruler was buried with an appropriately vast quantity of funerary offerings which included dozens of sacrificed young women as well as chambers full of ceramics, weavings and jewellery. Today's visitor sees only a huge area of crumbling mud walls, some decorated with marvellous friezes. It is, as advertised, the largest mud city in the world. The treasures are gone – although a few remnants can be seen in museums. The nine Royal Compounds have been named mainly after archaeologists and explorers. The Tschudi compound, named after a Swiss naturalist who visited Peru in the 1800s and published *Peruvian Antiquities* in Vienna in 1851, has been partially restored and is open to visitors. You can spend hours wandering around these ruins.

Chan Chan is about five km west of Trujillo. To get there take the white, yellow and orange colectivo which passes the corner of España and Mansiche every few minutes and costs about 10c. Most of these buses continue to Huanchaco so ask the driver to let you off at Chan Chan. Tschudi lies to the left of the main road and you reach it by walking about 500 metres along a dusty dirt road. As you walk you'll see the crumbling ruins of the other compounds all around you. At the Tschudi complex there is the entrance booth, a snack/souvenir stand, and a third booth where guides are available. There is usually a pair of Tourist Police on duty. Entrance is from 8 am to 4 pm daily and costs 40c plus a 15c camera fee. The ticket can also be bought at either the Huaca Esmeralda or the Huaca Arco Iris ruins and is valid for all three sites but must be used within one day. You can hire a local guide for about US$1.50 to make sure you don't miss anything and to be shown the original as opposed to the restored friezes and decorations. The complex is well marked by arrows, however, so you can see everything without a guide if you prefer.

Tschudi complex Entry is through a thick defensive wall. Inside, you turn right and almost immediately enter the huge and largely restored Ceremonial Courtyard. All four interior walls are decorated with geometric designs, most of which are new. Just to the right of the massive doorway as you enter you'll see a few designs at ground level which, I was told, are unrestored. They're slightly rougher looking than the modern work and consist of the three or four nutria (furry aquatic mammals) which are closest to the door. The design is repeated all the way around the Ceremonial Plaza and is topped by a series of lines which represent waves. Note the ramp joining the two levels at the far side of the plaza. Stairways were not a frequent feature of the major Chimu structures. Note also the great restored height of the walls in this plaza. All of the walls of Chan Chan have crumbled with time but, at the height of its occupancy, the highest of Tschudi's walls stood over 10 metres high.

Following the arrows, you leave the Ceremonial Plaza through a door to the right and make a sharp left hand turn to walk along the outside wall of the plaza. This is one of the most highly decorated and best restored of Tschudi's walls. The adobe friezes consist of waves of fish rippling along the entire length of the wall with a line of seabirds below. See if you can tell where the original mouldings end and the restored ones begin. As before, the rougher-looking fish are the originals but despite their time worn appearance they still retain a fluidity and character somehow lacking in the modern version. Nevertheless, the modern restoration has been done with care and succeeds in recapturing the entirety of the wall.

At the end of this wall, the arrowed path goes through a labyrinthine section known as the Sanctuaries. It is not clear exactly what these sanctuaries were for but their importance is evident in both the quantity and quality of the decorations. Though less restored than the waves and fish wall, they are the most interesting section of friezes in Tschudi. Their square and diamond-shaped geometric designs represent – quite simply – fishing nets. After all, being so close to the ocean, the Chimu based much of their diet on seafood and the importance of the sea reached venerable proportions. As we have seen, fish, waves, seabirds and sea mammals are all represented throughout the city and here, in the Sanctuaries, you can find all of them interspersed with the fishing nets. Not only was the sea venerated, but also the moon. This is shown in the Sanctuaries by several series of full moon symbols. For the Chimu, the moon and the sea were of religious importance, unlike the Incas who worshipped the sun and venerated the earth.

Detail from a Tschudi wall

From the Sanctuaries, arrows lead the visitor into a second ceremonial plaza similar in shape but smaller in size than the major ceremonial plaza. It also has a ramp joining the two levels. Behind this plaza a view is gained of a huge rectangular depression which looks like a drained swimming pool. In fact it was once a water cistern which supplied the Tschudi royal compound with its daily needs. The water level was reached by a series of ramps from the surface and each of the compounds had its own cistern. The Tschudi cistern is the largest in Chan Chan and measures 130 by 45 metres.

To the left of the cistern is an area of several dozen small cells which have been called the military sector. Perhaps soldiers lived here, or possibly the cells were used for storage. These constructions are not very well preserved. Leading back from the military sector, a straight path takes you almost back to the main entrance. A series of storage bins are passed and the final area visited is the Assembly Room. This is a large rectangular room with 24 seats set into niches in the walls. The acoustic properties of this room are such that speakers sitting in any one of the niches can be clearly heard all over the room. Try it.

You are back by the main entrance but you are free to wander around again to inspect more thoroughly the areas of particular interest to you.

Chan Chan has eight other compounds similar to Tschudi. Unfortunately, it is not as worthwhile or easy to visit the others. They are in much worse states of repair and there are no guards. It is possible to be robbed in these remote and dusty old ruins and so it's recommended that those seriously interested in seeing the less developed areas of Chan Chan do so in a group or with a guide who knows what he's doing. Particularly notorious for robbery and mugging is the path behind Tschudi leading down to and along the beach. If you stay on the dirt road joining the main road with Tschudi you shouldn't have any problems.

La Huaca Esmeralda

This temple was also built by the Chimu about the same time as Chan Chan. The site is open daily from 8 am to 4 pm and entrance costs 40c plus a 15c camera fee. The ticket is valid for entrance into Chan Chan and the Huaca Arco Iris on the same day. Huaca Esmeralda lies at Mansiche which is half way between Trujillo and Chan Chan so you can take the same bus as to Chan Chan or walk. If returning from Chan Chan to Trujillo the huaca is to the right of the main road, about three blocks behind the Mansiche church.

The site was buried by sand and was discovered by accident in 1923 by a local landowner. He made an attempt to uncover the ruins but the El Niño of 1925 began the process of erosion which was exacerbated by the floods and rains of 1983. Little restoration work has been done on the adobe friezes but it is still possible to make out the characteristic designs of fish, seabirds, waves and fishing nets. The temple consists of two

stepped platforms and an on-site guide will take you around for a tip.

La Huaca Arco Iris

This is the third Chimu site which can be visited at the same time and with the same ticket as Chan Chan and Huaca Esmeralda. Huaca Arco Iris (the Rainbow Temple) is also known locally as the Huaca del Dragon. It is located just to the left of the Pan-American Highway in the suburb of La Esperanza which is about four km north-west of Trujillo. Red, blue and white minibuses for La Esperanza pass the corner of España and Mansiche; the driver can drop you right outside the ruin.

This is one of the best preserved of the Chimu temples simply because it was covered by sand until the 1960s. Its location was known to a handful of archaeologists and huaqueros but excavation did not begin until 1963. Unfortunately, the El Niño of 1983 has caused damage to the friezes.

The excavation of the temple took about five years and the upper parts were rebuilt. It used to be painted but now only faint traces of yellow paint can be seen. The temple consists of a defensive wall over two metres thick which encloses an area of about 3000 square metres. There is only one entrance in this rectangular wall and within is a single large structure, the temple itself. This covers about 800 square metres and consists of two levels with a combined height of about 7½ metres. The walls are slightly pyramidal and covered with repeated rainbow designs, most of which have been restored. Ramps lead the visitor to the very top of the temple from where he or she can look down into a series of large storage bins which almost surround the structure and which have openings only at the top. There are good views from the top level of the temple.

There is a tiny on-site museum and local guides, some of whom speak a little English, are available to show you around the ruin and the museum. A tip is expected. There is a souvenir stand near the entrance where you can buy inexpensive and well-made reproductions of Chimu ceramics.

Las Huacas del Sol y de la Luna

The Temples of the Sun and the Moon were not built by the Chimu. They are about seven centuries older than Chan Chan and are attributed to the Moche period. Their location is on the south bank of the Río Moche, about 10 km south-east of Trujillo by rough road. To get there take one of the blue and white minibuses which leave about every ½ hour from Calle Suarez. The 20-minute ride costs 15c. These buses are among the most dilapidated that I have seen on the coast! The site is officially open from 8 am to 2 pm but there's no entrance booth and so you can freely go in any time you want. It's best to go in the mornings, however, because the wind tends to whip the sand up in the afternoon and the buses run less frequently later in the day. There are usually a couple of Tourist Police near the site in the morning.

The two huacas are both roughly pyramidal in shape and are usually visited together. The Huaca del Sol is the largest single pre-Columbian structure in Peru. Estimates of its size vary depending on the points of reference used, but recent measurements give a maximum length of 342 metres, breadth of 159 metres and height of 45 metres. The structure was built using an estimated 50 million adobe bricks (although I have read reports of three times as many). At one time the pyramid consisted of several different levels connected with steep flights of stairs, huge ramps and walls sloping at 77° to the horizon. A millennium and a half have wrought their inevitable damage and today the pyramid looks like a giant pile of crude bricks partially covered with sand. Despite this, the brickwork still remains very impressive from some angles. It appears that there are few

graves or rooms within the structure and its main purpose was as a huge ceremonial site. Certainly it is an awesome structure because of its size alone and the views from the top are excellent.

The smaller Huaca de la Luna is about half a km away across the open desert. This open area has dozens of pottery shards lying around. Although less impressive in size than the Huaca del Sol, the Huaca de la Luna has yielded many more artefacts. Unlike the almost solid sun pyramid, the moon pyramid is riddled with rooms which contained ceramics, precious metals and some of the beautiful polychrome paintings which the Moche were famous for. Unfortunately, the site is in an extremely bad state of repair and the murals are either badly damaged or covered with rubble.

Climbing either pyramid is fairly straightforward but attempting to enter the chambers of the Huaca de la Luna is both difficult and dangerous because of the loose stonework. It is still done, nevertheless, so if you decide to try bring a torch and be careful.

HUANCHACO

This fishing village is about a 15-km bus ride north of Trujillo and is developing a name as the best beach resort in the Trujillo area. You won't find expensive high-rises, though. Huanchaco is still very low key and retains its fishing village ambience.

Of particular interest are the tortora reed boats which look superficially like those found on Lake Titicaca in the southern highlands. They differ from the highland version by not being hollow and so the fishermen ride on them rather than in them. Hence these high-ended, cigar-shaped boats are called *caballitos*, or little horses, and are similar to those depicted on Moche ceramics 1500 years ago. The inhabitants of Huanchaco are among the few remaining people on the coast who still remember how to construct and use these precarious-looking craft and you can always see some stacked up at the north end of the beach. When the surf is good, the fishermen paddle the boats beyond the breakers to fish and then surf back to the beach with their catch. It's well worth seeing.

Apart from walking the beach and waiting for the *caballitos* to go into action, there's not much to do in Huanchaco and that's one of its attractions. It's a quiet, laid-back and relaxing sort of place. You can swim in the ocean but it's a little cold for most of the year; the El Niño current warms the water from January to March and Huanchaco gets a little busier then. You can climb the tower of the massive church at the north end of the village for a good view of the surroundings.

Warning

The beach of Huanchaco is no more dangerous than anywhere else but people have been mugged when walking a long way away from the village. Whilst it is possible to walk from Huanchaco to Chan Chan and on to the Trujillo beach at Buenos Aires, it is not recommended unless you are in a large group. You'll be OK if you stay in Huanchaco and use the bus to get to Trujillo.

Places to Stay

The *Hostal Bracamonte* is popular, friendly and secure. They have small bungalows in a walled compound a few blocks back from the beach and there is a cafeteria. The *Hotel Sol y Mar* is also set back from the beach but has some rooms with balconies and ocean views. Both these hotels charge about US$2 per person in clean rooms with private baths (cold water) and are recommended.

The *Caballitos de Tortora* is on the beachfront road and slightly more expensive. There is a swimming pool. Cheaper accommodation can be found by asking around: for example, there's a house with no sign opposite the Guardia Civil on the beach. They rent rooms for

US$1.50 per person and there are other families who have cheap rooms.

Places to Eat

There are several seafood restaurants especially (but not only) near where the tortora reed boats are stacked at the north end of the beach. None are luxurious but several are adequate – take your pick. Some places occasionally offer entertainment of sorts – they usually advertise in the hotels a few days in advance.

Getting There

The orange, yellow and white bus which leaves from the corner of Mansiche and España in Trujillo goes past Chan Chan and on to Huanchaco about two or three times an hour. Fare is 15c. The bus can drop you off near the hotel of your choice – ask the driver or you'll end up driving through the village to the north end which is away from the hotels. To return, just wait on the beachfront road for the bus as it returns from the north end, picking up passengers along the way. This bus service stops soon after sunset.

PUERTO CHICAMA

This small port is famous for its surf; it has the longest left-handed wave in the world. Not being a surfer, I have no idea what that means but I guess it is pretty important.

Places to Stay

Puerto Chicama is a surfer's hangout and has a couple of basic hotels and restaurants and no electricity at night. The 'best' hotel is the *Sony* which has two of its rooms facing the ocean. It's US$1 per person. Cheaper and really basic is the *El Hombre*. I've also heard that you can camp.

Getting There

To get to Puerto Chicama, wait for a bus near the Mansiche stadium in Trujillo. A few buses go direct but it may be easier to take a bus about 40 km north along the

Pan-American Highway to Paiján and change there for a local bus to Puerto Chicama, a further 16 km away.

I once met an Australian surfer who was just travelling from beach to beach along the Pacific coast. He had his board with him and seemed to think there was no problem in transporting it on the buses.

PACASMAYO & PACATNAMÚ

The small port of Pacasmayo is 105 km north of Trujillo on the Pan-American Highway. The turn-off to Cajamarca is 15 km beyond Pacasmayo. A few km further along the Pan-American, just before the village of Guadalupe, a track leads towards the ocean. The little visited ruins of Pacatnamú lie several km along this track. The site has been inhabited by various cultures; the Gallinazo, Moche and Chimu all have left their mark.

Places to Stay

There are a couple of cheap, basic but clean hotels in Pacasmayo. These include the *Ferrocarril* and *Panamericano*.

CHICLAYO

The next major coastal city north of Trujillo is Chiclayo, just over 200 km away on the Pan-American Highway. Chiclayo is not a historic city, being no more than an outlying district of the older town of Lambayeque during the 1800s. Today, Lambayeque is small and almost forgotten whilst Chiclayo has become one of the fastest growing modern cities in Peru. It is now an important commercial centre and the capital of the coastal desert Department of Lambayeque. With a population of about 350,000, it vies with Huancayo for the position of fourth largest city in Peru.

Because there's little to see of historical or archaeological interest, I'd always thought of Chiclayo as one of those cities that you travel through as quickly as possible. One traveller I met, however, put Chiclayo in a different perspective.

He told me that he considered Chiclayo one of the most interesting cities in Peru because it is full of life and vitality. It isn't a colonial city using its faded past to attract tourists; it isn't a resort town with beaches or beautiful scenery; it isn't conveniently located near a set of superb pre-Columbian ruins; it's simply a thriving Peruvian city with no tourist pretensions and good opportunities to meet ordinary Peruvians making Peru work. The next time I travelled north along the coast, I deliberately spent a couple of days in Chiclayo and found that my informant's perspective was surprisingly accurate. It's not such a boring place at all.

Information

Tourist Information The Tourist Information Office is at Avenida Saenz Peña 838. They are helpful in locating bus companies for you if you want to travel to unusual destinations.

Money Exchange The Banco de Crédito and the Banco de Nor Peru on the 600 block of Balta by the Plaza de Armas are currently giving the best exchange. There are several other banks nearby.

Other *Time, Newsweek* and other magazines can be bought from many of the bookstalls on the south side of the Plaza de Armas.

Market

If you're in Chiclayo, don't miss the huge market. Despite being a modern affair, it is one of the most interesting in Peru. Wander around and see the herbalist and *brujo* (witch-doctor) stalls with their dried plants, bones, bits of animals and other healing charms. Other things to look for include heavy woven saddlebags called *alforjas* which are a typical item of the area; they can be worn over the shoulder with a bag on your front and back as well as used as saddlebags. Woven straw items such as hats, baskets, mats and ornaments are also popular. And, of course, there is the usual cacophonous section of animals and a food market.

Coastal Area

There are three coastal villages serving Chiclayo. These are, in order from north to south, Pimentel, Santa Rosa and Puerto de Etén. All three can be reached quickly from Chiclayo by public transport although the service to Puerto de Etén is relatively infrequent. It's suggested that you go to Pimentel or Santa Rosa first and then change there for local transport to Puerto de Etén.

Pimentel is a straight 14 km run from Chiclayo and is the closest of the three villages. There is a good sandy beach here but it gets very crowded during weekends in the summer (January to March) but is quiet during the off season. A few km south of Pimentel is Santa Rosa, a busy fishing village where a few *caballitos* (tortora reed boats described in the Huanchaco section) may still be seen. There is an inexpensive hotel here. From Santa Rosa you can get colectivos to the small port of Puerto de Etén.

Places to Stay - bottom end

Many of the cheapest hotels are along the main downtown street of Avenida Balta, north of the Plaza de Armas. Some of them are very cheap but they are also extremely basic and have little to recommend them. The cheapest cost as little as 60c per person in not particularly clean rooms with cold water communal showers. These basic hostals include the *Ronald, Lima, Unión, Balta, Estrella, Adriatico* and *Chimu*. I wouldn't stay in any of them except in an emergency.

One of the best cheapies is the *Hotel Royal* on the Plaza de Armas – a building full of character. They charge US$1.30/2 for singles/doubles with bath (cold water) and have some cheaper rooms without private showers. The *Hotel Madrid* is similarly priced and clean. For US$2/2.70 you can get reasonably clean rooms with private cold water baths at the *Hostal*

Venezuela or *Hostal Americano*. The similarly priced *Hostal Cruz de Galpon* is much worse.

Places to Stay - middle

A good, clean, comfortable and reasonably priced mid-range hotel is the *Hotel El Sol* at US$3.30/4.70 for singles/doubles with bath and hot water. More centrally located is the *Hostal Costa de Oro* at US$4/5.30 with bath. At about this price is the *Hotel Obby* also with rooms with bath and hot water. Of the three, I prefer the *El Sol*.

Places to Stay - top end

The best hotel in town is the government-run *Hotel de Turistas* which can be reserved in Lima by telephoning ENTURPERU at 721928. They have a restaurant and swimming pool and charge US$10/15 for singles/doubles with private baths and also have some cheaper rooms with communal bathrooms. A continental breakfast is included.

Places to Eat

The best restaurant downtown, with a wide and surprisingly inexpensive variety of food, is the *Restaurant Roma*. The *Restaurant Imperial* across the street is cheaper but still quite good. *Mario's*, nearby, is a 24-hour restaurant. One of my favourites is *Restaurant Cordano* on the Plaza de Armas. It's cheap and friendly and the food is good. There are plenty of other cheap but unremarkable restaurants on Avenida Balta.

Getting There

Air Both AeroPeru and Faucett have offices in downtown Chiclayo. The airport is two km south-east of town. Between them, the two airlines provide two or three flights a day to Lima (US$36). There are six flights a week to Trujillo (US$10), mainly with Faucett. Each airline has two flights a week to Rioja/ Moyobamba (US$27). AeroPeru has two flights a week to Piura (US$12), two flights a week to Tarapoto (US$35) and one flight a week to Chachapoyas (US$26). Schedules change frequently so you are advised to check with the airlines.

Buses There is a large cluster of bus companies near the south exit of town at the corner of Saenz Pena and Bolognesi. This is often the best place to start looking for a long distance bus, especially to Lima. Buses for local destinations tend to leave from other parts of town.

Empresa Chiclayo has the most frequent service to Piura with buses leaving throughout the day at two-hour intervals and charging US$2.50 for the three-hour ride. Be warned that their buses rarely stay on schedule. Empresa Piura has two early morning buses to Piura. TEPSA offers a direct service to Tumbes but it's expensive – about US$8 for the 10-hour trip leaving daily at 2 pm. Transportes El Aguila has a cheaper daily bus which isn't

1	Emp Nor Pacifico
2	Emp Diaz
3	Emp D Olano
4	Exp Continental & Trans Izusa
5	Trans El Aguila
6	Chiclayo Express
7	Trans Piura, Trans Chinchaysuyo & Emp El Cóndor
8	Peru Express
9	Peru Express (Lima)
10	Roggero
11	Cruz de Chalpon
12	Emtrafesa
13	Tepsa
14	Hotel Obby
15	Cine Oro
16	Hotel de Turistas
17	Hotel El Sol
18	Post Office
19	Emp Chiclayo
20	Emp D Olano
21	Trans San Pablo
22	Taxis to Pimentel
23	Aero Peru
24	Comité 1
25	Comité 2
26	Emp San Pedro
27	Cine Colonial
28	Cathedral
29	ENTEL
30	Cine Tropical
31	Hotel Royal
32	Restaurant Cordano
33	Banco de Crédito
34	Banco de Nor Perú
35	Faucett
36	Restaurant Roma
37	Restaurant Imperial
38	Mario's 24 hour Restaurant
39	Hostal Costa de Oro
40	Tourist Information
41	Hostal Ronald
42	Hostal Lima & Hotel Unión
43	Hostal Balta & Hostal Estrella
44	Hostal Adriatico
45	Hostal Americano
46	Hostal Cruz de Galpon
47	Hostal Chimu
48	Emp Norandina
49	Emp Panamericana
50	Hostal Venezuela
51	Hostal Madrid

The mestizo offspring of the priests are being taken to Lima (Waman Puma)

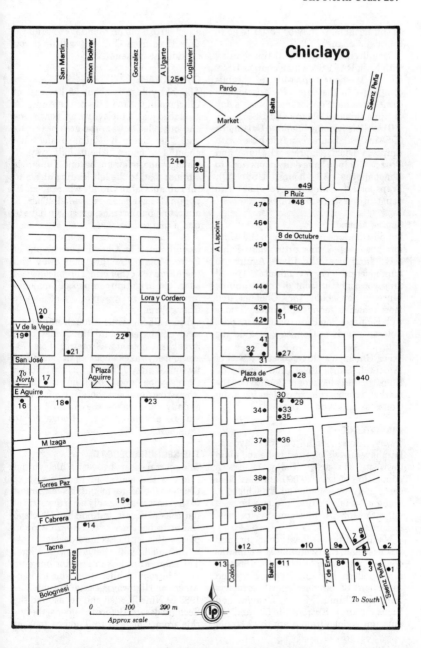

Chiclayo

as comfortable. It may be easier to go to Piura and change.

Trujillo is served several times a day with EMTRAFESA which charges US$2 for the 3½-hour trip. Most of the bus companies in the Saenz Pena/Bolognesi corner area have one or more buses a day to Lima (about 11 hours and US$7).

Travellers heading inland to Cajamarca (US$3.50, six hours) can find buses with Empresa Diaz. Empresa D Olano and Cruz de Chalpon have daily departures to Chachapoyas (18 hours, US$11.50). Transportes Chinchaysuyo has two departures a week to Tarapoto.

Getting Around

For destinations near Chiclayo the white minibuses of Transportes San Pablo leave from near the Plaza Aguirre to Lambayeque every few minutes. They'll drop you right in front of the Brunning Museum for about 15c. Cheaper and more crowded service to Lambayeque is with Empresa San Pedro near the market. Colectivo taxis of Comité 2 also do the trip.

For Chiclayo's three coastal towns of Pimentel, Santa Rosa, and Puerto de Eten, try the colectivos of Comité 1 by the market or the colectivos leaving from Gonzalez and V de la Vega.

LAMBAYEQUE

Twelve km north of Chiclayo is Lambayeque which used to be the main town in the area. Today it has a population of only 20,000 and has been completely overshadowed by Chiclayo. Some colonial architecture can be seen but the town's museum is its best feature.

Named after a local collector and businessman, the Brunning Museum was opened on its present site is the 1960s. It is a modern building housing a good collection of archaeological artefacts from the Chimu, Moche, Chavín, and Vicus cultures. Entrance is 50c and the museum is open from 8 am to 12.30 pm and 2.30 to 5 pm on Mondays to Fridays. Colectivos from Chiclayo will drop you outside the museum.

CHONGOYAPE

This old village is about 65 km east of Chiclayo in the foothills of the Andes. A good road joins Chiclayo with Chongoyape and buses leave from the area of P Ruiz and 7 de Enero in Chiclayo and take about 1½ hours. About half way to Chongoyape, a few km beyond Tumán, is a minor road to the left leading 31 km to the ruins of Batan Grande where about 50 pyramids have been excavated. There is almost no public transport so you have to find a taxi to take you.

In Chongoyape there is a cheap and basic hotel. The Chavín Petroglyphs of Cerro Mulato are three km away and there are a few other minor archaeological sites. The irrigation complex of Tinajones forms a large reservoir just before Chongoyape.

From Chongoyape a rough but scenic road climbs east into the Andes until it reaches Chota at 2400 metres. This 170-km journey takes about eight hours and two buses a day go from Chiclayo through Chongoyape and continue to Chota where there are basic hotels. From Chota a daily bus makes the rough journey via Bambamarca and Hualgayoc to Cajamarca.

THE SECHURA DESERT

The coastal desert between Chiclayo and Piura is the widest in Peru. South of Chiclayo the Andes mountains fall almost to the coast, leaving only a narrow strip of flat coastal desert, but north of Chiclayo this strip becomes over 150 km wide in places; this is the Sechura desert.

Two roads join Chiclayo with Piura. The shorter but less interesting one goes via Mórrope whilst the longer Pan-American Highway goes via Motupe. The 1983 El Niño flooded and devastated the Sechura desert. Before the floods, the bus ride from Chiclayo to Tumbes took as little as eight hours but for several months in 1983 the roads were washed away and impassable in places. A year after the floods the journey was still taking twice as long as before, but the roads are improving. The longer Pan-American Highway is in better condition and therefore is used by buses although the shorter route may reopen soon.

The Pan-American Highway linking Chiclayo with Piura and crossing the Sechura desert passes a few sites of interest. The first is Tucumé, about 25 km north of Chiclayo, near which is the little visited archaeological site of El Purgatorio where there are pyramids from the Chimu period. Near Motupe, almost 80 km north of Chiclayo, are the pre-Inca irrigation canals of Apurlec. None of these places are much visited.

PIURA

Piura, with a population of nearly 300,000, is the sixth largest city in Peru and the capital of its department. Intense irrigation of the desert has made it a major agricultural centre with rice being the main crop. Cotton, corn and plantains (bananas) are also cultivated. The department's petroleum industry is as valuable as its agriculture with the coastal oil fields near Talara producing the bulk of the oil.

Piura's economic development has been precarious, trying to survive extreme droughts and then devastating floods. The department was among the hardest hit during the disastrous El Niño floods of 1983 which destroyed almost 90% of the rice, cotton and plantain crops as well as causing serious damage to roads, bridges, buildings and oil wells in the area. Piura was declared a disaster area – with crops destroyed and land flooded, the inhabitants had no food to eat, no homes to go to and no jobs available. The area is now recovering although some flood damage can still be seen.

The city is referred to as the oldest colonial town in Peru. Its original site was called San Miguel de Piura and was founded on the north banks of the Chira River by Pizarro in 1532, before he headed inland and began the conquest of the Incas. The settlement was moved three times before construction of its present location began in 1588. Piura's cathedral dates from that year and the city centre still has a number of colonial buildings although many were destroyed in the earthquake of 1912. Today, the centre of the city is the large, shady and pleasant Plaza de Armas.

Roughly 30 km east of Piura was the centre of the Vicus culture which existed around the time of Christ. Although no buildings remain of the Vicus sites, tombs have yielded a great number of ceramics which can be seen in the museums of Piura and Lima.

Information

Tourist Information Tourist information is available from 8 am to 4 pm on Mondays to Fridays at the MITI office.

Money Exchange The Banco de Crédito, just off the Plaza de Armas, is the best place to change cash and travellers' cheques.

Museums

The archaeological museum is on the top floor of the *Municipalidad* on the Plaza de Armas and is open from 8 am to 12 noon on Mondays to Fridays. Admission is free. There is a good collection of Vicus ceramics which are characterised by the stumpiness and disproportion of their arms, legs and heads. Artefacts from other Peruvian cultures can also be seen.

Next door to the *municipalidad* is an art gallery in the Banco Central Hipotecario. The gallery is open during banking hours.

The house where Admiral Miguel Grau was born on 27 July 1834 has been turned into a naval museum. The house was almost completely destroyed by the

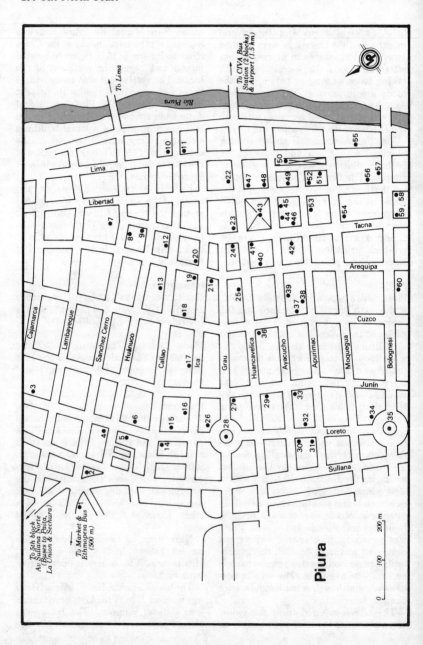

Piura

To Lima

To CIYA Bus
Station (2 blocks)
& Airport (1.5 km)

Río Piura

Lima

Libertad

Cajamarca

Lambayeque

Sánchez Cerro

Huánuco

Callao

Ica

Grau

Huancavelica

Ayacucho

Apurímac

Moquegua

Bolognesi

Tacna

Arequipa

Cuzco

Junín

Loreto

Sullana

To 5th block
Av Sullana Norte
(Buses to Paita,
La Unión & Sechura)

To Market &
Ethmopesa Bus
(500 m)

0   100   200 m

1	Empresa Chiclayo, Trans El Dorado & Comité 1 to Tumbes & Chiclayo	31	Hostal San Jorge
2	Empresa Petrolera Bus	32	Hostal Palmeras
3	ENTEL & Hotel Esmeralda	33	Hostal Continental
4	Ethmopesa Bus Office	34	Tepsa
5	Hostal Terraza	35	Bolognesi Monument
6	Eppo Bus	36	Tacos Mexicanos
7	Carmen Church	37	Café Concierto Coffee House
8	Hostal El Sol	38	Hostal Amauta
9	Aero Peru	39	Las Tradiciónes Restaurant
10	Tourist Office	40	Hotel Eden
11	San Francisco Church	41	Heladería Chalan
12	Hostal Oriental	42	Casa Grau
13	Hotel Tambo	43	Plaza de Armas
14	Comité 2 to Sullana	44	Archaeological Museum
15	Hostal Cristina	45	Art Museum
16	Hostal Ica	46	Banco de la Nación
17	Hotel Hispano	47	Restaurant Orion
18	Comité 24	48	Hotel de Turistas
19	Choppería Munich	49	El Gaucho Steak House
20	Hotel Tangara	50	Plaza Pizarro
21	Restaurant Tres Estrellas	51	Trans Piura & Colectivos to Catacaos
22	Faucett	52	Heladería Venecia
23	Cathedral	53	Las Redes Bar
24	Banco de Crédito	54	San Sebastian Church
25	Alex Chopp	55	Emp Sudamericano
26	La Carreta Chicken Restaurant	56	Chinchaysuyo Buses
27	Cine Variedades	57	Roggero Bus Terminal
28	Grau Monument	58	Comité 1 to Sechura
29	Hostal Lalo	59	Cruz de Galpon Buses
30	Residencial Piura	60	Residencial Bolognesi

earthquake of 1912 and was later restored by the Peruvian navy. Admiral Grau was a hero of the War of the Pacific against Chile (1879-80) and captain of the British built warship *Huascár*, a model of which can be seen in the museum.

For most of the year the museum is open from 8 am to 1 pm and 3.30 to 6 pm on Mondays, Wednesdays, Fridays and Saturdays and from 8 am to 12 noon on Sundays. From January to March, opening hours are from 7.30 am to 1.30 pm on Mondays, Wednesdays, Fridays, Saturdays and Sundays.

Churches

The oldest church in Piura is the Cathedral on the Plaza de Armas. Although parts of the cathedral date from 1588, the main altar was built in 1960. The side altar of the Virgin of Fatima is the oldest; it was built in the first part of the 17th century and was once the main altar. The famed local artist, Ignacio Merino, painted the canvas of Saint Martin of Porres in the mid-19th century.

Other churches worth seeing in Piura are the 17th century Church of Carmen and the Church of San Francisco which is where Piura's independence was declared on 4 January 1821.

Jirón Lima

This street, a block south-east of the

Plaza de Armas, has preserved its colonial character as much as any in downtown Piura.

Catacaos

This village is 12 km south-west of Piura and is famous both for its craft market and for its typical restaurants which are recommended for lunch. It can be reached by colectivos from the Plaza Pizarro in Piura.

The craft market sells a good variety of products including gold and silver filigree ornaments, wood carvings, leatherwork and panama hats.

There are dozens of little *picanterías* or local restaurants serving the maize beer (*chicha*) and typical dishes of the area. Most of the picanterías are only open two or three days a week but there are so many of them that you won't have any difficulty in finding several open, whichever day you visit. They are open for lunches rather than dinners and live music is sometimes played. Typical *norteño* (northern) dishes include *seco de chabelo* – a thick plantain-and-beef-flavoured stew; *seco de cabrito* – goat stew; *tamales verdes* – green corn dumplings; *caldo de siete carnes* – a thick meat soup with seven types of meat; *copus* – made from dried goats' heads cured in vinegar which are then stewed for several hours with vegetables such as turnips, sweet potatoes and plantains; *carne aliñada* – dried and fried ham slices, served with fried plantains; and many other dishes including the familiar seafood *cebiches* of the Peruvian coast.

Catacaos is also famous for its holy week celebrations.

Places to Stay – bottom end

For some reason, I found that hotels in Piura were slightly more expensive than elsewhere along the coast. The best value hotels started at over US$2 per person.

Budget travellers often stay at the *Hostal Terraza* which charges US$1.30 per person and is clean although I found the staff bored and rude when I visited the hotel. Also in this price range is the *Hotel Continental* which doesn't look too bad, the *Hostal Lalo* which looks basic but is reasonably clean, and the *Hotel Hispano, Eden* and *Ica* – none of which look particularly good. A little more expensive, but old-fashioned and interesting to look at, is the *Hostal Cristina* which charges US$2/2.70 for singles/doubles with shared showers and an extra 30c for rooms with private bath.

If you can afford a little more money, I recommend the very clean and pleasant *Hostal Palmeras* which charges US$2.20 per person in rooms with private showers, fans and hot water. If this hotel is full, try the *Hostal San Jorge* across the street which is clean and modern looking and charges about the same for rooms with private bath. Similarly priced is the *Hotel Oriental* which has only cold water but is very clean. The *Residencial Bolognesi* is a huge and ugly looking building with plenty of rooms with private hot showers for US$3.70 double. It has no singles. The *Hostal Amauta* charges the same and also has no singles.

Places to Stay – middle

All hotels in this section have rooms with private bath and hot water. The *Residencial Piura* is in a pleasant building and charges US$3.30/5.30. The *Hotel Tambo* is clean and good with singles/doubles at US$4/6. The modern looking *Hotel Esmeralda* has a cafeteria and charges US$4.70/6.70 and the recommended *Hostal El Sol* is similarly priced. The new *Hostal Tangara* charges US$6/8.70 and has a cafeteria.

Places to Stay – top end

The best in town is the government run *Hotel de Turistas* which charges US$11.30/15.70 for singles/doubles, including a continental breakfast. The hotel is in an attractive building on the Plaza de Armas.

Places to Eat

Piura gets very hot and dusty and so there are several pleasant snack and beer bars. On the main plaza is the *Heladería Chalan* which has a good selection of juices, cakes and ice creams, as well as sandwiches and other snacks. Also good for its variety of ice cream and sweets is the *Heladería Venecia*. If you prefer a beer, you can try Peruvian draught beer at one of the *Chopp* bars marked on the map – personally, I can't tell the difference between draught and bottled Peruvian beer. *Las Redes* has a pleasant patio to relax in and there is a bar and an Italian restaurant. The *Cafe Concierto* is a coffee house which occasionally has cultural entertainment.

For cheap restaurants, walk along Avenida Grau and you'll find several such as *La Carreta* which is an inexpensive fried chicken restaurant. The *Restaurant Orion* is a good place for light meals on the Plaza de Armas. If you're looking for something unusual, try the *Mexican Tacos* café. Don't forget that the nearby village of Catacaos (see above) is recommended for inexpensive and typical lunches.

The better restaurants include the *Restaurant Tres Estrellas, Las Tradiciones Restaurant* and *El Gaucho Steak House*. These tend to be open only in the evenings.

Getting There

Air The airport is on the south-west of the River Piura and about two km from the centre. Both Faucett and AeroPeru have offices downtown. There are daily flights to Lima (US$44) in the evenings with AeroPeru and three times a week in the mornings with Faucett. Faucett also has four morning flights a week to Talara (US$7) and three a week to Tumbes (US$15). These flights all originate in Lima so seats are limited.

Buses & Colectivos For the nearby towns of Sullana, Paita and Sechura, people often take the faster and more expensive colectivo taxis. Comité 1 to Sechura leaves from the intersection of Bolognesi and Libertad and charges US$1.20 for the one-hour drive. Comité 2 has cars to Sullana (45 minutes, 80c).

Buses, cars and trucks for various local destinations leave from the fifth block of Avenida Sullana Norte. Empresa Petrolera has five buses a day to Talara via Sullana and ETHMOPESA has several daily buses on the same route. Note that the ETHMOPESA office downtown is closed more often than not and so it's easiest to go direct to the departure point at the corner of Sanchez Cerro and the market, in front of the Goodyear Tyre dealer. EPPO has three buses a day to Talara (US$1.70, two hours) and more frequent departures for Sullana.

There are two routes into Ecuador. The most frequently used one is via Tumbes but the rarely taken route via La Tina is a possibility. ETHMOPESA has a daily bus service at about 7.30 am from the Piura market to La Tina (five hours, US$3). Roggero and Empresa Petrolera both have a daily bus to Tumbes but a better place to leave from is near the junction of Sullana and Sanchez Cerro where Empresa Chiclayo, Transportes El Dorado, and Comité 1 all have their offices. Between them, they provide frequent service to Tumbes which costs US$4 and takes six hours by bus and US$8 and 4½ hours by colectivo taxi. These companies also provide frequent transportation to Chiclayo (US$2.50, three hours).

If you're heading east into the mountains, then try CIVA which has a daily 9 am bus to Huancabamba (US$4.70, eight hours). ETRANCH, half a block away from CIVA, has buses to Chulucanas (90c, 1¼ hours) several times a day. For Cajamarca and across the northern Andes, it's best to go to Chiclayo and change. Chinchaysuyo has a daily departure to Huaraz (US$11.80).

Several companies go to Lima and the

length of the journey, number of stops, crowding of the buses and comfort of the seats vary with their prices. The cheapest is Cruz de Galpon which had a recent special price to Lima of US$6.70 for the 18-hour (they said) trip. Expreso Sudamericano is also cheap but usually slow and charges US$8.20 for the trip. TEPSA are probably the best and charge US$10.70 for the 16-hour trip. Other companies going to Lima include CIVA, Roggero, Transportes Piura and Chinchaysuyo. Most of these companies will sell you pro rata tickets to intermediate destinations. As you can imagine, their prices and schedules vary from month to month. If you're in a great hurry, you can go on an overnight colectivo taxi with Comité 24 which charge US$16.50 and claim to do the trip in 13 hours.

SECHURA

The fishing village of Sechura is on the estuary of the Rio Piura about 54 km by road to the south-west of Piura. It is famous for its 17th century cathedral and for its nearby beaches which get crowded with Piurans during summer weekends (January to March). The most interesting of the beaches is at San Pedro which is 11 km along a dirt road which branches right from the Piura-Sechura road about 10 km before you reach Sechura. Here, there is an excellent beach and a lagoon – the haunt of many seabirds including flamingoes.

There are few facilities at these beaches. Sechura has a basic and usually full hostal and a few simple restaurants. Camping is possible. Carry plenty of drinking water with you.

PAITA

Piura's main port is the historic town of Paita, 50 km due west by paved road. Paita is attractively situated on a natural bay surrounded by cliffs and its protected location did not miss the seafaring eyes of the conquistadors; Pizarro landed here in

1527 on his second voyage to Peru. Since then, Paita has had an interesting history. It became a Spanish colonial port and was frequently sacked by pirates and buccaneers.

According to local historians: 'In 1579, Paita was the victim of the savage aggression of the English filibuster, Francis Drake. Apparently, he heard that the Spanish galleon *Sacafuego* was in the area, laden with treasure destined for the Spanish crown. With shooting and violence, he attacked the port, reducing its temple, monastery and houses to ashes, and fleeing with his booty.' And to think that my teachers in England told me that Sir Francis was a hero! Drake wasn't the only one who made life miserable for the Spaniards. Privateer after privateer arrived during the centuries that followed. Another notable episode occurred in the 18th century when the buccaneer George Anson, in a fit of protestant pique, tried to decapitate the wooden statue of Our Lady of Mercy. The statue, complete with slashed neck, can still be seen in the Church of La Merced. The feast of La Virgen de la Merced is held annually on 24 September.

Paita is also famous as the home of the influential mistress of Simón Bolívar, the liberator. She was an Ecuadorian, Manuelita Sáenz, who arrived here upon Bolívar's death in 1850 and, forgoing the fame and fortune left her by her lover, worked as a seamstress until her death over 20 years later. Her house still stands and in front of it is *La Figura* – a Paitan landmark consisting of the wooden figurehead of a pirate ship.

The port has a population of some 50,000 and there are good beaches to the north and south. It is popular with Piuran holidaymakers during the season. A few km to the north is the good beach of Colán. There is a church here which is reputedly the oldest colonial church in Peru. The beach of Yasila, some 12 km to the south, is also popular.

Places to Stay

Despite Paita's beaches and historic interest, there are only two hotels. The cheapest is the *Hotel Pacífico* on the Plaza de Armas. Also there is the attractively restored wooden colonial building which now houses the *Hostal Miramar* at Avenida Jorge Chávez 418.

SULLANA

Sullana is a modern city 38 km north of Piura. It is an important agricultural centre and has a surprisingly high population of about 150,000 inhabitants. Despite its size and importance, most travellers find it of little interest and prefer to visit nearby Piura. There is nothing in particular to see in Sullana except the hustle and bustle of a Peruvian market town.

There are half a dozen cheap hotels and plenty of restaurants. One of the best hotels is the friendly and reasonably priced *Hostal San Miguel* at Avenida Farfán 208, near the Plaza Grau. There are several bus offices nearby.

HUANCABAMBA

The eastern side of the Department of Piura is mountainous, has few roads and is infrequently visited by travellers. Huancabamba, 210 km east of Piura by rough road, is one of the most important and interesting of the department's highland towns.

The western slopes of the Piuran Andes are an important fruit and coffee growing area. As you travel east from Piura, first over the asphalt Pan-American Highway and then, after 64 km, along the dirt road to Huancabamba, you pass citrus groves, sugarcane fields and coffee plantations. At Canchaque, you have covered two thirds of the distance between Piura and Huancabamba. There are a couple of simple hotels here, if you want to break the journey. Beyond Canchaque the road climbs steeply over a 3000-metre pass before dropping to Huancabamba at 1957 metres. This last 70-km stretch is very rough and there may be long delays in the wet season (December to March).

Huancabamba is an attractive country town located at the head of the long and very narrow Huancabamba River valley and is surrounded by mountains – a lovely setting. It is interesting to note that the Huancabamba River is the most westerly major tributary of the Amazon. Although only 160 km from the Pacific Ocean, Huancabamba waters empty into the Atlantic, some 3500 km away as the macaw flies. The banks of the Huancabamba are unstable and constantly eroding away. The town is subject to frequent subsidence and slippage and so has earned itself the nickname *la ciudad que camina* or 'the town which walks'.

The town has a long history. In Inca times it was a minor settlement along the Inca Andean Highway linking the important town of Cajamarca with Ecuador. Although the Inca town is lost, it is still possible to see remnants of Inca paving along the Huancabamba River.

Not only is Huancabamba geographically, geologically and historically interesting, but it is also one of Peru's major centres of *brujería* which can be loosely translated as witchcraft or sorcery. These superstitious traditions are used for both influencing the client's future and for healing and curing. The use of local herbs or potions is combined with ritual ablutions in certain lakes said to contain waters with curative powers. People from all walks of life and from all over Peru (and other countries) visit the *brujos* (witch doctors) or *curanderos* (healers) and pay sizeable sums in attempts to cure ailments which have not responded to more conventional treatments or to solve such problems as unrequited love, bad luck or infertility.

Although a few curanderos can be found in Huancabamba, the ones with the best reputations are to be found in the highlands north of the town in a lake region known as the Huaringas, at almost

A *brujería* doll used for bestowing abundance

4000 metres. The main lake is Shumbe, about 35 km north of Huancabamba. Nearby is the Laguna Negra which is the one most frequently used by the curanderos. Trucks can go as far as Sapalache, about 20 km north of Huancabamba, and after that you can hire mules. Many people visit the area, so finding information and guides is not difficult. However, the tradition is taken very seriously and gawkers or sceptics will meet with a hostile reception.

Places to Stay

There are three cheap and basic hotels of which the best is the clean and centrally located *Hotel El Dorado* on Medina 118. They also have a decent restaurant. The other hotels are the *Medina* on Medina 208 and the *Andino* on Grau 310.

Getting There

CIVA runs a daily bus from Piura which takes eight hours if the going is good, but the trip can easily take twice as long in the wet season. The CIVA office in Huancabamba is on the Plaza de Armas.

AYABACA

Ayabaca is a small highland town at 2715 metres in the north-eastern part of the Department of Piura, close to the Ecuadorian border. It is in an isolated and rarely visited region but is of interest to the adventurous traveller.

There is an Inca ruin at Ayapata, several hours away on foot. The site contains walls, flights of stairs, ceremonial baths and a central plaza, but is overgrown. Other Inca sites can be found in the region – many have not been explored. There are also a variety of pre-Inca ruins, as well as mysterious caves, lakes and mountains, some of which are said to be bewitched. An expedition to reach unexplored ruins could be mounted by those with time; mules and guides are indispensable.

The time to visit the area is the dry season (late May to early September) when the trails are easily passable; the wet months, especially December to April, are to be avoided. It is not a region you should attempt to visit alone as it is easy to become lost and there are drug smugglers in the area. A recommended and knowledgeable guide is Señor Celso Acuña Calle who lives at Cáceres 161 and can provide you with mules and information.

The religious festival of *El Señor Cautivo* is held from 12 to 15 October and is very colourful and rarely seen by tourists.

Places to Stay & Eat

There are three small and basic hotels. The *Hotel Señor Cautivo* is at Cáceres

109, the *San Martín* at Cáceres 192, and the *Alex* at Bolívar 112. They are not well signed.

There are a few simple restaurants and shops, but if you plan on an expedition bring what you will need with you as supplies in Ayabaca are both limited and basic.

Getting There

There is no regular bus service from Piura at this time and the best way to get to Ayabaca is to take the morning ETHMOPESA bus to La Tina and get off at the Ayabaca turn-off at Santa Ana de Quiroz, about three hours from Piura. From here, a dirt road leads the 83 km to Ayabaca and you can usually find a truck from Santa Ana if you arrive in the morning. Enquire in the Piura tourist office to find out if a better service has started recently.

LA TINA

This small border post is not large enough to qualify as a town. There are no hotels and it is suggested that you cross the border to Macará in Ecuador where there are better facilities. La Tina is reached by daily bus with ETHMOPESA from Piura. This international route continues to the Ecuadorian mountain town of Loja and is much less frequently travelled but more scenic than the desert route via Tumbes and Huaquillas.

Crossing the Border

Border crossings are from 8 am to 6 pm daily with irregular lunch hours. Formalities are fairly relaxed as long as your documents are in order. There are no banks and few money changers but if you ask around you'll find someone who will change cash but not travellers' cheques.

Travellers entering Ecuador are rarely asked to show onward tickets or money. Normally, only a valid passport is required and you are given a tourist card at the border which you must surrender when leaving the country. It is about an hour's walk from the border to the town of Macará and there are trucks doing the journey. In Macará there are four hotels of which the best is the *Parador Turistico* on the outskirts. Rooms are US$3.50/6 for singles/doubles with private bath. There are cheaper hotels in the town centre. Also in the town centre is Transportes Loja which has three buses a day to Loja, seven hours away, and daily buses to Guayaquil (15 hours) and Quito (22 hours). See the Lonely Planet book *Ecuador & the Galapagos Islands – a travel survival kit* for further information.

Travellers entering Peru are occasionally asked for a ticket out of the country, especially those who require a visa. If you don't require a visa you probably won't be asked. If you are, and you don't have an airline ticket, you can usually satisfy the exit ticket requirement by buying a round trip bus ticket to Sullana or Piura. The unused portion is non-refundable. Most nationalities, however, need only a valid passport and a tourist card which is obtainable from the border authorities. 'Gringo' exceptions are Australians, New Zealanders and French citizens who do require visas. There is a Peruvian consul in Macará. If you arrive at Macará in the afternoon, it is best to stay the night there. The ETHMOPESA bus from La Tina to Piura leaves in the early afternoon.

TALARA

Talara lies in the centre of Peru's major coastal oil-producing region. During the 120-km desert drive along the Pan-American from Piura, you'll see plenty of *lufkins* – automatic pumps used for oil extraction. Talara is on the coast and although there are some good beaches nearby, it is not of much interest to the tourist, particularly since the floods of 1983 severely damaged the town and hotels. Nevertheless, the authorities are trying to promote the beaches to attract tourists although the few hotels in town are often full of oil workers. The beach at

Las Peñitas, three km to the north, is one of the better ones.

Forty years ago, Talara was a small fishing village. Today it has a population of 45,000 and is the location of Peru's largest oil refinery with a production of between 60,000 and 100,000 barrels of petroleum per day. It is a desert town and everything, including water, must be imported.

Eleven km south of Talara by road is Negritos on the Punta Pariñas, the most westerly point on the South American continent. On the Pariñas Peninsula are the tar pits of La Brea where Pizarro dug tar to caulk his ships.

On the north side of Talara are the Pariñas Woods which, according to a local tourist information booklet, 'are perhaps the city's major tourist attraction, where one can encounter magnificent examples of wild rabbits and squirrels, etc as well as a diversity of little birds which belong to the fauna of the place.' Don't miss it!

Places to Stay

The five or six hotels are recovering after heavy flood damage in 1983 but are still often full and not very cheap. I haven't stayed in any of them and so can't recommend one in particular. There are plenty of restaurants, cafeterias and bars.

Getting There

Air Both AeroPeru and Faucett have flights to Talara. There are daily or twice daily flights to and from Lima (US$46). There are four flights a week from (but not to) Tumbes with AeroPeru and from (but not to) Piura with Faucett.

Buses There are plenty of buses from Piura or Tumbes.

CABO BLANCO

From Talara, the Pan-American Highway heads north-east for 200 km to the Ecuadorian border. The road parallels the ocean and beach views are frequent.

About 30 km north of Talara is Cabo Blanco, famous for its sport fishing. Ernest Hemingway fished here in the early 1950s. The largest fish ever landed on a rod was taken here by Alfred Glassell Jr in 1953; it was a 710 kg black marlin. The angling is still good although it has declined somewhat. One can camp by the fishing club and they can usually provide accommodation.

MÁNCORA

This small fishing village is about a further 30 km north and has the next well-known beach. It is a surfers' beach which has recently become popular with Brazilian surfers. It's been described as 'quite a scene' and the surf is particularly good from November to March. There are two or three medium priced hotels.

TUMBES

Soon after Máncora you enter the Department of Tumbes, Peru's smallest department. This area of Peru's northern coast has tolerably warm water year round, even in the cooler months of April to December when swimming is rarely done further south. The Pan-American Highway passes several more beaches en route to Tumbes. These include Punta Sal, Zorritos and Caleta Cruz. The latter two are reachable by local buses from Tumbes.

Tumbes used to be an Ecuadorian town until the 1940-41 border war which Peru won. It is now about 30 km away from the border and there is a strong military presence in this garrison town. With a population of about 50,000, it is also the capital of its department. Take care with photography in the Tumbes area as it is illegal to photograph anything remotely concerning the military.

History

Most travellers pass straight through Tumbes without realising that the city has a long history. The small and dusty town library on the Plaza de Armas displays a few ceramics which were discovered by workmen on the site of the Hotel de Turistas. These pottery vessels have been tentatively dated as being about 1500 years old.

At the time of the conquest, Tumbes was an Inca town on the coastal highway. It was first sighted by Pizarro in 1528 during his second voyage of exploration (the first voyage never reached Peru) and he invited an Inca noble to dine aboard his ship and sent two of his men ashore to inspect the Inca city. They reported the presence of an obviously well organised and fabulously rich civilisation. A few years later Pizarro returned and began his conquest of Peru.

Present day Tumbes is about five km north-east of the Inca city which is marked on maps as San Pedro de los Incas. The Pan-American Highway passes through it but there is little to see.

Information

General Information There is an office of the Ministry of Tourism in Tumbes. Their hours seem irregular and they are often closed. There is also an Ecuadorian Consulate which is open from 9 am to 12.30 pm and 4 to 6 pm on Mondays to Fridays. There is one cinema but otherwise there is little to do in the evenings apart from hang out in one of the pavement cafés on the spacious Plaza de Armas.

Travellers arriving in Peru should know that long distance and international phone calls can be made from the ENTEL office in any Peruvian town. They are normally open from 8 am to 10 pm daily.

Money Exchange There are exchange facilities both in Tumbes and in Aguas Verdes on the border. Generally, I've found that you can get better exchange rates at the border but you have to know the exchange rate and *bargain* with the money changers (recognised by their black briefcases). If you don't bargain, especially in Ecuador, they'll cheerfully tell you that the exchange rate is anywhere from 5% to 50% lower than it really is! Try and find out what the dollar is worth in both Ecuador and Peru by exchanging information with travellers going the other way.

A new bank has just opened up in Aguas Verdes and they give good rates, better than the banks in Tumbes. Banks are normally only open in the morning and are the only places to change travellers' cheques. A travel agent in Tumbes (see map) can change cash if the banks are closed. It is best to change intis to dollars in Peru and then dollars to sucres in Ecuador (or vice versa) to get the best rates.

Beaches

The two popular beaches at Zorritos and Caleta La Cruz, south-west of Tumbes, are easily reached by local transport. Colectivos to Zorritos (one hour, 60c) leave from the market as do cheaper, slower buses. The road goes past banana plantations until it reaches the sea at Caleta La Cruz, about 20 km from Tumbes. There are a couple of basic restaurants there.

All the way along the coast from La Cruz to Zorritos the beaches are sandy and there are many surf fishermen catching shrimp larvae in red nylon hand nets. These larvae are then transferred to commercial shrimp farms for rearing. Both villages also have picturesque fishing fleets. The water is fairly warm (around 18°C, about 70°F) year round although few Peruvians – except for the fishermen – venture into the sea outside of the hottest months of January to March. Women are advised not to go to the beaches alone.

A further 10 km brings you to Zorritos. On the outskirts of town, about four km before the town 'centre', is the government-run *Hotel de Turistas* which charges about US$5/8 for singles/doubles with bath and has a restaurant. There are other more basic restaurants in the town.

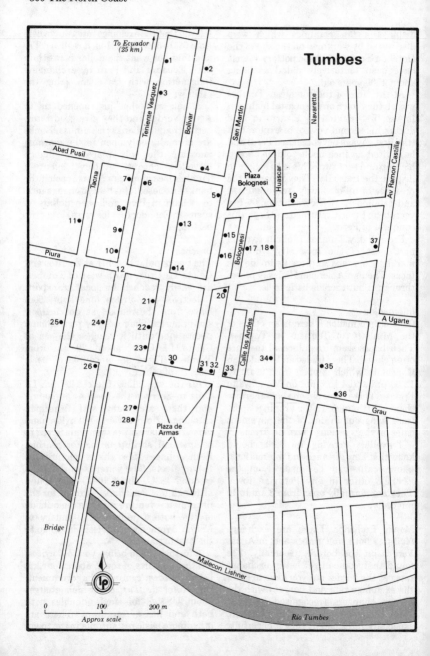

To Ecuador
(25 km)

Tumbes

Plaza
Bolognesi

Plaza de
Armas

Bridge

Abad Pusil

Piura

Tacna

Teniente Vasquez

Bolivar

San Martin

Navarette

Av Ramon Castilla

Huascar

Bolognesi

Calle los Andes

A Ugarte

Grau

Malecon Lishner

Rio Tumbes

0   100   200 m
Approx scale

1   Expreso Sudamericano
2   Hostal Kiko's
3   Hostal Toloa
4   Hostal Cordova
5   Hotel de Turistas
6   Restaurant Menova
7   Empresa D Olano
8   Restaurant El Huerto de mi Amor
9   Hostal Amazonas
10 Travel Agent & Money Change
11 Hostal Elica
12 Bus Terminal Corner (Expreso
    Continental-Ormeño, Roggero,
    Exp Nor-Pacifico, Trans El Dorado,
    Trans El Aguila, Comité 6,
    Piura Cars) & Hostal Los Once
13 Hostal Jugdem
14 Colectivos to Border
15 ENTEL
16 Post Office
17 Residencial Gandolfo
18 Ministry of Tourism
19 Residencial Internacional
20 Aero Peru
21 Banco de Crédito
22 Cine Tropical
23 Banco de la Nación
24 Hostal Premier
25 Faucett
26 Tepsa
27 Restaurant Mediterraneo
28 Ecuadorean Consulate
29 Restaurant Curich, Restaurant
    Europa & Hotel Bolívar
30 Cathedral
31 Library
32 Hotel Pilsen
33 Hostal Roma
34 Hostal Cesar
35 Hostal Lourdes
36 Hostal Italia
37 Colectivos to Zorritos,

bus stations and charge 40c. At Puerto Pizarro, the character of the ocean front changes from the coastal desert which stretches north from central Chile for over 2000 km to northern Peru. Here begin the mangrove swamps which now start to dominate the coastline throughout much of the Ecuadorian and Colombian coasts. This change of environment attracts a different variety of birdlife, too.

Although the water is a bit muddier, it is still pleasant enough to swim in and it is less crowded with fishermen than in Zorritos. You can stay at the *Motel Pizarro* on the beach (US$4.50/7 with bath). It is quite pleasant and has good meals at its restaurant although the service is desperately slow – there's not much to do but wait and watch the tide go out. The motel can arrange fishing boat and water-skiing trips (skis can be hired) if you have the time, money and inclination.

There is also the cheaper and basic *Hotel Venecia*. Many people stay in Tumbes and just come out on a day trip.

Fiestas

Tumbes' fiestas usually take the form of international trade fairs with Ecuador. The major ones are the International Integration Fair in the first week in August, the Festival of the Patroness of Perpetual Help in the first 10 days of September, and the Regional Fair of 8 December which takes place during the first two weeks of that month. There is also a moveable Tumbes Tourist Week in August.

Places to Stay – bottom end

There is a large amount of border traffic and hotels do tend to fill up. During the major holidays and trade fairs hotels are often full by early afternoon. During the rest of the year single rooms can be difficult to find by the afternoon although doubles are usually available. Most

Both villages are interesting both for their fishing activities and for their coastal bird life. You can see frigate birds, pelicans, egrets and many migratory bird species.

Another side trip is to Puerto Pizarro, about half an hour to the north of Tumbes. Colectivos leave from near the hotels have only cold water but that's no problem in the heat. Fans are available in all but the most basic of hotels – ask at the front desk.

Among the cheapest hotels a good choice is the *Hotel Italia* which has clean rooms with private showers for US$1.20/1.90 for singles/doubles. Similarly priced is the *Residencial Gandolfo* which is clean but a little more basic and noisier. They also have some cheaper rooms with communal showers. The basic but friendly *Hotel Pilsen* is in an old and rambling building on the corner of the Plaza de Armas; they charge US$1/1.60 for rooms with communal showers. The *Hotel Bolívar* is also cheap, basic and reasonably clean and the *Hotel Premier* is the most basic of all.

The *Hostal Los Once* is clean and conveniently situated for the buses and so tends to be noisy; they charge US$1.70/2.30 for singles/doubles with private shower. Similarly priced but quieter is the *Hostal Cordova*.

There are several clean, simple and thoroughly acceptable hotels which charge about US$2/3 for rooms with private bath. These include the good *Hostal Amazonas* which is very convenient for most buses although the front rooms are a little noisy; the friendly and recommended *Hostal Elica*; the *Hostal Toloa* which is in an ugly building but is clean and has plenty of rooms; and the *Hostal Kikos, Hostal Jugdem, Residencial Internacional, Hostal Lourdes* and *Hostal César* all of which are quite good. The last named has only double rooms.

Places to Stay – middle & top end

The new *Hostal Roma* is on the corner of the Plaza de Armas and looks good. They charge US$4.30/6 for singles/doubles with bath.

The best in town is the government-run *Hotel de Turistas* which has a good restaurant and a garden. They charge US$11.70/17.30 for rooms with bath, including continental breakfast.

Places to Eat

There are several bars and restaurants on the Plaza de Armas and many of them have shaded outside tables and chairs – a real boon in the hot weather. It's a pleasant place to sit and watch the world go by as you drink a cold beer and wait for your bus. One Sunday lunch time I was doing just that when I noticed a big crowd gathering in the plaza. Upon enquiring what was going on, I was told that a Peruvian air force paratrooper was going to land in the Plaza de Armas. The plaza has several tall trees and, worse still, a couple of very sharp looking flag poles in the centre. The thought of jumping onto one of those by accident was so unpleasant that I had to order another beer. An hour later the paratrooper made his appearance with smoke canisters marking his descent. Despite the hazards of flag poles, trees, and spectators, he made a perfect landing right in front of the restaurant where I was sitting. Viva Peru!

The best restaurants on the Plaza seem to be on the west side. The *Mediterraneo, Curich* and *Europa* are all reasonably priced and serve a variety of good food including excellent local seafood. Travellers arriving from Ecuador should try the *cebiche* – this marinated raw seafood dish is much spicier than the Ecuadorian version and goes down very well with a cold beer.

If you're in a hurry to catch a bus or you're looking for something very cheap, then try the *Restaurant Menova* or the *Huerta de mi Amor* both of which are within a block of most bus terminals and sell good, cheap food.

It's unlikely that you'll be in Tumbes very long, but if you are there are plenty of other inexpensive places to choose from.

Getting There

Air Both AeroPeru and Faucett have offices in Tumbes. There are daily flights to Lima (US$47) via either Talara (US$8) with AeroPeru on Mondays, Wednesdays, Fridays and Sundays or via Piura (US$14) with Faucett on Tuesdays, Thursdays and Saturdays.

Buses Most bus companies have their offices on Avenida Teniente Vasquez especially around the intersection with Avenida Piura. Services are improving since the devastating floods of 1983 washed away parts of the Pan-American Highway but the section to Piura is still rather slow. You can usually find buses leaving to Lima within 24 hours of arrival in Tumbes but sometimes they are booked up for a few days in advance. In that case, take a bus to any major city south that you can get to and try again from there. Carry your passport with you as there are several passport controls south of Tumbes.

Buses to Lima take 22 to 24 hours and fares vary but about US$14 is average. Most of the major companies have two departures a day and TEPSA (which is usually the fastest but most expensive) has four daily departures. TEPSA also has a non-stop 'Presidential' service daily at 2.30 pm taking 18 to 20 hours and costing US$20 per seat. Expreso Sudamericano is usually the slowest and the cheapest.

Most companies will sell you tickets to the intermediate cities at pro rata prices. Transportes El Dorado and El Aguila have buses to Piura for US$4 taking seven hours and there are colectivo taxis in front of their offices which take you to Piura in five hours for US$8.

Getting Around
Airport Transport The airport is north of town and a taxi charges about US$1.

Local Transport For Puerto Pizarro, use Comité 6 which have a stand on Avenida Piura near the main stations. For the beaches of Zorritos and Caleta La Cruz you'll find colectivos departing from the junction of Avenidas Piura and Ramon Castilla in front of the market. The market area is a good place to find colectivo taxis, buses and trucks going to most other local destinations.

Colectivo cars for Aguas Verdes at the border leave from the corner of Avenidas Bolívar and Piura and charge about 70c for the 26-km journey. Ask around for the exact price as the drivers aren't all honest. One of them tried to charge me US$2 for the trip (though he wasn't successful!). If there's a group of you, hire a car to take you to the *Migraciónes* office and on to the border. If you go alone, the drivers are usually reluctant to wait for you at *Migraciónes* and so you have to walk from there to the border which is almost two km. You may be able to persuade the driver to wait for you. Some want to charge you extra for stopping.

GOING TO ECUADOR
Peru has recently built a new *Migraciónes* (immigration) Office in the middle of the desert about two km from the border at Aguas Verdes. This has made the border crossing a little more time consuming than before.

Travellers leaving Peru must surrender their Peruvian tourist cards and obtain an exit stamp from the Immigration Office first. Exit formalities, assuming your documents are in order, are usually fairly quick. The Immigration Office is open daily from 8.30 am to 12 noon and from 2 to 6 pm.

Aguas Verdes is basically a long street full of stall holders selling consumer products. There is a bank, a few simple restaurants and no hotels. Colectivo taxis between Aguas Verdes and Tumbes leave and arrive on the main street about 300 metres from the border. Everyone knows where to go.

An international bridge across the Río Zarumilla links Peru with Ecuador. The long market street of Aguas Verdes continues into the Ecuadorian border town of Huaquillas with similar stalls. The Ecuadorian Immigration Office is on the left-hand side of the street, about 200 metres beyond the international bridge and it is identified by the yellow/blue/red striped Ecuadorian flag. It is open from 8 am to 12 noon and from 2 to 5 pm daily and all Ecuadorian exit and entrance formalities are carried out here. There is sometimes an hour's time difference when Peru goes on daylight savings time, so ask.

Entrance formalities into Ecuador are usually straightforward. No tourist needs a visa but everyone needs a T3 tourist card, available free at the immigration office. You must surrender your T3 upon leaving the country, so hold on to it. Exit tickets and sufficient funds (US$20 per day) are legally required but very rarely asked for. Up to 90-days stay are allowed but usually only 30 are given. Extensions can easily and freely be obtained in Guayaquil or Quito. Note that you are allowed only 90 days per year in Ecuador. If you've already been in the country for 90 days and try and return, you will be refused entry. If you have an international flight from Ecuador you can usually get a 72-hour transit visa to get you to the airport and out of the country.

There are some basic hotels on the main street of Huaquillas but most people take a bus for the two-hour journey to the city of Machala where there are much better facilities. See *Ecuador & the Galapagos Islands – a travel survival kit* for further information.

There are plenty of people who will offer their services as porters and guides. They usually overcharge and can be very insistent. Unless you really need help, they're more of a hassle than they're worth.

Travellers arriving in Peru must first surrender their Ecuadorian T3 card at the Immigration Office in Huaquillas and obtain an Ecuadorian exit stamp in their passports. Cross the international bridge (guards usually inspect but don't stamp your passport) and continue for about 300 meters to the colectivo taxi rank. It is a further ½ km to the Immigration Office where you get your entry stamp. Colectivo drivers will drop you there but won't normally wait unless a group of you get together and hire a vehicle.

Most European nationalities (except the French) don't need a visa for Peru. Neither do North Americans. Australians and New Zealanders do. Visas are not available in either Aguas Verdes or Huaquillas and you have to go back to the Peruvian consul in Machala to get one. Other nationalities normally just need a tourist card, available at the Peruvian immigration office. Remember to look after your tourist card – you will need to surrender it upon leaving Peru. Although an exit ticket out of Peru is officially required, gringo travellers are rarely asked for this unless they look thoroughly disreputable. Latin American travellers are often asked for an exit ticket, however, so if you're a non-Peruvian Latin American (or travelling with one) be prepared for this eventuality. There is a bus office in Aguas Verdes which sells (non-refundable) tickets out of Peru. The immigration official will tell you where it is – a *colaboración* may help here.

Once entrance formalities have been observed, you can usually find someone to take you into Tumbes if you wait long enough. Most of the cars that come through are full but the local buses will squeeze you on even if they are. If you get fed up with waiting, then go back into Aguas Verdes and get a colectivo from there.

The Huaraz Area

Huaraz is the most important climbing, trekking, and backpacking centre in Peru and, I would venture to add, in all of South America. Huaraz is a historic city but has been demolished several times by massive earthquakes and so it is not particularly attractive. The surrounding mountains, however, are exceptionally beautiful and many travellers come to Peru specifically to visit the Huaraz area.

Although the mountains are certainly the main attraction, there is much more. There are glacial lakes and hot springs. There are Inca and pre-Inca ruins, including the fascinating centre of the 3000-year-old Chavín feline-worship cult at Chavín de Huantar. There are friendly and interesting people living in remote villages reached only by mule or foot. And there is fascinating flora and fauna which includes the 10-metre-high *Puya raimondi*, the tallest flower spike and largest bromeliad in the world, and, of course, the magnificent Andean Condor, the heaviest flying bird in the world.

THE ANDES AROUND HUARAZ

Huaraz lies at 3091 metres on the Santa River valley, flanked to the west by the Cordillera Negra and to the east by the Cordillera Blanca. The valley between these two mountain ranges is popularly referred to as *El Callejón de Huaylas* after the district of Huaylas at the north end of the valley. A road runs the length of this valley, linking the main towns and providing spectacular views of the mountains. The Callejón de Huaylas is roughly 300 km north of Lima, about eight hours by bus.

The western Cordillera Negra is an attractive range in its own right, but it is comparatively low and snowless and completely outshone by the magnificent snowcapped mountains of the Cordillera Blanca. The lower range is relatively unvisited except by road from the coast en route to the Cordillera Blanca.

The Cordillera Blanca is about 20 km wide and 180 km long. In this fairly small area are over 50 peaks 5700 metres or higher. By contrast, North America has only three peaks in excess of 5700 metres (Orizaba in Mexico, Logan in Canada, and Denali in Alaska) and Europe has none. Only in Asia can higher mountain ranges than the Andes be found. Mt Huascarán, at 6768 metres, is the highest mountain in Peru and also the highest peak in the tropics anywhere in the world. But this string of figures does not do the Cordillera Blanca justice. Its shining glaciers, sparkling streams, awesome vertical walls and lovely lakes must be seen to be appreciated.

South of the Cordillera Blanca is the smaller, more remote but no less spectacular, Cordillera Huayhuash. It contains Peru's second highest peak, the 6634-metre-high Yerupaja, and is a more rugged and less frequently visited range. The main difference between the two ranges, for the hiker at least, is that you walk *through* the Cordillera Blanca, surrounded by magnificent peaks, and you walk *around* the smaller Huayhuash, one of the most spectacular mountain circuits in the world. Both ranges are highly recommended for climbers and hikers.

HUASCARÁN NATIONAL PARK

The idea of protecting the beauty of the Cordillera Blanca was first suggested by the well known Peruvian mountaineer César Morales Arnao, in the early 1960s. The idea did not become reality until 1975, when the Huascarán National Park was established, encompassing not only the highest peak in Peru, but also the entire area of the Cordillera Blanca above

4000 metres, except Mt Champará at the extreme northern part of the range.

The objectives of the park are to protect and conserve the flora, fauna, archaeological sites and scenic beauty of the Cordillera Blanca; to promote scientific investigation of its natural resources; to publicise its natural and historic attractions on regional, national and international levels; to stimulate and to control the development of tourism in the park; and to help raise the standard of living of the people living within its boundaries.

Visitors to the park should register with the park office (see under *Huaraz*) and pay a small fee for use. This is about US$2 but may change in the future. You can also register and pay your fee at one of the control stations located on the main trails entering the park. This money is used to help maintain trails, pay park rangers (there are a few), and regulate user pressure in the area. There are those who are against regulation; however, the number of visitors to the Cordillera Blanca, whilst still relatively small by western standards, is increasing sufficiently fast that some sort of regulation must be enforced if the inherent attraction of the mountains is not to be damaged. It seems to me that foreign visitors are the ones who get the most joy out of the Cordillera Blanca and, whether they like it or not, are among the ones who create the greatest change within the area. Hence they should also be the ones who contribute to the financing of the National Park with their user fees.

Present park regulations are largely a matter of courtesy and common sense. 'Do not litter' is the most obvious one; obvious, that is, to almost all of us. There are always a small number of visitors who leave a trail of yellow film cartons, pink toilet paper, green broken bottles and jagged tin cans to mark their path. This is thoughtless, rude, unnecessary and illegal. It is true that the local people are among the worst offenders, but 'When in Rome . . .' is not a sensible reason for imitating the offence. It is also true that people tend to litter more where litter already exists and so each candy wrapper contributes to the overall problem by beginning or continuing this chain reaction. Don't do it.

Other park regulations are: don't disturb, feed or remove the flora and fauna; don't cut down trees or live branches for fires or other use; no hunting; no fishing during the off-season (May to September); no fishing with explosives, nets or taking of fish below 25 cm in length; no off-road vehicle use; don't destroy or alter park signs.

Visiting the Mountains

Basically, there are two ways to go. One is to stay in the towns of the Callejón de Huaylas and take day trips by bus or taxi. A casual glance at the map will show that the summit of Peru's highest peak is a mere 14 km from the main valley road and so spectacular views can certainly be obtained simply by using public transport. For many people, that is enough. The more adventurous will want to take their backpacks and hike, trek, camp or climb in the mountains. This book will give details of public transport but it does not pretend to be a trail guide.

Weather

The best months for hiking, climbing and mountain views are the dry months of June, July and August. May and September are usually quite good. The rest of the year is the wet season and hiking can be difficult, especially from December to March, because the trails are so boggy. Despite the wet weather, you may be lucky and get some spectacular mountain views between the clouds.

Mountain Guide Services

Guiding services range from a single *arriero* (mule driver) with a couple of pack animals for carrying your camping gear, to a full fledged trekking expedition with *arrieros*, burros, cooks, guides, food and all equipment provided. In addition, high altitude porters and guides for mountaineering expeditions can be hired.

As with tourist agencies, there are several guide services available. One of the best, although certainly not the cheapest, is *Pyramid Adventures* run by the five Morales brothers (Marcelino, Pablo, Eleazar, Eudes, and Néstor). They are knowledgeable, hardworking, honest and friendly and can provide you with every level of service at fair prices. They are accomplished mountaineers and have been involved in new ascents as well as mountain rescue activities. They specialise in providing trekking and climbing groups with full services but can also put you together with a couple of arrieros if that's all you want. Eudes Morales speaks English. They are at Avenida Americas 330 or can be contacted in advance by writing to Casilla 25, Huaraz, Ancash, Peru (tel 721864).

Mountaineers should also check out the *Mountain Guide Association* opposite the Hotel de Turistas in Huaraz. They have some Swiss-trained mountain guides available for about US$30 per day.

Some cheaper guide services are available if you shop around but try and get references from other travellers before contracting with them. The cheapest way to go is to hire arrieros directly, although this involves being able to speak Spanish and perhaps some bargaining. Again, get references first. The National Park office has a list of arrieros and will tell you what the going rate is – usually in the region of US$5 per day for driver and burro. You can't hire a pack animal for yourself; the arrieros will not send out burros without experienced drivers. Horses and mules for riding purposes are also available. Bear in mind that it is far easier to make arrangements in Huaraz than anywhere else in the area and that in some towns and villages it is very difficult to find arrieros.

Of course, plenty of experienced back-packers go camping in the mountains without any local help. Just remember that carrying a backpack full of gear over a 5000 metre pass requires a lot more effort than at low altitudes.

Equipment Rental

The better guide services will be able to provide you with everything you need from tents to ice axes. There are also rental agencies in Huaraz which will rent equipment without your having to hire guides. Everything you need is available here. There are plenty of rental agencies along Luzuriaga so if the first one you try doesn't have what you want, don't give up. The rental prices are fairly similar but the quality of the equipment varies a good deal so check around before you rent.

If you bring your own equipment, remember that *kerex* (kerosene) is available in gas stations while *bencina* (white gas) is more difficult to find, though hardware stores and pharmacies do carry it. Camping Gaz canisters are usually, but not always, available. There isn't much firewood available and what there is shouldn't be indiscriminately burned so it's best to come prepared with a kerosene-burning stove. It often freezes at night so you'll need to bring a warm sleeping bag – a lightweight tropical one won't do. It can rain even in the dry season so rain gear and a waterproof tent are needed. Sun protection is also essential. Wear a brimmed hat and sunglasses and bring strong suntan lotion with you as it is difficult to find in Huaraz. The same applies to effective insect repellent.

Food is no problem. Expensive, light-weight, freeze-dried food is occasionally left over from mountaineering expeditions and can be bought at the trekking and rental agencies. You can easily make do with oatmeal, dried soups, fast cooking noodles and the usual canned goods, all of which are readily available in Huaraz.

Other Guidebooks

One book is particularly recommended for those of you who wish to camp or hike in the mountains. This is Jim Bartle's *Trails of the Cordilleras Blanca & Huayhash of Peru* which details 18 different hikes in the Cordillera Blanca and the complete circuit of the Cordillera Huayhuash.It has a wealth of background information and plenty of detailed maps and photographs.

Also recommended is *Backpacking & Trekking in Peru & Bolivia* by George and Hilary Bradt. Three Cordillera Blanca hikes are included in this book which also has plenty of background information including a useful natural history section.

John Ricker's *Yuraq Janka*, is recommended for mountaineers. It is a sensitively written and well-illustrated guidebook which gives fascinating historical, geological, meteorological, linguistic and sociological information about the region and so is of interest to non-climbers too. Prospective climbers should be aware of the fact that this book offers only very broad outlines rather than detailed and complete descriptions of the routes.

HUARAZ

The Santa River valley, on which Huaraz lies, has long been a major Andean thoroughfare and the Incas' main Andean road passed through here. Little remains of the valley's archaeological heritage, however, because a series of devastating natural disasters has repeatedly destroyed the towns of the Callejón de Huaylas.

The major cause of the natural disasters that have affected the Huaraz area is the build up of water levels in high mountain lakes which causes them to breach and cascade down to the valley below. The high lakes are often held back by a relatively thin wall of glacial debris which can burst when the lake levels build up. This can occur suddenly, as when an avalanche falls from high above the lake,

or more slowly with rain and snow melt. Earthquakes can also cause the lakes to breach. When this happens, a huge wall of water, often mixed with snow, ice, mud, rocks and other matter, flows down from the lakes, wiping out everything in its path. Such a mixture of avalanche, waterfall, and landslide is referred to as an alluvion.

Records of such alluvions date back almost 300 years and three recent ones have been particularly devastating in terms of lives lost. The first was in 1941, when an avalanche in the Cojup valley to the west of Huaraz caused the Laguna Palcacocha to break its banks and flow down onto Huaraz, killing about 5000 of its inhabitants and flattening the centre of the city. Then, in 1962, a huge avalanche from Huascarán roared down its western slopes and destroyed the town of Ranrahirca, killing about 4000 people. The worst disaster occurred on 31 May 1970, when a massive earthquake measuring 7.8 on the Richter scale devastated much of central Peru, killing an estimated 80,000 people. About half of the 30,000 inhabitants of Huaraz died and only 10% of the city was left standing. The town of Yungay was completely buried by an alluvion and almost every one of its 18,000 inhabitants was buried with the city. Evidence of the disaster is still to be seen throughout the valley.

Since these disasters, a government agency had been formed to control the lake levels by building dams and tunnels and so the chance of similar catastrophes has been minimised. The agency concerned is the *Instituto Geológico Minero y Metalúrgico* which is known by the acronym INGEMMET.

Most of Huaraz has now been rebuilt and it is a modern but not especially attractive city of over 50,000. It is the capital of the Department of Ancash. Its renown as the centre for visiting the Cordillera Blanca has led to the development of a thriving tourist industry with a multitude of hotels and other facilities.

Information

Tourist Information The tourist information office on Avenida Luzuriaga is open from 9 am to 12.30 pm and 1.30 to 4 pm, Mondays to Fridays. It is a good source of general information about the area.

The Huascarán National Park office is in the Ministry of Agriculture building at the east end of Avenida Raymondi. Working hours are from 7 am to 2.15 pm on Mondays to Fridays, but avoid arriving just before they close. They can help you with information about visiting the national park.

The INGEMMET office is useful for their dye line maps of the Cordillera Blanca which are among the most detailed available. Sometimes you have to give them 24 hours advance notice to print the maps you need. The *Instituto Geográfico Nacional* and the South American Explorers Club, both in Lima, are also sources of maps and information.

Money Exchange There are several banks on the north side of the Plaza de Armas and the 600 block of Luzuriaga. The Banco de Crédito gave the best rates with the least hassle. Many of the better hotels and tourist agencies will also accept cash US dollars for reasonable rates. I suggest you shop around because rates seem to vary more in Huaraz than in other cities.

Acclimatisation Huaraz's altitude of 3091 metres will mean that you feel a little breathless and perhaps have a headache during your first day or two so take it easy and don't over-exert yourself. The surrounding mountains are high enough to ensure that you will definitely get altitude sickness if you venture into them without spending at least a couple of days acclimatising in Huaraz. See the introductory Health section for more information.

Hot Showers Some of the cheaper hotels have only cold water but you can get a good hot shower at the *Duchas Raimondi* which are open to the public from 8 am to 6 pm daily and charge 20c for 20 minutes.

Museum

The Archaeology Museum on the Plaza de Armas is small but quite interesting. There are a few mummies, some trepanned skulls, and a garden of stone monoliths from the Recuay culture (400 BC to 600 AD) and the Wari culture (800 to 1200 AD). The museum is open every day, except Monday, and entry is about 20c.

Huaraz

0   100   200 m

Approx scale

To Peruvian Guides
Association
Hotel de Turistas (200 m)
& Caraz (66 km)

Confraternidad

Río Quilcay

Río Santa

Corongo

M Melgar

F de Zela

Pomabamba

Villazón

V Veles

Ranrapalca

Fitzcarrald

Centenario

Yungay

Guzman Barron

Patron

Recuay

Huaylas

Fanning

Carhuaz

L Pallicer

Villar

S Alliste

S Cristobal

Hualcan

Huascaran

Huandoy

Handov

• 1
• 18
• 17   • 16
• 15
• 13
• 14
• 21
• 22
• 19
• 20
• 23

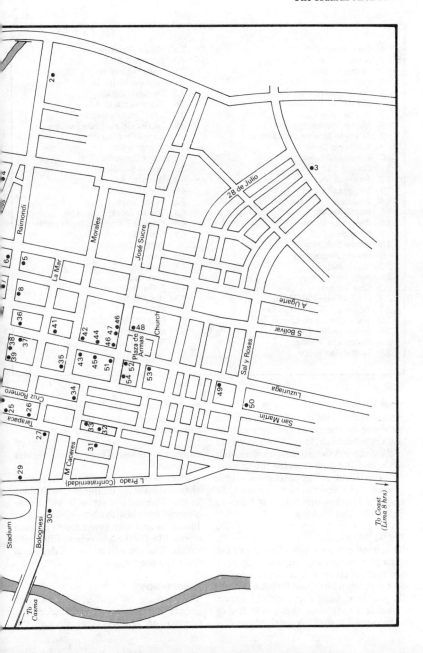

1	Trout Hatchery	29	Hostal Alpamayo
2	National Park Office	30	Edward's Inn
3	Hostal Andino	31	Trans Rodriguez
4	Pyramid Adventures	32	Pensión Maguina
5	Hot Showers	33	Pensión Galaxia
6	Hostal Los Portales	34	Alojamiento Quintana
7	Hostal Tabariz	35	Las Puyas Restaurant
8	Hostal Raimondi	36	Tourist Office, Chifa Familiar
9	Buses to Monterrey, Carhuaz		& other restaurants
	Yungay & Caraz	37	Imantata Bar
10	Empresa Ancash	38	Hotel Cataluña
11	Comité 11	39	Hostal Barcelona
12	Empresa Moreno	40	Discotec Any
13	Empresa Huaraz	41	Hostal Huaraz
14	Empresa 14	42	Pablo Tours
15	Hostal Yanett	43	Chavín Tours
16	Recreo La Unión	44	Pizzería Ticino & Hostal Premier
17	Pacccha'k Pub	45	Hostal El Pacifico &
18	Hostal Colomba		Peña El Dorado
19	Pio Pio Restaurant	46	Banks
20	Ingemmet	47	Hostal Landauro
21	Peña La Pascana	48	Cine Radio
22	Cine Soraya	49	El Palomar Bar
23	Hostal Pinos del Puente	50	Hotel El Tumi
24	Trome & Trans Huascarán	51	ENTEL
25	Trans Cóndor de Chavín	52	Post Office
26	Empresa Nor-Pacifico	53	Museum
27	Hostal Los Andes	54	Police Station
28	Hostal San Isidro		

Trout Hatchery

An unusual and interesting excursion can be made to the trout hatchery on the eastern outskirts of town. The best way of getting there is to walk east on Raimondi to the end and then cross the Río Quilcay on a small bridge. The hatchery is a little beyond and is open to visitors 9 am to 12 noon on Sundays and from 2 to 5 pm on Saturdays and Sundays.

Ruinas Wilcahuaín

This small pre-Inca ruin is in quite a good state of preservation and lies about eight km north of Huaraz. It can be reached on foot or you can hire a taxi for a few dollars. To get there, head north out of town on Avenida Centenario and you'll find a signposted dirt road to your right almost a

km past the Hotel de Turistas. From here the dirt road climbs six or seven km to the ruins and continues another 20 km to Laguna Llaca, where there are excellent mountain views. There is no regular transport.

The site dates to about 1000 AD and is an imitation of the temple at Chavín done in the Tiahuanacu style. It is a three-storeyed temple with a base of about 11 by 16 metres and with seven rooms on each storey. Most of these have been filled with rubble. The site can be visited daily and there is a 50c fee.

Places to Stay

The increase in tourism over the last decade has meant an increase in the number of hotels, especially of the cheaper variety. Often they have only a few rooms and are family run and very friendly. Hotel staff may meet the buses as they arrive at the main bus offices and generally these people will give you straight answers to questions about price, availability of hot water or private showers, and distance from the bus station. If arriving after dark when you're tired, this is very useful.

Places to Stay - bottom end

Probably the cheapest place in town is the basic but adequate *Hostal Tabariz* which charges 70c per person and sometimes has hot water in the communal showers. Two small, family-run places are the *Alojamiento Quintana* and the *Pensión Galaxia*. Both charge about US$1 per person and have hot water in the communal showers. They are basic, but clean and friendly and are recommended. Also about US$1 per person is the friendly *Hostal Alpamayo*, which has hot water in the mornings, and the *Pensión Maguina*, which has a very small sign but is right opposite the Rodriguez bus terminal. They also have hot water some of the time. These prices may be slightly higher at the height of the tourist season.

For about US$1.30 per person you can stay at the *Hotel Premier* which has spacious rooms, some with private bath, but an erratic hot water supply. There are no singles. Similarly priced but not as good is *Hostal San Isidro*. The *Hotel Barcelona* has great mountain views from the balconies but only cold water. They charge from US$1.50 per person and more in rooms with showers.

Edward's Inn is friendly, has hot water, laundry facilities and a cafeteria, and is popular with international backpackers. It is slightly out of the way and quiet. Edward speaks English and is a source of tourist information. Rooms are simple but clean and cost US$2 per person with private shower and a little cheaper without. Also friendly and with hot water and laundry facilities is the similarly priced *Hotel Los Andes*.

The *Hostal Huaraz* is rather run down but does have hot water. They charge US$1.70/3 for singles/doubles or US$2.30/4.30 with bath. The *Hotel Landauro* charges US$2.70 for a double room with cold water in the communal shower and has more expensive rooms with private shower. The *Hotel Cataluña* is US$2/3.30 for singles/doubles with bath. The rooms are small but the beds comfortable. Hot water is available although it tends to be a bit brown and you must ask to have it turned on. There are excellent views from the balconies.

The *Hostal Yanett* is clean, friendly, has a small garden and is recommended. They have double rooms with private bath for US$3.70 and there is hot water in the mornings and evenings. Also good, friendly and clean is the *Hostal El Pacifico* which charges US$2.30/4.30 for singles/doubles with private bath and hot water - but try to avoid some of the viewless inside rooms. The last hotel in this price range is the *Hostal Raimondi* which has a pleasant courtyard and is a clean and long-established Huaraz hotel. They charge US$3/4.40 for rooms with private bath and hot water and about a third less for rooms with shared showers.

Places to Stay - middle

The *Hostal Los Pinos del Puente* is an interesting looking stone and wood building on the banks of the Río Quilcay. It is clean and quiet and charges US$5 for a double with bath and hot water.

The *Hotel Tumi* is clean, comfortable and quiet and has great mountain views from many of its rooms. There is a good and inexpensive restaurant. Rooms with private bath and hot water are US$3.70/5.30. Closer to the centre is the *Hostal Portales* which is bare and modern looking and has clean singles/doubles with private bath and hot water for US$4.30/7.

Places to Stay - top end

The modern government-run *Hotel de Turistas* has clean spacious singles/doubles for US$8.30/11.30 with bath and including breakfast. Similarly priced is the *Hostal Colombo* which has comfortable bungalows set in a large pleasant garden. The best in town is the *Hostal Andino* which is Swiss run and has great views of the mountains. They charge US$18/26 for rooms with bath. Hotels in the upper price brackets are often full during the busy season.

Places to Eat

There are several restaurants around the major crossroads in town (Raimondi and Luzuriaga) of which the best is the reasonably priced *Chifa Familiar*. Slightly away from the centre, the *Pio Pio* chicken restaurant is inexpensive, simple and frequently recommended by travellers. For a cheap and typical local lunch try the *Recreo La Union*. It's not fancy but it is quite authentic. For good Italian food, the place to go is the *Pizzería Ticino* which is more expensive than most of the other restaurants but nearly always has a line of people waiting outside. They can't all be wrong!

The *Ebony 84* on the Plaza de Armas has been recommended although I've never eaten there because it often seems deserted. *Las Puyas* has very large and inexpensive meals and is popular with budget travellers – although you're going for quantity rather than quality. For top quality, the *Hostal Andino* has a Swiss-run kitchen and delicious food. It's primarily for guests of the hotel but non-guests will also be served if there's room, particularly if you make a reservation.

Entertainment

There are two cinemas in town – English language movies are sometimes shown. There are also several bars, discos and peñas. One of my favourites is the *Imantata Bar* which is a peculiarly low-roofed establishment for drinking and dancing. It gets underway at about 10 pm and is popular with trekkers and climbers as well as locals.

A new bar which quickly became one of the main climbers' hangouts is the *Tasco Bar* at Lucar y Torre 380, the small street off Morales and a block east of Luzuriaga. For a more typically Peruvian evening, you might want to try the *Peña El Dorado*, a couple of blocks away. There is sometimes some good live music here. The *Peña La Pascana* is another possibility.

For dancing try the inexpensive *Discotec Any* or the fancier *El Palomar Bar*. The promisingly named *Pacccha'k Pub* looks good but is very quiet most nights. Bear in mind that there is much less entertainment out of the tourist season.

Getting There

Air The Huaraz area airport is at Anta, about 23 km to the north of the town. Scheduled air service from Lima was suspended in the early '80s and there is occasional talk of restarting this service. I think it's unlikely to happen.

Buses & Colectivos - Local Buses and colectivo taxis heading north along the length of the Callejón de Huaylas leave from the corner of Fitzcarrald and Raimondi. Local transport goes as far as Caraz, 67 km north of Huaraz. The bus journey takes about two hours and costs 80c. Colectivo taxis take about 1¼ hours and charge US$1.25. There are frequent departures throughout the day but none after nightfall so plan to travel early.

Buses & Colectivos - Long Distance Several companies have departures for Lima (US$4, eight hours). These include Transportes Rodriguez with one day bus and two night buses, Empresa Ancash (the subsidiary of Ormeño) with two or three buses a day, Empresa Huaraz with three daily departures, Empresa 14 with one departure in the morning and one at night, and TROME with a daily bus. Comité 11 has colectivo taxis to Lima for US$6.50 per person but they don't leave every day. Many of these buses start from or continue to Caraz, 67 km north of Huaraz.

There are three main bus routes to Chimbote (US$4, eight hours) on the north coast. One goes north along the Callejón de Huaylas and then through the narrow and spectacular Cañón del Pato before descending to the coast at Chimbote. This is a spectacular route, but unfortunately most buses travel this journey by night. A route more frequently taken by day goes over the 4100-metre-high Punta Callán, 30 km west of Huaraz where spectacular views of the Cordillera Blanca are obtained. This road comes out at Casma and continues north along the coastal Pan-American to Chimbote. Finally, some buses take the road to Pativilca (the same route as Lima-bound buses) and then take the Pan-American north. Of the three choices, the Punta Callán route is the best at present because the views are excellent, the journey can be done in daylight and it avoids retracing your steps if you've come from Lima. Transportes Moreno has both daily and nightly departures. Empresa Huaraz has night buses via Pativilca.

Buses for Chavín de Huantar (five hours, US$2.20) continuing to Huari (seven hours, US$3) run every other day with Cóndor de Chavín. Transportes Huascarán also provides this service.

To get to Chiquián by bus it's best to go directly from Lima on TUBSA. There is no direct service from Huaraz and if you want to reach Chiquián you should head south along the Callejón de Huaylas on the earliest bus you can find. Get off the bus at Conococha, a high and cold lake with a little huddle of buildings nearby. Wait here for any transport to Chiquián, a further 32 km by dirt road.

Transportes Huascarán has two vehicles a week to La Unión, about nine hours away to the east. From here it is possible to find daily trucks to Huánuco.

Getting Around

There are several tourist agencies in Huaraz which provide vehicles for local tours. The three most popular trips each take a full day. One visits the ruins at Chavín de Huantar, another goes through Yungay to the beautiful Lagunas Llanganuco where there are spectacular views of Huascarán and other mountains, and the third tour is through Catac to see the giant *puya raimondi* plant. These destinations are described in greater detail in the appropriate sections later in the chapter.

There are many tour agencies in Huaraz and you'll find several along Avenida Luzuriaga. Two companies which generally give good services are Pablo Tours and Chavín Tours. Prices vary but are about US$6 per person for a one-day trip. This includes transportation (usually in minibuses) and a guide but the guide doesn't necessarily speak English. You should bring a packed lunch, warm clothes, drinking water and sun protection. There are departures almost daily during the high season but at other times departures depend on if there are enough passengers.

Things to Buy

There is an outdoor craft market along Luzuriaga every evening during the tourist season. Thick woollen sweaters, scarves, hats, socks, gloves, ponchos and blankets are inexpensively available for travellers needing warm clothes for the mountains. Tooled-leather goods are also popular souvenirs.

NORTH OF HUARAZ

The Callejón de Huaylas road north of Huaraz follows the Santa River valley and is paved for 67 km as far as Caraz. This road comes within 14 km of Peru's highest peak and links the departmental capital with the other main towns of the area. Buses for all towns mentioned below leave from the corner of Fitzcarrald and Raimondi.

MONTERREY

Just five km north of Huaraz is the small village of Monterrey, famous for its natural hot springs. The bus terminates right in front of the *Baños Termales* (hot springs) so you won't have any difficulty in finding them. The hot springs are divided into two sections; the lower pools are cheaper (10c) and more crowded while the upper pools cost 25c and are within the grounds of the Hotel de Turistas. Tickets for both levels are sold at the lower entrance.

Places to Stay

The government-run *Hotel de Turistas* is a pleasant building set in gardens right next to the hot springs. There is a simple but good restaurant with outdoor dining (overlooking the pool) and meals for under US$2. Both pool and restaurant are open to non-residents of the hotel. Singles/doubles are about US$6/9 with bath. Reservations may be made in Lima by phoning ENTURPERU at 721928. There is nowhere else to stay.

Getting There

Monterrey is reached by local buses which pass the Huaraz Plaza de Armas and continue north along Avenidas Luzuriaga, Fitzcarrald and Centenario. Try and get onto the bus early in the route as it soon fills up. The fare is 10c for the 15-minute drive.

CARHUAZ

The road north of Huaraz passes the rarely used Anta airport after 23 km. A few km beyond is the small village of Marcará from where trucks and buses go to the hot springs of Chancos, three km to the east, and occasionally a further four km to the ruins at Vicos. Beyond Vicos the Quebrada Honda trail continues across the Cordillera Blanca (for hikers only). The Chancos hot springs are popular at weekends when they tend to be crowded. They are not in a good state of repair.

The small town of Carhuaz lies 31 km north of Huaraz. It is not a particularly interesting place but you might stay here if you want to trek into the Cordillera Blanca via the beautiful Quebrada Ulta. Vehicles from Carhuaz to Shilla and Llipta (in the Quebrada Ulta) are frequent on Sunday, which is market day, but there's usually only one truck in the morning on other days.

Carhuaz has an annual fiesta for *La Virgen de La Merced* which is held on and around 24 September. There are processions, fireworks, dancing, bullfights and plenty of drinking. This is the most interesting time to visit Carhuaz.

Places to Stay & Eat

There are several small, basic and cheap hotels in Carhuaz. Expect to pay between 60c and US$1.30 per person. None of these hotels have hot water or private bathrooms.

On the Plaza de Armas is the clean and friendly *Hotel La Merced*. The not so good *Hotel Peru* is on the corner of the plaza on Avenida Progreso. Also on Progreso, a block away from the plaza, is the *Hotel Carhuaz* which has a pleasant courtyard and is perhaps the best hotel in town. At the north exit of town is the *Hostal Delicias* which actually advertises hot water but don't expect too much. There is also the *Hotel Victoria*.

There are a few cheap and basic restaurants. The *Palmeras* and the *Hotel Peru* restaurants on Avenida Progreso are OK.

YUNGAY

Continuing north from Carhuaz, the road goes through the village of Mancos from where excellent views are had of Huascarán at the head of the Mancos River valley. Shortly beyond is the newly rebuilt village of Ranrahirca (devastated in the 1962 earthquake) followed by the rubble-strewn area of old Yungay, site of the worst single natural disaster in the Andes. It was near here that the earthquake of 31 May 1970 loosened some 15 million cubic metres of granite and ice from the west wall of Huascarán Norte. The resulting alluvion picked up a speed of about 300 km per hour as it dropped over three vertical km on its way to Yungay, 14 km away. The town and almost all of its approximately 18,000 inhabitants were buried. The earthquake also killed about 60,000 people in other parts of central Peru. Today, the site is marked by a huge white statue of Christ on a knoll overlooking old Yungay. The path of the alluvion can plainly be seen from the road. (The November 1985 alluvion which swept through Armero, Colombia, had the unfortunate distinction of killing more people – 23,000 – than the Yungay alluvion, although the Yungay disaster was in itself just a small part of a greater catastrophe.)

New Yungay has been rebuilt just beyond the alluvion path, about 59 km north of Huaraz. A stark, hastily built town, it has no attractions in itself but it is from here that you begin one of the most beautiful and popular excursions in the Cordillera Blanca.

Information

Almost everything of tourist importance happens around the Plaza de Armas. There is a small tourist office here but it may well be closed outside of the high season and hours are erratic at other times.

Places to Stay & Eat

There are several cheap places to stay in Yungay, although there's little point in spending more than a night here en route to the mountains. One of the best hotels is the *Hostal Gledel*, a block from the plaza. They charge about US$1.50 per person, are friendly and have hot water and meals available. Also popular is the *Hostal Turistico Blanco* which is a tiny rustic hotel about 10 minutes from the plaza, behind the maternity hospital. It is quietly situated in a grove of eucalyptus trees, friendly, but has only cold water.

Cheaper hotels include the *Yuly* and the *Yungay*, both on the plaza, and the *Confort* on the road south of town. Hotels may close in the off-season and private homes often offer accommodation during the high season.

There are no particularly noteworthy restaurants but you'll find several cheap and simple *comedores* in the market next to the plaza.

Getting There

There are frequent minibuses from the Plaza de Armas to Caraz (20c, 15 minutes) and buses en route from Caraz will pick up passengers to Huaraz (70c, 1½ hours) from the south-west side of the plaza.

Empresa TROME has an office on the plaza for buses to Lima (7 am, 11 am and 7 pm) and Empresa Moreno has buses to Chimbote (day bus via Casma and night bus via Cañón del Pato). Other companies pass the Plaza en route from Caraz to Lima.

LAGUNAS LLANGANUCO

A dirt road goes up the Llanganuco valley to the two lovely lakes of the same name, about 28 km east of Yungay. There are great views of the giant mountains of Huascarán (6768 metres), Chopicalqui (6354 metres), Chacraraju (6112 metres), Huandoy (6395 metres) and others, particularly if you drive up a few km beyond the lakes. The road has recently been completed over the pass beyond the lakes and down to Yanama on the other side of the Cordillera Blanca and in the mornings there is often a truck between the two towns.

Yungay is also the town from where the walker begins the Llanganuco-Santa Cruz loop, the most popular and spectacular trek of the Cordillera Blanca. This takes an average of five fairly leisurely days (although it can be done in three) and is a good hike for everybody, but especially for beginners because the trail is relatively well defined. The Llanganuco road is also the access route to the Pisco base camp from where the ascent of Nevado Pisco (5800 metres) is made. This is considered one of the most straight-forward snow ascents in the range, although it is not to be taken lightly and requires snow and ice climbing equipment and ability.

To get to the Llanganuco lakes you can go on a tour from Huaraz or you can take buses or taxis from Yungay. During June – August, the height of the dry season, minibuses carrying 10 or more passengers leave from the Yungay Plaza de Armas. They charge about US$2 for the round trip which allows about two hours in the area of the lakes. A National Park admission fee of about US$1 is also charged. Taxis carrying up to five passengers charge about US$15 for the round trip. It is best to go in the early morning for clear views; it's often cloudy in the afternoon. Outside of the tourist season it is more difficult to find mini-buses as they don't want to go with less than 10 passengers, but you can find taxis to take you.

CARAZ

The pleasant little town of Caraz lies 67 km north of Huaraz and is the end of the road as far as regular and frequent transportation is concerned. Caraz is one of the few places in the area which, whilst suffering some damage, has managed to avoid being totally destroyed by earth-quakes or alluvions. There is an attractive Plaza de Armas, several hotels and restaurants, and you can take pleasant walks in the surrounding hills. Caraz is the end point of the popular Llanganuco-Santa Cruz trek as well as being the point of departure for excursions by road to the beautiful Laguna Parón and also the Cañón del Pato.

Excursions to both places can be made from the Plaza de Armas. Pick-up truck drivers will charge about US$20 (bargain) for either round trip and you can easily fit

half a dozen people in the back of the pickup.

The bright blue Laguna Parón is 32 km east of Caraz and is surrounded by spectacular snowcaps of which Pyramide (5885 metres) at the end of the lake looks particularly magnificent. The drive to the lake goes through a canyon with granite walls a 1000 metres in height. Although this excursion is further from Huaraz than to the Llanganuco lakes and hence not as popular and less crowded, it is as attractive as the Llanganuco tour.

The Cañón del Pato is at the far north of the Callejón de Huaylas and is its narrowest point. There used to be buses every day en route to Chimbote but now they go only at night so if you want to see the canyon you have to take a pickup truck or taxi from Caraz. It is a spectacular canyon but the hydro-electric plant at Huallanca is now out of bounds to visitors and the area has become sensitive of late. Terrorist activities have threatened to close this trip to tourists so make local enquiries about the situation. There is a cheap and clean hotel in Huallanca.

If you spend any time in Caraz you might want to check the two cinemas in town.

Getting There

Caraz is often the final destination of

1	Municipalidad & Cine Muni
2	Empresa Moreno
3	Hostal Suizo Peruano
4	Hostal Chavín
5	Cine
6	Pensión Caraz
7	Hostal Morovi
8	Residencial El Rosedal
9	ENTEL
10	Post Office
11	Ancash Buses
12	Empresa Cribillero
13	Empresa Rodriguez
14	Empresa Nor-Pacifico

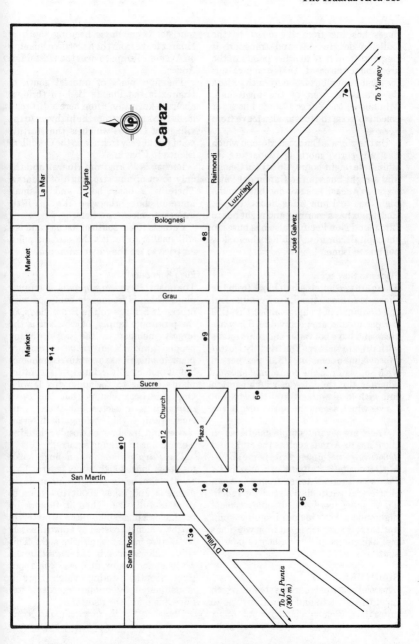

buses heading from the coast to the Callejón de Huaylas and transport is frequent from here to other points in the area and to the coast. Taxis and pick-ups for local excursions leave from the Plaza de Armas in front of the town hall. Minibuses to Yungay and buses or colectivo taxis to Huaraz also leave from here.

On the plaza is Empresa Moreno which has an early morning departure to Chimbote (eight hours, US$4) via Casma and a night bus via the Cañón del Pato. Expreso Ancash has two day buses and a night bus to Lima (nine hours, US$4), Rodriguez has a morning and night bus to Lima, and Nor-Pacifico also has buses to the capital. Empresa Cribillera has a slow old bus to Lima.

Places to Stay & Eat

There are two hotels a half block from the Plaza de Armas – the *Suizo Peruano* and the *Chavín*. They charge about US$1.50 per person and are good value. They are clean and have hot water and some rooms with private shower. The friendly *Hostal Morovi* has rooms at US$1 per person with hot water in the communal shower. There is also the *Rosedal* which is often full with local workers and the *Pensión Caraz* which seems the most basic of the lot.

There are several simple cafeterias on the Plaza de Armas such as the *Paris* and *Jeny's Bar* – nothing to write home about. My favourite restaurant in Caraz is *La Punta*, a short distance from the town centre and particularly good for lunch. They serve very cheap and typical highland dishes (including guinea pig) and there is a garden to eat in. If you don't feel like guinea pig, try a hearty bowl of soup.

SOUTH OF HUARAZ

The road south of Huaraz is the one which most travellers to and from Lima use to enter the Callejón de Huaylas but, apart from this, the road is little travelled by

tourists. Local buses heading south of Huaraz leave from the *frigorífico* bus stop on Avenida Tarapaca near the Hostal Los Andes.

The first place of interest south of Huaraz is the Puente Bedoya (bridge) about 18 km away. From here a dirt road leads two km east from the highway to the village of Olleros which is the starting point for the easy trek across the Cordillera Blanca to Chavín.

Recuay is 25 km from Huaraz and the only town of any size south of Huaraz. There is a basic hotel and a small museum but otherwise it's of little interest to most travellers.

Catac is 10 km south of Recuay and is a still smaller town. It's the starting point for trips to see the *Puya raimondi*.

Puya Raimondi

The giant *Puya raimondi* is a strange plant which is frequently confused with others. It belongs to the Bromeliads, or the pineapple family, of which it is the largest member in the world. Many people think it's an *agave* or century plant, to which it has a certain resemblance but is not closely related; the century plants belong to the amaryllis family. One guidebook claims that the *Puya raimondi* is a cactus but there is no comparison – they belong to different classes and are about as closely related as a chicken is to a flying squirrel!

The *Puya raimondi* is a huge spiky rosette of long, tough, waxy leaves. This rosette can be two metres or more in diameter and takes about 100 years to grow to full size. Then it flowers by producing a huge spike, often 10 metres in height, which is covered by approximately 20,000 flowers – a magnificent sight. This spiky inflorescence is the largest in the world and remains in flower for about three months, during which time it is pollinated by hummingbirds. After flowering once, the plant dies.

Obviously, with flowering occurring only once at the end of a century, most of

Top: Author trekking by Huascarán (6768 m) & Chacraraju (6112 m), Cordillera Blanca (RR)
Bottom: Keystone head at Chavín (RR)

Top: Cupola of Belén Church, Cajamarca (RR)
Left: Wood carving of tired Christ, Belén Church, Cajamarca (RR)
Right: Entrance to Kuelap ruins (RR)

the plants you'll see won't be flowering. When they do flower they tend to do so in groups and this occurs about every three or four years; it is not known why this happens. You should make local enquiries if you hope to see the *Puya raimondi* in flower – even when not flowering it is still a fascinating sight. The spiky rosette offers protection to a variety of birds and you may find several nests within the leaves of one plant.

The giant bromeliad is also considered to be one of the most ancient plant species in the world and has been called a 'living fossil'. It is rare and found only in a few isolated areas of the Peruvian and Bolivian Andes. The sites in the Cordillera Blanca are two of the best known ones and they receive protection as part of the Huascarán National Park.

Getting There

There are two ways to visit the *Puya raimondi* sites. One site is on the southern slopes of the upper Quebrada Queshque, about 20 km south-east of Catac. You can hike on a trail from Catac, as described in Bartle's book.

The other site is at the intersection of the Quebrada Raria with the Río Pachacoto and can be reached by road. You drive a further 10 km south of Catac on the main road and turn left at the Río Pachacoto where there is a National Park sign reading *Sector Carpa*. Follow the dirt road for about 18 km to the Quebrada Raria where the puyas are to be seen. These areas are also the best place in the Cordillera Blanca to watch for the beautiful vicuña, an infrequently seen wild relative of the alpaca and llama. Camping is possible in both areas.

Tour companies in Huaraz make trips to the second site and charge about US$6 per head. If travelling by public transport, take any early morning Lima-bound bus to the *Carpa* turn-off (60c) and wait for a truck going along the Río Pachacoto road. There are usually several trucks a day – start heading back by early afternoon if you don't want to spend the night. These trucks act as buses for the locals and you are expected to pay a bus fare (it shouldn't be more than about 50c).

The road continues as far as La Unión, a town several hours away. In La Unión you can find basic hotels and transportation on to Huánuco.

CHIQUIÁN

This small town is the centre for visiting the small but spectacular Cordillera Huayhuash, the next mountain range south of the Blanca. It has basic hotels and restaurants, but hikers should bring what they will need with them because few supplies are available.

Chiquián is at 3400 metres and there are good views of the Cordillera Huayhuash to be had as you drive to the village. The highest mountain in the range is Yerupajá which, at 6634 metres, is also the second highest mountain in Peru. Hiking in the Huayhuash usually involves making a circuit of the entire range – this is fairly strenuous and takes almost two weeks. Bartle's book describes the trail in detail.

Places to Stay & Eat

The best hotel in Chiquián is the *Hostal San Miguel* which charges a little over US$1 per person per night and is basic but clean. They are at Comercio 211. There are a couple of other even more basic places if this is full, and people have slept in the church when all else failed.

There are a couple of simple restaurants.

Getting There

There is no regular direct bus service from Huaraz to Chiquián, although trucks do make the journey two or three times a week. Despite this, it is not too difficult to get here from Huaraz. Simply take any early morning Lima-bound bus to Laguna Conococha, about 80 km south of Huaraz. At the lake there is a small huddle of houses and the turn-off to Chiquián, 32 km away. Several vehicles a day go along this road so if you get to Conococha in the morning you shouldn't have any difficulty in continuing to Chiquián.

TUBSA and Landauro bus companies have daily service to Lima (US$4.50, 10 hours). Their offices are on the Plaza de Armas in Chiquián. In Lima, TUBSA is at Leticia 633 and Landauro at Ayacucho 1040, near the Parque Universitario.

CAJATAMBO

This is the only other village on the Cordillera Huayhuash trek which has access by road. Empresa Espadín runs an old and slow bus between Lima and Cajatambo on a daily basis. In Lima the company is found opposite the Ormeño bus station. There are two basic hotels in Cajatambo.

CHAVÍN DE HUÁNTAR

This small village is of little interest in itself, but the ruins of Chavín on the southern edge of the village are well worth a visit.

Archaeology

The Chavín culture is named after its type site at Chavín de Huántar and is the oldest major culture in Peru. It existed from about 1300 to 400 BC, predating the Incas by about 2000 years. The major period of influence was from about 800 to 400 BC – and the Chavín certainly was an influential culture. They didn't conquer surrounding peoples by warfare, they simply influenced the artistic and cultural development of all of northern Peru. This cultural expansion is referred to as the Chavín Horizon by archaeologists. Signs of Chavín influence have been traced in ruins ranging from the present day Ecuadorian border to as far south as Ica and Ayacucho. None of these sites is as well preserved or as frequently visited as Chavín de Huántar.

The principal Chavín deity was feline (jaguar or puma) and lesser condor, snake and human deities also existed. Highly stylised representations of these deities are found carved in Chavín sites. The experienced eye can see similarities in the precise yet fluid lines of these carvings; the non-expert can tell that any culture capable of such fine work 3000 years ago must indeed have been well advanced.

The artistic work of Chavín is much more stylised and cultist than the later naturalistic art of the Moche and Nazca cultures. Because of this, archaeologists lack an accurate picture of what life was like in Chavín times. However, excavations of middens (garbage dumps) indicate that corn became a major staple and agriculture improved with the introduction of squashes, avocados, yucca and other crops. Better agriculture meant less reliance on hunting, fishing and gathering and, more importantly, allowed leisure time. Thus art and religion could develop and so the Chavín horizon, linking art and religion in its feline-worship cults, was able to influence a large part of Peru.

Visiting the Ruins

At first glance, the site at Chavín de Huántar is not a particularly prepossessing one. There are two reasons for this: many of the most interesting parts of the site were built underground and most of the site was covered by a huge landslide in 1945. To visit the site properly and to gain the most out of your visit you should enter the underground chambers. Although these are supposedly lit, the lighting system is rarely functioning and so you are advised to bring your own torch (flashlight). It is also worthwhile hiring a guide to show you around.

The site contains a huge central square, slightly sunken below the ground. An intricate and well engineered system of channels provides drainage for this square. From the square, a broad staircase leads up to the only entrance of the largest and most important building in Chavín de Huántar, the *Castillo*. It is about 75 metres square, up to 13 metres high, and built on three different levels. Each level is of dry stone masonry and the walls were once embellished with 'key' stones consisting of large projecting blocks carved into a stylised human head. Only one of these remains in its original place but others can be seen inside the Castillo in the underground chambers to which they have been moved.

The underground tunnels are an exceptional feat of 3000-year-old engineering; they are all so well ventilated that no mustiness of the air exists and yet there are no external windows or doorways except for the main entrance. In the heart of the underground complex is an exquisitely carved rock known as the *Lanzón de Chavín*. It is a thrilling and distinctly mysterious experience to come upon this four-metre-high dagger-like rock stuck into the ground at the inter-

Lanzón de Chavín

section of four narrow passageways, deep within the Castillo.

Travellers interested in the Chavín Horizon are advised to visit the Museum of Anthropology & Archaeology in Lima. Two carved rocks, the Raimondi Stela and the Tello Obelisk, smaller but similar to the Lanzón de Chavín, may be seen in the museum. The museum also has several of the large carved head 'key' stones which once decorated the Castillo. All of these exhibits are originally from the Chavín de Huántar site.

The site is open daily from 8 am to 12 noon, and from 2 to 4 pm. Entrance is about 60c, with a small extra fee for photography. A small tip will probably ensure entrance into the site during the lunch break. Spanish-speaking local guides are available to show you around and charge about US$1 for this service. There is a soft drink and snack stand.

Places to Stay & Eat

Hotels in the village of Chavín de Huántar are very basic and cheap. The best of a not particularly good lot is the *Montecarlo*. There are also the *Inca* and *Gantu*. The hotels are found on or near the Plaza de Armas.

There is also the *Albergue de Turistas Chavín* which is charges about US$5/8 for singles/doubles with bath and hot water. It is reportedly pleasant but I've never been there. It is about two km north of the town and reservations can be made in Lima by phoning 270323.

There are some basic *comedores* in town but they have a reputation for closing about sunset. Camping is reportedly possible at the hot springs about three km south of town.

Getting There

Hikers can walk to Chavín from Olleros in about three days (see Bartle's book). Tour buses make day trips from Huaraz for about US$6 per passenger. Public transport from Huaraz (US$2.20, five hours) is provided by Transportes Cóndor de Chavín or Transportes Huascarán on a daily basis. Cóndor de Chavín has buses to and from Lima (US$6, 11 hours) every day. Their office in Lima is at Montevideo 1039 near Nicolas de Pierola.

The drive across the Cordillera Blanca from Catac is an attractive one. The road passes the Laguna Querococha at 3980 metres from where there are good views of the peaks of Pucaraju (5322 metres) and Yanamarey (5237 metres). The road deteriorates somewhat as it continues climbing to the Cahuish tunnel at 4178 metres above sea level. This tunnel cuts through the Cahuish pass which is over 300 metres higher. The road then descends to Chavín at about 3145 metres.

HUARI

Many of the buses bound for Chavín continue to Huari, a small town about 40 km and two hours to the north. There are a couple of small hotels here. This is the end of the road as far as regular daily bus services are concerned.

NORTH OF HUARI

The road north of Huari goes through the villages of San Luis, Piscobamba, Pomabamba and Sihuas. The further north you go, the more difficult transport becomes and it may stop altogether during the wet season. Basic accommodation is available in these towns which may be the end of various cross cordilleran hikes. From Sihuas it is possible to continue to Huallanca via Tres Cruces and thus return to the Callejón de Huaylas. This round trip is scenic, remote and rarely made by travellers. It shouldn't be too difficult to find transport during the dry season if you really want to get off the beaten track.

Across the Northern Highlands

The traveller heading into the mountains north of the Cordillera Blanca is unable to do so conveniently without returning to the coast. Then he or she must travel north along the coast before returning inland and into the mountains again. The next major city north of Huaraz is Cajamarca, reached by three roads from the coast. The dirt roads from Trujillo and Chiclayo are both rough and difficult routes, while the road leaving the Pan-American between these two cities is paved all the way to Cajamarca. All three routes will be described in this chapter.

From Cajamarca, a very poor road continues north-east across the Andes to Chachapoyas, capital of the Department of Amazonas, but there is a better road to Chachapoyas via Bagua from the Pan-American north of Chiclayo. Beyond Chachapoyas, this road continues down the eastern slopes of the Andes to the jungles of the Department of San Martín. Crossing the northern Andes through Cajamarca and Chachapoyas is the subject of this chapter.

Note
Money exchange facilities throughout this area are limited and not very good. It is suggested that you change enough money on the coast to last for your entire inland trip.

CAJAMARCA
Cajamarca, capital of its department, is located at 2650 metres above sea level and five hours east by paved road from Pacasmayo on the coast. It is a traditional and tranquil colonial city with a friendly population of some 70,000 inhabitants. The surrounding countryside is green and attractive.

Cajamarca and its surroundings are steeped in history and pre-history. It was a major Inca city and played a crucial role in the Spanish conquest of the Incas. It was in Cajamarca that Pizarro tricked, captured, imprisoned for ransom and finally assassinated the Inca Atahualpa. Not only is the city historically important – it remains important today and is the major city in Peru's northern Andes. It has impressive colonial architecture, excellent Andean food and interesting people and customs. Despite this, it is not a major centre of international tourism because it lies some way inland from the 'gringo trail'. Perhaps this makes it more attractive still. I consider Cajamarca to be the second most interesting Peruvian Andean city after Cuzco.

History
Various pre-Inca sites have been discovered in the Cajamarca area but little is known about them. They are generally believed to be sites of the Chavín-influenced Cajamarca culture. The most visited site is the water channels of Cumbe Mayo. Around 1460 the Incas conquered the Cajamarca people and Cajamarca became a major Inca city on the highway linking Cuzco and Quito.

After the death of the Inca Huayna Capac in 1525, the Inca Empire, by then stretching from southern Colombia to central Chile, was divided between the half-brothers Atahualpa and Huascar. Atahualpa ruled the north and Huascar ruled the south. Civil war soon developed and Atahualpa, who had the support of the army, gained the upper hand. In 1532 he and his victorious troops marched southward towards Cuzco to take complete control of the Inca Empire. During this southbound march, Atahualpa and his army stopped at Cajamarca for a few days rest. The Inca emperor was camped at the natural thermal springs, today known as Los Baños del Inca, when he heard the news that the Spanish were nearby.

By 1532 Atahualpa was certainly aware of the existence of the strange bearded white men. In 1528, during his second voyage, Francisco Pizarro had invited an Inca noble from Tumbes to dine aboard his ship and word of this would undoubtedly have been passed on to Atahualpa. Atahualpa, supported by his army and flushed with victory in his civil war, would not have considered the small ragged force of Spaniards as a threat, let alone a fully-fledged invasion.

Pizarro and his force of about 160 Spaniards arrived in Cajamarca on 15 November 1532. They found a temple of the sun, the Inca fortress, some well-made buildings housing the Inca's chosen women and a central square surrounded by assembly halls called *kallankas*. The city was almost deserted; most of the approximately 2000 inhabitants were with the Atahualpa at his encampment by the hot springs, six km away. Pizarro sent a force of about 35 horsemen and a native interpreter to Atahualpa's camp with the purpose of asking the Inca emperor where the Spaniards were to stay. They were told to lodge in the kallankas surrounding the plaza and that the Inca would join them the next day.

The small force of Spaniards spent an anxious night, fully aware that they were severely outnumbered by the Inca troops which were estimated as being between 40,000 and 80,000 strong. The Spaniards plotted throughout the night and decided to try and entice Atahualpa into the plaza and, at a pre-arranged signal, capture the Inca emperor should the opportunity present itself. If this did not occur, they were to maintain a 'friendly' relationship and hope for another chance to capture the Atahualpa in the future. The next morning Pizarro stationed his troops in the kallankas, which were perfect for his plans. The kallankas surrounded three sides of the plaza and each had about 20 doorways so that a large number of the Spaniards could emerge and attack at the same time.

Atahualpa kept the Spaniards waiting all day, much to their consternation. He didn't break camp until the afternoon and didn't reach Cajamarca until early evening. His vast army came with him. Upon arriving at the outskirts of the city, the Inca emperor ordered the majority of his troops to stay outside while he entered the plaza with a retinue of nobles and about 6000 men armed with slings and hand axes. He was met by the Spanish friar, Vicente de Valverde. The friar, bible in hand, attempted to explain his position as a man of God to Atahualpa and presented the Inca with the bible. Atahualpa angrily threw the book to the ground and Valverde took this as an

The conquest of Peru showing the scene in the Plaza at Cajamarca - Pizarro, the priest Valverde and Atahualpa in his litter.

insult to Christianity and provided the excuse he needed to absolve the Spaniards in advance for an attack upon the Inca. He rushed back to the kallankas and prevailed upon Pizarro to order the firing of his cannons into the midst of the Indians. This was the pre-arranged signal for attack.

The cannons were fired and the Spanish horsemen attacked amidst much trumpeting and yelling. The Indians, who had never seen cannon or horses before, were both terrified and completely bewildered by the fearsome onslaught. Their small hand axes and slings were no match for the well-armoured Spaniards swinging razor-sharp swords from the advantageous height of horseback. The Indians tried to flee but the entrance to the plaza was too narrow to allow escape. By sheer weight of numbers, they knocked down a section of wall two metres thick and swarmed out of the plaza in total disarray. Pizarro's horsemen charged after them, chopping and hacking down as many Indians as they could. Meanwhile, Pizarro himself led a small contingent of men and succeeded in capturing Atahualpa. As the sun set over Cajamarca on the evening of 16 November, the course of Latin American history was changed forever. With an estimated 7000 Indians dead and Atahualpa captured, the small band of Spaniards had succeeded beyond their wildest hopes. Now they literally were *conquistadores*.

Almost immediately after he was captured, Atahualpa became aware of one of the weaknesses of the Spaniards – namely, a lust for gold. Accordingly, he offered to fill a large room once with gold and twice with silver in return for his freedom. The conquistadores were astounded by their good fortune and quickly agreed to Atahualpa's offer. They led Atahualpa to believe that they would not only release him after the ransom was paid, but also would return him to his northern lands around Quito.

This was a wily move on the part of Pizarro. By promising Atahualpa's return to Quito, he effectively controlled the northern part of the Inca Empire. And by holding Atahualpa captive Pizarro also maintained control of the southern half of the empire because the inhabitants of this region, having just been beaten by Atahualpa in a civil war, considered him an enemy and looked upon Pizarro as a liberator rather than an invader. This playing off of one Inca faction against the other was Pizarro's strongest weapon. If the Inca Empire had been united when the Spaniards arrived, the story of the conquest would have been an entirely different one.

The gold and silver slowly began to arrive at Cajamarca. Pizarro sent some of his men to Cuzco to ensure the collection of the ransom. Meanwhile, Atahualpa was held as a royal prisoner, with the servants and comfort he was accustomed to. The Spaniards were in no great hurry to collect the ransom; they were also waiting for reinforcements. On 14 April 1533 Diego de Almagro arrived from the coast with 150 soldiers, thus almost doubling the Spanish force at Cajamarca. Atahualpa began to suspect that the Spaniards were lying to him and that he wouldn't be released and returned to Quito when the ransom was paid.

Finally, in mid-June of 1533 the ransom was complete and Pizarro ordered the melting down and distribution of the treasure. Careful records were kept of these procedures and it is known that about 6000 kg of gold and 12,000 kg of silver were melted down into gold and silver bullion. At today's prices, this is worth roughly US$75 million but the artistic value of ornaments and implements which were melted down is impossible to estimate or recover. This treasure was distributed among the conquistadores in strictly controlled quotas.

Atahualpa was still a prisoner and now he knew that he was not going to be released. He sent desperate messages to his followers in Quito to come to Cajamarca and rescue him. The Spaniards heard of this rescue attempt and became panic-stricken. Although Pizarro was not anxious to kill the Inca emperor, thinking to further his own aims by continuing to hold Atahualpa hostage and using him as a puppet ruler, the other leading Spaniards insisted on the Inca's death. Despite the lack of a formal trial, Atahualpa was sentenced to death for attempting to have himself rescued. On 26 July 1533 Atahualpa was led out to the centre of the Cajamarca plaza to be burnt at the stake. At the last hour, Atahualpa accepted baptism and his sentence was changed to a more humane death by strangulation.

Immediately after Atahualpa's death, the Spaniards crowned Tupac Huallpa, a younger brother of Huascar, as the new Inca emperor. With this new puppet ruler, the Spaniards were free to march into Cuzco as liberators. During the march the new Inca emperor died of an unknown illness and the Spanish arrived in Cuzco on 15 November without an Inca ruler.

Today, little remains of Inca Cajamarca. Most of the great stone buildings were torn down to be used in the construction of Spanish homes and churches. The great plaza where Atahualpa was captured and later killed was roughly in the same location as today's Plaza de Armas, although in Atahualpa's time it was a much larger plaza. The ransom chamber, which Atahualpa had filled once with gold and twice with silver, is the only building which still stands.

For a much more detailed description of the momentous events which took place in Cajamarca in 1532 and 1533 see John Hemming's excellent *The Conquest of the Incas*.

Information

Tourist Information The tourist information office is in the *Conjunto Belén* – a complex consisting of the the colonial church and hospital of Belén and the present *Dirección de Turismo*.

Cajamarca Tours, next to the Hotel Cajamarca, provides tourist information and guided tours of the city and surroundings.

Money Exchange The Banco de la Nación will change money, though it's a slow process and rates are not good. Other banks nearby are no better, change money in Trujillo or Chiclayo for better rates and service.

Communications The post office at Lima and Galvez is open from 8 am to 8 pm daily except Sunday when it's open from 8 am to 12 noon. Long distance telephone calls can be made every day from 8 am to 10 pm at ENTEL on the Plaza de Armas.

The Ransom Chamber

El Cuarto del Rescate, as the Ransom Chamber is known in Spanish, is the only Inca building which remains standing in Cajamarca. Although called the Ransom Chamber, the room shown to visitors is where Atahualpa was imprisoned and not where the ransom was stored. It is only a small room with three trapezoidal doorways and a few trapezoidal niches in the inner walls – a typical sign of Inca construction. Although it is well constructed, it does not compare with the Inca buildings to be seen in the Cuzco area.

In the entrance there are a couple of modern paintings depicting Atahualpa's capture and imprisonment. The site is open from 9 am to 12 noon on weekends, closed Tuesdays, and open from 8 am to 12.30 pm and 2 to 5.15 pm on the other days of the week. Entrance is 30c and the ticket can be used to visit the Church and Hospital of Belén.

The Belén Complex

The building of the church and hospital of

Belén began in the latter part of the 17th century. The hospital (which is being restored) was run by nuns. Inside the hospital, the visitor can see the 31 tiny cell-like bedrooms lining the walls of the T-shaped building. Next door is the church with a fine cupola and a well-carved and painted pulpit. There are several interesting wood carvings including an extremely tired looking Christ sitting cross legged on his throne, propping up his chin with a double jointed wrist, and looking as if he could do with a pisco sour after a hard day of miracle working.

The outside walls of the church are lavishly decorated. Local guides tell you that the facade of the church has strange carvings of women with four breasts, although I couldn't find them.

Opening hours are the same as for the Ransom Chamber and the admission fee of 30c covers both sites. The Tourist Office in the complex can be visited for free.

Plaza de Armas

The plaza is pleasant and has a well-kept topiary garden. There is a fine central fountain which dates to 1692 and thus commemorates the 200th anniversary of Columbus's landing in the Americas. The town's inhabitants congregate in the plaza every evening. Strolling and discussing the day's events are traditionally popular activities – more so in this area of northern Peru than anywhere else in the country.

Two churches face onto the Plaza de Armas: the Cathedral and San Francisco. Both are often illuminated in the evening, especially at weekends. The Cathedral is a squat building which was begun in the late 1600s and only recently finished. In common with most of Cajamarca's churches, the Cathedral has no belfry. This is because the Spanish crown levied a tax on finished churches and so the belfries were not built, leaving the church unfinished and thereby avoiding taxes. One exception to this rule is the Church of San Francisco, whose belfries were finished this century – too late for the Spanish crown to collect its tax!

San Francisco

The church and religious art museum of San Francisco is open from 2 to 5 pm daily except Sunday. Admission is about 7c. The intricately sculpted chapel of La Dolorosa (to the right of the church) is considered one of the finest chapels in the city.

Archaeological Museum

This small but well-stocked museum is well worth a visit. There is a remarkably varied collection of ceramics from several cultures including a few examples of Cajamarca pots and an unusual collection of Cajamarca ceramic ceremonial spears. The Cajamarca culture existed in the area before the Inca Empire but it is a little studied and not very well known culture. The archaeology museum also has black-and-white photographs of various historic and prehistoric sites in the Cajamarca area. The director of the museum is both knowledgeable and willing to talk about the exhibits.

The museum is run by the University of Cajamarca and there is a token admission charge (6c when I was last there). Opening hours vary and you often have to knock on the door to get in. The museum is open from 8 to 11.30 am on Saturdays and Sundays. It is closed on Tuesdays. During the rest of the week, it is open from 8 am to 12.15 pm and 3 to 5.45 pm except in January to March when it is open only in the mornings.

Cajamarca plate

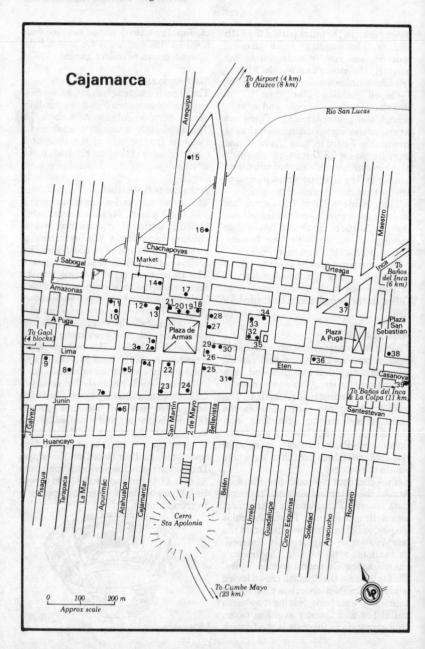

1   Cathedral
2   Hotel de Turistas
3   Aero Peru
4   Hostal Atahualpa
5   Hostal Bolívar
6   Teatro Cajamarca
7   Cine San Martín
8   Banco de la Nación
9   Post Office
10 Hotel Delfort
11 Hotel Prado
12 Hotel Amazonas
13 Hotel Becerra
14 Archaeological Museum
15 Local Buses to Airport & Otuzco
16 Hostal Turismo
17 Hostal Yusovi
18 Hostal 2 de Mayo
19 Hostal Plaza &
    Restaurant El Palacio de la Luna
20 Restaurant Salas
21 Chifa Zarco
22 ENTEL
23 Cine los Andes
24 Hotel Cajamarca & Cajamarca Tours
25 Cine Ollanta
26 Hotel Casa Blanca
27 San Francisco Church
28 La Taberna Restaurant
29 Peña La Rescate
30 Cuarto del Rescate
31 Conjunto Belén (Church, Hospital
    & Tourist Office)
32 Hostal Sucre
33 Hotel San Francisco
34 Empresa El Cumbe Buses
35 Trans Atahualpa
36 Cine Aurora
37 Empresa Diaz Buses
38 Recoleta Church
39 To TEPSA Bus Terminal
    & Restaurant La Namorina (1 km)

Cerro Santa Apolonia

This hill overlooks the city from the south-west and is a prominent Cajamarca landmark. It is easily reached by climbing the stairs at the end of Jirón 2 de Mayo. There are some pre-Hispanic carved rocks at the summit; they are mainly Inca but their origins are thought to date back to the Chavín period. One of the rocks is carved into the shape of a seat and is known as the seat of the Inca from where he was said to have reviewed his troops.

Fiestas

Cajamarca, like the majority of Peruvian Andean towns, is famous for its carnival – this one is a particularly wet affair with water fights being worse (or better, depending upon your point of view) than usual. The Corpus Christi processions are also very colourful. Both are Catholic feast days and vary each year, depending on the dates for Easter. Carnival is the week before Lent (which in itself is 40 days before Easter). Corpus Christi is the the Thursday after Trinity Sunday, which is the Sunday after Whitsunday, which is the seventh Sunday after Easter. Confused fiesta goers would do well to buy a Catholic calendar for the year they plan on being in Peru.

Tourism week in Cajamarca is around the second week in August. There are various cultural events such as art shows, folk music and dancing competitions, beauty pageants and processions.

Places to Stay – bottom end

There are several places which cost less than US$1 a night to stay but they all have cold water only. The *Hotel Plaza* is an old building on the Plaza de Armas and has some rooms with balconies and plaza views. They charge US$1/1.60 for singles/doubles. Similarly priced is the more modern *Hotel Amazonas* which has rooms with private shower and cold water. A few cents cheaper is the *Hostal Sucre* which has a sink and toilet in the rooms. Cheapest of all is the otherwise unrecommended *Hostal Bolívar*.

Several hotels offer two prices depending on whether or not you want a private bathroom. A good choice is the *Hotel Casa Blanca* – a thick-walled, creaky-floored, interesting old building right on the Plaza de Armas. They have an excellent 24-hour hot water supply and charge US$1.40/2.35 or an extra dollar per room with private bath. All the rooms are very spacious and some rooms have up to five beds which works out very cheaply if you are travelling with a group. There is a cafeteria which opens at 8.30 am.

The *Hostal Prado* is new, looks good and costs a few cents less than the *Casa Blanca*. It also has hot water and communal or private bathrooms. A third good choice in this price range is the *Hotel Becerra*. The new and good, although bare-looking, *Hotel Turismo* costs a few cents more. All rooms are clean, carpeted and have comfortable beds and private hot showers. They charge about US$2.50/3.75 for singles/doubles with bath.

The following hotels have hot water only in the mornings. The *Hostal Yusovi* is clean, but the water pressure leaves something to be desired. They charge US$1.80/2.80 for singles/doubles with private bath. The *Hostal 2 de Mayo* charges US$1.25/2.10 in rooms having toilets but no showers. The new *Hotel Delfort* charges US$2.25/3.75 for singles/doubles with private bath. Similarly priced is the clean and good *Hostal Atahualpa* on a pleasant pedestrians-only street. The *Hotel San Francisco* is clean but overpriced – cold water only in the private bathrooms.

Places to Stay - top end

The clean and pleasant *Hotel Cajamarca* is in a colonial house and is recommended for reasonable comfort. It has a good restaurant and they charge US$5.50/7.50 for singles/doubles with private bath and hot water.

The government-run *Hotel de Turistas* is in a newer building right on the Plaza de Armas. As well as being one of the best positioned hotels, this is also the most comfortable hotel in Cajamarca. It costs US$8/12 for rooms with private bath.

If you want quiet country comfort, go to the Baños del Inca (six kms away) where the excellent *Hostal Lago Seco* will

charge you US$12/18 for pleasant rooms with private bath. They also have bungalows sleeping four for US$36. They have a warm swimming pool and the hot water in all of the rooms is fed by the nearby natural thermal springs. There is a pleasant garden and good restaurant.

Places to Eat

My favourite restaurant is the *Salas* on the Plaza de Armas. It's a big barn of a place, popular with the locals, and serves various local dishes such as *cuy* (guinea-pig), delicious corn *tamales*, and *sesos* (cow brains) which I must admit I've never tried. You can eat well here for a dollar or so. Similar to the *Salas*, but a little cheaper, is the *Chifa Zarco* which serves Chinese as well as local Peruvian food. The *La Taberna* is more modern and serves good 'international' food at prices a little higher than the others. The restaurant in the *Hotel Cajamarca* is also good though again, a little pricier.

For breakfast the *Palacio de la Luna* café is good. For a typical local lunch try the *La Namorina*, about 1½ km away from the centre on the road to the Baño del Inca. It is an inexpensive and authentic highland restaurant.

Entertainment

Cajamarca has five cinemas and there's usually a reasonably good English language film playing at one of them. There are a few bars which have live music on Friday and Saturday nights; the best of these is *Peña La Rescate* on Avenida A Puga and there are others in this area.

Getting There

Air Only AeroPeru has an office or air service in Cajamarca. Local buses for Otuzco pass by the airport. There are three morning flights per week to and from Lima (US$41) via Trujillo (US$16). Two of these flights connect in Trujillo for Tarapoto.

Buses Cajamarca is on an ancient

crossroads dating back many centuries before the Incas. Today, daily buses leave Cajamarca on roads heading for all four points of the compass.

The most important road is the west-bound one, which is paved all the way to the Pan-American Highway near Pacasmayo on the coast. Here you have the choice of heading north to Chiclayo or south to Trujillo and Lima. The best buses serving Trujillo (US$4, seven hours) and Lima (US$8, 15 hours) are with TEPSA which has a daily departure at 6 pm except Sundays when it goes at 4 pm. The TEPSA terminal is located about a km south-east of town on the road to the Baños del Inca. To save you the walk you can buy tickets from the La Colmena store on the Plaza de Armas at A Puga by the San Francisco church. Transportes Atahualpa has older buses for Trujillo and Lima leaving at 2 pm and Empresa Diaz has the oldest buses of all which leave daily at 1 pm and 9 pm and go only as far as Trujillo. Empresa El Cumbe has daily buses at 11 am and 3 pm to Chiclayo (US$3.50, six hours). Empresa Diaz has a Chiclayo departure at 2 pm.

The southbound road is the old route to Trujillo via Cajabamba and Huamachuco. It is a rough gravel or dirt road and takes three times as long to Trujillo as the newer paved road via Pacasmayo, despite the fact that it is only 60 km further. Although the scenery is supposedly prettier than the shorter route, most buses beyond Cajabamba travel at night so you can't see a thing. Transportes Atahualpa has a noon bus to Cajabamba (US$2.50, seven hours) and Empresa Diaz leaves at 11 am for the same route. The Diaz buses are older and more likely to breakdown, but the Atahualpa buses pass through Cajamarca half full with passengers from Lima and Trujillo and the best seats are already taken.

The rough northbound road goes through wild and attractive countryside via the towns of Hualgayoc (US$2.20) and Bambamarca (US$2.50) to Chota

(US$2.90, nine hours). Hualgayoc is an attractively located mining village and Bambamarca has a colourful Sunday morning market and a basic hotel. More hotels are found in Chota from where buses go to Chiclayo along a very rough road. Buses from Cajamarca to Chota leave daily at 7 am with Empresa Diaz.

Finally, the eastbound road heads to Celendín and on across the Andes, past Chachapoyas, and down into the Amazon lowlands. The road is very bad between Celendín and Chachapoyas and trans-portation is unreliable, so travellers to Chachapoyas are advised to go from Chiclayo via Bagua unless they have plenty of time and patience. Buses to Celendín (US$2.30, 5½ hours) leave Cajamarca daily at 12 noon with Empresa Diaz and 1 pm with Transportes Atahualpa.

Getting Around

It is easy to find transport to the Baños del Inca. There are colectivo taxis leaving frequently from in front of the church of San Francisco. The fare is 15c. For about 10c you can take a Comité 3M bus which comes down Jirón Lima and goes through the Plaza de Armas.

The bus for the Ventanillas de Otuzco leaves frequently from the end of Jirón Arequipa, about ½ km from the Plaza de Armas and two blocks past the bridge. The fare is 10c and the bus goes by the airport and on to Otuzco, leaving you within a ½ km of the archaeological site.

Other local places are not served by public bus, although it is worth checking with the tourist office to see if this has changed. Walk, hitchhike, take a taxi, or join a tour.

Things to Buy

The market on Calle Amazonas is lively and interesting. Local products to look for include *alforjas* (heavy wool or cotton saddle bags) which are worn over the shoulder as well as being used on horseback. Woven baskets and leatherwork are also local crafts; the latter can be bought cheaply from the prisoners in the gaol which is just past the arch on Jirón Lima. They are open from 8 to 11.30 am and 2 to 4.30 pm. The local eucalyptus honey sold at the market is worth trying.

AROUND CAJAMARCA

There are several places of interest in the environs of Cajamarca. Some of them can be visited by public transport while others must be visited on foot, by taxi, or with a guided tour. The major tour company in town is Cajamarca Tours but there are others. They advertise in hotels or from their minibuses on the Plaza de Armas and are usually cheaper than Cajamarca Tours.

Baños del Inca

These natural hot springs are six km from Cajamarca. The water is channelled into many private cubicles, some large enough for up to half a dozen people at a time. They are available for a few cents per hour. There is no public pool.

Atahualpa was camped by these hot springs when Pizarro arrived in the area, but there is nothing to see today except for the springs themselves.

Cumbe Mayo

According to the locals, the name of this site is derived from the Quechua *kumpi mayo*, or well-made water channel. The site has some extraordinarily well engineered pre-Inca channels running for several km across the bleak mountain tops, about 23 km from Cajamarca by road. Nearby are some caves containing petroglyphs. The countryside is high, windswept and slightly eerie. Locals tell superstitious stories about the eroded rock formations in the area which look like groups of shrouded figures climbing the mountain.

The site can be reached on foot from the Cerro Santa Apolonia via a signposted road. The walk takes about four hours if you take the obvious short cuts and ask every passer-by for directions. Tours for about US$3 per person are offered in Cajamarca.

Ventanillas de Otuzco

This pre-Inca site is a necropolis, or graveyard, consisting of hundreds of funerary niches built into the hillside – hence the name *ventanillas* or windows. The site is in beautiful countryside and it is possible to walk here from either Cajamarca or from the Baños del Inca. There are also local buses. Further away are the larger Ventanillas de Combayo but these are rarely visited because the road is in bad shape.

Llacanora & Hacienda La Colpa

The picturesque little village of Llacanora is 13 km from Cajamarca. Some of the inhabitants still play the traditional *claríns* which are three-metre-long bamboo trumpets. A few km away is the Hacienda La Colpa which is usually visited on a tour combined with Llacanora (about US$2 per person). The Hacienda is a working cattle ranch and in the afternoons the cattle are herded into their stalls one by one; the ranch-hands call each cow by name. This is a locally famous tourist attraction. Perhaps these are the most intelligent cows in the world!

The Road from the Coast

The new highway to Cajamarca from the coast is paved all the way and therefore quite fast. About 46 km from the Pan-American the traveller passes through Tembladera which is named, interestingly enough, not after the tremors of earthquakes, but after the trembling and shivering of malaria victims. The disease was once common in this rice growing area. A further 41 km takes you to the mining village of Chilete, where there is a basic hotel.

On a side road 34 km north of Chilete is the village of San Pablo where there is a basic hotel and two or three buses a day to

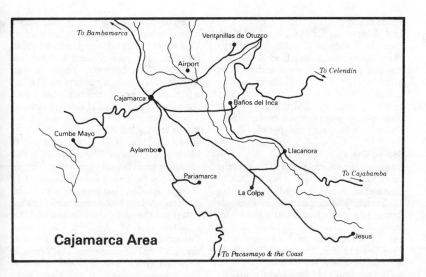

Cajamarca Area

Chilete. An hour's walk from San Pablo is the Chavín site of Kuntur Wasi where stone monoliths are to be seen. You can also walk from San Pablo to Cumbe Mayo and on to Cajamarca; the walk takes about three days and is described (in reverse) in the Bradt's book *Backpacking & Trekking in Peru & Bolivia*.

CAJABAMBA

The old route from Cajamarca to Trujillo is the 22-hour journey along the 360-km-long dirt road via Cajabamba and Huamachuco. Although this route passes through more interesting scenery and towns than the new road, the Huamachuco-Trujillo section is presently unrewarding because buses travel at night in both directions. From Cajamarca via Cajabamba to Huamachuco, however, is possible during the day. Check with the bus companies in case they've changed their schedules for daylight hours all the way.

Cajabamba is a very quiet but pleasant small town with a 19th century atmosphere. You'll see more mules than

motorcars in the streets and the whitewashed houses and red-tiled roofs give the place a colonial air. There is a cinema on the pretty Plaza de Armas. The feast of the Virgin of the Rosary is celebrated around the second week of October and there are bull fights, processions, dances and general bucolic carousing. Hotels, especially the best, tend to be full during this time.

Places to Stay

All hotels suffer from periodic water shortages and dim light bulbs. The best place to stay is the *Hostal Flores* on the Plaza de Armas next to the Banco de Crédito. There is a very small sign on the door and they charge US$1 per person. Try and get a room with a balcony onto the Plaza.

On the street behind the *Flores*, at José Sabogal 692 is a basic hotel without a sign (knock on the door) which charges 60c per person. At Grau 624 is the *Hotel Ramal* (75c per person) and the similarly priced *Hostal Bolívar* is at Ugarte 603. Both are within a block of the plaza.

Places to Eat

The *Restaurant La Peña* is a half block from the Banco de Crédito, just off the Plaza de Armas. It has loud music and passable food. Just beyond is the *El Cid* which has the brightest lights for reading and writing and serves a limited but tasty menu. A meal and a drink at either of these places will cost you under US$1. There are other, still cheaper places.

Getting There

Empresa Diaz at Balta 132 on the outskirts of town has a daily bus to Cajamarca at 5 am and Transportes Atahualpa (one block from the Plaza de Armas at Alfonso Ugarte 601) has better maintained buses leaving daily at 5.30 am for Cajamarca and continuing to Trujillo and Lima. The fare to Cajamarca is US$2.50 for the six-hour trip.

On the corner of Lloza and Caceres by the main market is Empresa Antisuyo which has a daily 5 pm bus to Huamachuco (US$1.25, 2½ hours) and Trujillo. If you want to travel to Huamachuco by day, there is usually a truck leaving from the market in the morning.

HUAMACHUCO

This village is about 50 km beyond Cajabamba and 190 km from Trujillo. There are two or three places to stay and the Plaza de Armas is impressive.

During the dry season you can find transport east to Pataz which is the starting point to mount an expedition to the little explored ruins of various cities in the jungle, including the recently discovered Gran Pajaten. This is an undertaking for explorers and archaeologists only. One ruin lies within reach of Huamachuco itself – the pre-Inca hilltop fort of Marcahuamachuco, about two to three hours away on foot.

CELENDÍN

This pleasant village is 118 km away from Cajamarca and at approximately the same elevation, yet it takes about five hours to make the journey by bus which indicates how rough and hilly the road is. There's not much to do here and most travellers are just passing through en route to Chachapoyas. There is one cinema which was inappropriately playing a film about the resurrection when I was there in October. Market day is Sunday.

Places to Stay & Eat

There are three basic hotels on the 300 block of 2 de Mayo. The *Maxmar* is the cheapest and just acceptable for 70c per person – some rooms even have private, though smelly, bathrooms with cold showers. A few cents more and slightly better are the *Hotel José Galvez* and the *Amazonas*. Best of all is the *Hostal Celendín* on the Plaza de Armas which charges US$1.25 single and US$2 double in rooms with a toilet and sink. There is hot water available in the communal shower.

The best restaurant (though nothing to get excited about) is the *Jalisco* on the Plaza de Armas.

Getting There

Transportation from Celendín to Chachapoyas is by infrequent trucks because buses are unable to negotiate the very demanding but beautiful 228-km journey between the two towns. There has been talk of two buses a week. The road drops steeply from Celendín at 2625 metres to the River Marañon at Balsas, only 46 km away but 1600 metres lower than Celendín. From Balsas, the road climbs through spectacular rain and cloud forest to emerge at the 3678 metre high point of the drive, the aptly named Abra de Barro Negro or Black Mud Pass, which gives you an idea of the road conditions.

From here the road descends to Leimebamba (2280 metres) at the head of the Utcubamba River valley and follows the river as it descends past Tingo (near the Kuelap ruins) and on to Chachapoyas at 1834 metres above sea level.

Top: Passing the Chicha & playing the Clarín, Llacanora (RR)
Bottom: Air view of east slope of Andes near Tarapoto (RR)

Top: Traveller meets Jabiru stork (RR)
Bottom: Ucayali area from the air (RR)

When trucks do leave for this journey, they often go in convoy, so you can be stuck in Celendín for several days waiting for the next convoy. One trucking company which does the 12 to 20-hour trip is Transportes Gueverra, at 2 de Mayo 211 (a private house). They usually know when the next truck is leaving. The road may be impassable during the wet season. The route to Chachapoyas from the coast at Chiclayo via Bagua is a much more frequently travelled one, although not as spectacular as the Celendín route.

Both Empresa Diaz on the Plaza de Armas and Transportes Atahualpa at 2 de Mayo 630 (one block from the plaza) have daily 6.30 am departures to Cajamarca (US$2.30, five hours). The latter company connects with and sells tickets for their 2 pm bus leaving Cajamarca for Trujillo and Lima.

CHACHAPOYAS

This quiet and pleasant little town of 18,000 inhabitants stands at 1834 metres on the eastern slopes of the Andes. It is the capital of the Department of Amazonas which, despite its name, is a mainly Andean department. It receives its name from the River Marañon which is one of Peru's two major tributaries of the Amazon and the one which reaches furthest west into the Andes. The Marañon bisects the department and forms most of its western border with the Department of Cajamarca.

The Department of Amazonas has long been difficult to reach and even today it remains one of the least visited areas of Peru. Along with the neighbouring Department of San Martín, it contains vast tracts of the little-explored cloud forest of the east slopes of the Andes. Within these highland forests are found some of Peru's most fascinating and least known archaeological ruins. The ravages of weather and time, combined with the more recent attentions of grave robbers and treasure seekers, have caused damage to many of the ruins but some have survived remarkably well and can be visited by the adventurous traveller. The best known and one of the most accessible is the magnificent ruin of Kuelap (see below. Chachapoyas provides an excellent base for visiting ruins and has been called 'the archaeological capital of Peru'.

Information

Chachapoyas is a military zone and foreign travellers are requested to register with the PIP (see city map for location). They simply check to see if your passport and tourist card are valid – it only takes a minute.

There is a small museum at the Instituto Nacional de Cultura and a Tourist Office around the corner. A useful booklet (in Spanish only) is available here; *Guia Arqueológica del Departamento de Amazonas* by Victor M Zubiate Zabarburu, (Chachapoyas, 1984). Those people seriously interested in visiting the remoter ruins can talk to the director of the Cultural Institute, Dr Carlos Torres Mas. General information on visiting the more accessible ruins is available at the Tourist Office. Practical information such as maps and letters of introduction to people living in remote regions can be obtained from Padre Pedro Rodríguez Arista, Calle Santo Domingo 643.

Useful books about the region include *Antisuyo – The Search for the Lost Cities of the Amazon* by Gene Savoy (New York, 1970). The British edition is entitled *Vilcabamba – The Lost City of the Incas* (London, 1971). This book gives his account of explorations in the region during the 1960s. Most professional archaeologists pooh-pooh his rather unscientific account but it makes entertaining and informative reading. A more text-book approach can be read in the well illustrated *The Peoples & Cultures of Ancient Peru* by L G Lumbreras, translated by B J Meggers (Smithsonian Institution Press, 1974).

A visit to the ruins of Kuelap is definitely the most rewarding and representative of the possible trips to ruins in the area. Travellers or archaeologists who want to visit one of the scores of other sites in the Chachapoyas area should look for further information in Chachapoyas. Most trips will require at least sleeping bags and sometimes tents and food as well. One good centre for exploration is Levanto, a small village about three hours away on foot.

It is not easy to change money in Chachapoyas and so you should change as much as you need before getting here. There is a reasonably well-stocked market and several general stores and most basic supplies can be obtained here. Specialised foods, camera gear and film, sun tan lotion, etc is best brought with you.

Chachapoyas is a quiet and friendly town. The traditional evening pastime of socialising and strolling around the Plaza de Armas is a favourite way of relaxing. There is also one cinema.

Places to Stay & Eat

Chachapoyas suffers from water shortages and all three of its hotels had no water when I was last there. Buckets of water were available for washing. The new *Hostal Johumaji* costs about US$1 per person in small clean rooms with good light and a private bath (but no water!) Also good is the similarly priced but older *Hostal Marañon* – they have cheaper rooms without private bath as well. Also cheap is the *Hotel Amazonas* on the main square. Some rooms have a view over the plaza.

My favourite restaurant is the *Kuelap* which is cheap, friendly, and has a fairly good selection of dishes – but arrive before 8 pm as they start running out of food by then. For a change you can try the *Chacha* which is more expensive although it's hardly any better. There are other places.

Getting There

There are two routes from the coast. The one through Cajamarca and Celendín is

more difficult but also more spectacular – it is described in the Celendín section earlier in this chapter. The more frequently travelled route is from Chiclayo via Bagua and takes about 20 hours. This is described below.

The route follows the Pan-American Highway north for 100 km as far as Olmos. Here a rough unpaved road heads east into the Andes and climbs over the Porculla Pass which, at 2145 metres, is the lowest pass which crosses the Andes in Peru. The road then drops to the Marañon River valley. Jaén is reached about 190 km from the Pan-American turn-off; there are a couple of basic hotels and restaurants, but it is a few km off the main road so not all buses go there. From Jaén there is a northbound road to San Ignacio near the Ecuadorian border, about 100 km away. Because of the 1942 border dispute, it is not possible to enter Ecuador and there is no transportation.

About 50 km beyond the Jaén turn-off is the village of Bagua. The bus usually goes through Bagua Grande, which is on the main road. Bagua, at 522 metres, is in the Marañon valley and can claim to be Peru's most westerly jungle town. There is basic accommodation and from here a long and difficult trip can be made by road and river to Iquitos (see the chapter on the jungle). Pick-up trucks and buses make the journey from Bagua to Moyobamba. The road climbs and follows the Utcubamba River valley for about 70 km as far as the crossroads town of Pedro Ruiz, which is not marked on most maps. From here, a southbound road branches down to Chachapoyas, 54 km away.

Air A new airport has been built and service began in 1985 with AeroPeru. They have an office on the Plaza de Armas but I expect them to change both their office location and air schedule before long – that's what tends to happen with new services. There was one flight a week to and from Lima (US$44) via

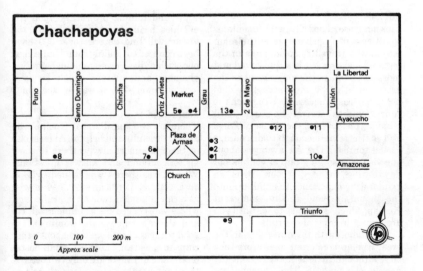

Chachapoyas

1. Hotel Amazonas
2. Olano Buses
3. Chacha Restaurant
4. Aero Peru
5. Cine Central
6. Instituto Naciónal de Cultura
7. Tourist Office
8. PIP
9. ENTEL
10. Post Office
11. Hostal Marañon
12. Hostal Johumaji
13. Restaurant Kuelap

Chiclayo (US$25). There was an attempt to start a service to Rioja but it has been suspended. Maybe AeroPeru will start it again.

Buses Olano is the main bus company and they have daily (except Sunday) departures via Bagua for Chiclayo at 10 am (20 hours, US$8).

Small minibuses and pick-up trucks leave the Plaza de Armas for various destinations. About three a day go to Tingo (1½ hours, US$1) and on to Leimebamba (three hours, US$1.50). They usually leave between 8 am and 1 pm. This is the service for Kuelap. A couple of times a week there are truck departures going through Leimebamba and on to Celendín – ask around.

To continue further down the eastern slopes of the Andes into the Amazon basin, you must first take a bus to the cross roads at Pedro Ruiz (US$1, 1½ hours). The first departure of the day is usually with the Olano bus to Chiclayo and they'll drop you off at Pedro Ruiz if they aren't full of passengers travelling further. After the Olano bus leaves, there are usually two or three minibuses which will make the journey. There are no direct buses from Chachapoyas to Moyobamba at the time of writing and so you have to wait in Pedro Ruiz to continue eastwards.

Other local destinations are served by pick-up trucks from the Plaza de Armas or from the market. It's a matter of asking around. The tourist office can help.

KUELAP

This immense ruined city in the mountains south-east of Chachapoyas is the main reason why travellers spend time in the region. Kuelap is the best preserved and most accessible of the major ruins in the area – note that by 'most accessible' I do not mean 'easily accessible'. To reach the ruins requires several hours of hard climbing on foot from the village of Tingo and so it is remote enough to discourage casual tourists. The site averages about one visitor or small group of visitors per day during the dry season. It is an exhilarating experience to climb up into the mountains and finally emerge at Kuelap, which is not easy to see until you are almost in front of the ruins.

In common with the other sites in the area, Kuelap is referred to as a pre-Inca city, although little is known about the people who built it. The Chachapoyas area was the centre of a highland people known variously as the Chachapoyans or the Sachupoyans – they were incorporated into the Inca Empire by the Inca Huayna Capac in the late 1400s. They left massive walled cities and fortresses on many of the mountain tops of the area. The stonework of these sites is somewhat rougher looking than Inca stonework but it is embellished with patterns and designs which are missing from the Inca work.

Kuelap is located at about 3100 metres above sea level on a ridge high above the left bank of the River Utcubamba. It is an oval-shaped city about 600 metres long and entirely surrounded by a massive defensive wall about six to eight metres high. There are three entrances piercing this wall. The principal entrance, which is the one used today to gain access to the site, leads into an impressive bottle-shaped and high-walled passageway. This is a highly defensible entrance; it would have been well-nigh impossible for attackers to run the narrow gauntlet of the high entrance walls without being repulsed by defenders perched on the walls and raining projectiles upon the enemies' heads. Once inside the site, the visitor will find dozens (over 300 have been counted) of mainly round buildings, one of which has a mysterious underground chamber and another which forms a lookout tower. The views are excellent.

Information

There are two guardians at Kuelap who are very friendly and helpful. At least one of them is almost always there to show visitors around and answer questions. When I was there I was helped by Don José Gabriel Portocarrero Chávez who gave me a guided tour of the ruins and whose wife cooked me a simple meal. He and the other guardian, Domingo, are good sources of information about other ruins in the area. There is a small hostal on the site but there are only two beds. If there are more than two of you there's no problem about sleeping on the floor. The two beds have blankets but it's worth bringing your sleeping bag if there are more than two of you. Camping is also possible if you have a tent. You should carry or purify water although soft drinks are sometimes for sale. Only very basic food is available so bringing your own isn't a bad idea.

Entrance to the site is about 20c and use of the hostal is about 40c. A small tip or present for the guardians is appreciated – flashlight batteries, a magazine or newspaper, chocolate or canned food goodies are all good gifts.

Getting There

There are several vehicles a day from Chachapoyas to Tingo. In Tingo there is a Guardia Civil post at the entrance to town. They will be happy to point out the path to you. There are a couple of very basic hotels and restaurants. Mules can be hired to take you or your gear up to the ruins, but most people walk.

The trail climbs from the south end of Tingo at 1900 metres to the ruins about 1200 metres higher. There are some signposts on the way and it is not very difficult to follow the trail, the main difficulty is the steepness of the climb. About five hours are needed to climb to Kuelap and so it's best to spend the night there. If you leave Chachapoyas in the morning, it's straightforward to reach the ruins by mid-afternoon.

PEDRO RUIZ

This is the small village at the junction of the Chachapoyas road with the Bagua-Moyobamba road. You have to wait here for vehicles to Rioja/Moyobamba if travelling from Chachapoyas. The earliest vehicle to Pedro Ruiz does not leave Chachapoyas until 10 am and so it's almost 12 noon before you get to the junction. It's a good idea to spend the night at Pedro Ruiz before continuing the rough journey eastward. There is the cheap, basic, but adequate *Hostal & Restaurant El Marginal* which is within a few metres of the junction.

From Pedro Ruiz very crowded and uncomfortable pick-up trucks go to Rioja every one or two hours throughout the day. These vehicles come from Bagua and are often full to overflowing when they arrive (I counted 33 people in the back of the Datsun pick-up I rode on). They claim the journey takes six hours but it's often more like nine or longer in the wet season when landslides can close the road. The fare is about US$3. Large trucks do the journey in about 15 hours. If you are very lucky, you might get on to one of the daily buses plying this route from the coast but they are often full. Ask the locals what time the buses are expected to come through.

The journey eastwards from Pedro Ruiz is spectacular as the road climbs over two major passes and drops into fantastic high jungle vegetation in between. It's definitely worth travelling this section in daylight, though it may be difficult to appreciate the landscape because of the very rough road and overcrowded, uncomfortable conditions.

About two hours east of Pedro Ruiz is the Laguna Pomacocha where a government-run *Hotel de Turistas* has recently opened. Rooms are about US$6/10 for singles/doubles and this is the only place with facilities to break the journey until Nueva Cajamarca, about five hours (minimum) beyond Pedro Ruiz.

Nueva Cajamarca is a brand new town built in the 1970s and inhabited by colonists from the highlands. There are two basic hotels, the *Peru* and the *Carrazon*, both of which charge under a dollar per person. From Nueva Cajamarca pick-up trucks and minibuses leave frequently for Rioja on the improved road. The fare is about 50c for the one-hour trip.

RIOJA

Rioja is the first town of importance on the road heading inland from the Pan-American Highway across the Andes. It is a small but busy and friendly town. Nearby is the airport which serves both Rioja and nearby Moyobamba, the capital of the Department of San Martín.

Places to Stay

There are two or three basic hotels along Avenida Grau of which the *Hostal San Martín* at Grau 540, about a block from the Plaza de Armas, is reasonable for about US$1 per person.

Getting There

Air AeroPeru and Faucett each have two flights per week to and from Lima (US$45) via Chiclayo (US$27). AeroPeru attempted to run a service to Chachapoyas but it has been suspended because of lack of passengers. Taxis to the airport can be found from the Plaza de Armas.

Buses Pick-up trucks leave from the corner of the Plaza de Armas for Pedro Ruiz and Bagua. Both pick-up trucks and plenty of minibuses leave from the plaza for Moyobamba (50c, 45 minutes) and Tarapoto (US$4, four to six hours).

MOYOBAMBA

From Rioja at 1400 metres there is a good road down to Moyobamba at 860 metres. This small town is the capital of the Department of San Martín. The town was the first to be founded in the Peruvian eastern lowlands, soon after the conquest. There isn't a great deal to see but it is a quiet and pleasant town nonetheless. Despite its capital status, Moyobamba doesn't have proper foreign exchange facilities and travellers should try and change money on the coast before getting here.

Museum

The Instituto Nacional de Cultura has a small office with an even smaller display of local stuffed animals, many of which are stuffed frogs in little costumes. Photographs are allowed if you have strange tastes.

Hot Springs

The local hot springs are about an hour's walk from town near Alto Mayo. A taxi will cost about a dollar. Alto Mayo is out along the Rioja road – almost anyone can give you directions to the Baños Termales. There are both hot and cold swimming pools.

Places to Stay & Eat

There are several cheap and basic places to stay. Try the *Hostal Monterrey* on the main plaza, which charges 70c per person and has a few rooms with private bath. The basic *Mesia*, *Los Andes* and *Weninger* cost 60c and have cold water in the communal showers.

A bit more expensive and good value is the clean *Hostal Cobos* which charges US$1.25/2.25 for singles/doubles with private bath (cold shower) and less with communal bath. They'll help you arrange transport to the nearby hot springs. The

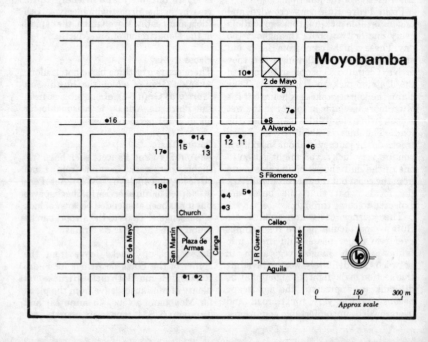

Moyobamba

Hostal Inca is a clean and relatively modern downtown hotel and the *Albricias* has a garden and is a few blocks from downtown. Both are good and cost US$2/3.50 for singles/doubles with private bath and cold water.

The best hotel in Moyobamba is the government-run *Hotel de Turistas* which can be reserved in Lima by telephoning ENTURPERU at 721928. The hotel is about two km out of town on Calle Sucre (take a taxi) and rates are about US$6/9 including continental breakfast.

There are plenty of restaurants, all inexpensive. My recommendation is the *Restaurant Moscu*.

Entertainment
Nightlife is limited to a couple of cinemas and the *La Tapala* bar which occasionally has music.

Getting There
Air There are both Faucett and AeroPeru offices in Moyobamba but all flights leave from or arrive in Rioja. You can get taxis to the hot springs and direct to Rioja airport.

1	Hostal Monterrey
2	Cine Viena
3	Bar/Peña La Tapala
4	Hostal Cobos
5	Pensión Weninger
6	Instituto Naciónal de Cultura
7	ENTEL
8	Faucett
9	Cine Verde
10	Bus stop
11	Hostal Mesia
12	Hostal Los Andes
13	Taxi (Colectivo) stand
14	Hostal Inca
15	Banco de la Nación
16	Hostal Albricias
17	Restaurant Moscu
18	Aero Peru

Buses & Colectivos To go to Rioja or Tarapoto go to the taxi-rank marked on the city map – colectivo cars leave as soon as they have five passengers. (Rioja – 60c, 45 minutes; Tarapoto – US$4.30, 3½ hours.) Slightly cheaper minibuses leave from the bus stand on J R Guerra but take a long time to fill up and go only to Rioja unless a group of passengers want to go elsewhere. For cheaper transport to Tarapoto, hang out by the taxi rank until a minibus or pick-up truck comes by with the driver yelling 'Tarapoto!'.

TARAPOTO
From Moyobamba the road drops still further down the Mayo River valley to Tarapoto on the very edge of the eastern Andean foothills at 356 metres above sea level. It is a 116-km journey but the road is one of the best in the department. Tarapoto is the largest and busiest town in the Department of San Martín and is the centre for the expanding agricultural colonisation of the lowlands of the northern part of the department. It has the best accommodation and air services in the region but it is also the most expensive of the towns here.

Information
Money Exchange This is one of the few towns in the region where money exchange is usually possible although the rates are not very favourable. It is said that this is because Tarapoto is on the fringe of the drug growing and smuggling area which is a major industry to the south along the Huallaga river valley. Be that as it may, you can try both the Banco de Crédito and the Sanchez Money Exchange for changing cash dollars (travellers' cheques with persuasion) but expect to receive almost 20% lower than Lima or Iquitos.

Things to Do
There's not much to do in Tarapoto itself apart from hang out in the Plaza de Armas, swim at the Hotel de Turistas pool, or go to the cinema.

The nearby village of Lamas is worth a day trip. It is an interesting Indian village with an early morning market, a small museum, and a reasonable restaurant. It is well off the normal tourist circuit and there are no hotels.

Places to Stay - bottom end

The best of the cheap hotels is the *Hostal Juan Alfonso* which charges US$1.30/2 for basic singles/doubles with communal cold showers and an extra 30c for rooms with private showers. Other basic hotels charging the same in rooms with communal showers are the acceptable *El Dorado, Melendez, Las Palmeras* and *Gran*. Cheapest of all is the very basic *Hostal Pasquelandia*. Many of the cheaper hotels have water available at only certain times of day so enquire about this if you're desperate for a shower.

The *Hostal Viluz* is new and clean and charges US$2/3.50 for rooms with private showers. Similarly priced is the older but centrally located *Hostal America* which provides towels, toilet paper, soap and a fan in all its rooms – very civilised. The *Hotel Tarapoto* is a little more expensive but also good.

Several hotels charge US$2.75/4.75 for singles/doubles with private bath. Of these, the *Hostal Miami* is good and clean and the *Edinson* is also recommended. The similarly priced *Hostal San Martín* will give you a discount if you stay for a few days and finally the *Hotel Misti* charges the same but doesn't look as good.

Places to Stay - middle

The best hotel near the centre is the *Acosta* which has comfortable rooms for US$4.75/6. Most expensive is the government-run *Hotel de Turistas* with singles/doubles for US$8/12 including continental breakfast. Reservations can be made in Lima by telephoning ENTURPERU at 721928 or in Tarapoto by telephoning 2225. The hotel is almost two km out of town on Jirón Pablo Cruz. There is a

swimming pool which is free for hotel residents and open to others for a small fee.

Places to Eat

The best of the cheaper restaurants is the *La Cajamarquina*. Slightly more expensive is the good *La Mesón* on the Plaza de Armas. Also on the plaza is the *La Terraza* which is a pleasant place for a snack or cold drink. There are plenty of other places to choose from.

Getting There

Air The airport is two or three km out of town and there are no buses. A taxi will cost about US$1. Tarapoto airport is a busy one. Both AeroPeru and Faucett have flights but they are often booked well in advance. Both airlines have offices downtown. In addition, smaller airlines have offices at the airport and have frequent flights in light aircraft to several jungle destinations.

Between them, AeroPeru and Faucett provide one or two flights a day to Lima (US$37.50). There is a flight to Iquitos (US$32) every day except Sunday. AeroPeru has two flights a week to Trujillo (US$29) and Chiclayo (US$35). Faucett has two flights a week to Yurimaguas (US$12) and Pucallpa (US$21).

AeroTaxi Iberico has an office at the airport. They fly light aircraft to Yurimaguas (US$14), Juanjui (US$17), and Tocache (US$24). These are good alternatives to the difficult journeys by road but remember that there isn't much room for baggage. You may have to pay for an extra seat if you're lugging a huge backpack around. AeroTaxi Iberico doesn't take reservations – just go to the airport in the morning and they'll leave as soon as the plane is full. Most of their planes have five passenger seats and so it doesn't take long for them to fill up. Flights start about 9 am and continue all day – it's a great way to see some of the jungle from the air. I flew from Tarapoto to Tocache and the

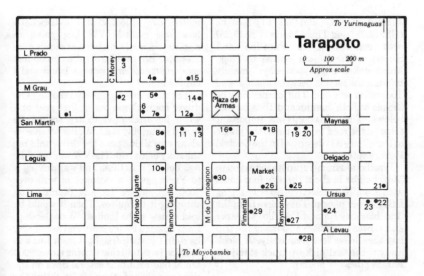

1	Post Office
2	Hostal Acosta
3	Hostal Misti
4	Hotel Tarapoto
5	Hostal Las Palmeras
6	Sanchez Money Exchange
7	La Cajamarquina Restaurant
8	Comité 1 Colectivos
9	ENTEL
10	Transport to Lamas
11	Aero Peru
12	Hostal America
13	Cine Central
14	La Terraza Café
15	Hotel Gran
16	Restaurant La Mesón
17	Hotel Edinson
18	Banco de Crédito
19	León de Huánuco Buses
20	Faucett
21	Trucks to Yurimaguas
22	Hostal Melendez
23	Hostal El Dorado
24	Ministerio de Turismo
25	Hostal Juan Alfonso
26	Hostal Miami
27	Minibus to Juanjui
28	Hostal Viluz
29	Hostal Pasquelandia
30	Hostal San Martín

pilot pointed out what he claimed were clandestine airstrips used by drug runners.

In addition, you can charter an aeroplane to other jungle destinations. You have to pay for all five passenger seats but that's no problem if you can get a group together.

If you end up having to spend a few hours at the airport, there is an inexpensive snack bar selling sandwiches and ice-cold beers.

Buses Tarapoto is an important junction with roads heading west to Moyobamba, south to Juanjui, and north into the Amazon basin at Yurimaguas – in descending order of the quality of the road.

The 145-km southbound journey via Bellavista to Juanjui takes five to eight hours in colectivo taxis (US$5.50) and minibuses (US$5) leaving from the corner of Raymondi and Levau. Vehicles supposedly leave throughout the day as soon as they are full but it's advised that you go in the morning. León de Huánuco buses leave at 9 am on Tuesdays and Fridays to

Juanjui (US$4) and on to Tocache (US$12.75) and Tingo María (US$13.25) with connections to Pucallpa and Huánuco. The 485-km journey to Tingo María takes about two days, mainly because the section between Juanjui and Tocache is very bad. The journey may be broken at both Juanjui and Tocache (see below). Tingo María is an important town on the road from Lima to the jungle at Pucallpa – it is described in the Central Peru chapter.

Westbound from Tarapoto takes you to Moyobamba in about three to four hours with Comité 1 colectivo taxis charging US$4.30 per person. They leave from the first block of Ramon Castillo. Cheaper and slower minibuses also make the trip but they leave less frequently. A block away is the taxi/pick-up truck stand for Lamas (75c, 1½ hours).

THE ROAD TO YURIMAGUAS

The 130-km road which climbs over the final foothills of the Andes, emerges onto the Amazonian plains, and continues on to Yurimaguas, is both one of the most beautiful and one of the worst roads in the area; it is almost impassable during the rainy season. There is no regular bus; pick-up trucks and other vehicles leave almost every morning (if the road is open) from the end of Jirón Ursua. The journey costs about US$5, takes from seven to 14 hours (perhaps averaging less than 10 km per hour!) and is usually very crowded and uncomfortable. There are no set departure times and vehicles usually leave anywhere between 4 and 10 am. If you're lucky you might get the front seat of a jeep – if not it might be standing room only in the back of a truck.

I had a memorable trip from Tarapoto to Yurimaguas. I was waiting at the usual departure point when a man asked me if I wanted a ride to Yurimaguas. I looked around but couldn't see any trucks or jeeps and so I asked him 'When?'. He told me that he was ready to go right away and pointed at a new VW bug standing a few

metres away. I looked at it in disbelief – how was a little VW bug going to negotiate a road which buses didn't dare attempt? But the idea of riding in comfort soon overcame any worries I had and I climbed in.

The road was absolutely terrible. The driver couldn't get out of first gear and when he attempted to try second he would invariably stall. Whilst we moved along at walking pace the driver told me the story of his trip. The VW was new – he had bought it in Lima and was driving it to Yurimaguas, a distance of well over 2000 km, where he was planning on shipping it to Iquitos. Then it would be sold as new at the Iquitos VW dealership. I was amazed by the story and asked why he didn't just air freight it from Lima to Iquitos. I was told that driving it over 2000 km of bad road plus several days on the river was cheaper than air freighting the car.

Finally, we managed to get over the last pass and were on the flat final 60 km stretch to Yurimaguas. The driver became very confident and we even managed to get into third gear. There were a few puddles in the road but we just splashed through them while the driver happily began telling me that the worst part was over and that we were as good as there. Unfortunately, one of the puddles turned out to be extremely deep and as the driver was blithely telling me how close we were to Yurimaguas the vehicle sank almost up to its windows and the engine stopped. Despondently, the driver opened the door to see how bad the situation was and a foot high wall of water came gushing into the car.

So much for delivering a new car to the Iquitos dealership! We tried pushing it out but to no avail – we were well and truly stuck. After about two hours a large truck came along (which gives you an idea of the frequency of traffic along this road) and pulled the car out. Another two hours were spent drying the starter and engine and finally we managed to get the car started and limped into Yurimaguas. Here, the driver dried out and cleaned up the car as best he could before arranging river transportation to Iquitos. I guess the moral of that story is 'Don't buy a new car in Iquitos'.

For more information about Yurimaguas and river travel into the Amazon Basin, see the chapter on the jungle.

TOCACHE

The Tocache area is one of the most expensive in Peru and the story circulates that everything is priced in dollars. It is near here that much of Peru's clandestine coca and marijuana crops are produced. Tocache is a new but growing town on the verdant and fertile Huallaga River. From here there is a fairly good road south to Tingo María and a terrible road north to Juanjui and Tarapoto. Unless you actually like gruelling bus trips, you might want to fly if you're heading to or from Tarapoto.

Places to Stay

There are four basic hotels and none of them are up to much. The showers don't always work. Despite this they are often full. The hotels are the patriotic sounding *Bolívar, Sucre* and *San Martín* and also the *Comercio*. Try and get into town early or you'll end up sleeping on the floor of the lobby of one of the hotels. They all charge about US$2 per person.

Getting There

Air The airport is about a km from town. AeroTaxi Iberico has flights to Juanjui or Tarapoto every day. Their office is at the airport and you just show up and wait for a plane. If you can't get to Tarapoto, there are basic hotels in Juanjui and frequent minibuses from there to Tarapoto, about five to eight hours away.

Buses & Colectivos Comité 1 on the main plaza has buses and cars to Tingo María (US$6.30, five hours). There are a couple of buses a week to Tarapoto with León de Huánuco. These take almost two days and are often full with passengers from Tingo María – it is better to fly.

The Amazon Basin

About half of Peru is in the Amazon Basin, yet it merits only one chapter in this book. Why is this? The answer is 'inaccessibility'. Few roads penetrate the rain forest of the Amazon Basin and therefore few towns of any size have been built. Those that do exist started as river ports and were connected with towns further down river, usually in Brazil or perhaps Bolivia. Only a few decades ago, the traveller from Peru's major jungle port of Iquitos had to travel down thousands of km of Amazon River to the Atlantic and then go either south around Cape Horn or north through the Panama Canal to reach Lima – a journey of several months. With the advent of roads and airports, these jungle areas have slowly become a more important part of Peru. Nevertheless, they still only contain about five percent of the nation's population.

There are five main jungle areas accessible to the traveller. Starting in the south-east, near the Bolivian border, is Puerto Maldonado which lies at the junction of the Tambopata and Madre de Dios rivers. Puerto Maldonado is most easily reached by daily flights from Cuzco or by an uncomfortable two-day journey by truck on an atrociously bad dirt road.

In central Peru, almost due east of Lima, is the area known as Chanchamayo which consists of the two small towns of San Ramón and La Merced, both easily accessible by road from Lima. There are several other villages in the area.

A new jungle road has almost been completed from La Merced as far north as Pucallpa, the capital of the Department of Ucayali and the third region described in this section. Because Pucallpa is a major port connected with Lima by daily flights or by a 24-hour bus journey, this region is one of the easiest to reach for the traveller wanting to get a quick glimpse of the Peruvian jungle.

Further north is the small port of Yurimaguas, reached by the difficult road journey described in Across the Northern Highlands or by flights from Lima.

Finally, Peru's major jungle port is Iquitos, reached by river boats from Pucallpa and Yurimaguas or by air from several cities including Lima. It is impossible to reach Iquitos by road.

PUERTO MALDONADO

Founded at the turn of the century, Puerto Maldonado has been important as a rubber boom town, a logging centre and more recently as a centre for gold and oil prospectors. It is also important for jungle crops such as Brazil nuts and coffee. Because of the logging industry, the jungle around Puerto Maldonado has been almost totally cleared – there is some ranching.

The various commercial enterprises centred on Puerto Maldonado have made it the most important port and capital of the Department of Madre de Dios. It is an unlovely fast-growing town with a busy frontier feel. It is interesting to experience this boom town atmosphere but otherwise there isn't much to see. Puerto Maldonado can be used as a starting point for trips into the jungle. The best of these are to the nearby jungle lodges. It is also possible to continue into the Brazilian or Bolivian jungle or to Manu National Park, but these trips aren't straightforward.

Information

Immigration If you're leaving Peru via Iñapari (for Brazil) or Puerto Heath (for Bolivia) you should first check with immigration officials in Puerto Maldonado or Cuzco because recently exit stamps were not obtainable at the borders. In Puerto Maldonado, *Migraciones* is found in the riverside complex opposite the Hotel Moderno. If flying from Cuzco to Iñapari, check Migraciones in Cuzco. There is no Bolivian or Brazilian consul in Puerto Maldonado.

Money Exchange The Banco de Crédito will change cash dollars at the unfavourable official rate; 20% more can be obtained in Cuzco at the favourable financial rate. There are no casas de cambio but the lawyer at Velarde 140 will sometimes give you a better rate for cash dollars if he has intis available. You might be able to get rid of Brazilian cruzeiros in the Banco de Crédito but changing any travellers' cheques or Bolivian pesos is difficult.

Motorcycles Motorcycles can be rented to see some of the surrounding countryside but it's best to go in pairs in case of breakdowns. One place which has rental motorcycles is marked on the map. They charge about US$1.50 per hour and the machines are mainly small 100 cc bikes. Bargain for all day discounts.

Other There are two cinemas which have shows irregularly; one Saturday night when I was there neither had a film playing, but you might get lucky. There are many pool halls but not much else to do. Personal items such as film, soap and batteries are expensive so buy them before you arrive.

Places to Stay - bottom end
There are about 10 hotels in town but they tend to start filling up by late morning and single rooms, especially in the cheaper hotels, may be hard to find. There are several cheap hotels which provide your basic four walls, a bed and a cold communal shower. Of these, the *Moderno* for US$1/1.50 singles/doubles is a good choice; it is quiet, clean and they have many rooms. The similarly priced

Oriental is a typical, basic Amazonian hotel with a tin roof and rough wooden walls painted an unappealing green. Despite its unprepossessing appearance it's OK in a pinch. Other cheapies to try are the *Mary* or the *Chavez*, neither of which is up to much. For US$1.30/2.30 singles/doubles, there are the *Hotel Tambo de Oro* and the *Central*.

For a better room with a private cold shower and fan you can try the new *Hotel Rey Port* for US$2.30/3.30 singles/doubles. The *Hotel Wilson* has long had a reputation for being the best run, downtown hotel. It has clean rooms with communal showers for US$1.30 per person and rooms with private cold shower and fan for US$2.80/4.30. They have a basic cafeteria and pool room on the premises.

Places to Stay - top end
About a km south-west of downtown, pleasantly located above the banks of the Río Tambopata, is the government-run *Hotel de Turistas* which charges US$7.50/11.50 singles/doubles in clean rooms with private cold showers and fans. There is a restaurant which opens on demand.

Places to Stay - jungle lodges
There are two jungle lodges both of which are reached only by boat. Reservations should be made in Cuzco or Lima as there are no offices in Puerto Maldonado.

The *Cuzco Amazonico Lodge* is more expensive, more comfortable and easier to reach. It is located on the Madre de Dios river about 15 km or 45 minutes from Puerto Maldonado. The *Explorer's Inn* is a little cheaper but less comfortable, and it takes three hours by boat to reach the lodge, 70 km from Puerto Maldonado on the Tambopata river. There is a better chance of seeing more wildlife at the *Explorer's Inn* as this lodge is in the Tambopata Wildlife Reserve which holds the world record for bird species sighted in one area (over 500 species) and other

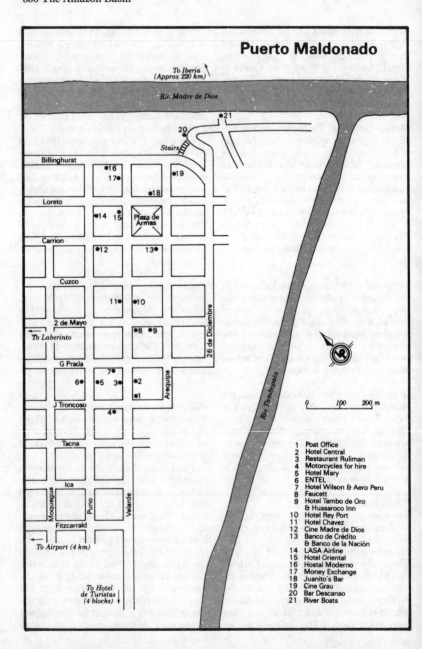

Puerto Maldonado

To Iberia (Approx 220 km)

Río Madre de Dios

Stairs

Billinghurst

16
17

19

18

Loreto

14 15

Plaza de Armas

Carrion

12

13

Cuzco

11 10

2 de Mayo

To Laberinto

8 9

26 de Diciembre

G Prada

7

6 5 3

2

Arequipa

J Troncoso

1

4

Tacna

Ica

Moquegua Puno

Velarde

Fitzcarrald

To Airport (4 km)

To Hotel de Turistas (4 blocks)

Río Tambopata

0   100   200 m

1 Post Office
2 Hotel Central
3 Restaurant Ruliman
4 Motorcycles for hire
5 Hotel Mary
6 ENTEL
7 Hotel Wilson & Aero Peru
8 Faucett
9 Hotel Tambo de Oro
   & Huasaroco Inn
10 Hotel Rey Port
11 Hotel Chavez
12 Cine Madre de Dios
13 Banco de Crédito
   & Banco de la Nación
14 LASA Airline
15 Hotel Oriental
16 Hostal Moderno
17 Money Exchange
18 Juanito's Bar
19 Cine Grau
20 Bar Descanso
21 River Boats

similar records for plants and animals including over 1000 butterflies. Naturalists are on hand to identify and explain the wildlife.

It's difficult to give exact prices as they tend to vary with the season and whether you book from the Cuzco office or from abroad. It's usually cheapest to book in Cuzco or Lima. Prices start at about US$30 per person a day, including meals and boat transfer from Puerto Maldonado. Check to find out what other boat trips or tours are included.

Reservations for the *Cuzco Amazonico Lodge* can be made at Andalucia 174, Lima (tel 462793) or Procuradores 48, Cuzco (tel 232161).

Reservations for the *Explorer's Inn* can be made at Garcilazo de la Vega 1334, Lima.

Places to Eat

There are no fancy restaurants in Puerto Maldonado and most of them are fairly basic. My favourite is *Rulman's* which is clean and has fruit juices and a good selection of food for a dollar or less per plate. It's the most reliable in Puerto Maldonado – other restaurants are often out of everything, except chicken, or they serve only beer. A recently opened restaurant/bar that you can also try is the *Huasaroco Inn* next to the Hotel Tambo de Oro. It's a bit more expensive and has a more limited menu than Rulman's but the food is good and they show English language videos on TV. It seems to be a hangout out for Puerto Maldonado's 'in' set.

It gets very hot and so you need to keep your liquid intake high. Two bars which I like are the *Descanso* and the *Juanito*. The first is a very basic, rickety old wooden bar whose sole charm is that it gives the best vantage for watching the Madre de Dios river flow by – as good a way as any of spending an afternoon when the temperature hits 38°C (100°F). They only serve cold beer or soft drinks. It gets a bit rowdy as the sun goes down and the

empty beer bottles pile up. *Juanito's* is a quiet and clean place on the Plaza de Armas where you can get a cold beer or coke and sometimes a meal.

Madre de Dios Ferry

A cheap way of seeing a little of this major Peruvian jungle river is to cross it. Even the most impecunious traveller can afford this trip – it costs about 15c each way. The crossing takes about five minutes and peki-pekis leave from the dock several times an hour. The Madre de Dios is about 500 metres wide at this point and on the other side you can continue by motorcycle or on foot.

GOING TO BRAZIL

There is a track open to Iñapari on the Brazilian border but it is in very bad shape and I don't know of any vehicles taking this route. It is possible to get through on a motorcycle if you just happen to be travelling on one. You can reach the Iñapari road by crossing the Madre de Dios on the ferry. There are a few small settlements of people involved in the Brazil Nut industry. The road is merely bad for the first 100 km and absolutely terrible after that. Iberia is reached after some 200 km and there is a basic hotel here. People in Puerto Maldonado told me that Iberia can be reached in one long day by motorcycle and I've read newspaper reports that a vehicle reached there in 1982.

To go onto Iñapari it's another 70 km by motorcycle or on foot. Few, if any, vehicles have done this section. The story here is 'Watch for snakes' which is a typical response to any question you have about travelling off-the-beaten-track anywhere in the Amazon basin.

From Iñapari it is possible to cross the Río Acre to Assis in Brazil but I've heard that the river must be waded. At Assis there is a basic hotel and a dry season road which connects to Brasiléia and Río Branco but there is no regular transportation. Travel along the Río Acre is possible. There is no immigration in Iñapari and you should see the police instead. (More information on Brazilian visa and entry requirements can be found in the Iquitos section.) Let me know if you travel this way – it'll be worth a free LP book. And good luck!

You can also fly to Iberia or Iñapari.

Getting There

Most people fly from Cuzco which is cheap and convenient. The road or river trips are only for adventurous travellers prepared to put up with both delay and discomfort.

Air The airport is about 4 km out of town. A colectivo costs about 70c and leaves from the airport after plane arrivals and from near the AeroPeru or Faucett offices before departures. Taxis are about US$2.

There are daily scheduled flights every morning to and from Lima via Cuzco with either AeroPeru or Faucett but these may get cancelled because of rain so allow some flexibility in your schedule. Cuzco flights cost about US$21 and Lima flights about US$57.

Grupo 8 (the military airline) has one flight a week to Iberia on Thursdays and they fly to Iñapari occasionally. Flights are subject to delay, cancellation or overbooking. It is a seven-km walk from the Iñapari airstrip to the village. Grupo 8 can be contacted at either Cuzco or Puerto Maldonado airport. If you want to fly you have to get to the airport early on the day of the flight and be persistent. Cost is about US$13 to Iberia. Grupo 8 also has a flight to Lima most weeks but it's not much cheaper than the daily commercial flight.

LASA has an office downtown and you can charter light aircraft to anywhere but you have to pay for five seats and the return trip. The office is often closed but you can try at the airport in the mornings.

Trucks Trucks to Cuzco during the dry season leave from outside the *Hotel Wilson*. The drivers sometimes stay at this hotel. Although it's only about 500 km, the trip takes three days depending on road and weather conditions, which gives an idea of how rough the road is. A Peruvian road engineer who I met in Chiclayo told me that this was undoubtedly Peru's worst road to link two major towns. The journey costs roughly US$10, though for a few dollars more you can talk the driver into letting you ride in the cab if you don't want to stand up in the back.

River Boat If you're heading to one of the lodges your boat trip should be provided.

You can hire boats at the Madre de Dios ferry dock. A pleasant jungle lake, Lago Sandoval, is about 1½ hours away down the Madre de Dios. Half the trip is by boat and the other half on foot. Bring your own food and water. A boat will drop you at the beginning of the trail and pick you up later for about US$15 and several people can go for this price. The boatman will also guide you to the lake if you wish. There are possibilities of seeing cayman, turtles, exotic birds and perhaps other wildlife if you are lucky. You can arrange various other trips to local lakes, beaches and islands.

A boat to the Bolivian border at Puerto Pardo costs US$80 for the half-day trip, and will take several people. With luck you may find a cheaper ride on a boat that's going there anyway. You can continue down the river to Puerto Heath in Bolivia, but this is difficult to arrange and isn't cheap. It's best to travel in a group to share costs. Basic food and accommodation (bring a hammock or sleeping pad) can be found. From Puerto Heath you can continue as far as Riberalto in northern Bolivia, where road and air connections can be made.

Just before the border is Lago Valencia which is reportedly a good trip for fishermen.

Getting to Puerto Maldonado by boat is rarely accomplished these days.

LABERINTO

There is a regular bus service from Puerto Maldonado to the nearby gold rush town of Laberinto (US$1.30, 1½ hours) which leaves several times a day from in front of the Hotel Wilson. This is the only local bus journey which you can take to see the countryside around Puerto Maldonado; you can leave in the morning and return in the afternoon but don't miss the last bus as the one hotel in Laberinto is a real dive and usually full of drunk miners. Laberinto itself is just a shanty town but you can take trips up and down the Madre de Dios river to various nearby communities, some of which are involved in gold panning.

Manu National Park

It is difficult to find boats which will go up the Madre de Dios (against the current) to Manu. It is possible to fly to Boca Manu on chartered light aircraft but this is more frequently done from Cuzco. Because Cuzco is a better place than Puerto Maldonado from which to reach Manu, the National Park is described at the end of the Cuzco section.

CHANCHAMAYO (La Merced & San Ramón)

The jungle region east of Lima which is most accessible from the capital is known as Chanchamayo, comprised of the two towns of La Merced and San Ramón which are entry points for further excursions into the jungle. San Ramón is about 300 km east of Lima and La Merced a further 11 km.

All buses to the region terminate in La Merced, which is the centre for ground transportation in the region and is the more important town. It has a population of over 10,000 and is a major coffee marketing centre. La Merced has a greater choice of hotels and restaurants although the region's best hotel is found in the smaller and quieter San Ramón. Although less important, San Ramón boasts the regional airport nearby. The two towns are linked by frequent colectivo service and locals consider them to be one unit.

La Merced is the centre for vehicles north to Oxapampa and Pozuzo, north-east to Puerto Bermudez, and south-east to Satipo.

Information

Money changing is difficult in Chanchamayo (you can try the Banco de Crédito). It is best to change money in Huancayo or Lima.

There is a colourful daily market in La Merced and the weekend market at San Luis de Shuaro, 22 km beyond La Merced, is interesting – local Indians visit it. There is a basic hotel here. Campa Indians occasionally come into La Merced to sell handicrafts.

Avenida Dos de Mayo is good for views of La Merced. The stairs at the north end give a good view of the town and the balcony at the south end gives a wonderful view of the river – excellent for photography.

There is an interesting botanical garden on the grounds of the *El Refugio Hotel* in San Ramón.

Places to Stay

La Merced

This is the most convenient place to stay if you are continuing on by road rather than air. There are several cheap and very basic hotels charging about US$1 per person. They are not particularly clean and the water supply is erratic in most of them, though you can always go for a bath in the river as the locals do. The cheapest are the *Hostal Roca*, *Hostal TB Palermo*, *Hostal Básico Chuncho* and the *Hostal Básico San Felipe*. The last of these, at US$1.40/2.25 singles/doubles, is the most expensive of the cheap hotels.

Similarly priced to the San Felípe but marginally better looking are the *Hostal Santa Rosa*, *Hostal Lima* and the *Gran Hotel* (formerly the *Romero*).

If you want something a little better

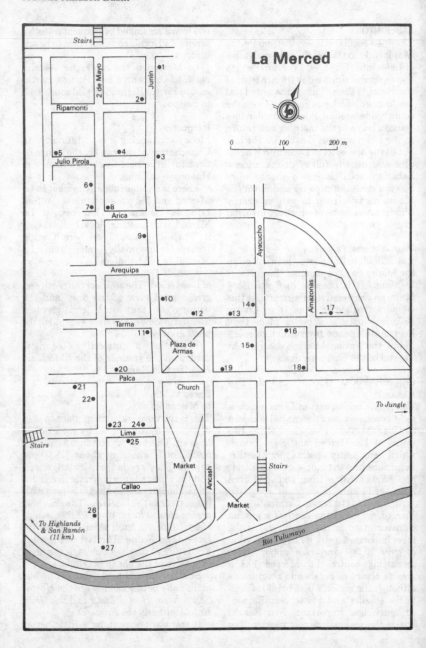

1 Hostal Rey
2 Trans Chanchamayo
3 Etucsa Buses
4 Banco de la Nación
5 Hotel Cosmos
6 Post Office
7 Turismo Chanchamayo
  (Minibuses to San Ramón)
8 Expreso Lobato
9 Cockfighting Stadium
10 Banco de Crédito
11 Chifa Roberto Sui
12 Restaurant Shambari Campa
13 Cinema
14 Hostal Roca
15 Hostal TB Palermo
16 Hotel Cristina & Hostal Mercedes
17 Minibuses & cars to Huancayo
   & the jungle
18 Transportes Los Andes
19 Gran Hotel
20 ENTEL
21 Trans Arellano
22 Hostal Basico San Felipe
23 Hostal Santa Rosa
24 Hostal Lima
25 Hostal Basico Chuncho
26 Trans Andahuayllas
27 Viewpoint of river

San Ramón

Most of the hotels here are clustered within a block of Avenida Paucartambo where it crosses the main street of Avenida Progreso. The cheapest are the *Hotel Progreso* and *Hotel Colón*. Neither look up to much, although the *Colón* was receiving a new coat of paint last time I was in town. The *Hotel Chanchamayo* is good value for about US$1.75 per person in rooms with private baths. Not any better but more expensive is the *Hostal de la Selva* which charges US$2.20/3.50 singles/doubles. The *Hotel Conquistador* is a good hotel and worth the US$4 single and US$6 double.

The best hotel in the Chanchamayo region is the *El Refugio* (also known as the *Albergue de la Selva*) which is about 10 minutes walk from the town centre. The hotel grounds are also a small but well-laid out botanical garden. I was impressed by the enthusiasm and pride that the owner displayed for his garden – the various exotic plants are labelled and tend to attract butterflies and birds. A nice place. Rooms are in comfortable bungalows which even boast hot showers; rates are about US$20 for a double. There is a restaurant.

Places to Eat

The 'best' place in San Ramón is the *Tumi* below the *Hotel Chanchamayo*. There are a few other chifas and cafeterias along the main street. None of these are especially noteworthy. Guests at the *El Refugio* will do best to eat at the hotel.

La Merced has many more restaurants. The best is definitely the *Restaurant Shambari Campa* which is down a little alley just off the main plaza. They serve both Chinese and Peruvian dishes and meals are good and not very expensive. There is an outdoor area where you can dine under thatched roofs. There are also several chicken restaurants and chifas of which *Chifa Roberto Sui* on the plaza is OK.

than basic try the *Hotel Cristina* at US$2/3.20; their rooms have private baths. The *Mercedes* next door is similar and costs a few cents more. Unfortunately, both hotels are quite small and tend to be full.

Bigger, but with snotty desk staff when I stopped by, is the *Hotel Cosmos* which charges US$2.80/4.50 singles/doubles in clean rooms with private bath. The best in La Merced is the *Hostal El Rey* which goes as far as providing towels, soap and toilet paper in your bathroom – but you must still put up with cold showers. There are telephones in the rooms and a top floor cafeteria that has good breakfasts. Climb up onto the roof for a good view of the town. Rooms are US$3.60/5.50.

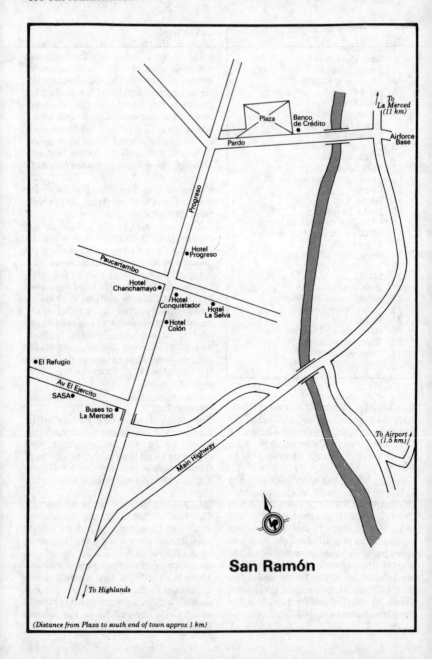

San Ramón

(Distance from Plaza to south end of town approx 1 km)

Getting There

It is possible to find buses which go all the way to and from Lima but most travellers find it more convenient to break the journey at Tarma. The 65-km stretch from Tarma to San Ramón (at 850 metres above sea level) drops 2200 metres and so it is worth trying to travel on this section in daylight hours for the views. Since 1984, a project to pave this road has kept it closed during working hours daily except on Sundays – the project was scheduled to finish by the beginning of 1987, although I wouldn't rely on that. Vehicles from Tarma were leaving between 4 to 6 am and 5 to 7 pm during construction.

Buses La Merced is where all the buses leave from. Buses to Tarma, La Oroya and Lima are available with Expreso Lobato, Transportes Arellano, Transportes Los Andes and Transportes Chanchamayo. During the road paving project only night buses were available. Fares varied from US$5.50 to US$7 for the 10 to 12-hour journey.

For Huancayo, the same applies – night buses only during the reconstruction. Expreso Lobato or ETUCSA charge about US$2.20 per person for the roughly five-hour journey. Colectivo cars from Avenida Tarma at Amazonas are faster and charge about US$3.30.

Transportes Andahuaylas have three buses a week for the long and gruelling ride to Andahuaylas – I haven't the faintest idea why anybody would want to go direct from La Merced to Andahuaylas.

If you are looking for transportation further into the jungle, go to the east end of Avenida Tarma where you'll find all kinds of trucks, cars, minibuses and jeeps. Larger buses don't travel on the narrow jungle roads. Minibuses will take you to Satipo (US$5, six hours), Oxapampa (US$3, four hours) and Puerto Bermudez (US$6.50, eight hours) as well as intermediate towns such as San Luis de Shuaro en route to Oxapampa. Colectivo taxis are more expensive. Schedules are haphazard – go down there as early as you can and start asking around. Sometimes you can buy tickets the night before but things are generally disorganised and you may have to rely on luck and persuasiveness.

Turismo Chanchamayo (*not* Transportes Chanchamayo) has frequent minibuses linking La Merced and San Ramón; fares are about 15c.

Air The Chanchamayo airstrip is about a ½-hour walk from San Ramón. Colectivo taxis leave irregularly from the plaza but are not reliable. You can hire your own taxi for about US$1.

The local airline is SASA which operates daily flights into the jungle. AeroPeru and Faucett do not fly into this airstrip. Although SASA has an office in San Ramón, it is rarely open and you are better off just turning up at the airport early (before 9 am) and waiting for a plane. Planes take between five and nine passengers and leave as soon as they are full. There are flights to Puerto Bermudez on most days – the fare is US$17. There are also flights to other jungle villages on a less regular basis – the staff at the airport can tell you when a plane may be leaving. If you are travelling in a group you can charter your own plane to almost anywhere in the region (you can charter a plane by yourself, too, but must pay for the empty seats).

There is a simple cafeteria which serves snacks and cold drinks, including beer.

SATIPO

This small jungle town lies about 130 km by road to the south-east of La Merced. Satipo is the centre of a small fruit producing region but its main claim to fame at this time is as the southernmost town on the *Carretera Marginal de la Selva* (the Marginal Jungle Highway).

This huge road project was devised by the Peruvian architect and President for two terms, Sr Fernando Belaúnde Terry. Belaúnde's dream was to open up the Amazon Basin, not by a road cutting across it, but by a road encircling the entire western boundary of the Amazon Basin. The scheme called for a road beginning in Asunción, the capital of Paraguay, and going through the jungle lowlands of Bolivia, Peru, Ecuador and Colombia before terminating at the Caribbean near Caracas, the capital of Venezuela. Only relatively small sections of this highway have been built and it is unlikely that the project will ever be completed. The section from Satipo to La Merced is fairly well-established – further north there are long breaks in the highway.

Satipo is also linked by a road into the highlands of Huancayo and so a round trip is possible by public transport. The scenery on this trip is spectacular but it is rarely done by foreigners. The buses are reasonably reliable.

Places to Stay

For such an isolated little town, Satipo has a surprising number of hotels. The best is the *Hotel Majestic* at Plaza Principal 408. They charge about US$6 for a double with bath. About half that price will get you a room with private bath at the *Hostal Palermo* at Manuel Prado 228. There are several other cheap and basic hotels.

OXAPAMPA

About 75 km north of La Merced is the ranching and coffee centre of Oxapampa. It used to be important for logging but most of the trees have been cut down now. Look around at your fellow passengers as you take the bus north from La Merced – you'll see some blond heads and blue eyes. This is because several hundred German settlers arrived in the area in the mid 1800s. Their descendents live in Oxapampa or in Pozuzo, about four hours north of Oxapampa by daily minibus. They have preserved many of their customs; buildings have a Tyrolean look to them, Austrian-German food is prepared, and an old-fashioned form of German is still spoken by some families. Although the area has been settled for over a century, it is still remote and rarely visited. The people are friendly and interested in talking with visitors. There are simple hotels in both towns; the *Bolívar* is the best in Oxapampa and the *Tirol* the best in Pozuzo. It makes an unusual and interesting trip.

PUERTO BERMUDEZ

Puerto Bermudez is a sleepy port on the Río Piches about nine hours north-east of La Merced by bus. Looking at the huddle of dugout canoes tied up to the mud bank of the small river flowing past the town, it is difficult to imagine that one could embark here on a river journey which would eventually take you down the Amazon to the Atlantic. Until recently, this was the only way to continue past Puerto Bermudez, but in the mid 1980s the new Carretera Marginal de la Selva was opened up as far as Pucallpa. I thought it would be interesting to try and travel this new section of road and see how Peru was opening up its frontier.

Places to Stay

There are two basic hotels right by the river which provide a bed, four walls and a river view. They are the *Hotel Tania* and the *Hotel Prusia* and they both charge about 70c per person. You get what you pay for. At least the river view is pretty, especially at dawn and dusk. If these two are full, there are a couple of other even more basic hotels a few streets away from the river. There is one main street where there are places to eat.

CIUDAD CONSTITUCIÓN

Constitution City is a recently conceived major town which is to be built in the middle of the jungle along a particularly unpopulated stretch of the new highway. Schools, a hospital, a cathedral, political offices, many blocks of streets with shops and housing have all been mapped out and an area of the jungle has been cleared. That's about as far as the project had got when President Belaúnde's second term of office came to a close. Now, with a new president and different political priorities, it is entirely possible that Ciudad Constitución will remain a forgotten and fly blown huddle of huts on the Río Palcazu with the new road passing by a km away.

Although the road has been pushed as far as Ciudad Constitución, only heavy trucks and road building equipment were able to get through when I did the trip. So I went down to the river at Puerto Bermudez and found someone heading down to 'Constitución' to give me a ride in his peki-peki. The journey cost me US$5, took seven hours and was much pleasanter than grinding my way over the newly churned mud of the highway. If you're lucky, you might be able to find a boat with an outboard motor which will do the trip in about four hours. From where the boat drops you off to the huts comprising the 'town' is a two or three-km walk.

There is a place to stay which consists of a hut with mud floors and rooms with no locks on the door. There is a small store where cold drinks are available and a simple meal can be ordered.

THE ROAD TO PUCALLPA
On most days there is one vehicle from Pucallpa which gets to Constitución late in the morning and turns around after a quick lunch stop. The return trip takes about seven hours and costs US$5. This section of the new highway is, for the most part, gravelled and in reasonable shape. You'll pass occasional small communities and the closer you get to Pucallpa the more open the country becomes – signs of the logging followed by ranching, which is typical of the opening up of the Peruvian rain forest.

About 1½ hours beyond Ciudad Constitución a small river is crossed by raft. There is a village here, **Zungaro**, and a basic hotel and restaurant can be found. From Zungaro there are both road and river communications with **Puerto Inca** on the Río Pachitea, about 10 km away. During the wet season the road is often closed and during the dry season the river between Zungaro and Puerto Inca is too low, so ask around for the best way to go. At Puerto Inca ask for Don José who is an old Czech gentleman who has lived in the area for many years and is a great source of local information. He is somewhat of a local figure and owns a simple hostal pleasantly situated on the river.

Beyond Zungaro, there is a stretch of about an hour when little except for forest is seen but soon the scenery gives way to ranch land and small homesteads. Alternatively, you can get to Pucallpa by boat from Puerto Inca.

PUCALLPA
With a population approaching 100,000, Pucallpa is the fastest growing of Peru's jungle towns and also the biggest to be linked directly with Lima by road. Until 1980, it played second fiddle to Iquitos, capital of the huge Department of Loreto. Since 1980 a new Department has been formed and now Pucallpa is enjoying political and economic growth as the capital of the new Department of Ucayali.

Despite a few pleasant modern buildings such as the Hotel de Turistas, Pucallpa is not a particularly attractive city. Many of its buildings are hastily constructed with concrete and tin roofs. Its roads are slowly becoming paved but many of those away from the centre are still red mud quagmires in the wet season and choking dust in the dry. One of the most startling of sights in Pucallpa is the huge flocks of vultures which lazily circle over the markets, plazas and dock areas. The roofs of the buildings around the food market are often crowded with scores of the huge black birds silently waiting for scraps to be thrown out. Yet there is a palpable feeling of civic pride, progress and growth. This is more than just another sleepy jungle port; this is Peruvians working to make Peru work.

Nevertheless, after feeling the pulse of the city and watching the languid flapping of the vultures, the visitor is not left with much to do. When you are ready to leave town, there are two good choices. One is to take the short bus trip to nearby Yarinacocha, a lovely oxbow lake where you can take canoe rides, observe wildlife, visit Indian communities and purchase their handicrafts, and stay in pleasantly rustic, lakeside jungle lodges. Yarinacocha is the 'tourist area' of Pucallpa and yet it is far from touristy – hotel, restaurant and boat services are provided in a casual and easy going atmosphere. It's worth spending a couple of days here. (Full description after the Pucallpa section.) Finally, when you are ready to move on, go down to the Pucallpa docks to find a river boat heading down to Iquitos and whilst you're looking you can experience at first hand the rough and tumble atmosphere of a busy and hard working river port.

Information

Pronunciation Just as you've become used to remembering that 'll' is always pronounced 'y' in Spanish, you come to one of the very few exceptions to this rule. Pucallpa is pronounced 'pukalpa'.

Money Exchange Cash dollars and travellers cheques can be changed at the Banco de Crédito for a 1% commission. Some stores also change money; one is marked on the map. The better hotels and the airlines normally change money for their clients but make sure you are getting the favourable financial rate and not the unfavourable official rate.

Medical The Clínica Santa Rosa is quite good for stool, urine or blood tests if you get sick.

Tourist Agencies & Guides There are

several tourist agencies near the AeroPeru office but I would go to Yarinacocha and look there for guides for trips to the jungle – fewer middlemen. Of the guides in Pucallpa, Marco Antonio Menendez is knowledgeable and honest. You can find him by asking at the *Hotel Mercedes* or writing to Apartado 83, Pucallpa, Ucayali.

Other The Plaza de Armas isn't up to much – the intersection of Raymondi and Ucayali is considered to be the main centre of town. There are a couple of cinemas which occasionally show English language films.

Places to Stay

Many hotels are full by early afternoon so start looking as soon as you arrive. Many travellers prefer to stay at Yarinacocha, although there are fewer hotels there.

Places to Stay - bottom end

The cheapest in town is the *Hostal Donita* which charges 75c single and US$1 double. It is often full, not very clean and cannot be recommended.

Several hotels charge US$1 single and US$1.70 double. The *Hotel Europa* used to be popular with budget travellers but it is now dirty and run down. Other cheapies in improving order of appearance are the *Hostal Alex*, *Hostal TB Ucayali*, *Hostal Excelsior* and *Hospedaje Mori*, but none of them are particularly recommended. The best of the cheap hotels are the small but friendly *Hostal Residencial Barbtur* and the *Hostal Peru* which also has some triples, as well as rooms with private baths for an extra 50c. The *Hostal Peru* has the advantage of having more rooms than the other hotels and so you stand a better chance of getting a bed here if you arrive late. Their single rooms and rooms with private baths are the first to go; their water supply is erratic.

Places to Stay - middle

The *Hostal Sun* is new and clean and charges US$2.30/3.70 for singles/doubles with private bath. Similarly priced are the *Hostal Confort* and the *Hostal Amazonia* which are OK. The *Hostal Toriri* charges US$4/6.50 for singles/doubles with bath and has a reasonable restaurant. There was also a new hotel opening when I was last in town – it's marked on the map and looks like it will be in this price range.

There are two hotels which charge US$5.30/8 in rooms with private bath. Both are recommended. The *Hotel Mercedes* downtown was the first good hotel to open in Pucallpa and has a certain dated charm and character. A few blocks away is the new *Hotel Komby* which boasts a swimming pool.

Places to Stay - top end

Conveniently located downtown is the modern government-run *Hotel de Turistas* which has a swimming pool, bar, restaurant, room telephones, etc. They charge US$12/15 for singles/doubles with private baths. This includes continental breakfast. Reservations may be made at EnturPeru in Lima (tel 721928). New, good and similarly priced is the *Hotel Inambu* which is air-conditioned but is some way out of town – take a taxi.

Places to Eat

It's usually hot in Pucallpa and so 'Places to Drink' is as important as eating. The best place in town for a huge variety of cold, freshly squeezed fruit juices is *Don José's*. There are two locations, called simply *Don José 1 & 2* and 1 is marginally cheaper. Apart from their excellent juices, they serve a wide variety of good and reasonably priced meals. Because of the heat in the middle of the day, restaurants tend to be open early (by 7 am) for breakfast. Several slightly cheaper restaurants are shown on the map if you want a change but I always ended up eating at Don José's.

The local beer, *San Juan*, has the distinction of being the only beer brewed in the Amazon – whether that is the entire Amazon or just the Peruvian Amazon is open to discussion. At any rate, because it is brewed locally it is cheaper than the coastal beers and for a light bottled beer it is good and refreshing.

If you want to splash out a little, go to the *El Establo* steak house which is out of town on the road to the airport (best to take a taxi). It serves the best steaks in town.

Getting Around

The green No 6 bus leaves from Atahualpa at 2 de Mayo for Yarinacocha. There are several buses an hour and the fare is 10c for the 30-minute trip. The No 1 bus goes north-west along Ucayali to the airport – 10c and 20 minutes. Taxis will take you to the airport for about US$1 and to Yarinacocha for about US$2 but you'll probably have to bargain.

Getting There

The easiest way to get to Pucallpa is with the daily flights from Lima or Iquitos but it is much more interesting to travel overland. A direct bus from Lima takes about 24 hours but you can break the journey in several places; Huánuco and Tingo María are the best of these. A journey from coastal Lima takes you up the steep western slopes of the Andes to a breathless 4843 metres above sea level. It continues along the Andes at an average of over 4000 metres for several hours before beginning the dizzying descent down the cloud-forested slopes of the eastern Andes to Pucallpa at a mere 154 metres. This incredible change of scenery and altitude gives the traveller an exceptional look at Peru in cross-section and is one of the most exciting, if demanding, 24-hour intercity bus journeys on the continent.

The journey as far as Tingo María is described in the chapter on Central Peru. From Tingo, the road climbs over a final

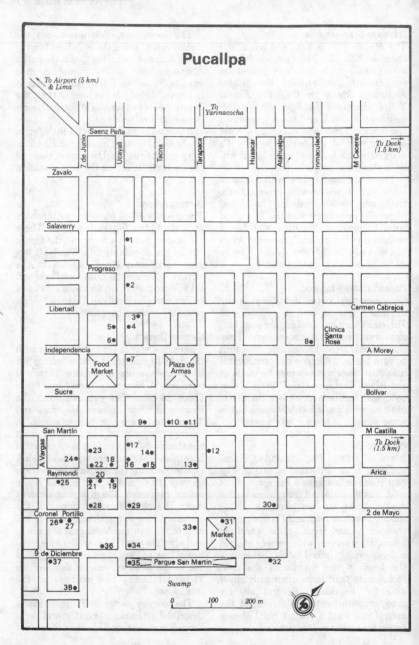

Pucallpa

To Airport (5 km) & Lima

To Yarinacocha

Saenz Peña

7 de Junio
Ucayali
Tacna
Tarapaca
Huascar
Atahualpa
Inmaculada
M Caceres

To Dock (1.5 km)

Zavalo

Salaverry

●1

Progreso

●2

Libertad

Carmen Cabrejos

●3
5● ●4
6●
8●

Clinica Santa Rosa

Independencia

A Morey

Food Market
●7
Plaza de Armas

Sucre

Bolívar

9●
●10 ●11

San Martín

M Castilla

To Dock (1.5 km)

A Vargas
●17
24● ●23
●14
●12
●22 18
16● ●15
13●

Raymondi
20
●25
21● 19
●28
●29
30●

Arica

Coronel Portillo
26● ●27
33●
●31 Market

2 de Mayo

●36
●34

9 de Diciembre
●37
●35 Parque San Martín
●32

38●

Swamp

0   100   200 m

1	ENTEL	21	Tepsa Buses
2	Empresa Sol de Oriente	22	Hostal Residencial Barbtur,
3	Cine Ucayali		Chifa Hong Kong & Restaurant Raymondi
4	Hostal Donita	23	Faucett
5	Hotel Komby	24	Trans Ucayali & Hostal Excelsior
6	Hostal Sun	25	Hostal Tariri & Hospedaje Mori
7	PIP	26	Hostal Confort, Aero Peru
8	Grupo 8		& various travel agencies
9	Hotel de Turistas	27	Hostal Amazonia
10	Banco de la Nación	28	Shop (will change $)
11	Post Office	29	Cafeteria Restaurant Roma
12	New Hotel	30	Comité 6 Bus to Yarinacocha
13	Banco de Crédito	31	Hostal Alex
14	Arellano Buses	32	La Capitanía
15	Etposa Buses	33	Hostal TB Ucayali
16	Don José 1 Restaurant	34	Guardia Civil
17	Cine Rex	35	Clock Tower
18	Hotel Mercedes	36	SASA Airline
19	Don José 2 Restaurant	37	León de Huánuco Bus
	& Pizza Restaurant	38	Hostal Europa
20	Hostal Peru		

pass in the eastern Andes before descending to Pucallpa in the Amazon Basin proper. There is an interesting story connected with building the road over this pass. Until the 1930's, the road reached only as far as Huánuco and engineers were carrying out surveys to assess the easiest route for the road to continue to Pucallpa. They were unable to find an obvious pass over the last range of the Andes and were preparing for an expensive road building project. One of the engineers had been studying historical documents and maps of the region, some of which had been made as long ago as the 1700s by Franciscan missionaries exploring the area. One document recounted a 1757 expedition by Father Abad and this led to the rediscovery of an extremely narrow, steep-walled gorge which cut through the final mountain barrier. The road was built through this pass, saving much time and money, and reached Pucallpa in 1941. The pass is now named after Padre Abad.

Driving through the pass is spectacular and should be done in daylight. The vertical walls are covered with waterfalls and clinging exotic vegetation and there are several natural pools where you could swim. The bird life is prolific and the careful observer may see troops of monkeys scurrying along the cliff ledges. Unfortunately, there is no public transport to the pass, only through it. Ideally, you could take a Tingo-Pucallpa bus and get off at the pass, walk through it (it's about a four-km walk along the road) and flag down a later bus. Otherwise, you'll have to be content with tantalising glimpses through the bus windows.

Buses Although service between Pucallpa and Lima is supposed to take 24 hours, during the rainy months (especially January to April) it can take two or three days if the road has been closed by mud slides. During the rest of the year, TEPSA usually provides the best service and has been known to do the trip in as few as 20 hours. They charge just under US$10 for the trip and leave two or three times a day. Other companies are cheaper but slower and these include

ETPOSA and León de Huánuco. The last mentioned also has three buses a week for the gruelling two-day trip to Tarapoto (US$11). Intermediate towns are served by these companies. Empresa Sol de Oriente only goes as far as Tingo María. Transportes Ucayali has a daily bus to Huancayo (US$8).

Some maps show roads continuing east of Pucallpa to Cruzeiro do Sul in Brazil. This is wishful thinking in the extreme because there isn't even a jeep track part of the way there. Absolutely nothing.

Air Pucallpa's airport is a small but busy one. Faucett and AeroPeru both have offices downtown and at the airport and between them provide daily service to Iquitos and Lima (US$36 either way). Services to jungle towns other than Iquitos are provided but schedules change frequently. Recently, Faucett had two flights a week to Tarapoto but you should check to see what is available now.

SASA has an office downtown but it is frequently closed and you're better off going to the airport to make enquiries about their services. They have flights to Atalaya fairly often and services to places like San Ramón less frequently – you'll have to ask.

Grupo 8 (also called TANS) is the military airline and provides occasional service to Lima and Iquitos but their office downtown is often closed, the flight is not much cheaper than the commercial airlines and it's generally not worth the hassle. TANS and Alas del Oriente also have a float plane service leaving from Puerto Callao in Yarinacocha that goes down the Ucayali to Iquitos stopping off at various river ports along the way. This service usually leaves on Saturday mornings, is always full and preference is given to locals. However, if you get down to the float plane dock very early on Saturday morning and get yourself onto the waiting list you might, with a good deal of luck and persistence, get yourself a seat. It would be an interesting trip.

Despite rumours to the contrary, there is no air service to Brazil.

River Boat Pucallpa's port is called La Hoyada and it is about 2½ km north-east of the town centre along unpaved roads. You can get river boats along the Río Ucayali from here to Iquitos, about five days away. Fares are about US$30 and it's much easier to get a passage when the river is high. Towards the end of the dry season (July to November) the river is too low for many of the boats. It is easier to get boats to the ports of **Contamana** and **Requena**. Accommodation is difficult to find in Contamana and onward passage is not any more frequent than from Pucallpa. Requena, on the other hand, has a couple of very basic hotels and boats to Iquitos leave on most days, taking about 12 hours.

Because air fares are not much more expensive than river boats, there are fewer passenger boats than there used to be and travel conditions are rough. Food is provided but it is very basic and travellers often get sick – bring some of your own food. Hammocks and mosquito repellent are essential but not provided. The *Capitanía* should be able to provide you with a list of boats and their destinations but in fact their information is rarely reliable until after the boat has gone!

Passengers from Pucallpa to Iquitos normally need to have their passport inspected by both the PIP and the Capitanía before beginning the trip. If you are heading on to Brazil, it is more convenient to fly as far as Iquitos and then begin your river journey from there.

Jungle 'guides' approaching you on the Pucallpa waterfront are usually not reliable and sometimes dishonest. There isn't much to do in the way of jungle trips from the dock anyway. If you are looking for an excursion into the jungle, you should look in Yarinacocha for reliable service. If you are looking for a passage on a river boat, ask for information on any likely looking boat, but don't give any money until you and your luggage are actually aboard the boat of your choice. Then pay the captain and no one else.

Don't wander around the docks with your luggage looking for a boat. Arrange a trip beforehand and then return with your luggage. Boats are sometimes delayed for some days before the cargo is loaded, but captains will often let you sling your hammock and stay aboard at no extra cost whilst you wait for departure.

YARINACOCHA

This attractive oxbow lake was once part of the Ucayali River but is now entirely landlocked, although a small canal links the two bodies of water during high water in the rainy season. Yarinacocha lies about 10 km north-east of Pucallpa. The road from Pucallpa goes to the small port of Puerto Callao which is the main centre of population on the lake. There are two cheap hotels and three more expensive jungle lodges, plenty of bars and restaurants, and boats are available for trips around the lake. You can visit Shipibo Indian villages and buy handicrafts or watch for wildlife in and around the lake. On a recent trip, my wife and I saw freshwater dolphins in the lake, a sloth and a metre-long green iguana in the trees around the lake, and plenty of exotic birds ranging from the curiously long-toed Wattled Jacana which walks on lily-pads and other floating vegetation, to the metallic green flash of the Amazon Kingfisher.

The Shipibo Indians live along the Ucayali and its tributaries in small villages of simple, thatched platform houses. They are a matriarchal society and the women make fine ceramics and textiles which are decorated with highly distinctive, geometric designs. Some Shipibo women come into Pucallpa to sell their pottery

and material but it is easy enough to buy direct from their villages. San Francisco at the north-west end of the lake is one such village which is commonly visited.

The Shipibo are also involved in a very fine co-operative craft store which collects work from about 40 villages. The store is called Maroti Shobo and is on the main plaza of Puerto Callao. Here, there are literally thousands of ceramics to choose from and because each piece is hand made it can be considered unique. Lengths of decorated cloth and other handicrafts are also available but it is the ceramics which make the place really worthwhile. The pieces range from small pots and animal figurines to huge urns. The staff is friendly and helpful and will arrange international shipping for you if you buy a large piece. Prices are fixed (no bargaining) but I found the work to be very fairly priced. I also was impressed by the easy going non-commercial ambience of the place. Although it is a well-run business, there is no one breathing down your neck to buy and it is a delight to just browse. I have a really soft spot for Maroti Shobo – I bought my favourite piece of South American handicraft here and every time I look at my sensitively moulded, two-headed, ceremonial drinking pot, I am reminded of Peru.

Arranging Tours

Whether your interest lies in birding, photography, visiting Indian villages or just relaxing on a boat ride around the lake, you'll find plenty of peki-peki boat owners ready to oblige. Take your time in choosing your boatman; there's no point in going with the first offer unless you are sure you like your boatman. Ask around. A good place for general information is *La Brisa Lodge* which is described under places to stay. A boatman for the trip to San Francisco and back might charge less than US$10 whilst a guide who goes with you and shows you around will charge twice as much. It is always worth bargaining over the price but the best way to do it is to set a price for the boat and then ask the boatman if you can bring a couple of friends. As long as there are only two or three of you they don't normally complain, so you can split the cost three ways. There are also guides available for walking trips into the surrounding forest including some overnight trips. I feel that a trustworthy guide is worth the money.

A good afternoon trip is up the north-east arm of the lake (to your right as you look at the lake from Puerto Callao). Ask the boatman to float slowly along to look for bird life at the water's edge or sloths (*perezoso* in Spanish) in the trees. Sunset is a good time to be on the lake. A day trip up the north-western arm is a good way to visit San Francisco and perhaps another Shipibo village. Fishing trips can also be organised.

Money Exchange

With persistence one can change money but don't expect favourable rates. The short bus ride into Pucallpa will provide much better facilities.

The Mission

There is a large and modern American missionary base on the outskirts of Puerto Callao which is affiliated to the SIL (Summer Institute of Linguistics). These missionaries have made contact with various Amazonian tribes and have worked to translate the Indian languages into English and Spanish and to make a workable alphabet for these previously unwritten languages, with a final goal of translating the New Testament into the many different Indian languages of the area.

I realise that to the unsympathetic ear this work sounds like proselytising and unacceptable meddling in traditional societies. Many people think that whether you are a missionary, oil prospector, tourist or logger, the end result for the Indians tends to be disease, starvation, misunderstanding and lack of care. This is not always true, however, and I feel that

the Summer Institute of Linguistics does have a genuine care for the people they work with and are concerned with physical needs such as improved living conditions, basic medical and schooling facilities, and an acceptance of the Indians into the Peruvian system. It is unrealistic to hope that in today's world, the Indian tribes can be totally left alone to continue traditional ways of life unchanged. Missions like the SIL, though far from ideal, do more good than harm for the Indians in the long run and their approach is more practical than any other solution proposed to solve the 'Indian Problem'.

Isolation is an ideal solution but the modern world is incapable of allowing it. Asking a poor third world country to leave its oil rich areas undisturbed so that the Indians can continue their traditional ways of life is impractical – the other citizens of the country want to improve their lot too. Idealism cannot work when there are slum dwellers starving in cities which could be improved by revenue from the jungle development of oil and other resources. The traditional approach has been (and in some remote areas appears to continue to be) a policy of wiping out the Indian tribes that stand in the way of progress. This cannot be condoned in any way whatsoever. The only viable alternative seems to be a gradual integration and the Summer Institute of Linguistics seems closer than others in achieving this aim.

Places to Stay – bottom end

There are two hotels within one block of the terminus of the No 6 bus from Pucallpa. To the right as you arrive is the *Hotel El Pescador* on the waterfront. At US$1.50/ 2.50 for singles/doubles this is the cheapest place to stay. Its main attraction is the waterfront location; otherwise it's a pretty basic hotel with erratic water supply in the none-too-clean bathrooms.

If you turn left from where the bus drops you off, a short dirt road leads to the

Hostal El Delfin which is not visible until you are there. Rooms here are better and only a little more expensive than *El Pescador*. Some rooms have a private bath, though they're not up to much. The *El Delfin* is full more often than the *El Pescador*. By asking around, you can sometimes find a room in people's houses.

Places to Stay - top end

There are three jungle lodges around the lake. The newest is the French-run *Ucayali Lodge* which charges US$25 a double with bath. It is near the north end of the lake, very quiet and out of the way. The owners are friendly. You have to get a peki-peki to take you there and the ride takes an hour. There is a restaurant on the premises. Reservations can be made at Casilla 133, Pucallpa or by Telex 95450 PECP Pucallpa. Tours can be arranged.

The oldest of the lodges is the German-run *La Cabaña* which is a 15-minute peki-peki ride across the lake from Puerto Callao. It also is good and quiet and has a restaurant. They charge a little more here than the other lodges.

Closest to Puerto Callao is *La Brisa Lodge* which was opened in 1978 and is owned and operated by Connor and Mary Nixon, from the US. It can be reached on foot from Puerto Callao by following the sign at the end of the village; it's about a ½-hour walk. The dirt road to the lodge closely follows the lake and is often flooded during the wet months of January to April but you can take an eight-minute ride by peki-peki from Puerto Callao. *La Brisa* is a great favourite of mine; the owners are not only knowledgeable about the area but they are friendly and helpful to everyone, whether you are staying there or not.

The lodge's central building – containing restaurant, bar, reception area and lounge – is an incredible structure. A huge central pole made of a 17-metre-high Cannia tree trunk supports a beautiful cone-shaped roof made of palm fronds.

The whole building is raised off the ground and screened to keep insects out. It allows cooling breezes in and there is a wonderful view of the lake. The well-stocked bar will provide you with a cool beer or other drink whilst you watch an Amazonian sunset. The furniture is beautifully carved into snakes, fish, birds and other jungle wildlife by a renowned local sculptor, Augustín Rivas. Shipibo handicrafts are on display. It's almost like dining in an art gallery. The food is the best in the area and it's reasonably priced.

The Nixons are usually in residence and happy to provide you with information. There are maps on the wall and they can help you set up trips ranging from a short sunset cruise or day trip to a Shipibo village, to a trip of several days. They know most of the local boatmen and guides and can tell you which are trustworthy and recommended.

Accommodation at the lodge consists of five comfortable double rooms which between them share two bathrooms. The double rooms have both a double bed and a single one. There are also some family-style bungalows with private baths. The rustic buildings blend in with the environment. Rates are US$15 single, US$25 double and US$35 for a bungalow with four beds. The Nixons are sympathetic to less well-heeled backpackers and young travellers and if there is space available a discount can usually be arranged if you are a member of the South American Explorers Club or have a student card.

There is an exchange library and the lodge also publishes a booklet entitled *Yarinacocha* which gives information on the wildlife, native groups and history of the area.

Places to Eat

There are several restaurants and lively bars lining the waterfront of Puerto Callao. They are all inexpensive and you can just wander around until you find one that seems OK. The best restaurant is at *La Brisa* lodge but they are open only from about 9 am to dusk so get there early. Their bar is open later. Their cook usually takes Monday off.

YURIMAGUAS

Locals nickname Yurimaguas 'the pearl of the Huallaga'. It is the major port on the Río Huallaga and boats to Iquitos can be found from here. Reaching Yurimaguas can involve a long and adventurous road trip of several days (see Across the Northern Highlands) or a simple flight from Lima. With a population of about 25,000, Yurimaguas is a quiet but pleasant little town, quite different from the bustling boom town atmosphere of Pucallpa. There are signs of the rubber boom days, for example the expensive imported tiles which decorate the walls of the buildings at the end of Avenida Arica. But generally it is a sleepy port in which you may have to wait for a week or more before finding a river boat to Iquitos. Bring a couple of good books.

Information

The Banco Amazonico will change cash dollars and travellers' cheques. There are a couple of cinemas where English language films are sometimes shown.

Places to Stay

My favourite is the *Cheraton Hotel* which has a few simple but spacious rooms with private bathroom and a balcony looking out onto the Plaza de Armas – not all the rooms are this good. Rates are about US\$2/3 for singles/doubles.

Other hotels include the new *Gran Hotel Yurimaguas* where drivers heading back to Tarapoto often stay. Rooms with bathrooms are about US\$1.75 per person. Similarly priced is the *Hostal Florindez* which has some rooms with air-con for an extra 50c. For about US\$1 per person try the *Hostal Jauregui* which is basic but adequate, or the *Hostal Estrella* and *Hostal Florida*.

Places to Eat

The *Restaurant El Naranjo, Copacabana* and *Cheraton* are among the best, though none of them are anything special.

Getting There

Air Faucett and AeroPeru each have two flights a week to and from Lima (US\$47) via Tarapoto (US\$12). In addition, AeroPeru has two flights a week to and from Iquitos (US\$30). Aero Taxi Iberico, which has an office opposite the airport, has light aircraft to various nearby towns – enquire at their office.

Trucks The only road out of Yurimaguas is the very rough one to Tarapoto and there are no scheduled transport services along it. Trucks and jeeps do leave for Tarapoto on most days, however, and you can find out who is going by asking in hotels and restaurants. The *Gran Hotel Yurimaguas* is a good place to start.

River Boat Cargo boats ply from Yurimaguas down the Huallaga to the Río Marañon and on to Iquitos. The trip usually takes about three to five days and there are departures once a week on average. Passages should cost less than US\$20. As with other river trips, bring a hammock, mosquito repellent, purified water or tablets and a supply of food, unless you're prepared to eat the very basic and monotonous food available on board. Because Yurimaguas is not as well served with air and road services as is Pucallpa, the river link is more important and the cargo boats are used to taking passengers. The journey could be broken at **Lagunas**, just before the Huallaga meets the Marañon. There is a basic hotel here and onward boats can be found to Iquitos.

SARAMERIZA

Sarameriza is a tiny port on the upper Marañon and the most westerly point to start a river journey down the Amazon, although it is very rarely done.

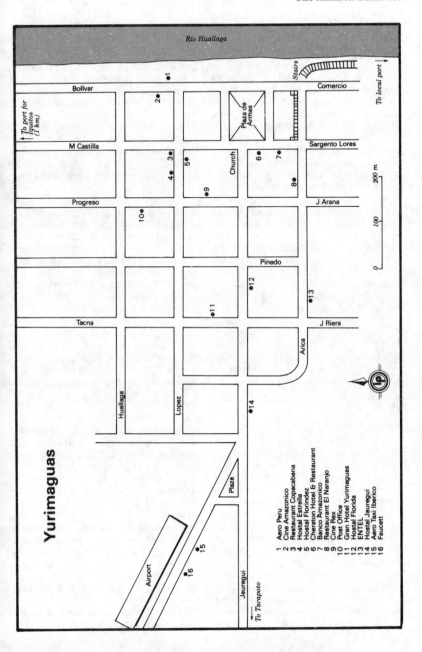

Yurimaguas

1 Aero Peru
2 Cine Amazonico
3 Restaurant Copacabana
4 Hostal Estrella
5 Hostal Florindez
6 Cheraton Hotel & Restaurant
7 Banco Amazonico
8 Restaurant El Naranjo
9 Cine Rex
10 Post Office
11 Gran Hotel Yurimaguas
12 Hostal Florida
13 ENTEL
14 Hostal Jauregui
15 Aero Taxi Iberico
16 Faucett

To get to Sarameriza (or Puerto Delfus, a few km away), you must first get to Bagua on the Chiclayo-Chachapoyas route in the northern Andes. From Bagua the going gets rough. There are daily trucks going to Nazareth about 80 km to the north-east and on to Imazita about 30 km further. There is a police checkpoint about half way between the two where your documents are checked. Bear in mind that you are close to the disputed Ecuadorean border here and so police may be sensitive to anyone wearing a 'Galápagos' T-shirt or even having an Ecuadorean stamp in their passport.

From here a road branches off to Sarameriza, about 150 km to the north-east. This road is in very bad shape and you have to hitchhike (expect to pay) on any vehicle which comes along. Vehicles do the trip about two or three times a week and it may take days depending on the state of the road. Be self sufficient with food and sleeping gear.

From Sarameriza, there are cargo boats leaving for Iquitos about every 10 or 15 days so be prepared to wait. The river journey takes about five days. Obviously, this is a trip for someone with a spirit of adventure, plenty of common sense and self sufficiency, and a lot of spare time. Good luck!

IQUITOS

With a population of over 200,000 (one local guide book claims 350,000 but I am unable to substantiate this) Iquitos is Peru's largest jungle city and capital of the huge Department of Loreto, the largest of Peru's 24 departments. Iquitos is linked with the outside world by air and the Amazon River – it is the largest city in the entire Amazon basin which is not connected by outside roads.

Iquitos has had a varied and interesting history. It was founded in the 1750s as a Jesuit mission, fending off attacks from Indian tribes who didn't want to be missionised. The tiny settlement survived and grew very slowly; by the 1870s the population had reached some 1500 inhabitants. Then came the great rubber boom and the population increased about 16-fold by the 1880s. For the next three decades, Iquitos was the scene of ostentatious wealth and abject poverty as the rubber barons became fabulously rich and the rubber tappers, mainly local Indians and poor mestizos, suffered virtual enslavement and sometimes death from disease or harsh treatment. Signs of the opulence of those days still remain in some of the mansions and tiled walls of Iquitos.

The bottom fell out of the rubber boom as suddenly as it had begun. A British entrepreneur smuggled out some rubber tree seeds from Brazil and plantations were seeded in Malaya. The orderly rows of rubber trees in the plantations made it much cheaper to collect the rubber than from the wild trees scattered in the Amazon Basin and by WW I Peru's rubber industry was at an end.

Iquitos suffered a period of severe economic decline during the ensuing decades, supporting itself as best it could by a combination of logging, agriculture (Brazil nuts, tobacco, bananas and *barbasco* – a poisonous vine used by the Indians to hunt fish and now exported for use in insecticides) and the export of wild animals to zoos. Then, in the 1960s, a second 'black gold boom' revitalised the area. This time the black gold was oil and this has made Iquitos a prosperous modern town. In recent years, tourism has also played an important part in the economy of the area.

Information

Tourist Information The tourist office is on the Plaza de Armas in the *Municipalidad* (town hall) and is open from 8 am to 12 noon on weekdays. There is no sign so ask one of the guards. The tourist office can give you maps of the area as well as up-to-date information.

There are various commercial jungle guides and jungle lodges which give tourist information. This is obviously biased towards selling their services – fine if you are looking for guides, tours or jungle lodges.

Money Exchange Rates for exchange of cash dollars and travellers' cheques vary from place to place and so it is worth checking two or three places before you change a large sum. There are several banks within a block or two of the Plaza de Armas on Raymondi and I found the Banco de Crédito gave the best rate, although the nearby Banco Amazonico was also quite good. You can also try the casas de cambio of which there are a couple on Fitzcarrald and elsewhere. Their rates may be lower than the bank but they are open longer hours.

Things to See

Although most travellers use Iquitos as a base for excursions into the jungle or as a place to wait for river boats along the Amazon, there are interesting places to see in and around the city itself.

The Iron House Every guidebook tells of the 'majestic' Iron House designed by Eiffel (of Eiffel Tower fame). It was imported piece by piece into Iquitos to beautify the city during the opulent days of the rubber boom. Unfortunately, no one knows exactly which building it is – during my research I have read of three different buildings which are supposedly the famous Iron House. Even the people at the Tourist Office were vague when I questioned them! The most likely building seems to me to be the one on the north-east corner of Putumayo and Raymondi on the Plaza de Armas. It looks like a bunch of scrap metal sheets bolted together and certainly nothing to get excited about. I can't help wondering if the famous Iron House is a myth perpetrated by generations of guides who felt that stretching the truth to make a good story was better than no story at all!

Azulejos There are some impressive remnants of those boom days, however. The best are the *azulejos*, hand made tiles imported from Portugal and used to decorate the mansions of the rubber barons. Many of the buildings along Raymondi and the Malecón (literally, dike or seawall) are lavishly decorated with azulejos. Some of the best are *Cohen's Cafeteria* and various government buildings along the Malecón.

Belén A walk down Raymondi (which turns into Prospero) and back along the Malecón is interesting, not only to see some of the tile faced buildings, but also to go to the Belén market area at the south-east end of town. Belén itself is a floating shanty town which has a certain charm to it (the locals call it an Amazonian 'Venice' but other people would call it a slum). It consists of scores of huts built on rafts which rise and fall with the river. During the dry months these rafts sit on the river mud and are dirty and unhealthy but during most of the year they float on the river creating a colourful and exotic sight. Several thousand people live here and canoes float from hut to hut selling and trading jungle produce. For a fee, someone will row you around. Although it is a very poor area it seems fairly safe – at least in daylight.

Within the city blocks in front of Belén is the city market – the usual raucous, crowded affair common in all Peruvian towns. All kinds of strange and exotic products are sold here among the mundane bags of rice, sugar, flour and cheap plastic and metal household goods. Look for the bark of the Chuchuhuasi tree which is soaked in rum for weeks and is used as a tonic drink served in many of the local bars. All kinds of other medicinal and culinary offerings are for sale: piles of dried frogs and fish, armadillo shells, piranha teeth and a great variety of tropical fruits. It makes for exciting shopping or watching, but remember to watch your wallet.

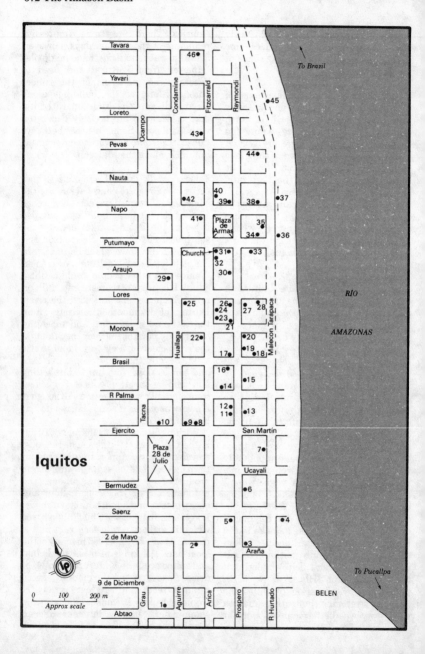

Iquitos

To Brazil

RÍO

AMAZONAS

To Pucallpa

BELEN

Tavara

Yavari

Loreto

Pevas

Nauta

Napo

Putumayo

Araujo

Lores

Morona

Brasil

R Palma

Ejercito

Bermudez

Saenz

2 de Mayo

9 de Diciembre

Abtao

Ocampo

Condamine

Fitzcarrald

Raymondi

Huallaga

Tacna

Grau

Aguirre

Arica

Prospero

R Hurtado

Malecon Tarapaca

San Martin

Ucayali

Araña

Plaza 28 de Julio

Plaza de Armas

Church

46

45

43

44

42

40

39

38

37

41

35

34

36

31

32

30

33

29

25

26

24

23

27

28

21

22

20

17

19

18

16

14

15

12

11

13

10

9

8

7

6

5

4

3

2

1

0   100   200 m
Approx scale

1	Local Buses & Trucks
2	Colectivo to Moronococha
3	Cine Iquitos
4	Hostal Alfert
5	Alojamiento el Amazonico
6	Hostal Internacional
7	Pensión Anita
8	Several Chifas
9	Cine Bolognesi
10	Several Chifas
11	Faucett
12	Hostal María Antonia
13	Hostal San Antonio
14	Hotel Acosta
15	Hostal Lima
16	Moises Torres Viena (Jungle Guide)
17	Hotel Europa
18	Hostal Isabel
19	Hostal Camino Real
20	Cohen's Cafeteria
21	Maynas Hostal
22	Post Office
23	Hostal Libertad
24	Cine Excelsior
25	Grupo 8 (Airforce)
26	Hostal Peru
27	Hostal Loreto
28	TANS Airline
29	Hostal Acosta
30	Aero Peru
31	Banco de Crédito
32	ENTEL
33	Tour & Lodge Operators
34	Don Giovanni's Restaurant
35	Hotel de Turistas
36	Maloka Restaurant
37	Boats upriver (Chalk boards)
38	El Mesón Restaurant & Hotel Safari
39	Municipalidad (Tourist Information)
40	Casa de Cambio
41	Hostal Amazonas
42	Pax Discotheque
43	Casa de Cambio
44	Hostal La Pascana
45	Boats to Brazil (Chalk boards)
46	Regional Museum

The Regional Museum The museum is open daily except Sundays from 8 am to 7 pm. Entrance is 10c. The main exhibits are stuffed animals of the region. As one might expect in the heat and humidity, they are not in a very good state of repair but it's worth a look if you're interested in Amazonian wildlife.

Laguna Moronacocha This lake forms the western boundary of the town. To get there take the colectivo which departs from 2 de Mayo and leaves downtown along Ejercito. It's a 15-minute ride and costs 10c. There really isn't much to see but I enjoyed going in the afternoon to have a cold beer and watch the sun set over Moronacocha. There are a couple of very basic bars with views of the lake.

Laguna Quistacocha This lake lies roughly 15 km south of Iquitos and makes a pleasant day trip. Buses and trucks leave several times an hour from the corner of Abtao and Aguirre. There is a small zoo of local fauna and also a fish hatchery where you can see two-metre-long paiche fish swimming around. This huge river fish is one of the tastiest I've eaten but it appears that its popularity has caused a severe decrease in its numbers. An attempt to rectify the situation is being made by the breeding programme at the fish hatchery. People swim in the lake (though it looks rather unsavoury) and paddle boats are for hire.

Nightlife

For a large and busy international port, Iquitos has surprisingly little nightlife. There are several cinemas, three of which are downtown and marked on the map. There are a few discotheques, mainly along the northern end of the Malecón, but they are usually short lived affairs which close down every few months. The *Pax* disco near the Plaza de Armas was recently popular. Wander around this area and you'll find bars blaring out music, but there isn't much in the way of typically Peruvian music.

Jungle Trips

Basically, excursions into the jungle can be divided into two types: visits to jungle lodges or more demanding camping and walking trips.

The majority of the operators have their offices on Calle Putumayo between the Plaza de Armas and the river, so it is easy to visit several before you choose. Because the lodges are some distance from Iquitos, river transportation is included in the price and a short trip of two or three days can be expensive.

A typical two-day trip involves a river journey of two or three hours to a jungle lodge with reasonable comforts and meals, a 'typical jungle lunch', a guided visit to an Indian village where crafts may be bought and perhaps dances seen (although tourists often outnumber Indians), an evening meal at the lodge, perhaps an after dark canoe trip to look for caymans by searchlight and a walk in the jungle the following day to look at jungle vegetation and perhaps, if you are lucky, monkeys or other wildlife. A trip like this will set you back about US$60 to US$120 depending on the operator.

The further away from Iquitos your lodge is, the better your chance of seeing more wildlife. Operators in Iquitos include Explorama Tours (who have three different lodges), Amazon Lodge Safaris, Jungle Amazon Inn, Amazon Sinchicuy Lodge and Tamshiyacu Lodge. All of these have good reputations and will detail what you get for your money.

Cheaper and less comfortable tours can also be arranged. Carlos Grandéz, who speaks English, runs Amazonia Expeditions and his emphasis is on jungle walks, wildlife observation and conservation. He doesn't take you to Indian villages. He is trying to set up the 20,000 hectares around his camp as a wildlife reserve. He charges about US$30 per day but will give discounts if you do chores or odd jobs at his camp. There are screened bungalows and dining rooms, an outhouse and cold shower, but no electricity.

Freddie Valles Wing runs Amazona Adventure Tours where he teaches jungle survival courses. He speaks English. His six-day introductory course for five people costs US$180 per person. You provide suitable jungle clothing and he provides the rest. It's a tough trip and involves a lot of walking through the jungle without trails. Sleeping shelters are built in a different place every night and food is fished or hunted. If you do OK in the introductory course he'll do a 15-day trip for five people at US$350 per person. If you're interested you can find him at Calle Yurimaguas 754 (six blocks south of and parallel to Abtao in the south end of town) or telephone 23 7305 or 23 3940. You must be fit.

Somewhat less demanding and cheaper than Freddie's tours are the jungle expeditions led by Moises Torres Viena at Brasil 217. His courses also include long walks in the jungle and catching your own food. Some river travel is involved and overnights are in Indian villages rather than completely roughing it in the wilderness. Moises doesn't speak English. I have heard good reports about all of these operations.

Places to Stay

There are plenty of hotels to choose from but the nicest cheap ones tend to fill up early, so look as soon as you arrive for the best choice. Most of the cheapest places are near the Belén area and most of them suffer from erratic or non-existent water supply. Even some of the mid-priced hotels suffer from a water shortage and so it is important to look at your room and check the water supply before taking the room. Almost all the hotels, even if they have water problems, provide a private bathroom – this can be a hindrance if you can't flush the toilet. Mosquitoes are rarely a serious problem and so mosquito netting is not provided although a fan always should be. If there isn't one in your room ask the management to give you one.

Places to Stay – bottom end

The basic *Hostal Alfert* is friendly and this is why it's popular with travellers on a tight budget. Rooms with private bathroom and a fan cost US$1/1.50 singles/doubles but unfortunately all water for washing and toilet flushing must be hauled by bucket. Other similarly priced basic hotels with erratic water supplies include the *Hostal Internacional*, *Pensión Anita* and *Hostal San Antonio*.

The *Maynas Hotel* is very good value with clean rooms with private bath and fans going for US$1.90/3.30 single/doubles. It's often full. A similarly priced alternative is the *Hostal Lima* which is a bit more basic but clean and the *Alojamiento El Amazonico* which is also clean but tends to have water only at night. The *Hostal Camino Real* is in this price range.

For US$2.70/3.30 singles/doubles you can get good clean rooms with private bath and fan at the *Hostal Isabel* which is popular with travellers. For a few cents more you get similar facilities at the *Hostal Peru* or at the *Hostal La Pascana* which is slightly out of the way and quiet.

Places to Stay – middle

The *Hostal Loreto* is quite good for US$3/4.50 singles/doubles in rooms with private bath and air-con; they have some cheaper rooms without air-con. The *Hostal Libertad* also has air-conditioned rooms with private bath for US$3.70/5. The *Hostal María Antonia* used to be quite a good hotel but is getting rather run down; it is still probably worth the US$4/5.50 for rooms with private baths and air-con. Cheaper rooms with fans are available.

The *Hostal Amazonas* has been recently refurbished and charges US$5.30/6.70 singles/doubles with bath and air-con. Also with private bath and air-con are the quite good *Hotel Safari* and *Hotel Europa* for US$6/8.

Places to Stay – top end

The government-run *Hotel de Turistas* is a good one with many of its clean air-conditioned rooms looking out over the Amazon which alone makes it worth the US$10 single and US$14 double. The price includes a continental breakfast and they also have cheaper rooms with fans.

The fanciest place in town is the new and good *Hotel Acosta* which provides all modern conveniences, including a mini refrigerator in the rooms, for US$21/28 singles/doubles. They also run the *Hostal Acosta* which, although much cheaper at US$7.50/10.50, is also very good.

There are two 1st class hotels a little way out of town that are reached by taxi. The *Amazon Bungalows* are out by the Río Nanay about four km west of town. Air-conditioned bungalows run about US$20 for a double; there is a restaurant and swimming pool. About half way to the airport is the *Amazonas Hotel* (formerly the Holiday Inn) which charges about US$50 for a double room and has the amenities you'd expect from a Holiday Inn.

Places to Eat

For those wishing to economise, you can eat at small restaurants and stalls in the market area but this is not recommended if your stomach is not used to Peruvian food. There are several chifas on and near the Plaza 28 de Julio. They vary in price from fairly cheap to moderately expensive.

There are several good restaurants between the Plaza de Armas and the waterfront. The *El Mesón* is a favourite haunt of locals, especially during lunch. Their set lunch is quite cheap and the other meals are good and reasonably priced. A block away is *Don Giovanni's* which, as its name suggests, serves good Italian food. My favourite place is the *Maloka* which is a floating restaurant on the Amazon. Considering its pleasing location, the prices are very reasonable and the food is good. If you are on a strict budget, you can always go for just a beer and watch the river flow by. After all, you're not on the Amazon very often!

Along Raymondi, the main drag, there are several cafeterias which serve juices, ice cream and other snacks. The most attractive of these is *Cohen's* with its ornate, tiled exterior. It is also the highest priced of the cafeterias and there are several others along the same street which serve similar food for less money.

Getting There

Airplane or river boat are your only two choices – all roads into the jungle stop within 20 km or so.

Air Iquitos has Peru's second most important airport. Before the 'air war' described in the Getting There section, there were almost daily arrivals and departures for Miami. Now, there are fewer international flights but you can still fly from here to Brazil. Of course, there are local flights as well.

Both AeroPeru and Faucett have offices in town and between them they have three or four flights a day to Lima (US$52). There are also flights to Tarapoto (US$32) and Pucallpa (US$36) on most days and flights to Yurimaguas (US$30) about twice a week.

Grupo 8 operates military flights to Lima and TANS has military flights to Requena, Contamana and Pucallpa as well as Islandia by the border with Brazil. Flights to Lima and Pucallpa cost about 20% less than the commercial airlines but leave only once a week, are often full and are subject to cancellation or postponement. The flight to the border, if you are lucky enough to get on it, is the best value because it costs only about US$16. Schedules, destinations and fares change very frequently but the last I heard was that flights to Contamana, Requena and Pucallpa left on Fridays and to Islandia on Tuesdays.

The most regular international departure is with Varig which charges US$77 to Tabatinga (on the Brazilian side of the border) and US$208 on to Manaus. There are two flights a week. Airport departure tax is US$10 for international flights. Other international flights are sometimes possible, or you can connect to many points from Manaus.

River Boat Iquitos is Peru's largest and best organised river port, quite capable of accepting ocean going vessels which it did in the rubber boom days. Most boats today, however, ply only Peruvian waters and you have to change boats at the border.

The Iquitos docks have a chalkboard system which tells you which boats are leaving when, for where and whether they are accepting passengers. Note that there are two different chalkboard locations marked on the map – one for upriver boats and the other for downriver.

Passages to Pucallpa or Yurimaguas (against the current) take from six to ten days respectively and cost about US$20 to US$30 per person. Boats leave about once a week – less often if the river is low. There are more frequent departures for the closer intermediate ports. Boats to Islandia or Ramón Castilla on the Peruvian side of the border with Brazil and Colombia leave about twice a week and take two days. Fares are US$15 to US$20 per person. Read the River Boats section in the Getting Around chapter for more detailed descriptions of what these journeys are like.

Getting Around

A distinctive local taxi is the two passenger motorcycle rickshaw. These strange looking contraptions charge a little less than a taxi and they're fun to ride.

Most buses and trucks for nearby destinations, including the airport, leave from the area between Grau and Aguirre at the south end of town.

Taxis tend to be rather more expensive

than in other Peruvian cities – a trip to the airport will run you about US$3 or US$4 but a motorcycle rickshaw will charge about US$2 to US$3 for the 10-km ride.

GOING TO COLOMBIA & BRAZIL

Before leaving Peru you need to get an exit stamp in your passport and you can't get an exit stamp if your entry stamp has expired. Don't think that just because you are in the middle of the Amazon jungle nobody will care. On the contrary, border officials have very little else to do other than refuse you passage if your documents are not in order, so make sure that you have enough days left on your visa or tourist card before attempting the trip.

Exit formalities change frequently. When I last left Peru for Brazil, I received my exit stamp at a Peruvian guard post just before the border (the boat stopped there long enough for travellers to do this; make sure that the captain agrees to this before you depart Iquitos). It's worth checking with the *Migraciones* office at Arica 477 in Iquitos to make sure that an exit stamp will be available near the border. The office is open from 9 am to 1 pm on weekdays.

Travellers crossing into Brazil or Colombia have different entry requirements according to their nationalities and again, formalities change and so it is worth checking with the Brazilian or Colombian embassy at home or in Lima before you go. There is also a Brazilian consul at Morona 283 in Iquitos and a Colombian consul at Malecón Tarapaca 260.

The most recent Brazilian regulations require consular visas for citizens of the US, France, Canada, Australia and New Zealand whilst most other citizens of Europe and Latin America need only their passport to obtain a tourist card (valid for 90 days) at the border.

Colombian regulations require visas costing US$20 for New Zealanders, Australians, Canadians and US citizens as well as citizens of some other countries. Visas for French citizens cost US$5. Citizens of the UK, Ireland and almost all western European countries, as well as most Latin American countries, do not require visas and can get a tourist card upon presentation of a valid passport at the border.

There are several ports at the tri-border. They are several km apart and connected by motor boats which act as public ferries. The biggest town is Leticia in Colombia which boasts the best hotels and a hospital. From Leticia you can take one of the infrequent boats to Puerto Asis on the Río Putumayo – the trip can take almost two weeks. From Puerto Asis you can take buses into Colombia. Alternatively, you can fly from Leticia to Bogotá on almost daily commercial flights. If you are looking for a boat up or down the Amazon, it is better to stay in Brazil or Peru, although accommodation is poorer.

There are two small ports in the Brazilian section: Tabatinga and Benjamin Constant. Both have basic hotels and money changers who will change your intis or cash dollars at unfavourable rates, so cash only enough to get to Manaus. Tabatinga has an airport with flights to Manaus and Iquitos. Benjamin Constant is the better place to find boats for Manaus.

In the Peruvian section are the small ports of Ramón Castilla and Islandia. Most boats from Iquitos will drop you at Islandia from where a motor canoe can take you to Benjamin Constant, literally a stone's throw away (well, maybe two throws). This is the best place to be to look for boats to Manaus. Ask at the port, the hotel, the restaurants, the money changers or the stores. Everyone will have an opinion and you can soon figure out which boat is going where and when.

If you are arriving from Colombia or Brazil, again, Benjamin Constant is a good place to stay when looking for boats from Islandia to Iquitos. There are no hotels in Islandia.

Bear in mind that the border hotels and restaurants will be fairly basic and slightly more expensive than other parts of Peru. Also remember that however disorganised things may appear, you can always get meals, beds, money changed, boats, etc simply by asking around. The locals are used to the different way of doing things on the river so ask them. As my Polish mother used to tell me, 'Koniec jezyka za przewodnika' – which perhaps is an appropriate way to finish this book. Roughly translated, it means 'Use your tongue as your guide'.

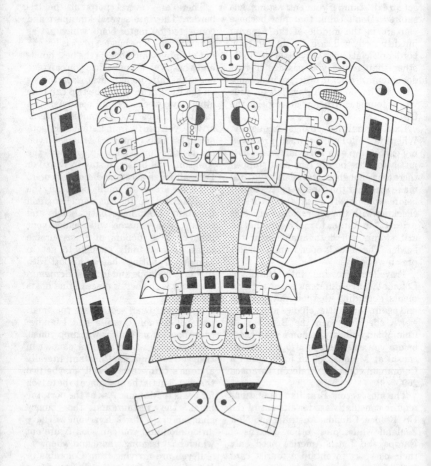

INDEX

Map references are in **bold** type.

379

Temperature

To convert °C to °F multipy by 1.8 and add 32

To convert °F to °C subtract 32 and multipy by 5/9

Length, Distance & Area

	multipy by
inches to centimetres	2.54
centimetres to inches	0.39
feet to metres	0.30
metres to feet	3.28
yards to metres	0.91
metres to yards	1.09
miles to kilometres	1.61
kilometres to miles	0.62
acres to hectares	0.40
hectares to acres	2.47

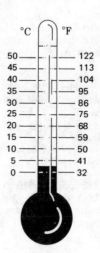

Weight

	multipy by
ounces to grams	28.35
grams to ounces	0.035
pounds to kilograms	0.45
kilograms to pounds	2.21
British tons to kilograms	1016
US tons to kilograms	907

A British ton is 2240 lbs, a US ton is 2000 lbs

Volume

	multipy by
imperial gallons to litres	4.55
litres to imperial gallons	0.22
US gallons to litres	3.79
litres to US gallons	0.26

5 imperial gallons equals 6 US gallons
a litre is slightly more than a US quart, slightly less
than a British one

Lonely Planet Newsletter

We collect an enormous amount of information here at Lonely Planet. Apart from our research there's a steady stream of letters from people out on the road. To make the most of all this info we produce a quarterly Newsletter (approx Feb, May, Aug, and Nov).

The Newsletter is packed with down-to-earth information from the pens of hundreds of travellers who write from first-hand experience. Whether you want the latest facts, travel stories, or simply to reminisce, the Newsletter will keep you in touch with what is going on.

Where else could you find out:
- about boat trips on the Yalu River?
- where to stay if you want to live in a typical Thai village?
- how long it takes to get a Nepalese trekking permit?
- that Israeli youth hostel stamps will get you deported from Syria?

One year's subscription is $10.00 (that's US$ in the USA or A$ in Australia), payable by cheque, money order, Amex, Visa, Bankcard or MasterCard.

Order Form

Please send me four issues of the Lonely Planet Newsletter. (Subscription starts with next issue. 1987 price – subject to change.)

Name and address (print) ....

....

....

Tick one

☐ Cheque enclosed (payable to Lonely Planet Publications)
☐ Money Order enclosed (payable to Lonely Planet Publications)
Charge my ☐ Amex, ☐ Visa, ☐ Bankcard, ☐ MasterCard for the amount of $.............

Card No .... Expiry Date ....

Cardholder's Name (print) ....

Signature .... Date ....

Return this form to:
Lonely Planet Publications   *or*   Lonely Planet Publications
PO Box 2001A   PO Box 88
Berkeley   South Yarra
CA 94702   Victoria 3141
USA   Australia

Guides to the Americas

South America on a shoestring
An up-dated edition of a budget travellers bible that covers Central and South America from the USA-Mexico border to Tierra del Fuego. Written by the author The New York Times called "the patron saint of travellers in the third world".

Alaska – a travel survival kit
A new edition of a definitive guide to one of the world's most spectacular regions – including detailed information on hiking and canoeing.

Canada – a travel survival kit
Canada offers a unique combination of English, French and American culture, with forests mountains and lakes that cover a vast area.

Mexico – a travel survival kit
Mexico has a unique blend of Indian and Spanish culture and a fascinating historical legacy. The hospitality of the people makes Mexico a paradise for travellers.

Ecuador & the Galapagos Islands – a travel survival kit
Ecuador is the smallest of the Andean countries, and in many ways it is the easiest and most pleasant to travel in. The Galapagos Islands and their amazing inhabitants continue to cast a spell over every visitor.

Chile & Easter Island – a travel survival kit
Chile has one of the most varied geographies in the world, including deserts, tranquil lakes, snow-covered volcanoes and windswept fjords. Easter Island is covered, in detail.

Lonely Planet travel guides

Africa on a Shoestring
Alaska – a travel survival kit
Australia – a travel survival kit
Bali & Lombok – a travel survival kit
Bangladesh – a travel survival kit
Burma – a travel survival kit
Bushwalking in Papua New Guinea
Canada – a travel survival kit
China – a travel survival kit
Chile & Easter Island – a travel survival kit
East Africa – a travel survival kit
Ecuador & the Galapagos Islands
Egypt & the Sudan – a travel survival kit
Fiji – a travel survival kit
Hong Kong, Macau & Canton – a travel survival kit
India – a travel survival kit
Indonesia – a travel survival kit
Japan – a travel survival kit
Kashmir, Ladakh & Zanskar – a travel survival kit
Kathmandu & the Kingdom of Nepal
Korea & Taiwan – a travel survival kit
Malaysia, Singapore & Brunei – a travel survival kit
Mexico – a travel survival kit
New Zealand – a travel survival kit
North-East Asia on a Shoestring
Pakistan – a travel survival kit kit
Papua New Guinea – a travel survival kit
Philippines – a travel survival kit
Raratonga & the Cook Islands – a travel survival kit
South America on a Shoestring
South-East Asia on a Shoestring
Sri Lanka – a travel survival kit
Tahiti – a travel survival kit
Thailand – a travel survival kit
Tibet – a travel survival kit
Tramping in New Zealand
Travel with Children
Travellers Tales
Trekking in the Indian Himalaya
Trekking in the Nepal Himalaya
Turkey – a travel survival kit
West Asia on a Shoestring

Lonely Planet phrasebooks

Indonesia Phrasebook
China Phrasebook
Nepal Phrasebook
Papua New Guinea Phrasebook
Sri Lanka Phrasebook
Thailand Phrasebook
Tibet Phrasebook

Lonely Planet Distribution

Lonely Planet travel guides are available round the world. If you can't find them, ask your bookshop to order them from one of the distributors listed below. For countries not listed, or if you would like a free copy of our latest booklist write to Lonely Planet in Australia.

Australia
Lonely Planet Publications, PO Box 88, South Yarra, Victoria 3141.
Canada
Raincoast Books, 112 East 3rd Avenue, Vancouver, British Columbia V5T 1C8.
Denmark, Finland & Norway
Scanvik Books aps, Store Kongensgade 59 A, DK-1264 Copenhagen K.
Hong Kong
The Book Society, GPO Box 7804.
India & Nepal
UBS Distributors, 5 Ansari Rd, New Delhi - 110002.
Israel
Geographical Tours Ltd, 8 Tverya St, Tel Aviv 63144.
Japan
Intercontinental Marketing Corp, IPO Box 5056, Tokyo 100-31.
Netherlands
Nilsson & Lamm bv, Postbus 195, Pampuslaan 212, 1380 AD Weesp.
New Zealand
Roulston Greene Publishing Associates Ltd, Private Bag, Takapuna, Auckland 9.
Papua New Guinea see Australia.
Singapore & Malaysia
MPH Distributors, 601 Sims Drive #03-21, Singapore 1438.
Spain
Altair, Balmes 69, 08007 Barcelona.
Sweden
Esselte Kartcentrum AB, Vasagatan 16, S-111 20 Stockholm.
Thailand
Chalermnit, 108 Sukhumvit 53, Bangkok, 10110.
UK
Roger Lascelles, 47 York Rd, Brentford, Middlesex, TW8 OQP.
USA
Lonely Planet Publications, PO Box 2001A, Berkeley, CA 94702.
West Germany
Buchvertrieb Gerda Schettler, Postfach 64, D3415 Hattorf a H.